W9-CLG-172

COLLECTED WORKS OF ERASMUS

VOLUME 43

COLLECTED WORKS OF
ERASMUS

NEW TESTAMENT SCHOLARSHIP

General Editor Robert D. Sider

PARAPHRASES ON
THE EPISTLES TO THE CORINTHIANS
THE EPISTLES TO THE EPHESIANS,
PHILIPPIANS, COLOSSIANS, AND
THESSALONIANS

edited by Robert D. Sider

translated and annotated by

Mechtilde O'Mara and Edward A. Phillips Jr

University of Toronto Press

Toronto / Buffalo / London

The research and publication costs of the
Collected Works of Erasmus are supported by
University of Toronto Press.

© University of Toronto Press 2009
Toronto / Buffalo / London
Printed in Canada

ISBN 978-0-8020-9296-0

Printed on acid-free paper

Library and Archives Canada Cataloguing in Publication

Erasmus, Desiderius, d. 1536
[Works]
Collected works of Erasmus

Each vol. has special t.p. ; general title from half title page.
Translation of : Paraphrasis in epistolam Pauli ad Corinthios priorem, etc.
Includes bibliographical references and index.
Contents: v. 43. Paraphrases on Corinthians, Ephesians, Philippians,
Colossians, Thessalonians / translated and annotated by
Mechtilde O'Mara and Edward A. Phillips Jr ;
editor, Robert D. Sider.
ISBN 978-0-8020-9296-0 (v. 43)

1. Erasmus, Desiderius, d. 1536–Collected works. I. Title.

PA8500.1974   199'.492   C740-06326-x rev

University of Toronto Press acknowledges the financial assistance to its
publishing program of the Canada Council and the Ontario Arts Council.

University of Toronto Press acknowledges the financial support for its
publishing activities of the Government of Canada through the Book Publishing
Industry Development Program (BPIDP).

Collected Works of Erasmus

The aim of the Collected Works of Erasmus
is to make available an accurate, readable English text
of Erasmus' correspondence and his
other principal writings. The edition is planned
and directed by an Editorial Board, an Executive Committee,
and an Advisory Committee.

Contents

Preface

For the composition and publication of Erasmus' *Paraphrases*, 1519 was a signal year. The first of the *Paraphrases* – that on Romans – had been published in November 1517, and had become an immediate success. Less than six months later Erasmus confided to Cardinal Grimani that the *Paraphrase on Romans* had been 'received with applause in learned circles,' and that many who were 'anxious to learn' were encouraging him to provide a similar exposition of the other Epistles.[1] The encouragement of friends had its effect. During the summer of 1518 Erasmus was in Basel deeply engaged in the preparation of the second edition of his New Testament, but immediately on its completion late in October, Erasmus, now back in Louvain, expressed his intention 'to finish the paraphrases, if Christ so please.'[2] Soon thereafter he turned to the two letters to the Corinthians for his next *Paraphrase*, following the canonical order of the Pauline Epistles. Erasmus perhaps began the work in the last weeks of 1518, but it would appear that much of the *Paraphrase* was composed in January of 1519. Printing was completed by late February.[3]

The year 1519 was, however, one of generally troubled times for Erasmus. At the University of Louvain he found both open and covert hostility to his ideal of humanistic learning as a foundation for theological study. This was an ideal presupposed in his editions of the New Testament and sharply articulated in the *Ratio verae theologiae* published in November of 1518. The ideal was also embodied in the curriculum of the Collegium Trilingue founded in 1517 in Louvain for the study of the three biblical languages, an institution for which Erasmus had been from the beginning

* * * * *

1 Ep 835:4, 11–13 (26 April 1518)
2 Ep 886:32–3
3 For the time of composition and the date of publication, see Bateman *Textual Travail* 220.

both advisor and advocate. Throughout 1519 there were distracting disputes, many of them related to Erasmus' advocacy of the humanities. The *Paraphrase* on the two Corinthian Epistles had barely been published when Jacques Masson (Latomus) published a book challenging the value claimed for languages in theological education.[4] A month before, Jan Briart of Ath, the vice-chancellor of the university, had by insinuation attacked Erasmus' *Encomium on Marriage*, bringing a response from Erasmus so swift that his *Apologia* could be added to Martens' edition of the *Paraphrase* on the two Corinthian Epistles.[5] A nasty quarrel with Edward Lee became full-blown in the course of 1519, resulting in Lee's publication of a book with accusations against Erasmus ranging from plagiarism to heresy.[6] It was a year in which, to his dismay, Erasmus found his name eventually associated with that of Luther. Aside from the distraction of controversies, Erasmus was also engaged in the preparation of an edition of the *Opera* of Cyprian.[7]

In spite of all, Erasmus was nevertheless able to complete the *Paraphrases* on the Pauline Epistles: the *Paraphrase on Galatians* was published in May; late in the year, and curiously out of canonical order, the *Paraphrases* on the Epistles from 1 Timothy through Philemon appeared; then, finally, in early 1520 the *Paraphrases* on the Epistles from Ephesians through 2 Thessalonians. Thus, in Erasmus' endeavour to publish *Paraphrases* on all the 'genuine' Pauline Epistles, the *Paraphrases* in this volume stand, after the *Paraphrase on Romans* in which the project had been only tentatively begun, as beginning and end.[8] Given the political context in which he wrote, the reader may expect to hear in these *Paraphrases* echoes of the controversies that engaged Erasmus during this tumultuous year.

The two sets of *Paraphrases* were dedicated to figures of ecclesiastical importance. After his arrival in Louvain in 1517, Erasmus frequently spoke of the great men who might become his patrons. On more than one occasion he associated in this way the names of the archbishop of Mainz, Albert

* * * * *

4 For the significance of Masson's book in Erasmus' relation with the theologians of Louvain in 1519, see the Introductory Note to the *Apology against the Dialogue of Latomus* CWE 71 32–6.
5 Cf Bateman *Textual Travail* 220. Briart gave the offending address on Feb 21; Erasmus' *Apologia* is dated 1 Mar 1519; cf Ep 946 introduction.
6 For the controversy, see CWE 72 xi–xxv.
7 Cf Ep 1000 introduction.
8 For Erasmus' perception that the *Paraphrases* on Ephesians through 2 Thessalonians marked the completion of his work on a well-defined corpus of New Testament literature, ie the genuine Pauline Epistles, see the dedicatory letter to Campeggi nn125, 126.

of Brandenburg, Erard de la Marck, prince-bishop of Liège, and Philip of Burgundy, prince-bishop of Utrecht.[9] To Albert he had dedicated the *Ratio verae theologiae*, published, as we have seen, in November 1518. De la Marck would receive the *Paraphrase* on the Corinthian Epistles.[10] Erasmus had made the first overtures to the bishop of Liège early in the autumn of 1517.[11] In December of that year he had sent the bishop a copy of his newly published *Paraphrase on Romans*, to which de la Marck responded warmly by inviting Erasmus to visit him.[12] Erasmus had come to believe not only that the bishop would offer patronage, but that de la Marck was committed to the principles of a liberal education as a foundation for theological studies. On October 21, 1518 Erasmus had written to his friend Hermannus Buschius that 'the bishop of Liège has a special love for scholars,' and a few days later he observed that 'that noble prince and saintly bishop Erard of Liège [seeks] to have none about him so much as those who have learning and purity of life to recommend them.'[13] Thus, in early 1519, Erard de la Marck would have seemed to Erasmus, who had so recently articulated his principles of theological education in the *Ratio*, an ecclesiastical prince entirely worthy to receive the dedication of the *Paraphrase* on 1 and 2 Corinthians.

As the hostile atmosphere in Louvain became increasingly threatening, Erasmus looked not only for generosity in patrons but for defence as well. When, in May of 1519, he took the initiative to establish by letter a relationship with Cardinal Campeggi, the papal legate in London, he may indeed have hoped for a voice to speak on his behalf for preferment in England.[14] His letter, however, is one of self-exculpation, pointing an accusatory finger at those who 'leave no stone unturned to suppress the humanities,' a campaign 'they conceal behind splendid maxims – Down with heresy, the church is in danger.'[15] Campeggi replied with a sympathetic and highly supportive letter, promising that if he could do anything to help Erasmus or his reputation, his assistance would not be found wanting in any respect, and sent Erasmus a diamond ring as a pledge of his good will. Erasmus was elated and promptly replied, observing that he had full

* * * * *

9 Cf eg Epp 783:22–5, 809:152.
10 Philip would have to wait until year's end for the dedication of the set of *Paraphrases* on 1 Timothy through Philemon.
11 Cf Ep 674:27–9.
12 Cf Epp 738, 746.
13 Cf Epp 735:5–7, 884:9, 894:10–12.
14 Cf Ep 961 introduction.
15 Ep 961:18–20

confidence in the cardinal, in whom he found a 'capital marriage of learning and wisdom.'[16] Campeggi, recalled to Rome that very summer, invited
Erasmus to dine with him when he passed through Bruges on his way to
Italy in late August. Little more than two weeks before this dinner meeting, Erasmus had, with the hostility of Louvain in mind, written to Pope
Leo x to request that he order the supporters of the old scholastic and the
new humanistic learning to cease their hostile wrangling and to replace it
with respectful dialogue.[17] Erasmus became increasingly insecure in Louvain after the condemnation of Luther's views by the faculty of theology
on 7 November 1519,[18] and in his mind it became ever more urgent that
the hostile voices of opponents be suppressed. Hence, he took the occasion
of the publication of his *Paraphrases* on Ephesians through 2 Thessalonians
to seek through the dedicatory letter the support of a powerful friend in
Rome, a cardinal sympathetic to the new learning, who might be induced
to plead once more with the pope to quell the hostilities in Louvain.[19]

The *Paraphrases* are, as Erasmus acknowledged, a kind of commentary,
in which the biblical text is clarified by a process of expansion.[20] Inevitably,
in the process of expansion and clarification, the interpretation of the paraphrast emerges. Indeed, for the modern reader it is the interpretation of
Erasmus that will in the first instance command our attention. We are likely
to read the paraphrases in this volume asking how Erasmus speaks to his
contemporaries, perhaps even how he speaks to us. In the biblical text the
two letters to the Corinthians touch on a wide range of subjects with unavoidably practical implications, and they do so with the deep personal in-
volvement of both author (Paul) and addressee (the Corinthian Christians).
They are consequently fertile ground for the paraphrast to clarify the text
in a way that draws the text into the reader's contemporary world. Thus
we can detect the Erasmian voice speaking on a rich array of subjects significant in his own day, and not irrelevant to ours. In this *Paraphrase* we
observe Erasmus' familiar analysis of discord perceived as an evil arising
from the passions, which Erasmus understands as diseases – avarice, ambition, lust, and slander. We learn of the prescription for the healing of these
diseases: to have one's understanding purified through faith, one's emotions corrected through love. The problem of marriage in the Corinthian
church invited an interpretation of 1 Corinthians 7 that anticipates Eras-

* * * * *

16 Cf Epp 995:72–4, 996:13.
17 Cf Ep 1007:121–32.
18 Cf Ep 1030 n7.
19 On the dedicatory letter see the Translators' Note xvii.
20 Cf CWE 42 xv–xvi, and the Translators' Note xviii and xxiv.

mus' response to criticisms of his own publication in 1518 of the *Encomium on Marriage* : celibacy is to be extolled; nevertheless, celibacy is only for those who have the strength for it. On the question of the meaning of the Eucharist, a subject that would within a decade hold a central place in theological debate, the interpreter's ambiguity leads to no definitive answer, but offers instead a collage of images: the Eucharist is presented as a mystery, a mystical feast, a memorial, a fellowship meal. We find in this *Paraphrase* subtle indications of Erasmus' proclivity to rationalize: in 'clarifying' the gifts of the Spirit, for example, there is a suggestion that the gift of tongues is a gift of languages learned for the exposition of Scripture. Here, too, we recognize one of the chief foci of Erasmian theology, for the paraphrases on the two Corinthian letters repeatedly reinforce Erasmus' deeply held conviction that the church is the body of Christ, into which the members are grafted through baptism, and who are intended to practice here the immortality they will eventually share with the immortal Christ, the head to which the members are united.

The image of the church as the body of Christ, the images of 'head and members' and of 'grafting' become thematic likewise in the *Paraphrases* on Ephesians through 2 Thessalonians. In these *Paraphrases* also we hear frequently of the indispensable theological virtues of faith and charity. The text of these Epistles required Erasmus to articulate a theology of the Trinity to some degree, and one can observe the care with which the co-equality of Father, Son, and Holy Spirit is expressed without sacrificing the Erasmian insistence that the Father is the source of all, including the Son, through whom, along with the Holy Spirit, the Father works. The great Christological passage in Philippians 2 reflects in paraphrase the Erasmian insistence on the humanity of Christ. Of equal interest in the *Paraphrases* on these Epistles is the portrayal of the apostle Paul as the suffering servant. He is, to be sure, portrayed also in the *Paraphrase* on the two Corinthian letters as the apostle who suffers, but there biographical details tend to come to the fore, and the suffering apostle jostles alongside the accommodating Proteus, the triumphing warrior, the mystic visionary. In the Ephesians– 2 Thessalonians set of *Paraphrases*, we are given to understand more fully the theological rationale of suffering: to suffer is the mark of an apostle, as an imitator of Christ; moreover, since head and members share the same life, the Apostle's suffering in some way ·complements the suffering of Christ.

If the *Paraphrases* in this volume offer a rich field for the exploration of Erasmus' theology, they also provide the devotee of Scripture with interesting, sometimes imaginatively fertile, interpretations of problematic images and expressions in the Pauline text. What, for example, are the 'gold, silver, precious stones,' the 'wood, hay, straw' that might be used to build upon the foundation of Christ (1 Cor 3:12)? How does a believing spouse consecrate an unbelieving partner (1 Cor 7:14)? What was effected by the 'baptism for the dead' (1 Cor 15:29)? What is the 'thorn in the flesh' that afflicted Paul (2 Cor 12:7)? What is the 'mystery' that in marriage 'refers to Christ and the church' (Eph 5:32)? What was the 'equality with God' that Christ refused to grasp (Phil 2:6)? Who is the 'restrainer' in the apocalyptic events foretold in the second letter to the Thessalonians (2:7)? Erasmus could not escape these questions in the course of paraphrasing. His solutions to the problems arrest, if they do not always satisfy.

Finally, the *Paraphrases* in this volume, as in others, are enhanced as a literary endeavour by the occasional intrusion of the paraphrast in a manner so abrupt and with a voice so clear that the paraphrast becomes quite unmasked. The effect is to bring to the narrative an element of surprise, and to the reader delight in the evident humour. The fictional names of divisive parties in the paraphrase on 1 Corinthians 3 point unmistakably and with a certain mocking humour to the monastic orders of Erasmus' day. More subtly, perhaps, the interpretation of 'making melody to the Lord with all your heart' (Eph 5:19) as 'raising psalms not with the unbecoming shouts usual with intoxicated people' may be read as a sly jab at the contemporary church music that Erasmus elsewhere so roundly berated.[21] And the modern reader will not refrain from a genial smile at the anachronism when the paraphrastic Paul reminds the Corinthians (1 Cor 14) that 'tongues' belonged especially to the period of the 'primitive church,' and so were no longer to be prized by them!

I take this opportunity to express my thanks to Professors O'Mara and Phillips for their careful and conscientious work over a period of some years, and for their exemplary cooperation with their editor in working through difficult problems in translation and annotation. I have greatly appreciated the generous support for my work given by both Dickinson College, Carlisle, Pennsylvania and the University of Saskatchewan, and I join with the translators in gratefully acknowledging the many and outstanding services of the University of Toronto Press in bringing this volume to completion and publication.

RDS

* * * * *

21 See the paraphrase on Eph 5:19 with n30.

Translators' Note

The *Paraphrases* contained in this volume represent two separate publications of Erasmus in his larger project of paraphrasing the New Testament. The *Paraphrase* on 1 and 2 Corinthians, dedicated to Erard de la Marck in a prefatory letter,[1] was first published in February 1519 by Martens in Louvain. The *Paraphrases* on Ephesians, Philippians, Colossians, and 1 and 2 Thessalonians probably appeared early the next year. In the dedicatory letter to Lorenzo Campeggi, 5 February 1520, Erasmus refers to his *Paraphrases* on 'the five Pauline Epistles which remain out of all his genuine letters, completed in one recent spell of work.'[2] This collection was, perhaps, first published by Martens also although no copy of such an edition has come to our attention. Two Froben editions from March 1520 are the earliest of the versions we have included in our collation.[3]

* * * * *

1 Ep 916 (2–18 below).
2 Ep 1062:189–91 (cf 295–6 below). The *Paraphrases* on the Epistles to the Romans and Galatians appeared in 1517 and 1519 respectively and are translated in CWE 42.
3 The exact date and the printer of the first publication of the *Paraphrases* on Ephesians to Thessalonians remain uncertain. The earliest known editions are those of Froben printed in March 1520, but some scholars suppose that an earlier edition was published by Martens. Of the two Froben editions of 1520, the earlier is the quarto edition in roman type; the later an octavo in italics, dated by a colophon at the end of Colossians to March 1520. It corrected some errors of fact and grammar that appeared in the other gathering, evidence that it is the later of the two. Bietenholz (CWE 7 195) thinks that a Martens first edition is probable, but that one produced 'elsewhere in the Netherlands' is also possible. Martens was subsequently able to produce the first edition of the remaining *Paraphrases* on 1 and 2 Peter and Jude (later in 1520), and Hebrews (early 1521). For a fuller discussion of the date of composition and the history of the printed text of the *Paraphrases*, see Sir Roger Mynors 'The Publication of the Latin *Paraphrases*' CWE 42 xx–xxix; also John Bateman CWE

Prefaced to each *Paraphrase* is an 'Argument' or summary by Erasmus. In his *Novum Instrumentum* (1516) Erasmus had printed the same meagre Latin Argument as appears in some Vulgate copies and in some commentaries before the text of the relevant book. These were traditionally brief, elementary summaries. See for example the Argument of Colossians in *Novum Instrumentum Faksimile-Neudruck* ed Heinz Holeczek (Stuttgart-Bad Cannstatt 1986) 101 or that prefaced to Philippians in Nicholas of Lyra's *Postilla*. But Erasmus published his own lengthy Argument for the *Paraphrase on Romans* in 1517 and composed a set of Arguments for the rest of the Epistles in the fall of 1518. These were published first with the *Ratio verae theologiae* in November 1518 and printed in the 1519 edition of his *Novum Testamentum*, each as a preface to its Epistle. Only the *Paraphrasis in Romanos* had been published by the fall of 1518; consequently the new Arguments were available for all his other *Paraphrases*, and were usually published with them. The 1520 *Paraphrases* on Ephesians through 2 Thessalonians are exceptional in not having Arguments prefixed to each Epistle; the Arguments for the *Paraphrases* on these Epistles appear in the first 'collected' edition of 1521: *The Paraphrases of Erasmus of Rotterdam on all the authentic Epistles of Paul and on all the Canonical [Epistles] carefully revised by the author and enhanced by marginal notes.*

In accordance with the editorial practice of CWE, we have translated the 1532 Froben text of the *Paraphrases*,[4] the last edition published during Erasmus' lifetime with significant editorial revision. Against this 1532 edition we collated Martens' *editio princeps* of 1 and 2 Corinthians, Froben's 1520 editions of Ephesians through Thessalonians, and five subsequent editions by Froben of the collected *Paraphrases* on the Epistles that appeared during Erasmus' lifetime, including the 1534 octavo, which, although subsequent to the 1532 folio, reveals only minor alterations from it.[5] In our notes

* * * * *

44 xiii–xiv, ASD VII-6 9–12, and 'Textual Travail' 213–63.

4 *Tomus secundus continens Paraphrasim D. Erasmi Roterodami in omneis epistolas apostolicas* (Basel 1532). This *tomus secundus* (ie volume two) was a revision of the 1523 Froben edition of Erasmus' *Paraphrases* on the New Testament Epistles; its companion, volume one, the *Paraphrases* on the Gospels and Acts, appeared in 1535.

5 While the 1538 and 1540 editions were printed after Erasmus' death, they may include some changes proposed by him. See Bateman 'Textual Travail' 247. Hence these editions have not been excluded from our attention. The translators consulted the following versions identified where possible according to the catalogue of Irmgard Bezzel *Erasmusdrucke des 16. Jahrhunderts in bayerischen Bibliotheken* (Stuttgart 1979) 36, 394–430:

we have recorded all significant variants and additions; the most important
by far are the clarifications and expansions that appeared in the 1532 revision itself. We have also noted the few variants or corruptions that appeared after Erasmus' death in the 1538 edition, the 1540 Basel *Opera omnia*, or in the Leiden edition of 1703–6 (commonly referred to as LB), which,
although it has no textual authority, is at the moment the most easily consulted edition of the Latin text of Erasmus' *Paraphrases*.[6]

Since each new edition constituted a new typesetting, minor changes
could be introduced at every step. Some of these seem deliberate, consistent, and minor, for example, ways of spelling certain words such as *car-
itas/charitas, desiderium/desyderium*; punctuation marks; replacement of one
demonstrative pronoun by another. Slight emendations in grammar and the
insertion of conjunctive adverbs for the sake of clarity or emphasis also fall
into this category. Many of the changes included in Froben's first collected
edition in 1521 are of this deliberate and minor type.

There is, however, one significant exception: the dedicatory letter (Ep
1062) addressed to Cardinal Lorenzo Campeggi. A first sketch in the form
of a shorter letter was published in the 1520 editions. It appears as an appendix in this volume (475–8). The longer and more elaborate 1521 version
of the dedication is printed, with italics added to indicate changes in the
text, immediately before the *Paraphrases* on Ephesians through Thessalonians. Allen acknowledges that the differences between the two versions are
so great that 'it is not possible to fuse them satisfactorily' (Allen Ep 1062
introduction).

Other changes result from typesetters' errors – either misreading or
'correcting' copy texts – or they are necessitated by previous typesetters'
mistakes.[7] For the purposes of this volume, such minor changes have been

* * * * *

a/ Louvain: Martens (1 and 2 Corinthians only) 1519 4° (Bezzel 1434);
b/ Basel: Froben (Ephesians–Thessalonians only) 1520 4° roman type (Bezzel
1445); 1520 8° italic type (Bezzel 1446);
c/ Basel: Froben (Corinthians and Ephesians–Thessalonians) 1521 8° (Bezzel
1526); 1522 2° (Bezzel 1469a = 1528); 1523 (*Paraphrases* II) 8° (Bezzel 1499a);
1523 (*Paraphrases* II) 2° (Bezzel 1500); 1532 (*Paraphrases* II) 2° (Bezzel 1505);
1534 (*Paraphrases* II) 8° (Bodleian Antiq. f.G.S. 1534); 1538 (Paraphrases II) 2°
(Bezzel 1508); 1540 *Omnia opera* VII 2° (Bezzel 11); 1703–6 *Omnia opera* LB VII
6 With the publication in 1997 of ASD VII-6, critical editions of the *Paraphrases*
have begun to appear.
7 Eg the typesetter(s) for the 1520 editions of the *Paraphrase on Colossians* apparently misread (or 'corrected') *mens* for *meus* at 4:8; the 1521 edition emends
properly to *meus*. On the other hand, a corruption apparently takes place in

briefly noted wherever they produce a difference in English translation; otherwise, they have been ignored.

Major changes both in content and in style appear primarily in the 1532 edition. Modifications in diction that Erasmus here introduces seem directed to a more pleasing literary style. There is, however, a number of longer additions, some extending to several lines, that appear to be doctrinally based and may have been suggested by Erasmus' work in related studies.[8] They are often aimed at clarifying or emphasizing the orthodoxy of a paraphrase that has been brought under suspicion by Erasmus' critics.

Erasmus describes the paraphrase as a more discursive statement of Paul's message in which he intended to convey what Paul might have written if he had been addressing mature Christians in pure Latin. Instead, Erasmus says, Paul's audience consisted of recent converts incapable of understanding anything more than hints of the Christian mysteries, since Paul wrote in a Greek highly affected by the Hebrew idiom. Erasmus notes the concentrated, almost elliptical, even strange language of the Epistles and hopes to make the good news more accessible. He aims, that is, to make Paul's text clearer by elaborating the Apostle's thoughts, and to make it more attractive by having Paul convey his thoughts in a smoother and more highly embellished Latin style.[9] The paraphrase can function, then, as a kind of commentary on the biblical text – or, rather, as an expansion of the text in what is ostensibly Paul's own 'voice,' but a highly amplified

* * * * *

the paraphrase on Col 1:22 when *sui* (in all editions from 1519 to 1534) is misread as (or 'corrected' to) *filii* in *1538*. The change is retained by LB. Sometimes variants were produced simply from careless typography, as when *domum* was set for *donum* in the 1520 editions of the paraphrase on Eph 2:19–20 and then corrected in 1521. In our notes, italicized dates referring to the *Paraphrases* and *Annotations* are an abbreviation for 'the edition(s) of' the years(s) designated.

8 See, for example, a *1532* addition to the paraphrase on 1 Thess 4:15 and chapter 4 n25, which may be related to the fact that Chrysostom's homilies (as distinguished from the excerpts quoted in Oecumenius or the *Catenae graecorum*, and the abridged version contained in the exposition by Theophylact) were published at Verona in 1529. There is, however, no conclusive evidence that Erasmus used the Verona edition for the 1532 *Paraphrases*. See n21 below.

9 See Ep 710 CWE 42 2–3, the dedicatory letter for the *Paraphrase on Romans*. For fuller discussion of the aims and style of Erasmus' *Paraphrases*, see 'The *Paraphrases* of Erasmus: Origin and Character' CWE 42 xi–xix; Bateman 'From Soul to Soul' 7–16. The dedicatory letters prefacing the separate publications are fruitful sources of evidence for Erasmus' objectives in publishing the *Paraphrases*.

and eloquently Latin one. The Paul of the *Paraphrases* writes Erasmian Latin.[10]

The *Paraphrase* on Paul's first letter to the Corinthians provides an exceptional case in point for the way the voices of Paul and Erasmus merge. First Corinthians is notable for its condemnation of divisive pride and its consistent call for harmony and cooperation within the early church, in particular for the accommodation of different roles, needs, and gifts. These were precisely the emphases Erasmus found useful in his perception and criticism of theological quibbling, pharisaical legalism, and moral failure in early sixteenth-century Christianity. The dedicatory letter prefacing the Corinthian *Paraphrase* points frequently to the extreme contrast between Paul's self-effacing ministry to the needs of early congregations and the corrupt, self-serving actions of many churchmen in Erasmus' own day.[11] Occasionally the Paul of Erasmus' *Paraphrase* even appears to address sixteenth-century Christendom directly, as in an only slightly veiled allusion to contemporary monastic orders as examples of ecclesiastical division.[12] More often the *Paraphrase* simply magnifies both Paul's critique of philosophical quibbling and pharisaical legalism, and his corresponding praise of Christian unity and agreement. Thus, the simple greeting of 1 Cor 1:3 becomes in paraphrase an eloquent homily on Christian concord and irenicism, perhaps even more appropriate for the sixteenth century than for the first.[13]

The pastoral and theological elaborations of Erasmus' *Paraphrases* are everywhere grounded in the scholarship of his *Annotations* on the text of the New Testament. The *Annotations*, first published in 1516 and then gradually and extensively expanded in four subsequent editions, discuss and correct passages in the Vulgate translation and defend the changes Erasmus made in his new Latin translation of the Greek text.[14] These changes

* * * * *

10 On *persona* in the *Paraphrases* – Paul's or Erasmus' – see CWE 42 xvi–xvii; CWE 44 xvii–xviii; Sider 'Historical Imagination'; and Jane E. Phillips '*Sub evangelistae persona*: The Speaking Voice in Erasmus' *Paraphrase on Luke*' in Pabel and Vessey *Holy Scripture Speaks* 85–109 and 127–50.

11 This contrast is a theme throughout Ep 916, the dedicatory letter, but reaches something of a climax near the end. See 15–16 below.

12 See the paraphrase on 1 Cor 3:4 with n10.

13 See the paraphrase on 1 Cor 1:3. For Erasmus' insistence on harmony and consensus among believers, see Hilmar M. Pabel, 'The Peaceful People of Christ; the Irenic Ecclesiology of Erasmus of Rotterdam' in *Erasmus' Vision of the Church* ed Hilmar M. Pabel, Sixteenth Century Essays and Studies 33 (1995) 57–93.

14 For the text of Erasmus' Latin and Greek *Novum Testamentum* containing the

sparked numerous theological and ecclesiastical controversies into which the *Paraphrases* were immediately drawn.[15] We have attempted to identify in our notes significant parallels in language and thought between the paraphrases and the annotations on specific verses, especially where Erasmus' interpretations triggered controversies. The *Annotations* on 1 Corinthians, for example, parallel the *Paraphrase* with frequent condemnations of divisive factions and legalism within the church.[16] Controversies involving both the *Annotations* and the *Paraphrase* arose concerning, among other topics in 1 Corinthians, the nature and language of the Eucharistic liturgy, the efficacy of the baptismal rite, the relative virtues of marriage and celibacy, the prohibition of divorce, the nature and purpose of dietary regulations, the remuneration of clergy, and the character and time of the resurrection.[17]

* * * * *

Epistles paraphrased in this volume, see ASD VI-3; for the Latin text of the *Annotations*, see LB VI; for the annotations on 1 and 2 Corinthians, see also ASD VI-8. The *Annotations* were greatly expanded in four subsequent editions as Erasmus noticed further insights relevant to the text in his readings of the Fathers, or as he required further patristic sources to substantiate his own defence. In *Erasmus' Annotations on the New Testament: Acts–Romans–I and II Corinthians* ed Anne Reeve and M.A. Screech, Studies in the History of Christian Thought 42 (Leiden 1990) and *Erasmus' Annotations on the New Testament: Galatians to the Apocalypse* ed Anne Reeve, introduction M.A. Screech, Studies ... Thought 52 (Leiden 1993), the first four editions appear collated against a facsimile edition of the final 1535 edition, with changes and additions marked. For a discussion of their origin, sources, purposes, style, and repercussions, see Rummel *Erasmus' Annotations* and P.F. Hovingh ASD VI-6 1–35.
More generally, on Erasmus within the context of the theology of his time, see also Erika Rummel 'Theology of Erasmus' in *The Cambridge Companion to Reformation Theology* ed David Bagchi and David C. Steinmetz (Cambridge 2004) 28–38.

15 The controversies fill the final two volumes (IX and X) of the LB *Opera omnia*. For a survey of the attacks by Erasmus' critics and his responses, see Erika Rummel 'A Reader's Guide to Erasmus' Controversies' *Erasmus in English* 12 (1983) 13–19; also Rummel *Catholic Critics*. In the *Responsio ad epistolam Alberti Pii*, Erasmus' response to the criticisms of his *Paraphrases* includes the restatement both of his purpose and of the precedents for biblical paraphrase that justify his work in this genre. See CWE 84 74–83.

16 See eg the annotations on 1 Cor 1:10 (*ut idipsum dicatis*), 3:12 (*foenum, stipulam*) and 15:51 (*omnes quidem resurgemus*), and 1 Cor chapters 3 n20, 9 n6, and 15 n71.

17 On the Eucharist eg see 1 Cor chapters 10 n28 and 11 nn29, 31, and 34; on baptism, see 1 Cor Argument n5 and 1 Cor chapter 6 n26; on marriage and divorce, see 1 Cor chapter 7 nn26 and 73; on dietary regulations, see 1 Cor chapter 8 n25; on priests' remuneration, see 1 Cor chapter 9 n22; on the resurrection, see 1 Cor chapter 15 n71.

Nowhere in the *Paraphrase* on this Epistle does Erasmus back away from the points he defends in the *Annotations*, although he frequently makes partial accommodation for words and phrases of the Vulgate text that have specifically been rejected in the *Annotations*.[18]

In suggesting sources, controversies, and parallels connected with Erasmus' *Paraphrases*, we have been guided in the first place by his *Annotations*, where Erasmus establishes the scholarly evidence for the Greek text and reveals his growing familiarity with the extant and available commentaries on Paul's letters. The *Annotations* also reveal Erasmus' extensive knowledge of classical Greek and Latin literature and his conviction that the classical texts reflect not only a language but also a world of thought that is relevant to the interpretation of the Scriptures. The *Paraphrases* contain many echoes of Aristotle and Cicero among others; the most obvious and apparent of these echoes are indicated in the notes.

The most pervasive influences on the *Paraphrases*, however, seem to have been Erasmus' favorite patristic commentators. The Latin authority who seems to inform the paraphrases in this volume most frequently is the fourth-century commentator 'Ambrosiaster'[19] whom Erasmus, following tradition, at first identified with Ambrose. On the Greek side a comparable service is rendered by Theophylact,[20] whose teaching is largely an

* * * * *

18 See eg 1 Cor chapters 5 n11, 6 nn2 and 30, and 14 n52. The *Paraphrases* differ from the *Annotations* in being primarily for non-specialists: to enable the ordinary reader to engage in direct conversation with the biblical author as with a friend. Because the paraphrase is continuous, the paraphrast may not omit anything of substance, nor may he simply restate opposing positions, without choosing between them, as is possible in the *Annotations*. Recent scholarship has sharpened attention to the word 'paraphrase,' distinguishing between the explanatory / exegetical function and that of emulation / imitation. In Erasmus' *Paraphrases* both purposes are present as he reformulates the substance, in the 'voice' of the biblical author, in order to clarify the meaning of the biblical text. See Jean-François Cottier 'La paraphrase latine, de Quintilien à Erasme' *Revue des études latines* 80 (2002) 237–52.

19 Throughout his *Annotations* Erasmus refers to the writer of a set of commentaries on Paul's letters as 'Ambrosius,' although in the preface to the fourth volume of his 1527 edition of Ambrose, he questions the ascription of these commentaries to Ambrose. The name 'Ambrosiaster' has been used since Erasmus' time. On Ambrosiaster, see H.J. Vogels ed CSEL 81/1 ix–xvii and A. Souter *The Earliest Latin Commentaries on the Epistles of St Paul* (Oxford 1927) 37–49.

20 The Greek commentary on the Pauline Epistles by the eleventh-century Bulgarian bishop Theophylact (whom Erasmus at first called Vulgarius) was available to Erasmus in Basel when he was preparing his 1516 edition of the New Testament. See ASD VI-3 3. Erasmus also knew this commentary through a Latin

abridgement and systematization of material drawn from the *Homilies* of John Chrysostom. For 1 Corinthians Erasmus had, in Basel, access as well to Chrysostom's homilies at least as early as 1516, when he was preparing his first edition of the New Testament. However, he apparently did not have Chrysostom ready to hand either in Greek or in Latin translation while he was working on the early editions of the *Paraphrases*.[21] Thus, it might be safe to assume that Chrysostom's influence on the early editions of the *Paraphrases* was largely indirect, that is, through the commentary of his follower and systematizer, Theophylact. That Erasmus exercises independence in following these sources can be seen, for example, in his devotional treatment of Philippians 2 as compared with the theological arguments directed against heretics that are set forth in both Ambrosiaster and Theophylact.

In addition to these two pervasive influences, there are close parallels in specific passages to Jerome (whose commentary on Ephesians, for example, is the main source for much of Erasmus' *Paraphrase* on that Epistle), to Augustine (whose Letter 149 is an important source for the *Paraphrase* on chapter 2 of Colossians) and to Origen among the Fathers, as well as to the *Gloss*[22] and to the *Postilla* of Nicholas of Lyra among authors of the medieval

* * * * *

translation by Porsena, which had been published among works attributed to Athanasius, but recognized by Erasmus as early as 1518 as Theophylact's. See CWE 56 15 n25 and Rummel *Erasmus' Annotations* 36–7. See also Ep 916:450–5 (18 below).

21 Erasmus attests that for his *Novum instrumentum* (1516) he had access in Basel to a manuscript of Chrysostom's *Homilies* on 1 Corinthians; cf the annotation on 1 Cor 1:2 (*ipsorum*). By 1527 he had acquired manuscripts of the *Homilies* on both 1 and 2 Corinthians (Ep 1195:17–18). It is possible that for the 1532 edition of the *Paraphrases* he also had a copy of the *Homilies* on the Pauline Epistles published by Gian Matteo Giberti in Verona in 1529, although he had still not seen the book by August 1531 (Allen Ep 2526:9–12). On the availability of Chrysostom's homilies as a source for Erasmus see Robert D. Sider '"Searching the Scriptures": John Chrysostom in the New Testament Scholarship of Erasmus' in *Within the Perfection of Christ: Essays ... in honor of Martin Schrag* ed Terry L. Brensinger and E. Morris Sider (Nappanee, IN 1990) 83–105.

22 *Glossa Ordinaria*, the major scriptural commentary that arose during the twelfth and thirteenth centuries, is a compilation of shorter (interlinear) and longer (marginal) comments on biblical texts drawn from the writings of earlier patristic and medieval Christian exegetes. 'Always a library text,' it was 'surprisingly stable' as the 'definitive reference edition' of the Bible, according to Margaret T. Gibson 'The Glossed Bible' in *Biblia Latina cum Glossa Ordinaria* Facsimile Reprint of the *editio princeps* by Adolph Rusch of Strassburg 1480/1 (Turnhout 1992) vii–xi. For the sequence of printed editions detailing some of their features, see Karlfried Froehlich 'The Printed Gloss' ibidem xii–xxvi.

period. In synthesizing the teaching of his sources, Erasmus often manages to include what is presented in them as interpretations that differ from one another, and sometimes are even mutually contradictory.[23]

In accordance with the objective of CWE to produce a reliable and readable translation, we have endeavored to be faithful to the tone and style as well as to the content of Erasmus' text. Some of his longer Latin sentences, if they could not be managed easily and clearly in English syntax, have been broken up into shorter units. Wherever Erasmus uses particular Latin words or phrases with consistent theological or ecclesiastical significance, we have attempted to imitate his consistency. Our notes discuss the most important of these terms, such as *mysterium* 'mystery,' *sacramentum* 'sacrament,' and *professio* 'profession.'[24]

Among the other features of his *Paraphrases* to which we have paid particular attention is his use of personal pronouns. Erasmus' annotations at several points indicate that he is careful to note exactly the reading of the Greek text, particularly in reference to the persons of the Trinity.[25] For this reason we have observed the same care. On occasion Erasmus elaborates over an extended passage an image latent or adumbrated in the Pauline text (or suggested in its Chrysostom-Theophylact exposition). In these situations his delight in language and his art in expression are manifest.[26] Paraphrasing for Erasmus is essentially an art of amplification, clarification, and elaboration – an art he learned from his study of rhetorical theory and from his wide reading in Greek and Latin authors, and which he describes fully in his own work on rhetoric, *De copia*.[27]

* * * * *

In the annotation on Phil 4:9 (*haec cogitate et agite*), Erasmus reports with remarkable precision that at a time when he was residing in the countryside near Brussels for the sake of his health he was provided with a very early, perhaps a first edition, of the ordinary and interlinear *Gloss* from a particular Carthusian monastery nearby.

23 See eg his paraphrases on Phil 4:3 with n3; 1 Thess 1:3 with n7; and 2 Thess 2:10 with n19.
24 See the Index of Greek and Latin Words Cited.
25 Regarding Erasmus' concern with accurate translation of texts denoting relationships among the persons of the Trinity and his awareness of possible ambiguities in the Greek text, see eg the annotation on 1 Cor 1:3 (*a deo patre nostro et domino Iesu*).
26 Note eg the image of running a race in the paraphrase on Phil 3:12–16.
27 See *De copia* 1–8 CWE 24 295–302. Jacques Chomarat has studied the rhetoric of Erasmus' *Paraphrases* in connection with *De copia* in *Grammaire et rhétorique chez Erasme* (Paris 1981). Where Chomarat comments specifically on Erasmus' rhetorical style in the *Paraphrase on First Corinthians*, an indication will be found in the notes to those passages.

In our translation we have endeavoured to respect the figures of speech and of thought that illumine Erasmus' *Paraphrases*. Not all of the figures of speech transfer readily into non-inflected English. Nevertheless, where it is evident that Erasmus was adorning his text with rhetorical highlights, we have attempted to imitate his foray into the grand style.

Within a paraphrase on a passage, the proportion devoted to developing an idea sometimes reflects the extent of controversy the passage has engendered in times past; more often, it shows Erasmus' perception of the importance of the passage to intelligent living of the gospel faith. A third determinant of length may be related to time constrictions on the work of paraphrasing. It seems that as he nears the end of each *Paraphrase* and perhaps each collection of *Paraphrases*, Erasmus exercises greater economy in his expression.[28]

Our notes have several purposes: to point out (and occasionally explain) major textual variants and additions; to indicate the most important patristic and medieval sources that seem to have suggested interpretations to Erasmus; to cite biblical, classical, and later sources and parallels for language and ideas; to point, although not exhaustively, to parallels in Erasmus' other works and in those of some of his contemporaries, including Valla's *Collatio* as well as the later *Annotationes* that was discovered and edited by Erasmus; to note the passages that have given rise to public and dangerous criticism or in which Erasmus has attempted to respond to criticism and debate; to examine in context the connotations and denotation of specific words. Sometimes Erasmus launches out on what appears to be a tangent having only a tenuous connection with the text he is paraphrasing; we have endeavoured to tease out the connection in Erasmus' thinking that prompts such apparent digressions. We have not endeavoured to reproduce the information of a modern scriptural commentary; however, when Erasmus' paraphrase on a particular passage touches upon an issue of longstanding dispute concerning the biblical text or its interpretation, we have not hesitated to refer the reader to representative modern commentaries.

References in the notes are generally adapted to the chapter and verse numeration of the *Revised Standard Version* of the Bible. For the *Paraphrase*

* * * * *

28 In this regard we might note that, although Paul's Thessalonian Epistles closely approximate in length the Epistle to the Ephesians, the length of the *Paraphrase on Ephesians* is over eighteen LB columns, while that of the *Paraphrases* on 1 and 2 Thessalonians is only twelve LB columns. Similarly, although 2 Corinthians is approximately two-thirds as long as 1 Corinthians, the *Paraphrase* on 2 Corinthians is less than half the length of the *Paraphrase* on 1 Corinthians.

on Ephesians, citations from Jerome's commentary are identified by both the traditional divisions of his text in PL and the RSV reference. We assume that the *lemmata* in Erasmus' *Annotations* point to a contemporary Vulgate text he was following.[29] Translations of substantial passages in classical texts are taken from the Loeb Classical Library.

Both translators have read the entire translation and the notes at several stages. Edward A. Phillips translated and annotated the *Paraphrase* on 1 Corinthians; Mechtilde O'Mara, the *Paraphrases* on Ephesians, Philippians, Colossians, and 1 and 2 Thessalonians. The *Paraphrase* on 2 Corinthians was translated and annotated jointly by O'Mara and Phillips.

ACKNOWLEDGMENTS

In the course of the research and writing of CWE 43, assistance has come in many forms and the translators of this volume are grateful for it all. We acknowledge the help of colleagues and friends who have provided resources or discussed issues arising from the text, in particular we wish to thank James K. McConica, R.M. Schoeffel, John J. Bateman, Richard M. Toporoski, and especially Robert D. Sider, the editor of this volume, who has kept up a lively correspondence full of learned suggestions.

Institutional support too has come from a variety of sources: from the University of St Michael's College and the Pontifical Institute of Mediaeval Studies, which have fostered our research and provided study space for both contributors to this volume; from the Librarians Jonathan Bengtson, James K. Farge, and their respective staffs, especially Noël McFerren and Carmen Cachia, Caroline Suma and William Edwards; and from the Directors and Curators of the Centre for Reformation and Renaissance Studies at Victoria University. In addition, the University of Toronto Classics Department has facilitated visits to the Libraries of Cambridge University, the Vatican Library, and the Bibliothèque Nationale by granting the Norwood Award for Travel to Mechtilde O'Mara. Edward A. Phillips benefited from access to special collections at the University of Chicago's Regenstein Library, the Folger Shakespeare Library, and the Catholic University of Amer-

* * * * *

29 Exactly what Vulgate text Erasmus used is not known. References to the Vulgate in this volume refer to the text of the Vulgate printed in his 1527 edition of the *Novum Testamentum*. The lemmata of his *Annotations*, however, do not always match this text, as Andrew J. Brown noted in ASD VI-2 4. See Jane Phillips' note 'Erasmus Biblical Text' CWE 72 xvii–xix. See also CWE 44 Translator's Note n20. For lists of the biblical manuscripts Erasmus consulted, see ASD VI-2 10, VI-3 18, VI-5 5–8, ASD VI-6 2–4.

ica's Mullen Library, from research space at Grinnell College's Burling Library, and from the college's funding for research travel and leaves.

On a personal level, I thank my family and friends, the Congregation of the Sisters of St Joseph of Toronto of which I am a member, and especially the late Sister Geraldine Thompson CSJ who shared with me her enthusiasm for the study of Erasmus.   (Mechtilde O'Mara)

I am most grateful as well to the Grinnell College Classics Department for fostering a supportive community within which both teaching and learning thrive, and to my family for its nurture and patience during the many months apart that this project has required.   (Edward A. Phillips Jr)

In preparing the text Carla DeSantis and George Bevan provided valuable assistance. Finally the volume owes much to the careful eye and sound sense of style of our copyeditor Douglas Adamson and to the helpful advice of Mary Baldwin; and it is a pleasure to acknowledge the highly professional work of the typesetters, Lynn Browne and Philippa Matheson.

MO'M and EAP Jr

PARAPHRASE ON FIRST CORINTHIANS

Paraphrasis in epistolam Pauli ad Corinthios priorem

translated and annotated by
EDWARD A. PHILLIPS Jr

DEDICATORY LETTER

TO THE RIGHT HONOURABLE PRINCE AND RIGHT REVEREND PRELATE ERARD DE LA MARCK,[1] BISHOP OF LIÈGE, NOW A CARDINAL,[2] FROM ERASMUS OF ROTTERDAM, GREETING

Often had I heard your Highness' praises sung, both in letters from many correspondents and in conversation, as of a person richly endowed with every quality and every gift that could be thought worthy of a prince; but while enjoying a few days of your society[3] I found you such that my friends seemed to have given a niggardly and stinted – I would almost call it a jealous – account of your felicity or (it would be truer to say) ours. And so the situation was reversed. You, who had long been fired by the kind words of several friends with an excessive wish to meet me, must (I think) once we had met have begun to modify your high opinion and will take the first opportunity of protesting to those who had tried to sell you a small fly like myself as a great elephant;[4] I on the other hand, who felt already a considerable desire to see you, once given the opportunity to observe you at close quarters was quite carried away by love and admiration for your great qualities and was soon making my protest to those who had given me such a niggardly picture of you.

This is not the place to tell of the historic eminence of your family and your pedigree of illustrious ancestors, of the wide extent of your territories, or of the heroic aspect of your physical presence, which bespeaks a splendid prince even from afar, although I know full well that things like these help to set off your gifts of personality. I would more gladly dwell on

* * * * *

1 Erasmus' dedicatory letter (Ep 916) for the *Paraphrase on the Two Epistles of Paul to the Corinthians* is addressed to Erard de la Marck, Bishop of Liège (on whom see CEBR II 382–5), and dated 5 February 1519. The translation is that of R.A.B. Mynors (CWE 6) with minor revisions by EAP; the notes are those of Peter Bietenholz (also CWE 6), amplified and numbered by EAP.
2 now a cardinal] Added in 1532. De la Marck had been made a cardinal in 1521.
3 This meeting had been planned for some time. See Epp 748, 867:89–91, 198–9.
4 Cf *Adagia* I ix 69.

the qualities which are more essentially yours: the incredible charm of your character; the courtesy so readily open to all comers, which makes everything more cheerful whichever way you turn; that wonderfully supple and wholly versatile intelligence, which is always certain of itself and always ready; that exceptional judgment in affairs of every kind which, unerring in its own nature, is rendered more so by wide experience of business; that unparalleled vigour in counsel, on account of which I reckon our prince so fortunate too, and our court to which you have recently been joined;[5] besides these, your uncommon propensity towards piety and sound learning, in both of which you are yourself pre-eminent; above all, your unbroken pursuit of peace, for after all those warlike prelates you have shown such incredible wisdom in ruling a people in other respects ready to rush headlong into war that they have never fallen a prey to anyone and never taken the offensive. Difficult and exceptional as it is to be a good prince, it is even more exceptional to be an upright and untainted prelate. You alone fill both positions with a completeness which any other man could scarcely achieve in one alone and are no less a religious leader than you are a head of state.

But there will perhaps be a more appropriate occasion to dwell on this elsewhere, and it will be better done, I think, in other ears than yours. Meanwhile, that I may not a second time meet such a prince, who has laid me under so many obligations, empty-handed and without a gift, and that you may not think this most flourishing university of yours has nothing to offer you except spiced wine,[6] in the last few weeks I have made ready this modest present in the literary way, a *Paraphrase* on the two Epistles to the Corinthians, so that having Paul, the supreme interpreter of our religion, in this form, you can carry him round with you wherever you please and have him speak to you in future in clear and familiar language without a lengthy commentary.[7] Nor do I doubt that you will gain as much profit as pleasure from what he says. For in the first place much is revealed in these two

* * * * *

5 to which ... joined] Added in *1521*. The clause acknowledges the political realignment of de la Marck. In 1518 Hapsburg diplomacy had succeeded in winning the de la Marck family over from their alliance with France (cf Epp 748:29n, 956 introduction). The realignment marked the beginning of an era of peace and prosperity for the territory of Liège.
6 A hint at the litigation over the right of nomination to certain benefices in the diocese of Liège that continued to trouble the relations between the University of Louvain and Prince-Bishop Erard. Cf Paul Harsin *Etude critique sur l'histoire de la principauté de Liège* II: *Le règne d'Erard de la Marck 1505–1538* (Liège 1955) 230–3, 248. For a comparable dispute, see Ep 762 introduction.
7 See Ep 710 introduction.

Epistles about the beginnings of the infant church, on which I am surprised to find almost nothing recorded by serious historians and such as one can safely trust.[8] Luke alone touches on a few points relating to a few of the apostles in the course of conducting Paul as far as Rome. Dionysius, who in his second Hierarchy gives a fairly full description of the early rites of the church, is thought by the learned to be someone more recent than the celebrated member of the Areopagus who was a disciple of Paul.[9] I have read a liturgy of the Greeks attributed by them to Chrysostom,[10] to whom they are willing to attribute almost anything; that does not make it seem likely to me.

If only the liturgical matters which Paul touches on here and shows us as it were through a lattice[11] had been handed down by him somewhat more fully and more clearly! How concise is his mention of the eucharist or synaxis,[12] as though he were afraid of saying something that he ought not to say about that great mystery, on which certain moderns hold forth at length and issue pronouncements without pausing, as the saying goes, to wipe their feet![13] If only he had told us one thing at least: the persons, the time, the vestments, the rite, the wording customarily employed to consecrate the mystic bread and the cup that contains the Lord's most holy blood, from the unworthy handling of which, Paul tells us, spring frequently disease and death[14] – words that should make

* * * * *

8 The Paris theologian Noël Béda (CEBR I 116–18) censured this statement. Erasmus' response points out that he had not questioned the reliability of the Acts of the Apostles and that among the later historians even Eusebius is not always fully credible. See *Divinationes ad notata Bedae* LB IX 472B ; also *Supputatio* LB 675F–676A.

9 The *Hierarchies* attributed to Dionysius, Paul's convert on the Areopagus at Athens (Acts 17:34), are Neoplatonic treatises of the early fifth century. The first *Hierarchy* explains the ranks of angels, while the second deals, as here mentioned, with the rites of the church. Prior to Erasmus there had been little questioning of the traditional attribution; as a result he was more than once attacked because of this statement. In the *Declarationes ad censuras Lutetiae vulgatas* (LB IX 916–17), he pointed out that his view was independent of any Lutheran teaching and was shared by Lorenzo Valla and William Grocyn. See also *Divinationes ad notata Bedae* LB IX 472B–C and *Supputatio* LB IX 676A–B.

10 A mass which Erasmus himself had translated into Latin (cf Ep 227:2n; PG 63 901–22; PG 64 1061–8). Erasmus' doubts about the authorship are justified.

11 Cf *Adagia* III i 49.

12 1 Cor 11:23–31

13 Cf *Adagia* I ix 54.

14 Cf 1 Cor 11:29–30. The first part of this paragraph was criticized on several occasions by Noël Béda and the Paris faculty. Erasmus repeatedly defended the piety of his wish that Paul had written more fully about the Eucharist. If he had, Erasmus suggested, the church would now be suffering less contention

us too consider with more circumspection whether this could be the source of the pox that has been spreading everywhere for some years. And it is handled unworthily, not only by the man who approaches it when polluted by lust, but much more by him who is befouled with envy, hatred, and malice, with scandalmongering and a passion for revenge, and other faults of the kind which by their own nature are diametrically opposed to the Christian charity which in this mystery we set forth. He speaks rather more fully of the gift of tongues, of interpretation, of prophecy, and other gifts the place of which was later taken by church music, the reading of Scripture, and preaching. For the gifts of healing and apocalyptic vision have long since left us, since charity grew cold, faith languished, and we learnt to depend on human resources rather than on the help of heaven.

He has something too to say about ecclesiastical jurisdiction, when he forbids recourse to gentile judges and gives instructions that financial disputes must be settled by Christian arbitrators. He even claims some right of judicial enquiry for himself when he says 'When I come, in the mouth of two or three witnesses shall every word be established.'[15] And again in the execution of judgment he leaves his authority as an apostle in no doubt when he delivers unto Satan the man who has associated with his father's wife,[16] the place of which is now filled by excommunication – a weapon which in these days is to my mind used rather too readily: this terrifying thunderbolt is aimed indiscriminately and for the most frivolous reasons, and never with more energy than when some contemptible sum of money is at risk, while Paul (if I mistake not)[17] besides Hymenaeus and Alexander delivered unto Satan one person only.[18] Those two he condemns for their obstinate opposition to the gospel although they passed for Christians – and although we read of their condemnation, we do not read that they were ever reinstated; the other man for his open and notorious abomination. And yet even against him he did not pronounce sentence except in accordance with a unanimous vote, nor did he ever give the man's name. When condemning him, he was satisfied with denouncing his offence; in readmitting him, he does not even mention the offence, whence one can perceive it was the

* * * * *

and ridicule. See *Divinationes ad notata Bedae* LB IX 472C–D and *Elenchus in N. Bedae censuras* LB IX 506B–C, and for fuller defences *Supputatio* LB IX 676B–677C and *Declarationes ad censuras Lutetiae vulgatas* LB IX 849C–853A.

15 2 Cor 13:1
16 1 Cor 5:1–5
17 if I mistake not] Added in *1521*
18 Cf 1 Tim 1:20; 1 Cor 5:5.

sin and not the sinner that was the target for his severity. Nor did being delivered unto Satan in those days mean more than being shunned for a time by everyone, so that shame might bring one to repentance.[19] For Paul adds to his sentence 'for the affliction of the flesh, that the spirit may obtain salvation in the day of the Lord'; so that even the severity with which he cures the evil breathes the charity of the Apostle. But not long after, see with what zeal he recommends the man to the Corinthians, telling them to receive him kindly into their society after correction, for fear lest he be overwhelmed by grief too heavy for him.[20] This penalty was at that time enough to satisfy the merciful Apostle.

Besides which, although there were many who had sinned, he preferred to take steps against one alone as a warning to the others, but with a mild penalty which should be not so much a punishment as a remedy. The rest he menaces in his letters with repeated threats, to make them repent, as though he would have no right to be severe against those who had repented of their own free will. But now look at the ferocity with which we rage against the common folk, although we have more grievous crimes on our own consciences! But at the same time the case of this man guilty of abomination, who is condemned and then received back again, makes nonsense of the doctrine of Montanus and Novatianus, who refuse to receive into Christ's flock anyone who has lapsed seriously after baptism.[21] Not but what in the days of Augustine only a single opportunity for public penance was allowed, that the remedy might not lose its value by frequent use; although he does not deny to those who have relapsed into the same offence the hope of forgiveness in the presence of God, in his long discussion of the point in the letter to Macedonius, which now bears the number 54.[22] The same precedent gave rise to the retributions authorized

* * * * *

19 In connection with this sentence, Béda evidently charged Erasmus with misunderstanding Paul, misrepresenting church doctrine regarding excommunication, and promoting himself. Erasmus responded in *Elenchus in N. Bedae censuras* LB IX 506C–D and *Supputatio* LB IX 677C–678A. For the citation in the next sentence see 1 Cor 5:5.

20 Cf 2 Cor 2:5–11. See also the paraphase on 1 Cor 5:2 with n5.

21 These were second and third century founders of sectarian movements characterized by eschatology and severe asceticism. See Eusebius *Historia ecclesiastica* 5.14–19 (Montanism) and 6.43–6 (Novatianism). For the position on post-baptismal sin maintained by these two movements see J.N.D. Kelly *Early Christian Doctrines* 5th ed rev (San Francisco 1978) 199 (Montanism) and 436–7 (Novatianism).

22 Augustine Ep 153.3.7 PL 33 655–6

by canon law, which were once very severe,[23] as appears from the decrees
of the early popes. From these again arose, it is clear, what are now commonly called indulgences, out of which I only wish it were as much our
good fortune to grow rich in religion as it is certain other persons' to fill
their coffers with coin. First[24] of all, some relaxation was allowed in the regular penalties inflicted by the bishop, but sparingly, and only for weighty
and religious reasons; but nowadays the remission of the torments of pur-
gatory is openly hawked up and down, and not merely sold for money but
forced upon those who do not want it, for reasons which in these days I
will not mention. You remember the false apostles whom Paul knew to be
a grievous plague,[25] but none the less he lets them be for a time, for fear
that severity directed against a few men may bring the general state of the
church into jeopardy; for he does not dissent from Augustine's view that
some men should be set right in secret and not openly, for fear of rousing
them to greater madness and turning mere criminals into tyrants or leaders
of heresy.[26]

Besides which, he lays down the law as befits his apostolic office, on
marriage lawful and unlawful, equal and unequal, on remarriage, and on
divorce, recommending some things as being valuable and requiring others
as being necessary. Of these precepts we retain some quite inflexibly enough
in my opinion, not to say too much so – for example, on divorce;[27] some
have been abandoned entirely, for instance, Paul's advice that a Christian
wife should continue to live with a gentile husband if he does not seek a
divorce.[28] He lays down rules also about meat sacrificed to idols, on which
decisions are given in the Acts as well by James and Peter;[29] and this perhaps
has no relevance now, for no one sacrifices to demons nowadays. Although
this decree too has now lost its force, inasmuch as it is not now thought an

* * * * *

23 The early church required public penance and other forms of chastisement.
Cf 'Satisfaction' in *Dictionnaire de théologie catholique* ed A. Vacant et al XIV-1
(Paris 1939) 1135–50, 1152–60.
24 First ... mention] Added in *1532*
25 Cf 2 Cor 11:13–19.
26 Cf *Sermones* 262 *De poenitentia*, (falsely) attributed to Augustine (PL 39 2229–
30).
27 In response to Béda's criticism of this observation, Erasmus defended both
his support for more lenient divorce practices and his respect for the church's
teachings. See *Divinationes ad notata Bedae* LB IX 472E–F, *Elenchus in N. Bedae
censuras* LB IX 506D, and *Supputatio* LB IX 678A–B. See also 1 Cor chapter 7 n73.
28 1 Cor 7:13–15
29 Cf 1 Cor 8:4–13; Acts 15:20 and 29, 21:25.

abomination to eat an animal that has been strangled or an animal's blood. But Ambrose interprets the prohibition of the blood as forbidding us to eat all living creatures that have blood in their veins and thinks for this reason that the 'things strangled' are a superfluous addition by the Greeks, because he who expressly forbids the eating of animals forbids us at the same time to eat anything strangled. But whether one should subscribe to Ambrose's opinion is for others to decide.[30] It seems to me more like pure Christianity and more in keeping with the teaching of the Gospels and the apostles to lay down for no man any specific form of food, but to instruct all men to eat in accordance with their habit of body, whatever is most conducive to each man's good health, with a view to moderation and not self-indulgence, with thanksgiving and a lively desire to think aright.[31]

But, to let my pen run on, the Apostle teaches us here in passing how far we ought to condescend to weaker brethren and how far to avoid any cause of stumbling: whenever, that is, there is an immediate threat to their faith and the occasion of stumbling is scarcely to be overcome, being newly identified and a survival from a former way of life, not originating in us and deliberately introduced. For whether we should agree with Augustine, who in a letter to Publicola in which he treats of various questions in this field expresses the simple view that it is better to starve to death than to eat sacrificial meat discovered by accident, if you know it to be sacrificial,[32] I leave for others to determine; Paul finds nothing wrong in this, unless it is a cause of stumbling to the weak, and openly protests that neither idols nor

* * * * *

30 This statement reflects Erasmus' allusion to Ambrosiaster in his annotation on Gal 2:6 (*nihil contulerunt*) in *1516*. In slightly modified form, the statement was shifted in *1519* to an annotation on Gal 2:2 (*qui videbantur aliquid*), where it remained unchanged through *1535*. Erasmus expresses doubt (from *1516*) about the value of Ambrosiaster's opinion. On Ambrosiaster, see Translators' Note n19.

31 Béda and the Paris faculty criticized this sentence as encouraging disregard for church rules about eating and fasting and as agreeing with Lutheran and other heretical beliefs. In response, Erasmus maintained that he had never scorned the practice of fasting and charged that Béda had purposely ignored the context of the sentence. He pointed as well to Paul's preference for the spiritual over the corporeal, but suggested that he would not criticize the contemporary church for resorting out of necessity to 'Judaistic vestiges' in order to help those of weak faith. See *Divinationes ad notata Bedae* LB IX 474A, *Elenchus in N. Bedae censuras* LB IX 506D–507A, *Supputatio* LB IX 678B–E, and *Declarationes ad censuras Lutetiae vulgatas* LB IX 827A–829B. See also 1 Cor chapters 8 n25 and 9 n6.

32 Augustine Ep 47.6 PL 33 187

meat offered to idols are anything, indignant that he should be criticized in respect of something for which he himself gives God thanks. Once that scruple has been removed, why need a Christian starve to death? For there is no similarity in the things which Augustine compares in his *De bono coniugii*, parenthood and death by starvation.[33] Nor does Paul confuse the issue like this; on the contrary, he instructs us to refrain for the time being, since there are other sources on which you can draw in order to silence your ravening stomach.[34] If I am allowed to steal food in order to preserve life, why am I told to die rather than arouse another man's misgivings? And all this was at that time the mere rudiments of ecclesiastical legislation, when as yet dignities and prebends, the pallium and the wearing of the pallium,[35] and tithes predial[36] and personal and annual dues were not yet the central questions.

Besides this, he opens to some extent the question of the property and pay of priests when he plainly lays it down as right that those who are servants of the gospel should live of the gospel;[37] but his word is 'live' – nothing about growing rich and faring like a prince, and no living either unless they serve and attend constantly upon the altar. Not but what, while maintaining this right for others, he does not take it up himself, although labouring more than them all in the cause of the gospel. Such is Paul's noble and truly generous spirit, and in all the centuries since then I see no one keen to emulate him. Nothing is done free; on the contrary, a price is asked for everything, and no one does it as his bounden duty and service, while the apostles used what was freely offered to them and Paul would not use even that. They collect money too, but it was the freewill offerings of those who had more than they needed, and not exactions; moreover they collect for the benefit of the faithful who were in want and not to give the rich more luxury, and the terms of the collection were such that neither Paul nor Titus, who were in charge of the business, got anything

* * * * *

33 In *De bono coniugali* 16.18 CSEL 41 210–12, Augustine compares eating and sexual union in terms of virtue and vice and concludes that, just as it would be better to die from starvation than to eat forbidden food ie food sacrificed to idols, so it would be better to die without children than to seek to gain them through illicit sexual relations.
34 Literally 'barking' – a reminiscence of Horace *Satires* 2.2.18. Cf the paraphrase on 1 Cor 8:7.
35 The pallium is a vestment worn around the shoulders by the pope; it is granted by the pope to archbishops as an indication of their authority over other bishops, and to certain bishops as an honour.
36 A predial tithe is paid from the produce of an estate (*praedium*).
37 Cf 1 Cor 9:14.

whatever out of it. Hence, it is clear, it came about afterwards that many men entrusted their wealth to the church, to be expended on the needs of widows and the aged amongst others; from which the selfishness of certain people later diverted it to support their own personal rule. Representatives are sent this way and that, and they are given due honour both on arrival and on departure; but I fancy less was spent on ceremony than we see now. About the business entrusted to them I raise no questions. One can but rejoice at this great increase in the church's wealth, if religion has grown in proportion to the grandeur and the turmoil. Not that in those early times the apostles lacked their proper dignity and standing, nor did they lack resources. Paul boasts that his forces are not carnal but spiritual, owing their power not to troops clad in iron but to the protection of God, and intended not for the destruction of cities, for the plundering of common people and the slaughter of human beings, but for the overthrow of every thought that raises its head against the providence of God. The nature of those forces is explained even more clearly by Ambrose in his *De viduis*. 'It is not by the weapons of this world,' he says, 'that the church overcomes hostile powers, but by the spiritual weapons which owe their strength to God.' And a little further on, 'The church's weapon,' he says, 'is faith; her weapon is prayer, which overcomes the adversary.'[38] This opinion finds support in Pope Nicholas,[39] whose words are recorded in the *Sentences* book IV, distinction 37, in the paragraph beginning '*His adiiciendum.*'[40]

These were the weapons and these the forces, such was the equipment of the troops, with which Paul, that invincible warrior, conquered Greece and a great part of Asia Minor and proceeded to attack and take possession of the Roman empire, which at that time was more than the weapons of any monarch could defeat. But all the territory that he subdued, he subdued for Christ and not himself; with Christ to support him he proved himself invincible by the very fact that he depended on no support from men. He maintained the rights of the kingdom of heaven with heavenly weapons and fought the battles of the gospel with the resources that the gospel supplies – tentmaker and pontiff, offscouring of the world and chosen instrument of Christ, who wished by the Apostle's sublime humility and tongue-tied eloquence and stammering flow of words to spread the glory of his name through superstitious Jewry, clever Greece, and Rome, the queen of earthly kingdoms. Of him it is true, as was once said of Pericles, if I mistake not, that

* * * * *

38 Ambrose *De viduis* 8.49 PL 16 262–3. For 'Paul's boast' see 2 Cor 10:4–5.
39 Cf Gratian *Decretum* c 33, q 2, c 5–6 (citing Nicholas the Great, pope 858–67) in *Corpus iuris canonici* ed A. Friedberg, 2 vols (Leipzig 1879–81) I 1152.
40 Peter Lombard *Sentences* PL 192 931–2

with thunder and lightning he confounded, not Greece alone like Pericles, but the whole round world.[41]

There is another thing which it occurs to me to marvel at from time to time: the danger that faced the gospel teaching at the start in its early stages, had not Paul put his best foot forward, as they say,[42] to withstand it, much as the life of some unborn babies is in danger before they have ever come forth into life. Such a mass of weeds sprang up, which almost overwhelmed Christ's sowing while it was young and still in the blade; nor was it long before worldly philosophy and Jewish superstition, as though they had deliberately joined forces, were conspiring against Christ. Philosophy threw doubt on the resurrection and began to some extent to spoil the simplicity of the gospel with quibbles of men's making. Judaism would have imposed on us the whole of Moses and even the crowning indignity of circumcision and would have reduced that heavenly philosophy to a matter of coarse and lifeless ritual, had not this valiant Isaac of ours opened so many wells of the authentic gospel, so many springs of living water against the Philistines, who would fill all with dirt.[43] Philosophy at that time, led by sage fools with tongue and pen and even by tyrants with the sword, was advancing against Christ's small and innocent flock and has left traces which remain to this day. Judaism, acting through men disguised as apostles, was creeping in still more perilously under a false mask of piety and occupied Christ's whole cornfield to such an extent that even now it cannot be weeded out.[44] Saint Augustine at any rate, in a letter to Januarius which now bears the number 119,[45] witnesses that in Africa vessels used for washing the feet, which Juvenal also mentions,[46] used to be kept with such superstitious respect that a graver rebuke was in store for the man who had touched the earth

* * * * *

41 Erasmus adapts the description of the oratory of the Athenian statesman Pericles (c 495–29 BC) in Aristophanes *Acharnians* 531. For 'offscouring' and 'chosen instrument' in the preceding sentence, see 1 Cor 4:13 and Acts 9:15, respectively.

42 Cf *Adagia* III i 34, from Quintilian 12.9.18.

43 Paul is compared to Isaac. For the allusion, cf Gen 24:62, 26:12–22.

44 For Erasmus' attitudes towards Jews, see CWE 44 60 n20 and 46 8 n18; also 1 Cor chapter 9 n6.

45 Augustine Ep 55.19.35 PL 33 221. Augustine refers to a regulation that bare feet should not touch the earth during the period set aside for foot-washing lest the sanctity of the foot-washing vessels be compromised. In chapter 18 he had explained that since some Christians did not wish to confuse foot-washing with baptism, they chose the third or the eighth day of Easter for foot-washing.

46 The allusion to Juvenal is ambiguous. Juvenal nowhere speaks of *pelluvia*, but a marginal note in all editions of the *Paraphrase* from 1519 cites Juvenal 6.159: 'Where barefooted kings keep the Sabbath as their feast day.'

with his bare foot during their octaves than for one who had drowned his wits in drink; for he was most indignant that the church of Christ, which God in his mercy willed should be free and have very few sacramental rites, should be loaded with the slavery of so many burdens that the state of the Jews might seem preferable in that, although they had not recognized their day of freedom, yet they were subjected to the burdens of the Law and not to human innovations.

Tares of this kind among the wheat he somehow tolerates, although reluctantly; what he finds quite unbearable, as openly contrary to the faith and wholly inconsistent with sound doctrine, is the way some people carry abstention from meat-eating to the length of regarding those who do eat it as unclean. Of this superstition likewise clear traces survive to our own day, for most people think that a good part of religion lies in the choice of foods, which God created of equal value that we might eat and give him thanks. Their judgment on this point is no less preposterous than the view of those Africans on the washing of feet, nearly everyone regarding it as a more serious crime to eat meat on a Saturday than to attack their brother's reputation with virulent falsehoods[47] or even to cut a fellow-creature's throat. As Paul foretold, some were found to forbid marriage entirely.[48] It seems to be a relic of this superstition when even St Gregory lays down as the practice of the Roman church and proper to be observed that a man who has had commerce with his own wife should abstain for some time from entering a church and should not enter until he has had a bath[49] and, as the poet puts it, has cleaned away the night's thoughts in river water,[50] and for this piece of superstition he produces a reason on which I will express no opinion: to wit that, although matrimony is an honourable estate, yet pleasure, without which there can be no intercourse between man and woman, cannot possibly exist without guilt. What I say will be found in the *Sentences* book IV, distinction 31, in the paragraph beginning '*Si forte aliquis.*'

* * * * *

47 This passage, beginning at 'Of this superstition' above, was rebuked by Béda as Lutheran and hostile to church regulations. Erasmus defended it in *Divinationes ad notata Bedae* LB IX 473A–B as all too true and lamentable. At greater length in *Supputatio* LB IX 678E–679C he defends his support for church regulations, ridicules the charge that his views are Lutheran, and points to Béda himself as an eminent example of one who would keep dietary rules religiously while viciously attacking an innocent neighbour's reputation.
48 Cf 1 Cor 7:8–9, 25–40.
49 Cf Gratian *Decretum* C 33 q 4 c 7 (citing Gregory the Great, pope 590–604) in *Corpus iuris canonici* (see n39 above) I 1248–9.
50 Persius 2.16

And[51] the defence excogitated at that point by the Master of the Sentences, that we should understand this to refer to copulation provoked by incontinence, is a broken reed;[52] the man who says 'cannot possibly' allows no room for exceptions.[53]

There are other heresies too,[54] the names of which have disappeared, but their vestiges and, so to say, the scars of them can be detected even now[55] – those, for example, of the so-called Essenes, Ebionites, Apostolics, Psallians, or Euchites, to say nothing of the Simoniacs, a word[56] that has long been classed as obsolete. But disputes between sects of this sort, which later set almost the whole world on fire (especially under the leadership of Arius, when things were so uncertain that it was not clear which way the world would go), multiplied even during Paul's lifetime – disputes not about indulgences or applications or other questions of the kind, which we now drag by the scruff of the neck into the substance of the faith, but about the resurrection of the dead, which is the foundation and the crown of our belief. Against this plague Paul fights with all his might,[57] but even so I fear that this viper still lives in some men's hearts; for in Italy every year in sermons before the people they try to defend the resurrection,[58] thinking that they will be home and dry[59] on this question, once they can show that Aristotle did not entirely abolish the immortality of the soul. I say nothing for the moment about their conversation at table. In any case, what other

* * * * *

51 And ... exceptions] Added in 1532
52 Literally 'a prop of figwood,' which was proverbially weak and useless (*Adagia* I vii 85)
53 'Master of the Sentences' is a sobriquet for Peter Lombard. Cf PL 192 921–2 (quoting Gregory the Great)
54 For brief descriptions of the sects mentioned here, see *The Oxford Dictionary of the Christian Church* ed Frank L. Cross, 3rd ed rev by E.A. Livingstone (Oxford 2005). The names may have been chosen at random and from memory. Simoniacs apart, a connection with the problems of the church of Erasmus' own day is not immediately apparent. See eg Augustine *De haeresibus* 1 (on Simoniacs), 40 (on Apostolics), 57 (on Euchites) CCL 46 290, 307, 326. Cf Ep 901:10n. On Essenes, see CWE 44 24 n2.
55 Reading *hodieque*, altered in Allen to *hodie quoque*, apparently in error, but with no change in meaning.
56 a word ... obsolete] Added in 1532
57 Cf 1 Cor 15.
58 The position here outlined is reminiscent of Paduan philosophers such as Pietro Pomponazzi. See E. Garin *Italian Humanism, Philosophy and Civic Life in the Renaissance* (Oxford 1965) 136–50.
59 Literally 'in harbour'; cf *Adagia* I i 46.

men believe it is not my business to conjecture; one thing at any rate is obvious, that there are men, and particularly men in high worldly station, who live as if they have no belief whatever in a future life.

And would that here too Paul had given us somewhat more light – whether souls exist separate from the body and where they exist; whether they enjoy the glory of immortality; whether the souls of the wicked are in torment even now, whether our prayers or other good actions are of any service to them, whether an indulgence from the pope frees them all of a sudden from punishment;[60] for I observe that many men are in doubt on these points, or at any rate dispute about them, which would have been needless had Paul left us clear definitions.[61] Besides which, although those who are born again in Christ ought to put off the old man with his deeds and his affections, we see nevertheless that while the gospel, under Paul's leadership, was still fresh, lust, avarice, strife, ambition, discord, and other pests of religion and morality had crept in among the people, while certain vices left over from their former life it had not been possible altogether to root out. Let no one therefore be surprised if in our own day some men abound in iniquity because their love has grown cold. Even in Paul's lifetime false apostles had made their way in, ready to turn the gospel enterprise to their own profit, to divert the glory of Christ into their own personal rule, and to preach themselves rather than God; to teach the world in place of Christ and the flesh in place of the Spirit; to gloss over[62] heavenly teaching

* * * * *

60 Cf the doubts raised by Luther's Ninety-five Theses, Ep 785:39n. Erasmus' writings frequently reflect the controversy over indulgences. See CWE 39 63 n26, and 7 above.

61 The extended wish expressed in the first sentence of this paragraph was censured by Béda and the theological faculty at Paris as impious, futile, and dangerous, since it might encourage doubt among the wavering. The Scriptures, they argued, were sufficient on all questions raised here by Erasmus except on indulgences, and on this subject the church had spoken clearly. Erasmus responded in *Divinationes ad notata Bedae* LB IX 473C that he merely wished for Pauline authority to use against those who resisted the church's teachings. In *Declarationes ad censuras Lutetiae vulgatas* LB IX 849E–853A, he elaborates this defence with a catalogue of points of contention among the church Fathers, calling attention also to the ambiguity within the Scriptures, and inconsistency within ecclesiastical tradition and practice. Images from the Bible are reflected in the sentence that follows: 'born again' (John 3:3 and 7; 1 Pet 1:23), 'put off the old man' (Eph 4:22; Col 3:9).

62 to gloss over] The verb was added in 1532 ; prior to that, the verb of the next clause would presumably have been taken with this clause as well: 'to build on heavenly teaching the teachings of men and on Christ . . .' This passage is

with the teachings of men and build on Christ our foundation a structure unworthy of him. And they were made more dangerous enemies of the church because they did all this under the pretext of Christ's name and recommended by the title of apostles, whose mask they wore.

If only the church of Christ had no false apostles today! If only all those who have succeeded to the office of preaching the gospel would follow Paul's example and preach Jesus Christ not for profit, not for advancement, not for the favour of the great, not to wreak hatred or earn favour among men, but in sincerity and truth! Paul himself when in chains boasts that the Lord's word is not chained.[63] But now – and a sorry sight it is! – we can see men who have been virtually hired by salaries from the great for that very purpose and preach what tends not so much to Christ's glory and to true religion as towards the hunt for benefices, the setting of snares to entrap preferment, and the spreading of nets to catch bishoprics; vigorous and vocal when flattery is not only safe but profitable, and where truth would mean loss, more dumb than fish. If salt has lost its savour, what else is there with which ordinary folk that taste of nothing can be salted? If the light be turned to darkness, what can dispel the shadows of the uneducated public? If shepherds become wolves, what hope for the flock? If the leaders on the path are blind, who will call them back from a wrong turning? If men are buying and selling who ought to be the fathers of their people, where else can we look for honesty?

Has terror of men so much more power over us than the fear of God? Are we more moved by men's rewards than God's? Can it be that we first indulge our own self-love in order with more disastrous results to flatter the self-love of others? Paul does not allow any mortal man to be acclaimed, he does not suffer the praise due to the gospel to be transferred to men. But some men nowadays, as though Christ were outmoded, introduce a new species of idolatry, making gods, if I may so put it, out of men. And all the time humble folk are misled, all the time the multitude lie under a tyranny of more than one description. This most of us can see; and we hold our peace. We not merely hold our peace; we help the other side. 'I admit,' we say, 'that this is right, but it is not safe.' If among Christians it is not safe to preach the gospel unadulterated freely, where then will it be safe? Had this fear always equally prevailed, who would have passed the gospel down to

* * * * *

replete with biblical echoes eg 'love grown cold' (Matt 24:12), 'false apostles' (2 Cor 11:13), 'preach themselves' (2 Cor 4:5), 'Christ our foundation' (1 Cor 3:11).
63 Cf Col 4:18; 1 Cor 9:12.

us? Perhaps the ears of princes do not take kindly to sincere advice because
we have made them too familiar with smooth words.

I do not say this to find fault with anyone. Would God there were
no one at whom it might be fairly aimed! I shall not give them away; but
by the books they publish and the sermons they deliver they daily give
themselves away, with such shameless compliance that their very apes hold
them in scorn. The voice that should be dedicated to religion is the slave
of gain; it ought to teach the kingdom of heaven and it is enslaved to the
kingdom of the world; it should expound the mysteries of Christ and it
recounts the dreams of men. The trumpet of the gospel, which Isaiah bids
sound to publish forth the glory of God, is turned into a lyre to tickle the
ears of men. As for the tongue, while Isaiah boasts that he has been given the
tongue of the learned to root out the nurseries of vice and plant the seeds
of religion,[64] it is adapted to a very different purpose, teaching what it
ought not to teach and attacking what it ought to praise. The dog's tongue,
which ought gently to lick the wounds of those who have done wrong,
often attacks the reputation of the innocent and, what is more disgraceful,
of those who have done it a service. We use it as a weapon with which we
attack anyone who offends us or even, without offending us, has done us a
service unasked. The tongue of healing, one might think, has changed into
the tongue of a viper. Why can we not imitate instead a tongue like Paul's,
which can utter nothing except the Lord Jesus? Why can we not bear in
mind that a preacher is an angel of the Lord, from whose mouth the people
expect to hear the law of God, and not abuse of fellow-members of the body
of Christ; and that there is a world of difference between hierophant and
sycophant, between godliness and gossip, between teaching and treachery?
At this point we need the bishops to play their part; for it is their business to
see that opportunity to preach to the people is not given casually to the first
comer. And[65] let us not suppose it sufficient for performing this apostolic
office that a man wears a cowl. Not all who have a tongue have heart and
brains.

But to speak of these questions there may be a more convenient opportunity elsewhere; let me now return to my subject. This Paul of ours is

* * * * *

64 Cf Isa 58:1, 50:4. The little disquisition on the tongue that follows has parallels
   in eg the paraphrases on James 3:1–12 CWE 44 153–6 and Acts 2:4 CWE 50 14–
   15, and in Erasmus' large work *Lingua* CWE 29. The allusion to Isaiah in the
   preceding sentence may recall several passages; cf eg Isa 27:3, 60:1–3, 66:18–
   19.
65 And ... brains] Added in 1532

always skilful and slippery, but in these two Epistles he is such a squid, such a chameleon – he plays the part of Proteus or Vertumnus[66] to such a tune that in dealing with the Corinthians, who are more than Greeks, he seems somehow to exemplify the old proverb 'Cretan with Cretan stand,'[67] turning himself into every shape that he may shape them anew for Christ; with such freedom does he himself twist and turn like a man who threads the windings of a maze, and appearing to us in a fresh guise every time.[68] How humble and ingratiating he sometimes is, as he beseeches them by the mercy of Christ and begs them to bear with his foolishness for a space! Then again he cries in harsh and threatening accents 'Do ye seek a proof of Christ speaking in me?' Elsewhere he abases himself and calls himself an offscouring, misbegotten and unworthy of the name of Apostle; and then becomes grand and exalted and sets himself even above the greatest of the apostles, crawling upon the ground at one moment, and the next appearing to us out of the third heaven.[69] Now he praises the piety of the Corinthians, now thunders against their faults. Some things he demands openly; others he suggests by a kind of underground approach. Sometimes he is an unready speaker who knows nothing save Jesus, and him crucified; sometimes he speaks wisdom among them that are perfect. In one place he acts the part of an intelligent and sober man; in another he dons the mask of one who is foolish and beside himself.[70] Now he boldly claims his own rights, now

* * * * *

66 For the comparisons, see P.G. Bietenholz *History and Biography in the Work of Erasmus of Rotterdam* (Geneva 1966) 86–7. Vertumnus is the old Roman god of the seasons, constantly changing his shape. For Proteus, cf 1 Cor chapter 9 n33.

67 The Cretans were proverbial for quarrelling amongst themselves yet standing by each other when assailed by misfortune or by other people. Cf *Adagia* I i 11.

68 Béda objected to Erasmus' characterization of Paul in this sentence as *vafer* 'crafty' or, as translated here, 'a squid.' In defence, Erasmus reiterates more or less what he says here about the usefulness of this versatility for promoting the gospel, and he cites the words of Paul himself and of Jerome on the positive connotations of the characteristic. See *Divinationes ad notata Bedae* LB IX 473D and *Supputatio* LB IX 679E.

69 For Paul's claim of apostolic standing, cf 1 Cor 9:1–3; for his self-abasement, 1 Cor 4:13, 15:9; for the 'third heaven,' 2 Cor 12:2–5; for 'bearing with his foolishness,' 2 Cor 11:1; for 'Christ speaking in him,' 2 Cor 13:3.

70 In defending this sentence against Béda's censure, Erasmus points out that donning the mask of a fool is not the same as being a fool; the characterization highlights, rather than obscures, Paul's glory. See *Divinationes ad notata Bedae* 473E and *Supputatio* 679F. There are, again, numerous biblical echoes in this

courteously resigns them. In one place he speaks from the heart, sometimes resorts to irony, with 'Forgive me this wrong.' You may find that
he gives an appearance of inconsistency; but he is most like himself when
he seems unlike, and most consistent when he seems the reverse. Always
Christ's business is his main concern; always he thinks of the well-being of
his flock, like a true physician leaving no remedy untried that may restore
his patients to perfect health.

The greatest scholars labour to explain the intentions of poets and orators; but in this orator far more toil is required if you are to understand
what he has in mind, what he aims at, and what he is avoiding; so full of
tricks is he everywhere, if I may so express it.[71] Such is his versatility, you
would hardly think it is the same man speaking. At one time he bubbles
up gently like a crystal spring, at another pours roaring down like a great
torrent, carrying many things before him; now flows peacefully and gently, now spreads himself as though into a spacious lake. Again, he sometimes plunges underground and reappears suddenly in another place; then,
when it suits him, meanders unexpectedly, caressing now this bank and
now that; sometimes fetches a long digression and turns back again upon
himself. I am the more amazed at some people who, although they have
hardly a smattering of grammar and no idea what it is to write, yet suppose an understanding of Paul's language to be an easy and almost childish thing. What I have achieved it will be for others to decide. Ambrose
and Theophylact the Bulgarian bishop[72] have been my chief guides; and although the latter is more recent, he read commentaries of the early Greek
Fathers which are now lost to us. But although I have always had these
two as my advisers, I have always adopted the solution that seemed closest to Paul's meaning. That I have tried to be faithful, I call Paul himself to
witness.

My preface, I perceive, is longer than it should be, nor have I any
excuse except that I share this fault with many other writers in our own age
especially, and that my affection for you has made me run on. May your
Highness be preserved for us as long as possible in health and wealth by
our Prince and Master, Jesus Christ.

5 February 1519. Louvain

* * * * *

passage. Cf eg on the foolishness of Paul, 1 Cor 1:21; on 'Christ crucified,' 1
Cor 2:2; on speaking wisdom, 1 Cor 2:6–7; for the citation that soon follows,
'forgive me this wrong,' see 2 Cor 12:13.
71 if I may so express it] Added in 1532
72 For 'Ambrose' and Theophylact, see the Translators' Note nn19, 20.

THE ARGUMENT OF THE FIRST EPISTLE
OF PAUL TO THE CORINTHIANS
BY ERASMUS OF ROTTERDAM

Corinth, once the capital city of Achaia, was, on account of the convenience
of its harbours (for it is an isthmus), both the most frequented and also
the wealthiest trading centre for all of Asia.[1] It generally happens, moreover, that the morals of such cities are by far the most corrupt because
there is typically an influx not so much of good morals as of vices from
all parts and every race, and traders as a class adopt for themselves an
exceedingly licentious way of life.[2] Accordingly, although the Corinthians
had some time before received the teaching of the gospel through Paul's
preaching, nevertheless there still remained some traces and remnants of
their former character and life – to such an extent that there was a danger
they would be made strangers to the purity of Christ by philosophers who
were disdaining the preaching of the cross as base and unlearned, and by
false apostles who were inviting them towards Judaism. It is such an arduous task[3] to be transformed into another person – from those conditions

* * * * *

1 'Achaia' was the name of the Roman province that constituted the southern
 part of what is now Greece. Corinth was its administrative centre at the time
 of Paul. The city had been completely destroyed by the Romans in 146 BC and
 reconstructed a century later under the sponsorship of Julius Caesar and the
 emperor Augustus. Its harbours – Cenchreae on the Saronic Gulf to the east
 and Lechaeum on the Corinthian Gulf to the north – gave Corinth access to
 the two seas on either side of the isthmus and thus to trade routes both east
 and west.
2 Cf Cicero *De re publica* 2.4.7 on port cities and the dangers posed by their
 importation of foreign morals. Cicero congratulates Romulus for not locating
 Rome on the seacoast, and attributes the decline of cities like Corinth and
 Carthage to the temptations and corruptions associated with proximity to the
 sea.
3 Perhaps an echo of Virgil *Aeneid* 1.33 or 12.646. Cf the similar characterization
 of conversion in Erasmus' Argument of Romans CWE 42 9, where the allusion
 to *Aeneid* 1.33 is more explicit.

both in which you were born and to which you have long been habituated. Indeed, Saint Jerome in the preface of the second book of the commentary he wrote on the Epistle to the Galatians confirms that among the people of Achaia even in his own time there were still remnants of those faults which Paul charged against the Corinthians,[4] although today we think it sufficient for you just to be washed with a bit of water in order suddenly to become a perfect Christian.[5] Paul, therefore, knowing that it is just as worthy a deed to keep possessions secure as it is to have obtained them, calls his children back to Christ with a zeal equal to the great zeal with which he had begotten them in Christ – for he had spent a year and a half with them. And he strengthens them in the gospel's teaching, now with apostolic authority venting his anger, rebuking, scolding, and, finally, threatening, now coaxing with fatherly affection, and also encouraging, and softening the harshness of the necessary reprimand by mixing in praise. Thus, in the manner of wise physicians, he sweetens the bitter drug of wormwood with a dab of honey,[6] and applies suitable remedies to individual evils.

First, as the habitual companions of wealth there are prideful swelling and insolence, and among the insolent very often factions arise when no one is willing to yield to another, and each one thinks himself more important. In addition to these, overindulgence accompanies wealth, and a devotion to the appetite. Overindulgence draws in lust as its companion, and avarice is the besetting sin of traders. But the Corinthians swelled in pride not only from wealth, but also from the arrogance of Greek philosophy; they despised as barbarians the others who were utterly deficient in this.[7] Swollen as they were, they exalted themselves on the prestige of the apostles by whom they had each been baptized. From this came those divisive cries: I am a follower of Apollos, I of Cephas, I of Paul. It was also from pride, moreover, that

* * * * *

4 Jerome *Comm in Gal* II PL 26 356A
5 A panel of Spanish theologians criticized this passage as an attack on the sacrament of baptism. Erasmus responded that Paul, Peter, James, and John all agreed that baptism needed to be followed by newness of life. See *Apologia adversus monachos* LB IX 1060F–1061C. See also chapter 6 n26.
6 Cf Lucretius 4.11–17. Chrysostom and Theophylact frequently observe that Paul softens the severity of his message for the sake of persuading his audience. See eg Chrysostom *In 1 Cor hom* 2.1 (on 1:7) PG 61 18, 3.1 (on 1:10–12) PG 61 21–4, 13.1 (on 4:10–12) PG 61 107–8, 44.1 (on 16:12) PG 61 374; Theophylact *Expos in 1 Cor* (on 11.1) PG 124 693A–B.
7 who were utterly deficient in this] First in 1532; earlier editions read 'without this.'

not even when they came together in religious assemblies was there much accord among them, since they were all priding themselves on their own spiritual gifts. And when in respect to the same gift they were loath to yield to each other, commotion and disorder arose so much that even the women were speaking in public assembly, and teaching too. Further, it was from overindulgence as well as from pride that whenever they assembled for the hallowed supper, which Paul calls the Lord's,[8] whereat it was especially proper to display Christian concord, the rich, not waiting for those less well off, would take the food and gorge themselves to a state of drunkenness while the rest went hungry. What resulted now was not only division and intemperance at that meal, but even a certain disgraceful inequality, which was unknown at the Lord's supper.

Now it was partly the fault of pride and partly that of philosophy that certain of them were disdaining Paul as poor and lowly, and then as ineloquent and ignorant. But it was the particular result of philosophy alone that they were calling into doubt the resurrection of the dead, the foundation of our faith.[9] It was from overindulgence that they were indiscriminately eating meat being sacrificed at that time to images of demons,[10] and did not avoid a stumbling block for weaker ones. It was from lust, which nowhere in the world reigned with more impunity than at Corinth,[11] that in addition to the other problems there was found among them a person who defiled with shameful intercourse his father's wife (that is, his own stepmother), and they did not cast out the author of this outrage from their fellowship, and it was from lust that they kept company with other scandalous Christians, as if countenancing their vices.

Related to this is the unseemliness by which men went long-haired, and women did not fear to be seen with their heads uncovered when in a church meeting, as if the men were parading by the very deportment of

* * * * *

8 1 Cor 11:20
9 See the paraphrase on 15:1 with n1.
10 Ie images of the pagan gods. Paul calls the pagan gods 'demons' in 10:20. See chapter 10 n35. Erasmus elaborates the idea in the paraphrases on 8:4–6 and 10:19–21.
11 Cf the paraphrases on 7:2 and 9:1 and the annotation on 6:9 (commisceamini fornicariis), where Erasmus describes Corinth as a city 'most corrupted with pleasures of this sort.' He makes similar references in the paraphrase on Acts 18:1 CWE 50 112; Institutio christiani matrimonii CWE 69 389; and De vidua christiana CWE 66 198: 'What place has there ever been more decadent than the city of the Corinthians?' See also n2 above. For Corinth's reputation for wealth and sexual license, see Strabo Geography 8.6.20.

the body their womanish behaviour, and the women their charms. It was from avarice that they brought lawsuits against each other, not because of damage to reputation, or danger to life, but for monetary interests. The devotion to money was growing to such a degree that Christians, who had professed contempt for matters of this sort, were disputing before heathen and ungodly judges to the great shame of the Christian name, and so far were they from disregarding the loss of a bit of money that instead they were willfully defrauding others in dealings of this sort. Finally, about marriage they disagreed among themselves in that even then some of them were claiming that Christians ought to refrain from marriage altogether since they saw that the apostles held off from their wives.[12]

I have disclosed the diseases of the Corinthians, not of all the Corinthians, but of certain ones, to whom Paul offers the following remedies lest they infect the whole flock with the contagion. In the first place, having declared at the beginning his own confidence that they would persevere in the gospel of Christ, he scolds and teaches them rather sternly not to glory in humans through human contentiousness, but through concord and unanimity to glory in Christ, to whom alone all things ought to be credited, incidentally pointing to swelling pride as the source of such dissension. Therefore, from the arrogance of worldly philosophy, he calls them back to the humility of the cross, which although it has no ostentation, nevertheless has power and effectiveness. He also identifies as the authors of this evil the false apostles who rushed in after Paul's departure, and declares that he has laid the proper foundation. They should beware lest they build upon it something that a little later will have to be torn down, that is, that the Corinthians do not learn something they will soon need to unlearn. Then, like a father to his children, he complains that they have advanced to a point of such high standing that they now scorn their founder as a lowly man who endures all manner of suffering for the sake of the gospel. For this very reason it would have been proper to show him all the more favour. He urges his children, moreover, not to fall away from the character of their father, nor of their own volition to enslave themselves

* * * * *

12 See chapter 7 n4 for Erasmus' interpretation that the issue raised by the Corinthians is abstinence from marriage altogether rather than just from sexual intercourse. For Erasmus' view that most of the apostles maintained celibacy and that this was a state suitable for those early times of urgent apostolic mission, see the 'Encomium' on marriage in *De conscribendis epistolis* CWE 25 136–7; also the annotation on 7:39 (*liberata est a lege*) ASD VI-8 158:11–15; and Payne *Theology* 110.

to pedagogues.[13] These are the points especially that he treats in the first, second, third, and fourth chapters.

Now, to my mind, the end of the fourth belongs to the beginning of the fifth.[14] He gives directives concerning the man who committed incest, and he decrees, by means of a public council, that intimacy with the man ought to be avoided, partly so that, reformed through shame, he may repent,[15] partly lest through contact with this man the rest be infected. He warns them, moreover, to avoid not only this man, but also all who, falsely called Christian, were in disgrace because their scandalous behaviour was clearly evident. Yet there is not so much need to avoid disreputable[16] pagans – either because what sort of people they are is of no importance to us, or because disreputable people are everywhere, so that someone wishing to escape them would need to avoid everyone. These matters he treats in the fifth chapter.

In the third place, he warns about lawsuits. If any disputes of this sort arose among them (although to be fighting on account of money, which ought to be of very little value to us, would itself seem shameful among Christians), the matter should not progress to the point where they resort to heathen judges. Instead, they should conclude the matter among themselves through some arbiter or other. This subject he treats in the sixth chapter, a great part of which, in my opinion at least, pertains to the seventh,[17] namely, from the place where, about to discuss matrimony, he condemns

* * * * *

13 A pedagogue (Greek παιδαγωγός) in the Graeco-Roman world was usually a trusted slave who acted as governor for his master's son, conducted him to and from school, and in general oversaw the boy's education and conduct.

14 Erasmus thus takes Paul's suggestion that he might come to the Corinthians with a punishing rod (4:21) as a threat appropriate to the serious sin treated in chapter 5. Accordingly, the final sentence of the paraphrase on chapter 4 emphasizes the moral innocence Paul demands in chapter 5.

15 'Repent': resipiscat. On Erasmus' use of resipiscere 'to come to one's senses' to designate repentance see CWE 44 13 n5 and his annotation on Matt 3:2 (poenitentiam agite). See the Index of Greek and Latin Words Cited.

16 disreputable] In all editions from 1519 to 1532; in 1534 the word is omitted.

17 The 'great part' Erasmus has in mind begins at 6:9 and continues to the end of the chapter. In 6:9 Paul's concern shifts from lawsuits before pagan judges (6:1–7) and acts of injustice within the Christian community (6:8) to other forms of unrighteousness that preclude inheritance of God's kingdom (6:9–20). In verses 9–20 those issues predominate that arise from the immoral use of the body rather than the immoral quest for gain, and Erasmus evidently sees Paul's diatribe against the former as a kind of prelude to his treatment of sexuality within marriage in chapter 7.

among other vices fornication, adultery, and sodomy, and this he pursues up to the beginning of the next chapter: Do you not know that your members are the temples of Christ?[18]

In the fourth place he gives directives about matrimony, widowhood, mixed marriage, divorces, virginity, incidentally warning that the outward[19] condition of one's life ought not to be changed because one has become a Christian. In this whole discourse he urges celibacy and continence in such a way that he does not, nevertheless, deny the remedy of marriage to those who need it. This is treated in the seventh chapter.

In the fifth place he teaches that flesh sacrificed to idols differs in no real way from other flesh, and yet it ought to be shunned if there is a danger that some pagan or a weaker Christian might suppose from what you eat that you approve of the worship of idols. From these and similar vices he discourages through Old Testament examples.[20] And this he treats in the eighth chapter and again in the ninth.[21] For in between[22] he digresses into a commendation of himself, implicitly advancing himself above the other apostles, even the foremost ones, in that he was the only one of them all to impart to the Corinthians the teaching of the gospel free of charge.

In the sixth place he teaches what ought to be observed in the common assembly of Christians: that men not wear their hair long, that women not appear with their hair uncovered; furthermore, that fellowship and equality be preserved at the banquet of the Lord. His point is that they are not tending there to the stomach's interests (which are more properly addressed at home), but that by the mystical[23] feast the Lord's supper is represented. In addition, he warns that no one should flatter himself on account of a spiritual gift, but each one should confer his gift for the common good. By the example of the members of the body, he urges them to use properly

* * * * *

18 Erasmus cites from 6:19, thus a verse near the end of chapter 6. He appears to be citing the Vulgate reading of the verse, a reading he corrects in his annotation on 6:19 (*an nescitis quoniam membra vestra templum sunt*) by replacing *membra* 'members' with *corpora* 'bodies.'

19 outward] Added in 1532

20 Cf 1 Cor 10:1–11.

21 ninth] The discussion of sacrificial meat continues in the tenth chapter, not the ninth. The Martens text of 1519 reads *novo* 'new' rather than *nono* 'ninth.' The change to 'ninth' (whether a mistake or a 'correction') appears in 1521, is repeated thereafter, and may have caused the mistaken addition indicated in n26 below.

22 Ie in chapter 9. See previous note.

23 'Mystical': *mysticis*. On *mysticus* see chapter 10 n7.

the other gifts they have received, but especially to strive towards charity, without which the others, far from providing a benefit, actually hinder.

In turn, although he assigns to charity the first place among the Spirit's gifts,[24] he assigns the next to prophecy for this is what he calls the exposition of the mysteries of Scripture.[25] In this part he admonishes that commotion and disorder ought to be avoided – that it will be avoided if few speak and in turn. Meanwhile women are bidden to keep silent to the extent that not even for the sake of learning are they permitted to ask questions in an assembly. These[26] matters he treats in the eleventh, twelfth, thirteenth, and fourteenth chapters.

In the seventh place he builds up with various arguments the resurrection of the dead, showing of what sort and in what ways it will be – and this in fact in the fifteenth chapter. In the final chapter he appends certain matters of a more personal nature: the collection of money for the relief of the poor, his own return to the Corinthians. Finally, he commends Timothy and several others to them.

St Ambrose thinks this is not the first Epistle Paul wrote to the Corinthians,[27] basing that conjecture, I suppose, on what Paul says in the fifth chapter, 'I wrote to you in my Epistle' [5:9], as if he had written to them about this matter earlier in another letter, although the Greek interpreters disagree.[28] Some think the present letter was sent through Timothy, whom he mentions several times, and together with him, through Stephanas, Fortunatus, and Achaicus, whom he commends to them. Again some think it was sent from Ephesus because he writes at the end, 'But I shall remain at

* * * * *

24 among the spirit's gifts] Added in 1532
25 For this definition of 'prophecy,' see chapter 12 n30; also the paraphrase on 13:2 with n4.
26 These ... chapters] All editions from 1519 to 1538. So also LB VI, where the Argument precedes the *Annotations* on 1 Corinthians. In the 1540 *Opera omnia* and LB VII, however, the sentence reads, 'These matters he treats in chapters X, XI, XII, XIII, and XIV.' The addition of chapter 10 to the list may have resulted from the Argument's mistaken assignment of the discussion of sacrificial meat to the ninth, rather than the tenth, chapter. See n21 above.
27 Ambrosiaster *Comm in 1 Cor* (on 5:9) CSEL 81/2 57:5–9. On the attribution of this commentary to Ambrose, see Translators' Note n19.
28 Eg Chrysostom *In 1 Cor hom* 16.1 (on 5:9) PG 61 129 and Theophylact *Expos in 1 Cor* (on 5:9) PG 124 625B, who assume that Paul is referring to an earlier place in the current letter. See chapter 5 n19. For the scholarly debate concerning the number, sequence, and unity of Paul's letters to the Corinthians, see Orr and Walther 18–24, 120–2; Conzelmann 2–5; and Barrett 11–17. On 2 Corinthians in particular, see Furnish 29–48; see also the Argument of 2 Cor n1.

Ephesus until Pentecost' [16:8]; others, from Philippi, for the Greek manuscripts have this subscription.[29] But I cannot guess on what basis those who
thought so have made this inference, unless they conclude that it was written en route because Paul writes: 'But I shall come when I have passed
through Macedonia, for I shall pass through Macedonia' [16:5]. And next:
'For I do not want to see you just in passing' [16:7].

The End of the Argument[30]

* * * * *

29 For the subscription and manuscripts that carry it, see A. Robertson and A.
Plummer *A Critical and Exegetical Commentary on the First Epistle of St Paul to
the Corinthians* International Critical Commentary (Edinburgh 1914) xxvii. AV
carries the subscription (of κ, ʟ, and the *textus receptus*). See Metzger 504.
30 In this volume concluding statements such as this, as well as the titles for the
Arguments and the *Paraphrases*, are translated as they appear in the edition of
1532.

THE PARAPHRASE ON THE FIRST EPISTLE OF PAUL TO THE CORINTHIANS BY ERASMUS OF ROTTERDAM

Chapter 1

Paul, not a false apostle, nor a usurper of the apostolic office (although such is the case with some among you),[1] but summoned to this role to be Christ's ambassador,[2] not an ambassador of men; summoned, moreover, not because of my own merit, but only because it pleased God the most merciful Father that by my ministry the glory of the Son might be spread abroad. [I say this] lest perchance you are in some way dissatisfied with this apostle or desire others. Therefore, Paul, no stranger to you, and together with me Sosthenes, my brother in religion and partner in the fellowship of the office, write this letter, not to factions and those fighting divisively, but to the congregation of the church,[3] which the goodness of God has bonded

* * * * *

1 Cf Theophylact *Expos in 1 Cor* (on 1:1) PG 124 564A: 'Observe that the preface immediately attacks false teachers.' On 'false apostle,' see 2 Cor chapter 11 n19. Chomarat I 603 discusses Erasmus' method of amplification in this opening paragraph. See also Translators' Note xviii and xxiv, and *De copia* CWE 24 342–3.
2 'Ambassador': *legatus*, from *legare* 'choose as an envoy.' *Legatus* and its cognate *legatio* 'office' or 'duties of an envoy' are the Latin terms Erasmus regularly uses in the *Paraphrases* to elaborate on the Greek ἀπόστολος 'apostle,' 'one who has been sent.' On the meaning of 'apostle,' see Orr and Walther 141 and Furnish 99; cf 2 Cor chapters 8 n32 and 11 n19, and CWE 50 167 n98. For *legatus* 'ambassador' or 'emissary' and its cognates, see the paraphrases on 2 Cor 1:1 with n1; Eph 1:1; Phil 4:6 with n8; Col 1:1; 1 Tim 1:1 (CWE 44 5); 2 Tim 1:1 (CWE 44 41); Titus 1:1 (CWE 44 57); 1 Pet 1:1 (CWE 44 81); and 2 Pet 1:1 (CWE 44 111).
3 'Congregation of the church': *ecclesiae congregationi*, paraphrasing ἐκκλησία. Although in his translation of 1 Corinthians Erasmus always renders the Greek ἐκκλησία 'church' by its Latin transliteration *ecclesia*, in representing the term in the *Paraphrase* he uses *congregatio* 'congregation' as often as *ecclesia*, and

firmly together[4] at Corinth in singleness of mind and heart and, as is fitting
for Christians, in mutual love. It is at God's bidding that I undertake this
embassy; he has built a new and heavenly city on the old one, and in place
of a human community has set up a heavenly one, namely, one cleansed
from old vices and passions, from the pride of riches, from the arrogance
of philosophy, and from the other diseases which usually give rise among
mortals to divisions and disputes. Far removed from these ought they to be
whom the same God, the same advocate Christ, the same baptism, the same
religion, the same reward unite and tie together in so many ways. Christ
once freely removed the offences of your former life so that thereafter by
living holy lives you might preserve the innocence he restored to you. For
not through your own merit have you obtained this, nor do you owe it to
wealth or to philosophy[5] or to the keeping of the Mosaic law, but to Christ
Jesus, who once and for all cleansed you by his own blood and then called
you to a never-failing and perpetual wholeness and holiness of life.[6] And
what I say does not apply to you alone; it applies to all people anywhere
on earth who profess the name of our Lord Jesus Christ and, having no
trust in their own resources, rely on his protection, whether they be among

* * * * *

here combines the two. On the special sense *congregatio* sometimes conveys,
see chapter 16 n13; also CWE 44 71 n7 and CWE 50 40 n20. In this translation
of the *Paraphrase*, *ecclesia* is always rendered by 'church' and *congregatio* by
'congregation.'
4 'Has bonded firmly together': *conglutinavit*. This is the verb Erasmus uses
frequently to express the action of the Holy Spirit in establishing the church's
peace and harmony. Cf eg the paraphrases on 6:5 with n10 and 6:19: 'You have
imbibed this spirit in baptism, and by it you are firmly bonded to Christ';
also on 16:24 with n16, Phil 2:2 with n2, and John 14:27 CWE 46 174: 'The
peace I leave you, attaching you to each other in mutual harmony ...' In the
paraphrase on 1:3, *concordia* 'concord' or 'singleness of heart' is introduced by
Erasmus as the central idea in his paraphrase on 'peace,' an idea elaborately
developed as the essential counterpart of *gratia* 'grace.' See Chrysostom *In 1
Cor hom* 1.1 (on 1:2) PG 61 13 and Theophylact *Expos in 1 Cor* (on 1:2) PG 124
564B for similar emphasis on Paul's concerns with unity and close bonding. On
Erasmus' view of the church and the importance of ecclesiastical concord and
consensus, and for the verb *conglutinare* in particular, see James K. McConica
'Erasmus and the Grammar of Consent' 82–7.
5 Cf Theophylact *Expos in 1 Cor* (on 1:2) PG 124 564B–C: 'through baptism namely,
not through wisdom or wealth, on account of which you are puffed up.'
6 See the annotations on Rom 1:1 ('called an apostle') and 1:7 ('called saints')
CWE56 5–6and 30–1, where Erasmus similarly defines the Christian 'vocation'
as a calling to 'holiness of life' and contrasts it with both the Greek reliance
on human wisdom and the Jewish observance of Mosaic law. See also the
paraphrase on Rom 1:7 CWE 42 16.

the Jews or among the gentiles.[7] There is the same church for all, the same
fellowship; all are equally under obligation to Christ alone because they
have been delivered from the most hideous slavery of their sins and have
been chosen to make a profession[8] of holiness. Neither locality nor race
divides the cause of the gospel; Christ is common to all equally; equally
free is whatever he gives to anyone at all.

* * * * *

7 This sentence and the next two illustrate Erasmus' attempt to incorporate
   within his paraphrase differing interpretations of the biblical text. A literal
   translation preserving the word order of the Greek text at the end of 1:2
   might read as follows: 'called as saints together with all those who call upon
   the name of our Lord Jesus Christ, in every place, both theirs and ours.' At
   issue is the reference of the possessive pronouns 'theirs and ours' placed ambiguously at the end of the verse. Erasmus discusses three possible interpretations in his original (1516) note in the annotation on 1:2 (ipsorum). The first
   applies the possessives to 'Lord' as a rhetorical reinforcement of Christian
   unity: the one Lord belongs to all. This is the interpretation Erasmus discovered in Chrysostom In 1 Cor hom 1.1 (on 1:2) PG 61 13 and Theophylact Expos
   in 1 Cor (on 1:2) PG 124 564C–565A, and is the prevailing modern interpretation: '. . . all those who in every place call on the name of our Lord Jesus
   Christ, both their Lord and ours' (RSV; so also AV and NEB). Erasmus calls
   this reading affectata 'strained' or 'affected.' In a second interpretation, the
   pronouns are taken as a simple expansion on 'in every place': 'whether in
   their own places, where they are active, or in these in which we are' and is
   perhaps represented in the Douay translation: '. . . all that invoke the name
   of our Lord Jesus Christ in every place of theirs and ours.' Erasmus recommends a third interpretation, a variation on the second, as argutior 'more striking' and 'Pauline': 'in whatever place, whether theirs or ours.' Here also, the
   pronouns are taken with 'place,' but with, he argues, the special nuance of
   showing that Paul 'considers every place in which people invoke the name
   of the Lord to be his own since among Christians charity makes all things
   common.' It is in Ambrosiaster Comm in 1 Cor (on 1:2) CSEL 81/2 5:20–6:2,
   however, that Erasmus finds an additional fourth interpretation (incorporated here in the paraphrase and mentioned in the Annotations for the first
   time in 1519): that 'theirs and ours' may be specifically intended to designate both gentile and Jewish Christian communities. The paraphrase point-
   edly avoids the personal possessives and manages within its emphasis on
   both universality and unity to accommodate all the interpretations mentioned
   in the annotation.
8 'Profession': professionem. Erasmus uses the word in several related senses,
   specifically, a baptismal vow; more generally, the profession of faith and devotion that distinguishes Christians from non-Christians; most generally, any
   claim to some skill or quality, as the philosophers' claim to wisdom; similarly
   the verb profiteri 'profess.' In the paraphrase on 7:12–14, Erasmus uses prof-
   itentes (or professi) Christum 'professing Christ,' initiati Christo 'initiated into
   Christ,' and baptizati 'baptized' synonymously. Cf 1 Thess chapter 5 n9.

Therefore, for them as well as for you I wish a common grace and concord, neither of which will any one else provide except the one to whom you owe all things, God the Father, from whom all our happiness springs forth as from a fountain, and our Lord Jesus Christ, through whom alone the Father willed that all things be conferred.[9] Grace will protect your innocence; concord accompanies it. Grace reclaims you from your sins and restores you to God's favour; concord restores you to each other's favour. Through grace the kindness is so perceived that its author[10] is not unknown; through concord it is made evident that you have embraced Christianity not just in name only, but also in actual fact. Through the one you share in the heavenly beneficence; through the other what you have received from heaven you pour out in turn on one another to the best of your ability.

There is, through God's generosity, something on which I congratulate you and for which I also give thanks to God. But there is in turn something that I find lacking in you, and would prefer to see corrected.[11] Among you there are some who live up to their profession and some in whom you recognize remnants and traces of their former life. I say this because, just as I consider your welfare my own, so, if anything is amiss, I count it my business. Therefore, I do not cease to thank my God on your account since by his goodness the munificence of Christ has become so fruitful

* * * * *

9 Erasmus is paraphrasing the rather typical Pauline salutation: 'Grace to you and peace from God our Father and the Lord Jesus Christ.' What follows in the paraphrase is an effective rhetorical expansion in which the terms 'grace' and 'peace' (the latter Erasmus represents by *concordia* 'concord') are clarified and defined in relation to each other by a series of balanced and increasingly complex sentences. For Erasmus' technique in defining theological terms in this passage and others, see Sider 'Grace' 16–25.

10 'Author': *auctor*, a frequent term in this *Paraphrase* for God as creator, prime mover, initiator, or source, from whom all goodness springs. The term will soon be contrasted with *minister* 'minister,' 'assistant,' 'steward.' See the paraphrase on 1:7. The contrast will be further developed in the paraphrase on 1:13–14. The pairing of divine *auctor* and human *ministri* provides a continuing and unifying focus for Erasmus' amplification of the letter's first four chapters: the Corinthian 'problem,' ie the division and dissension within the church that results from confusing the stewardship of apostles with the authorship of God, from taking assistants for authors, stewards for masters. The distinction is one between the proper owner of a business or estate and the manager appointed to oversee it. *Auctor* is rendered variously in this translation as 'master,' 'author,' 'source,' and twice as 'initiative.' See also nn14 and 17 below.

11 Here in the paraphrase on 1:4 Erasmus anticipates the rebuke that is to begin in verse 10, as did Ambrosiaster. See *Comm in 1 Cor* (on 1:4) CSEL 81/2 6:20–7:3.

in you that you who previously were hunting the unstable and transitory riches of the world have now been amply provided through the kindness of Christ with the imperishable riches of heaven. These alone render you truly blessed. For there is no gift either of speech or of knowledge that you have not fully acquired. Not long ago you were swollen with the arrogance of your worthless philosophy, but now, embracing true wisdom instead of false, you cultivate modesty.[12] Formerly you were pleased with yourselves, trusting to your human eloquence, but now that your tongues have been inspired from heaven, you speak of heavenly matters. And you have also persevered firmly in what you know is best. As a result, both the truth of the gospel and faith in Christ have through you been made more resplendent and more certain, while from the evidence itself it has been made clear[13] to all that what has been accomplished in you has not been accomplished with human patronage, but through God's initiative.[14] By adding his gifts he has confirmed our preaching. For although you have seen neither Peter nor James, whom some consider either the only or the chief apostles,[15] nevertheless in none of those things by which God is accustomed to confirm the ministry of apostles do you seem inferior to the others.[16] As a result it may clearly be seen that although ministers may be different, yet the author is the same since the same effect follows.[17]

* * * * *

12 you cultivate modesty] Added in *1521*. In *1519* the participle *amplexi* 'having embraced' functioned as a finite verb, and the sentence ended: 'But now you have embraced true wisdom instead of false.'

13 'From the evidence itself it has been made clear': *ipsa re declaratum est* – a variation on *res indicabit, res ipsa loquitur,* or *res ipsa declarat.* On this idiom, see *Adagia* III iv 49; also CWE 46 45 n5, 60 n57, and 139 n53. Cf the paraphrase on 3:3 with n6; also 2 Cor chapters 3 n1 and 7 n14.

14 'Initiative': *auctore.* See n10 above.

15 Cf Gal 2:9; also the paraphrase on 9:5 with n14. Chomarat I 612 notes the enrichment here of 1:7 with relevant historical context and refers to Erasmus' discussion of this technique in *De copia* CWE 24 575-6.

16 By 'those things' that confirm the effectiveness of an apostle's ministry, Erasmus evidently has in mind the specific transformation of the Corinthians' formerly 'human' wisdom and eloquence into the spiritual endowments of true wisdom and divinely inspired speech. Cf Paul's more general claim in 9:1-2 that winning Corinth for Christ is the sign of his apostleship; also the paraphrase on 9:1-2. For the signs of apostolic legitimacy, see also Rom 15:18-19; 2 Cor 12:11-13; Gal 3:5.

17 In the distinction between ministers and authors, Erasmus anticipates 1:12-13 and 3:4-9. On this technique, see Chomarat I 611-12. See also nn10 and 11 above.

Now as you hold these gifts of yours as securities for an everlasting life to come, so from these things that you see acquiring a trust in those you do not see,[18] you await that day on which Christ, who now seems yet to be suffering in his members, shall openly reveal his majesty, separating the ungodly from the godly and driving out every affliction from his people. In your longing for this day you suffer hardships; the fear of it keeps you dutiful. For although[19] people wrongly condemn or acquit, surely that day shall with unerring reckoning either consign to eternal punishment or appoint to everlasting life. And there is no reason for you to be distrustful. The one who will someday be your judge is now the one present to assist you. It is by his favour that you have been restored to innocence from the errors of your former life. It is by his favour also that, just as you have begun to lead a godly and pure life, so will you persevere in your blameless conduct. Thus the dreadful day of our Lord Jesus Christ will not find in you anything meriting the black stone.[20] That this will be so I am confident, relying not on my own resources or on yours, but on the goodness of God, who deprives no one of his hope and defaults on nothing that he promises.[21] Since by his own good will he has freely adopted you and admitted you into partnership with his only Son, our Lord Jesus Christ, he will support you also as you struggle to persevere in the honour of adoption[22] and not to be deprived of the inheritance, of which you already hold payment in earnest.[23]

* * * * *

18 For the progress from knowledge of things seen to faith in things unseen, see Rom 1:19–20 and Heb 11:1–3. Cf the paraphrase on 1:21 with n46, where Erasmus also seems to have the passage from Romans in mind.

19 although] *ut*; first in 1521; previously *ne*, 'lest [people wrongly condemn . . .]'

20 'Black stone': *atrum calculum*, referring to an ancient voting procedure by which a white stone meant acquittal, and a black stone a condemnation. Cf Ovid *Metamorphoses* 15.41–4.

21 For a similar definition of God's 'faithfulness,' see Chrysostom *In 1 Cor hom* 2.2 (on 1:9) PG 61 19 and Theophylact *Expos in 1 Cor* (on 1:9) PG 124 569B. Chomarat I 595 uses this sentence as an example of Erasmus' amplification through definition. See also *De copia* CWE 24 332.

22 Cf Ambrosiaster *Comm in 1 Cor* (on 1:9) CSEL 81/2 8:21–4: 'So may we be found not faithless and distrustful, but persevering in our adoption.'

23 Erasmus may be borrowing the metaphor of adoption and inheritance from Romans 8:15–17. See the paraphrase on this passage CWE 42 47–8, where Erasmus calls God's Spirit a pledge (*pignus*) or sign of inheritance: 'This pledge, so to speak, and symbol of paternal love, gives confidence to our spirit that we are the sons of him who gave the pledge.' The image of the earnest or guarantee may be taken from 2 Cor 1:22, 2 Cor 5:5, or Eph 1:14. Erasmus uses it again in the paraphrase on 1 John 5:12–13 CWE 44 199. See also the note on that passage (199 n18), explaining the distinction Erasmus makes between *arrabo* 'the earnest' and *pignus* 'pledge.'

Up to this point I have spoken about matters for which I rejoice on your behalf – both those in which I wish you to remain constant and those in which I should like you to go on making progress. Now hear what I find lacking in some of you, what needs to be changed, and in what I very much want you to be unlike yourselves. It is not necessary that I teach you what befits your profession, for you know that well enough. I only beseech you, dearest brethren, through the name of our Lord Jesus Christ (which, as is perfectly right, is most holy to all those who have once been initiated into it), that your harmony not be split apart by shameful divisions, but that you agree in minds and tongues alike so that you may truly be one body, whole in that all its parts cling mutually together.[24] Worldly wisdom is split apart because of differing beliefs and doctrines, and from this comes the eternal contention of its schools and sects.[25] But the beliefs of Christian philosophy are the same among all people, and it does not know those little rivulets of human sects and opinions. There is one instructor and author of all. For that reason, just as the initiates of this philosophy are joined together by the agreement of their minds, it is right that they refrain also from words that speak dissension. To disagree in mind[26] is ungodly; to fight with words is shameful.

And lest you think I infer these things from groundless suspicion, they were reported to me by those whose piety and integrity deserve trust. You know Chloe, a woman noted[27] for her devotion; you know that the

* * * * *

24 The paraphrase here reflects Erasmus' New Testament translation and his annotation. The Greek verb καταρτίζω has the meaning 'to make sound,' 'complete.' In the Greek of 1:10 the verb appears as a perfect participle passive with the verb 'to be,' ἦτε κατηρτισμένοι, which Erasmus renders not by the Vulgate's *sitis perfecti* 'that you be perfect' but by *sitis integrum corpus* 'that you be a whole body.' See the annotation on 1:10 (*sitis autem perfecti*): 'For Paul warns that they should not only be harmonious in language, speaking the same thing, but also that, just as the members of a whole body are driven by the same spirit, they should likewise have the same mind.' The paraphrase on 1:10 here anticipates the later metaphor of the Corinthians as members of Christ's body (12:12–27). Cf Chrysostom *In 1 Cor hom* 3.1 (on 1:10) PG 61 23. For Erasmus' technique of anticipation, see nn11 and 17 above.
25 and sects] Added in 1532. Cf n29 below.
26 'In mind': *intus*, literally 'inwardly.' Erasmus' paraphrase places rather more emphasis than his patristic authorities placed on outward harmony, the necessity of avoiding discordant speech as well as dissentient minds. See eg Chrysostom *In 1 Cor hom* 3.1 (on 1:10) PG 61 23 and Theophylact *Expos in 1 Cor* (on 1:10) PG 124 569C–570A.
27 'Noted': *spectatam*. On this word, which carries the sense of 'tested' or 'proven,' see CWE 50 46 n7 and 98 n54. See also 2 Cor chapter 8 n26.

members of her household are not unlike their mistress.[28] I have heard from them (as they both devote themselves to your welfare and attend to my concerns) that there are disputes among you in the manner of parties contending among themselves. For what else do these words mean, which are everywhere heard among you, as for example when this one says, 'I belong to Paul'; and that one on the other hand, 'I belong to Apollos'; another, 'I to Cephas'; another, 'I to Christ'? What? Are these not the names of parties and sects? It is the same way with those who pursue the foolish wisdom of this world: one boasts of Pythagoras, another of Plato, one of Aristotle, another of Zeno, one of Epicurus,[29] another of now this master and now that one, and each battles with the other on behalf of his own master. We have only one master; we have the same doctrines, the same target.[30] From where, then, do these different names come? Has Christ been carved up,[31] and does he disagree with himself? Why do we parcel out among

* * * * *

28 Chrysostom *In 1 Cor hom* 3.1 (on 1:11) PG 61 23 comments similarly on the trustworthiness of the informants; also Ambrosiaster *Comm in 1 Cor* (on 1:11) CSEL 81/2 9:22–4: 'To some ... [Chloe] seems to have been a woman devoted to God; with her there would have been many worshippers of God, whose trustworthiness would not be questioned.' Ambrosiaster, however, appears uncertain whether the proper name refers to people, a place, or a woman. Erasmus, in the annotation on 1:11 (*ab his qui sunt Chloes*), argues on grounds of syntactic propriety and from the example of Horace *Odes* 3.9 that 'Chloe,' being a woman's name, identifies a Corinthian household, not a geographic locality.

29 one of Epicurus] Added in 1532. Erasmus elsewhere also lists the names of the major philosophers of antiquity and their schools. Cf eg the *Paraclesis* Holborn 140:19–23 and the annotation on Rom 1:16 ('for I do not feel ashamed of the gospel') CWE 56 41. Cf the paraphrase on 1 Cor 3:4, where Erasmus uses a similar list to illustrate the disunity and divisiveness of human loyalties and then extends the illustration to include the religious orders of his own day. Cf also the annotation on 1:10 (*ut idipsum dicatis*), where the list is that of scholastic theological sects. For an expansive patristic version of the comparison between Christian unity and pagan multiplicity, see Augustine *De civitate Dei* 19.1–4 CSEL 40/2 362–80, where the unity of Christian faith is contrasted with Varro's classification of 288 schools of classical philosophy. Cf also Ambrosiaster *Comm in 1 Cor* (on 1:13) CSEL 81/2 10:17–22 for a catalogue of Christian heretical loyalties. For the importance of unity and consensus in Erasmus' thought, see McConica 'Erasmus and the Grammar of Consent,' especially 80–9 and 95–9.

30 the same target] Added in 1532. *Scopus*, here translated 'target,' might also be translated 'sighting' or 'focal point.' See the paraphrase on Phil 3:14 with n43.

31 'Has ... been carved up': *sectus est*. Erasmus may intend a pun on the similarity (in sound only) between the participle *sectus* 'cut' and the unrelated noun *secta* 'sect' or 'school of philosophy.'

humans the glory of this profession, making stewards into masters,[32] when all the glory is owed to him alone? To whom do you owe your innocence? Is it not to the one who washed you with his own blood? Why, therefore, do you allege for yourself some other name than the name of the one whose kindness this is? Or (and I speak this way for the sake of teaching) was Paul crucified on your behalf? If you all owe this kindness to Christ alone – and all of you equally, since he died for all alike – why do you adopt for yourselves the titles of different men, as if allotting to them what you ought to have credited to Christ alone? Through baptism we are grafted onto Christ, and we are baptized in his name, from whom proceeds all the force of baptism.

But how is it right for you to be called Paul's rather than Christ's, when you were baptized not in Paul's name, but in Christ's? If through this favourable opportunity glory, which is owed to God, is claimed for the names of men, then I thank God that I baptized none of you except Crispus and Gaius, who, if I am not mistaken, claim from this no glory for themselves and recognize that I was the minister, but Christ the author.[33] Now if I had baptized many, there might possibly be some who would wish to be called Paulines rather than Christians. Meanwhile, however, it occurs to me that I did baptize the household of Stephanas. I do not remember clearly enough whether I baptized anyone else. I am more mindful of things that are more important. In baptism the part contributed by the human agent is very small. Anyone can pronounce the customary words. And to wash[34] a willing and ready person with water is not only easy to do, but safe as

* * * * *

32 For Erasmus' repeated contrast between steward (*minister*) and master (*auctor*), see n10 above, and cf the paraphrase on 1:14 (next paragraph) with n33.

33 Erasmus has John the Baptist elaborate on this distinction in the paraphrase on John 1:34 CWE 46 31–2. Cf the paraphrase on Acts 11:16 CWE 50 78 and especially n23. See also Payne *Theology* 156 and n9 for Erasmus' emphasis on Christ, and not the minister, as the source of baptism's power.

34 'To wash': *tingere*, literally 'to wet,' 'to moisten,' or 'to dip.' *Tingere* seems to have been the Latin word early Christians used for 'baptize' before *baptizare* was adopted from Greek. See Alexander Souter *A Glossary of Later Latin to 600 A.D.* (Oxford 1949) 421. The word probably suggests immersion, rather than aspersion. For Erasmus' depreciatory comments on the latter method, see Payne *Theology* 157 and n15. For Erasmus' use of *tingere* for baptism elsewhere in the *Paraphrases*, see the Argument 20 and the paraphrase on 6:8; see also the paraphrases on John 1:33 CWE 46 31 ('For a human being washes with water'); Mark 1:10 CWE 49 19 ('The body is bathed with water'); and Luke 3:16 LB VII 313D ('I wash the body with water').

well.[35] To lead someone, however, through efficacious discourse away from sins that have long since become habitual, away from ancestral ceremonies and ordinances, into both a religion and a life far different – and this not without great danger to one's life – this truly is a service worthy of an apostolic man.[36] From this would come a more just reason for boasting if it were right to claim anything for ourselves. It is not that I disapprove of baptism, but that I give precedence to more important things, particularly when this task above all has been assigned to me. For Christ did not destine[37] for me this mission among the gentiles so that I might be only[38] a minister of baptism, but so that through my office as herald I might make the glory of his name shine among all people, and join as many as possible to him through the teaching of the gospel. Yet even here there is nothing of which I may humanly boast. For he did not wish this to be accomplished by the resources of human wisdom or eloquence – resources that could provide nothing of this sort – but he wanted so arduous an exploit[39] to be carried out by simple and unadorned speech[40] so that all the praise for the feat

* * * * *

35 as well] Added in 1532. For similar references to baptism, see the Argument 20 and the paraphrase on 6:8–10. For Erasmus' disparagement of the sufficiency of formal baptism, see the following note and especially chapter 6 n26.

36 The comparison between baptizing and preaching in this passage seems to draw on Chrysostom *In 1 Cor hom* 3.3 (on 1:17) PG 61 26 and on Theophylact *Expos in 1 Cor* (on 1:17) PG 124 576C. Cf eg Theophylact's explanation of the verse: 'To proclaim the gospel was more laborious and also required a soul of iron. For to change a person's persuasion and to take the person away from ancestral teachings – and that, in the midst of dangers – that is the work of a great and noble soul.' See also Paul's preference for prophetic preaching over other spiritual gifts in chapter 14 and Erasmus' paraphrase on John 4:2: 'Yet Jesus himself was not baptizing, even then showing that the work of preaching is more important than baptizing,' where see CWE 46 53, where see n2. For Erasmus on preaching, see CWE 50 10 n85. On ceremonialism and legalism, cf the paraphrases on 3:12–15 and 8:8 with n25, and chapter 9 n6.

37 'Destine': *destinavit*. On this word and its compound *praedestinare*, see Erasmus' commentary in the annotation on Rom 1:4 ('who was predestined') CWE 56 10–11 and especially nn10 and 17.

38 only] Added in 1532

39 Cf the Argument 19–20 with n3.

40 'By simple and unadorned speech': *incomposito simplicique sermone*. The paraphrase follows Erasmus' own translation of 1:17 (*non erudito sermone*) rather than the Vulgate's (*non in sapientia verbi*). See the annotation on 1:17 (*non in sapientia verbi*), where Erasmus argues, first, that the Greek term σοφία conveys not

may be assigned to God, whom it pleased to renew all the world through the despised and dishonoured cross of Christ.

The cross of Christ seems a low and worthless affair, but this lowliness subdues all the loftiness of this world. This crude and unpolished speech, by which we proclaim that Christ was fixed to the cross and died on the cross, seems to be a foolish and ignorant thing, but to whom, may I ask, does it seem so? Surely to those who, blinded by their old vices, do not hear the gospel word inwardly, and therefore perish because they have rejected that from which their salvation could arise. Those, however, who attain eternal salvation from this source understand indeed that it is no feeble thing, but one that is more efficacious than all human deployments and that proceeds directly from God. By this new and least known method, it seemed good to him to restore all the world. That he would do this he once had promised through the prophet Isaiah, where he speaks thus: 'I will destroy the wisdom of the wise, and the cleverness of the clever I will thwart' [29:14]. Has he not fulfilled what he promised? Do we not see the world being renewed? Do we not see people distrusting their former religion, their former philosophy, and embracing the cross of Christ? Do they not now understand that what previously was regarded as pious devotion is impious, and what formerly seemed wise is very foolish? Where, meanwhile, is the wise man swelling up with his knowledge of the Law? Where is the scribe haughty with his exposition of the Law? Where is the philosopher who explores the secrets of nature and, unmindful of the maker, marvels at created things? They all made big promises, but they have both deceived

* * * * *

only 'wisdom' (the Vulgate's *sapientia*), but also 'elegance' and 'erudition'; and second, that *sermo*, rather than the Vulgate's *verbum*, best renders the Greek λόγος. (On Erasmus' preference for *sermo*, see CWE 46 15 n16; also 1 Thess chapter 2 n20.) In a *1519* addition to the annotation, he refers to speech (*sermo*) about the cross as 'simple and unadorned' (*simplex et incompositus*) – quite different from the beautified, embellished speech of philosophers and rhetors. Cf the paraphrase on 2:1–5 with n6; also the paraphrase on Gal 4:13–14 CWE 42 117 and the Argument of the Epistle to the Romans CWE 42 12. For the tradition of humble speech in Christian preaching, see Augustine *De doctrina christiana* 4.6.9, 4.9.23–10.25, 4.15.32, 4.18.35, 4.26.56 CSEL 80 123–4, 134–6, 140–1, 144, 163–4, and the discussion of Augustine's rhetoric in Erich Auerbach 'Sermo Humilis' *Literary Language and Its Public in Late Latin Antiquity and in the Middle Ages* trans Ralph Manheim (New York 1965) 27–66. For Erasmus' relation to this tradition, see Marjorie O'Rourke Boyle 'Weavers, farmers, tailors, travellers, masons, prostitutes, pimps, Turks, little women, and Other Theologians' *Erasmus in English* 3 (1971) 1–7 and Bateman 'From Soul to Soul' 7–16.

and been deceived. They were promising righteousness[41] and happiness; meanwhile they themselves were unhappy and buried in sins.[42] God has allowed them through their blindness (and so did their presumption deserve) to go headlong into every kind of disgrace,[43] so that he might show them to themselves, and in repenting[44] they might at last understand that their claim[45] to wisdom was hollow and powerless. Has God therefore not shown the wisdom of this world to be foolish?

Earlier as well he had shown his own wisdom through this most beautiful spectacle of the world created by the highest reason in order that from their admiration for the work human beings might be swept into love for the maker of the work. But because of their own sin this matter turned out quite differently. They admired and worshipped created things, but scorned the author as if he were unknown,[46] and so they lived as though God either approved vices or did not govern what he had created. Therefore, he undertook to achieve the same purpose by a different path. It seemed best that those for whom the wisdom shown through creation had turned out for the worse should be restored through the preaching of a message that would seem foolish and base to mortals: that those who as philosophers were worshipping dumb stones for gods should now as believers obtain

* * * * *

41 'Righteousness': *iustitiam*. By this term, which might also be translated 'justice,' Erasmus seems to mean a condition of innocence or sinlessness. See Phil chapter 3 n22; also CWE 42 xxxvii, CWE 44 xvii with n40, and CWE 50 7 n36 and 23 n105. On the meanings of *iustitia* in Erasmus' New Testament scholarship, see Sider 'The Just,' especially 4–8.

42 Cf Erasmus' treatment of philosophers' and lawgivers' futile promises of happiness at the opening of the *Paraphrase on Mark* CWE 49 13.

43 Cf Rom 1:21–32 and Erasmus' paraphrase on this passage CWE 42 18–19, where he similarly uses *passus est* 'he allowed' or 'suffered' in order to clarify God's relationship to human blindness and sin. See in particular CWE 42 18 n20.

44 'Repenting': *resipiscentes*. On this word, see the Argument n15.

45 'Claim': *professionem*. Erasmus' use of the word is deliberate in order to contrast the philosophers' claims to wisdom with the Christians' profession of Christ. On *professio*, see n8 above.

46 Erasmus perhaps alludes to Paul's mention of an altar 'to an unknown god' at the beginning of his speech to the Athenians (Acts 17:22–30). There are in fact many echoes here in the paraphrase on 1:20–1 of that speech and also of Rom 1:19–23, 25 (cf nn18 and 43 above), in particular the failure of the world's wise to know the invisible God through the glories of the visible creation, and their worship of idolatrous images instead of the true God. The first of these is noted as well by Chrysostom *In 1 Cor hom* 4.2 (on 1:21) PG 61 32 and Theophylact *Expos in 1 Cor* (on 1:21) PG 124 580B–C in explaining the folly of the world's wisdom.

true salvation through the cross of Christ, and now having come to distrust the defences of human philosophy should through faith trust in God's goodness. For there was no hope of salvation, had they not understood the source from which it had been right to hope for salvation. Of first importance, therefore, was the need for all people to do away with the confidence they had in themselves – not only Jews, but also gentiles. In fact, just as the Jews demand wondrous signs and pride themselves on their ancestors' miracles, so do the Greeks strive for erudition and for the knowledge of philosophy, assuring themselves that from this will come happiness and glory. Both have been deceived in their thinking. For the Jews through confidence in the Law have fallen away from Christ, and the philosophers, bloated with their belief in wisdom, do not accept the outwardly humble preaching of the cross.

But[47] we do not preach the conversations Moses had with God,[48] or the angels who received hospitality from Abraham,[49] or the sun that was ordered to stand still[50] – or any such thing as the Jews preen themselves on. Nor on the other hand do we preach the movements of heavenly spheres or the influence of constellations or the causes of lightning. Knowledge of such phenomena leads to arrogance in the Greeks. What then? We preach a message that looks at first sight to be foolish and lowly, namely, Christ crucified, whose lowliness offered the Jews a cause for falling – people who marvel at the prodigy of Jonah, yet disparage the deeds of Christ although he is so much greater than Jonah.[51] To the Greeks, however, who investigate all things with human reasoning, it seems foolish that by heavenly power a maiden conceived a child, that God lay hidden under human form, that life has been restored by death, that he who was once dead has come to life again.[52] Thus to both, Christ seems worthy of contempt, but only to

* * * * *

47 Chomarat I 603–4 uses this paragraph (paraphrasing 1:23) to illustrate Erasmus' techniques of amplification.
48 Such conversations are recorded frequently in Exodus. See eg 5:22–6:13 and 33:12–23. Ambrosiaster *Comm in 1 Cor* (on 1:22) CSEL 81/2 16:16–18 refers to the episode of the burning bush (Exod 3:2–4:17).
49 See Gen 18.
50 See Josh 10:12–14.
51 Cf Matt 12:41; Luke 11:32. Ambrosiaster *Comm in 1 Cor* (on 1:22) CSEL 81/2 16:14–15 also cites the prodigies involving Jonah among the signs sought by the Jews.
52 Ambrosiaster *Comm in 1 Cor* (on 1:23) CSEL 81/2 16:26–17:3 similarly cites the virgin birth and the resurrection of the dead as things 'incongruous to worldly reasoning.'

those who still trust wrongly in their own defences. Yet those whom divine inbreathing[53] has called to faith and who have already been transformed through the preaching of the gospel – whether Jews or Greeks – perceive that the same lowly Christ who was crucified is the power of God and the wisdom of God as well. And so now neither do Jews long for miraculous signs since they discover greater ones in Christ, nor the Greeks for wisdom, once they discover Christ, the fountain of all wisdom.

God has in a way[54] cast himself down from his sublime height to our lowliness;[55] from his wisdom he came down to our foolishness. Nevertheless what seemed foolish in him surpasses all the wisdom of the world, and what seemed feeble in him has been sturdier than all human strength. What is more humiliating than to be hanged on a cross as a criminal between criminals? And yet in this way he alone completely conquered death, which had been conquered by no one. What is more artless or belongs more to ordinary people than the teaching of the gospel? It has renewed all the world, a feat that before this nothing the philosophers professed was able to accomplish, to the end that none of the praise for this deed should be assigned to human supports. That would have happened if the affair had been conducted with the auxiliary props of wealth or erudition, through those in power or distinguished by their profession of wisdom. Because, now, through uneducated folk and fishermen the pinnacle of human wisdom has been taken by storm,[56] we realize that the glory of this whole work

* * * * *

53 What Erasmus has in mind by *divinus afflatus*, the 'divine inbreathing' or 'inspiration' that calls one to faith, may not be immediately clear to the reader. For a fuller description of the Spirit's secret instruction of a wisdom otherwise inaccessible, see the paraphrase on 2:7–16. Cf also the paraphrases on 2:4, 3:7, 6:11, and 7:18, and chapter 2 nn6, 9, and 13.

In the twofold description that begins this sentence, there is perhaps an allusion to a scholastic distinction between 'infused faith' and 'acquired faith' – the former coming through an infusion of grace, the latter gained through the 'hearing' of Scripture or preaching as well as through other means. See Oberman *Harvest* 68–74. 'Divine inbreathing' here may also suggest the category of grace called *auxilium speciale*, a special aid or grace that supplements an individual's natural gifts ('natural grace') and merits in order to initiate the soteriological process. See Payne *Theology* 76–85, and cf the phrase 'infused habits of grace' CWE 56 154 n13. Cf also 2 Cor chapter 4 n12. For the medieval traditions regarding the categories of grace, see Oberman *Harvest* 135–45.

54 in a way] Added in *1532*

55 Erasmus amplifies God's 'folly' and 'weakness' by alluding to Phil 2:5–8.

56 Erasmus' military metaphors and his juxtaposition of fishermen and the unlearned with the world's philosophers and rulers find a parallel in Chrysostom *In 1 Cor hom* 4.3–5 (on 1:22–5) PG 61 34–7: eg 'How greatly did [Plato]

belongs to God alone, whose secret power has brought forth opposites from opposites.[57]

Now what I am saying is not only applicable to Christ or to the apostles; the same condition appears among your flock, those whom God has called to this grace. You yourselves, brethren, see how few persons there are among you endowed with human learning, how scarce are those judged in popular opinion to be powerful, how few are renowned for their distinguished line of ancestors.[58] Through the lowly the glory of the gospel sprang forth; through the lowly it is being spread abroad so that, contrary to the normal course of events, lowliness overwhelms loftiness, and simplicity refutes human cunning. Therefore those things that seem before the world unrefined and ignorant, these especially God has chosen so that the professors of human wisdom may be the more ashamed of their trifling effort. And things that in the opinion of most people seem weak, these especially he has chosen in order to laugh the more at[59] those who, because of factions and wealth, or tyranny, or any other capability think themselves powerful. And things that to the world are humble and despised – yes, even those that are regarded as nothing – these chiefly has he chosen so that he might make obsolete[60] whatever used to seem most important, so that mortal flesh, or

* * * * *

labour to show that the soul was immortal; yet he said nothing clear, and in this way he died, having persuaded none of his hearers. But the cross persuaded by means of unlearned men; yes, it persuaded even the whole world. ... Rustics and the unlearned – it made philosophers of them all. ... it overran the whole world, and took all people by force. ... For the upright deeds that publicans and fishermen were able to accomplish through the grace of God, these deeds, philosophers and rhetoricians and tyrants and, in short, the whole world, running about on countless paths, could not even imagine' (34–5). For Erasmus' use of the metaphor 'taking by storm' in similar contexts, see CWE 46 60 with n56, CWE 49 94 with n25, and CWE 50 7 with n37.

57 Chrysostom *In 1 Cor hom* 4.3 (on 1:22–4) PG 61 33–4 elaborates on God's achievement of opposites by means of opposites.

58 'Distinguished line of ancestors': *maiorum imaginibus,* literally 'the images of their ancestors.' Roman nobles displayed in a conspicuous place in their homes the busts or waxen images of their ancestors as a show of aristocratic distinction. The *imagines* might also be paraded publicly in elaborate funeral processions. See Polybius 6.53–4.

59 'Laugh at': *irrideat.* On this word, as used of God, see CWE 50 36 n55.

60 'He might make obsolete': *antiquaret.* The word indicates the cancellation or annulment of an agreement or legislation. Erasmus uses *antiquare* again in a similar context in the paraphrases on 2:6 (where see n12) and 13:8. See also the paraphrases on 2 Cor 3:11 and 14; Eph 2:15; and Col 2:14. Erasmus glosses the word in his annotation on Heb 8:13 (*veteravit prius*), where it translates πεπαλαίωκε and is glossed as *fecit antiquum* 'he has made it old.' See the

human understanding may have no cause to trust in itself before God as judge. For boasting is futile before human beings; between divine matters and human ones there is no comparison.[61]

Moreover, although in this world's judgment you are cheap and worth very little, yet you have attained the true and highest rank of honour by the kindness of God the Father, who has adopted you into partnership with his Son, through whom by a different means he has bestowed on you all of the rewards that the haughty world was fraudulently promising. Through him has come true and saving wisdom, so that you have no need of philosophy; through him has come innocence, so that you no longer have reason to long for the aid of Moses' law; through him you have received holiness of life, lest any impute this to their own merits; through him has come freedom, in that by his blood we have been redeemed from the tyranny of sins. In short, to Christ alone we owe the sum total of happiness, and to its source, the Father, so that what Jeremiah wrote may clearly come to pass: 'Let not the wise pride himself on his own wisdom, or the powerful trust in his own strength, or the rich be puffed up through trust in his wealth; for these possessions do not grant happiness. But if anyone should wish to boast rightly, let him boast on this account: that he recognizes God as the author and the fountain of all true goods.'[62] Yet[63] let him boast in such a way as not to claim for the world's resources any portion of this enterprise.

* * * * *

paraphrase on that verse CWE 44 234 where *antiquatur* is translated 'is becoming obsolete.' See also CWE 56 92 n1 and CWE 48 97 n19.

61 Erasmus' style here is paratactic, and the connection among the clauses somewhat unclear; he uses no connecting word to indicate whether the second clause is meant to be essentially adversative with reference to the first (granted, there *is* a kind of hollow boasting possible before the world, *but* God's ways are totally different from the world's), or explanatory (there *is* a kind of hollow boasting possible before the world since God's ways are totally different), or copulative and reinforcing (*even* before the world boasting is a hollow activity, *and* God's ways are totally different). Any of these interpretations seems plausible. Although Coverdale chose the second for the 1549 *Paraphrase of Erasmus* (fol vi verso), the last seems most direct and requires the least interpretation on the part of the reader. It has been chosen for this translation. For Coverdale's role in this early English translation, see CWE 42 xxxiii.

62 In 1:31 Paul quotes (inexactly) from the Septuagint of Jer 9:24. Erasmus' annotation on 1:31 (*ut quemadmodum scriptum est*) identifies the allusion as from Jeremiah and quotes the fuller context (Jer 9:23–4), citing the Vulgate. Here he freely paraphrases this larger passage.

63 Yet] *at* in all editions from 1519 to 1540; in LB *aut* 'or,' or possibly 'at least.'

Chapter 2

Let them consider, therefore, in what way they are superior to you,[1] those people who are ashamed of Christ's humility, but vaunt themselves before you by reason of their Law, their wealth, and their wisdom. I surely did not convert you to Christ by such means. For when I first came to you, intending to teach you the secret and hidden wisdom of the gospel,[2] I did not come equipped with the power of some eloquence for you to marvel at, or deserving your respect for some exceptional acquaintance with philosophy, although I knew that you had the highest regard for people of this kind. So far was I from proclaiming any of these qualities that the world deemed excellent that among you I considered myself to know nothing other than Jesus Christ, and him indeed crucified.[3] The one[4] whom I preached was a human being, but one anointed by God and promised by the prophets for the redemption of the human race. It was from what was most lowly in him that I began the preaching of the gospel.

Although my preaching took effect in you, nevertheless from this I claimed no praise for myself. I lived among you not as someone powerful, but as one weak and low in rank; not as one grasping a kingdom, but as one subject to the snares of the ungodly and to perils of every

* * * * *

1 in what way they are superior to you] *quare vobis praestantiores sint;* first in 1532; previously the similar *quid vobis praestent,* 'in what respect they surpass you'

2 'The secret and hidden wisdom of the gospel': *arcanam et reconditam evangelii sapientiam.* The paraphrase seems to favour Ambrosiaster's reading of 2:1 ('mystery of God') rather than that of Erasmus' own text and translation ('testimony of God'). See the annotation on 2:1 (*testimonium Christi*) and Ambrosiaster *Comm in 1 Cor* (on 2:1) CSEL 81/2 21:17–20. Ancient sources are divided on 'testimony' and 'mystery,' but the latter is now favoured. Cf RSV, NRSV, and Metzger 480. On a second textual point, Erasmus' annotation on the verse also corrects the Vulgate's 'testimony of Christ' to 'testimony of God.' The paraphase's 'gospel' would appear to accommodate either reading. Erasmus frequently applies the adjective *arcanus* 'secret,' 'hidden' to Scripture and to matters that may require spiritual interpretation to reveal hidden meanings. Cf n13 below, chapters 11 n38, 12 n15, 14 nn2 and 7, 15 n70, and Phil chapter 1 n34.

3 Cf similar language in the paraphrase on Gal 4:13–14 CWE 42 117, where, in amplifying Paul's description of his first preaching in Galatia, Erasmus borrows from 1 Cor 2:1–4 and also from his paraphrase on 1 Cor 1:17. See chapter 1 n40.

4 The one ... race] Added in 1532

kind.[5] Through patience I overcame the strength of the powerful. Moreover, the character of my life was matched by my style of speaking. Just
as my life had been fortified against the violence of the wicked by no human defences, but by the protection of God alone, so my speech had not
been furnished in any way with the ornaments of the rhetoricians or the
arguments of philosophers that it might show how much I myself could do
either with eloquence or with erudition. Nevertheless, it had the efficacy to
transform you, not through its display of learning, but through the Spirit
and power of God, who through inspiration and miracles was adding persuasive force to the speech, unpolished as it was.[6] That you have been transferred out of the darkness of your earlier life into the light of the gospel[7]
is a fact very difficult to believe, yet firmly established deep within. But
no one should think that you owe this to human teaching or to eloquence,
which we do not claim to have, but to divine power, through which our language was more effective than the philosophers' discourse, however subtly
argued and embellished it might be.

You[8] were swollen with human wisdom, but unacquainted with God's,
when we set before you teachings that are quite simple, yet necessary for
salvation. We have as well teachings about Christ that are more difficult to
understand, but these we discuss among the mature.[9] Strive, therefore, to

* * * * *

5 Erasmus' patristic sources similarly attribute Paul's 'fear and trembling' in 2:3
   to the persecution his preaching elicited. Cf Theophylact *Expos in 1 Cor* (on
   2:3) PG 124 585C: 'persecuted and put to the test and subjected to countless
   terrors'; also Chrysostom *In 1 Cor hom* 6.1 (on 2:3) PG 61 49 and Ambrosiaster
   Comm in 1 Cor (on 2:3) CSEL 81/2 22:19–21.

6 John Bateman, quoting this passage, notes that Erasmus has shifted Paul's
   emphasis from God's power to the contrast between two kinds of discourse.
   See 'From Soul to Soul' 13–14. Cf Origen's quotation of 2:4 in his comparison
   of beautiful but unprofitable philosophical speech with the simple, practical,
   and inspired speech of Scripture in *Contra Celsum* 6.2 PG 11 1289D. On humble
   speech appropriate for preaching, see also chapter 1 n40 and the paraphrase
   on 10:13 with n26. Cf also the paraphrase on 2 Cor 11:6 with n12. See also
   Erasmus' statements in *Ecclesiastes* I and IV ASD V-442:165–74 and V-5 330:383–
   92 about the preacher's dependence upon inspiration, rather than rhetorical
   skill, for effectiveness; also the paraphrase on 1 Pet 4:11 CWE 44 103. For
   Erasmus' interest in effective preaching, see CWE 50 10 n85.

7 Erasmus echoes Col 1:13.

8 you ... mysteries] Added in 1532. With this addition and possibly that indicated in n14 below, Erasmus appears to anticipate 3:1 and the theme of differing levels of maturity among Christians. See also the following note and
   chapter 3 n1.

9 'The mature': *perfectos*. The word also has the sense of 'complete,' 'perfect.' By
   'the mature' who are 'fit for the mysteries,' Erasmus probably means those

be mature so that you may be fit for the mysteries. Now among unbelievers we seem to teach foolishness when we preach the cross of Christ, but
among those who fully believe we seem to preach an exceptional wisdom,[10]
but one far different from that which vainly explores through human reasoning the causes of this world. Nor is it the human wisdom on the basis of
which those who are commonly considered illustrious[11] vaunt and adver-
tise themselves. Their authority, along with their wisdom itself, is through
Christ made null and obsolete[12] since their foolishness has been disclosed.
But we speak a heavenly wisdom, one not exhibiting qualities on the outside

* * * * *

Christians who have ceased all reliance on human wisdom and have imbibed or
been infused with God's Spirit. Cf the paraphrases on 1:24 and 2:7–14; see also
chapter 1 n53, and n14 below. See also Erasmus' discussion of *perfectus* (Greek
τέλειος) in relationship to God's will in the annotation on Rom 12:2 ('what is
the good and the well-pleasing and the perfect will of God') CWE 56 324–5.
Paul's own intention, however, when he says in 1 Cor 2:6 that he imparts
wisdom 'among the mature,' remains uncertain. He may be implying stages
or levels of spiritual progress within the Corinthian Christian community, or
he may be distinguishing Christians from non-Christians. Modern scholarship
is divided on this issue; for the former view, see Conzelmann 60–1 and Barrett
68–9; for the latter, see Orr and Walther 163–4. It is this latter interpretation
that the *1519* text of Erasmus' paraphrase on 2:6–7 appears to expound ie a
differentiation of believers ('the mature') from non-believers. But the *1532*
additions (see n8 above and n14 below) introduce the former sense as well
ie the differentiation of the mature from the immature within the believing
community itself. That Erasmus understands Paul to distinguish the initial
public preaching of the cross from a deeper level of preaching suitable for
advanced believers seems clear from his annotations on 1:25 (*quod stultum est
Dei*) and 2:6 (*sapientiam autem*).

10 Likewise Chrysostom *In 1 Cor hom* 7.1 (on 2:6–7) PG 61 54–5 explains that only
believers recognize that what Paul had earlier called 'foolishness' is in fact
'wisdom' ie salvation by the cross.

11 See the annotation on 2:6 (*neque principum huius seculi*), where Erasmus interprets 'the rulers of this age' to be 'philosophers, orators, and other learned
men who once reigned in the commonwealth,' and he cites the scribes and
Pharisees as the Jewish equivalent of these pagan leaders. He follows Chrysostom *In 1 Cor hom* 7.1 (on 2:6–7) PG 61 55 and Theophylact *Expos in 1 Cor* (on
2:6) PG 124 588C in this interpretation. Ambrosiaster *Comm in 1 Cor* (on 2:6)
CSEL 81/2 24:25–25:5 argued instead that Paul meant here not only Roman and
Jewish leaders, but also spiritual powers of wickedness. Note, however, that,
when Erasmus paraphrases the next reference to these same *principes* in 2:8,
he includes 'the demons themselves' along with the Jewish leaders and specifies 'philosophers' only in a *1532* addition. See n15 below. For modern views
on this issue see Orr and Walther 156–7, 164 and G.B. Caird *Principalities and
Powers* (Oxford 1956).

12 'Made obsolete': *antiquatur*. On this word, see chapter 1 n60.

it does not possess within, but powerful and effective because of its hidden strength.

This wisdom has no arrogance, nor is it accessible to just anyone; it is secret, and it is perceived through secret inbreathings,[13] by those only whom God deems worthy to become partakers of this secret. We[14] do not toss out its more hidden elements to the crowd, but share them in secret with those who are suitable. Although it has been revealed at last in these times, nevertheless God in his eternal design had prepared it for his people before all time so that just as the world, holding its head high, has until now been foolishly boasting of its human wisdom, so after this the lowly may have a far superior wisdom on which to congratulate themselves. This wisdom takes its delight in simple and pure souls, and for that reason not one of the rulers of this age has attained it, not the magi,[15] nor the philosophers, nor

* * * * *

13 'Through secret inbreathings': *arcanis afflatibus*. See the paraphrase on 2:9–12 for a description of how the Spirit secretly instructs. See also the paraphrase on 1:24 with n53 for a similar use of *divinus afflatus* as an infusion of grace that brings perception otherwise unavailable. On *arcanus*, see n2 above.

14 We ... suitable] Added in *1532*, apparently to clarify the paraphrase here on 2:7: 'But we speak the wisdom of God in a mystery, even the hidden wisdom' (AV). The addition corresponds to an addition to the paraphrase on 2:6. See nn8 and 9 above. By using the comparative 'more hidden,' Erasmus may, as in the preceding addition, be referring to levels of Christian maturity and stages of Christian instruction, a theme he elaborates frequently, particularly in the paraphrase on 3:1. See chapter 3 n1. Or perhaps Erasmus has in mind here, not a distinction between more and less advanced Christians, but the more basic distinction between believers and unbelievers. In this case, the addition may allude to the doctrine of reserve ie that Christianity's sacred mysteries should be withheld from the unholy. Erasmus' *1519* annotation on 2:7 (*in mysterio quae abscondita*) amplifies the verse similarly, although without apparent reference to levels of maturity among believers: 'We speak, [Paul] says, not openly, or indiscriminately, lest we be a stumbling block, but in secret, and not among just any sort of people, lest we toss out roses to swine, but among the mature [or perfect], and not just any wisdom, such as other philosophers publicly profess, but one that is secret and hidden, and, so to speak, thrust out of sight.' Chrysostom *In 1 Cor hom* 7.1 (on 2:6–7) PG 61 55 similarly elaborates Paul's point in a negative comparison with those 'who make a show of their preaching and divulge pearls and doctrines to all indiscriminately, and holy things to dogs and swine.' For the doctrine of reserve, cf CWE 50 55 n69, and see Salvatore R.C. Lilla *Clement of Alexandria: A Study in Christian Platonism and Gnosticism* (Oxford 1971) 142–58.

15 not the magi ... philosophers] Added in *1532*. Erasmus uses *magus* in the sense of 'magician' in his paraphrase on Acts 8:18–19 CWE 50 59 (identifying the Samaritan Simon), but here he clearly intends *magi* to mean something

Pilate, nor Annas or Caiaphas,[16] nor the Pharisees, nor the demons themselves. Otherwise, if they had known that the cross of Christ, however lowly
and foolish it was, would by its radiance darken the glory of the world, and
that however feeble it was, it would overthrow the tyranny of death and
sin, never would they have fixed the prince and source of all glory to the
cross. However learned they were in their comprehension of visible things,
however swollen in their knowledge of the Law, nevertheless, they failed
to perceive this mystery, which was to be shared only with those whom
humility of mind had reconciled to God. That this would be, Isaiah had
foretold when he declared that this wisdom about which we are speaking was breathed secretly into minds: 'Things,' he said, 'that have never
been seen with human eyes, nor heard with human ears, nor understood
by the reflection of any human being, God has prepared for those who genuinely love him,'[17] who base their philosophic disputation on faith, not on
syllogisms.[18]

Exalted rulers were not worthy of this mystery, nor were pompous
philosophers. To us, as if to friends, God has revealed it, not through human
teaching, but through the secret inbreathing of his Spirit. Since this Spirit is
divine and has proceeded from God, it probes even the most deeply hidden
and remote of God's secrets, where human curiosity[19] does not reach. The

* * * * *

like 'learned men of the East.' Cf the annotation on Matt 2:1 (*in Bethlehem
Iudae*), where Erasmus states that those whom the Greeks call 'wise men' or
'philosophers' the Chaldeans call *magi*.

16 For Pontius Pilate (Roman governor of Judea, AD 26–36), see Matthew 27; Mark
15; Luke 23; John 18–19. For Annas (high priest in Jerusalem about AD 6–15
and evidently still powerful at Jesus' death), see Luke 3:2; John 18:13–24; Acts
4:6. For Caiaphas (son-in-law of Annas and high priest AD 18–36), see Matt
26:3, 57; John 11:49–52, 18:14, 28; Acts 4:6. Chrysostom *In 1 Cor hom* 7.2 (on
2:8) PG 61 57 and Theophylact *Expos in 1 Cor* (on 2:8) PG 124 589A name Pilate
(John 19:7–9) and Herod (probably Herod Antipas; Luke 23:7–12) as rulers
who did not know the significance of Jesus.

17 Erasmus paraphrases and, incidentally, completes the syntax of Paul's loose
citation of Isa 64:4. In the annotations on 2:9 (*quod oculus non vidit* and *his qui
diligunt illum*), Erasmus suggests that Paul probably drew the sense but not the
exact words from the Hebrew text of Isaiah rather than from the Septuagint,
which differs considerably.

18 Theophylact *Expos in 1 Cor* (on 2:9) PG 124 592A briefly identifies those loving
God as the 'faithful'; similarly Ambrosiaster *Comm in 1 Cor* (on 2:9) CSEL 81/2
27:5–6.

19 'Curiosity': *curiositas*. Erasmus elsewhere opposes useless human speculation
to evangelical piety or godliness; the one springs from doubt and contentiousness, the other from faith and constancy. Cf the paraphrase on 2:16 with n30

outer appearance of people is available for anyone to see, but no mortal observes what lies hidden in the innermost retreats of the soul. Only the spirit itself and the soul of a person, being inwardly aware of itself, knows that. Likewise, many people search out and contemplate created things, but no one knows matters deeply hidden in the mind and purpose of God except the eternal Spirit, which is innermost in God and on that account is inwardly aware in him of all things. A person imparts secret thoughts to another by a quiet whispering; God imparts his purpose to the godly through the Spirit; not through a human spirit, which, outside of human affairs, can contribute nothing except through God's. A spirit teaches such things as match its nature. This world also has its own spirit, and those who are possessed by it not only savour of worldly things, but love them as well. But the inspiration of the divine Spirit feeds us with heavenly things so that we may understand how great are the blessings God has bestowed on us through the cross of Christ.

This is the philosophy which, as we have drawn it from the Spirit of Christ, so we, in turn, impart it to simple and godly persons, not with artfully embellished words in the way those professing philosophy impart what they profess, but with words which, although indeed they are unpolished, yet impart spiritual teaching. It is fitting that just as the kind of wisdom is entirely different, so also is the method of teaching different. Human matters are taught in a human manner; heavenly and spiritual matters needed to be taught in a new way, and that not to every sort of person certainly, but only to those who by imbibing the Spirit of Christ are now fit for spiritual teaching, since in fact they are spiritual themselves.[20]

* * * * *

and on 15:35. On the terms *curiosa* 'fruitless speculations' and *curiositas* 'curiosity' or 'speculation,' see CWE 44 66 n15 and CWE 50 8 n38, and cf 2 Thess chapter 3 n13.

20 The Greek text of the final phrase in 2:13 is ambiguous and may be translated in at least three ways: 'interpreting spiritual matters to spiritual persons' (so RSV, NEB, and also Ambrosiaster *Comm in 1 Cor* [on 2:13] CSEL 81/2 29:20–4); 'interpreting spiritual matters by spiritual words' (so Orr and Walther, Conzelmann); and 'comparing spiritual matters with spiritual matters' (so AV, DV). Erasmus rejects the first interpretation in the annotation on 2:13 (*spiritualia comparantes*), where he argues that the participle should be translated 'comparing' and that *spiritualibus* refers to things or matters (eg events), not to people. He appears to favour the third interpretation, and in a 1535 addition to the note cites with approval the explanation of Chrysostom *In 1 Cor hom* 7.4 (on 2:13) PG 61 59 that the truth of New Testament events, eg resurrection, is best confirmed by comparison with or reference to Old Testament events, eg Jonah's deliverance. These may be called 'spiritual' because whatever is in the Scriptures has come from the same Spirit. The paraphrase, as often, appears

For a spiritual pupil is suited to a spiritual philosophy in that[21] understanding has been purified through faith and emotion corrected through love. The gross[22] and natural person, who swells in pride from his knowledge of visible things and is governed by human emotions does not accept things that belong to the divine Spirit; he counts as folly and ridicules whatever differs from his way of thinking. He does not believe anything except what he has either confirmed by experience or proven by human reasons. And he does not observe that this philosophy, which teaches that Christ was born of a virgin; that he was true God and true man equally; that by dying he conquered death, and from death rose to life again; that what he has fulfilled in himself he will also fulfil in his members; that the path to true happiness lies through tribulations; that the attainment of immortality comes through death[23] – this[24] is not grasped by human reasoning, but by

* * * * *

designed to accommodate and harmonize all the possibilities: spiritual matters are taught 'in a new way,' ie not through syllogistic disputation or fancy rhetoric but through simple, unembellished language that 'imparts spiritual teaching,' and through the comparison or illustration of spiritual matters with spiritual matters, but also only to people who are 'spiritual themselves.' It is clear throughout this passage, moreover, that Erasmus intends 'in a new way' to refer primarily to the idea that Christian wisdom is imparted 'spiritually,' not through human reasoning or eloquence, but through the inbreathing or imbibing of the Holy Spirit. Cf the paraphrases on 2:6–12 with n13 above and especially the paraphrase on 2:16.

21 in that ... through love] Added in 1532
22 'Gross': crassus. Erasmus frequently uses this adjective, suggesting the heaviness and density of the body, in distinguishing the carnal disposition from the spiritual. For other uses and variations in meaning, see chapters 3 n2 and 7 n5; 2 Cor chapter 3 n20; Eph chapter 1 n46; CWE 42 16 n9, CWE 44 231 n10, CWE 46 86 n68, CWE 48 32 n16, and CWE 50 13 n4. That Erasmus here clarifies Paul's description in 2:14 of the 'natural' person ($\psi\nu\chi\iota\kappa\acute{o}s$ / animalis) with this adjective reflects his concern that animalis is not quite adequate to describe both the body and the soul, ie two of the three parts of human nature in Erasmus' understanding of Pauline anthropology. See the annotation on 2:14 (animalis autem homo), and cf the paraphrase on 1 Cor 15:43–9 with nn62–8 for the treatment of the natural body as a gross and sluggish impediment to the soul. Erasmus describes the components of human nature in Enchiridion CWE 66 38–54 (especially 51–2). For a discussion of Platonist influence on Erasmus' anthropology, see Payne Theology 35–43 or 'The Hermeneutics of Erasmus' 17–23. See also the paraphrase on 1 Thess 5:23.
23 Cf Ambrosiaster Comm in 1 Cor (on 2:14) CSEL 81/2 30:7–9 for a similar, although briefer, listing of Christian teachings for which human wisdom is unsuited.
24 this] Added in 1532, producing a partial anacolouthon (change of grammatical construction within a sentence). Prior to 1532 the sentence reads: 'And he does not observe that this philosophy, which ... death, is not grasped ...'

the Spirit's inspiration. You need not, I think, bring to this task a sharp and cunning intellect; bring instead[25] simple and pure faith. This is an instrument fit for the handiwork of the Spirit: one that offers itself wholly to it[26] to be fashioned and formed.

Still, there is nothing that the spiritual person does not judiciously examine, having no regard for temporal matters, and longing for eternal ones. Nevertheless, he cannot himself be examined by any of the carnal persons, for they are ignorant of this heavenly and secret wisdom. For[27] as a human being does not judge divine matters, so a carnal person does not judge a spiritual one. I say this because the matters that are being taught here have been drawn from the innermost secrets of the divine mind, not from human syllogisms. As Isaiah said,[28] 'What mortal of himself[29] knows the mind of the immortal God so that he can be in God's council,' as if privy to his secrets? The divine mind wished to lay claim to its own people by a new method that would elude all human speculation.[30] We, however, have hold of the mind of Christ because we have imbibed his Spirit.

Chapter 3

This philosophy has rudiments; it has stages of advancement; it has a sum- mit.[1] Discourse must be accommodated to each person's capacity. There-

* * * * *

25 instead] Added in *1532*

26 to it] Added in *1521*

27 For ... a spiritual one] Added in *1532*

28 As Isaiah said] Added in *1532*

29 of himself] Added in *1532*. In his annotations on 2:16 (*sicut scriptum est, quis enim cognovit* and *aut quis instruxit eum*), Erasmus discusses textual difficulties and variants in Paul's free quotation of Isa 40:13. The form of the quotation given here differs somewhat both from the Vulgate and from the version Erasmus quotes in his Latin translation.

30 'Speculation': *curiositatem.* Cf n19 above and chapter 15 n49. The term sug- gests the specious reasoning and quibbling logic Erasmus often associates with scholastic theology.

1 The idea that there are stages of maturity within the philosophy of Christ is a common theme in Erasmus' exposition of Scripture, and one by which he adds unity to the disparate parts of this Epistle. The theme appears later in the paraphrases in connection with the eating of sacrificial meat (on 8:7), the perils of excessive confidence (on 10:12), the superiority of love to prophecy and knowledge (on 13:11), and the hierarchy of spiritual gifts (on 14:20). For the theme in other works, see the paraphrases on Mark 4:28–9 CWE 49 60–1, Luke 2:52 LB VII 308C–309A, and 1 Pet 2:1–3 CWE 44 88–9; *Concionalis interpretatio in psalmum 85* CWE 64 55–6; *Ecclesiastes* III ASD V-5 250:153–65; and the letter to

fore, when I first came to you, I could not teach you the highest truths, as
if you were fully spiritual, but I lowered my speech to the level of your
weakness. Among the simple I used simple language; to the unspiritual[2] I
spoke quite unspiritually; and I babbled as if I were among infants.[3] For
faith also has its own stages of advancement. Since I saw, therefore, that
you were still infants in the philosophy of Christ,[4] I fed you with the milk,
so to speak, of less spiritual teaching, not with the solid food of more mature teaching. The reason was not that we could not have taught you greater

* * * * *

Paul Volz Ep 858:321–4, in which the reference to levels of maturity appears
as part of Erasmus' discussion of three concentric circles of Christian social
order. For the related idea that divine discourse accommodates itself to the
level of its audience, see n3 below.

2 'Simple' translates *rudes*; 'unspiritual,' *crassis*. The first denotes Christians who
are as yet uninstructed; the second, the immature, whose perception is dull
or thick because of their carnal condition. Both terms are amplifications of
Paul's characterization of the Corinthians as σαρκικοί (Vulgate *carnales*) 'people
of the flesh.' For Erasmus' use of *crassus*, especially in describing a carnal, as
opposed to a spiritual, disposition, see chapter 2 n22.

3 'I babbled ... among infants': *apud infantes balbutii*. Cf *Concionalis interpretatio
in psalmum 85* CWE 64 20–1: 'Instead, Scripture, by lisping indistinctly with the
words of men so that it may be understood in a less forbidding way, accommodates itself to men's weakness, like a nurse or mother using baby language
to her child to make herself understood.' The idea of divine condescension
in language also appears in *Enchiridion* CWE 66 35, *Commentarius in psalmum 2*
CWE 63 102–4, and *De libero arbitrio* CWE 76 14. Cf Erasmus' advice concerning
adapting standards of correct pronunciation 'to locally established usage' in
De recta pronuntiatione CWE 26 472: 'It is better to lower one's standards [*bal-
butire cum balbis*, literally 'to babble among babblers'] than to raise laughs at
one's own expense and be misunderstood into the bargain.'
John Bateman discusses rhetorical and theological *accommodatio* in Erasmus'
Paraphrases in 'From Soul to Soul' 13–14. See also Manfred Hoffmann *Rhetoric
and Theology: the Hermeneutics of Erasmus* (Toronto 1994) 106–12. Payne 'The
Hermeneutics of Erasmus' 40 cites Origen and the patristic tradition in general as sources for Erasmus' concern with accommodation. See also Ambrosiaster *Comm in 1 Cor* (on 3:2) CSEL 81/2 32:12–33:2, where Paul's rhetorical
accommodation is justified by the example of Jesus, who spoke differently
among his disciples from the manner in which he spoke among people in
general, and even made distinctions among the disciples themselves. See also
'accommodation' in the indexes of CWE 42, 50, and 56; see in particular CWE
42 72 n9 for the broader applications of the principle of accommodation in
Erasmus' thought.

4 The term 'philosophy of Christ,' suggesting a life of godliness informed by
the moral teachings of Christ, occurs frequently in Erasmus' writings. See the
numerous references in Phil chapter 2 n6. For the importance of this motif in
Erasmus' thought, see CWE 66 xxii–xxv.

things, but that you were not yet ready to understand higher teaching because of your carnal disposition and the mists from your former life. And not even now are all of you ready. For there are some among you, who, although through baptism they have enlisted in Christ's service,[5] nevertheless have not yet shaken off all their human affections. Such persons are at least to this extent carnal, not spiritual. What need is there of words or why should I be afraid to make this pronouncement about you when the very facts of the case cry out?[6]

The nature of a thing is known from its effect. Since the Spirit of Christ produces concord, while on the contrary envy, strife, and divisions arise only from human feelings, does not the detection of these faults among you prove conclusively that you are still involved in gross[7] and human affections? Otherwise, from where do those voices come that are heard speaking discord among you, if not from a debased mind? Although there is a common source and ruler of all, still one of you says, 'I am a Pauline,' and another, 'I am an Apollonian.' For the students of human philosophy contend among themselves with labels of this same sort: 'I am an Aristotelian,' 'I a Platonist,' 'I a Stoic,' 'I an Epicurean.'[8] It is not that anything of this sort has arisen from my name or Apollos', but I wanted to use these names so that you might sense more clearly the impropriety of the matter.[9]

If it is improper for you to transfer to us the glory and authority that is owed to Christ, even though we are true apostles and have passed on to you nothing except what we drew from the Spirit of Christ, who would bear it should you adopt the names of any sort of men whatsoever – perhaps of false apostles – and attribute to puny men the authorship of salvation and religion when you owe this to Christ alone? If, for instance, some Frangilius or Benotius or Augulius or Carmilius[10] or someone else of

* * * * *

5 Cf chapter 6 n26. For the image of baptism as military enlistment, see the paraphrase on Acts 5:13 CWE 50 41 with n22.
6 'The very facts of the case cry out': *ipsa res clamitet* – a variation on the common phrase *res ipsa declarat*, 'the very facts of the case show.' Cf chapter 1 n13; also 2 Cor chapter 3 n1.
7 'Gross': *crassis*; on the connotations of this word, see n2 above and chapter 2 n22.
8 Cf the paraphrase on 1:12 with n29.
9 Erasmus anticipates 1 Cor 4:6. See chapter 4 n5.
10 In amplifying Paul's condemnation of divisions and sects in the early church here in 3:4, not only does Erasmus cite the 'sectarianism' of competing philosophic schools among the Greeks – as Paul could have done, and Augustine did do (cf the paraphrase on 1:12–13 with n29) – but he also alludes provocatively

any name at all – for these names may serve as examples – has devised some
human rule of life, will you right away take pride in their names, engage in
shameful contention among yourselves and, consigning the name of Christ
to oblivion, make human beings the authors of true religion when its one
and only author is Christ? What is left except that, just as you have done
with your manufactured names, so with dress as well and diet and with
your whole manner of life, you both reveal and nourish the disagreement
of your minds? What is left except that, just as satraps' attendants attest
to the different deputies they serve[11] – some by the colour yellow, others
by red, some by a mosaic of different colours, others by other identifying
marks of this sort – so you in like manner (since you are devoted to men in
the same way, as if you have received life and liberty from them) glory in
their names – as though it were not glorious enough to be called Christians?
Are you ashamed of this name? Or is it not enough to profess him by the
innocence[12] of your life? You cut apart that which is one, and divide up the
glory of Christ piecemeal among puny men.

* * * * *

to differing religious orders of his own day. Frangilius, Benotius, Augulius,
and Carmilius are transparent disguises for the eponymous patrons (including our Lady of Mount Carmel!) of the Franciscans, Benedictines, Augustini-
ans, and Carmelites. Chomarat 1 613–14 uses this passage to exemplify Erasmus' penchant in the paraphrases for making applications from Paul to his
own contemporaries. Cf Erasmus' annotation on 3:8 (*unum sunt*): 'But if Paul
is so incensed at the Corinthians because they took for themselves the names
of those who had baptized them and first initiated them into the mysteries
of Christ, what would he say about the factions of our own time, in which
those who are called "religious" are divided among themselves by a thousand names, a thousand cults, ceremonies, rules?' For similar Erasmian attacks on the religious orders and their mockery of 'true religion,' see *Moria*
CWE 27 130–5, *Querela pacis* CWE 27 298, and *Ecclesiastes* III ASD V-5 190:797–
191:823.

11 The satraps were provincial governors or vassals of the Persian king. Darius I
(521–486 BC) eg is reported in Herodotus 3.89 to have divided his empire into
twenty satrapies. The comparison of the factious Corinthians with followers of
men, ie the satraps, who were merely glorified servants themselves, reinforces
the element of mockery in Erasmus' treatment of 3:4. The use of coloured
apparel to show slavish devotion completes the *reductio ad absurdum*. I have
not discovered a source for Erasmus' use of this detail. On Paul's ridicule of
his rivals as self-glorifiers, see Sider 'Historical Imagination' 93–4.

12 On Erasmus' fondness for the term *innocentia* 'innocence' to denote righteousness, see CWE 44 xvii. For the necessity of a Christian's perseverance here and
now in the life of virtue and innocence, cf the paraphrases on 6:14 with n40,
15:49 with n69, 15:58 with n77. See also Eph chapter 4 n3.

What sort of people[13] these are I do not yet say. But suppose they are the Apolloses, suppose they are the Pauls, suppose they are even[14] the apostles of the highest rank[15] – what else are they but stewards of the Christ in whom you believe? They are not the masters,[16] but at their own risk they serve as stewards for the business of another, and to Christ they owe this very ability to be stewards. With him as their common master, different ones perform different duties, as God has given to each an assignment. I, for example, first planted the seedling[17] when I laid the foundations of the gospel's teaching. Apollos watered and with devoted admonitions fostered what we began. But as to the fact that the little tree grows up, that it becomes great and pours forth a rich yield of fruit, for that we must credit God, not ourselves. For the planter would labour in vain, and the waterer in vain, if heaven did not breathe its hidden force upon the plant – a force all the more effective because it is hidden.[18] If this force forsakes the farmer, neither the planter nor the waterer accomplishes anything; but if it lends support, the whole yield is owed to heaven and to God. As far as the praise that comes with this tree is concerned, both the planter and the waterer are in the same situation since both alike perform another's business and will receive the reward for their service, not from you, but from God, for we are his labourers.

Like hired workers[19] we toil in the work of God; you are his field, which we cultivate for him, not for ourselves; you are a building which

* * * * *

13 'What sort of people': *quales* in all editions from 1519 to 1540; mistakenly given in LB as *qualis* 'what sort of person'.

14 even] Added in 1532

15 'Apostles of the highest rank': *summates ... apostoli.* Cf the paraphrase on 9:5, where Erasmus uses a slight variation of this phrase (*apostolorum summates* 'the highest rank of apostles') for the leading apostles, including those whom he designates by the term 'the brothers of the Lord.' On his use of the latter term, see chapter 9 n14. For designations like 'highest apostles' in the Corinthian paraphrases (sometimes used in straightforward fashion, sometimes ironically and derisively), see the paraphrases on 4:7 with n6, 2 Cor 5:12 with n12, 2 Cor 11:5 with n11, and 2 Cor 12:11.

16 On *ministri* as 'stewards' and *auctores* as 'masters,' see chapter 1 n10.

17 Erasmus borrows this planting metaphor for his paraphrase on Gal 4:19 CWE 42 118: 'I had sown good seed, from which genuine Christians ought to have been born. But by some kind of witchcraft you are degenerating into Jews.'

18 because it is hidden] Added in 1532. Cf Erasmus' description of the 'secret inbreathing' of the Holy Spirit, upon which true faith and wisdom depend. See in particular the paraphrase on 2:7–16 with n13.

19 'Hired workers': *operarii;* Augustine suggests this word when he cites 3:6–9 in commenting on God as 'farmer' in *Enarrationes in psalmos* 67:1 CCL 39 857:32.

rises for him, not for us. We owe him our labour; let each one examine
what kind of labour he offers God: if it is faithful and genuine, then he
is going to receive an honourable reward; but if otherwise, then either his
labour will come to nothing, or he will collect the wages he deserves. Let
me illustrate with an analogy: just like a well-trained architect, I have laid
the foundation for the building, not by my own strength, but by the help
of God, who had assigned me this responsibility. Different people have
built on the foundation I laid, but let each be constantly mindful of what
he is building. For the foundation set down by me cannot be changed.
In whatever name those who follow me come preaching, if they do not
preach Christ Jesus and him crucified, they are not to be heeded. But if
they judge the foundation sound, then it remains for them to build over
it a structure worthy of such a foundation. It is a heavenly and spiritual
foundation; a structure of carnal and earthly teaching does not suit it.[20]
While an empty and counterfeit structure may deceive the judgment of
humans, it will not escape the judgment of God. Upon this foundation,
therefore, if anyone should erect substantial and extraordinary materials,
like gold, silver, precious stones or, on the contrary, if anyone should add
cheap and paltry materials, like wood, hay, and even stubble, the result
itself will show what sort of labour each has contributed.

Let me speak more bluntly so that you may better understand. I placed
before you Christ as your focal point.[21] If anyone should teach by his

* * * * *

Valla *Annot in 1 Cor 3* (I 863) cites the Augustinian precedent and corrects
the Vulgate's *adiutores* 'helpers' to *cooperarii* 'co-workers': 'Who can give help
to God? Can God need help?' Erasmus uses *cooperarii* in his Latin translation
and similarly defends it in his annotation on 3:9 (*Dei enim adiutores sumus*).

20 Following Ambrosiaster *Comm in 1 Cor* (on 3:12) CSEL 81/2 36:17–22, Erasmus
interprets the metaphorical structures built on the foundations to be good
and bad teaching; thus the paraphrase focuses on the motives and messages
of teachers. Similarly, Erasmus argues in a *1519* addition to his annotation on
3:12 (*foenum, stipulam*): 'To me the simplest sense is most pleasing, that we understand [the passage] as about the teaching of the apostles who succeeded
Paul.' Erasmus proceeds, in both the paraphrase on the verse and the annotation, to identify false teaching with pharisaical legalism and ceremonialism.
Cf chapters 8 n25 and 9 n6. On Erasmus' frequent contrast between the gospel
as spiritual and the Law as carnal, cf the paraphrase on Acts 1:4 CWE 50 6 with
n23.

21 'Focal point': *scopum* 'target'; see chapter 1 n30 and Phil chapter 3 n43. Cf
Enchiridion CWE 66 61: 'Let this be your fourth rule: place Christ before you as
the only goal [*scopum*] of your life, and direct to him alone all your pursuits,
all your endeavours, all your leisure time and hours of occupation'; also the
paraphrase on Matt 6:22 CWE 45 122: 'If the eye of the mind directs its vision

example that one ought to live an innocent life, treat even enemies well, not trust in wealth, despise honours, abhor like the plague base pleasures, refer all things to the glory of Christ, hope for no reward for righteous deeds except everlasting life, even choose death if it should be necessary to die for Christ, then this person adds a structure worthy of Christ, its foundation. But if he adds trivial human regulations concerning dress, diet, frigid ceremonies, and similar customs, which humans typically devise not for the good of Christ, but for their very own glory, or even for profit, with the result that people who began from so excellent a foundation degenerate from being godly to being superstitious,[22] then he has imported wood, hay, and stubble. Each person's work, when it has been brought nearer to the light of truth and the gospel's standard, will have its character plainly revealed. If the teaching that has been added should make you invincible against all human affections, its effectiveness is plain to see; but if it makes you incapable of enduring misfortunes, if it makes you irritable, peevish, contentious, quick to disparage or dissemble, from this it is clear enough that the teaching is adulterated.[23]

* * * * *

only to the true goal [*scopum*], whatever is done in one's life is pleasing to God.'

22 The contrast between being godly (*pius*) and being superstitious (*superstitiosus*) may initially seem unlikely, but see CWE 44 xvi–xvii on Erasmus' sense of *pietas* as the state of true and complete devotion to God. This state is frequently contrasted by Erasmus with the overscrupulous observance of rules and ceremonies. See eg CWE 42 78 and 122. See also n20 above, and cf Erasmus' paraphrase on Paul's instructions regarding sacrificial meat in 8:7. There the strength of mature Christian piety is contrasted with the weakness of immature Christians influenced by ancestral superstitions. Cf the paraphrase on 2 Cor 3:6 with n8. On Erasmus and dietary regulations in particular, see chapter 8 n25. On *pietas*, the meanings of the term, and its centrality in Erasmus' theology, see John O'Malley's Introduction to CWE 66 ix–xxxiii.

23 These disagreeable emotional states may represent to Erasmus conditions that are particularly likely to lead to disagreement and division within a human community. As Erasmus seeks through the elaborations of the paraphrase to bring coherence and order to Paul's difficult and often elliptical train of thought, it is not surprising that the paraphrast should highlight here (as the effects of faulty teaching) emotional states that undermine the unity and concord he sees as Paul's primary emphasis so far. Compare these emotional states eg with the effects that concord produces within a community in the paraphrase on the letter's opening salutation in 1:3 ('Grace to you and peace from God'). For Erasmus' views on the role of concord and consensus in determining authoritative doctrine, see McConica 'Erasmus and the Grammar of Consent' 81–9.

Those who have been summoned to appear on a given day before a human judge often get off; but the judgments of God are as exact as if you were putting something to the test by fire. In peaceful times, a useless substructure is perhaps not noticeable, but as soon as the storm-winds of persecutions attack, or the goads of passion,[24] then as you totter you show in fact that the Spirit is not drawn from ceremonies or human doctrines. For people endowed with the Spirit endure all these things for Christ's sake even with joy. This is the fire[25] that will examine the nature of each person's work.

If, therefore, in this conflagration one or another's building endures, he will claim for himself no praise before the world on this account, but he will obtain his wages from God, for whom he toiled. If, however, the work of one or another is consumed by the fire, then the labourer will have lost his labour and be cheated of his reward, even though he himself will be unharmed. Like those who escape with nothing from a fire,[26] there remains

* * * * *

24 Cf Matt 7:24–7 and Erasmus' paraphrase on Matt 7:24 CWE 45 138: '... when the sky is serene any building whatever stands easily, but winter proves a structure's strength.' It is perhaps the influence of Matt 7:24–7 (about rocky and sandy foundations) that suggests to Erasmus the surprising word *substructio* ('substructure' or 'foundation') for this sentence in the paraphrase on 3:13, where we might rather expect a word denoting a structure built on top of a foundation.

25 In 1 Cor 3:13–15 Paul refers to the 'day' that will reveal the nature of each builder's work and the 'fire' that will test it. In the annotations on 3:12 (*foenum, stipulam*) and 3:13 (*dies enim domini*), Erasmus argues against those who interpret the 'day' as Judgment Day and the testing 'fire' as eschatological or purgatorial fire. Instead Erasmus suggests that 'day' and 'fire' are Paul's metaphors for the clear inspection and the exact examination of one's work that occur especially in times of affliction and persecution and that result in acknowledgement of error and in the sufferings of penitence. In support of this view, he cites in particular Ambrosiaster *Comm in 1 Cor* (on 3:13–15) CSEL 81/2 36:23–38:11.

26 'Escape with nothing from a fire': *ex incendio nudi subducunt sese*. Paul's figure in 3:15, 'he himself will be saved, but only as through fire' (RSV), suggests a common expression for avoiding calamity, 'scarcely to escape a fire' (see Conzelmann 77). In Erasmus' elaboration, to pull oneself out of a fire *nudus* 'bereft,' 'destitute,' or 'without property,' there is perhaps an echo of Juvenal 3.210 or even of Livy 22.35.3 and 40.3, where L. Aemilius Paullus is said to have escaped the fire of popular disapproval *prope ambustus* 'nearly scorched' and *semustus* 'half-burnt.' Cf also Chrysostom *In 1 Cor hom* 9.3 (on 3:12–15) PG 61 79: 'For he does not speak here about persons truly burned, but rather in order to inspire fear and to show that one who lives in vileness is bereft of [*nudum*] defenses and security.'

nothing left for him to do except to erect at new expense a structure which fits its foundation. The best and most desired policy would have been to pass on to those who had been initiated into Christ nothing but what is worthy of Christ. If this has not been done, the labour of both has been doubled – both for those who have taught what must be untaught and for those who have learned what must be unlearned. Still there is hope of salvation as long as Christ has remained the foundation.[27]

How is a filthy life consonant with that profession you made? How are frigid ceremonies consonant with Christ's fiery love?[28] In these matters those who corrupt you with their teaching will receive just punishment from God. Do you not remember that you are a temple consecrated to God, a temple that the indwelling Spirit of God sanctifies? But if someone who defiles a temple that has been dedicated by a human agent suffers punishment, is not God going to destroy the one who pollutes God's own temple?[29] Since God by his own Spirit once caused this temple to be pure and holy, we must strive to keep it pure and holy. It is kept so by innocence and conduct worthy of Christ; it is defiled and polluted by ambitious striving, lust, dissension, and similar feelings and maladies.[30] Since, therefore, you are the temple of God, built from living stones,[31] whoever imports into your company any conduct, feelings, or teaching unworthy of Christ is acting wickedly against God.

Christ deceives no one who leans upon him. But let each take care lest in wrongly relying on human resources he deceive himself. There is no reason why you should look to the resources of philosophy or the Law for your happiness. Nor should anyone value himself above the others because he excels in human learning. Rather, whoever deems himself wise in the estimation of the world, let him wisely become foolish so that he may truly become wise. Let him cease being the pompous professor of a foolish

* * * * *

27 So all editions from 1519 to 1540, but LB places a question mark at the end of the sentence, turning the affirmation into an inappropriate question: 'Still is there hope of salvation . . . ?'

28 On frigid ceremonies, see nn10, 20, and 22 above.

29 For the punishment of temple-polluters in the biblical record, see 2 Chron 36:14–21, where the punishment is destruction. Cf also the story of Paul and his companions in Jerusalem (Acts 21:27–36).

30 'Feelings and maladies': *affectibus ac morbis*. On this terminology, see Erasmus' annotations on Rom 1:26 ('to passions of shame') CWE 56 56 and nn2–3, Rom 1:31 ('without disposition') CWE 56 64–5 and n2, and Rom 8:7 ('because the wisdom of the flesh') CWE 56 204–5 and n4.

31 Cf 1 Pet 2:4.

wisdom, and he will be fit to be a student of the wisest folly. Even as this world's wealth does not make a person truly rich, as the world's honours do not cause one to be truly distinguished, as the world's pleasures do not make one truly happy, so this world's wisdom does not make one truly wise in the sight of God,[32] whose judgment no one escapes, even if one should claim for oneself a reputation for wisdom in the sight of the world. God mocks such wisdom while showing that far from promoting salvation it actually blocks salvation from being obtained[33] since it makes people headstrong and proud and therefore hard to teach. This was long ago foretold, moreover, in the book written about the patience of Job, where Job says of God: 'He catches the wise through their very own cunning' [5:13]. And again in Psalm 63: 'The Lord knows the thoughts of those who think themselves wise, that [their thoughts] are empty and incapable of providing what they promise' [94:11].[34] Since this work of our salvation is wholly divine, there is no basis for human beings to claim any part of it for themselves, and no reason for you to assign any portion of the glory to a man, as if he were the author, since all the glory is owed to God.

Now since you are one body, united by your love for one another, there is no cause for one or another of you to make special claims for yourselves when all things are yours in common. If Paul has any influence, or Apollos,

* * * * *

32 Erasmus' expansion of the Pauline paradox in 3:18–19 recalls Chrysostom *In 1 Cor hom* 10.1 (on 3:18–19) PG 61 82: 'Therefore, just as poverty is, according to God, the cause of riches, humility the cause of exaltation, and scorn for glory the cause of glory, so also to become a fool makes one wiser than all. For our affairs rest upon opposites'; similarly Theophylact *Expos in 1 Cor* (on 3:18) PG 124 605C.

33 Cf Chrysostom *In 1 Cor hom* 10.1 (on 3:18–19) PG 61 83: 'For not only does [worldly wisdom] contribute nothing, but it even gets in the way'; similarly Theophylact *Expos in 1 Cor* (on 3:19) PG 124 605C.

34 The quotation is an expansion of Ps 93:11 in the Vulgate; however, all editions from 1519 to 1534 of the *Paraphrase* (and LB as well) read 'LXIII,' ie 63. Erasmus evidently intended this paraphrase on the psalm as an explanation of the terse citation from Job. Cf his comments on the words 'in their very own cunning' in the annotation on 3:19 (*in astutia eorum*): 'Those foolishly wise have been caught and convicted by their very own cunning, in that they discover that their wisdom has contributed nothing towards the attainment of true happiness.' Cf Theophylact *Expos in 1 Cor* (on 3:19) PG 124 605C–608A: 'Not only did [their wisdom] not help them or lead them to true wisdom; it actually hindered ... They thought they had no need of God, but could understand everything themselves. But God showed them ... that their cleverness and cunning were of no avail at all.'

or Cephas, by the goodness of God they have equal influence for your advantage; if the world offers any hindrance, it turns out for your good; if we are granted life, we live in order to encourage you by our teaching; if death strikes, we die in order to strengthen you by our example;[35] if present concerns face you, they must be treated with neglect for they are fleeting; if future concerns, then you must struggle courageously towards those things which, although you do not see them with the eyes of the body, nevertheless you do see with the eyes of faith.[36] Have done, therefore, with the names of divisions and factions, since through the one chief source, all things are yours equally, even though you do not belong to yourselves in such a way that you can transfer title over yourselves to a human being, but you belong to Jesus Christ, to whom you owe yourselves just as we do, too. Moreover, for Christ you are indebted to God, the supreme source of all things, who wished through Christ to lavish all things upon us.

Chapter 4

Whoever truly wishes to boast, therefore, should boast of Christ. We, on the other hand, should be evaluated in this way: not as masters or lords, but as it is proper for those to be evaluated who as stewards manage the interests of Christ, and who distribute goods entrusted to them by another, the mysteries not of human beings, but of God. Since, therefore, it is generally known that all of them (of whatever sort they are) administer a business – and although the most important business, still one belonging to another – let nothing else for the moment be looked for in them, as far as your judgment about them is concerned, except that in good faith they manage what has been entrusted by God and look nowhere else than to the glory of Christ.[1] Those who teach human matters in place of divine, who

* * * * *

35 In 3:22 Paul includes life and death in his listing of 'all things' that belong to the Corinthian Christians because they belong to Christ. Erasmus, however, appears to follow Chrysostom *In 1 Cor hom* 10.2 (on 3:22) PG 61 83–4 and Theophylact *Expos in 1 Cor* (on 3:22) PG 124 608c in interpreting 'life' and 'death' in the list as the continued life or possible death of the apostles, which the apostles enjoy or suffer for the benefit of Christian communities.
36 For the image of the mind's, heart's, or faith's 'eyes' elsewhere in Erasmus' paraphrases, see CWE 46 121 n2 and cf 170 n14; also 2 Cor chapter 3 n29.

1 Theophylact *Expos in 1 Cor* (on 4:2) PG 124 609B similarly interprets a trustworthy steward as one who maintains the distinction between master and servant: 'What is sought in a steward is that he not appropriate for himself his master's goods, that he administer affairs not as a master, but as one managing

for profit and pride abuse your readiness to obey, who under the pretence of the gospel pursue their own interests, who under the shadow of Christ's glory aim at tyranny – these are managers who act in bad faith, and however much they mislead human judgment, they do not deceive God, whose approbation is the highest good.

It is of very little importance to me whether I am approved or not in your judgment alone – or indeed in any human judgment. It is, in fact, so unlikely that a person can judge rightly about the conscience of another that I should not dare to pass judgment even on myself, as to whether I deserve praise before God, or not. To be sure, I have striven with all my strength to fulfil my appointed responsibility, and I am not conscious of any deceit, but not on this account would I dare claim the praise of righteousness. For it[2] is possible that I have inadvertently done something otherwise than I ought, whether by overstepping or by falling short. Since God alone knows this, I hold him as the sole judge of my service. To him, therefore, whose eyes see all things clearly, let us yield all judgment about hidden matters. He will pronounce judgment about each matter individually when he thinks the time right.

As servants, therefore, you must keep from anticipating the decision of the Lord and judging before the proper time. For it is not time to pronounce a verdict on these matters until the Lord comes to judge what is in heaven and on earth and under the earth.[3] Then will he bring into light whatever now lies buried in darkness, and he will make visible to the eyes of all what is now hidden in the intricate recesses of the human heart and escapes human consciousness. Then from him whose judgments are sure will come rewards according to merits. Whoever sincerely discharges his duty will secure eternal praise from God, even if he has found scant favour among human beings. But one who does otherwise will suffer shame and punishment under God's condemnation, no matter how highly prized he has been in human estimation.[4]

* * * * *

the affairs of someone else and indeed his master's, not saying that his master's goods are his own, but on the contrary, that his own are his master's.' See also Chrysostom *In 1 Cor hom* 10.2 (on 4:2) PG 61 84.

2 For it ... falling short] First in *1521*. Previously 'For it is possible that I have inadvertently done something – too much or too little – otherwise than I ought.'

3 An echo of Phil 2:10 – although there is no indication in Erasmus' paraphrase on that verse or in his annotation on it that he understands it eschatologically. Cf also Isa 45:23.

4 Erasmus seems to be elaborating on Ambrosiaster's interpretation. See *Comm in 1 Cor* (on 4:5) CSEL 81/2 43:22–4: 'One who was looked down upon may

But don't misunderstand: in this discourse so far I have used Apollos and myself metaphorically, not because we are the occasion for any such sects (for neither do we claim anything for ourselves, nor does anyone among you boast of being Pauline or Apollonian); rather, knowing that there are among you various partisan attachments, and fearing that I might provoke someone to anger, I preferred to introduce the matter with names disguised so that when the letter is read in public, each one may quietly recognize himself.[5] And it is out of consideration for you that our names have been used in discussing the unpleasant matter so that without any public disturbance you might learn how unseemly are the boasts that some make over the names of false apostles, disdaining others in comparison with themselves, and wickedly attributing to human beings what belongs to God.

* * * * *

happen to appear worthy, and one who was thought important may be found to be counterfeit.'

5 Erasmus interprets 4:6 to mean that Paul has used his own name and Apollos' not as examples, but as disguises, ie primarily as a way not to name other apostles, who, unlike Paul and Apollos, had been objects (and perhaps encouragers) of divisive loyalties among the Corinthians. In his annotation on 4:6 (transfiguravi in me et Apollo), he explains that Paul has shifted the role or identity of others onto himself and Apollos in order to speak about bad 'stewards' under cover of his own person. The Greek verb μετασχηματίζειν, when used in the middle voice, does denote disguise or dissemblance (as in 2 Cor 11:13–15), but its use here (in 1 Cor 4:6) in the active voice is recognized by modern commentators as difficult. See Conzelmann 85–6 and Barrett 105–6. Erasmus replaced the Vulgate's transfiguravi 'I have changed the form of' or 'transformed' to transtuli 'I have transferred' or 'applied.' English translations vary: 'I have in a figure transferred' (DV, AV); 'I have applied' (RSV); 'into this general picture I have brought' (NEB); 'I have exemplified by reference' (Conzelmann); 'I have made [these things] seem to apply' (Barrett). There appears to be no clear consensus as to whether Paul was using loyalties to himself and Apollos as examples or as disguises and thus, by the latter, exempting himself and Apollos from the situation, as Erasmus' paraphrase here suggests.

Erasmus' patristic sources appear to encourage the idea of disguise. Thus Chrysostom In 1 Cor hom 12.1 (on 4:6) PG 61 95–7 speaks of hiding the identities of others under the names of the revered Paul and Apollos in order to make the medicine easier to take; Theophylact Expos in 1 Cor (on 4:5) PG 124 612A–B notes Paul's common practice of teaching by applying to himself something that belonged to another; and Ambrosiaster Comm in 1 Cor (on 4:6) CSEL 81/2 44:11–17 attributes to Paul the same three purposes Erasmus articulates in this and the next sentence: by criticizing false apostles under the cover of his own and Apollos' names, Paul seeks to avoid public discord, to encourage silent recognition, and to warn against false human pretensions.

The only reason they each exalt the high status of their own apostle is to make themselves more eminent in the process, and they are no less foolish in judging themselves than they are in judging those whose reputations elevate them. This conduct could perhaps have been tolerated if it were only foolish, but now since it gives rise to ruinous divisions, the matter cannot be ignored. For more should not be ascribed to men of apostolic office than, as I just said, is right to ascribe to managers of someone else's estate; nor should anyone boast of the name of this or that person since even the very thing contributed through them is owed to God.

When I weigh these considerations carefully, I cannot but wonder what the source is for such despicable ambition among you, be it the ambition of apostles who foolishly claim for themselves what belongs to Christ, or that of disciples who prefer to boast of a human steward rather than the divine master.[6] I am addressing you, whoever you are, who are either pleased or displeased with yourself on account of the counterfeit glory of the one from whom you received the easy gift of baptism.[7] Who is the author of this distinction whereby this one seems to have received less, that one more?[8]

* * * * *

6 In speaking of both 'disciples' and 'apostles,' Erasmus identifies two addressees for 4:6–8: the Corinthian Christians on the one hand, and the leaders whom they followed on the other. The patristic exegetical tradition had noted the problem of 'audience' in these verses (including Paul's switch from second-person plural in verse 6 to second person singular in verse 7 and then back to plural for verses 8–13), but had come to differing interpretations. Theophylact in *Expos in 1 Cor* (on 4:6–7) PG 124 612D–613A notes the shifting target of Paul's words: although he speaks to the people in 4:6, he shifts focus in 4:7 and directs the question 'Who sees anything different in you [singular]?' at the individual leaders and teachers; similarly Chrysostom *In 1 Cor hom* 12.1 (on 4:6–7) PG 61 97–8. Ambrosiaster in *Comm in 1 Cor* (on 4:7) CSEL 81/2 44:18–45:8 assumes instead that the question is directed at a part of the people, in particular those who supposed that certain of them had gained more through baptism or instruction than others because of the prestige of their baptizers. Erasmus lends support to both interpretations in his annotation on 4:7 (*quis enim te discernit*). For modern interpretations see Conzelmann 86 and Orr and Walther 181. Here at the beginning of the paraphrase on 4:7, Erasmus is careful to have Paul address both 'audiences,' giving precisely equal attention to each – first to the followers, then to the leaders – and introducing each section with the declaration 'I am addressing you [singular], whoever you are, who...' For the distinction between human stewards and divine masters, see the paraphrases on 1:6–7, 1:12–14, and 2:4–5. See also chapter 1 n10.
7 On baptism as an easy gift, cf the paraphrase on 1:16–17 with nn34, 35, and 36.
8 Erasmus, in explaining Paul's first question in 1 Cor 4:7, 'For who sees anything different in you?' (RSV), echoes Ambrosiaster *Comm in 1 Cor* (on 4:7)

If anyone should be baptized in a golden or jewelled basin under the sponsorship of satraps,[9] and that [done] by an apostle, or if this is not enough,
by the foremost apostle, one who with all his fanfare would surpass the
opulence of kings, would anyone dare proclaim that more was conferred
on him than if he had been baptized in a fig-tree trough by some assistant of Peter, a fisherman, or of me, a leather-worker?[10] In turn,[11] I
am addressing you, whoever you are, who implant this most foolish error in the minds of the simple, or at least take improper advantage of
an error that you ought to have corrected. What, pray tell, is the pretext for this pluming of yourself? Do you teach your own doctrine, or
another's? If your own, then you proclaim yourself, not Jesus Christ. But
if another's, then with what cheek do you usurp what you have received
from God, as if it had sprung from yourself? If you believe that what
comes as a gift from God is your own, then what is blinder than you?
But if you do understand, and you still vaunt and recommend yourself on
its merits, just as if it were your own, then what is more shameless than
you?

To what great heights have you come, O Corinthians, from such a
humble foundation? When we were with you, we were so hungry, poor,
and needy that we made a daily living for ourselves by stitching leather.[12]
Humble and suffering in ways undeserved, we preached Christ to you

* * * * *

CSEL 81/2 44:18–20: 'That is, there are some who, receiving more in baptism
or teaching, maintain that the others have gained less.' Cf Erasmus' annotation on 4:7 (*quis enim te discernit*), and see n6 above. For Erasmus' treatment
of baptism, see chapter 6 n26.

9 Cf chapter 3 n11. The Persian satraps appear to supply Erasmus with a convenient hyperbolic and derisive image for false apostles – an example of lavish, prideful display by individuals who were essentially servants rather than
masters. Here perhaps Erasmus also has an eye to Corinth's own wealth and
reputation for indulgence. Note that Paul's ironic passage on the Corinthians'
wealth and power (4:8) follows shortly. See the paraphrase on that verse; also
(for Corinth's reputation) the Argument n11 and (for prideful display) the
paraphrase on 2 Cor 10:7.

10 For Peter's occupation, see Matt 4:18. Paul, however, usually gives Peter's
name in its Aramaic form, Cephas; he uses 'Peter' only at Gal 2:7. For Paul's
trade, see Acts 18:3; also G. Kittel and G. Friedrich eds *Theological Dictionary
of the New Testament* trans G.W. Bromley (Grand Rapids 1964–74) 7 393–4.

11 'In turn': *rursus*, which may also be understood as 'on the other hand.' Erasmus
here shifts the focus of Paul's critique from the Corinthian Christians to the
leaders they variously followed. See n6 above.

12 See Acts 18:1–4.

without adulteration. Have you now come to the point where you despise us through the influence of other apostles, and are so headstrong from being sated, and so swollen from being rich, and so factious from having power? Do you possess such a rich storehouse of possessions, while we, who have carried out the most difficult portion of this work, have been shut out? See for yourselves whether you have procured any great thing. I should wish indeed that you had truly obtained a kingdom worthy of Christ. Then we would thrust ourselves into some portion of this kingdom so that we who established its beginnings might rule it along with you. For I do not think that you would be so utterly uncivil as to shut out completely from sharing your good fortune those from whom its initial stages had arisen, unless we have been born with precisely this misfortune, that[13] while others get for themselves such great glory with their dishonest teaching, we carry off no reward beyond scorn, hunger, disgrace, imprisonment, beatings, and threats of death.[14] If apostolic service ought to be compensated with human rewards, then I think the chief rewards are owed to us, who at the cost of such great perils were the first to implant Christ in you.

If, however, it is right for such people to reign among you – ones who have built anything at all upon the excellent foundation laid by us – then I suppose the reason we alone are unfortunate is that we have angered God. While wealth and reputation for wisdom gain for them influence and domination among you, I suppose Christ summoned us last of all[15] to the apostolic office in order to throw us to punishment and death, like those who because of their evil deeds are thrown to beasts as a spectacle for the people.[16] Into what praetorium have we not been dragged?[17] What prison is there that is not privy to our torment?[18] What marketplace is there in which we have not been made a public laughingstock to the point that we have

* * * * *

13 that] *ut* in all editions from 1519–1538; *1540* and LB, however, read *aut* 'or.'
14 Cf 2 Cor 11:23–7. See Acts 14:19, 16:22–3.
15 'Last of all': *omnium postremos*. The paraphrase here on 4:9 seems to echo 15:8 ('he appeared to me last of all') and suggests Paul's chronological relationship to the other apostles. Cf the same phrase in the paraphrase on Mark 9:35 CWE 49 116.
16 The spectacles presented as public entertainment in Roman amphitheatres constituted a regular form of punishment and execution for criminals. See eg Tacitus *Annales* 12.56.5; Paulus *Sententiae* 5.22.1–2; Seneca *Epistulae morales* 7.2–5; and J.P.V.D. Balsdon *Life and Leisure in Ancient Rome* (New York 1969) 288, 308–12.
17 See Acts 23:33–5.
18 See Acts 16:23–4, 21:33; Phil 1:7.

been a spectacle,[19] not only to this world, which condemns Christ, not only
to people who savour earthly things, but even to the demons themselves,[20]
who delight in our misfortunes?

Oh, how the fortunes of life are turned and overturned! We, as fools,
are despised for Christ's sake because we have preached him crucified and
lowly; you, as sages, have grown proud through confidence in Christ. We,
being weak, have abased ourselves for Christ's glory; you, being powerful,
grow insolent. We are scorned and overshadowed; you distinguished and
illustrious. For us there has been no return except hard work and trouble;
all the harvest goes to you. For what reward has come to us in return for
so many perils and evils? Even up to this day we are so far from reigning,
unlike some who recommend themselves as apostles, that often we lack
something to eat, something to drink, something to clothe ourselves with
– so far have we been from getting rich on the gospel. Nay, we are even
repeatedly battered and beaten, so far have we been from winning honour.
Even now we wander about with no sure dwelling – and it is indeed[21] a sign
of extreme indigence to have not even a little house of your own in which
you might bear poverty more easily if only[22] because it is more hidden. So
far are we from fleecing anyone that we make our living with the work of
our hands; so far from hunting for human praise that we pray for those who
curse us, that we return blessings for the abuses we continually endure; so
far from overpowering anyone that we suffer the cruelty of our persecutors
in silence. What more need I say? Others possess glory in your eyes; to this
very day for your sake we are regarded as the refuse of this world, and
nothing can be more worthless or contemptible than that.

If, as some do, I wanted to claim credit from you for my toils, my perils, my services, would I not have a most just cause for complaint? I am not
writing this now, as one estranged from you because of your ingratitude, in
order to shame you. No, rather like a very loving father, I am admonishing

* * * * *

19 See Acts 16:17-23.
20 Paul says in 4:9 that the apostles 'have become a spectacle to the world, to
   angels and to mortals' (NRSV). For 'angels' paraphrased as 'the demons themselves,' cf Ambrosiaster's suggestion in Comm in 1 Cor (on 4:9) CSEL 81/2 46:23–
   47:2 that the angels here are evil angels, like those mentioned in Ps 78:49, where
   God employs destroying angels to punish Israel and Judah. Theophylact Expos in 1 Cor (on 4:9) PG 124 613D explains that Christians struggle not only
   against humans, but also against perverse angels. Cf chapter 11 n20 and Eph
   chapter 3 n14.
21 indeed] Added in 1521
22 if only] Added in 1532

my dearest[23] children, not for my own sake, but for yours. For if your situation were being improved by the misfortune that I alone[24] am suffering, I would regard my own disadvantage as of no consequence and would be rejoicing for you. For your advantage I would not hesitate even to lay down my life.[25]

Now since I see that you through the influence of new apostles are falling into a worse condition,[26] my devotion towards you compels me to warn you of your peril, which I surely[27] regard as my very own. You ought not to reject this affection, Corinthians, for it is the affection of a true and genuine father. There is a vast difference between a pedagogue and a father. The pedagogue exercises severity for a time on the innocence of youth, and does his duty – if he does it – either[28] for the sake of payment or out of fear of punishment. But a father considers the welfare of his children, even to his own misfortune, on account of a devotion deeply implanted by nature.[29] Although you happen to have even ten thousand pedagogues, surely you will find few among them to be fathers. Why then should I not call myself a father, and you my children, since I was the first of all to preach the gospel to you, since through me you were born again in Christ? Did I not in a manner give birth to you? What mother endures so much pain in childbirth as I suffered when I laboured to bring you forth for Christ?[30] Therefore, if you acknowledge this man as father, if you are truly

* * * * *

23 'Dearest': *carissimos*. Here in the paraphrase on 4:14 Erasmus follows the Vulgate's practice of translating the Greek ἀγαπητός 'beloved' by the Latin *carissimus* rather than *dilectus* 'beloved,' the equivalent he uses in his Latin translation and recommends in the annotation on 4:14 (*charissimos*). Cf the paraphrases on 2 Cor 7:1 and 12:19 with n22; also CWE 56 311 and 342.

24 alone] Added in *1532*

25 Cf John 15:13.

26 Cf Ambrosiaster *Comm in 1 Cor* (on 4:13) CSEL 81/2 49:3–6: 'Since he saw that his own humility was benefiting them not at all, he complains ... that such great submissiveness and injuries have been able to yield no profit; but what is even less desirable, they have brought about a worse condition.'

27 surely] Added in *1532*

28 either] Added in *1532*

29 Erasmus develops the thought from his annotation on 4:15 (*si decem milia*): 'There is a great difference between a pedagogue and a father. The pedagogue rages imperiously; the father lays down even his life if necessary.' Cf the contrasting images of threatening pedagogue and encouraging father in Erasmus' paraphrase on Gal 3:24 CWE 42 113–14. On 'pedagogue,' see the Argument n13.

30 Echoing Gal 4:19 and Erasmus' paraphrase on that verse CWE 42 118

his children, I beseech you by our mutual devotion to express your father in your life and character.[31] Why, when you are our children, do you prefer to seem like others? Consider where those things come from that are reported to me about you. Surely you did not draw them from me?

But in case you have forgotten any of our teaching, since I may not yet come myself, I am sending Timothy to you, as if he were my second self, truly in no way an unworthy son,[32] but by God's kindness a faithful one. As he first imbibed Christ through me, so he nowhere departs from his father's steps. He will recall to your memory the rule by which I order my life, and which, according to the example of Jesus Christ, I both follow myself and teach,[33] not only to you, but to every assemblage that professes Christ. Just as Christ is the source shared by all, so must all keep to the same plan of living. Whoever is a true child performs his duty from the heart, not from fear of punishment. But among you there are some who because of my absence have banished shame and behave so arrogantly, as if I were never going to return. They will be disappointed; for I shall be with you very soon, if the Lord allows, and then shall I in fact find out, not how powerful in talk these people are who advance themselves so arrogantly, but how powerful in deeds. For the strength of the gospel is not placed in splendid words, which may come to anyone, but in a heavenly force or power made evident by the endurance of evils, by concord, by the innocence of one's whole life, and by miracles. Do you want me to come to you? I shall come indeed. Take care that you receive me as you ought. It rests with you to make me come either with a severe and terrifying aspect or with one gentle and mild. I have the authority passed on by Christ[34] to restrain and overcome the rebellious and unmanageable with the rod of punishment. But I should prefer not to use it; I would prefer that your character be such that as a devoted, gracious, and gentle father either I might rejoice in your

* * * * *

31 For the idea of the son's likeness to his father, see Eph chapter 5 n1. See also CWE 46 46 n16 and 115 nn60 and 61. Erasmus' paraphrase at this point follows his Greek text and Latin translation of 4:16 in omitting 'as I [am an imitator] of Christ,' with which the verse ended in the Vulgate. See the annotation on 4:16 (*sicut et ego Christi*): the clause 'seems to be borrowed from the eleventh chapter of this letter.'

32 Erasmus elaborates on Timothy as Paul's 'true son' at the opening of the *Paraphrase on First Timothy* CWE 44 5–6.

33 Similarly Ambrosiaster *Comm in 1 Cor* (on 4:17) CSEL 81/2 50:17–18: 'He wants them to turn back to the rule of truth taught by himself.'

34 Paul claims this authority in Gal 1:11–17. See also Acts 9:3–6 and 1 Cor 9:1 and 15:8–9, and cf the paraphrase on 7:25 with n53.

innocence, or if you have any slight faults, these might be corrected with a soft and fatherly reproof.[35]

Chapter 5

It is a fact too well known to be denied, too serious to be borne, and too ruinous to be conveniently put off, that there is a foul rumour of immoral passion among you, for whom, as a temple[1] sacred to God, complete purity was proper. This is a kind of passion whose scandalous report is not even found among pagans and those who are strangers to Christ, namely, that someone has his own stepmother for a wife.[2] How great, do you think, is the shame that comes to the Christian name when the common talk about you broadcasts outrageous acts of this sort? Meanwhile, just as if such dishonour to your profession had nothing at all to do with you, you are pleased with yourselves and swollen with a worthless belief in your wisdom,[3] when it would be more appropriate for you to cast out the doer of such wickedness from your company and to witness with public mourning that the most shameful deed is totally abhorrent to you. You ought to do this, in the first place, so that you do not seem to countenance base crimes by welcoming as intimate friend and associate one who has not yet shown he is sorry for his outrage; then, so that the deadly infection, once it has gained access, may not gradually spread among you more widely; finally, so that the doer of the abominable wickedness might, if you avoid him as one condemned by the common judgment of all, be touched by shame and come to his senses.[4] And he should be avoided until sure indications of his remorse show the man fit to be received into the fellowship of saints.[5] You ought to have

* * * * *

35 Erasmus echoes Ambrosiaster *Comm in 1 Cor* (on 4:21) CSEL 81/2 51:24–52:3: 'If they truly longed for the apostle's presence, they would prepare themselves to welcome him, ie they would wash themselves from every stain of guilt so that when he came he would take delight in them as with his dearest children.'

1 See 1 Cor 3:16 and the paraphrase on that verse. Cf also 6:19.
2 Ambrosiaster *Comm in 1 Cor* (on 5:2) CSEL 81/2 53:4 uses the same idiom for the sin: 'He had his own stepmother for a wife.'
3 Chrysostom *In 1 Cor hom* 15.1 (on 5:2) PG 61 122 and Theophylact *Expos in 1 Cor* (on 5:2) PG 124 621B speculate that the fornicator was a respected sage and that the mention of the Corinthians' arrogance in 5:2 refers to their pride in some teaching he had given them.
4 'Come to his senses': *resipiscat*. See the Argument n15.
5 There is ample evidence for the practice of penance and the remission of sins in the early church, but little information about specific procedures. Cf the

taken this action immediately when through ugly rumour the man (for I still hold back his name)[6] stood accused of the wicked offence.

I myself was going to do this if I had been present with you. Now in my absence – granted, I am not totally absent, for although I am absent in body, yet I am present in the authority of the spirit – in my absence, therefore, but just as if I were present, I render my judgment, with which you also need to comply, so that you pronounce the judgment in public meeting and in full assembly lest anyone privately usurp this authority for himself.[7] This assembly should come together without any human prejudice,[8] but having in view nothing other than the glory of our Lord Jesus Christ; in this assembly I will be present with you in spirit only, as I said. And the authority of our Lord Jesus Christ will not be lacking; in his name you will come together; by his own power he will render my judgment effectual: that the one who has so foully committed this wickedness be thrown

* * * * *

dedicatory letter n23 above, and see Furnish 161 for several relevant citations from Qumran documents. For a concise discussion of attitudes in the pre-Nicene Church towards the remission of sin, see Kelly *Early Christian Doctrines* 198–9. Modern commentators generally agree that the text of 5:2–5 does not seem to allow for the possibility of receiving this sinner back into fellowship. See Orr and Walther 186–9, Conzelmann 97–8, and Barrett 125–6. Erasmus, however, follows the traditional interpretation that 2 Cor 2:5–10 (where Paul encourages the Corinthians to become reconciled with an unnamed offender) records the aftermath of this case of incest. In the dedicatory letter 5–6, in the paraphrase on 2 Cor 2:1–10, and in the annotations on 2 Cor 2:8 and 10 (*ut confirmetis in illum* and *quod donavi*), Erasmus clearly identifies the penitent and forgiven man of the second letter with the fornicator of the first. Chrysostom *In 1 Cor hom* 15.4 (on 5:8) PG 61 126 makes the same identification and suggests that in 1 Corinthians 5 Paul purposefully withholds from the fornicator the hope of restoration in order to make the motivation for repentance more compelling. See also n9 below. For a vigorous argument against identifying the sinner of 1 Corinthians 5 with the one in 2 Corinthians 2, see Furnish 163–8.

6 Chrysostom *In 1 Cor hom* 15.1 (on 5:1–2) PG 61 122 notes that the omission of the man's name follows the church's custom in matters 'exceedingly offensive.'

7 The emphasis on assembly and public meeting in this elaboration on 5:4 may be intended to invite reflection on the conciliar debates of the fourteenth and fifteenth centuries, in which the supremacy of papal authority was at issue. For conciliarism see Roland Bainton *Christendom: a Short History of Christianity and Its Impact on Western Civilization* (New York 1966) I 234–42 or Martin Marty *A Short History of Christianity* (Cleveland 1959) 190–5.

8 Cf Theophylact *Expos in 1 Cor* (on 5:4) PG 124 621D–624A: 'The assembly should meet not in accordance with any human prejudice, but in accordance with God.' Similarly Chrysostom *In 1 Cor hom* 15.2 (on 5:4–5) PG 61 123.

out from your company and delivered to Satan so that he may be afflicted in the flesh and shamed by human judgment, in order that his spirit and soul may be unharmed in the presence of the judge Jesus Christ, when he comes to judge all things, not these only, or this man only. In the meantime it is also to the man's benefit to anticipate that precise and severe judgment of God, and be vexed by temporal correction rather than sentenced to everlasting punishments. It is our place to provide remedy rather than penalty.[9] For we ought to deal with an offender in such a way that he may be one who can be corrected. We do not do away with the person, but we destroy the sin and save the person. With this punishment Christian gentleness ought to be satisfied. It is the Jewish way to stone a person to death; the Christian way is to heal.

None of this was of concern to you; neither the common shame nor the common danger discomforted you, but you exalted yourselves as if over a deed well done. There is a great difference between the boasting of worldly people and the boasting of Christians.[10] That boasting of yours is a disgrace to you, and not only a disgrace, but also perilous. Granted, you say, there is one person who has sinned; what is this to the whole? Do you not know that a little bit of yeast affects a huge quantity of dough and makes it sour? The yeast is what remains from the spoiled lump of dough.[11] If, therefore,

* * * * *

9 Erasmus interprets Paul's instruction to 'deliver this man to Satan for the destruction of the flesh' (RSV) in terms of penance rather than physical death. Chrysostom *In 1 Cor hom* 15.2 (on 5:5) PG 61 123–4 similarly sees Paul 'opening up the doors of repentance to him and delivering such a person as if to a tutor ... And so [Paul speaks] more as one administering a cure and healing than as one simply cutting down or punishing rashly and senselessly. For the profit is greater than the punishment since the latter is for a time only, but the profit is forever.' For Erasmus' views on penance, see Payne *Theology* 181–216 and Richard DeMolen *The Spirituality of Erasmus of Rotterdam* (Nieuwkoop 1987) 57–63.

10 Cf the paraphrase on 1:29 with n61.

11 'The spoiled lump of dough': *corrupta massa* ie leavened or soured dough. The idea is that yeast is what remains in the Corinthians from the leavened dough that was their former life. In this passage Erasmus accommodates both the Vulgate's diction and that of his own Latin translation. In his translation, as in his annotations on 5:6 (*modicum fermentum totam massam corrumpit*) and on the identical sentence in Gal 5:9 (*totam massam corrumpit*), Erasmus follows Jerome *Comm in Gal* III (on 5:9) PL 26 402B–C in expressing the yeast's action by the verb *fermentare* 'to leaven,' rather than by the Vulgate's *corrumpere* 'to corrupt' or 'spoil.' He also replaces the Vulgate's *massa* with *conspersio* for 'dough.' Here in the paraphrase, however, *corrupta massa* 'the spoiled [or leavened] lump of dough' follows closely after *ingentem farinae conspersae vim* 'a huge

anything of your old life still lives in you and conflicts with the simplicity of Christ, it is yeast, and you must be utterly purified of it so that through newness of life you may be new dough, and that in the whole batch there may be nothing of your former wickedness mixed in. For as Christ rendered you free from your sins once, so must you take care that no pollution from your former life creep back into you, and corrupt the genuineness of your Christian innocence. God loves those who are free from this yeast.

Was this not foreshadowed long ago in mystical[12] figures? When the Hebrews had, by passing through the sea, been freed from their Egyptian bondage, they were ordered as a token and memorial of this event to sacrifice a year-old lamb every year at an appointed time, and for seven days to eat bread that was not adulterated with any leaven, just as they had done when preparing their flight from Egypt.[13] Meanwhile they brought out with themselves pure flour and left behind all the yeast for the Egyptians.[14] And no one is considered worthy to eat of the paschal lamb unless for seven days he has abstained from yeast.[15] In fact it was considered a sin during that period[16] for any leaven to be found anywhere in the homes of the Hebrews.

* * * * *

quantity of dough,' and *universa massa* 'the whole batch' after *nova conspersio* 'new dough.'

12 'Mystical': *mysticis*. Erasmus sometimes uses this term to identify Old Testament passages or events that require spiritual ie Christological, interpretation for full understanding. Cf the paraphrase on 10:3-4. On *mysticus* 'mystical,' see chapter 10 n7; for other uses of the term in this volume, see the Index of Greek and Latin Words Cited. On Pauline typology, see n17 below and chapter 10 n4; also Eph chapter 5 n39.

13 This Hebrew precedent is recorded in two versions: Exod 12:1-24 and 13:1-13. The passage through the Red Sea is recorded in Exod 14.

14 Exod 12:34, 39

15 Regarding this sentence, Erasmus had to defend himself against the charges of Noël Béda that he misunderstood the Hebrew observance of Passover, namely, that he thought the seven-day avoidance of yeast preceded the eating of the paschal lamb. Erasmus, although he considered the discussion a waste of time, responded that the sentence in question did not assert a temporal scheme and that the larger context of the passage clearly revealed his understanding of Hebrew practices. See *Divinationes ad notata Bedae* LB IX 474A-B. Cf *Elenchus in N. Bedae censuras* LB IX 507B-D and *Supputatio* LB IX 680D-F.

16 during that period] Added in 1532. The logic of the narrative suggests that this phrase refers to the seven-day period in which the eating of unleavened bread was forbidden. Since, however, a comma follows the phrase, Erasmus may intend that it be taken with 'it was considered' rather than with 'to be found.' If so, the addition may be influenced by Chrysostom *In 1 Cor hom* 15.4 (on 5:8) PG 61 126: the removal of yeast 'was done among them in the recent

They had the shadows of things, but we hold the true Passover,[17] the lamb wholly without spot. This is Christ Jesus, sacrificed on the altar of the cross in order to free us from the most hideous tyranny of death and sins. It was not for nothing that he was sacrificed. We have escaped Egypt once; it remains for us to celebrate this feast continually, by no means rejoicing and priding ourselves upon those things to which we were formerly captive, when yet the bondage, both shameful and harsh, held us. This is to say that we are to celebrate the feast not with the yeast[18] of the Mosaic law, nor with the yeast of our old wickedness and craftiness, but with cakes and breads spoiled by no yeast, that is, with conduct that is blameless, straightforward, genuine, and free of pretence and dissembling.

But lest you make any mistake about my instruction a little earlier[19] for you to avoid association with those defiled by disgraceful and immoral passion, I do not mean by this that I require you to avoid all the immoral people of this region without exception, and not to associate with anyone who suffers disgrace from greed or swindling, or who is devoted to the worship of idols, for if you attempted this, you would have to abandon Greece entirely since such people turn up everywhere.[20] And yet I would

* * * * *

past, but now no longer. For leaven is found everywhere that a Jew is found. For the feast of unleavened bread is celebrated in the middle of cities, and indeed now more in play than as law. For since the truth has come, the types no longer have a place.'

17 Cf the paraphrase on 10:1–11 with n4 for Erasmus' similar elaboration on Paul's use of Hebrew events as 'types' of Christian experience.

18 In 1 Cor 5:8 Paul exhorts the Corinthians to 'celebrate the feast,' not ἐν ζύμῃ παλαιᾷ 'in the old yeast.' Erasmus preserves the preposition in his Latin translation (in fermento veteri). His omission of the preposition at this point in the paraphrase suggests that he interprets the Greek ἐν in this phrase as instrumental rather than locative. Cf his annotation on Rom 1:4 ('in power') CWE 56 16 and n8.

19 Erasmus seems to follow Theophylact Expos in 1 Cor (on 5:9) PG 124 625B in referring the verse ('I wrote to you in my letter') to the preceding instruction in 5:7. See also Chrysostom In 1 Cor hom 16.1 (on 5:9) PG 61 129. Ambrosiaster in Comm in 1 Cor (on 5:9) CSEL 81/2 57:6–9, however, and most modern commentators explain 5:9 as referring to a previous letter in which Paul issued a general warning to the Corinthians not to associate with sexually immoral people. See Orr and Walther 190. See also Erasmus' comment in the Argument 25 with n28.

20 Cf the annotation on 5:10 (commisceamini fornicariis), where Erasmus comments that by 'this world' Paul means Greece 'particularly Corinth, which was very much corrupted by pleasures of this sort.' Cf also Chrysostom In 1 Cor hom 16.1 (on 5:9–11) PG 61 130: 'For he names as "fornicators of the world" those

wish this also,[21] if it might be done; now since it cannot be done, I do not demand it. What I do demand is that if anyone called a Christian should be known to be infected with the kinds of vices that are farthest from Christian practice, such as whoring[22] or greed or the worship of idols or the disease of slander or drunkenness or swindling, you so completely avoid the person's company that you deign not even to eat with him until he repents. It is of greatest importance to you that your assembly be pure and undefiled. As for what sort of people non-Christians are, let them see to that themselves; their vices neither corrupt you nor bring dishonour upon the Christian name.

Consequently, once a charge is out in the open among you,[23] you ought not to allow such people to go unpunished. This for me is sufficient. For what is the purpose of my passing judgment on those also, who as strangers to Christ do not concern us? Is it not the case that each one acts as judge and critic in his own home, and thinks that what goes on in others' houses is not his business? If any offence is committed in his own home, he considers it the business of the whole household. It is sufficient for us, therefore,

* * * * *

who were among the Greeks.' On Corinth's reputation for sexual immorality, see the Argument n11.

21 The paraphrase here reflects Erasmus' interpretation, and indeed his translation, of the last clause of 5:10, 'since then you would need to go out of the world.' He thought the Greek verb, in his reading ὀφείλετε 'would need,' expressed not only an impossible condition, but also a wish, and he translated, 'Otherwise would that of course you had withdrawn from the world.' See the annotation on 5:10 (alioqui debueratis): 'But so that I may add something on my own to the studies of earlier commentators, it seems to me that ὀφείλετε in this place is the indication of someone wishing, and has been used instead of εἴθε, ie "would that" or "if only."' Thus in 5:10 Paul would not be merely correcting the erroneous and unrealistic assumption that he was forbidding association with immoral non-Christians (an impossibility without departing from Greece entirely), but also expressing the optimal situation of avoiding such associations entirely by withdrawing from the world.

22 'Whoring': scortatione is a word Erasmus prefers to the Vulgate's fornicatio because he thinks it represents more precisely the Greek πορνεία 'illicit sexual intercourse' or 'prostitution.' See his annotation on 5:1 (inter vos fornicatio), where he notes that he has not found fornicatio used by 'approved' authors, and indicates his preference for either stuprum 'disgrace,' 'illicit sexual intercourse' or scortatio 'whoring.' Typically he translates the Greek πόρνος 'one who engages in illicit sexual intercourse' as scortator 'whoremonger' rather than the Vulgate's fornicarius. See eg the annotations on 5:9 (commisceamini fornicariis) and 6:9 (neque fornicarii), and cf the paraphrase on 6:9 with n27. See also 1 Thess chapter 4 n4.

23 among you] Added in 1532

if we Christians pass judgment on Christians. Those who are strangers to
the profession of the Christian name we leave to the judgment of God.
But if no one allows in his home a wicked and unwholesome person, you
too must drive out from your company the perpetrator of such wickedness;
this action serves both his interest and your own, and it befits the honour of
the Christian name. For not only will he be stricken with shame and come
to himself again, but also you will ward off from yourselves the danger
of infection as well as any suspicion, and everyone will know that these
offences are not acceptable to Christ, who taught and practised a life of
innocence. I have shown thus far that the unwholesome yeast of divisive
strife and of base passion should be utterly cast out from within your midst.

Chapter 6

Elsewhere also I find in you remnants of your former life that smack of
the yeast of avarice. Just as it is not your business to pass sentence on those
who are strangers to the fellowship of the church, so it is most unseemly for
Christians to be judged by non-Christians. In the first place, I am amazed
how anyone who has professed Christ can, if some dispute arises about
money matters,[1] bring himself without misgiving to appeal to a judge, and,
what is more serious, to an ungodly judge rather than a Christian. Will
someone judge rightly who is unrighteous in all that his life professes?
Do you not see how absurd it is that the world, whose ungodliness must
someday be condemned from the faith and life of the saints, should now
pass sentence on the saints and resolve their disputes, as if the world were
more virtuous and just than they? But if so great a matter is entrusted[2] to

* * * * *

1 Cf the annotation on 6:3 (*quanto magis secularia*): 'for he means cases involving
  money matters.' Theophylact in *Expos in 1 Cor* (on 6:1) PG 124 628C similarly
  assumes the lawsuits are disputes about money matters.
2 is entrusted ... is condemned] First in 1532; previously 'will be entrusted ...
  will be condemned.' Cf the annotation on 6:2 (*de hoc mundo iudicabunt*), where
  Erasmus argues (from 1516) against the Vulgate's future (*iudicabitur* 'will be
  judged') in 6:2b, and notes that Paul used the present tense to make clear that
  the world was at that time being judged by the lives of Christians. Erasmus
  cites Ambrosiaster (first in 1519), Theophylact (first in 1527), and Chrysostom
  (first in 1535) in support of his position. He admits, however, that Augustine
  read the future tense here and referred it to the final judgment. Erasmus concludes that Paul's statement can apply both to the present (when 'the ungodly
  world may be condemned by the innocent lives of the godly') and to the future ('when all the deeds of the godly and the ungodly will be revealed'). It

you that through you the life of the whole world – that is, of all the ungodly – is condemned, do you think you are quite unfit for judging the slightest and most trivial of matters? For[3] you are the light of the world,[4] [the light] which is to convict the errors of the ungodly. How is this to happen if in you yourselves there should be darkness,[5] if there should be something worthy of reproof? Now[6] you take your lawsuits to ungodly judges, as if they either were wiser than you or possessed more fairness.

Do you not know that someday you are going to judge not only people devoted to the world, but also wicked angels, the tyrants of this world?[7] So do not think it a great accomplishment if you settle among yourselves trivial suits over matters that concern the enjoyment of physical life. Your ready belief will condemn their unbelief, your godliness their ungodliness, your innocence their impurity, and condemns them even today, if you lead a life worthy of Christ. And do you, having forgotten your own status, set up as judges over your affairs people who will all receive sentences of condemnation issued through you? But if you are so quarrelsome, if you are so enamoured of transient things (although you profess your contempt for them) that you not only are divided among yourselves about such things, but are so divided that it is absolutely necessary to appeal to judges, then you should take[8] cases of that sort to anyone at all in your fellowship – even the most despised and lowly.

* * * * *

appears that prior to 1532 Erasmus adopted the Vulgate for his paraphrase, but that from 1532, he accommodated the paraphrase to both the Vulgate and his own translation. See nn3 and 6 below. Note, however, that from 1519 onward the paraphrase on 6:3 affirmed an at least hypothetical present condemnation of the world (parallel to the predicted future condemnation).

3 For ... reproof] Added in 1532, apparently to clarify the potential for pagans to be judged by the lives of Christians in the present as well as in the future. See the preceding note.
4 Matt 5:14
5 Cf Luke 11:34–5.
6 Now] First in 1532; prior to that 'But'
7 LB punctuates to read, 'but also the angels, the wicked tyrants of this world' – a reading the editions from 1519 to 1540 permit, but do not require. For the idea of angels exercising a tyranny, see Eph 6:12 and Erasmus' paraphrase on that verse. Chrysostom In 1 Cor hom 16.3 (on 6:3) PG 61 133 explains that Paul 'speaks of those angels about whom Christ says: "Go into the fire that has been prepared for the devil and his angels"' (Matt 25:41). See also Theophylact Expos in 1 Cor (on 6:3) PG 124 629B, and cf the paraphrase on 4:9 with n20.
8 'You should take': deferatis. The main verb in 6:4, καθίζετε 'do you lay ... before,' can be read as either imperative or indicative. Modern interpreters

I do not say this because I would have it done this way, but I speak like this[9] to make you ashamed of yourselves when you fight it out before heathen judges. If you live up to what you profess, then one who is the most worthless among you is better than those who are most highly regarded among the ungodly. Do you really despise yourselves to such a degree? Is there really no one among you who is wise enough to sit in judgment concerning such trivial matters, and to settle a lawsuit between two Christians? Since Christians are bound firmly together[10] by fraternal love and by the sharing of all things, they ought to reach agreement very easily.[11] But now

* * * * *

generally prefer to take it as an indicative question, in which Paul chastises the Corinthians either for entrusting internal disputes to the judgment of outsiders (so Conzelmann 103–5, NEB) or for not choosing as judges the most competent persons within the church community (so Orr and Walther 194–5). Erasmus, however, follows patristic tradition in taking the verb as an imperative; so also the Vulgate, AV, DV. See the annotation on 6:4 (*illos constituite ad iudicandum*), where Erasmus cites Augustine *Contra Faustum Manichaeum* 5.9 PL 42 226, Theophylact *Expos in 1 Cor* (on 6:4) PG 124 629B–C, and Chrysostom *In 1 Cor hom* 16.3 (on 6:4) PG 61 133 in support of a hyperbolic imperative: better to set up the least respected Christian as judge than to go before a heathen.

9 'Like this': *sic*. Erasmus' paraphrase of 6:5 reflects an ambiguity he saw in the Greek, where it is possible to take the Greek word οὕτως 'thus' or 'in this way' either with the sentence that precedes – 'I speak in this way to your shame' – or with the question that follows – 'Is it so, that there is not a wise man among you?' (AV). Erasmus himself, the Vulgate, and most modern translations adopt the second reading. Erasmus, however, found a few Greek manuscripts that adopted the first, and the ambiguity interested him. In the annotation on 6:5 (*sic non est*), he notes that the effect of the first reading is to explain the manner of Paul's speech: I speak like this so that you can understand how unworthy your behaviour is, not because I actually want the most contemptible serving as your judges. The effect of the second reading, which he prefers and adopts in his translation, is to stress the measure of disdain implied by 'so': Do you so despise yourselves that a wise man cannot be found? Characteristically Erasmus has accommodated both interpretations in the paraphrase on this verse.

10 'Are bound firmly together': *conglutinantur*. On this verb, see chapter 1 n4. Note that Erasmus has extended his use of the verb here to underpin the idea of *consensus* among Christians as determinative in matters of judgment. Cf McConica 'Erasmus and the Grammar of Consent' 84–9.

11 In his annotation on 6:5 (*qui possit iudicare inter fratrem suum*) Erasmus notes in passing that *fraternus affectus* 'fraternal affection' eliminates the need for judicial exactitude in such cases and makes reconciliation easy. Cf Chrysostom *In 1 Cor hom* 16.3 (on 6:5) PL 61 134: arbiters in lawsuits between Christians need no great skill or understanding 'since disposition and relationship assist greatly towards the resolution of such a dispute.'

there is so little agreement that Christian goes to court against Christian, and what is more shameful, before those who are strangers to Christ, as if they by the standard of human laws can pronounce what is just, but you by the standard of the gospel cannot.

Consider in how many ways you sin here. First, this very thing is a disgrace to you, that you yourselves do not resolve such disputes among yourselves without a public disturbance or settle any quarrel either[12] by mutual concession or at least through arbitrators. But there has come to be so much obstinacy that, while neither party gives way to the other nor gives anything up, the case must be argued before the public judges for all the people to see.

There would be no lack of fault if these matters were being argued before ecclesiastical judges. Now how vile a spectacle is it to contend before ungodly judges about matters of no importance! Our religion is peace, and since we have been grafted into one body through Christ,[13] we have become more than genuine kin.[14] Moreover, it is our disregard of these base things, for which this world eagerly battles, that makes us Christians.[15] But when you vie for these very things so fiercely that Christian is not ashamed to drag Christian into court, and make accusation before an ungodly judge, what do you suppose enters the thoughts of those who observe this? Will they not think to themselves something of this sort: Where is there shame among these Christians? Where brotherly love?[16] Where the sharing of all possessions?[17] Where the peace which they always have on their

* * * * *

12 either ... arbitrators] Added in 1532
13 Erasmus is perhaps borrowing the image from Rom 11:17–24, where Paul asks the gentile Christians, as branches grafted onto the tree of the true Israel, not to be proud at the expense of natural branches which have been broken off (unbelieving Jews) and may well yet be restored. Here in the paraphrases on 1 Cor 6:7, emphasis is instead placed upon a new unified Christian body whose members, through being grafted onto Christ, are more closely related than natural siblings. For the image of grafting, see also the paraphrases on 6:8, 2 Cor 5:17 and, in a pejorative sense, 2 Cor 11:13.
14 Cf Ambrosiaster *Comm in 1 Cor* (on 6:7) CSEL 81/2 62:7–9: 'They ought to make every effort to be harmonious, like genuine kin, especially since our faith is eager for peace.'
15 In this claim Erasmus may be alluding to the contrast in 1 John 2:15–16 and 3:13–20 between one's love for God or neighbour and one's concern with worldly goods.
16 For 'brotherly love' as a Christian characteristic, see Rom 12:10; 1 Thess 4:9; Heb 13:1; and cf the paraphrase on 6:5.
17 See Acts 2:44–5, 4:32–5.

tongues?[18] Where their scorn for money?[19] Where that evangelical meek-ness, by which they are ordered to give up even their tunic willingly if anyone has taken away their cloak?[20] Look how despicably they duel, and over what a small matter – not only with us, but also among themselves.

How does it happen, O Corinthians, that even now you esteem money so highly that for its sake you draw such great shame upon the Christian name? Someone will answer: Unless I pursue my rights, I shall not avoid injury; unless I claim what is mine, I will suffer loss. But take constant care lest, while you fear a slight financial loss, you cause serious damage to your innocence and good reputation, and likewise bring serious loss to the gospel. It would be preferable not to recover your property rather than to give unbelievers this handle for disparaging Christ. It would be better to ignore the slight injury than, while prosecuting it in this way, to display publicly a mind desirous of revenge.[21]

But now so far are you from enduring loss in the mild manner of Christians, or injury without retaliation that you yourselves without provo-cation inflict injury on others; without provocation you deceive and cheat others, not only unbelievers, but even those who are your true kin through the fellowship of religion. Do these things not smack of the yeast of your former life? Are they not harshly out of harmony both[22] with what you have learned and with what you have professed? Whoever professes Christ, professes innocence, and to such conduct the kingdom of heaven has been promised.[23] For it is not enough to have been washed in water,[24] not enough

* * * * *

18 See John 14:27; Acts 10:36; Eph 2:17. Erasmus may also be alluding to the prominence of 'peace' in Christian liturgy eg in the *Gloria* and *Agnus Dei* as well as the formal *Pax*, or kiss of peace.

19 See eg Matt 6:19–20; Mark 6:8; Acts 8:18–21; 1 Tim 6:10.

20 See Matt 5:40; Luke 6:29. Tertullian *Apologeticum* 39 CCL 1 150–3 offers an in-teresting reverse parallel to this series of hypothetical pagan reactions to the conduct of the Christian community. Tertullian sarcastically catalogues the ways Christian displays of brotherly affection and humble piety may become occasions for disparagement by uncomprehending and uncharitable pagan observers.

21 Theophylact in *Expos in 1 Cor* (on 6:7–8) PG 124 632A states the principle in more general and Socratic form: 'It would be good, he says, neither to do nor to suffer injury; but in the end it is better to suffer it.' Cf Plato *Republic* 358E–359B, 444C–445B, *Apology* 30A–B, *Crito* 49A–D; Cicero *De re publica* 3.13.23.

22 both ... professed] First in the folio edition of 1523; previously, 'both with what we have taught and with what you have professed'

23 Cf Matt 5:3, 19–20 and 18:1–4.

24 'To have been washed in water': *tinctos esse liquore*. Cf the Argument 20 and

to have been grafted onto Christ, unless one's whole life measures up to the teaching of Christ. For this reason you have been released from the world and admitted into the body of Christ, so that after this in the integrity of your life you might measure up to Christ your head.[25] Or does it escape you that people living unrighteously, however much they have been baptized,[26] are to be shut out from the inheritance of the heavenly kingdom? Lest anyone be fooled, over and again I speak, and speak plainly to you: neither whoremongers,[27] nor worshippers of idols, nor adulterers, nor effeminate men, who, like the emasculated,[28] are devoted to an unnatural lust, nor those who use males in place of women, nor thieves, nor the covetous, nor drunkards, nor slanderers, nor those who forcibly seize the possessions of others – none of these will share in the kingdom of God. Their new title[29] will do them no good if their life is defiled with old vices; rather, to these Christ becomes an occasion for harsher condemnation.

* * * * *

the paraphrase on 1:17; on *tingere* 'to wash,' see chapter 1 n34. For Erasmus' disparagement of the outward rite of baptism, see n26 below; also the Argument n5.

25 Here Erasmus anticipates 6:15 and 12:27, but the explicit reference to Christ as 'head' of the body comes from Eph 1:22–3, 4:15–16, and Col 1:18. See also the paraphrases on 1:10, 6:13–17, 15:13, 15:16, and 15:20–3.

26 Cf the paraphrase on Gal 5:21 CWE 42 126 for a similar disclaimer regarding baptism's efficacy before a similar Pauline list of sins. Erasmus frequently refers to the bonding of the individual to Christ through baptism in his paraphrases on passages in which, as here, Paul makes little or no direct mention of baptism, eg in the paraphrases on 1:1–2, 3:3, 4:7, 6:19, 10:1–12, and 15:17. Cf also the paraphrase on 2 Cor 5:9. This practice is noted by Albert Rabil in 'Erasmus's *Paraphrases of the New Testament*' in *Essays on the Works of Erasmus* ed Richard L. DeMolen (New Haven 1978) 154. These amplifications typically involve a disparagement, not of baptism itself, but of the adequacy of the outward rite, if it is not accompanied by a change in living, ie the real practice of the philosophy of Christ in one's life. Cf *Enchiridion* CWE 66 71; also n24 above. For a more thorough discussion of Erasmus' views on baptism, see Payne *Theology* 155–80, especially 166–9.

27 'Whoremongers': *scortatores*. See chapter 5 n22.

28 'The emasculated': *evirati* 'unmanned' or 'unmanly.' Erasmus may have eunuchs in mind, although it is not clear why eunuchs are associated *ipso facto* with unnatural lust. In comparing *molles* 'the effeminate' with *evirati* 'the emasculated,' Erasmus may be remembering Martial 5.41.1–2, where the epigram's addressee is accused of being 'more unmanned (*eviratior*) than a flaccid eunuch and more effeminate (*mollior*) than the Phrygian catamite' (ie Attis, Cybele's young consort, who castrated himself).

29 Ie as 'Christians' or 'the baptized'

And indeed[30] these disgraces, which I have just mentioned, once belonged to you before you were reborn through Christ. I do not reproach you with what you were, provided you do not fall back to the same condition. You have been washed clean of your former transgressions, washed at no cost to you; beware lest you again become defiled. Not only has he restored innocence to those washed with his own blood, but of his own accord he has even granted holiness and righteousness, and that, not with the aid of the Law or your own merits,[31] but through Jesus Christ, in whose name you were baptized, and through the Spirit of our God, by whose secret inspiration the sacraments of the church are efficacious.[32] All the more should you strive not to lose through your sin so great a kindness, and one which comes freely, for in this you would be at the same time showing ingratitude towards your benefactor and acting in your own worst interests.

In matters that have to do with natural needs, all things are permitted me.[33] For no one forbids me to enjoy the same rights the other apostles enjoy. But perhaps it does not always benefit you for me to use my rights. Those who live on your food, who fleece you, as though bought by your generosity, dare not freely admonish you for your immorality, lest you

* * * * *

30 'Indeed': *quidem*. Here Erasmus follows his copy of the Vulgate: 'And there was a time, indeed, when you were these things.' In the annotation on 6:11 (*et haec aliquando quidem*), however, he corrects to *quidam* 'certain ones' or 'some' and attributes to scribal error the Vulgate *quidem* in the majority of the manuscripts he had seen. His translation reads: *Atque haec eratis quidam* 'And some of you were these things.' Note that the Clementine Vulgate and most modern editions also read *quidam*. See *Novum Testamentum Latine secundum editionem Sancti Hieronymi* ed John Wordsworth and Henry J. White *editio minor* (Oxford 1911) 404.

31 Cf Rom 3:21–8; Gal 2:16.

32 On secret inspiration, cf the paraphrases on 2:7–16 and 3:7. Erasmus consistently finds the efficacy of a sacrament not so much in the formal ceremony itself, as in the power of Christ and the mysterious working of the Spirit which accompany the sacrament and which the participant receives inwardly. Cf also the paraphrases on Mark 1:10 CWE 49 19 and Acts 11:16–17 CWE 50 78 with n23. For Erasmus' views on the causal or symbolic nature of the sacraments in general, see Payne *Theology* 97–103 and 220–3; for baptism, see the references in n26 above; for the Eucharist, see Payne *Theology* 134–5.

33 Here Erasmus follows Ambrosiaster *Comm in 1 Cor* (on 6:12) CSEL 81/2 64:16–65:4 in referring the statements in 6:12 not to Christian freedom in general or to the freedom to eat sacrificial offerings in particular (which will be the subject of chapters 8 and 10), but to Paul's apostolic rights and to his voluntary restraint (chapter 9). Eulalius prefers the same interpretation of 6:12 in Erasmus' colloquy 'The Godly Feast' CWE 39 189–91 and n182.

take offence and confer your bounty upon another. I had the right also to burden you with my expenses, the right to receive payment for the effort I spent, especially since I laboured more than anyone else.[34] I did not lack the power to exercise these rights, but I did not want by using this power to give an occasion for being brought under another's power,[35] and to seem to be bound to any of you. My intent is that it might be clearer to you that if I teach anything, I attend your interests, not my own, and that if I offer some chastisement, you should hear me out patiently. For the free speech of a counsellor does not easily offend if he is not bound under any obligation to the one he is correcting.

In any case, it does not matter so much whose food you eat since food is a universal necessity. Foods were intended for the belly, and the belly in turn was set apart for foods; come, then, for the time being let needs be satisfied as circumstances require.[36] Soon God will destroy both the belly and foods; that is, neither will the stomach torment us with hunger, nor will there be any use for foods. But although we who have been initiated into Christ must obey necessity – a characteristic we share with pagans – still there should be no sharing in their vices. Concerning foods I prohibit nothing; let each person eat whatever he wants. But I do forbid immoral passion. For although the belly has been designed for foods, the body has not been similarly destined for filthy passion. Rather our body has been consecrated to the Lord Jesus, and he in turn has been bonded closely to us. For it seemed right to him that we should perform the role of the members, and he that of the head,[37] and together we should make up the mystical body. This bonding is not temporary: death removes the need for eating, but it does not sever our union with Christ. For just as God the Father raised up the Lord Jesus, our head, from death, so will he raise us up also, his members, along with him, and will bestow immortality upon us together with him.[38] For he is able and

* * * * *

34 Cf 1 Cor 15:10.
35 Cf the annotation on 6:12 (*omnia mihi licent, sed ego sub nullius*), where Erasmus notes the Greek text's pun on similar sounding verbs and his own attempt to imitate the pun in his Latin translation through the repetition of *potestas* 'power' in different grammatical cases.
36 This deduction from the slogan in 6:13 is closely echoed in the colloquy 'The Godly Feast' CWE 39 190–1.
37 Both Chrysostom *In 1 Cor hom* 17.1 (on 6:13) PG 61 140 and Theophylact *Expos in 1 Cor* (on 6:13) PG 124 633D similarly at this point introduce the metaphor of Christ as head and church as body. See also n25 above.
38 Cf the importance Erasmus, following Origen, places on 'the same resurrection of the head and of the members' in the annotation on Rom 1:4 ('from the

sufficient[39] to perform this deed although some find it difficult to believe. Therefore, since our soul will not share in that immortality unless it has practised it here through devotion to perpetual wholeness, so the body, when raised up again, will not share in that glory unless here it has been free from the infection of sins.[40]

Yet what an unnatural sight is it to behold, if the members of a body should seem to have no correspondence to the perfectly innocent head. Does it not occur to you that, as I said,[41] your bodies are members of Christ? What then? Shall I become so demented that, although I know these things, still with extreme insult to the head, I take away a member of Christ and make of it a member of a harlot? Pray God, may such a thing never happen! And yet what else does the man do, who consorts with a harlot? Do you fail to see what is perfectly obvious: one who is bonded firmly to a harlot becomes one and the same body with her? For thus we read in Genesis about husband and wife: 'From two there will be made one flesh and the same body' [2:24]. For as in lawful marriage honourable agreement[42] makes one

* * * * *

resurrection of the dead of Jesus Christ') CWE 56 20, and see also the paraphrases on 1 Cor 15:16 and 20 with nn19 and 28.

39 and sufficient] Added in *1521*. Cf the extended defence Chrysostom *In 1 Cor hom* 17.2–3 (on 6:14) PG 61 141–3 gives at this point to the credibility of God's power to raise the dead. See also the paraphrases on 15:1 and 15:34. The defence of bodily resurrection against philosophic scepticism was a common topic in early Christian writings. See chapter 15 nn1 and 48; also CWE 50 142 n6.

40 In 6:14 Paul's reference to resurrection is brief; Erasmus seems to elaborate here on the basis of Rom 6:8–23 and 1 Cor 15:12–57. Cf, in particular, the paraphrase on 1 Cor 15:42–52 for similar language and for amplification on the necessity of practising immortality now in order fully to inherit it later. On the necessity of rehearsing in the present for a goal that can only be realized in the life to come, cf the paraphrase on 13:11. Cf also n26 above for the related emphasis on the insufficiency of baptism alone, ie if not accompanied by godly conduct, for guaranteeing salvation.

41 Erasmus (but not Paul) has already introduced the idea of Christians' bodies as members of Christ's body. See the paraphrase on 6:13.

42 'Agreement': *consensus*. In *Institutio christiani matrimonii*, Erasmus associates the 'formal cause' of marriage, 'union and partnership of life' [*coniunctio et societas vitae*], with the mutual consent of the marriage partners: 'There can be no marriage unless there is agreement [*animorum consensus*] between the partners' CWE 69 220. He defines the nature of marriage by analogy with the Incarnation, in which two natures come together in one indissoluble union. Thus 'true marriage' is that which 'is cemented [*conglutinatur* 'bonded firmly together'] between equals in virtue by true affection' CWE 69 227. On *conglutinare*, see chapter 1 n4. For further discussion of these passages and their background in canon law and scholastic theology, see Payne *Theology* 116–21.

soul out of two, and likewise[43] the legitimate coupling of bodies produces one body from two, so in unlawful sexual intercourse each one becomes one with that to which he foully attaches himself. But if it is considered vile for a wife to deceive her husband and couple her body sexually with an adulterer, so it is an abomination to couple a body once consecrated to Christ with a disgusting harlot. Because of the mutual participation of body and head, whoever is firmly bonded to the Lord Jesus is made one spirit with him; and this spirit, since it is wholly pure, is wholly unsuited for filthy passion, which takes away one's use of the mind, and virtually turns a human being into a senseless beast.[44]

With all your energy, therefore, flee from forbidden passion. Nearly all the other wicked deeds that the ungodly commit, although they stem from the body, nevertheless seem associated with injury to someone else's body and do not, as it seems, pollute the whole person.[45] But he who sins from lust is abusive against his very own body, which he defiles and infects with a foul coupling. Indeed, the adulterer does not pollute the adulteress without at the same time polluting his own body, apart from which the wicked act is not committed. The murderer who pierces someone with a spear injures the body of someone else but keeps his own unharmed, and seems defiled in only one part of himself.[46] Lustful passion pollutes the whole person, as even the common crowd seems to understand. For after

* * * * *

43 likewise] Added in 1532
44 The paraphrase here, in contrasting passion and reason, beasts and human beings, resembles conventional Stoic teaching. See eg Seneca *Epistulae morales* 124 on the faculty of reason as the prerequisite for morally good action and as the distinguishing factor between human nature, which has the capacity for goodness, and dumb animals' nature, which does not. See also Cicero *De officiis* 1.30.107 and cf the paraphrases on Acts 1:15 CWE 50 10 with n76, Acts 2:2 CWE 50 14 with n12, and Acts 8:20 CWE 50 60 with n38.
45 Ambrosiaster *Comm in 1 Cor* (on 6:18) CSEL 81/2 67:20–68:4 distinguishes similarly between fornication and other sins against the body, and even suicide, which he calls a sinful act of violence against one's soul (presumably as the seat of life), but not a sin against one's body.
46 Cf Chrysostom *In 1 Cor hom* 18.1 (on 6:18) PG 61 146: a murderer does indeed pollute his hand, but Paul emphasizes the seriousness of fornication by saying that it makes the 'entire body ... defiled. For, as if fallen into a vat of filth and soaked in impurity, it is thus polluted.' Theophylact *Expos in 1 Cor* (on 6:18) PG 124 637A adds that 'it is conceivable to assault someone with a rock, plank, or some such instrument and not incur pollution of one's body, but impossible to engage in fornication without using one's body and consequently polluting it.'

sexual intercourse people normally make use of the baths so that they may wash away the filth incurred from the coupling of bodies.[47] It is a wicked act to cause harm to the body of someone else. But it seems very much like madness to involve one's own body in disgrace.

Do not think the guilt incurred by lustful passion is inconsequential, even if lust were polluting the body most of all. Even the body ought to have its proper honour because it is the dwelling of the immortal soul, and once it has been cleansed with holy water, it also has itself been consecrated to God so that it is the temple of the Holy Spirit. You have imbibed this Spirit in baptism,[48] and by it you are firmly bonded[49] to Christ, never to be severed from him. But if it does not seriously trouble you that you abuse yourselves, surely it should trouble you that such conduct causes grievous injury to Christ. Once and for all you have passed completely under the authority of the one into whose body you have been admitted. He ransomed you from death and made you his own so that after this you might not have authority over yourselves. Authority over a body that has been purchased belongs to the purchaser; if someone transfers this right to another or handles it otherwise than the master wishes, he injures the one to whom he owes his very self. Christ truly did not purchase you cheaply, but spent his priceless blood in reclaiming you.

Therefore, since you have been wholly dedicated to God, do not dishonour him by defiling your bodies, but carry around in yourselves, in chaste bodies as well as innocent minds,[50] the divine presence that dwells within, and make it shine before the world. Both mind and body are God's; keep both pure lest on account of your disgraces Christ, by whose name

* * * * *

47 Theophylact *Expos in 1 Cor* (on 6:18) PG 124 636D makes the same point; similarly Chrysostom *In 1 Cor hom* 18.1 (on 6:18) PG 61 146, explaining more fully that after acts of greed or robbery people do not generally take care to visit the baths, but return home as if nothing were out of the ordinary.

48 See n26 above.

49 'You are firmly bonded': *conglutinamini*. On this verb, see chapter 1 n4.

50 See the annotation on 6:20 (*glorificate et portate Deum*), where Erasmus follows Chrysostom *In 1 Cor hom* 18.2 (on 6:20) PG 61 147 and Theophylact *Expos in 1 Cor* (on 6:20) PG 124 638D–640A in adding to 'Glorify God in your body' the words 'and in your spirit, which are God's.' This continuation, although it appears in AV, is not included in the Vulgate or in modern versions. See Metzger 487–8. In the annotation, Erasmus also rejects the Vulgate's addition of *et portate* in this sentence: 'Glorify *and bear* God in your body.' The paraphrase, however, accommodates the Vulgate on this latter point with the jussive subjunctives of both *illustretis* 'make shine' and *circumferatis* 'carry around.'

you are known, should receive a bad reputation among the ungodly. For as the renown of masters belongs to their servants as well, so does the baseness of servants bring infamy to their masters.[51] Therefore, although God can be rendered neither more renowned by praise nor more ignoble by reproach, nevertheless, as long as he is judged by the masses according to the life of his people, he is in a way both defamed before the world by the misdeeds of his people and honoured by the purity of their conduct and the holiness of their life.

Chapter 7

But I have not said these things because I think the body is befouled by any sexual intercourse at all, as some are trying to convince you in order that, being hypocrites, they may promote for themselves a reputation among you for holiness.[1] There is a use of marriage that is both chaste and lawful,[2] but unlawful intercourse must be avoided equally by all. Each person should make use of lawful matrimony, or not make use of it, to the extent that it profits the work of the gospel, or impedes it. Therefore, in response to the concerns about which you asked my advice in your letter, I shall briefly say in reply what those who are now entangled in marriage ought to do;

* * * * *

51 The sentence has a proverbial character. Cf the paraphrase on 1 Tim 3:8 CWE 44 21: 'since the misconduct of servants brings their master's authority into disrepute.'

1 Ambrosiaster similarly sets up the context for chapter 7 in *Comm in 1 Cor* (on 7:1) CSEL 81/2 70:12–14: the Corinthians were 'stirred up by the perverse views of false apostles who, so that they might seem purer than the others, were hypocritically teaching that marriage ought to be rejected.'

2 Cf the paraphrases on 7:7 and 7:36; also *De vidua christiana* CWE 66 213, 218 and the *Institutio christiani matrimonii* CWE 69 386–7, where Erasmus allows the begetting of offspring and the remedying of incontinence as proper purposes for marriage and urges moderation in conjugal relations so that a marriage may be 'restrained, modest, and chaste, and, as far as is possible, like the state of virginity.' Cf Augustine *De bono coniugali* 5.5–6.6 CSEL 41 194–5: marriage makes something good out of sinful concupiscent nature by redirecting otherwise sinful desire towards the honourable purpose of procreation. Although Augustine considered marital intercourse still to be sinful if it was performed for reasons other than procreation, this was a venial rather than a mortal sin and a legitimate defence against much worse offences. For Erasmus' views on marriage, see Payne *Theology* 109–25 and Pabel 'Exegesis and Marriage' 175–209.

secondly, what those who live single and those who are widowed ought to do; likewise those who are involved in troubled marriages, or even mixed ones; and finally, virgins who are to be given in marriage or not to be given.[3]

First then, as conditions now stand it would for many reasons be beneficial to abstain entirely from conjugal relations,[4] so that there might be more freedom for devoting oneself to the work of the gospel and to a good purpose. No matter how honourable marriage is as an estate, nevertheless it envelops a man, however unwilling, in worldly cares, and whatever attention is given to these cares is taken away from holy matters. Then also, the conjugal relationship has a certain coarseness,[5] which for the moment devours the whole person, and restores him to his former state hereafter[6] less than he was.

* * * * *

3 Cf the annotation on 7:8 ASD VI-8 130:500–9 (*dico autem non nuptis*), where Erasmus supplies a similar outline for Paul's ordering of his thoughts relating to marriage in 1 Corinthians 7.

4 'Relations': *commercio*. In certain contexts *commercium* refers to sexual relations, but see the annotation on 7:1 (*mulierem non tangere*), where Erasmus argues that the issue here is clearly marriage itself, and not either sexual intercourse or contact in general with women: '*tangere* ... very often does not mean to touch by hand, but to have dealings [*negotium*] or relations [*commercium*] with someone.' He takes 'woman' here as 'wife,' and 'not to touch' as 'not to marry.' Most modern interpreters, however, refer the advice in 7:1 to the expedience of abstaining from sexual relations, not from marriage. See eg Orr and Walther 206–8.

5 'Coarseness': *crassum*. On this word, see chapter 2 n22. Cf Erasmus' *Responsio ad annotationes Lei* 1 (Concerning Note 19) CWE 72 118: '... sexual relations between spouses are allowed, but they have something lowly about them, and if I may say so, something *sordidum* compared with the purity of more sacred things.' There, in the dispute with Edward Lee (CEBR II 311–14) over his annotation on Mark 10:8 (*et erunt duo*), Erasmus defends himself against charges that he called sexual intercourse or marriage itself indecent or filthy. However, the general sentiment that sexual love ministers only to an inferior and cruder side of human nature and that one's desire might better be directed at worthier and more spiritual objects has ample precedent in both classical and Christian writings. See eg Socrates' speech in Plato's *Symposium*, especially 208C–212A: a young man, if he transcends the baser instincts and pleasures of physical love, may eventually fulfil his desire in union with Absolute Beauty itself and thereby procreate true goodness in himself. For a patristic parallel, see Augustine *Confessions* 8.1 and 8.6 CCL 27 113–14 and 126: the most tenacious obstacle impeding the future bishop's spiritual journey and conversion was his concupiscence. See also n2 above.

6 hereafter] *aliquando*, first in the folio edition of 1523; previously, *aliquanto* 'somewhat.' For the meaning 'hereafter,' see L&s *aliquando*. In either version

I see what course is most to be desired, but I should not dare to demand what I desire, lest you, in trying with too little success to reach what is best, slip into what is worse when you have the opportunity. I know how untamed and impetuous this passion is, and I have noticed how you are particularly inclined towards it.[7] Therefore, I think it a safer course for every man to have his own wife and every woman to have her own husband, so that through mutual service each may cure the intemperance of the other. Although elsewhere the husband's authority is greater[8] yet in this area each one has equal jurisdiction. For the husband is not master of his own body to this extent, that he cheat his wife of access to her conjugal rights and offer access to another.[9] Jurisdiction over the wife's body, in turn, belongs to her husband in the matter of marital rights, not to the wife; she should neither deny her husband access to herself nor offer it to another. The obligation is mutual and ought to be honoured on both sides in good faith, as the occasion requires. Let the husband, therefore, fulfil the obligation he owes his wife according to the law of marriage. Let the wife fulfil the obligation she owes her husband according to the right of

* * * * *

Erasmus alludes to the idea that sexual intercourse leaves the self spent and diminished. A *locus classicus* might be the description of coitus in Lucretius 4.1113–16: sexual intercourse results in the weakening and dissolution of the limbs. See also Aristotle *De generatione animalium* 725b or Tertullian *De anima* 27.6 CCL 2 823; in the latter post-coital exhaustion is associated with the drainage of body- and soul-producing seeds contained in seminal fluid. Cf the conceit common in Renaissance and later literature that sexual climax is a kind of dying, of which a famous example occurs in John Donne's 'Canonization,' lines 21, 26, 28.

7 A reference to the Corinthians' reputation for sexual passion. Cf the Argument nn2 and 11; also the paraphrase on 9:1.

8 Chrysostom *In 1 Cor hom* 19.1 (on 7:3–4) PG 61 152 similarly notes that the equality Paul declares in 7:3 is an exception to the norm. He quotes Gen 3:16 and Eph 5:25, 33 as examples of the husband's normal prerogative. In the *Institutio christiani matrimonii* CWE 69 386 Erasmus explains that this equality between husband and wife may seem difficult to accept, but it pertains only to conjugal relations and befits the proper ends of marriage: the begetting of children and the remedying of incontinence.

9 The paraphrase echoes patristic sources in suggesting that the equality of obligation in sexual matters arises from the equal necessity for both partners to avoid extramarital relationships. Cf Theophylact *Expos in 1 Cor* (on 7:4) PG 124 640C and Ambrosiaster *Comm in 1 Cor* (on 7:4) CSEL 81/2 71:8–9. In a 1535 addition to his annotation on 7:3 (*uxori vir debitum reddat*), however, Erasmus appears to suggest that Paul is stressing here simply the need for the married couple to fulfil for each other their sexual obligations.

matrimony.[10] In the other matters, perhaps, sovereignty and power belong to the husband; here each one is equally obliged to yield to the other. Not to comply with the other's request is cheating. For not only is the person who reneges on a debt of money a cheat, but also the one who refuses a debt of duty.[11]

Let neither one, then, out of eagerness for chastity cheat the other unless you come to an agreement, and both concur that you will abstain from sexual union for a time so that with your minds purified (since that coupling of bodies tends to blunt the mind's energy somewhat) you may be the more free to devote yourselves to holy prayers and the contemplation of heavenly matters.[12] Therefore, neither should abstain, or both should, but only by agreement; and not for just any reason, but out of eagerness for heavenly things; and not for too long, but for some period of time – and you should soon return to your former practice. I give this advice not because I do not understand that it is best to be free constantly for devotion, but because I see the danger that Satan, who is everywhere on the lookout for your destruction, may take advantage of your proclivity towards passion to entice you towards the worse. I would rather there be in you[13] something that is less perfect, provided it be secure, than something that is nobler, yet linked with the peril of great evil.

I do not mention this in order to force anyone to take a wife, or to forbid anyone to embrace constant chastity if sufficient strength for so great

* * * * *

10 It is not clear whether Erasmus intends to distinguish in some way between *lex coniugii* 'law of marriage' (for the husband) and *ius matrimonii* 'right of matrimony' (for the wife), or whether he is simply providing rhetorical variety at the end of a passage in which mutual obligations have been expressed in carefully balanced syntax. Each of the terms *lex* and *ius* has a wide range of meanings, some of which overlap; together they present marriage both as a contract between partners (*lex*) and as the legally sanctioned rights and obligations (*ius*) which this contract establishes.

11 Cf the financial analogy in Theophylact *Expos in 1 Cor* (on 7:5) PG 124 640D: 'For one of them [to abstain from sexual relations] against the other's will is cheating, just as we speak in reference to money matters also.'

12 The paraphrase follows the Vulgate of 7:5, '... give yourselves to prayer' (DV; so also RSV). However, in both his Greek text and his Latin translation, Erasmus reads '... give yourselves to fasting and prayer' (AV) – although he admits in the annotation on 7:5 (*ut vacetis orationi*) that Chrysostom and Theophylact probably did not read 'fasting' in this verse. See Metzger 488, where 'fasting and' is found to be an interpolation 'introduced in the interest of asceticism.'

13 in you] Added in 1532

a purpose should be available, and if mutual agreement should exist in the marriage; but being aware of your weakness, I give thought to your perils. Apart from this concern, I would wish all people, if possible, to be like myself, that either they would be completely free from marital bonds, or that they would treat their wives as sisters, and live together pure with pure, chaste with chaste.[14] But what Christ did not require of his followers I would not be so bold as to require of you. He declares blessed those who had castrated themselves for the kingdom of God,[15] but he does not scorn those who were practising the rights of marriage in a restrained and chaste way. Perpetual chastity, adopted in service to Christ, is an exceptional state.[16] But lawful marriage also is an honourable state, and God himself has initiated and hallowed[17] it. Indeed, there is an enormous diversity of

* * * * *

14 In the annotation on 7:8 (*dico autem non nuptis*) Erasmus discusses three possibilities for Paul's marital situation: married (but living with his wife as brother with sister), widowed, and never married. He concludes that the first two are the more likely, but that Paul is recommending not so much a particular marital status as the tranquillity that comes from continence. In his annotation on 7:7 (*volo autem omnes vos esse sicut meipsum*), Erasmus may be suggesting a preference for the first possibility when he notes that, since Paul offers to those who are married the specific example of his own continence, one might well conjecture that he himself had a wife. See also chapter 9 n12, and cf Phil chapter 4 n3.

15 See Matt 19:12.

16 Cf the discussion of three virtuous states for women – virginity, marriage, widowhood – in *De vidua christiana* CWE 66 201–3. All three states are 'gems,' each with its own strengths; virginity holds the first place of honour, but by little. Later in the treatise we read that 'though the virtue of continence is illustrious, still it is safer, albeit less glorious, to marry' (CWE 66 244). Cf Augustine *De bono coniugali* 8:8 and 13:15 CSEL 41 198 and 207: marriage and continence are both goods, but continence is better, and married couples who choose to be continent attain a higher level of holiness.

17 and hallowed] Added in 1532. Cf the 'Encomium' on marriage in *De conscribendis epistolis* CWE 25 130: 'If we seek the author of marriage, we discover that it was founded and instituted ... by the sovereign maker of all things, and from the same it received praise, and by the same it was made honourable and holy.' The addition to the paraphrase may reflect Erasmus' continued esteem for marriage despite the heated controversy in which he had been attacked for preferring marriage to celibacy. Cf n71 below. For the relation of the 'Encomium' in *De conscribendis epistolis* to the *Encomium matrimonii* published in 1518 and the controversy following its publication, see CWE 26 528–9 n1. For fuller discussions, see Payne *Theology* 109–12 and Emile Telle *Erasme de Rotterdam et le septième sacrement* (Geneva 1954) 315–45. For Erasmus' advocacy of marriage as a remedy for clerical incontinence,

bodies and souls, and God has not given equal gifts to all. It may perhaps be
beyond a human being's strength to abstain completely from intercourse.
Happy are those who have this strength from God, but he has loved this
diversity in his people, that different ones should excel in different gifts,
and that such diversity should wonderfully work towards the harmony and
decorum of the whole.[18] Therefore, neither should anyone condemn the
status of another, nor regret his own, but each one should according to his
own strength measure up to the gift received from God. There is a chaste
kind of marriage, and there is an unclean kind of virginity. Here you have
my advice about marrying and being married.[19]

Now hear my response to your question about remarriage. For there
are some, I understand, who, although they do not deny you the right of
marriage, nevertheless would not have you marry a second time once the
death of one spouse has freed the other.[20] This is my opinion on the subject:
if any man is single because of the death of his spouse, or any woman a
widow because of the passing of her husband, if they have the strength
for perpetual continence, it would be excellent if he would not seek a wife
again, nor she a husband, but both dedicate their freedom to the things
of God. What I judged best I myself have embraced, lest anything hold
me back from the work of the gospel. This work is so dear to me that in
my devotion to it I readily reject the pleasure associated with having a
wife.[21] Now if I knew that everyone shared a like disposition, I would not
hesitate to call everyone to follow my example. But in this matter, since
the condition of bodies and minds is not uniform, the same advice cannot
be given to everyone, but each one should consider his own strength, and

* * * * *

see the annotations on 7:1 (*mulierem non tangere*) and 1 Tim 3:2 (*unius uxoris
virum*).

18 Erasmus' amplification here of the 'gifts' of continence and normal marital
relations anticipates Paul's larger discussion of spiritual gifts in 1 Cor 12:11–
27. See in particular the paraphrase on 12:11: '. . . the diversity leads to harmony
and decorum, not to division.'

19 'Marrying and being married': *ducendis ac habendis uxoribus*, literally 'taking and having wives.' The Latin, it may be noted, assumes the husband's
perspective.

20 Likewise in the annotation on 7:8 (*dico autem non nuptis*) Erasmus argues that
the 'unmarried' whom Paul addresses here are not those who have never
married (whose status will be taken up later), but probably those who have
become unmarried through the death of a spouse.

21 For Erasmus' views concerning Paul's marital status, see n14 above. The language here could refer to any of the three possible states: unmarried, widowed, or married but treating his wife as a sister.

embrace that kind of life for which he is by nature most suited. Those who
have once tried marriage and feel that they are still no match for the fierce
goads of passion should seek remarriage – for in this way they may remedy
their incontinence by means of lawful intercourse – rather than wish, in a
state of celibacy grievously itching with lustful passion, to be subject to the
perils of a more grievous offence. Here, therefore, I neither urge marriage
nor forbid it, but I leave it to each individual to determine on the basis
of personal reflection what is beneficial. For I have received no instruction
from the Lord to hand down to you. That which has been commanded by
Jesus Christ, however, I would not hesitate to require of you. Those who
are not married are free, as I said, according to their own judgment, either
to embrace marriage or not, provided they aim at nothing other than Christ.

Once matrimony has been entered into, I should not want it to occur
that a marriage be broken off for just any cause, as commonly happens
among Jews and pagans.[22] For the Lord has forbidden a man to cast out his
wife for wrongs that are not serious[23] even though Moses once granted this
license to the Jews[24] not because he judged it right, but because he feared
that people naturally vengeful and stubborn, if denied the right of divorce,[25]
might commit offences more horrid than divorce.[26] The Lord allowed one

* * * * *

22 Cf the paraphrase on Mark 10:12 CWE 49 123: 'A Jew divorces his wife because
of bad breath, runny eyes, or similar faults ...' For Jewish laws and customs
relating to divorce, see Louis Epstein *The Jewish Marriage Contract: a Study in
the Status of Women in Jewish Law* (1927; repr New York 1973) 193–223 and
Elliot N. Dorff and Arthur Rosett *A Living Tree: the Roots and Growth of Jewish
Law* (Albany 1988) 440–563. For Roman laws and customs relating to divorce,
see Susan Treggiari 'Divorce Roman Style: How Easy and How Frequent Was
It?' in *Marriage, Divorce, and Children in Ancient Rome* ed Beryl Rawson (Oxford
1991) 31–46.
23 See Matt 5:31–2, 19:3–9; Mark 10:2–12; Luke 16:18. In 7:10 Paul does not mention the qualification (recorded by Matthew only) that divorce may be permitted in cases of adultery, but Erasmus includes it here and explains it in the
next sentence. Similar explanations appear in the paraphrases on each of the
Gospel passages cited above. For Erasmus' own lenient view towards divorce
see n73 below.
24 See Deut 24:1–4.
25 if denied ... divorce] Added in 1532
26 Cf the annotation on 7:39 (*liberata est a lege, cui autem vult, nubat*): 'On account of
hardness of heart Jews were permitted to divorce a wife for any cause lest they
commit a worse offence' ASD VI-8 172:232 – 6. See also the paraphrases on Matt
5:31–2, 19:9 CWE 45 104–6, 271–2; Mark 10:5–12 CWE 49 122–3; and Luke 16:18
CWE 48 97–8, where Erasmus has Jesus elaborate more fully on the 'hardness'
of the Judaic heart, the trivial reasons for which divorce might be permitted,

cause only – if a wife were having an affair with another man – whether because a woman who has pledged access to herself to one man, and then has had intercourse with another, has forfeited the rights of marriage, or because it seems unjust to compel anyone to share home, bed, hearth, and table with one who has betrayed the trust of marriage (than which nothing is holier) and involved herself with a vile adulterer. So firm and undivided has Christ wished this union to be. Therefore, unless something of this sort occurs, a wife should not leave her husband, nor a husband banish his wife. But if it should happen, when disagreement has sprung up as a result of other offences,[27] that a woman leaves her husband, she should refrain from marrying again lest she shut herself off from hope of reinstatement. If she has been chaste, her husband will perhaps take her back when he is more kindly disposed; but who will take her back if she has been adulterated? Now if a woman meanwhile cannot control herself so as to keep from intercourse, she should strive to return into her husband's favour.[28] If this attempt fails, she should bear in mind that her union with anyone at all is in fact adultery, although in name it be marriage.[29]

Now in answer to your questions about mixed marriage, I have nothing to say based on the authority of the Lord, but there is something that I do advise as in my own opinion more useful. Divorce is so disagreeable that once a marriage has been entered I would not have it broken off because of a difference in religion. If it happens that a Christian woman is joined in marriage to a husband who has not yet professed Christ, and he, although a stranger to the mysteries[30] of Christ, is nevertheless not so hostile

* * * * *

and the crimes to which Jews might turn if divorce were not available. In these paraphrases Jesus recommends a 'Christian mildness,' by which the faults of a spouse might be endured or gently corrected, as the proper alternative to ready divorce. But see also n73 below for Erasmus' controversial view on divorce.

27 as a result of other offences] Added in 1532
28 Ambrosiaster in *Comm in 1 Cor* (on 7:11) CSEL 81/2 74:22–4 and Theophylact *Expos in 1 Cor* (on 7:10–11) PG 124 644A similarly explain Paul's command in 7:11 that the woman be reconciled.
29 Cf Matt 19:9; Mark 10:12; Luke 16:18.
30 mysteries] *mysteriis*, first in 1521; previously *sacramentis*. Erasmus defines *mysterium*, in his annotation on Rom 11:25 ('brothers this mystery') CWE 56 308, as 'something hidden, and known to few, and which is to be shared only with initiates.' Through the change here from *sacramenta* to *mysteria* Erasmus probably seeks to avoid confusion with the use of *sacramenta* in its special and precise sense denoting the seven sacraments recognized by the Roman church. In classical Latin *sacramentum* is a military or legal term denoting an oath of alle-

as to think she ought to be repudiated because of a difference in religion, the wife will not leave her husband if she heeds my advice. Likewise, if it happens that a man initiated into Christ is joined to a wife who remains a stranger to Christ (for it is not right that anyone be forced to adopt a religion), and she does not seek divorce because of her dislike for a different religion, the husband on my advice will not put her out. For there is no reason for a Christian man or woman to dread becoming stained from union with someone who is a stranger to Christ. Although the religion of the other may be impure, nevertheless the marriage is lawful and pure which connects equally together those who are otherwise unlike. The ungodliness of the worse partner does not pollute the godliness of the other, but rather that element prevails which is better and more powerful.

Therefore, however unholy a husband is in his religion, he is nevertheless, in so far as the marriage is concerned, rendered holy through the fellowship of a Christian woman.[31] Likewise, a wife not yet initiated

* * * * *

giance, a sum of money deposited as a security, or in a more general sense a sacred obligation. In ecclesiastical Latin it assumes a variety of senses, from its most restricted meaning as one of the seven sacraments, to the broader senses of 'mystery' or 'secret.' In both the narrow and broad senses it corresponds to the Greek μυστήριον. See Alexander Souter *A Glossary of Later Latin to 600 A.D.* (Oxford 1949) 360; Kelly *Early Christian Doctrines* 193 and 423. Where the Vulgate translates μυστήριον in its broader sense by *sacramentum* Erasmus generally prefers *mysterium*. See eg the annotation on Col 1:27 (*sacramenti*) and especially the annotation on Eph 5:32 (*sacramentum hoc*), where he discusses the meanings of *sacramentum* and defends his preference for *mysterium* when translating μυστήριον in its general senses. For a possible exception to this practice, however, see the paraphrase on 10:16 with n29. On *mysterium*, see also Eph chapter 5 n38 and Col chapter 1 n48.

31 In 7:14 Paul offers the opinion that an unbelieving spouse is sanctified (ἡγία-σται) through a Christian wife or husband. Interpretation of the assertion is difficult especially in light of verse 16, where the salvation of an unbelieving partner appears still to be determined. Both ancient and modern commentators tend to limit the sanctification, as Erasmus apparently does here, to the marital relationship itself and the unbelieving spouse's role in the relationship. Thus Chrysostom *In 1 Cor hom* 19.3 (on 7:14) PG 61 155 notes that Paul does not say the idolatrous spouse is now 'holy,' but only that he has been 'hallowed.' Chrysostom interprets this to mean that the spouse remains ungodly and unclean in his belief, but that in the marriage itself and in the ungodly husband's conjugal relations with the Christian wife, there is no impiety or uncleanness. The uncleanness resides in the man's will and thoughts, not in the bodies that come together. See also Theophylact *Expos in 1 Cor* (on 7:14) PG 124 644D–645A, and for modern commentary Conzelmann 121–3 and Barrett 164–6.

into Christ is in some manner rendered holy and pure by the sexual
union with her Christian husband, on account of the lawful relations of
marriage. If this were not so, your common children would be considered unholy and impure, as born from sinful intercourse.[32] But it now is
well established that they are lawful and pure, as begotten from lawful
union. For when a wife who has been baptized has relations with a husband not yet baptized, she is not being contaminated with a pagan, but
is complying with a husband; it is not that she loves an ungodly man,
but that she patiently bears with a man who may become godly. He offers this hope concerning himself in that although he does not yet himself profess Christ, nevertheless he does not abhor in his wife her worship of God. For the man who tranquilly lives with a wife professing the
name of Christ, a man who tranquilly sees the symbol of the cross fastened over their common bed, is not wholly a pagan, but in some part a
Christian.[33] No couples stay together with more difficulty than those divided by a difference in religion. This hope, therefore, ought to keep a

* * * * *

32 Erasmus means intercourse outside the sanction of lawful marriage, as the next
   sentence suggests. Ambrosiaster *Comm in 1 Cor* (on 7:14) CSEL 81/2 76:15–16
   likewise explains that the children of these mixed marriages are considered
   clean 'because they are born from lawful marriage.' Illegitimate children suffered certain legal disabilities in the Roman world, but illegitimacy apparently
   involved little serious social stigma. See Susan Dixon *The Roman Family* (Baltimore and London 1992) 123–32; Beryl Rawson 'Adult-Child Relationships in
   Roman Society' in *Marriage, Divorce, and Children in Ancient Rome* ed B. Rawson (Oxford 1991) 26–7 and 'Children in the Roman *Familia*' in Rawson *Family*
   178–9; and Roger Just *Women in Athenian Law and Life* (London and New York
   1989) 45–62.
   Erasmus' paraphrastic explanation of the 'unclean' and 'holy' children of 7:14
   in terms of illicit and licit unions may reflect sensitivity to his own illegitimate
   birth. The papal dispensation he received in 1517 describes him (apparently
   in language he himself used) as suffering 'from a disability of birth being the
   offspring of an unlawful and (as he fears) incestuous and condemned union'
   (Ep 517:9–10). For a discussion of the issues involved in this dispensation and
   in the disability adhering to Erasmus' legitimacy, see James K. McConica's introductory notes to Epp 446, 447, and 517 and to Erasmus' *Compendium vitae*
   in CWE 2. See also R.J. Schoeck *Erasmus of Europe: The Making of a Humanist
   1467–1500* (Savage, Maryland 1990) 26–41 and *Erasmus of Europe: The Prince of
   Humanists 1501–1536* (Edinburgh 1993) Appendix C.
33 Ambrosiaster *Comm in 1 Cor* (on 7:14) CSEL 81/2 76:7–10 similarly elaborates
   on the sanctification that may occur regarding a pagan partner in a mixed
   marriage: '[Paul] shows that they have the benefit of the good will whereby
   they do not abhor the name of Christ. And he refers to the protection of a
   dwelling in which there appears the symbol of the cross, by which death is
   conquered.'

woman living with her husband when she has been the first to embrace Christ.

But if a divorce should be initiated by a man who has not yet believed, and he rejects his wife out of hatred for Christ, there is no reason for her to stay with the ungodly man any longer since in this case there is no hope of changing him. That man forfeits the right of matrimony who abhors God, the author of matrimony.[34] For the marriage vow does not to such an extent obligate a woman devoted to Christ that she is forced to put up with an ungodly husband who is continually quarrelling and reviling Christ. Let her take, therefore, the freedom to divorce, which he[35] has given, and let her serve Christ in peace. Indeed, God has not for this reason called us to the evangelical life, that we might live in quarreling, but in harmony and peace. Consequently, if those in a mixed marriage have no accord, and the unbelieving partner asks for divorce, the Christian wife should not stay with him against his will. But if there is accord, let the wife remain with her husband in hope of changing him, and likewise let the husband remain in hope of changing his wife. How can you know, wife, whether through words of encouragement at home,[36] or by unassuming and

* * * * *

34 Cf Ambrosiaster *Comm in 1 Cor* (on 7:15) CSEL 81/2 76:22–77:3: 'If an unbeliever leaves out of hatred for God, the believer is not responsible for the marriage's dissolution; for the cause of God is greater than that of marriage ... Regard for marriage is not owed to one who abhors the author of marriage.' Ambrosiaster goes on to suggest that the deserted spouse incurs no sin if he or she proceeds to marry another, for the marriage bond with the unbelieving spouse has been dissolved. This interpretation of 7:15, by which a marriage contracted between two non-Christians can be dissolved if one spouse becomes a Christian and the other refuses to cohabit in peace, has been common since the fourth century and is known as the 'Pauline Privilege.' The text of 7:15, however, speaks only of separation and not of dissolution or remarriage. See Canons 1143–7 in *The Code of Canon Law: a Text and Commentary* ed James A. Coriden, Thomas J. Green, and Donald E. Heintschel (New York 1985) 814–16, and the brief discussion in *The New Catholic Encyclopedia* 2nd ed (Detroit 2003) 11 38.

35 'He': *ille* – most likely a reference to the unbelieving partner, who by his offensive behaviour has made divorce in this situation acceptable. Cf Chrysostom *In 1 Cor hom* 19.3 (on 7:16) PG 61 155: 'For he has now provided the grounds for divorce, just as one who has committed fornication.' Theophylact in *Expos in 1 Cor* (on 7:16) PG 124 645C comments: 'If he is contentious, he has offered cause for divorce.' Coverdale, however, apparently took *ille* to refer to God as the granter of the freedom: 'Let her therefore use the lybertie of divorce geven unto her by God' (fol xx recto).

36 words of encouragement at home] *alloquiis domesticis*, the reading of all editions from 1519 to 1540 that I have seen. LB, however, gives in a marginal note a

agreeable behaviour, or by conjugal affection, you will cause your husband
to come to his senses and be saved along with you? How can you know,
husband, whether through such methods you will save your wife, and win
her for Christ? If you succeed, is this not a huge profit? If it comes to
nothing, God will nevertheless commend the good intentions that yearned
for it. Meanwhile, however, as long as it is uncertain whether it will succeed
or not, the marriage should be maintained in good hope, and the difference
in religion should not alter the condition of one's life.[37] For baptism releases
neither a wife from the authority of her husband, if he exercises it lawfully,[38]

* * * * *

variant reading from 'another edition': *colloquiis domesticis* 'conversations at
home.' Coverdale may have had access to this variant reading, for he translates
'by familiar communication' (fol xx recto).

37 Cf Theophylact *Expos in 1 Cor* (on 7:16–17) PG 124 645D: 'How do you know
whether you will save her or not? ... Since this is uncertain, the marriage
should not be dissolved.' With this sentence in the paraphrase Erasmus begins to develop a transition between 7:16 and 7:17a. He follows closely the
explanation of Paul's thought process which he gives in the 1519 annotation on 7:17 (*nisi unicuique sicut divisit dominus*), where he also summarizes at
length Theophylact's discussion of the difficulties associated with the transition. The specific problem involves the ambiguity of εἰ μή in the Greek (*nisi*
in the Vulgate; 'but' in AV, DV; 'only' in RSV; 'however that may be' in NRSV).
The question is whether εἰ μή (or rather the alternate reading found in some
Greek manuscripts, ἢ μή 'or not') should be taken at the end of 7:16 ('how
do you know, man, whether you will save your wife *or not*'), or whether
εἰ μή forms a transition at the beginning of 7:17, where Paul begins an excursus recommending that Christians remain in the outward condition they
had at the time of their conversion – specifically the conditions of circumcision or uncircumcision and of slavery or freedom. Erasmus argues for taking εἰ μή with 7:17 and suggests Paul is employing a common idiom used
for shifting from points that remain uncertain to ones that are sure and un-
ambiguous: 'Thus since Paul had proposed something uncertain – about saving a husband or wife who was not a believer – however this may be, he
says, let each one remain [in the condition] just as God has apportioned it
to him and just as he has been called, whatever outcome follows concerning
the saving of the spouse.' The transition between 7:16 and 7:17 remains problematic for modern commentators. See eg Orr and Walther 215 and Conzelmann 125.

38 Cf the paraphrase on 7:3–4 with n8 above. Erasmus introduces woman's subordinate status (anticipated from 11:3 and perhaps reflecting Eph 5:22–4) as a
way to reveal the continuity in Paul's thought process as he interrupts the discussion of marriage for an excursus (7:17–24) on the expedience of not changing one's outward condition, specifically in regard to slavery or circumcision.
See also the previous note.

nor a slave from the authority of his master, if he exercises it within rightful limits.

Whatever the lot God has given to each, let each serve Christ within it. Let each person persevere in that condition in which the teaching of the gospel found him. The newness of the religion abolishes the old life, but it does not remove the old condition, because Christianity accords with any kind of situation in life. It has been introduced, certainly not to disturb the general condition of human affairs, but that in every condition people may lead holy and godly lives.[39] I offer this as my opinion, and not for you alone, but also for all the churches. You will not find it burdensome to follow what all embrace. And so if, when God calls, his inspiration[40] finds you married, there is no reason on that account for you to break up your marriage; if it finds you circumcised, there is no reason for you to regret your lot and wish to summon a foreskin.[41] For the foreskin is no impediment to the new religion.[42] On the other hand, if it finds you a stranger to circumcision, this is no reason for you to wish to be circumcised.

* * * * *

39 Cf the paraphrase on Rom 13:1 CWE 42 74: 'I should not want you to throw into confusion what may indeed be but the shadow and outward form of justice which this world has, provided it does not plainly conflict with the righteousness of Christ.' See also the paraphrase on 7:24 with n51 below.

40 'Inspiration': *afflatus*. Cf the paraphrase on 1:24 and see chapter 1 n53 for Erasmus' concept of God's *afflatus* as a form of grace instrumental in the process of salvation. See also chapter 2 nn2 and 6.

41 In his Latin translation of 7:17 Erasmus similarly renders the Greek ἐπισπᾶσθαι by *accersere* 'summon' or 'fetch' rather than by the Vulgate's *adducere* 'draw up.' The Greek verb literally means 'to draw up to oneself'; as a medical term it can be used for 'pulling the foreskin over' (Soranus *Gynaecology* 2.34), but its use here to mean 'hide or remove the effects of circumcision' appears to be unique. See BDAG ἐπισπάομαι 3 and LSJ ἐπισπάω III. The Spaniard López Zúñiga (CEBR II 348–9) objected not only to *accersere*, but also to *asciscere* 'receive' or 'adopt,' which Erasmus had suggested in his annotation on 7:18 (*non adducat praeputium*) as a Latin equivalent for ἐπισπᾶσθαι. Zúñiga evidently found neither of Erasmus' verbs suitable for describing the medical procedure in question, arguing that they ineptly suggested the restoring of a foreskin for oneself from elsewhere. See *Apologiae contra Stunicam* (1) ASD IX-2 184:375–82 and 381n. Erasmus defended his translation as more modest than the Vulgate's; moreover, he considered it unlikely Paul had in mind a literal undoing of circumcision anyway, rather he was telling the Corinthians that neither the circumcised nor the uncircumcised should regret their condition.

42 Ie the absence of a foreskin is no impediment. Cf Chrysostom *In 1 Cor hom* 19.3 (on 7:17–21) PG 61 156: 'Such things [as marriage to an unbeliever, slavery, circumcision, uncircumcision] are not impediments to piety.'

For in regard to your new religion, it matters not at all whether you have been circumcised or not. What does matter equally for either condition is that the person who has been initiated into God live after this not according to carnal desires, but according to the commandments of God. It is sufficient that one's life be changed; it is not at all necessary that one's condition be changed, because this could not be done without disrupting the order of things.

The opinion I have expressed concerning marriage and circumcision must also be applied in the case of slavery. Those who are subject to slavery when the teaching of the gospel takes hold of them are to bear their lot calmly, and not think themselves emancipated from the legal rights of their masters because they have been emancipated from the tyranny of their sins.[43] Again, if a freeborn man has been called to Christ, that is no reason for him to wish his status altered, and to cast himself into slavery. But rather, should the opportunity arise, every effort should be made to seize freedom and exchange slavery.[44] If a master out of hatred for Christ casts out a slave, there is no need for the slave to seek a new owner, nor to be displeased with himself because he has no master, since he who was formerly a slave has become Christ's freedman, and has Christ as his patron.[45] On the other

* * * * *

43 Cf 1 Tim 6:1–2 and Erasmus' paraphrase CWE 44 34: 'Thus any who were in slavery when they were baptized are to remember that they have been emancipated from the lordship of sin, not freed from the masters' legal rights.'

44 Paul's verb χρῆσαι 'use' (AV) in 7:21b has no explicit object. Translations generally assume that 'freedom' (supplied from the context) is its intended object: 'Art thou called being a servant? care not for it: but if thou mayest be made free, use it rather' (AV); so also DV, RSV, NEB. On this interpretation, Paul urges the slave to seize an opportunity to change the current condition and become free. But it is possible to assume that the intended object is 'slavery,' reading the Greek thus: 'Are you called as a slave? Do not be concerned about it. But even if you are able to be free, use it (ie accept slavery) rather.' Cf NRSV: 'Even if you can gain your freedom, make use of your present condition now more than ever.' This interpretation finds support in both ancient and modern interpreters. See Chrysostom In 1 Cor hom (on 7:21) 19.4 PG 61 156: 'And why does he bid one who can become free remain a slave? He wants to point out that slavery does no harm, but even does a service.' See also Theophylact Expos in 1 Cor (on 7:21) PG 124 648C; Barrett 170–1; Orr and Walther 215–17; and Conzelmann 127. Erasmus, however, adopts the former interpretation in his paraphrase on the verse. This also appears to be the case in his Latin translation, although the Latin is somewhat ambiguous. See also nn48 and 52 below.

45 'Patron': patronum. Erasmus adopts a term from Roman social organization; a patronus was an influential man who looked after the legal and financial

hand, one who was born free, and through baptism has been reborn, should neither be displeased nor pleased with himself because of his condition, since through baptism he has become Christ's slave. Consequently, they have exchanged their fortunes: freedom has befallen the slave, and slavery has come to the freeborn in order that they each may bear their lot with greater moderation. For these are the kinds of concerns at which Christ may be said to wink. If slavery chafes, then you should seize a more agreeable handle;[46] comfort yourself on this account, that whatever legal rights your master may have over your body, nevertheless your soul has been released from its sins and emancipated for Christ.

If freeborn status makes you at all proud, remember that you have been purchased by Christ, and purchased for no ordinary price. You have a master who must be followed in every way; do not suppose that you are free to live according to the caprice of your feelings. And one who is bound in slavery to a human master has been set free through Christ to the extent that if his master should bid him do anything ungodly, he should heed Christ, his new patron, rather than his old master, for the latter has lost his rights by using them wrongly.[47] It would be right if those whom Christ

*　*　*　*　*

interests of individuals of lower social status with whom he established a reciprocal relationship and who became his 'clients' (*clientes*). On the pervasive patronage system of Roman society, see J.A. Crook *Law and Life of Rome* (London 1967) 93–4 and M.I. Finley *Politics in the Ancient World* (Cambridge 1983) 41. In the particular practice to which Erasmus alludes here, a Roman slave, when freed, continued to be legally bound in some way to the master who had emancipated him and who now became his patron. For the condition and rights of freedmen, see Thomas Wiedemann ed *Greek and Roman Slavery* (London 1981) 53–6; Jane F. Gardner *Being a Roman Citizen* (London and New York 1993) 7–51; and Susan Treggiari *Roman Freedmen during the Late Republic* (Oxford 1969).

46 'Handle': *ansa*. It is not perfectly clear to what Erasmus refers. In light of n44 above, the 'more agreeable handle' could be interpreted as an opportunity (should it arise) to be manumitted and enjoy freedom. The continuation of the current sentence, however, suggests that the 'handle' be interpreted instead as the consolation in knowing that Christ has emancipated the slave in mind and soul, if not in body. For the metaphoric use of 'handle' see *Adagia* I iv 4.

47 In this paragraph Erasmus develops his interpretation of Paul's injunction in 7:23 ('do not become slaves of men' [RSV]) in at least two directions: 1/ those who are enslaved to human masters need not commit sinful acts at the behest of their masters and are freed at least to that extent from their masters' dominion; 2/ slaves should avail themselves of opportunities for manumission. On the latter, see the following note. The former interpretation may derive from Theophylact *Expos in 1 Cor* (on 7:23–4) PG 124 649A, who

at the price of his own blood had set free were not oppressed by the rule of a human master. I favour freedom, if it becomes available;[48] I say this because servitude to Christ is genuine free birth.[49] It seems unbecoming for a Christian to be an ungodly person's slave. And it would be fitting for slaves to pass from a Christian master into the name and affection of brothers and sons because of the common master, who has redeemed both master and slave at a common cost.[50] But lest the Christian religion be a pretext for the disruption of the political order, let each one bear his lot and continue in it, but continue in such a way as to remember none the less that the commandments of God must have priority over the orders of human beings.[51] Obey your masters, but in a way acceptable to God, to

* * * * *

finds Paul here instructing Christians – whether slave or free – 'to do nothing for the sake of courting the favour of others and not to carry out the biddings of those who have enjoined perverse deeds.' Theophylact goes on to interpret the phrase 'with God' in Paul's exhortation in 7:24 ('So, brethren, in whatever state each was called, there let him remain with God' [RSV]) to mean that no one 'in obeying wicked masters should fall away from God' or 'obey masters beyond what is right.' Similarly Chrysostom *In 1 Cor hom* 19.5 (on 7:23–4) PG 61 156–8. See also n51 below.

48 In paraphrasing Paul's exhortation in 7:23 (see previous note), Erasmus reiterates his interpretation of 7:21, that slaves should take opportunities that may arise for manumission. See nn44 and 47 above. Erasmus reads this exhortation rather more literally than others in the exegetical tradition. Ambrosiaster eg *Comm in 1 Cor* (on 7:23) CSEL 81/2 81:1–2 interprets the phrase 'become slaves of men' as subjecting oneself to human superstitions, while Chrysostom *In 1 Cor hom* 19.5 (on 7:23) PG 61 156–7, interpreting the real slavery to be slavery to sin, applies this particular injunction to both slaves and free: the slave is a 'slave to men' when he performs his duties with false or selfish motives; the free person is a 'slave to men' when he performs some wicked service to satisfy the passions, whether gluttony, greed, or ambition.

49 Cf Chrysostom *In 1 Cor hom* 19.5 (on 7:24) PG 61 157: 'Christianity is such a thing: in slavery it imparts freedom.'

50 Cf 1 Tim 6:1–2.

51 As he paraphrases 7:24, Erasmus may have in mind Paul's discussion of the Christians' duty to the political state in Rom 13:1–7. Cf Erasmus' paraphrases on Rom 13:1 and 6 CWE 42 73 and 75: 'The state stands firm through order, it ought not to be disturbed under the pretext of religion ... But if they [rulers] order impious things, God must be obeyed rather than men.' For the likely influence of Theophylact on Erasmus' paraphrase on 7:24, see n47 above. For Erasmus' views on the relationship between Christianity and political order, see CWE 42 73 n1; also the annotation on Rom 13:1 ('those, however, which are from God') CWE 56 347 and the paraphrase on 1 Pet 2:13–17 CWE 44 91–2. Cf the paraphrase on 7:17 with n39 above.

whom you owe more since he ransomed you at a greater price than they paid for you.

What I have said about slavery and freedom also applies in some measure to matrimony and celibacy,[52] for the person who has taken on the yoke of matrimony is in some way a slave. But one who is celibate has the opportunity to live a freer life. One ought, therefore, always to aim at the more advantageous condition, if that should be possible. That is to say, freedom should not be pursued to such a point that in our eagerness for it we dash ourselves onto the rock of a greater peril.

Likewise in response to your question whether Christians ought to give their virgin daughters in marriage, or keep them at home, as sacred to Christ, in perpetual virginity so that they may serve him more freely – although I have no directive from the Lord from which to give you a sure answer, nevertheless I have advice to recommend as to what I think best. Nor should you, I think, spurn my advice since to me also apostolic authority has been delegated.[53] And, although I am unworthy, God's goodness has granted to me also to give trustworthy and salutary advice in accordance with his will, with an eye not to what serves my advantage, but to what promotes your advancement. I judge it desirable, therefore, for the sake of freedom, that a virgin bind herself to no one except to Christ; I advise this not because I deny that marriage is a holy and honourable state, but because it brings with it much suffering and anxiety on account of family relationships and the care of raising children.[54] One who abstains from marriage

* * * * *

52 Erasmus the paraphrast is rather more careful than Paul to develop the parallels between marriage and the two 'statuses' discussed in the excursus in 7:17–24: slavery and circumcision. In the paraphrase there are clear preferences for celibacy and freedom as less encumbered conditions, but parallel fears (incontinence and political disruption) recommend remaining in one's current condition, be it marriage or slavery.

53 Paul's explicit assertions of apostolic standing appear at 1:1 and 9:1–3. In his paraphrase on 7:25, Erasmus adds the assertion of 1:1, and perhaps the defensive tone of 9:1–3, to Paul's claim here to be giving trustworthy advice. Cf also the paraphrases on 4:21, 7:40 and 2 Cor 5:12.

54 The Greek phrase τὴν ἐνεστῶσαν ἀνάγκην in 7:26 has been understood either as 'present difficulties' or as 'impending distress' at the end of the age. Erasmus follows Theophylact in interpreting the phrase as a reference to worldly familial cares and not to eschatological disruption. See *Expos in 1 Cor* (on 7:26) PG 124 649C: 'It is best to abstain from matrimony on account of the annoyances in it and the troublesome features of marriage, not on account of uncleanness.' Ambrosiaster *Comm 1 Cor* (on 7:26) CSEL 81/2 82:6–8 interprets Paul's point similarly.

escapes this necessity and, if you will, bondage. It is better, therefore, to embrace freedom, if it is either possible or prudent to do so. It is not possible for those who are already entangled in the bonds of matrimony; it is not prudent for those who do not restrain themselves.

Accordingly, if you are already bound to a wife, do not use Christ as a pretext to seek divorce. If you are free, do not be eager for the halter of matrimony.[55] But if, because of distrust in your strength, you have taken a wife, there is no reason to be sorry, for you have done nothing wrong. The state you have entered is one subject to cares, but yet lawful. Not on that account – because you have a wife – will you be less acceptable to Christ, but you will be in greater distress and more subject to worldly cares. Furthermore, a virgin who would rather be mistress of a household[56] does not sin if she takes a husband lawfully. There is no harm in this, except that because of household cares, she is less free to attend to the reading of Scripture[57] and to prayers, or to other services of piety. And so, in leaving either condition open to you, I spare you in two ways: I provide for the freedom of one who can live without marriage; I relieve the peril of one who cannot. I praise celibacy as the happier state; I approve marriage as the more prudent. Therefore, let each person consider individually what decision to make about this matter. Neither do I compel nor do I forbid anyone, at least in these matters where the Lord has neither required nor prohibited.

There is something I shall require of you all without distinction, brethren, since this time is limited in that the last day draws near: you should hasten with all your strength towards the things that prepare us for that day, having cast off whatever detains us as we hurry towards it. It is uncertain when that day will be, but it is certain that it is not far off. Whoever is ever mindful that it is drawing near[58] will be little affected by fleeting affairs of the moment, whether what comes our way is annoying

* * * * *

55 'The halter of matrimony': *matrimonii capistrum.* Cf Juvenal 6.43.
56 'Mistress of a household': *materfamilias* – another term from Roman social economy. Cf n45 above and n63 below. The position of *materfamilias* normally derived from marriage to the *paterfamilias*, the eldest father and head of the household.
57 'The reading of Scripture': *sacrae lectioni* 'sacred reading.' Erasmus recommends *sacra lectio* as a valuable form of piety for widows in *De vidua christiana* CWE 66 246. Cf *Enchiridion* CWE 66 126–7 and the paraphrase on 1 Tim 4:13 CWE 44 26.
58 Or 'whoever is mindful that it is ever drawing near.' It is unclear which verb *semper* 'ever' or 'always' modifies: *cogitet* 'is mindful' or *instare* 'draws near.'

or desirable. For that final day will take away both from us. And death too will take them away if it should come before that day. What purpose does it serve, therefore, to agonize over such things as will soon perish, or to desire them greatly, when eternity is the matter at hand? Let those who want wives have them, but have them without care, exactly as if they did not have them; in this way the enslavement of marriage will trouble them less, and less also will the pleasure of wedlock hold them back.[59] Those whom fortune burdens with adversity, let them so weep as if they did not weep. Those upon whom the fortune of this world smiles, let them so rejoice as if they did not rejoice. Those who make purchases, let them purchase as if they did not possess what they have bought, seeing that it will soon be carried off and – whether you wish it or not – pass into another's hands.[60] And those who are by chance or necessity involved in worldly affairs, let them engage in these affairs as if they did not engage in them. Such matters as these should be the last concern; heavenly matters should be the first, if they cannot be the sole concern. This world holds only the shadows of goods and evils, in which there is nothing substantial, and nothing lasting;[61] to cling to these shadows wholeheartedly is not for those who strive after immortality.

I say this because I wish you to be distracted as little as possible by worldly cares, and to embrace most of all the kind of life that involves you as little as possible in secular dealings. In this respect the condition of the single person is preferable to that of the married one, for the single

* * * * *

59 In reference to Paul's admonition in 7:28 that those who marry involve themselves in worldly troubles, Theophylact in *Expos in 1 Cor* (on 7:29) PG 124 652A notes the possible objection that marriage brings pleasure as well as distress, but adds that the shortness of time brings all things to an end: 'Therefore even if there is also some pleasure in wedlock, nevertheless it is brief and short-lived, and this fact itself is an affliction.' Cf Chrysostom *In 1 Cor hom* 19.6 (on 7:29) PG 61 159 and Erasmus' annotation on 7:29 (*tempus*).

60 In paraphrasing 7:30 Erasmus could find numerous antecedents for the warning not to hoard up treasures that only one's heirs will live to enjoy. The warning is common in classical literature. See especially Horace *Odes* 2.3.17–20, 2.14.21–9, 3.24.61–4, and 4.7.17–20. For the same general idea, see Eccles 2:18 and Ecclus 14:3–5, and cf the paraphrase on 1 Tim 6:8 CWE 44 35 with n7.

61 For a fuller elaboration on heavenly goods and evils and their earthly shadows, see *De puero Iesu* CWE 29 67–70. Here the paraphrase echoes Theophylact *Expos in 1 Cor* (on 7:29–31) PG 124 652C: Paul 'lets it be known that the things of this present world are ... superficial, having no firmness and substance.' Cf the annotation on 7:31 (*praeterit enim figura*), which also cites Theophylact's interpretation.

man is not pulled apart among various concerns,[62]such as how to make his father-in-law, his mother-in-law, or the rest of his relations, or his wife and children happy; through what means to provide for the needs of a household that increases daily,[63] through what means to be worth more than his wife's dowry.[64] But he has all his time free for Christ; he has obtained his highest prayer if he pleases Christ alone. The man who has taken a wife,

* * * * *

62 In the annotation on 7:33-4 (*et divisus est*) Erasmus discusses the textual problem of whether μεμέρισται 'is divided' is to be taken with the preceding sentence and referred therefore to the married man, whose interests are 'divided'
(so the Vulgate, DV, RSV), or whether it is to be taken with the following sentence, which would then read as follows: 'The [married] woman and the virgin have different interests' (so AV). It was this latter reading that Erasmus
adopted (from 1516) for his own Greek text and Latin translation. He bases
his choice on the evidence of his Greek manuscripts and of the Fathers, especially Jerome and Ambrosiaster (both of whom, however, offer ambiguous evidence). For Ambrosiaster, see *Comm in 1 Cor* (on 7:33-4) CSEL 81/2
86:16-87:3. Here in the paraphrase Erasmus specifically expresses the Vulgate's reading, but in the rest of the paragraph he allows as well for the other
possibility. The Greek text is problematic; for the difficulties, see Metzger
490.
63 A Roman household (*familia*) was not limited to the modern conception of
a nuclear family, but included relations and slaves under the control of the
paterfamilias, and often former slaves as well, and might well change size on
a frequent, if not a daily, basis. See Beryl Rawson 'The Roman Family' in
Rawson *Family* 7-15 and R. Saller '*Familia, Domus*, and the Roman Conception
of the Family' *Phoenix* 38 (1984) 336-55.
64 The precise nature of the concern Erasmus has in mind in this clause is not
clear. In Roman custom, a woman brought to her marriage a dowry of money
(and sometimes property), which the husband then owned and managed during the tenure of the marriage, but which upon dissolution of the marriage
he would normally be required to return intact. The verb *evincere* 'to be victorious over' or 'surpass,' here translated 'to be worth more than' (so also
Coverdale [fol xxii verso]), might then suggest the husband's need to manage
his wife's dowry properly and to be financially secure without it. In special
legal contexts *evincere* can mean 'to recover possession through legal procedures (OLD 5),' but that sense is unlikely here since Erasmus is addressing
the concerns of a husband rather than those of a father who might need to
recover his daughter's dowry after a difficult divorce. For the worries that
attended the Romans' complicated dotal customs, see J.A. Crook 'Women in
Roman Succession' in Rawson *Family* especially 68-9 and Susan Dixon 'Family Finances: Terentia and Tullia' ibidem 93-120. For dowries in the Middle
Ages and Renaissance see Michael M. Sheehan *Marriage, Family, and Law in
Medieval Europe: Collected Studies* ed James K. Farge (Toronto 1996) 16-37; Jack
Goody and S.J. Tambich *Bridewealth and Dowry* (New York 1973); OER 3 22-3.

however, although he may devote part of his time to the Lord, nevertheless owes some part of himself to his wife and to matters that come with a wife. It is the same in a woman's case: since a wife is not entirely under her own authority, she cannot be entirely free for Christ, but, split apart among various concerns, half of her serves Christ, and half serves her marriage. On the other hand, the virgin or the woman who is otherwise single has only one concern, and that is to please Christ her betrothed, whom she pleases only if she keeps herself wholly chaste and undefiled, not in body only but also in mind. But the married woman necessarily divides herself between Christ and the world; she is busy trying to please Christ without displeasing the husband to whom she owes compliance.

Now lest anyone misinterpret, this whole discourse of mine, in which I extol celibacy, has this end: it is not that I would deprive you of the freedom to marry or not to marry, or drive you by constraint into a kind of life that may not sit well with someone's disposition; but with friendly counsel I am attending to your interests so that when you know that you may choose either path, you may incline rather towards that which, besides the virtue of honour, has the added advantage of freedom as well.[65] Through this freedom the single person may with constant zeal and devotion so cling to the Lord Jesus Christ as never to be torn from him by any earthly cares. Let each one weigh in his own mind whether what he sees as conducive to honour and freedom he likewise judges to be prudent for himself or even to his liking.

In the case of a man who is afraid that he will incur some shame or scandal if he keeps his virgin daughter[66] confined at home beyond the

* * * * *

65 Throughout this passage Erasmus draws on the terminology and distinctions of classical ethical philosophy. Here eg the distinction between honour or virtue (*honestum*) and advantage or benefit (*commodum*) reflects Cicero's division of his work on ethics, *De officiis*, into three books: one on the honourable (*honestum*), a second on the useful or beneficial (*utile*), and a third arguing the Stoic view that the honourable and the useful are congruous. Accordingly, marriage and celibacy each involve for Erasmus a congruence of virtue and utility. *Commodum*, Erasmus' term here for 'advantage,' is one closely associated by Cicero' with *utile*, for the principle of 'usefulness' pertains to the *commoda vitae* 'things advantageous to life' (*De officiis* 2.3.9.) Cf chapter 6 n44. On Erasmus' use of the language of Ciceronian moral discourse, see CWE 44 xvii–xviii.

66 The Greek text of 7:36 is unclear as to whether the 'virgin' is one's daughter or one's betrothed, but there is no indication that either Erasmus or his patristic sources knew of the latter interpretation. In the annotation on 7:36 (*turpem se videri existimat*), however, he rules out the possibility mentioned

proper time, although she is already old enough for a husband and not averse to marriage – and circumstances encourage marriage – I raise no objection to his doing what it seems necessary to do. For although we have said that marriage is associated with the disadvantages of servitude and worry, it is nevertheless not associated with sin. It is a lawful and honourable state,[67] and for some also a necessary one. Therefore, let him join his virgin daughter to a husband in an open and also a timely manner so that she does not commit in a furtive and shameful way an act that in marriage is free from reproach.[68] But if a father, knowing that he is free to marry off his virgin daughter or not to marry her off, and that he is not compelled by any necessity to do either, nevertheless has in good conscience resolved and decided to keep at home a girl who does not wish for marriage, he does the proper thing. For just as it is not prudent to bar from marriage one who desires it, so it is not godly to shake a girl's mind from its eagerness and longing for chastity. And so if anyone out of fear for the danger gives in marriage a daughter who wishes to be married, he does the proper thing. But if anyone does not urge marriage on a girl striving for perpetual chastity, but complies with her honourable wish, he does something more proper. For in addition to honour he gains this advantage also:[69] that the virgin will be free to devote herself wholly and undividedly to Christ, her betrothed.[70] Indeed, for no other use ought one to seek the freedom of the single life. In God's sight it is far better to devote to divine worship whatever in married life can be stolen away from the cares of essential business than it is to abuse the pretext of virginity in order to pursue wantonness, or idle leisure, and riotous living.[71]

* * * * *

with disapproval by Augustine that one's 'virgin' might refer to a man's own virginity. Most modern commentators interpret 'virgin' as 'betrothed.' For the critical debate, see Orr and Walther 223–4; Conzelmann 134–6; Barrett 182–5.

67 Cf the paraphrases on 7:1 with n2 and 7:7 with nn16 and 17.

68 Cf Ambrosiaster *Comm in 1 Cor* (on 7:36) CSEL 81/2 89:12–13: 'It is better for her publicly to marry according to lawful covenant than in secret to do foul deeds.' Cf also the 'Encomium' on marriage in *De conscribendis epistolis* CWE 25 137, where Erasmus presents a similar argument for granting marriage to priests and monks.

69 See n65 above.

70 Ambrosiaster in *Comm in 1 Cor* (on 7:38) CSEL 81/2 90:1–3 explains similarly that 'he does better because he both secures merit for her in God's eyes and also frees her from worldly care.'

71 Erasmus may be echoing Ambrosiaster's comments in relation to an earlier verse. See *Comm in 1 Cor* (on 7:35) CSEL 81/2 88:4–14: 'For we see unmarried people [*virgines*] thinking about the world, and married people being zealous

So far am I from denying a virgin her first marriage, therefore, that I do not take away even from a widow the right to be wed again, although not even the world grants honour to second marriages.[72] It is not my place to prescribe in detail what is right in individual cases. On this point people should individually seek their own counsel. What can be done short of transgression – that I point out. A virgin may marry because she is independent. Once a woman is married, she does not have the same rights for she has now ceased to be independent, but has bound herself to a husband by

* * * * *

for the Lord's works ... To the former, however, not only will virginity not be credited, but they will also be subjected to punishment since under the cover of a better ambition they have busied their lives and relations with worldly care and bother and rendered themselves lazy for doing God's works.' Erasmus' sentence, moreover, seems not so much a paraphrase on 7:38 as an expression of his concern about moral corruption among contemporary clergy. See also n17 above. Cf the 'Encomium' on marriage in *De conscribendis epistolis* CWE 25 137: 'I only wish those who conceal their vices behind the high-sounding name of castration, and under the pretence of chastity gratify worse lusts, were truly castrated ... In my view it would not be ill advised for the interests and morals of mankind if the right of wedlock were also conceded to priests and monks.' In the *Apologia de laude matrimonii* CWE 71 94 Erasmus argues that he was not, in the *Encomium matrimonii* (cf n17 above), speaking against the monastic way of life, but against corrupt moral behaviour: the majority of those embracing celibacy 'attach themselves to this way of life not so much through love of chastity as for the sake of gain or ease.'

72 Cf the paraphrase on 7:8, where Erasmus assumes that in that verse Paul is addressing specific opposition to remarriage within the Corinthian Christian community. In general, however, in Greek and Roman societies, although a woman who remained loyal to her deceased husband may have enjoyed special honour as *univira* ('married to only one man'), remarriage after divorce or the death of a spouse was certainly the norm and involved no dishonour. See Sue Blundell *Women in Ancient Greece* (Cambridge, MA 1995) 128 and J.A. Crook 'Women in Roman Succession' in Rawson *Family* 77–8. Erasmus, however, may be reflecting attitudes of later ages. In the article 'Widow' in the first edition of *The Catholic Encyclopedia* William H.W. Fanning shows that several decrees of early councils (Ancyra, canon 19; Laodicea, canon 1) declared second marriages less worthy than first marriages, and that the Council of Trent (session xxiv, canon 10) in 1563 declared widowhood to be a more honourable estate than remarriage because of its higher goodness. See *The Catholic Encyclopedia* (New York 1913) 15 618. Cf *De vidua christiana* CWE 66 245 where Erasmus speaks of remarriage as 'serial polygamy,' and Jennifer Tolbert Roberts' evaluation CWE 66 181 of Erasmus' suspicion both of widows who seek to remarry and of those who do not. For ambivalence towards remarriage in the Renaissance, see *Encyclopedia of the Renaissance* ed Paul F. Grendler (New York 1999) 54.

the marriage agreement, as long as he lives. Only death breaks off this bond;[73] for whoever enters matrimony enters with the intention that the knot be unsevered. But if a husband dies, the surviving wife has her freedom restored so that if she wishes to marry again, she may marry whomever she wants, provided that it is a Christian wedlock, that is, one not courted for the sake of indecent behaviour, and one contracted with a man of the same religion.[74] But yet, although I grant that she who enters a second time upon a permitted marriage is not guilty of sin, still I judge the woman happier who through her eagerness to devote herself to Christ keeps intact the freedom she has recovered. This, therefore, is not something I enjoin as in fact necessary, but I advise it as more advantageous. You are hearing the advice of a man, but it is not incompatible with the mind of Christ, who delivers many teachings through himself and some through his followers. Since I am his apostle[75] and have as well, if I am not deceived, received his Spirit, like the other apostles, there is no reason why my counsel should hold little weight among you.

Chapter 8

I believe the questions about marriage have been answered sufficiently, so that after this you should not clash with each other about these matters because of differing opinions. Now since I understand that you are also debating whether it is permissible for a Christian to eat the meat of an animal sacrificed to idols[1] when this meat is considered by pagans to be holy,

* * * * *

73 Erasmus himself thought the church's rules concerning divorce should be more lenient. In a treatise-length addition in 1519 to his annotation on 7:39 (*liberata est a lege, cui autem vult, nubat*), he argues for divorce as a remedy for the miseries of unhappy marriage. This controversial note is summarized by Payne *Theology* 121–5 and discussed by Emile Telle, *Erasme de Rotterdam et la septième sacrament* (Geneva 1954) 203–28. See also Erasmus' response to the criticism of the note by Edward Lee in *Responsio ad annotationes Lei* 3 (Concerning Note 17) CWE 72 377–92.

74 Cf Ambrosiaster's definition of marriage 'in the Lord' in *Comm in 1 Cor* (on 7:39) CSEL 81/2 90:15–16: 'This means both that she marry without suspicion of indecency [ie of marrying in order to gratify indecent desires] and that she marry a man of her own religion.'

75 See n53 above.

1 'Idols': *idolis*. In the paraphrase on 1 Corinthians Erasmus generally renders the Greek εἴδωλον 'image' or 'idol' by the classical Latin *simulacrum*, and this is always the case in his Latin translation of the Epistle. Occasionally, however,

hear my opinion about this matter as well. There are some among you who, because they understand that an idol is nothing more than wood or bronze or stone, therefore that the meat sacrificed to it is in reality no different from other meat, and that a human soul cannot be defiled by any kind of food, wrongly rely on their knowledge and everywhere gorge themselves indiscriminately on sacrificial meat.[2] They indeed judge the matter correctly, but are too little mindful of Christian charity, which likes to avoid every stumbling block and accommodate itself to those who are weaker until they gradually progress to a better state.[3] Where is the importance, moreover, in understanding that idols have no divine power? What Christian does not understand this fact, which even those who are a bit more thoughtful among the pagans understand?[4] But very often the more responsible action is to adhere to the dictates of charity rather than to the dictates of knowledge.

Knowledge frequently hinders in that it encourages swollen and arrogant pride. But charity is everywhere eager to benefit; it hurts no one. Yet a great part of knowledge seems lacking in those who do not know how knowledge ought to be used.[5] This is what charity teaches, as it measures

* * * * *

in the paraphrase, as here, he uses *idolum*, the Latin word borrowed from the Greek εἴδωλον, and the word used by the Vulgate throughout this chapter. In the annotation on 8:4 (*quia nihil est idolum*), Erasmus cites Ambrosiaster's practice in 1 Corinthians 8 of using the two words apparently without distinction. The one difference Erasmus notes is that *simulacrum* is etymologically associated with the idea of 'pretence' while *idolum* derives from the idea of 'form' or 'shape.'

2 Chrysostom *In 1 Cor hom* 20.1 (on 8:1) PG 61 159 similarly sets up the context for Paul's advice regarding sacrificial meat. See also Theophylact *Expos in 1 Cor* (on 8:1) PG 124 656C–D: 'There were some mature Corinthians, who, knowing ... that idols are stones and pieces of wood and not able to harm, indiscriminately entered the temples of idols and stuffed themselves on the sacrificial meat.'

3 'Accommodation' as a principle of the Christian community is prominently featured throughout the paraphrases on Paul's instructions regarding sacrificial offerings in chapters 8 and 10, and reappears in the paraphrase on 13:4. Earlier, in the paraphrase on 3:1, Erasmus had emphasized the application of the principle in apostolic speech. See chapter 3 n3. Soon (paraphrase on 8:3) he will cite the Incarnation as a theological analogy for the principle. On Paul as accommodator, see also chapter 9 nn28, 30, and 33.

4 So Chrysostom *In 1 Cor hom* 20.1 (on 8:1) PG 61 161 notes that Paul deflates the Corinthians' pride by declaring that knowledge is not their unique possession, but common to all.

5 Cf the annotation on 8:2 (*nondum cognovit*): 'This is the chief part of knowledge: to be acquainted with the principle of knowing (*rationem sciendi*), ie that

all things by a neighbour's advantage. Whoever wishes to seem truly endowed with knowledge needs to call in charity as counsellor; but whoever
lacks charity and swells with an empty belief in his knowledge is in fact so
far removed from knowledge that he has not even succeeded in knowing
how he should use his knowledge. Whoever is wise in God's sight is truly
wise. For when someone preens himself and strives after his own glory
while neglecting his brother's peril, his knowledge does not have God's approval. But the one who truly loves God necessarily loves his neighbour
as well.[6] Therefore, God acknowledges him as his own disciple, for just
as God accommodated his majesty to humans for their salvation, so such
a person subdues his knowledge and compels it to serve his neighbour's
advantage.[7]

To return, therefore, to the point I had begun to discuss, most of
us recognize that although an idol is worshipped by pagans just as if it
has divine power, it is nevertheless in reality nothing other than wood
or stone, and has no more divinity than any unhewn trunk of a tree or
any unchiselled stone; for this reason there is no more either of good or
of evil in meat sacrificed to it than in the meat sold in the marketplace.
With respect to the stone that you see sculpted according to the image of a
human or some other living being, since there is one God, and he has no
likeness (for he cannot be fashioned), what does the image represent if not
demons to whom the unfortunate sacrifice in place of God?[8] Food of this
type, therefore, defiles those people who take it as if it were truly sacred
although it is common; it does not defile a Christian, who does not eat it as
sacred, but as food granted by God for satisfying hunger. He eats because
of need, not because of religion, inwardly laughing at the ridiculous horde
of pagan gods, and certain as well that there is no other God besides the one
to whom all things are sacred. For although there are others who are called
gods, whether in heaven (pagans call these the heavenly dwellers) or on

* * * * *

knowledge must be employed with charity. Cf also the paraphrase on 13:3:
'Only charity fully shows how you should use your gifts.' In general Erasmus'
method in the paraphrase on 8:1–3 is to make explicit the connections the passage may have with Paul's discourse on charity in 1 Corinthians 13. See in
particular 13:4–7 and Erasmus' paraphrase on it.
6 Cf Prov 19:17; Matt 22:37–9, 25:40; Luke 10:27.
7 Cf Ambrosiaster *Comm in 1 Cor* (on 8:3) CSEL 81/2 92:21–2: 'The one who loves
   God is the one who for the sake of charity moderates knowledge in order to
   benefit a brother, on behalf of whom Christ died.'
8 On pagan gods as demons, see chapter 10 n35.

earth[9] (these they speak of as the gods below)[10] – and clearly there are many gods of this sort, and many lords also – yet they are gods and lords in name only,[11] and they are such only to those who through grossest error believe them to be such and who have adopted them into the status of gods and lords. To us Christians, however, there is none but the one and only God, namely, the Father of Jesus, the creator and author of the universe, from whom alone all things proceed to us, and being bound to him alone, we are eager to please him with pious worship. Likewise, there is one lord, Jesus Christ, through whom alone the Father has bestowed upon us all things, and by the kindness of him alone we acknowledge the true God so that now

* * * * *

9 'On earth': *in terra*. The Latin phrase can be translated either 'on the earth' or 'in the earth.' Since it corresponds here to the Greek ἐπὶ γῆς 'on earth,' the former translation seems more likely, but Erasmus may have in mind gods thought to be dwelling within or beneath the earth. See the following note.

10 'The gods below': *inferos*. Normally in Latin 'those below the earth,' especially 'the gods of the underworld' and so normally also in Erasmus' usage, where *inferi* 'those below,' and the related *inferni* 'those lower' or 'under' and *infimi* 'the lowest' or 'those at the bottom' generally identify beings residing below the earth, ie the dead or the underworld gods. See eg his Latin translations of Eph 4:19 and Phil 2:10, the annotation (*et infernorum*) explicating the latter, and especially the paraphrase on that verse, where he exploits the Latin symmetry balancing *inferi* (underworld beings) with *superi* (heavenly beings), and juxtaposes both with whatever is *in terris* 'on earth.' See also the listing for *inferus* in the index to Erasmus' works in LB X. For *inferi* as 'gods below' and the contrasting *superi* 'gods above' in classical usage, see Plautus *Cistellaria* 512 and Terence *Phormio* 687.
The Greek text of 8:5, however, refers to 'so-called gods in heaven and on earth' (RSV). Erasmus' identification of gods ἐπὶ γῆς 'on earth' as *inferi* here is thus puzzling. Elsewhere in the paraphrases and in his Latin translation, he translates ἐπὶ γῆς correctly as *in terra* or *in terris* 'on earth.' See eg, in addition to the paraphrase on Phil 2:10, his translation of Eph 1:10 and the accompanying annotation (*quae in terra sunt*); also his translation of Col 1:16, 20. Given his usual clear distinction between *in terra* as 'on earth' and *inferi* as identifying inhabitants below or within the earth, it is unclear what Erasmus intends here in the paraphrase on 8:5. My translation assumes that Erasmus is using *inferi* loosely to mean 'deities residing below' (ie in this case below the 'heaven-dwellers,' whether *in* the earth or *on* it).

11 Chrysostom *In 1 Cor hom* 20.3 (on 8:5) PG 61 163 explains Paul's concession in 8:5 similarly: 'So that he should not seem to be contradicting obvious facts, he goes on to say, "For although there are ones who may be called gods, as clearly there are," but [he does] not [mean] "there are" in the absolute sense, but [says] "they are called" [gods], having this [existence] not in reality, but in name.' Similarly Theophylact *Expos in 1 Cor* (on 8:5) PG 124 660A.

we have no dealings at all with the false and profane gods of the pagans and ought not to value them more than if they did not exist at all.

And so, whoever through Christian strength scorns an idol and what is sacrificed to idols holds the right opinion indeed, and might rightly eat sacrificial meat in the same way as any other meat. For if everyone were equally convinced and cognizant of what is utterly true, then no one would be offended. But now there are some reclining at feasts who as a result of ancestral practices from earliest childhood have been persuaded and deeply imbued with the idea that an idol is a sacred thing and that all who recline at banquets are participants in this sort of superstition; they do not believe that those things can be so greatly scorned which they themselves so greatly reverence and fear. What you do with discretion and in good faith, these people, speaking among themselves, will interpret this way: inasmuch as Christians do not shrink from our rites, the worship of idols is not so detestable a thing.[12]

Perhaps also there is some Christian reclining or standing by who, although he has been initiated into Christ, nevertheless has not yet matured in the strength of his faith, but suffers from the infection of his old practices, an infection received from his ancestors since traces were left behind as a result of long-standing, shared habitation. When he eats sacrificial meat, it is not without scruple; he has some hope or fear that the demon, whichever one it is, may somehow prove either helpful or hurtful. Indeed, why is it surprising if this happens among some of the Greeks when we see it happening among many of the Jews?[13] It is difficult to tear out from human minds completely and by the root what has been implanted there by the instruction of one's earliest years, by common use, by long habitation. No one suddenly becomes fully Christian. Just as nature has its stages of development, so also does religion.[14] And so, just as we who are stronger

* * * * *

12 Chrysostom *In 1 Cor hom* 20.4 (on 8:7) PG 61 165 also includes among those with a 'weak conscience' not only naïve Christian converts, but also pagan idol-worshippers who will acquire a false understanding of Christianity. For the danger in giving pagans false impressions of Christianity, cf the paraphrase on 10:27–9, and see chapter 10 n44.

13 Erasmus is referring to a certain ingrained character of belief – an obstinate adherence to law and custom – which he finds characteristic among the Jews and which he frequently identifies as superstition. Cf n17 below, chapter 9 n6, and CWE 42 8–10 and 77–8.

14 For this repeated motif, see the paraphrases on 3:1 with n1 and 13:11. Here, however, Erasmus gives the theme of gradual advancement towards Christian maturity a somewhat different point as he combines it with the equally

because of age bear with and foster the weak, following the bidding of nature, so, following the example of Christ, those who are more advanced in faith ought sometimes to oblige those less firm, until in the course of time they gather their rightful strength.

Yet just as today there are among the Hebrews some who have professed Christ, but because of the religion received from their ancestors are unable to treat things of this sort with disregard – even though it is clear both that the holy prophets foretold that it[15] would be, and that Christ himself ordered that it be done[16] – so, when the gospel was first coming to light, there were some among the Greeks (indeed, even today there are some) who although they acknowledge Christ, nevertheless have not yet driven out from deep within their minds their dread arising from their parents' religion.[17] And so they eat the meat of a victim sacrificed to idols not as meat suitable for appeasing a barking stomach[18] but as sacred meat, dedicated to this or that demon. When such a one sees you (whom he considers a person of excellent learning and judgment) reclining with pagans at sacred banquets, and he suspects that you eat with the same intent as he, he is made to stumble because of your example and wrongly imitates your deed as well, since he does not perceive your mind and judgment. Therefore, one who was wavering a little earlier, and was mildly superstitious, is through the occasion rendered more superstitious.

* * * * *

prominent theme of Jewish superstition, withdrawal from which may necessarily be slow and gradual. Cf the paraphrases on Acts 15:6 CWE 50 96 and Rom 14:1–4 CWE 42 77–8.

15 'It': *id*. Erasmus' use of the pronoun is imprecise here and in the next clause. I understand it to refer to the disregard Jews would come to have for their 'ancestral superstitions.' As to prophecies that foretold this, Erasmus may have in mind Isa 29:13–24, where the prophet condemns insincere or superficial worship and foresees God's establishment of true worship in a restored Israel; also the promise of a new covenant and a new community in Jer 31:31–4.

16 Erasmus may be alluding to Jesus' dispute with the Pharisees concerning traditional practices and the Law of Moses, as reported in Matt 15:1–20; Mark 7:1–23; and Luke 11:37–44.

17 Chrysostom *In 1 Cor hom* 20.4 (on 8:7) PG 61 165 similarly refers to the time of the gospel's introduction, when their ancestral religion continued for a time to instill fear in new gentile converts.

18 'For appeasing a barking stomach': *ad medendum latranti stomacho*; an allusion to Horace *Satires* 2.2.17–18: *cum sale panis / latrantem stomachum bene leniet* 'bread and salt will serve well enough to calm a barking stomach' – as well, that is, as meat. Cf the dedicatory letter n34.

I do not say these things because I approve either the superstition or the suspicion of this person. For in fact Christian charity teaches that weakness should not be commended or fostered, but that in some places it should for a time be suffered and pampered. Nor indeed do I think you ought everywhere to indulge the desires of the weak. For what else would this be than to feed superstition endlessly and to indulge the weak so much that you lose your own strength? The weak person ought to be instructed, to be admonished, to be reproved. For when, as the weaker one, he ought to listen to the stronger, he nevertheless privately judges and condemns one better than himself; and when it is appropriate for him to acquire strength of faith from the example of the strong, he intensifies the sickness of his own mind; and when it is more fitting for him to strive towards the perfection of the stronger, he forces the stronger to sink down to the weakness of another.

But if the one being warned is not yet[19] capable, it befits Christian piety, in my opinion, that the one who is stronger should for a while indulge the one who is feeble, yet on the verge of making progress. This is especially so in a matter of this sort, in which two particular considerations ought to be weighed: first, that the superstitious disposition,[20] which has been received together with mother's milk and strengthened by long-standing habitual practice, is well-nigh impregnable; and second, that no peril is more frightening than the peril of idolatry. But the case of the weaker ones[21] we shall deal with at another time.[22] Meanwhile we must rather deal with this, that we blunt the knowledge that is arrogant and lacks charity, since I see that this is the area where sinning more often occurs among you.

I approve what you say: food does not commend us to God. Indeed, since God has created all things for human use and does not demand

* * * * *

19 'Not yet': *nondum*; so all editions from 1519 to 1534. *1540* and LB, however, read simply *non* 'not.' LB indicates in a footnote that another edition reads *nondum*.

20 disposition] *affectus* in all editions from 1519 to 1534, apparently by mistake, since it does not construe properly with the syntax of the sentence. In the 1540 *Opera omnia*, followed by LB, *affectus* is corrected to *affectum*.

21 the weaker] First in *1523*; previously 'the weak.'

22 Erasmus perhaps has in mind chapter 10, where Paul returns to the question about eating sacrificial meat, but first prefaces his instructions with an exhortation to avoid temptations towards idolatrous practices (10:1–12 and 14–22) and with an assurance that God provides the strength to resist temptation (10:13). Cf Rom 14.

anything from us except a godly life, what does it matter to him whether we eat the meat of fish or of quadrupeds or of birds.[23] For nothing of these either adds anything to godliness or takes anything away. Distinguishing among these foods can make one superstitious, but by no means godly; Christ taught that there was no difference among them.[24] And so it would be ill-advised for some puny man to try to burden anyone with regulations of this sort. Let each person eat whatever is pleasing in accordance with his own physical disposition, provided he does it soberly and sparingly, in all things giving thanks to God,[25] and neither condemning anyone who eats different foods nor being proud of himself because in the interests of his physical health he does not eat this food or that. But, although in other matters there is not so great a danger, here, where it is greatest, some concession ought to be made to the weakness of some. If you eat meat that has

* * * * *

23 Perhaps an allusion to Peter's vision in Acts 10:9–16, recounted in Acts 11:5–10, in which Jewish dietary laws appear to be nullified, and all animals are declared clean.

24 See Mark 7:14–19; Matt 15:11, 17–18.

25 Cf similar passages in Erasmus' paraphrases on Rom 14:5–8 CWE 42 78–9 and on 1 Tim 4:3 CWE 44 24, in both of which giving thanks to God is similarly central to the Christian's freedom to eat anything at all.
The passage here, beginning above with 'distinguishing among these foods . . .' was attacked by Noël Béda, and later by the Sorbonne theological faculty as a whole, as heretical Lutheran undermining of the church's regulations regarding eating and fasting. Erasmus responded that the paraphrase remained true to Paul's sentiments and intentions, that Paul's words were directed against dietary restrictions that false apostles were at that time imposing on Christian freedom and could not be applied to ecclesiastical teachings of a later age, and, furthermore, that the passage addressed discrimination among foods and had nothing at all to do with fasting. See *Divinationes ad notata Bedae* LB IX 474B–E, *Elenchus in N. Bedae censuras* LB IX 507D–E, *Supputatio* LB IX 680F–681C, and *Declarationes ad censuras Lutetiae vulgatas* LB IX 829B–831D. Cf the annotation on 8:8 (*esca autem nos non commendat Deo*). Further distinctions between the true Christian and the superstitious 'Judaic' Christian appear in the fifth rule in the *Enchiridion*. See particularly CWE 66 79. See also the dedicatory letter at n31, where Erasmus recommends the wisdom of a sensible diet that accords with an individual's physical health. Erasmus' own health prompted him to disregard some of the church's dietary restrictions: in 1520 he received permission to eat meat during Lent (Ep 1079:6–8 with n1), and in 1525 he received a formal papal dispensation from restrictions regarding meat (Ep 1542:18–25). For similar controversies over fasting and the choice of foods in relation to Erasmus' annotations on Matthew 11 and Colossians 2 and his *De esu carnium* (ASD IX-1 19–50) see Rummel *Erasmus' Annotations* 146–52. On Erasmus' criticism of 'Judaizing,' see also chapter 9 n6.

been offered to idols, you will be no holier;[26] if you do not, you will be no less pure.

In the meantime you must guard against making such use of your right to eat anything you like that you furnish the weak with an opportunity to fall. Why would this not happen if someone who is still somewhat infected with this superstition notices you, who seem to excel in judgment and learning, reclining at a common banquet together with the others, who have sacrificed to an idol, and although you eat with a different understanding, nevertheless your eating does not have a different appearance. Will not his mind, predisposed on its own towards its previous superstition, be bolstered by your example and propelled towards idolatry, with the result that what you eat in secure and good faith and with an untroubled conscience as well he will eat with an impure conscience? What then is the consequence of this, you ask? Clearly there is danger that through the occasion offered by your strength a weak brother may perish; weak though he may be, yet still a brother, that is, a Christian, whom Christ himself was so far from disregarding that he did not hesitate to die in order to save him. Christ, on behalf of the weak, regarded his own life as cheap. Is your brother's salvation of so little moment to you that because of the cheapest food you have no regard for his peril, especially when there is no lack of food with which you can satisfy your belly's need without raising an obstacle for a brother?[27]

Do not suppose that the offence is trivial in that you are sinning merely against a human being; as often as you become an obstacle for the weak in this manner, wounding their weak conscience by your questionable example, you also offend Christ himself. No matter how weak they are, no matter how feeble, Christ nevertheless has acknowledged them as his

* * * * *

26 holier ... less pure] So read all editions from 1519 to 1540. LB, however, reverses the two adjectives, producing a more common and less complex sentiment: 'If you eat meat that has been offered to idols, you will be no less pure; if you do not, you will be no holier.' Paul's point, however, in 8:8 is that Christians who eat sacrificial meat in the knowledge that it is no different from any other meat do not thereby gain worthiness in God's sight; nor do those who lack such knowledge and therefore abstain diminish their worth before God.
27 Erasmus' paraphrase expands on Theophylact *Expos in 1 Cor* (on 8:12) PG 124 661C–D: 'And your completeness [or maturity] will become a cause of destruction for another, and that for one who is weak ... Christ in fact did not refuse to die on his behalf, but you do not even abstain from bits of food so as not to cause him to stumble?' Similarly Chrysostom *In 1 Cor hom* 20.5 (on 8:11) PG 61 167.

members;[28] in them he counts himself injured. Whatever service has been paid out to them, he permits to be accounted to himself.[29] And not without reason did he so often warn against becoming a stumbling block for the weak. No one knows more than I that in food there is no portion either of piety or of impiety; nevertheless, if I become aware of the danger that a brother who is still rather superstitious may be drawn by the occasion to eat food that will disquiet his conscience, sooner will I totally abstain from the eating of meat throughout my life than be guilty of endangering a member of Christ for my own sake. Food offered to an idol does not, I admit, pollute the steadfast conscience of one who eats it. But disregard for a brother's peril does pollute the person who eats in this way; for we are bidden to love our brother in just the same way as we love ourselves.[30]

Chapter 9

There is no reason, therefore, why anyone should complain that a right already granted is being taken away. One ought not always to look to what is permitted, but to what is expedient. Nor should one proceed right away upon any action that can be defended, but rather follow the course that has been urged by Christian charity, which does not seek its own advantage, but that of others. Indeed, how many cases there are in which I have not made use of my rights![1] It is not that I failed to discern them; I was fully aware of what I was permitted, but I preferred what was expedient for you. I did many things that I knew had no importance for the godly life; I did them to placate those whom I was not willing to see estranged from Christ.[2] I did not do many things I might have done if my concern for

* * * * *

28 For the idea of Christians as members of Christ's body, see 6:15 and 12:27. Cf Chrysostom *In 1 Cor hom* 20.5 (on 8:12) PG 61 167 and Theophylact *Expos in 1 Cor* (on 8:12) PG 124 664A. For Erasmus' use of the metaphor, see also chapter 6 n25.

29 Cf Matt 25:40. In his paraphrase on that verse CWE 45 339, Erasmus similarly draws on the vocabulary and imagery of accounting.

30 See Matt 22:39; Rom 13:8-10; also nn5 and 7 above.

1 Chrysostom *In 1 Cor hom* 21.1 (on 9:1) PG 61 169 and Theophylact *Expos in 1 Cor* (on 9:1) PG 124 664B similarly explain Paul's transition to the discussion of his apostolic rights in 1 Corinthians 9: Paul would feel compelled to follow up his claim in 8:13 (that he would abstain from meat) with evidence of his proven self-restraint in other areas.

2 This is probably an allusion to 9:20-3, where Paul cites Jews, gentiles, and 'the weak' as groups to whom he has accommodated himself.

your advantage had not urged a different course. Why so? Am I not an apostle, just as the others are who boast of this title? Have I not at Christ's bidding been sent to the gentiles?[3] But if I am an apostle just as much as the others, why do I have less apostolic power and authority? Has it not also been granted to me to see our Lord Jesus Christ? – if it seems important to anyone (as it is), that he was witnessed by others after the resurrection.[4] But if apostles are measured by the services they offer and by their noble deeds, what is there in which even here I am found wanting? Is it not an apostolic deed to gain Corinth for Christ, a city once so bound over to worldly desires?[5] And yet with the Lord's help it was through me that this deed was accomplished.

Whether I am an apostle to the Jews, let those decide who are eager to mix Christ with Moses.[6] Surely I am an apostle to you, who believe in Christ through my urging, who have perceived that divine power assists my speech. You, therefore, are my work if deeds are required (although any praise here is owed to Christ, not to me).[7] Are you not my certificate,[8]

* * * * *

3 See Acts 9:15, 22:21, 26:17–18; Gal 1:16. Cf Ambrosiaster in *Comm in 1 Cor* (on 9:1) CSEL 81/2 96:19–21 for the argument that Paul's mission to the gentiles demonstrates his apostolic standing. Cf the paraphrase on 9:2 with n7 below.

4 For Paul as witness to the resurrected Christ, see 1 Cor 15:8; Acts 9:3–6; Gal 1:15–16. Erasmus is echoing Theophylact *Expos in 1 Cor* (on 9:1) PG 124 664D: 'For it was of great importance to have been eyewitnesses of Christ.' For similar emphasis on this conventional sign of apostleship, see the paraphrase on Acts 1:22 CWE 50 12 with nn98, 100, and on Acts 10:39–41 CWE 50 74; also CWE 49 175.

5 Cf the Argument n11.

6 Ambrosiaster *Comm in 1 Cor* (on 9:2) CSEL 81/2 97:7–10 explained the 'others' of 9:2 to whom Paul was not an apostle as a reference to Jewish Christians who denied Paul's apostolic status because he scorned Jewish laws regarding circumcision and the Sabbath. Erasmus frequently elaborates on contemporary 'Judaizers' who would impose on Christian freedom a similar legalistic servitude to ceremonies and regulations. See especially the paraphrase on 8:8 with n25; also the paraphrase on 3:12–15 with nn20 and 22, and the paraphrase on Phil 3:2–3 with n3.

7 The phrase 'in the Lord' in 9:1, 'Are not you my workmanship *in the Lord?*' (RSV), is similarly interpreted by Chrysostom *In 1 Cor hom* 20.1 (on 9:1) PG 61 171 and Theophylact *Expos in 1 Cor* (on 9:1) PG 124 665A: Paul has accomplished his work not through his own power, but through God's.

8 'Certificate': *diploma;* in classical usage a letter of recommendation or authority, as might be given eg to one travelling on a mission for the Roman state. Such a document might instruct local officials to provide whatever assistance was needed for the journey (OLD).

by which I could show that the apostolic ministry[9] has been assigned to
me for the glory of Christ? This is the way I customarily answer those
who keep asking by what proof I show myself to be an apostle. Now if I
have accomplished in you whatever the highest apostles[10] have anywhere
accomplished in others, how am I less an apostle than they? But if either the
authority or the fruitfulness of my apostolic service is equal to theirs, what
would forbid me to enjoy rights equal to theirs? And if I am their equal or
perhaps their superior in labours,[11] why should I not be their equal as well
in rewards? Are we the only ones who lack the right to eat and drink at
the expense of those to whom we preach the gospel? Are we the only ones
who are not permitted to travel around with Christian matrons[12] to provide
us with the necessities of life at their own expense?[13] The apostles do this,

* * * * *

9 'Apostolic ministry': *apostolicam functionem.* By *functio* 'service' or 'performance,' Erasmus typically designates the actual fulfilment of an office or service, rather than the simple holding of the rank or office. See 2 Cor chapter 2
n18.

10 On the designation 'highest apostles' (*summos apostolos*), cf n14 below, and see
also chapter 3 n15. For a derisive use of a similar designation, cf the paraphrase
on 4:7 with n6; also the paraphrases on 2 Cor 11:5 and 12:11.

11 See 1 Cor 15:10. Erasmus repeats this boast in the paraphrase on 9:12 below.

12 'Christian matrons': *Christianas matronas.* Erasmus here is paraphrasing the
Greek phrase ἀδελφὴν γυναῖκα 'sister wife' or 'sister woman.' The exegetical
tradition has long debated Paul's meaning in 9:5: 'Have we not the power to
lead about a sister, a wife, as well as other apostles' (AV). At issue, first, is
whether γυναῖκα has here only its general sense of 'woman' or the more specific sense of 'wife.' Erasmus' use of the Latin *matrona* 'married woman' in
the paraphrase perhaps leaves the issue ambiguous, but the clause that follows ('to provide us ... life') clearly suggests that, for the paraphrase at least,
Erasmus accepts the interpretation that γυναῖκα here does not refer to a real
wife. A second issue concerns 'sister': should it be taken as 'in the manner
of a sister' ie referring to wives who accompany the apostles, but accompany
them 'as sisters,' or does it simply mean, as the paraphrase indicates, 'Christian,' ie identifying the women as believers. Erasmus addresses the various
interpretations in his annotation on 9:5 (*sororem mulierculam*), where he argues
strongly for 'sister' as 'Christian,' but does not choose clearly between 'wife'
and 'woman.' He does imply, however, through a quotation from Clement of
Alexandria, derived from Eusebius *Historia ecclesiastica* 3.30, a preference for
the view that Paul did in fact have a wife, but that she did not accompany him
on his journeys. For Erasmus' views on Paul's marital state, see also chapter
7 n14 and the paraphrase on Phil 4:3 with n3.

13 On the services and resources of these women, Erasmus follows Ambrosiaster
Comm in 1 Cor (on 9:5) CSEL 81/2 98:8–11 and Theophylact *Expos in 1 Cor* (on
9:5) PG 124 665B–C: 'Rich women were accompanying the apostles to supply

and not just any apostles, but the highest[14] rank of apostles, the brothers of
the Lord, who are called James and John, nay even Cephas himself, who
stands first in honour among the apostles. Or do I alone, and Barnabas,
because we do not do what they do, seem not to have the right to live free
from employment[15] and to preach the gospel at the expense of others? So

* * * * *

for them their daily needs ... so that the apostles were wholly engaged in
preaching alone.'

14 but the highest ... John] First in 1521. In the Martens edition of 1519, the
passage is punctuated to yield a slightly different reading: 'but the highest
rank of apostles, those who are called brothers of the Lord, James and John ...'
In either version Erasmus' paraphrase on 9:5 is a curious departure from the
biblical text: 'The other apostles and the brothers of the Lord and Cephas' (RSV).
Here in the paraphrase, 'brothers of the Lord' appears as a special designation
for the highest rank of apostles (apostolorum summates), and these are identified
as John and James. James here is not the brother of John (that James was
killed by Herod Agrippa [Acts 12:2]), but the leader of the Jerusalem church
mentioned in Acts 12:17, 15:13, and 21:18, and identified by Paul as a 'brother
of the Lord' in Gal 1:19. Erasmus identifies this James by the same designation
in the paraphrase on 15:7. Cf the paraphrases on Gal 1:19 CWE 42 101, Acts
12:17 and 15:13 CWE 50 82 and 97 with n41. Erasmus' specific naming of James
and John along with Cephas as leading apostles here in the paraphrase on 9:5
may derive from Paul's statement in Gal 2:9 that James, Cephas, and John
are 'reputed to be pillars' of the church. On the designation 'apostles of the
highest rank,' as used within the Corinthian paraphrases, see chapter 3 n15.
Biblical references to Jesus' 'brothers,' however, are usually interpreted in
prevailing Catholic tradition not to indicate a special apostolic designation,
but to denote the cousins of Jesus. This interpretation derives from Jerome
(De perpetua virginitate B. Mariae adversus Helvidium I 13–16 PL 23 [1845] 196A–
200B), who argued that the term 'brothers' in Hebrew custom can denote 'close
relatives' or 'cousins,' and that the 'brothers' of Jesus named in Mark 6:3 and
Matt 13:55 were actually the sons of the Mary who was wife to Clopas and
sister to Jesus' mother (John 19:25); thus they were Jesus' maternal first cousins.
In his paraphrases Erasmus generally follows the prevailing tradition. See eg
the paraphrases on Matt 13:55 CWE 45 219; John 7:3 CWE 46 91 with n7; and Acts
1:14 CWE 50 10 with n73. Cf 2 Cor chapter 5 n15. For the various interpretations
of biblical references to Jesus' 'brothers and sisters,' see ABD 3 819–21.

15 Note that Erasmus is paraphrasing here his preferred interpretation of the
Greek text of 9:6: οὐκ ἔχομεν ἐξουσίαν τοῦ μὴ ἐργάζεσθαι '[do we] have no right to
refrain from working for a living?' (RSV). This is also the sense adopted in AV
and most modern translations. In the annotation on 9:6 (hoc operandi), Erasmus
notes his preference (in 1516) and cites Theophylact Expos in 1 Cor (on 9:6) PG
124 665C (in 1519) and Chrysostom In 1 Cor hom 21.2 (on 9:6) PG 61 172 (in
1535) in support. He suggests as a possible translation potestatem non operandi
'the right not to work for a living.' However, at the end of the annotation

far are we from hunting wealth from the gospel that we have accepted as a gift not even a simple and thrifty living although it was in itself[16] perfectly just to do so. Who is there who ever serves as a soldier in war and pays his own wages? Who cultivates the vine without eating of the vine's fruit? Who pastures a flock and does not meanwhile feed on the flock's milk? In every occupation expenses are provided by the one for whom the work is performed.

What? Is it with merely human arguments that I make these assertions? That which natural reason dictates – does not sacred law bid the same thing? Indeed, Mosaic law forbids anyone to muzzle the mouth of an ox when it is being led around for threshing grain because it would be unjust not to provide fodder from its place of work. But someone may say: 'What has this to do with apostles?' Is it really likely that God by this law wished only oxen to be watched over and protected? Or rather does some deeper meaning lie hidden which pertains to us? So far is God from wishing the workers to be cheated of their living that he has not wished this to happen even to oxen. Therefore, this was written not so much for the sake of oxen as for our sake, so that whoever is employed at laborious cultivation in the grain-field of the Lord may not be cheated of the hope of due reward, and someone employed at threshing on the ground of the Lord may, besides the hope of eternal reward, lighten the labour with the comfort of present compensation as well. Indeed, do not think it a great thing if, when we have conferred upon you things that concern everlasting life, we should receive from you in turn what is pertinent to the needs of the present life, and if, when we have sown in you spiritual goods, we should receive your material goods. There is no reason why anyone exchanging the cheapest goods for the most precious ones should claim credit for an act of kindness. We are not indebted to you if we accept a living you have offered us, but you are ungrateful if you deny a living to those who sweat for your welfare.

* * * * *

Erasmus surprisingly yields to the widespread acceptance of the Vulgate's translation: *potestatem hoc operandi* 'the right to do this' (DV), ie have women accompany them on their journeys, as the others do. And in his translation he makes only a minor stylistic modification of the Vulgate rendering; thus his translation does not match his Greek text. Here, in the paraphrase, although he follows his preferred interpretation of the Greek text, he may be partially accommodating the Vulgate reading in the subordinate clause 'because ... what they do.'

16 in itself] Added in *1521*

But if apostles, such as they are (for I do not for the moment render judgment on them),[17] have used, and do use, this right among you, how much more justly could we have used it, who not only were the first of all to labour on your behalf but also laboured the hardest of all.[18] And yet we have consciously and prudently not used our right, not because we were not permitted to, or because we were supported from other sources, but rather in our severe lack of necessities there was nothing we did not endure lest anything arise to break off the progress of the teaching of the gospel. Otherwise, if we had not looked more to your salvation than to our own gain, we knew you were well aware that just as among the Greeks ministers of the sacred rites have their living from the sacrifice, so among the Jews those who serve at the altar are sharers of the altar.[19] And no differently did the Lord Jesus ordain, namely,[20] that those who preach and teach the gospel should have their living provided from the gospel.[21] For even one who performs the work of the gospel with diligence and zeal ought to be content with a simple living. Indeed, God forbid that anyone pile up wealth from that which teaches contempt for wealth.[22]

* * * * *

17 Chrysostom *In 1 Cor hom* 21.4 (on 9:12) PG 61 174–5, Theophylact *Expos in 1 Cor* (on 9:12) PG 124 668D–669A, and Ambrosiaster *Comm in 1 Cor* (on 9:12) CSEL 81/2 100:13–15 all suggest that the 'others' who Paul says 'share this rightful claim upon you' are the false apostles. See the paraphrase on 1 Thess 2:9, where the comparison with false apostles is explicit.
18 See 1 Cor 15:10. Cf the paraphrase on 9:4.
19 Deut 18:3–4 defines the rights of the Levitical priests to receive a share of the altar sacrifices. For the idea that the two halves of 9:13 refer to distinct gentile and Jewish practices, Erasmus seems to be following Ambrosiaster *Comm in 1 Cor* (on 9:13) CSEL 81/2 101:1–2. The distinction may have been encouraged by the Vulgate's imprecise rendering of the text. The Vulgate uses *sacrarium* ('shrine' or 'sanctuary') for the Greek ἱερά 'rites' or 'holy objects' in the first half of the verse and *altarium* [or *altar*] 'altar' for the Greek θυσιαστήριον 'altar' in the second half, and thus appears to be distinguishing between two differ- ent kinds of holy places. But in the annotation on 9:13 (*qui altario deserviunt*) Erasmus disparages the attempt to distinguish the two halves of the verse by reference to gentile and Jewish practice, since neither *sacrarium* nor *altarium* is a term restricted to a particular nationality, any more than 'house' is a term appropriate to the French or the English.
20 namely] Added in *1521*
21 See Matt 10:9–10 and Luke 10:7. Cf the paraphrase on 9:18 with n27.
22 This amplification of 9:13 arises from Erasmus' concern about priestly abuses in his own time. Cf the annotation on 9:13 (*qui altario deserviunt*), where he complains of contemporary priests who neglect altars, but share in the altars'

You see how many the reasons, how many the arguments that would
have permitted me to do what the others do, and yet none of these moved
me to accept anything from you. Nor do I have any intention ever to do this
in the future lest anyone think that I have marshalled so much evidence in
this matter so that what I have not heretofore done I may do with more
justification hereafter. I am so far from regretting this attitude that I would
sooner die of hunger than give anyone cause to take this glory[23] away from
me. Having once embraced it, I shall keep fast hold on it. For it does not
grieve me to endure these things; nay rather it gives me pleasure,[24] and I
consider it my glory that I preach the gospel free of charge when I see that
it promotes your well-being in such a way that following my example you
also restrain yourselves, sometimes even from things that are permitted
when the interest of others requires it.[25]

Indeed, if I should preach the gospel in the manner of the others, there
is no reason for me to boast. The Lord has imposed this duty, and whether
I wish to or not, I must obey. There is no ground for praise, therefore,
if I discharge an appointed duty; on the contrary, punishment awaits if
I am remiss in the preaching of the gospel. If, willing and unbidden, I
have preached the gospel, I will be rewarded by God for my ready and
willing disposition; if I am unwilling, I must nevertheless carry out the
task appointed. The gospel has been entrusted to me not so that I may keep
it concealed in my possession, but so that I impart it to the gentiles. If I share
it, it is the Lord's wealth that I share, not my own; if I do not, then I bring
injury to the Lord, because I keep his talent fruitless in my possession, a
talent he wanted to grow with interest.[26]

But, you say, if a penalty awaits one who does not discharge a duty,
and there is no reward for one who does, then, O Paul, on what grounds

* * * * *

wealth just the same. Chrysostom *In 1 Cor hom* 22.1 (on 9:13–14) PG 61 181–2
and Theophylact *Expos in 1 Cor* (on 9:14) PG 124 672A make a similar distinction
between receiving a living from the altar and getting rich from it.

23 'Glory': *gloriam*. In his translation, however, Erasmus corrects the Vulgate's
gloriam to *gloriationem* 'boasting.' See the annotation on 9:15 (*quam ut gloriam
meam*).

24 Chrysostom *In 1 Cor hom* 22.1 (on 9:15) PG 61 182 similarly emphasizes Paul's
pleasure, rather than distress, at not exploiting his rights: 'So far is he from
being grieved that he even boasts.' See also Theophylact *Expos in 1 Cor* (on
9:15) PG 124 672B.

25 Ambrosiaster in *Comm in 1 Cor* (on 9:18) CSEL 81/2 103:4–6 explains Paul's
reward as the benefit that comes to others when they take up his pattern.

26 See Matt 25:14–30.

do you boast? Just this, that if anyone in providing a service should go beyond what has been bidden, on these grounds praise is merited. The Lord instructed that the gospel be preached, but he did not instruct that it be preached free of charge and by our own means of support. No, he gave us the right to eat and drink from the provisions offered by those to whom we delivered the gospel.[27] Therefore, what he was willing to allow, I have not been willing to allow myself. And I have not used the power granted because I perceived it was more to your advantage and to the advantage of the gospel for the gospel teaching to be imparted free of charge to you. In this way I would have greater freedom to admonish you, and it would be transparently clear that I was not doing what some do, who teach for profit, acting in their own interest, not that of Jesus Christ.

Now just as here I have not used my right, so in other matters I have subjected myself as if I were liable for things for which I had no obligation. Indeed, although I am not accountable to gentile laws, and have through the grace of the gospel been freed from Mosaic law, nevertheless, of my own accord, as if under obligation, I make myself subservient to all so that I may gain more people for my Lord. And so I have accommodated myself to the Jews. At times I have taken a vow, shaved my head, likewise had Timothy circumcised,[28] just as if I truly were a Jew even though I knew that the Mosaic law had been abolished.[29] In this way I might by my deference gently lure to Christ those not yet able to free themselves from the superstition of their ancestral law, or at least I might not seriously offend them and drive them away from Christ.

Among those, therefore, who thought themselves subject to the Law, I acted as if I also were subject. On the other hand, among others, who are free and exempt from Mosaic law, I acted at times as if I also were under no law, although by no means before God am I without law, but am subject to the law of Christ, which I much prefer to that of Moses. And yet outwardly I accommodated myself to their capacity and feeling, just as

* * * * *

27 See Matt 10:9–10 and Luke 10:7. Cf the paraphrase on 9:14 with n21.
28 For vows and head-shaving, see Acts 18:18 and 21:23–6; for Timothy's circumcision, see Acts 16:1–3, and cf the paraphrase on Gal 5:11 CWE 42 123–4. Chrysostom *In 1 Cor hom* 22.2–3 (on 9:20) PG 61 183–4, Theophylact *Expos in 1 Cor*
(on 9:20) PG 124 673B–C, and Ambrosiaster *Comm in 1 Cor* (on 9:20) CSEL 81/2
103:25–104:2 likewise illustrate the text by alluding to the vow and Timothy's
circumcision. For the principle of accommodation in Erasmus, see chapter 8
n3. On Erasmus' presentation of Paul as an accommodator, see Sider 'Historical Imagination' 102–3.
29 Cf Eph 2:15, but also Matt 5:17.

among the Athenians I did not immediately arouse hatred by declaiming
against their gods, whom they were worshipping with much superstition,
but I snatched the opportunity offered by an altar inscription to introduce
Christ indirectly.[30] At first I moderated my speech about him in such a way
as to teach that he had been an outstanding individual, and as though he
were one who had been accounted among the gods because of his excellent
deeds. I did not claim that he was God as well as man, because I knew
they were not yet able to grasp this mystery.[31] Indeed, even from their
own authors I brought forth witnesses, trying everything to lure them to
Christ. But none of this did I do for my own sake, none through fault of
inconstancy, but through eagerness to spread the gospel.

I could have put my strength to use and acted like myself, but I preferred what was for me in fact less advantageous. Still, it profited the gospel
more that I tempered myself to the weakness of others, just as if I were held
by a similar frailty, so that I might win the weak.[32] To be brief, among every
sort of people I took on every sort of appearance[33] so that I would every-

* * * * *

30 Erasmus' verb here, *insinuare* 'to make one's way in' or 'to enter by indirect
means,' was used by classical rhetoricians to identify a subtle or indirect introduction to the cause at issue. In *Ad Herrenium* 1.4.6–7.11 eg a distinction
is made between two kinds of introductions: *principium*, the open, direct approach, and *insinuatio*, the subtle, indirect approach that may be advisable
when, for example, the audience is hostile to the cause. Erasmus is here sum-
marizing Paul's visit and speech to the Athenians (Acts 17:16–34). For an excellent illustration of 'Pauline' accommodation in practice, see Erasmus' paraphrase on that speech CWE 50 108–11, and on Athenian superstition, in particular, see CWE 50 108 n31.
31 Cf Theophylact in *Expos in 1 Cor* (on 9:21) PG 124 673C: '[Paul at Athens taught]
about Christ as if he were not teaching about God, but about a human being.
For [the Athenians] could not hear any such thing, but they thought he too
was one of the ones who had been deified among them, like Heracles and
Asclepius.' On *mysterium* 'mystery,' see chapter 7 n30, and for the importance
of 'mystery' in Erasmus' Christology, see Sider 'Historical Imagination' 96–7.
32 On the language of strength (here *firmitas*), weakness (*infirmitas*), and frailty
(*imbecillitas*), see the annotations on Rom 14:1 ('the weak, however'), 14:2 ('but
he who is weak'), and 15:1 ('we the more robust') CWE 56 366, 368, and 388.
33 Cf Erasmus' elaborate description of the Proteus-like nature of Christ's life
in the *Ratio* Holborn 211:28–31 and 214:31–3: 'The variety of Christ does not
confound [his] harmony ... In such a way has he become all things to all
people that nowhere nevertheless was he unlike himself ... Although nothing
is simpler than our Christ, nevertheless in some mysterious sense he represents
a kind of Proteus in the variety of his life and teaching.' For the image applied

where save some, stealing through compliance into the hearts and minds of all. This is not the compliance of a flatterer, by which some seek your favour, but it certainly would be so if I have either taken or sought to take any reward from you. I do the work of the gospel, not my own; I hunt profit for the Lord, not myself. From him alone do I await reward if I carry out the task according to his will. Noteworthy reward comes only to noteworthy achievement. Towards this end ought we to strive on the gospel's running-track: that not only do we seem to have discharged our duty, but also carry away the victor's palm and glory.

Do you not see that in the case of ordinary running-tracks, where contenders race after the reward has been posted, although many take part in the contest, only the one who comes first of all to the finish line is granted the reward. Let it not be enough for you, therefore, to discharge your duty in a perfunctory way, and escape punishment; you must strive for the highest goal with all your strength, and race on the gospel's running-track in such a way as to garner praise before God, the director of the contest.[34] There is nothing that one ought not both to bear and to do for the sake of this.[35] Many things, although harsh, must be endured provided they lead to this reward; from many things, although otherwise permitted, must we abstain if they delay the victor's palm. One who hastens to the finish line must avoid whatever stands in the way. It is shameful if we are more sluggish in contending for so great a prize than the common run of people are for a cheap reward. For whoever is a contender in those popular contests holds back from food, from pleasures, and many other inherently agreeable things because they contribute nothing to victory; he endures many things, although disagreeable, heedless of every aggravation provided the victor's palm becomes his; he aims at it alone. But if such people do everything, suffer everything, in order to win the silly applause of the masses, to obtain the praise of human beings, to carry off a cheap little reward, how much

* * * * *

to Paul, see the paraphrase on 2 Cor 12:19 with n23; also the dedicatory letter to de la Marck n66. See also *Enchiridion* CWE 66 49.

34 'Director of the contest': *agonothetam*, or 'superintendent of the games.' For this term, see the paraphrase on 1 Tim 6:12 CWE 44 37 with n12; also Phil chapter 3 n41.

35 'For the sake of this': *huius gratia* – or possibly 'for his [God's] sake' since the antecedent of *huius* 'of this' may be either *laudem* 'praise' or *agonothetam Deum* 'the director . . . God.' The emphasis on 'reward' in the rest of this paragraph argues for the former; Coverdale (fol xxvii verso), however, chose the latter.

more ought we to do the same in order to win applause from angels, praise from God, and the eternal reward of everlasting life? When such a matter is at stake, will food sometimes of the most worthless kind, or anything like that, hold us back from the race that has begun? Take heed yourselves how you conduct yourselves in this the finest contest.

I at least do not run a sluggish race as those usually do who are hurrying to no sure finish line. Likewise I play the boxer not as those usually do who beat the air with their fists for sport, but in all ways and with real afflictions I subdue my body, so habituating it that it is tamed and becomes obedient to the spirit,[36] and that, as often as the work of the gospel requires, it both easily abstains from things permitted and eagerly endures any hardship that arises. Thus, I would avoid what happens to some others: that when by my preaching I have called others to this contest, I would myself gain no praise in it, and when I have spurred others on to the pursuit of praise, I would myself depart without praise. It is in the surest hope of rewards that I strive, and whatever I teach others by my words I myself fulfil in my life.[37]

Chapter 10

Now this whole discourse of mine is directed at this: that for obtaining the prize of salvation we do not suppose it is enough to have been admitted through baptism[1] into the household of Christ, to have been delivered by his kindness from the tyranny of sins and restored to freedom[2] – unless we henceforth keep ourselves free from any association with base desires. Baptism is common to all, but the reward will not be common to all. Therefore, brethren, I would not have what has been disclosed in our books concealed from you. When Moses led our ancestors in flight from the tyranny

* * * * *

36 Cf Ambrosiaster *Comm in 1 Cor* (on 9:27) CSEL 81/2 106:24–5: the body 'is subjected to slavery while it is carrying out not its own will, but the Spirit's.'
37 Erasmus echoes Ambrosiaster *Comm in 1 Cor* (on 9:27) CSEL 81/2 107:3–8: 'He confirms the hope of his own preaching, therefore, when he shows by his deeds that he follows what he teaches.'

1 For the insufficiency of baptism without a consequent change of life, cf the paraphrases on 6:8–9 with n26 and 10:12.
2 Erasmus concisely summarizes here the two effects of baptism associated with salvation: grafting into Christ's body and rebirth to new life after death to sin. Cf the paraphrases on Rom 6:3–6 CWE 42 37 and Gal 3:28 CWE 42 114, and see Payne *Theology* 164–6.

of Pharaoh, they were all equally defended from the heat of the sun by
the protecting cover of a cloud spread over them by God's hand;[3] they all
equally journeyed on foot through the divided waters of the sea; and, indeed, nearly every gift conferred on us through Christ came previously in
some way to them.[4] We, with Christ as author,[5] are released through baptism from the tyranny of sins; they, under Moses' leadership and protected
by the cloud, were baptized in their own way (foreshadowing our baptism) while they were crossing the sea, which leapt apart at the stroke of
Moses' rod.[6] We, as many of us as have been cleansed through baptism, feed
equally on the food of the most blessed body, and all drink from the mystical cup.[7] In a similar way they too were all eating the manna sent down

* * * * *

3 In Exod 13:21–2 a pillar of cloud leads the Hebrews towards the sea, and in
  14:19–20 the cloud moves behind them to protect them from the Egyptians.
  No mention is made of protection from the sun, but see Ps 105:39: 'He spread
  a cloud for a covering.'
4 Cf the 1522 addition to the *Ratio* Holborn 209:10–13: 'There was almost nothing done by Christ that those divine [Hebrew] seers did not describe. There
  is nothing in his teaching that some passage of the Old Testament does not
  match.' In 10:1–5 Paul introduces his warning to the Corinthians against com-
  placence and overconfidence with a rudimentary form of typological interpretation. Here, events in Hebrew history – miraculous demonstrations of
  God's favour towards the Hebrews – are presented as precursors of, or analogies for, the Christian sacramental experience. Erasmus' paraphrase on these
  verses explicates the parallels that are only elliptically suggested in Paul's
  words. Cf Erasmus' paraphrase on Gal 4:21–31 CWE 42 119–21, another, more
  elaborate example of Paul's typological method. On the language of typology, see CWE 50 5 n6, CWE 44 236 n15, and CWE 46 55 n16. See also n10
  below.
5 'Author': *auctore*, ie for us the author and giver of baptism. See Matt 28:19,
  Mark 16:16, and John 3:5 for Jesus' institution of baptism. For the image, see
  the annotation on John 1:31 (*ego nesciebam eum*) ASD VI-6 62:724–32, where Erasmus (discussing the 'heretical' view that those baptized by unworthy bishops
  had to be rebaptized) identifies Christ as the author (*auctor*) of baptism, while
  the priest is merely the minister or steward (*minister*). On these terms, see
  chapter 1 n10. See also Erasmus' paraphrase on John 1:33 CWE 46 31, where
  John the Baptist points to Jesus as the source of a powerful baptism that would,
  through the Holy Spirit, confer upon 'all those who trusted him remission of
  all their sins.'
6 Moses' rod is not mentioned in the account of the crossing itself (Exod 14:19–
  22), but it does appear in God's instruction in Exod 14:16: 'Lift up your rod
  and stretch out your hand over the sea and divide it.'
7 Erasmus uses the adjective *mysticus* 'mystical' frequently to describe the Eucharistic meal and its elements of bread and wine. In the dedicatory letter (cf

from heaven;[8] they were all alike drinking from the water that Moses drew forth from the rock with a stroke of his rod. Yet these things were not done in an ordinary way or by chance; Christ was at that time[9] rehearsing among them things that for us he has openly and truly performed.[10] From Christ was that manna raining down; the power of Christ, which is nowhere absent from his people, took the dry and barren rock and made it abound with water. It was Christ who was deeming his people worthy of such great favours and of such great honour.[11]

The honour and favour were common to all, but not all reached the place of their destination. It did them no good to have escaped from Egypt if they carried Egypt out with them. It did them no good to have thrown off an old slavery if afterward they were more shamefully enslaved to their own desires than they had been to Pharaoh. Rather God hated them all the more because to their earlier faults they had added the offence of ingratitude as well. Therefore, stricken with various evils through God's avenging justice, they were cut down in the wilderness now by fire, now

* * * * *

4 with n14) eg it is the bread that he calls *mysticus* 'mystic' while the cup is identified as containing 'the Lord's most holy blood' – the reverse of his practice here in the paraphrase on 10:3-4, where the bread is 'the food of the most blessed body,' and the cup is 'mystical.' Cf the paraphrase on 11:25. The adjective refers in classical Greek and Latin to something connected to or used in secret mystery rites, and is also employed in the more general sense of 'secret' or 'mysterious' (LSJ, OLD). For Erasmus, it usually suggests something that cannot be understood fully on the literal or physical level, but points to, or carries, a spiritual, and specifically a Christological, meaning or reality. Cf chapter 5 n12; 1 Thess chapter 5 n18; and CWE 44 216 n12. In connection with the Eucharistic elements, the term *mysticus* seems clearly to include the sense of 'containing the Lord's body [or blood].' For Erasmus' views on the Eucharist, see Payne *Theology* 126–54, and cf n28 below and the paraphrase on 11:19–26 with nn29 and 37.

8 Erasmus' paraphrase on 1 Cor 10:2–4 closely follows Theophylact's explication of the Christian meaning of the early Hebrews' experiences. See *Expos in 1 Cor* (on 10:2–3) PG 124 680B–C, where eg he comments, 'Just as we after baptism eat the Lord's body, so they after crossing the sea ate manna.'

9 at that time] First in *1521*; previously 'only' or 'to such a degree'

10 'Was ... rehearsing': *praeludebat*. Erasmus presents Hebrew history as the rehearsal (*praeludium*) for Christian salvation. For the same typological idea, but applied to Jesus' miracle at Cana (as 'rehearsal' for later signs and events) and elaborately explicated, cf the paraphrase on John 2:11 CWE 46 40 with n20.

11 Theophylact *Expos in 1 Cor* (on 10:5) PG 124 680D similarly concludes that through these events 'God had shown many signs of his love for [the Hebrews] and deemed them worthy of such great benefits.'

by sword, now by pestilence, now by attack of serpents.[12] But just as their flight foreshadows our baptism, so is their punishment an example for us so that, relying on baptism, we might not lead a life unworthy of baptism, or through dissipation and in our craving for harmful flesh return to Egypt in our soul, just as they did to their own great ruin when they scorned the manna.[13] And let us not through stupidity and immoderation slip back to the worship of idols, or seem to have slipped back, as they did when they ignored God and worshipped the molten image of a calf in the manner of unholy gentiles. For thus it is written in the book of Exodus: 'When they had offered up the sacrifices, the people sat down to eat and drink, and when they were filled, they rose up to play' [32:6]. But soon, under the avenging hand of God, twenty-three thousand were slain.[14] And let us not shamefully have intercourse once again with the prostitutes of the ungodly, just as they had with the prostitutes of the Moabites. But they provoked God, and on one day twenty-four thousand people fell dead.[15] And let us not lack faith and through our impatience put Christ to the test, as some of them tested him,[16] when they were inciting to anger with

* * * * *

12 For God's punishment of Israelite rebellion, see Exodus 32 and Numbers 14 and 16; and for punishment specifically by fire, Lev 10:1–2 and Num 16:35; by sword, Exod 32:27–8 and Num 14:43–5; by pestilence, Exod 32:35; Num 14:12, 16:45–50, 25:8–9; and by serpents, Num 21:6–7.

13 See Numbers 11, especially verses 4–6, 33–4. Erasmus perhaps follows Chrysostom *In 1 Cor hom* 23.3 (on 10:7) PG 61 192 and Theophylact *Expos in 1 Cor* (on 10:7) PG 124 681B in suggesting gluttony as the point of comparison between the Corinthians' eating of sacrificial flesh and the ancient Israelites' craving for meat, and as the source of the idolatry in both cases.

14 For the incident of the Israelites' worship of the golden calf, see Exodus 32. Exod 32:28 reports that the Levites slew three thousand at this time. This is the number in the preferred reading of the Vulgate, but some medieval manuscripts and the Clementine edition of 1592 read 'twenty-three thousand.' Cf Weber 123 and 28n. Here, in the paraphrase on 10:7, the number may derive from Erasmus' Vulgate reading of Exod 32:28, or might have been introduced from the biblical text of 10:8, which also reports twenty-three thousand destroyed. See also n15 below.

15 See Num 25:1–9 and the aftermath of this incident in Num 31:1–20. In 1 Cor 10:8 the number Paul cites as slain after an unspecified incident of fornication is twenty-three thousand. Here in the paraphrase Erasmus identifies the incident (fornication with Moabite prostitutes) and corrects the number to twenty-four thousand to correspond to the text of Num 25:9. Erasmus makes no attempt in his annotations on the chapter to explain the discrepancy between the text of 1 Cor 10:8 and Numbers 25:9, to which Paul evidently refers.

16 The Vulgate of 10:9 reads: 'Let us not test Christ as some of them [*illorum,*

their impious murmuring,[17] and they were destroyed by fiery serpents sent
against them.[18] And let us not murmur against Christ and Christ's servants, just as some of them murmured against God and Moses when a con-
spiracy had been formed, instigated and led by Korah. At that time fourteen thousand perished besides those whom the gaping earth had devoured
alive.[19]

Now these things did in fact happen to those ancient people, and the
memory of them has been handed down through the chronicles of our ancestors. Yet whatever happened to them did not happen without purpose,
but rather to present for us who have fallen upon this final age of the
world an example of what we ought to strive for or what to avoid. Since
they kept returning to debauchery,[20] idolatry, base amusements, prostitution, and other diseases[21] which they had received from lodging with the

* * * * *

Greek αὐτῶν] tested.' Erasmus apparently found some manuscripts that justified reading αὐτόν 'him' for αὐτῶν 'of them': 'as some tested him.' In his annotation on 10:9 (sicut quidam eorum), he argues that the latter reading, in which
'him' definitely points to Christ, would prove the divinity of Christ, since it
shows him 'tested' prior to his birth as a man. Although Erasmus follows the
Vulgate reading in his Greek text and Latin translation, the paraphrase here
incorporates both readings ('as some of them tested him'), leaving unshaken
the argument for the divinity of Christ.
17 Erasmus is fond of the noun murmur 'murmuring' and the related verb mur-
murare 'to murmur' to denote impious resistance to, and criticism of, God's
servants. He uses it similarly in the Paraphrase on Acts. See 'murmur' in the
Index of Greek and Latin Words Cited and the General Index in CWE 50.
18 See Num 21:4–9.
19 Numbers 16 reports several rebellions against Moses and Aaron: first, a challenge by Korah and 250 leaders of the congregation to the special religious
status of the Levites (1–11); second, a rebellion against Moses' authority by
Dathan and Abiram (12–19); and third, the murmuring of the whole congregation of Israel (41–2). Three punishments are reported: Korah, Dathan, and
Abiram, along with their households, are swallowed by the gaping earth (31–
4); the 250 leaders are destroyed by fire (35); 14,700 from the congregation are
killed by plague (47–9).
20 'Debauchery': luxum. The word suggests immoderate, indulgent living and
in this volume has been translated variously according to context: 'self-
indulgence' (dedicatory letter 8), 'overindulgence' (Argument 20–1), 'wantonness' (paraphrase on 7:38), and 'dissipation' (paraphrase on 10:6 above).
21 Erasmus appears to have Rom 1:26–32 in mind. See in particular his annotation on Rom 1:26 ('to passions of shame') CWE 56 56, where he recommends
'diseases' (morbi) as a fitting term for the emotional and spiritual perversions
of the Jewish people. See also in the Argument 22 the phrase 'diseases of the
Corinthians.'

Egyptians, they fell from God's grace, and because they did not show themselves worthy of the kind actions of God, it did not help them to have been
redeemed. Indeed, today[22] there is no race of people cast off so far from
God as the Jews. As for ourselves, the more often the divine favours invite us to innocence, the more we must fear that Christ will punish us very
severely[23] if, when we have once escaped from Egypt through baptism, we
should under the label of Christ continue to exhibit morals worthy of Egypt
and not of Christ.

Therefore, let no one, falsely confident in his own strength, scorn the
weak or, confident in baptism, feel assured of his own salvation, unless he
adds to it a life worthy of baptism. They too were pleased with themselves
because they had been delivered out of so many perils and were the objects
of God's special care. And yet they were all the more severely punished because, although they had been separated from the unholy gentiles, they had
nevertheless fallen back into gentile ways. There is danger in trusting oneself. Rather one who is standing needs especially to guard against falling.
The safest course, however, is always to advance towards the better, and
not to trust in any one stage. Satan's wiles cause many things to occur that
estrange us from Christ.

I have not used these terrifying examples because I fear a similar
peril for you. Up to this time you have sinned and strayed somewhat from
Christian purity, but it is still a human and curable failing that I see.[24]
Indeed, I trust that God will not suffer you to slip so far that you become
utterly inadequate to meet the evils that trouble you; but even if he suffers
some evil to befall you, he will so temper the outcome[25] that you can bear it.

* * * * *

22 Perhaps Erasmus means to suggest his own time as much as Paul's. On Erasmus' attitudes towards Jews, see CWE 44 60 n20 and CWE 46 8 n18.
23 Chrysostom *In 1 Cor hom* 23.4 (on 10:11) PG 61 193 finds the same implication:
   Christians are at greater risk of punishment than their Jewish forebears because of the greater gifts they have received; similarly Theophylact *Expos in 1
   Cor* (on 10:11) PG 124 681D. Ambrosiaster warns that greater knowledge of the
   Law makes the disobedient more guilty. See *Comm in 1 Cor* (on 10:11) CSEL
   81/2 111:8–10.
24 Cf Erasmus' annotation on 10:13 (*tentatio vos non apprehendat*): 'For he hints
   that the Corinthians have already fallen into temptation, but a human – that
   is to say, an endurable and curable – temptation ... He had previously fright-
   ened them with terrifying examples, but soon, lest they lose hope, he relieves
   them.'
25 'Outcome': *eventum*. Cf the annotation on 10:13 (*proventum*), where Erasmus
   makes a philological emendation, criticizing the Vulgate's *proventum* as more
   appropriate for the issue or produce of something planted than for the

Perhaps there are some among you who disregard me on account of my plainness[26] and favour other apostles more on account of their fanfare and fawning speech, but you have not yet approached the sedition of Korah.[27] There are some who frequent too freely the sacred banquets of the ungodly, but not yet has your conduct slipped so far that you yourselves sacrifice to the idols; even so, in proximity there is danger.

Therefore, my dearest children, in all circumstances shrink back from the worship of idols. Whoever eats with them, although he may be unusually firm in his intention, nevertheless presents in himself the appearance of one who supports their superstition. There is no reason for me to go on at length persuading you of this since you yourselves in your good sense have a proper grasp of the matter. Judge for yourselves whether what I say is true. What can banquets that are so sacred as ours share with their profane rites? Whoever enjoys food in common seems to acknowledge a common religion. Does not that sacred cup, which we for the remembrance of Christ's death take up with thanksgiving and consecrate,[28] demonstrate a fellowship because we have all equally been redeemed through the blood of Christ? Again, that sacred bread, which by the example and ordinance of Christ we distribute among ourselves, demonstrates a covenant

* * * * *

provision of a way out or escape from temptation. In the annotation, as here in the paraphrase, Erasmus seems concerned with understanding how God can allow evils to befall us that tempt us to sin. Cf CWE 42 18 n20.

26 'Plainness': *tenuitatem*. Perhaps the word refers to the simple style of speech Paul claims for himself. Cf chapters 1 n40 and 2 n6. In ancient rhetorical theory, *tenuitas* implies 'lack of ornamentation' and is characteristic of the plain style of speech, the *genus humile* or *tenue*. See Cicero *Orator* 75-90. *Tenuitas* may also refer to Paul's unadorned way of life. See in particular the paraphrases on 2:1-4 and 9:12.

27 See the paraphrase on 10:9 with n19.

28 'Consecrate': *consecramus*. Erasmus cites his use of this word here in the paraphrase on 10:16 ('The cup of blessing that we bless [NRSV]) when he refutes the claim of the Zwinglian Leo Jud (CEBR II 248-50) that in the paraphrase on 1 Corinthians 10-11 Erasmus had shown an affinity with Zwinglian Eucharistic ideas. See *Detectio praestigiarum* ASD IX-1 248:347-71. Erasmus argues that, on the contrary, he might 'more justly be criticized' for adding 'on his own the word for consecrating,' as if deliberately to accommodate both senses in which the biblical (ie the Vulgate) *benedicimus* can be understood: 'we give thanks' and 'we consecrate.' Erasmus notes that 'the ancients' (cited as Chrysostom and Theophylact in the annotation on 10:16 [*cui benedicimus*]) preferred the former sense, and more recent interpreters the latter, thus referring Paul's words to sacramental consecration. See also chapter 11 nn29 and 37. For a related controversy involving Acts 2:42, see CWE 50 24 n118.

and perfect partnership among ourselves as initiates into the same myster-ies[29] of Christ.[30] Bread is made by bringing together countless kernels of grain in such a way that they cannot be distinguished.[31] A body is made up of different parts in such a way that among them all there is an insep-arable partnership. When we all partake of the same bread, therefore, we show ourselves, however many in number, to be nevertheless, through har-mony of minds,[32] one bread and one body. So those who partake of pa-gan banquets seem to acknowledge their partnership in superstition. Con-sider whether this is not also the case among those who still offer victims in sacrifice according to the law of Moses.[33] They admit to the eating of the sacrificed animal only participants in the Jewish religion, and whoever feeds on the sacrificial offerings seems likewise to approve of the Jews' sacrifices.

What, then, is the drift of your words, someone will ask. Are you denying, Paul, what you affirmed a little earlier,[34] that an idol is nothing, and what is offered to an idol is nothing? By no means do I deny it; but I am saying that the sacrifices that the gentiles offer are offered to demons, not to God. In the things themselves there is nothing different from the or-dinary, but the mind creates a difference. They regard demons as gods, and

* * * * *

29 'Mysteries': *sacramentis* in the general sense of the term, or perhaps 'sacra-ments' in the specific sense. Since Erasmus is at pains to allow 10:16–17 to re-fer either to the general context of common meals or to the specific context of the Eucharist proper, either translation can be defended. I have chosen 'mys-teries' here as the more inclusive of the two translations. Prior to 1527, Eras-mus had concluded his annotation on 10:14 (*et panis quem frangimus*) with his belief that this verse refers to the consecrated bread of the sacrament. In his 1527 addition, however, he modified this conclusion with an explanation of the more general alternative sense and expressed no preference between the two interpretations. See also the previous note. On *sacramentum* as 'mystery,' see chapter 7 n30.

30 This sentence is first punctuated with a period in Froben's folio edition of 1523; prior to that (the 1519 edition through the octavo of 1523) as a question: 'Again, does not that sacred bread ... Christ?'

31 Cf Chrysostom *In 1 Cor hom* 24.2 (on 10:17) PG 61 200: 'For just as bread, consisting of many kernels of grain, is united in such a way that nowhere are the kernels apparent ... so also are we joined both with each other and with Christ'; similarly Theophylact *Expos in 1 Cor* (on 10:17) PG 124 685B.

32 'Harmony of minds': *animorum consensu*. For this phrase in respect to marriage, cf chapter 6 n42 and for the importance of *consensus* 'harmony' or 'agreement' in Erasmus' thought, see chapter 1 nn4 and 29.

33 For Mosaic law concerning the eating of sacrificial victims, see Lev 7:6, 15–18.

34 1 Cor 8:4

they think these demons' power resides in statues.[35] Therefore, whoever eats sacrificial offerings with them seems to be a partner in their ungodly error. And I would not have you, who have once been consecrated to God, become the partners of demons. Whoever professes godliness rejects ungodly worship; it does not suit the same individual to practise such[36] conflicting religions. You cannot drink at the same time from the hallowed cup of Christ and from the accursed cup of demons. Nor can you partake of the table of the Lord and at the same time of the table of a demon, if you do it either[37] with your mind's consent or with serious injury to the weak. There is no accord between Christ and ungodly demons;[38] it is impossible to serve both at the same time[39] without marked dishonour to Christ. Do we on purpose, therefore, provoke him to anger by entering into fellowship with his enemies? There is no harsher insult. Are we then stronger than he, so that we do not fear the vengeance of an angered Lord? God forbid that anyone of you should be so minded. Idolatry is such an accursed thing that we ought to be farthest removed not only from the offence itself, but also from suspicion of the offence. The conviction is generally well established in the minds and hearts of all, that those who eat sacrificial offerings together share a fellowship of religion. The deed itself, I grant,[40] is without fault, but from the general impression a stumbling block arises, and this must here surely, if anywhere, be avoided.

As far as food is concerned, everything is lawful for me, yet not everything benefits my neighbour, for whose sake sometimes I must abstain even from lawful things. Nothing is unlawful for me, yet not everything is conducive to the godliness of others. Moreover, Christian charity prescribes

* * * * *

35 Erasmus also elaborates on the idea of pagan gods as demons in the paraphrase on 1 Cor 8:4–6. See also the Argument 21. Cf the paraphrase on 1 Thess 1:9 with nn22 and 23 and CWE 50 92 with n18. For other uses of the term 'demon,' see *daemones* in the Index of Greek and Latin Words Cited.

36 such] Added in *1532*

37 either ... weak] First in *1532*; earlier editions read simply 'with your mind's consent,' evidently referring to the willing adoption of idolatrous practices that Paul is warning against here in chapter 10. The change in *1532* recognizes the concern for the weaker Christian addressed in chapter 8.

38 Cf 2 Cor 6:15–16 and Erasmus' paraphrase on 2 Cor 6:16: 'Conflicting deities, conflicting religion, conflicting morals, conflicting hope! What agreement is there between the temple of God and profane images?'

39 Cf Matt 6:24 and Erasmus' paraphrase on that verse CWE 45 122–3. At this point Ambrosiaster *Comm in 1 Cor* [on 10:21] CSEL 81/2 115:3–4 cites the passage from Matthew directly.

40 itself, I grant] Added in *1532*

that one ought not to serve one's own individual advantages, but rather those of others. Each one should make use of his right, but if such use would place a brother in peril, then one should consider carefully what is expedient for the brother rather than what is lawful for oneself.

Otherwise, eat whatever is ordinarily for sale in the meat market without discriminating or inquiring whether or not it is a sacrificial offering – and that on account of conscience, for you ought to avoid a stumbling block, if one should arise, but not go looking for one. Nothing of this sort is inherently impure, because all things are the Lord's. And whatever has been fashioned by him for human use cannot be impure, just as the Psalmist also testifies: 'The earth is the Lord's,' he says, 'and with it everything that is anywhere contained in the earth' [24:1]. It is from minds that impurity arises, not from food.[41]

And so if anyone who is a stranger to Christ invites you to dinner, and it otherwise seems good to go, eat whatever is served on the table before you, making no judgments nor inquiring whether the dishes served are from sacrificial offerings or not, lest you raise an obstacle for conscience. But if anyone volunteers the information that this meat was offered to idols, then do not eat – not for your own sake, but for the sake of the one who has warned you it is a sacrificial offering, lest you raise an obstacle for conscience – not for your conscience, I say, which is pure and steadfast, but for the conscience of that other one, who apparently thinks it is not lawful for Christians to eat sacrificial meat. There is also the danger that this person may think you are either friends of demons or gluttons, and may think to himself: 'However much in their words[42] Christians despise our gods, nevertheless they do not disdain to eat sacrificial meat, and by no means[43] would they do this if they cursed our religion as much in their minds as they do in their words.'[44] It is the conscience of such a

* * * * *

41 For a similar appeal to Ps 24:1 (paraphrased in the preceding sentence) see Chrysostom *In 1 Cor hom* 25.1 (on 10:26) PG 61 205: 'But if the earth, the fruits, and the animals all belong to the Lord, then there is nothing unclean [in them by nature]; but the uncleanness comes in another way: from our intention and from our disobedience'; cf also Theophylact *Expos in 1 Cor* (on 10:26) PG 124 689B.

42 in their words] Added in 1532

43 and by no means ... words] Added in 1532

44 Erasmus assumes, along with Ambrosiaster *Comm in 1 Cor* (on 10:29) CSEL 81/2 117:17–118:2, Chrysostom *In 1 Cor hom* 25.1 (on 10:29) PG 61 206–7, and Theophylact *Expos in 1 Cor* (on 10:29) PG 124 692A, that the informant whose conscience is at stake in 10:28–9 is a pagan, not a weak Christian. Cf, how-

person, therefore, that must be considered, and it can be considered without great trouble. He is mistaken, but a mistake that you cannot do away with must for a time be indulged. In these matters Christ wished us to have utmost freedom; he neither prescribed nor proscribed any kind of food.

Why, therefore, is my freedom judged by someone else's conscience? Why is something that can rightly be done drawn into wrongful suspicion? If I eat food that the generosity of God[45] has granted us for the enjoyment of life, why on this account am I visited with someone's reviling words when for the enjoyment of this food I give thanks to God, not to demons? You will eat or not eat, therefore, according to this rule: that whether you eat, drink, or do anything else, you refer all to the glory of God. And in this way adjust all your life according to the condition of the times and the people so that there may be no reason for anyone to be justly offended, whether Jew or pagan or Christian – and that, by my example. In all things I accommodate myself to all people: eating, not eating,[46] receiving, not receiving,[47] living as a Jew, not living as

* * * * *

ever, the paraphrase on 10:23–4; there Erasmus finds Paul concerned about the interests of fellow Christians. Modern interpreters are divided on the focus of 10:28–9: Orr and Walther (255) and Conzelmann (177–8) think that it is a pagan's misunderstanding that concerns Paul here, and that the passage therefore extends the principle Paul established in 1 Corinthians 8 concerning indulgence of a weak Christian's conscience; Barrett (242) thinks it more likely that Paul has in mind here the conscience of a guest who is a fellow Christian, and that the passage thus simply reiterates the earlier principle. Erasmus evidently sees the two concerns as closely related: in the paraphrase on 8:7, he has already introduced the issue of the pagan's conscience as correlative with that of the weak Christian's conscience. See chapter 8 n12.

45 In his translation of 10:30 Erasmus follows the Vulgate in rendering χάριτι as '[if I partake] with thanksgiving'; here he reads it as instrumental dative, '[if I partake] by grace.' See the annotation on 10:30 (cum gratia participo), where Erasmus mentions 'by grace' as the preference of Chrysostom In 1 Cor hom 25.1–2 (on 10:30) PG 61 207 and Theophylact Expos in 1 Cor (on 10.30) PG 124 692A–B. They identify the 'grace of God' as the 'strength of mind of one who scorns an idol, and the goodness of God by which it happens that God's gifts are not tainted for the pure through the malice of the ungodly.' Another possibility, rejected by Erasmus, is Ambrosiaster's suggestion in Comm in 1 Cor (on 10:30) CSEL 81/2 118:4–5 that Paul means to say, 'if I share in grace.'

46 See 1 Cor 8:13.

47 Ie whether he receives or refuses support for his living. See 1 Cor 9:15; 2 Cor 11:8.

a Jew,[48] regulating whatever can either be properly done or properly disregarded according to circumstances not for my own personal benefit, but for the benefit of many. Through this compliance of mine, I hunt these people down not as prey for myself, but to lure them to salvation.

Chapter 11

You should not be reluctant to follow the example of your apostle since it is not so much my example as it is Jesus Christ's. In all things he accommodated himself to us in our weakness so that he might gain us for the Father.[1] I follow him as Lord and teacher; you children should follow your father, you disciples your apostle. And I think that what I have said about eating meat and avoiding the sacred rites of the ungodly is enough. Now I shall touch upon what you should observe or avoid in your assemblies so that here also nothing goes on which is either unbecoming or done through strife or overindulgence.

In the first place I praise you, brethren, because in the other matters you are mindful of me in all respects and hold fast what I had directed and what I had instructed you to observe in your solemn assembly. Let me mention a point that is, however, less weighty and can be adjusted to suit the time and place.[2] But still I would not in the meantime have you unaware that just as the head of every man is Christ, and the head of every wife is the husband,[3] so is the head of Christ God. Although the

* * * * *

48 See 1 Cor 9:20–1; cf Gal 2:14–15. The Latin *Iudaissans* 'living like a Jew' is apparently the participle of the unusual verb *Iudaissare*, formed on the adjective *Iudaeus* 'Jewish' by means of the intensive verb suffix -*isso* (-*esso*), and on the model of the Greek verb Ἰουδαίζειν 'to imitate the Jews' (from Ἰουδαῖος 'Jewish').

1 Cf 1 Cor 9:19 and Erasmus' paraphrase on that verse. On 'accommodation,' see chapters 3 n3, 8 n3, and 9 nn28 and 30.
2 Chrysostom *In 1 Cor hom* 26.1 (on 11:2) PG 61 211–13 and Theophylact *Expos in 1 Cor* (on 11:1) PG 124 693A–B similarly identify the subject of 11:1–16 (the roles and attire of men and women in the church) as less weighty than the concerns of previous chapters (immorality and idol worship in particular) and than the discussion of divisive and unruly conduct at the Eucharist that follows in 11:17–34.
3 Although in his Latin translation of 11:3–16 Erasmus preserves, in accordance with the Greek text and the Vulgate, the broader terms *mulier* and *vir* for 'woman' and 'man,' in the paraphrase he prefers the more specific *uxor* 'wife' and *maritus* 'husband.'

man rules his wife, nevertheless he acknowledges Christ as Lord; Christ
himself acknowledges the authority of the Father in all matters; each one
must serve the glory of the person to whom he is subject. In private you
may act in the way each thinks expedient,[4] but whatever man prays or
prophesies in a public gathering with his head covered dishonours his head
by concealing it as though it were a slave's[5] although he acknowledges no
master besides Christ; and for Christ's glory[6] it is reasonable that the man's
head be uncovered not only by removing his cap, but even by shaving

* * * * *

4 The distinction between private situations and public gatherings is Erasmus'
   addition to Paul's text. 1 Cor 11:4–5 simply forbids men to cover their heads
   and women to uncover theirs while praying and prophesying. Erasmus further defines the private/public distinction in the next paragraph when he suggests that a woman may in the privacy of her home uncover her head for her
   husband's pleasure. In this concession, he is perhaps departing from Chrysostom and Theophylact, who both observe that, while Paul does not require
   men always and everywhere to go bareheaded, but only in public worship,
   he does intend women to have their heads covered at all times. See Chrysostom *In 1 Cor hom* 26.3–4 (on 11:4–5) PG 61 217 and Theophylact *Expos in 1 Cor*
   (on 11:4–5) PG 124 696A–D.
5 Erasmus may derive the explanation that a covered head denotes servility
   from the patristic tradition. Theophylact *Expos in 1 Cor* (on 11:4) PG 124 696A–
   B eg notes that the covering of the head is a sign of subjection to the power of
   another. Theophylact may not be referring to contemporary custom but making a deduction based on 11:10. See also Theophylact *Expos in 1 Cor* (on 11:10)
   PG 124 697C; Chrysostom *In 1 Cor hom* 26.5 (on 11:10) PG 61 218; and Ambrosiaster *Comm in 1 Cor* (on 11:10) CSEL 81/2 122:15–16. It was not, however, normal practice in the Greco-Roman world for either free men or slaves to go
   about with their heads covered. See Ugo Enrico Paoli *Rome: Its People, Life, and
   Customs* (Westport, CT 1975) 105. Seneca *De clementia* 1.24.1 and Appian *Bella
   civilia* 2.120 both suggest that there was little distinction in clothing between
   free men and slaves. See also Thomas Wiedemann ed *Greek and Roman Slavery*
   (London 1981) 68.
6 The paraphrase here may reflect Theophylact's suggestion in *Expos in 1 Cor*
   (on 11:4) PG 124 696A–B that the head dishonoured may be either the man's
   physical head or his spiritual one, ie Christ: 'For just as a puny body shames
   its head, so also someone who has by God been made free and independent
   but nevertheless weakens himself [by wearing the sign of slavery] ... brings
   shame upon Christ, who is the head of this person, as if [the head] of a body.'
   Theophylact appears to be extending here the familiar Pauline metaphor of
   Christ as head and the believing community as body or individual Christians as members. Cf 6:15–17, 12:27; Eph 1:22–3, 4:15–16; and Col 1:18. For
   Erasmus' extension of the metaphor, see the paraphrase on 6:8–17 with n25.
   For modern treatment of Paul's use of the word 'head' in 11:4, see Barrett
   248–51.

his hair.[7] For the hair also is more truly a covering, than a part, of the body.[8]

A woman, on the other hand, if she should pray or prophesy in solemn assembly with her head uncovered, disgraces her head, which in private ought perhaps to be made visible to please her husband,[9] not in public assembly, where Christ is served, not husbands. For it is the same for a woman to cast off her wedding veil as it is for a man to be shorn or shaven. But if it is fitting for a woman, observing a man's practice, to cast off her head-covering, then by the same token let her follow the masculine fashion and be shorn also or shaven, so that she prays or prophesies openly with her head bald.[10] But if, as everyone agrees, this would be absurd and base, then let her witness by her covered head that she is subject to the man. To do the same, however, would not befit a man, who bears the image of God and is thus set over the woman just as Christ is over the church,[11] and it is through the man that God's glory, which ought not to be concealed, is illuminated.[12] Conversely, as a woman is subject to her husband, so is she attired for his glory; towards him she would be insolent if by baring her head openly she both witnessed to her own arrogance and, as if she were

* * * * *

7 Erasmus probably has in mind the short haircut which was the norm for men in the first-century Greco-Roman world, and which Paul recommends in 11:14. See also n8 below. But the verb used here for 'shave' (*deradere*) typically suggests a head shaved clean (OLD 2b), as does the reference in the next paragraph to a bald head (*calvum caput*). Erasmus may be using an exaggeration intentionally. See also n10 below.

8 Chrysostom *In 1 Cor hom* 26.4 (on 11:4–5) PG 61 217 and Theophylact *Expos in 1 Cor* (on 11:4) PG 124 696A similarly interpret 'headcovering' for a man as either a cap or long hair. See also the annotation on 11:4 (*velato capite*).

9 See n4 above.

10 There may be a faint, perhaps unlikely, allusion here to the monk's tonsure, or even to Apuleius *Metamorphoses* 11.10, where the male worshippers of the Egyptian goddess Isis at Corinth are described as celebrating her mysteries with heads shaved clean (*capillum derasi funditus*). Cf Juvenal 6.533 and Martial 12.29.19. Either of these allusions would heighten the *reductio ad absurdum* that Erasmus sees Paul using in 11:6. Chrysostom *In 1 Cor hom* 26.4 (on 11:6) PG 124 217 similarly notes Paul's use of absurdity in this verse.

11 Cf Eph 5:23. Erasmus may also have in mind Theophylact *Expos in 1 Cor* (on 11:7) PG 124 697A: the man's uncovered head 'is the sign that the man has not been placed under any earthly power, but that he himself rules all things, inasmuch as he is the image of God.'

12 Cf Ambrosiaster *Comm in 1 Cor* (on 11:5–7) CSEL 81/2 121:24–122:1: 'For it is incongruous for the image of God to be concealed; indeed it ought not to be hidden for the glory of God is seen in the man.'

free, repudiated the governance of the man. Christ is honoured if a man openly and without covering does service to him and proclaims his glory. A man is honoured if his wife by her propriety, silence, and reserved attire displays modesty together with obedience.[13]

But here someone might say: 'By what law is a woman forced to submit to her husband, and not the other way around?' The reason is that when God was first fashioning the human race, man did not come forth from woman, but, on the contrary, woman from man. First Adam was fashioned from mud, and mind was added by the divine inbreathing;[14] then from his side Eve was brought forth, as if she were a certain portion of the man. What[15] was more perfect was fashioned first – and that, contrary to the common order of nature – and then what was less perfect. For a husband plays in matrimony the same role reason plays in a person; a woman plays in marriage the same role feelings play in a person.[16] Furthermore, man was not fashioned for the sake of woman, but on the contrary, woman was added for the comfort of man, and[17] for assistance in procreation as well, where

* * * * *

13 For this description of a woman's proper behaviour and appearance, Erasmus draws on 1 Tim 2:9–12. Cf the paraphrase on this passage CWE 44 16–17. In recommending silence in particular, he anticipates 14:34 as does Ambrosiaster *Comm on 1 Cor* (on 11:8–9) CSEL 81/2 122:23–123:1. Cf the paraphrase on 14:34. In 1 Corinthians 11, Paul does not tell women to be silent in Christian worship, but indicates rather that women did pray and prophesy during the Corinthians' meetings (11:5), as both Chrysostom *In 1 Cor hom* 26.3 (on 11:4–5) PG 61 216–17 and Theophylact *Expos in 1 Cor* (on 11:5) PG 124 696C note was the case in Paul's time. The commendation of silence as a woman's glory was commonplace in antiquity. See eg Sophocles *Ajax* 293.

14 'Divine inbreathing': *divino afflatu*. See Gen 2:7. For Erasmus' use of this phrase in the context of salvation rather than creation, see chapter 1 n53.

15 What ... feelings play in a person] Added in 1532

16 For this commonplace association of man with intellect and woman with feelings, particularly in relation to the 'natural' rule of husband over wife in marriage, see Aristotle *Politics* 1254b2–10, 1259a37–b17, and 1260a9–24. For the different and in antiquity much less common philosophic opinion, that women have the same natural capacity for reason as men have, see the Roman Stoic Musonius Rufus 3, 4, and 13a (cited in Mary R. Lefkowitz and Maureen B. Fant *Women's Life in Greece and Rome: A Source Book in Translation* 2nd ed [Baltimore 1992] 50–4).

17 and ... the matter] Added in 1532. Cf *Institutio christiani matrimonii* CWE 69 226. For this view of sexual roles in procreation, see Aristotle *De generatione animalium* 716a5–23, 727a2–30, 765b8–20. Erasmus' language (*forma, actus, materia*) suggests Aristotelian formal, efficient, and material causes for sexual reproduction. Cf also Apollo's argument in Aeschylus *Eumenides* 658–61 and Theo-

the man supplies the pattern and the agency, and the woman the matter. It is right, then, that authority lies with him who was both fashioned earlier and fashioned for God alone, not for woman.

Since the very beginnings of nature, therefore, have given this right to the man, a woman ought to acknowledge her lot – and not only by her compliance, but also in her attire[18] to witness to the lordship of her husband. And just as a shorn crown reveals a state of freedom,[19] so the veiling of the head is a mark of subjection. But if a woman has become so shameless that she has no fear before the eyes of human witnesses, at least let her cover her head on account of the angelic witnesses, who are present at your meetings.[20] To this extent a woman acknowledges what befits her.

This is not to say that a husband ought to consider her of little value because she has been bidden to obey, or that a wife ought to be dissatisfied with herself because she has been made subject to her husband, for as far as their partnership in religion is concerned, they are both equal.[21] Often a husband needs the service of his wife, often a wife that of her husband.

* * * * *

phylact *Expos in 1 Cor* (on 11:12) PG 124 700A: 'The man, however, is through the woman; that is, the woman assists in human generation, but the working of the seed is more powerful, with the result that the man is not properly said to be from the woman, but from his father through the woman.' Chomarat I 596 cites this passage as an example of enlargement of the text with the 'judgments' or 'sentences' of famous writers or philosophers, a method described in *De copia* CWE 24 626–7.

18 'Attire': *cultu*, which Coverdale (fol xxxi recto) translates as 'reverente behaviour.' The context, however, suggests the more concrete meaning, 'adornment,' 'dress,' or 'attire,' as in the paraphrase on 11:7.

19 Cf nn7 and 8 above and Erasmus' annotation on 11:10 (*velamen habere*).

20 Why Paul argues that women should wear a veil 'because of the angels' (11:10) has been subject to much debate. For a brief summary of the various interpretations, see Barrett 253–5 and Conzelmann 188–90. For the idea of angels as witnesses of human conduct, cf 4:9, although in the paraphrase on that verse, Erasmus interprets the angelic witnesses as demons; cf chapter 4 n20. For the presence of angels with Christians, see Theophylact *Expos in 1 Cor* (on 11:10) PG 124 697C: 'So, to walk around with her head uncovered declares her shamelessness, which the angels also, who accompany Christians, curse.' On angels as guardians, cf CWE 50 82 n26.

21 Chrysostom *In 1 Cor hom* 26.5 (on 11:11) PG 61 218–19 and Theophylact *Expos in 1 Cor* (on 11:11) PG 124 697D similarly explain Paul's qualification in 11:11, but neither proceeds to suggest the equality of husband and wife as partners in religion. Cf, however, Ambrosiaster *Comm in 1 Cor* (on 11:12) CSEL 81/2 123:18–20: 'For they are one flesh and one body in the Lord.' Erasmus perhaps alludes to Gal 3:28. Cf his paraphrase on that verse CWE 42 114.

Moreover, although long ago woman was brought forth from man, now neither does a woman give birth without a man, nor can a man become a father without a woman. And yet there is no cause for anyone to feel either self-satisfaction or self-reproach in these matters since all things must be ascribed to God as author, who in this way governs the order of the universe.

To return to the point I had taken up: if by so many arguments I do not yet persuade you how unfitting it is for a woman to pray bare-headed in public, then let each of you at least weigh the matter carefully according to your own understanding and judgment. For I think no one is so dull-witted as to have lost the power of natural judgment. Does not even nature itself teach you that it is considered a disgrace for a man if he wears his hair long in the manner of women, or that, on the contrary, a woman gains honour if she wears her hair long? The reason is that nature has given to her a thicker and fuller head of hair than to a man so that she, who is subject to a man, might nowhere lack a veil for her head.

I have shown what seems to me more fitting. But if any among you seems rather contentiously to defend his own opinion about this matter, let him do as he pleases, provided he know that to do so is neither our way nor that of the other churches of God. Whether it is fitting for you to dissent both from the ordinances and example of your apostle and from the practice of the remaining congregations,[22] you yourselves may judge. There would be less harm if you were somehow to be of one mind in these matters. These[23] are external concerns and have very little to do with evangelical piety.

But the following I would not hesitate to require of you, and I am displeased that what I indeed[24] imparted is not being heeded. The fact that in the other matters you are mindful of my ordinances, I applaud;[25] that here, where it would be especially fitting to do likewise, you are not mindful, I do not applaud. I had ordained that you come together without disturbance, without overindulgence, without contention, with the utmost

* * * * *

22 'Remaining congregations': *reliquarum congregationum*. Although Erasmus sometimes prefers *congregatio* to *ecclesia* 'church' when the reference is to a 'household church,' here he seems to be using it as a substitute for *ecclesia* in order to vary his expression. In the previous sentence he has just referred to the same congregations as *ceteris ecclesiis* 'the other churches.' See also chapters 1 n3 and 16 n13; also CWE 50 40 n20 and CWE 44 71 n7.

23 these ... piety] Added in 1532

24 indeed] *quidem*, first in 1534; previously *pridem* 'long since'

25 See 1 Cor 11:2 and the paraphrase on that verse with n2.

equality, which most of all promotes harmony;[26] and your conduct when all are together was to be such that each one would return home a better person. Now your behaviour has degenerated so far that it would be better not to come together than to come together as you now do – and that for many reasons, since it is not in only one area that you sin.

In the first place, when you come together in solemn assembly, I hear that there are divisions among you. This is indeed an uglier report than I should like to believe, and yet considering your natural tendencies, I do in part believe it. It was unavoidable that divisions of this sort would arise among you.[27] And out of the evil comes the good result that hereby those who are truly virtuous become more clearly apparent. For while the others are raising an indecent uproar and gorging themselves, these are celebrating the holy feasts in which we represent that last supper of Christ with his disciples modestly and soberly in accordance with the apostles' directives as well as the ancient custom of the church.[28] We do this mindful of the covenant he initiated with us and to exemplify the mutual concord we have with each other.[29] But now there has crept in among you a practice unseemly beyond measure:[30] that as often as you come together, what seems to be engaged in is not the Lord's Supper such as he held with his followers but some tumultuous feast in which all are not treated equally

* * * * *

26 Cf n31 below.
27 Chrysostom *In 1 Cor hom* 27.2 (on 11:19) PG 61 226 and Theophylact *Expos in 1 Cor* (on 11:19) PG 124 701C explain the inevitability of divisions here not by reference to the Corinthians' particular tendencies, but to the weakness or depravity of human nature in general.
28 For apostolic directives regarding modest and sober conduct, see eg 1 Thess 5:6, 8; 1 Tim 3:11; 2 Tim 4:5; Titus 1:8, 2:2, 4–6; 1 Pet 1:13, 4:7, 5:8. Cf also Erasmus' annotations on 1 Pet 4:7 (*estote itaque prudentes*) and Rom 12:3 ('to be wise unto sobriety') CWE 56 327. If modesty and sobriety are prescribed generally, then by extension they may apply to the specific context of the Lord's Supper. For 'the ancient custom of the church,' Erasmus may have in mind passages like Acts 2:42–7. See in particular the paraphrase on that passage CWE 50 24–6, where Erasmus summarizes early church customs regarding the breaking and sharing of bread in memory of Jesus' passion and especially highlights the harmony, modesty, and gentleness of early church life. See also patristic descriptions of early Christian sobriety at the Lord's Supper, eg Tertullian *Apologeticum* 39.17–18 CCL 1 152–3.
29 On the language Erasmus uses here for describing the Eucharist (*repraesentamus* 'we represent' and *ad exemplum* 'to exemplify'), see n37 below. On the Eucharist as a sign of Christian unity see n31 below.
30 beyond measure] Added in *1532*

because through self-indulgence and unrestrained gluttony, without waiting for the others, you each grab your own supper. And so it happens that
the poor man goes hungry either because he has nothing to eat or because
he comes too late, while the rich man who has already grabbed his supper
is full and drunken, and that mystical feast is doubly dishonoured, first, because through the arrogance of the rich the poor are held in contempt, the
poor whom Christ did not contemn; and then because with intoxication and
indulgence the Lord's Supper is defiled. Here the mystery of Christian unanimity is concerned, not affairs of the belly or the gullet, which you should
have tended to not in public assembly, but in the privacy of your houses.[31]
If you wanted to fill your gut, do you lack homes in which you may do this
apart from others? Or do you so scorn the public congregation[32] of Christians that in its presence you serve your gullet, as if doing this meanwhile
with the intent of shaming the poor, who have nothing to bring, while you
make public display of your indulgence and pomp? What shall I say here,
Corinthians? Am I to praise you? I would indeed wish that were possible
and you were deserving – and in other things I surely do praise you, but in
this matter I cannot. Your conduct deviates too far from that Supper of the
Lord which ought to be the model for the holy feasts you observe among
yourselves.

　　I am at a loss to imagine who introduced these customs to you. For
I myself as an apostle received from the Lord what I then passed on to
you, namely,[33] that our Lord Jesus, on that night in which he was betrayed
through a disciple and taken prisoner, took bread, and having given thanks

* * * * *

31 Erasmus' language closely follows that of Ambrosiaster *Comm in 1 Cor* (on
　11:22) CSEL 81/2 126:15–16: 'These things ought to be done at home, not in
　church, where people gather for the sake of unity and the mystery, not for
　the sake of conflict and the belly.' Erasmus typically emphasizes unity and
　fellowship among participants in the Eucharist. Cf *Detectio praestigiarum* ASD
　IX-1 242:198–201. In the Eucharist 'there is signified the closest partnership of
　Christians with each other, either because from many kernels one bread is
　formed, and from many grapes one wine flows together, or because shared
　food and drink may be a symbol of friendship and association.' See also *In
　psalmum 22 enarratio triplex* CWE 64 162: ' And they become one not only with
　Christ their head, but since they share in the same meal and are animated by
　the same spirit, they become one among themselves'; also the paraphrase on
　John 13:2 CWE 46 160: at the Last Supper Jesus ratified 'the bond of a friendship
　that would never in any way perish.'
32 'Congregation': *congregationem*. For the terms Erasmus uses for the church, see
　chapters 1 n3 and 16 n13; also CWE 44 71 n7 and CWE 50 40 n20.
33 namely] Added in *1521*

to God, broke the bread and said: 'Take, eat; this is my body, which is broken[34] for you and is to be shared by all.[35] This which you see me do, you also are to do after this for the remembrance of me.' You see that they are all reclining together here with their teacher, that the table and food are shared by all, that not even Judas the betrayer has been removed from the fellowship of the table, that the same bread has been distributed among all equally. Did the Lord act thus with his disciples, and do you despise brothers and sharers in the same religion?[36]

In the same manner after distributing the bread, he took the cup also into his hands and, the meal now finished, said: 'This cup is the new testament through my blood; as often as you drink from it, do so for the remembrance of me.' Here, therefore, all were drinking from the same cup, and among you the rich are drunk while the poor thirst. Christ wished this feast to be a commemoration of his death and a symbol of an everlasting covenant,[37] yet now it is celebrated among you with self-indulgence and

* * * * *

34 Here and in his translation of 11:24 Erasmus replaces the prevailing reading of the Vulgate, *tradetur* 'will be given,' with *frangitur* 'is broken,' a change likewise made by Valla *Annot in 1 Cor* 11 (I 866). (For other variants, see Weber 1781.) In his annotations on 11:24 (*hoc est meum corpus* and *quod pro vobis tradetur*), Erasmus defends his reading against Béda and the Paris theologians, who apparently objected to referring to Christ's 'body' as being literally 'broken.' Erasmus cites the agreement of Greek manuscripts and the witness of Ambrosiaster, Chrysostom, Theophylact, Bede, and others, and he castigates Béda for refusing to read his explanation of the propriety of *frangitur*. See also Erasmus' brief defences in *Divinationes ad notata Bedae* LB IX 474E–F, *Elenchus in N. Bedae censuras* LB IX 507E, and *Declarationes ad censuras Lutetiae vulgatas* LB IX 877C–D, and the fuller response in *Supputatio* LB IX 681C–684B. For discussion of the controversies surrounding Erasmus' annotations on 11:24 and other Eucharistic passages (including Mark 14:22, Matt 26:26, and Acts 2:42), see Payne *Theology* 126–54 and Rummel *Erasmus' Annotations* 156–60.
35 In expanding 11:24 ('This is my body which is broken for you' [AV]) with 'and is to be shared by all,' Erasmus may have Matt 26:27 in mind.
36 Erasmus seems to be echoing the emphases of Theophylact *Expos in 1 Cor* (on 11:24) PG 124 705A: 'Recall that ... he had the betrayer himself as dinner companion; and do you judge your brother unworthy?'
37 The language Erasmus uses throughout this passage, eg the paraphrase on 11:19 and elsewhere, in reference to the Eucharist (*commemoratio* ' commemoration,' *symbolum* ' symbol' or 'token,' *repraesentatio* 'representation,' *exemplum* 'example') and the controversy that arose regarding his views on the Real Presence are discussed by Payne *Theology* 133–48. See also CWE 50 24 nn115, 117 and 118. Cf the paraphrase on Mark 14:22 CWE 49 160: 'Jesus commended to his disciples the sacred symbol of his death, of the lasting covenant with those who persevere in the evangelical faith.' Erasmus points out in his defences

division. It is mystical bread, and all ought equally to be partakers of it. It is a most holy cup, which belongs equally to all; in no way was it provided in order to appease the body's thirst, but to represent a hidden[38] matter so that you may not forget at what price you have been redeemed from the sins of your former life.[39] As often, therefore, as you come together to eat this bread or to drink of this cup, you do not engage in the business of the stomach, but you are mystically representing the death of the Lord Jesus so that the continual memory of him may keep you faithful in your duty until he comes again in person to judge the world.

And so whoever eats this bread or drinks from the Lord's cup in a way other than is worthy of the Lord renders himself guilty of a serious offence[40] because he has treated the Lord's body and blood in a way other than the Lord himself commanded that they be treated. Indeed, the matter that is of all things the most mystical ought to receive pure and reverent treatment, but, so that mistreatment may not occur, let each person first engage in self-examination and testing. And so one whose conscience is clear should eat of that bread and drink of the cup; one whose conscience is not so clear should rather abstain and make sacrifice to his gullet at home. For although the body and blood of the Lord bring salvation, nevertheless for anyone who eats and drinks unworthily they turn deadly and destructive because that person has approached so great a mystery without reverence and with an unwashed soul and has not pondered enough how fearfully one ought to receive the Lord's body.[41] These people will pay the penalty for profaning the mystery as soon as Christ comes.[42] Yet

* * * * *

that he never claims that the bread and cup 'represent' the body and blood of Jesus, but that the Eucharist itself represents Jesus' death and the covenant he made. See eg *Detectio praestigiarum* ASD IX-1 251:427–252:436, 254:504–6. See also chapter 10 nn7 and 28.

38 'Hidden': *arcanae*; Erasmus frequently applies this adjective to Scripture and to matters that may require spiritual interpretation to reveal hidden meanings. Cf chapters 2 nn2 and 13, 12 n15, 14 nn2 and 7 and 15 n70.

39 Cf 1 Cor 6:20, 7:23; 1 Pet 1:18–19; Acts 20:28.

40 'Guilty of a serious offence': *gravi crimine ... obnoxium*. On Erasmus' moral vocabulary and the importance in particular of 'innocence' (*innocentia*), see CWE 44 xvi–xvii, and cf chapters 1 n41 and 3 n12.

41 Chrysostom *In 1 Cor hom* 28.1 (on 11:29) PG 61 233 is similarly concerned with explaining how the Eucharist can lead to condemnation: 'What then? Does the cause of so many goods, the table pouring forth life, itself become judgment? Not from its own nature, he says, but from the will of the one approaching it.'

42 Ambrosiaster *Comm in 1 Cor* (on 11:27) CSEL 81/2 128:18–23 similarly identifies the judgment as the future final one. Each one approaching the Eucharist 'will render an account on the day of the Lord Jesus Christ.'

even in the meantime the penalty of their offence is burdening some, for this explains why so many of you are found to be in ill health, plagued with bad fevers and listlessness, and, yes, many are even dying before their time. These are some beginnings and portents of the judgment to come. But if we were judging ourselves with discernment before receiving [the Lord's body], by no means would we be suffering thus the judgment of the Lord. Yet it is better to be judged here in the meantime than to be condemned on that day. For when, under judgment by the Lord, we are stricken with slight evils, we are not utterly destroyed, but are chastened by the blows so that afterwards we may not be condemned for eternity along with the world.[43] Let none be foolishly deluded if, despite unworthy treatment of this mystery, they should remain physically hale and hearty.[44]

And so, my brethren, when you come together for this banquet, wait in turn for each other so that in accordance with Christ's example you may feast together in equality. But anyone who is so eager for food that a delay would be unbearable should eat at home, not at the mystical and public feast, lest what has been ordained for your salvation become instead an occasion for condemnation. And now about this matter enough has been said. About the other things that relate to it, I shall give guidance in person when I come.

Chapter 12

Now, to say something about the gifts of the Holy Spirit, since not even on these do you sufficiently agree. I want you to remember, brethren, that you were once pagans, and at that time[1] you simply went, however you were led, to dumb and lifeless idols in accordance with your ancestors' superstition.

* * * * *

43 In this passage there are echoes of Ambrosiaster's treatment of the present ills of the Corinthians as a portent of the harsher testing and punishment that will come in the last days to those who have scorned the warning. See *Comm in 1 Cor* (on 11:30) CSEL 81/2 129:13–21.
44 Chrysostom *In 1 Cor hom* 28.2 (on 11:30) PG 61 234 gives much the same warning: 'What, therefore, about those who continue in good health and reach a hearty old age, do they not sin? ... How, therefore, do they not suffer punishment? Because they will suffer there a more serious punishment.'

1 at that time ... superstition] First in 1532; previously: 'At that time you simply went, in whatever direction you were led, to the practice of idolatry in accordance with your superstition.' Erasmus discusses the syntactic difficulties of the Greek text here in his annotation on 12:2 (*cum gentes essetis*).

Then you had error as your leader, now the Spirit of Christ. Now[2] your
former error is not charged against you. Just as then your ungodly conduct
and ceremonies corresponded to your ungodly religion, so now it remains
for you to match your true and holy religion with godly conduct so that
whatever is done among you is done in such a way that it is seen to be
done by the inspiration of the Holy Spirit.[3] Whatever is said or sung[4] to
the glory of Christ has proceeded from his Spirit. Therefore, I would not
have you unaware that no one inspired by the Spirit of God the Father
curses Jesus his Son;[5] and no one is genuinely able to call Jesus Lord except
through the inspiration of the Holy Spirit. Whatever goodness is in you,
therefore, you owe to his beneficence, and for his glory it ought to be
employed.

Although the Spirit is the same for all, nevertheless its gifts are diverse;
through its inspiration it apportions some gifts to some, other gifts to others,
as it wishes. And the services performed through these gifts are variously
assigned, although the Lord who distributes the tasks is the same for all.
Indeed even the efficacy and power of the Spirit act and flourish[6] differently
in different people, yet there is nevertheless one God common to all, and
from him proceeds the power to do all things which, one way or another,
are accomplished in individuals. To God, therefore, the one author, we owe

* * * * *

2 Now ... against you] Added in 1532
3 Ambrosiaster *Comm in 1 Cor* (on 12:2) CSEL 81/2 131:1–8 similarly explains
   Paul's purpose in mentioning the Corinthians' pagan past.
4 For singing as well as speaking under the influence of the Spirit, see 1 Cor
   14:14–15.
5 The qualifiers 'Father' and 'Son' do not appear in the text of 12:3; Erasmus' use
   of them may reflect the exegesis of patristic authors, who saw a Trinitarian
   emphasis in the three verses that follow. See Chrysostom *In 1 Cor hom* 29.3
   (on 12:5–7) PG 61 243–4; Theophylact *Expos in 1 Cor* (on 12:5–6) PG 124 712C–D;
   and Ambrosiaster *Comm in 1 Cor* (on 12:4–6) CSEL 81/2 133:13–134:3.
6 See the annotation on 12:6 (*divisiones operationum*), where Erasmus notes that
   the Latin *operatio* 'activity' or 'working' is not quite adequate to render the
   Greek ἐνέργημα, which he explains as 'a certain force or effectiveness, by
   which God acts in us.' So in the paraphrase on the verse he avoids *operatio*
   and renders the notion of the efficacious working of God by *vis* 'force,' *effectus*
   'performance' or 'effectiveness,' and *actus* 'accomplishment' or 'action.' The
   paraphrase also avoids here the verb *operari* 'work,' which the Vulgate uses to
   translate the Greek verb ἐνεργεῖν 'work' both in 12:6 and also in 12:11. In the
   note on 12:6, Erasmus suggests instead *agere* 'act' or 'put in motion,' the verb
   he supplements here in the paraphrase with *vigere* 'flourish.' In his translation
   of both 12:6 and 12:11, Erasmus renders ἐνεργεῖν by *efficere* 'bring about' or
   'accomplish.' Cf the paraphrase on 12:11 with n16.

all the gifts,[7] whether they are ordinary or exceptional, and there is no reason why anyone on this account should be proud.[8] What he has is due to another's favour, and whatever has come by the inspiration of the Spirit has been conferred for the common good, not for private arrogance.

To one there has come through the Spirit of God the ability to give faithful and judicious counsel through wise speech. Again, to another has come by the kindness of the same Spirit the ability to promote the commonwealth's interest because of his knowledge of liberal learning and affairs;[9] to another by the inspiration of the same Spirit has come the strength of faith that moves even mountains from their place, according[10] to the promise of the Lord; to another through the same Spirit has come the power to heal disease. Someone has been given the remarkable power to perform miracles; someone has received the gift of prophecy for explaining things that are either still to come or in some other way difficult to

* * * * *

7 For Erasmus' emphasis on God as the source of grace, see Sider 'Grace' 21; also 'Χάρις' 250–1.

8 Cf, however, Chrysostom *In 1 Cor hom* 29.2–3 (on 12:4–12) PG 61 243–5 and Theophylact *Expos in 1 Cor* (on 12:4–7) PG 124 712B–713A, where Paul's emphasis on the diversity of gifts is interpreted mainly as consolation for recipients of lesser gifts rather than deflation of those who are proud of what they consider greater gifts.

9 Erasmus' reference to the Christian community as *respublica* 'commonwealth' is striking. The term was used by the Romans for the 'body politic,' the 'state' as the collective interests of its people. Erasmus' treatment of the gift of knowledge (12:8) suggests the influence of the Ciceronian principle that the state's interests are best served by men of broad learning, and the correlative principle that the proper use of learning lies in governing the state and serving the common good. See eg Cicero *De re publica* 1.2.2–8.13, 3.3.5–6; *De officiis* 1.6.18–19; *De oratore* 1.5.6–19, 3.21.80; and cf n32 below. The word translated 'affairs' here (*res*) suggests matters of public business. The word translated 'liberal learning' (*disciplinae*) probably refers to the subjects or 'disciplines' of learning or culture, but it also sometimes means 'instruction' (see chapter 14 n36), and sometimes 'orderly conduct' or 'way of living.' Thus, Coverdale (fol xxxiii verso) translates it here 'rules of good order.' Cf the paraphrase on 12:28 with n31, and the paraphrase on 13:2. Ambrosiaster *Comm in 1 Cor* (on 12:8) CSEL 81/2 134:9–13 applies the gift of knowledge (*scientia*) to 'divine matters,' while the previously mentioned gift of wisdom (*sapientia*) comes not from scholarship but from the Spirit's brilliance and enables one 'to discern what ought to be avoided and what followed.'

10 according ... Lord] Added in *1532*. The allusion to Jesus' promise in Matt 17:20 and 21:21 also appears in Chrysostom *In 1 Cor hom* 29.3 (on 12:9) PG 61 245 and Theophylact *Expos in 1 Cor* (on 12:9) PG 124 713B. Cf also 1 Cor 13:2 and Erasmus' paraphrase on it.

understand;[11] someone else has been given the ability to discern with prudent judgment whether instances of inspiration in human beings have proceeded from God or from elsewhere;[12] again, another has received this endowment, to speak in various tongues[13] although he is but a single person, a gift that makes no small contribution to the knowledge of the sacred books;[14] another, the gift either through inspiration or skill in the arcane writings[15] to interpret or explain what the former have spoken. For it is not the case that whoever commands a tongue also commands the hidden meaning of the speech.

There is no cause here for anyone either to feel self-satisfaction, since the things he has are not his own; or to feel self-reproach, since the distribution depends on the will of the Holy Spirit. This Spirit, as the one and only maker,[16] bestows all these different endowments, however diverse, upon

* * * * *

11 'In some other way difficult to understand': *alioquin abstrusa* ie the mysteries or hidden meanings of Scripture. For this understanding of the prophet's tasks, see n30 below.

12 Cf 1 John 4:1. On the word translated 'instances of inspiration' here, *afflatus*, see chapters 1 n53, 2 n13, and 11 n14.

13 Paul speaks in 12:10 of the gift of 'kinds of tongues,' probably meaning glossolalia or ecstatic speech, but understood by many patristic sources to be 'different foreign languages' such as the 'other tongues' spoken spontaneously at Pentecost by the disciples in Acts 2:4. See eg Chrysostom *In 1 Cor hom* 29.1 (on 12:1) PG 61 239 and 35.1 (on 14:1–3) PG 61 296, and Theophylact *Expos in 1 Cor* (on 12:10) PG 124 713C. That Erasmus uses the modifier *varius* 'different' or 'various' may indicate that he too is using *lingua* here in the sense of 'foreign language.' In his paraphrase on the fuller discussion of speaking in tongues in 1 Corinthians 14, moreover, Erasmus frequently describes 'tongues' as if they were 'foreign languages' even where Paul appears clearly to distinguish between the two types of speech. See chapter 14 nn10, 11, and 34. It is the practice of this translation, nevertheless, to render *linguae* as 'tongues' wherever it cannot be certain that Erasmus has foreign languages in mind.

14 With this clause Erasmus points unmistakably to the biblical languages, Hebrew, Greek, and Latin, whose importance for the interpretation of Scripture he stressed in his *Apologia contra Latomi dialogum* CWE 71 37–84. See also the paraphrase on 14:15 with n17.

15 'Arcane writings': *arcanarum litterarum*. By this term Erasmus may have in mind the Holy Scriptures; if so, then he appears to identify the gift of interpreting tongues with the gift of prophecy, which he regularly understands as the ability to explain the hidden meanings of Scripture. See n11 above and n30 below. On *arcanus* 'hidden' or 'concealed' as a term associated with Scripture, cf chapters 2 n2, 11 n38, 13 n3, and 14 nn2 and 7; also *Ecclesiastes* I ASD V-4 106:530 and CWE 50 99 n64.

16 'Maker': *opifex*. Cf the paraphrase on 12:6 with n6 above. In identifying the Holy Spirit as 'maker,' Erasmus may also be alluding to Gen 1:1–2.

different people, imparting to each as seems best to it, but in such a way that, because of your mutual charity towards each other, the endowments of individuals are common to all, and the diversity leads to harmony and decorum, not to division.

Why should what we see to be true of the physical body be any less true of the mystical body of Christ? Each person's body, although it be one, has nevertheless been joined together from different members, but in such a way that the same spirit[17] imparts the gift of life to all the members; and these members, although individually they are many and diverse, yet all together are one body. Christ wished it to be just the same in his body. Inasmuch as we are all equally partakers of baptism, we have been joined together through the same Spirit common to all into the same body, whether Jews or Greeks, slave or free, male[18] or female, married or single, powerful or humble. We have all drunk the same Spirit,[19] although it expresses its force differently in different people.

The body does not consist of one member only but of many, and these as diverse as can be. Now, if the foot, debasing itself, should say, 'I am not a hand and have nothing to do with the rest of the body,' is it therefore no part of the body? And if the ear, lamenting its lot, should say, 'I am not an eye and am not related to the rest of the body,' would it therefore be no part of the body? Difference in position[20] or use does not bring a member into ill repute since the variety itself leads to the well-being of the

* * * * *

17 The Latin word *spiritus* 'spirit' means, first of all, 'breath' and may refer here to the vital principle of life infused throughout the body's members and uniting them. Cf the paraphrase on 12:27 below. Cf also Gen 2:7 and Virgil *Aeneid* 4.336. For the role of *spiritus* in Erasmus' anthropology, see Payne 'The Hermeneutics of Erasmus' 23; also chapters 1 n24 and 2 n22.

18 male ... humble] Added in 1532. Cf Ps 49:2 and Gal 3:28. Erasmus may also have in mind here the equal treatment Paul gives Christian wives and husbands in 1 Cor 7:2–5, 10–16, 32–4.

19 'We have all drunk the same Spirit': *eundem spiritum hausimus omnes*. Although the reading of 12:13 in the texts of both the Greek and the Vulgate varies (cf Weber 1782), Erasmus follows here his own translation of 12:13 rather than his Vulgate. Erasmus translated (from 1519) 'we have all drunk one Spirit'; the Vulgate of 1527 reads 'we have all in one Spirit drunk.' In his annotation on 12:13 (*in uno spiritu potati sumus*), Erasmus notes that both Ambrose (ie Ambrosiaster) and Augustine support his translation.

20 Chrysostom *In 1 Cor hom* 30.2 (on 12:16) PG 61 252 summarizes with a similar statement: 'Whether or not [some part] belongs to the body does not arise from the fact that different parts are located in different places, for this constitutes a difference of place only.' See also Theophylact *Expos in 1 Cor* (on 12:16) PG 124 717A.

whole body. Whatever function is given to each member, this is given for aiding the whole body. The eye is a distinguished part of the body, but if the whole body were an eye, where will the ears be? Again, if the whole body were an ear, where will the nose be? Foreseeing this, God joined the body together out of diverse members and assigned to each member its proper place and proper function, not according to the members' merit, but according to his own decision.[21] If these members, now many and diverse, were reduced to one member, say a nose or an eye, where would the body's harmony be?

Now this is not the case; but although the members individually differ from each other, nevertheless because they share the same soul they are nothing other than one body so that no member can be disdained by the other members, no matter how humble it is. For the eye, as a superior part of the body, and as if a more intimate organ of the mind, cannot say to the hand, as if to a cruder[22] member: 'I have no need of your aid.' Nor again can the head, although it is the palace[23] of the mind, say to the feet, as if to the lowest parts: 'I care nothing for your service.' So far is any member of the body from being despised that on the contrary those that seem the feebler are the ones rather that we consider necessary and to which we devote special care. Those that are commonly regarded as less honourable are the ones we outwardly[24] more abundantly honour, and those that seem a little uncomely are the ones on which we bestow more comeliness, as if through courtesy compensating for what otherwise seems deficient; nor are we unaware that the whole body is dishonoured by the disgrace of any one member. For those of our parts that are inherently comely, such as a face or a hand, do not need additional adornment although our private parts are covered and adorned with clothing. By this design has God the creator tempered and blended the whole body with a certain harmony of the different parts so that any part that seemed to lack some honour (although

* * * * *

21 Erasmus' word for expressing God's will here is *arbitratus*, which denotes the 'power of choice' and the 'capacity for judgment.' Its contrast with *meritum* 'merit' perhaps hints at the theological debate over the role of merit or good works in salvation. For this debate, see Oberman *Harvest* 167–8 and 192–3. For a brief summary of Erasmus' views on the role of merit in justification, see Roland Bainton *Erasmus of Christendom* (New York 1969) 188–9.
22 On Erasmus' psychology and the role, in particular, of *crassus* 'crude' in it, see chapter 2 n22.
23 'Palace': *regia* ie the royal residence
24 outwardly] Added in 1532

no part of the body by nature is without honour)[25] might out of courtesy receive more honour. Clearly, the purpose was that the members should not become divided against themselves since there is not one whose use is not needed, but that all with equal care and a shared sense of responsibility might in turn watch over each other, lest through division the body collapse and all perish while each promotes its private interest.[26] Nay, rather, if any advantage or disadvantage comes to this or that member, they all think it belongs to themselves; or if anything afflicts one member, all members are afflicted together; or if any honour comes to any one member, they all rejoice for themselves.

Will you not at least from this example stop striving among yourselves, whom the Spirit[27] of Christ has joined together more tightly into one than the same physical breath has joined the members of a body? How can it be that nature has more power than grace? Are you not the body of Christ, or at least some part of its members?[28] He has arranged these members in his body, which is the church,[29] in such a way that he has assigned to each its proper place, to each its proper function. In the first place he has

* * * * *

25 Cf Theophylact *Expos in 1 Cor* (on 12:25) PG 124 721A: 'For nothing is by nature without honour or nobility.' Chrysostom *In 1 Cor hom* 31.1 (on 12:22–23) PG 61 258 similarly notes that Paul refers only to a seeming lack of honour, not one that springs from nature: 'Nothing in us is without nobility; for it is a work of God.'

26 Cf the explanation of Chrysostom *In 1 Cor hom* 31.2 (on 12:25) PG 61 259: 'If [those parts that lack honour] had not gotten from us great provision, they would have been reviled since they did not have assistance from nature, and having been reviled they would have perished; if they had perished, the body would have split apart; and with the body split apart, even the other parts that are far greater than these would have perished.'

27 Spirit] First in 1532; previously 'baptism.' Cf the paraphrase on 12:12 with n17. Erasmus' change here strengthens the analogy between the physical body and the church as the body of Christ by focusing attention on the life-giving and unifying power of 'spirit' in both.

28 Erasmus explains μέλη ἐκ μέρους 'individually members of it' (12:27 RSV) similarly in his annotation on 12:27 (*membra de membro*): Paul 'says this because the Corinthians were not all the members of the body, but some part of the members.' So also Chrysostom *In 1 Cor hom* 32.1 (on 12:27) PG 61 264: 'The church [at Corinth] is part of the Church which is everywhere in the world, and of the body which is constituted by all churches'; similarly Theophylact *Expos in 1 Cor* (on 12:27) PG 124 721D.

29 For the specific designation of the church as the body of Christ, see Col 1:18, 24 and Eph 1:22–3. Cf the paraphrases on 1 Cor 6:8 and 13 with nn25 and 37, and on Col 1:18 and 24.

stationed apostles, who as stewards of the gospel's grace perform the role of Christ; in the next place he has stationed prophets, either to disclose what is still to come or to explain what is hidden;[30] in the third, teachers endowed with erudition and liberal learning,[31] to bestow what they have for the common benefit; in the fourth place those endowed with the power to restrain the force of demons and to make the name of Christ illustrious through miracles; in the fifth, those who are capable of removing disease. Following these are others who by their authority and counsel can help the afflicted, those who by their good judgment have unusual ability to keep the multitude dutiful.[32] In the last place those who by their skill with tongues can be of use to the rest.[33]

This variety not only urges you, but even compels you towards mutual harmony in that you each in turn need the help of others. Not all are apostles, are they? Not all prophets? Not all teachers? Not all are endowed

* * * * *

30 Ambrosiaster *Comm in 1 Cor* (on 12:28) CSEL 81/2 141:5–12 explains the ecclesiastical roles of apostle and prophet similarly: 'He placed therefore apostles, who are the ambassadors of Christ, as head in the church ... We should understand "prophets" under a twofold category as both those who tell what is to come and those who reveal the Scriptures.' For Erasmus' conception of prophecy's role, cf the paraphrases on 12:10, 13:2 with n4, and 14:1 with n1. See also Eph chapter 4 n20 and CWE 50 99 n64.

31 'Erudition and liberal learning': *litteris ac disciplinis*. *Litterae* 'letters' suggests literary pursuits, scholarship and 'book learning,' or, more generally, 'culture'; *disciplinae* 'disciplines' suggests the subjects of academic learning, although Coverdale (fol xxxiv verso) again gives the word its moral sense, 'rules of good order'; see n9 above. Ambrosiaster *Comm in 1 Cor* (on 12:28) CSEL 81/2 141:23 describes these teachers as ecclesiastical instructors of children. Chrysostom *In 1 Cor hom* 32.1 (on 12:28) PG 61 265 and Theophylact *Expos in 1 Cor* (on 12:28) PG 124 724B distinguish teachers from prophets by the fact that the former draw material from their own minds whereas the latter draw from the Spirit alone.

32 Again, Erasmus seems influenced by Ambrosiaster's description of the spiritual callings. In *Comm in 1 Cor* (on 12:28) CSEL 81/2 142:9–10 Ambrosiaster describes the κυβερνήσεις (Vulgate *gubernationes*) 'administrators' (12:28) as 'governors who by spiritual reins serve as a lesson for the people,' ie serve as a restraining force upon the people through the example of their own self-restraint. Behind this image of the constraining and moderating 'governor' may be such classical descriptions of the ideal statesman as that of Cicero in *De re publica* 1.29.45 and 2.29.51 and of Virgil in the *Aeneid*'s first epic simile (1.148–53). Cf n9 above.

33 See the paraphrase on 12:10 above, where Erasmus considers the usefulness of both the speaker in tongues and the interpreter of tongues. See also nn13–15 above.

with the power [to work miracles], are they? Do all have the ability to heal?
Do all speak in diverse tongues? Do all have the gift of interpreting? By
no means, but they each have their proper gift. No one ought to be disdained, but nevertheless all must strive to merit access to the gifts that are
pre-eminent among these, and always to advance towards the better ones.
For nobody's endowment has been assigned with the stipulation that hope
of better ones is ruled out. These are gifts of the Spirit (lest we claim anything here for ourselves), but it is by our effort and our prayers that the
Spirit is usually called forth to give and[34] to protect and increase what it
has given. These are excellent gifts I have described, but ones that could be
found in people who are not particularly godly. But I shall disclose something that surpasses all these, and that should be the chief object of your
striving since without it these gifts of which I have spoken, and which you
pursue as if they were the only ones, have no power.

Chapter 13

It is a splendid thing to speak in tongues, and on this account you are especially pleased with yourselves. But although I should speak in all tongues
– not only in those of human beings, but also in those of angels (to use
an expression for the sake of emphasis)[1] – and yet should have no eagerness to benefit my neighbour and bestow God's gift for the common good,
I would be as useless as brass cleaving the air with hollow clatter, or a cymbal striking ears with useless clinking.[2] But if there should be granted as

* * * * *

34 and ... has given] Added in 1532

1 Cicero uses the same verb, *exaggerare* 'build up,' 'magnify,' 'make more important,' to describe the heightened rhetoric of the grand style of speech in
   contrast with the humble and moderate styles. See *De oratore* 3.27.105; *Orator*
   59.192; *Brutus* 17.66. See also the annotation on 13:2 (*charitatem non habeam*)
   ASD VI-8 252:659–60, where Erasmus discusses the figurative nature of Paul's
   . speech here: 'Angels do not have a tongue, but this has been added through
   supposition for the sake of emphasis [*exaggerandi gratia*].' The same point is
   made in Chrysostom *In 1 Cor hom* 32.3 (on 13.1) PG 61 268 and Theophylact
   Expos in 1 Cor (on 13:1) PG 124 725A–B.
2 The Latin style becomes heightened at this point with balanced phrases, allit-
   eration, and assonance: *aes* 'brass,' *aerem* 'air,' *aures* 'ears,' *inani strepitu* 'with
   hollow clatter,' *inutili tinnitu* 'with useless clinking.' By 'brass cleaving the air
   with hollow clatter,' Erasmus probably intends the percussive sound or din of
   a gong, or perhaps clinking armour. With the images here compare Erasmus'
   description of Dodonean bronze in *Adagia* 1 i 7. Erasmus explains the image

well something more splendid than this, say the gift of prophecy, through which to grasp all the hidden meanings[3] of divine Scripture[4] (if, that is, any one mortal has been granted a grasp of all things), if there were added a complete knowledge of all the fields of learning,[5] finally if such strength of faith were added that with its help I could also move mountains from their place, yet should charity be lacking, in vain are those things at hand that are of profit to no one. If there were available[6] so great a gift for offering assistance that I would expend the whole of whatever resources[7] I have to feed the needy, yes, and if for relieving the oppressed I would expose my body to all perils, even to the point of being burned, yet (if this is possible)[8] should charity be lacking, that is, a soul thirsting to do good

* * * * *

of the 'clinking cymbal' with reference to Dodonean bronze in an annotation on 13:1 (aut cymbalum tinniens). In the same note he emphasizes the constant and incessant nature of the sound and suggests applying Paul's comparison of speaking in tongues with 'clinking cymbals' to 'those who sing or recite in the churches sacred words that are unintelligible.'
3 'Hidden meanings': arcanos sensus. Cf chapter 12 n15.
4 For this understanding of 'prophecy,' see chapters 12 n30 and 14 n1. Chrysostom and Theophylact also consider the phrase 'and understand all mysteries' as explicative of 'prophecy.' See eg Theophylact Expos in 1 Cor (on 13:2) PG 124 725B: 'not simply "prophecy," but most of all the pre-eminent [form of prophecy], the one that knows all the mysteries'; similarly Chrysostom In 1 Cor hom 32.3 (on 13:2) PG 61 269.
5 'Fields of learning': disciplinarum. On this word see chapter 12 n31.
6 available] First in 1532; previously 'available to me'
7 whatever resources] quicquid facultatum, first in 1532; previously the less specific quicquid rerum 'whatever things.' The change acknowledges a correction Erasmus introduced in 1519 to his annotation on 13:3 (distribuero in cibos pauperum). In 1516 the annotation reads τὰ πάντα μου as the Greek text of 13:3 ('And though I bestow all my goods' [AV]) and explains it as omnia mea 'all my things.' This is the reading he appears to have in mind when he paraphrases quicquid rerum. In 1519 he corrects his annotation by noting that he finds πάντα τὰ ὑπάρχοντά μου 'all my means' or 'possessions' in some manuscripts. In fact, the Greek text printed with Erasmus' Latin translation reads (all editions) πάντα τὰ ὑπάρχοντά μου, and his Latin translation reads omnes facultates meas.
8 Cf the annotation on 13:2 (charitatem non habeam) ASD VI-8 252:668–254:737, where Erasmus argues that Paul does not mean that true faith and prophecy and the other spiritual gifts can exist without charity, but represents the supposition of spiritual gifts separable from charity only in order to heighten and exaggerate the necessity of charity; similarly Chrysostom In 1 Cor hom 32.5 (on 13:3) PG 61 270 and Theophylact Expos in 1 Cor (on 13:3) PG 124 728A. In the same note Erasmus suggests that sola fide may mean not 'by faith alone,' but

even without reward, then I draw no profit from my endowments. Only
charity fully shows how you should use your gifts, and it would be futile
to possess them if you did not know how to use them.

The other gifts suffer corruption from ambition, from malice, from
dissension; from all of these evils charity is far away. The other gifts each
have their own special usefulness, but charity cannot be corrupted, and
in use it has the widest application. Charity keeps a gentle disposition[9] in
the face of injuries sustained and is also accommodating and courteous
in the everyday associations of life.[10] Charity does not know how to envy
anyone, but pours out even its own goods upon others. It is not impudent,
but defers to all; it is not puffed up, but lowers itself before everyone;
it thinks nothing unseemly for itself provided it gives benefit;[11] it is not
eager for its own personal advantage; it is not provoked by injury, and
is so far beyond returning injury for injury that it does not even think
about revenge;[12] and it is so far removed from wickedness that not even

* * * * *

'by faith especially' or 'pre-eminently.' Thus charity and charity's works are
not excluded, even if it is not through them that Christians receive justification (cf ASD VI-8 254:737–256:793).

9 For charity's 'patience' (cf 13:4 AV, RSV) Erasmus uses *lenis animus* 'gentle
disposition' or 'mildness.' Cf the annotation on 1 Cor 13:4 (*charitas patiens
est*), where he prefers this Latin phrase to the more common *longanimis* 'long-
suffering' or *magnanimus* 'great-hearted.' *Longanimis* is Valla's preference. See
Annot in 1 Cor 13 (I 867).

10 This sentence paraphrases two words of 13:4: 'patient' (the first clause; see
preceding note) and 'kind' (the second clause). In his translation Erasmus follows the Vulgate in translating χρηστεύεται by *benigna est* 'is kind'; cf the annotation on 13:4 (*benigna est*): the Greek word suggests 'courtesy and considerate
behaviour ... True godliness does not know how to be arrogant.'

11 Erasmus follows his own translation of the Greek ἀσχημονεῖ 'act unseemly'
rather than the Vulgate *ambitiosa* 'ambitious,' which sense, he says in his annotation on 13:5 (*non est ambitiosa*), can scarcely be found in the Greek. He
does, however, allow that the end of the previous verse, 13:4 ('is not puffed
up' [AV]), seems to apply to 'ambition.' The opening of the current paragraph,
paraphrasing 13:4–7, may reflect that observation. Erasmus suggests his interpretation of ἀσχημονεῖ follows the Greek scholiast (PG 118–19 833D–835A) and
is not unlike that of Theophylact. See *Expos in 1 Cor* (on 13:5) PG 124 728C–D;
likewise Chrysostom *In 1 Cor hom* 33.2 (on 13:5) PG 61 278. On the scholiast as
Pseudo-Oecumenius, see CWE 56 13 n1.

12 This clause paraphrases the final clause of 13:5: οὐ λογίζεται τὸ κακόν '[charity]
thinketh no evil' (AV). In his annotation on 13:5 (*non cogitat malum*), Erasmus
(from 1516) accepts with Valla *Annot in 1 Cor 13* (I 867) the interpretation 'does
not impute evil to anyone or entertain evil thoughts about anyone.' In 1519 he

in someone else does it put up with unrighteousness,[13] but takes delight rather in sincere and undesigning behaviour. In its eagerness to help there is nothing it does not suffer, no matter how harsh; nothing it does not believe, so far is it from forming wrongful suspicions about anyone. It does not easily despair of anyone, but in unfaltering hope bears with all people and with the expectation of amendment most steadfastly endures.[14]

In short, charity ceases nowhere. Even[15] though after this life the need for service will be removed, charity towards souls will nevertheless remain. Here meanwhile, wherever you progress, charity everywhere attends you, as a gift always present and spread throughout the whole life of Christian people whether prophecy happens to be abolished, tongues cease, knowledge becomes obsolete[16] through the growth brought by greater progress. For what we understand from these gifts up to this time is imperfect; neither have we come to know the mysteries in full nor do we understand

* * * * *

adds the explanation, 'whether because it measures everyone by its own mind or because it does not strive for vengeance.' For the paraphrase here, Erasmus chooses this latter interpretation that the specific evil Paul has in mind is that of retaliation. This is also the interpretation of Theophylact *Expos in 1 Cor* (on 13:5) PG 124 729A. For Erasmus' concern with the sin of retaliation, cf his annotation on Rom 12:21 ('do not be overcome by evil') CWE 56 343–4.

13 This clause paraphrases the beginning of 13:6: '[Charity] does not rejoice at wrong' (cf RSV). The sequence of thought Erasmus has in mind seems elliptically expressed in the paraphase and might be filled out in this way: 'So far is charity from wickedness that not only do charitable persons not harbour it in themselves, but they do not put up with unrighteousness even in others.' So, in Coverdale's translation: 'So farre from doyng wrong herselfe, that she cannot in other abyde it' (fol xxxv recto). Erasmus departs here from the interpretation of Chrysostom *In 1 Cor hom* 33.5 (on 13:6) PG 61 281 and Theophylact *Expos in 1 Cor* (on 13:6) PG 124 729B, both of whom take the 'wrong' charity does not tolerate in 13:5 as an injury or injustice suffered, rather than committed, by another.

14 Theophylact makes a similar point in *Expos in 1 Cor* (on 13:7) PG 124 729C: 'It does not despair of the loved one, but hopes he is always advancing to something better.'

15 even ... meanwhile] Added in 1532. Cf the annotation on 13:13 (*maior autem horum*), where Erasmus added in 1535 a discussion of the word 'now' as it relates to the permanence of faith, hope, and charity: although the genuine love of God and neighbour will never cease, nevertheless the function of charity in which we benefit our neighbours 'will cease in the world above, where there will be no one who needs to be helped by the service of another, although in this life there is no one who does not need the help of a neighbour.'

16 'Becomes obsolete': *antiquabitur*. On this verb, see chapter 1 n60.

them in full through prophecy. Accordingly, when that which is perfect
has come, that which is now partial will in some way be abolished. The
Christian religion has its own stages; it has its own ages and progress of
ages, just as nature does.[17] When I was a child, I spoke as a child, I felt as
a child, I thought as a child. But when I became a man, I cast away childish
things, now applying my mind to better things, while gradually I advance
towards the highest. If this goal is not granted in this present life, nevertheless I must practise here in order to attain the goal in the life to come.
Indeed, it is an ever-so-small amount that we now perceive through these
endowments, and this, not at all clearly, but as if in the mirror of faith we
gaze upon only the images of heavenly things; and from the Scriptures, as
if through a veil of mystery,[18] we make inferences about the mind of God.
But when perfection comes, then shall we contemplate the realities themselves face to face. Now in some way I know in part; then I shall know
God in person, just as I am known by him. For to be known by him is to
be loved, and the more precious each one is to God, the more fully and
intimately shall each enjoy the ineffable knowledge of him.

But in the meantime, although the rest of the gifts, which serve the
propagation and strengthening of faith, will cease as if useless once faith has
been established firmly enough,[19] nevertheless in the meantime, faith, hope,
and charity remain – faith, by which we see from a distance the immortality
to come; hope, by which we trust that we will share in it; charity, by which
we return to God the love he so deserves from us, and for his sake love
our neighbour.[20] These three surpass all the other gifts, but nevertheless

* * * * *

17 See chapter 3 n1.
18 'Veil of mystery': *involucrum aenigmatis*. The same phrase is translated 'cover
of allegory' in the paraphrase on Mark 4:29 CWE 49 61, where Erasmus uses
it to describe Jesus' method in telling parables. On *aenigma* 'riddle,' see CWE
44 236 n15. Cf the discussion of the uses of scriptural allegory in *Ecclesiastes*
III ASD V-5 250:133–65. The last of these uses is to guide Christians by stages
to the perfect knowledge of God; nevertheless, Erasmus advises, without the
fiery inspiration of the Holy Spirit all things remain as if in dreams. For
allegory's role in Erasmian exegesis see Payne 'The Hermeneutics of Erasmus'
35–49.
19 Cf Erasmus' annotation on 13:13 (*maior autem horum*): 'Certain gifts that were
necessary in the beginning stages of the church now cease, such as the gift of
tongues, healings, foreknowledge of the future, and the remaining miraculous
powers, which are superfluous to people strengthened in faith since signs
were given to those without faith, not to those with faith.'
20 Cf Matt 22:37–9; Lev 19:18. See Augustine *De doctrina christiana* 1.22.20–1 and
3.10.16 CSEL 80 18–19 and 89 for the form of the commandment by which one

among these themselves, charity is foremost since to it we are indebted even for faith and hope, or at least without it not even they are efficacious for salvation.[21]

Chapter 14

Nevertheless, these things that we preach in such a grand style about the pre-eminence of charity do not mean that the remaining endowments are to be neglected or despised. You should strive after charity in such a way that meanwhile you approve and respect none the less the kinds of tongues or the interpretation of speech, although you should exert more effort for that which is more useful, namely, to prophesy, explaining the mystical sense[1] for the well-being of your hearers. Indeed, one who speaks only in a tongue does not speak to human beings, to whom he contributes nothing with his

* * * * *

loves one's neighbour for God's sake or loves God in the neighbour. Cf n15 above.

21 Cf, however, the somewhat different treatment Erasmus gives faith and charity in relation to salvation in two annotations – in effect short treatises of theological explication – added in the 1535 edition of the *Annotations*. In the annotation on 13.2 (*charitatem non habeam*), he considers two related questions: whether the other spiritual gifts, faith in particular, can really exist separate from charity, and what is meant by justification *sola fide* 'by faith alone.' The note argues that Paul speaks only figuratively, or by supposition, about the other gifts' existence apart from charity, that the doctrine of justification by faith alone is not meant to exclude love, but only to deny the efficacy of human philosophy, ceremonies, and laws, and that justification is indeed by faith and not by works, but Paul nowhere separates faith from charity and charity's works. See also n8 above and cf the paraphrase on Phil 3:10–11 with n35. In his annotation on 13:13 (*maior autem horum*), he considers, among other topics, the relative importance of faith and charity; he emphasizes the priority and necessity of faith (without which the other gifts, including charity, can be neither given nor received) but also the ubiquity and necessity of charity (without which no gift is pleasing to God). For a discussion of this latter note and a denial of Lutheran influence upon it, see Jerry Bentley *Humanists and Holy Writ: New Testament Scholarship in the Renaissance* (Princeton 1983) 190–1.

1 'Mystical sense': *mysticum sensum*. On *mysticus* 'mystical,' see chapter 10 n7. For the definition of 'prophecy,' see chapters 12 n30 and 13 n4, and cf Erasmus' annotation on 14:1 (*sectamini charitatem, aemulamini spiritualia*): 'Here, by prophecy Paul means not the prediction of the future, but the interpretation of divine Scripture.' Ambrosiaster *Comm in 1 Cor* (on 14:4) CSEL 81/2 150:22–5 similarly defines prophecy as the revealing of the Scriptures' hidden meaning.

voice, but speaks to God, whom he praises with words not understood. For as far as others are concerned, what difference does it make whether he remains silent or whether, although speaking, he is not understood? Like one inspired by the Spirit, he utters secrets,[2] which, although he personally may understand them, surely he communicates to no one, and although he may be of benefit, he benefits no one except himself alone. In vain,[3] therefore, does someone speak in the church, if he is heard by no one, and he is not heard if he is not understood. Spiritual discourse, moreover, is not understood unless you receive the more concealed meaning that the heavenly Spirit has signified to us by those words. But no human being can do that except by the special gift of the Spirit.

Conversely, one who performs the duty of a prophet speaks not only to God, but to human beings as well. And it is not just a single advantage that he brings them: at the same time as he is summoning the evil-doers to a better life,[4] he is also goading the sluggish towards vigilance, and lifting up and comforting the faint-hearted. See what a great difference there is between one gift and another. One who speaks in a tongue benefits only himself individually. But one who explains the mysteries of Scripture through the gift of prophecy benefits the whole congregation. Now the more widely available a good is, the worthier it is. And so let me repeat what I had just said: you should not despise the gift of tongues; in itself it is a great thing, and it comes from the Holy Spirit. I want all of you to speak in tongues if it seems right; nevertheless, I would rather you excel in the other, which is a worthier gift. For one who takes the prophet's role is greater than one who speaks sacred words in tongues, uttering words understood by no one unless perchance[5] the one who has earlier spoken in tongues should presently interpret what he has said so that the people may gain at least some profit. Indeed, there are some who do not even

* * * * *

2 'Secrets': *arcana*. On this word, see chapter 2 n2.
3 In vain ... of the Spirit] Added in 1532
4 Paul says in 14:3 that the prophet speaks to people for their 'upbuilding' (RSV) or 'edification' (AV). He evidently means at this point the edification of people within the church, as verses 4–5 go on to suggest. Erasmus interprets Paul to mean the reformation of sinners, and he may be looking ahead to 14:24–5, where Paul turns to prophecy's reformative effects upon outsiders or unbelievers. Cf the paraphrase on those verses.
5 'Perchance': *forte*. The adverb appears in the Vulgate text, but Erasmus omits it in his Latin translation and suggests in the annotation on 14:5 (*nisi forte interpretetur*) that the word neither appears in Greek commentaries nor adds anything to the sense of the passage.

themselves sufficiently understand the sounds they produce with their lyric tongue.[6]

On the other hand, from words that are understood some profit can in one way or another be taken. Imagine a different situation, where I have come to you now for the first time and speak nothing other than in tongues. What advantage would I bring you unless I speak and then immediately disclose the secret message[7] for you through the gift of revelation, or unless through the gift of knowledge I eruditely explain matters that pertain to the apprehension of the faith, or through the gift of prophecy disclose hidden meanings, or through the gift of teaching explain something pertinent to good moral behaviour? Indeed, even inanimate instruments, such as a pipe or a harp, although they have been designed for nothing other than making sounds, nevertheless unless they make definite and distinct sounds, which by definite harmonies and rhythms make known either the subject of the song or the disposition towards which the song invites – that is, if they merely make sounds – what profit or pleasure will the listener receive, since he will not discern what kind of song is being played on the harp or pipe, whether it is joyful or mournful? Again, if a trumpet gives an indefinite signal and does not distinguish by the playing itself whether it bids the troops to join battle or whether it sounds a retreat,[8] what does it matter that the trumpet blasts, when the soldier does not understand where he is being summoned?

It is likewise with you. When speaking in tongues, unless you utter a sound representing something definite to your listeners, you will speak without profit since what is said cannot be understood. And so the utterance of the speakers will not penetrate the minds of the listeners, but will only strike the air with the empty din of its words.[9] It is easy to see that

* * * * *

6 Cf Theophylact *Expos in 1 Cor* (on 14:5) PG 124 736D: the gift of interpretation 'was given to some who were speaking in tongues, but not to others.' Erasmus' reference to 'lyric tongue' (literally 'plectrum of the tongue') anticipates the musical analogy Paul introduces in 14:7–8 for unclear and incomprehensible utterance. In the annotation on 14:2 (*spiritus autem loquitur*), he cites Ambrosiaster's statement that speaking in an unknown tongue is a function of spirit rather than of reason or understanding. See *Comm in 1 Cor* (on 14:2) CSEL 81/2 150:7–10.

7 'Secret message': *arcanum*. On this word, cf n2 above.

8 Chrysostom *In 1 Cor hom* 35.2 (on 14:8) PG 61 298 and Theophylact *Expos in 1 Cor* (on 14:8) PG 124 737B similarly develop the analogy of the military trumpet.

9 Cf Erasmus' critique of liturgical chanting in his own day in the annotation on 14:19 (*quam decem milia*). In the first version of the note (1516) he complains that

there are a great many kinds of languages[10] in the world, and each of them has its own set of sounds.[11] The sounds can indeed be perceived by all, but if there is nothing but sounds, each of us will speak to the other in vain. Indeed, although each of us speaks his language correctly, nevertheless, since neither understands the other, it turns out both that I, who speak Greek, am a babbling foreigner to the African, and that he in turn is a foreigner to me since I am ignorant of African. Accordingly, you also, Corinthians, will at my urging (for of your own accord you pursue and exalt gifts characterized by miraculous speech) concentrate upon the greater gifts so that you may be of use to the whole congregation.

Whoever, therefore, has received the gift of tongues should entreat God with prayers that the gift of interpreting be granted also. Otherwise, if I should pray in a language unknown to the people[12] – Persian, say,

* * * * *

interminable chanting has virtually ousted healthful sermons so that 'only a jingling of voices strikes the ears.' In *1519* he adds the observation that nothing but 'a din of voices' fills most monasteries, colleges, and churches, and that the articulation is so bad that 'mere sound strikes the ears.' Cf also the paraphrase on 13:1.

10 'Kinds of languages': *linguarum genera*. In 14:10–11 Paul illustrates the problem of unintelligible speaking in tongues with the analogy of unfamiliar foreign languages. To refer to these languages he uses the word φωναί 'voices' (or sometimes 'languages') perhaps because in his discussion of spiritual gifts γλῶσσαι 'tongues' or 'languages' (Latin *linguae*), already refers to 'ecstatic speech' (Conzelmann 236). The usual Latin equivalent for φωνή is *vox* 'voice,' as Erasmus recognizes in the annotation on 14:10 (*genera linguarum*), and he corrects the Vulgate's *genera linguarum* to *genera vocum* in his own translation. The paraphrase, however, follows the Vulgate here in using *linguarum*. It should be noted, however, that the distinction between γλῶσσα/*lingua* and φωνή/*vox* for Erasmus is probably not a distinction between ecstatic speech and a foreign language (as it seems to have been for Paul), but between a foreign language and oral communication in general. Throughout the paraphrases on chapters 12–14, Erasmus seems to understand 'tongues' as unfamiliar foreign languages. See chapter 12 n13, and nn12 and 34 below. On the meaning of *vox*, see the next note.

11 'Set of sounds': *vox*. By this term (equivalent to the Greek φωνή) Erasmus seems to mean something like 'oral communication' or a system or set of vocal sounds broader and more basic than a 'language.' He explains in the annotation on 14:10 (*genera linguarum*) that Paul is speaking not only about languages (*linguae*), but about all kinds of vocal utterance, and that some peoples communicate by vocal means other than languages, eg hissing or shrieking sounds.

12 Paul, having introduced in 14:10–11 the analogy of speaking an uncomprehended foreign language (φωνή), returns in 14:13–14 to the discussion of the

among Greeks – or worse, if I[13] should utter speech which is unknown to me no less than to others (as some do, who enjoy singing the words of a song they have learned in a foreign language, although not even they themselves who sing it know what it means),[14] my spirit indeed and my breath produce the words of prayer, but my mind remains without profit. I benefit myself either not at all or very little, and to others as well I am vexing or even ridiculous,[15] and not only useless.[16] What then should I do? I shall pray with my voice when the occasion calls for it, but not content with this, I shall pray with heart and mind as well. I shall sing the praises of God with the instruments of the voice, but not content with this, by bringing knowledge of the language,[17] I shall sing with the mind as well.

Otherwise, if you chant the praises of God in speech that no one knows, how will someone taking the people's part[18] respond with the customary 'Amen' at the end of your thanksgiving? For the intonation of this

* * * * *

spiritual gift of ecstatic utterance (γλῶσσα). Erasmus, however, continues to amplify the text with reference to foreign languages, as if there were no distinction between tongues and foreign languages. Cf the previous two notes and n34 below, and chapter 12 n13. Erasmus' amplification of 14:14 is closely modelled on patristic interpretations. See nn14 and 16 below.

13 I ... to me] Corrected in 1521 from 'you ... to you.' The second person is obviously incongruous with the rest of the sentence.

14 Erasmus is apparently alluding to church music in the liturgy of his own day. Cf n9 above. Cf also Ambrosiaster *Comm in 1 Cor* (on 14:14) CSEL 81/2 153:6–7, which cites Latin-speakers who enjoy chanting in Greek without knowing what the sounds mean.

15 or even ridiculous] Added in 1532

16 Chrysostom *In 1 Cor hom* 35.3 (on 14:13–15) PG 61 299–300 calls those who speak only in an unknown foreign language useless not only to others, but to themselves as well: 'For if anyone speaks only in Persian or any other foreign language, but does not know what he says, he will then henceforth be a barbarian even to himself, not only to someone else'; similarly Theophylact *Expos in 1 Cor* (on 14:14) PG 124 740C.

17 Erasmus the philologist notes that 'praying with the mind' necessitates linguistic knowledge and skill. This amplification of 14:15 echoes Erasmus' frequent argument that proper study of the Scriptures required the study of Greek and Hebrew, as well as Latin. See eg Epp 149:22–30, 182:209–22, 337:653–7 (to Maarten van Dorp); *Ratio* Holborn 181:15–18; *Apologia contra Latomi dialogum* CWE 71 41–3. Cf chapter 12 n14.

18 This is the interpretation of τὸν τόπον τοῦ ἰδιώτου suggested in Chrysostom *In 1 Cor hom* 35.3 (on 14:16–17) PG 61 300 and Theophylact *Expos in 1 Cor* (on 14:16) PG 124 741A. In his annotation on 14:16 (*quis supplet locum idiotae*), Erasmus gives two meanings for ἰδιώτης: a common person not holding an office

word confirms what has been said in the prayers and hymns.[19] Indeed you know that this pageant,[20] so to speak,[21] is performed with various roles. The learned sing first; the unlearned and general populace, confirming their approval for what has been said, as if with one voice call out 'Amen.' Who, however, will call out [this response] if he does not know what you say? It is a holy thing that you pronounce, and for you perhaps[22] it has some value, but meanwhile the people are in no way made better. Yet it is for this that they assemble, that from the speech of the educated they may return home better, and that in a public setting they may learn how they ought to live in their private lives.

Now lest anyone suppose that I do not much favour the gift of tongues because I am unskilled in tongues[23] (just as everyone generally admires and extols the qualities in which his own strength lies, but scorns and belittles different ones),[24] I am grateful to God that in this gift I surpass all of you, who flatter yourselves on this point especially. For there is among you no kind of speech that I do not both speak and understand.[25] And so

* * * * *

and someone unlearned or uninstructed. Modern commentators offer various interpretations of the phrase; Orr and Walther eg take 'the uninstructed' as 'outsiders, nonmembers' (303); Conzelmann, as 'laymen,' ie those without the gifts of speaking in tongues or interpretation (239).

19 Similarly Ambrosiaster *Comm in 1 Cor* (on 14:16) CSEL 81/2 153:23–154:2

20 'Pageant': *fabula*. The word means 'story' (Greek μῦθος) or 'play' (Greek δρᾶμα). The word appears in the latter sense in the paraphrase on Mark's narrative of Jesus' 'triumphal entry' into Jerusalem, specifically in the paraphrase on Mark 11:7 CWE 49 36: 'The apostles played a supporting role in this act [*fabulam*]' – a passage attacked by Béda, apparently because of its associations with fictive narratives or enactments. See Erasmus' defences in *Elenchus in N. Bedae censuras* LB IX 504A–B and *Supputatio* LB IX 654A–C. In the latter, Erasmus explains that *fabula* does not necessarily imply fictitiousness but simply means in this context 'a sort of performance to be viewed, and consisting of various roles ... such as is customary in solemn festivals.' For the Incarnation as 'play-acting,' see Erasmus' annotation on Rom 8:3 ('after the likeness of the flesh of sin') CWE 56 201. Elsewhere the theatre provides Erasmus with a pejorative image for the vanity of pharisaical teaching and scholastic theology. See eg Ep 1062:36–8 and the paraphrase on Mark 4:2 CWE 49 56 with n4.

21 so to speak] Added in *1532*

22 perhaps] Added in *1532*

23 Or perhaps 'in languages.' See chapter 12 n13 and nn10 and 17 above.

24 This explanation paraphrases Theophylact *Expos in 1 Cor* (on 14:18) PG 124 741B.

25 Erasmus' paraphrase on 14:18 seems close to the Vulgate reading: 'I speak in the tongue of all of you.' In the annotation on 14:18 (*omnium vestrum lingua*

it is not through envy, but through good judgment that I prefer the gift
of interpretation to the gift of tongues, which it is more proper to use in
private than in solemn assembly. In the church and the company of saints I
would rather speak ever so few words, but in such a way that I understand
my message and cause the others as well to understand me, than to utter
ten thousand words in a way that not one of the others understands, and
perhaps not even I myself.

Therefore, brethren, since, as I have said,[26] godliness has, so to speak,
its own stages and progression of growth, endeavour to abandon lesser
gifts and advance to greater ones so that you may not seem perpetually
to be children. There are endowments that are suited to those newly consecrated to Christ; there are ones that befit those already more advanced.
Indeed,[27] I want you perpetually to be children in respect to the simplicity and innocence of your moral behaviour, but in the endowments of the
mind I would have you continually advance until you reach the highest
stage. It is not enough now for you not to harm anyone, but you must
strive earnestly, as adults now, also to be effective in being of help to
everyone.[28] It is natural for children to marvel at things ever so trivial, and
to be enormously pleased with them.[29] But age causes them later, when
they vie for greater goods, to care little for the things they used to boast
of earlier. Christian faith likewise has its elementary stages,[30] in which it
is unseemly to grow old. That this is so, even God himself once testified,
speaking in this manner through the prophet Isaiah: 'With various tongues
and different lips I shall speak to this people, and not even so will they
hear me'.[31]

* * * * *

loquor), however, he argues instead for the reading that is now generally accepted: 'I speak in tongues more than all of you' (NRSV).
26 See the paraphrase on 13:11 and chapter 3 n1.
27 Indeed] Added in 1532
28 A similar distinction between a 'negative' and a 'positive' goodness was developed by Cicero in his discussion of justice in De officiis 1.7.20–2 and 1.10.31.
29 After a similar comment on children's interests, Chrysostom In 1 Cor hom 36.1
(on 14:20) PG 61 305 adds that 'those who had the gift of tongues thought they
had the whole thing, although in fact it was the lowest of the gifts.'
30 Cf 1 Cor 3:1–3 and the paraphrase on 3:1.
31 Cf Isa 28:11–12. Erasmus notes in the annotation on 14:21 (in aliis linguis) that
Paul expresses the sense more than the actual words of Isaiah and in a form
closer to a Hebrew version than to that of the Septuagint. Note that Erasmus
also omits Paul's attribution of the statement to the 'Law,' which apparently
refers, not just to the Torah, but to the whole of the Hebrew Scriptures (Orr
and Walther 303 and Conzelmann 241–2).

Therefore, although the gift of tongues is of little concern to those who believe, it proved useful at the origins of the primitive church in order that by this wonder unbelievers might be stirred. But on the other hand, the gift of prophecy benefits not only unbelievers so that they may repent,[32] but also believers so that they may become daily more steadfast and in essence better people. It ought, therefore, to be very clear how little advantage there is in the use of tongues since sometimes it even causes obstruction and offence.[33] For suppose now that the whole congregation has come together, and all are talking at the same time in different, but unfamiliar languages[34] – one in Hebrew, another in African, a third in Asian – and meanwhile there come into your meeting other Christians who are unacquainted with the languages, or even unbelievers, likewise unacquainted with the languages. When they hear the great confusion and din of the different voices, understanding none of them, will they not declare that you have taken leave of your senses and in your crazed state are thus speaking absurdities? On the contrary, if through the gift of prophecy someone is teaching, another admonishing, another exhorting, another comforting,[35] and meanwhile there arrives at your meeting some uninstructed stranger, or even an unbeliever, and he both understands your speech and is understood in turn, does he not, as he recognizes true godliness in you, condemn the superstition he sees in himself and abhor his own ungodly ways when compared to your godliness? He is wholly revealed to himself while he

* * * * *

32 'They may repent': *resipiscant*. On this word see the Argument n15.

33 Erasmus' interpretation of 14:22 suggests Chrysostom *In 1 Cor hom* 36.1–2 (on 14:22–25) PG 61 307–8 and Theophylact *Expos in 1 Cor* (on 14:22) PG 124 744A–B. Chrysostom is at pains to explain the seeming contradiction between Paul's statements that speaking in tongues is a sign for unbelievers (14:22) and yet that unbelievers will also judge speakers in tongues to be mad (14:23). He concludes that the purpose of speaking in tongues as a 'sign' to unbelievers was to astonish the unbelievers, but that without interpretation it often served as an obstacle for their further progress, especially in the case of unbelievers who lacked knowledge or discernment. Chrysostom grants that for discerning believers, eg Cornelius in Acts 10, 'signs' could bring profit beyond mere astonishment. Chrysostom also argues that when Paul says prophecy is not for unbelievers, he does not mean that prophecy does not benefit both unbelievers and believers.

34 Cf Chrysostom *In 1 Cor hom* 36.3 (on 14:22–5) PG 61 309, where the speaking in tongues Paul depicts in 14:23 is also assumed to be a confusion of different languages. See also nn10, 11 and 12 above and chapter 12 n13.

35 Cf Paul's description of the effects of prophecy in 14:3 and Erasmus' paraphrase on that verse.

hears from you instruction[36] in true religion; he sees that until now he has remained far removed from it, and he is conscious of those faults that your speech abjures. The result at last is that, as he has been changed into a different man and repents, he falls face down upon the ground, acknowledging and openly witnessing that you have truly been inspired by the Spirit of God and do not speak[37] in the manner of pagan madmen[38] who have been seized by a demonic frenzy and utter voices understood neither by themselves nor by others, issuing sound without meaning.

What then, brethren, ought to be done? As often as you come together in a public meeting, each person brings with him his own gift: one has a mystical[39] psalm by which he is pleased to sing God's praise; another has a teaching by which he can educate people to order their lives; another has a revelation so that he may draw out the hidden and profound meanings in Holy Scripture; another has been endowed with the gift of a tongue.[40] None of these is to be despised, but all are to be applied to the public advantage in the public assembly, but in such a way that no disturbance or confusion arises. Let those who are endowed with the gift of tongues also be given their place, but in such a way that only two speak in any one meeting place, or at most three, and then not at the same time, but by turns. Again, let them not speak by themselves, but let there be someone present to interpret to the

* * * * *

36 'Instruction': *disciplinam.* For other senses of this word, see chapter 12 n9.
37 do ... speak] This verb was added in 1532.
38 'madmen': *phanaticorum* (= *fanaticorum*). The word derives from *fanum* 'shrine' or 'temple' and means 'inspired,' frenzied,' or 'demented.' Cicero refers to philosophers who defend the Delphic Oracle as *superstitiosi et paene fanatici* 'superstitious and half-crazed' (*De divinatione* 2.57.118). Livy uses it of bacchants drugged by sleeplessness, wine, and nocturnal clamour (39.15.9). Tacitus refers to Druids as *fanaticum agmen* 'a fanatical horde' (*Annales* 14.30). Erasmus' contrast between Christian prophets and pagan fanatics was suggested perhaps by Paul's earlier comparison of tongue-speakers to seeming madmen (14:23): unbelievers, coming upon a congregation of tongue-speakers, would think them insane (14:23), but coming upon a congregation of prophets, they would acknowledge their true inspiration.
39 'Mystical': *mysticum.* On this word, see chapter 10 n7. Here the word seems to refer to Erasmus' notion of a 'psalm' as a text allowing spiritual interpretation in order to reveal its soteriological, and specifically Christological, significance. Cf CWE 44 216 n12. For an example of this approach to the psalms see Erasmus' interpretation of Psalm 2 CWE 63 79–80. For the term 'mystical psalm,' see also the paraphrase on 2 Cor 4:13.
40 The paraphrase omits the final gift Paul lists in 14:26: 'an interpretation' (RSV).

people what they have said. One interpreter will suffice for two or three of those endowed with the gift of a tongue, because there is no need to utter many words in tongues. But if there is no interpreter skilled in tongues, there is no reason to speak in the assembly; let the one who has nothing except the gift of tongues use his gift, but in private where he may sing to himself and to God. In the assembly it is public business that is tended.

In the same way let not all the prophets speak, but two or three, and then by turns, but let there be present some who have the gift of discerning instances of prophetic inspiration, whether they be true or not,[41] so that they may challenge anything spoken that is unworthy of Christ's Spirit. But if while someone is speaking, one who is sitting nearby begins to interrupt as one inspired by God, let the earlier speaker become quiet so that there may be no confusion of voices. For it now appears that what the earlier one was seeking has been disclosed to the other since he has intervened through inspiration and under[42] the impulse of the Spirit. And if this be done, then you all can prophesy, provided that you do so in turns, and one yields the turn of speaking to the other. The teaching would then yield greater profit for all as, one by one, they report before the whole company what God has inspired. And all would be refreshed with a richer consolation while they each impart upon all what the Spirit of Christ has inspired.

There is no reason to allege in excuse that those who are divinely inspired are not in command of themselves, as we see to be the case with the frenzied. It is far different with the inspiration of Christ, which impels the mind in such a way that you remain none the less under your own power, whether it is speech that is called for, or silence. This is a healthy inspiration and nothing other than the impelling of a godly mind towards things that are seen to redound to the glory of God. All the more ought this inspiration to serve the common tranquillity and be all the farther removed from contentiousness because it proceeds from God, who is the author of peace, not of disturbance and division.[43] Since such freedom from contention is

* * * * *

41 Ie whether the inspiration comes from God or elsewhere. Cf the paraphrase on 12:10 with n12.

42 and under ... Spirit] Added in 1532

43 In 14:32–3 Paul connects the prophet's control over his spirit with God's encouragement of peace and harmony. Erasmus connects it as well with Paul's earlier admonitions regarding contentiousness and strife within the Corinthian church (1:10–13). Theophylact *Expos in 1 Cor* (on 14:32–3) PG 124 748B–D interprets the passage similarly.

observed in all the assemblies[44] of the saints,[45] it is right that it likewise be observed in your meetings, if you wish them to be seen as saintly, so that while you do not dissent from the rest in religious profession, you might not seem to differ from the rest in practices.

And for this very reason let your women keep silent in solemn assembly lest, since the sex is prone to the vice of garrulousness,[46] an unseemly disturbance arise. For indeed they have not been permitted to preach in public as authorities, but have been instructed to be subject to their husbands. For thus in Genesis God says to the woman: 'You will be dependent upon the man,[47] and he will have dominion over you' [3:16]. Therefore, let them acknowledge this law not only by covering their heads,[48] but also by keeping silence, which in that sex is a most seemly adornment.[49] Someone will say: 'Do you deprive women of their tongue to the extent that not even for the sake of learning or inquiring do they have the right to speak?' I utterly forbid it in public, but if there is anything that they do not sufficiently understand, and they wish to learn, they may ask their husbands at home. In this way neither will they be cheated of learning, nor will there be any unseemly conduct. For it is an utterly unseemly spectacle to see a woman speaking in a public gathering of saints, when even in the profane meetings of pagans this is considered disgraceful.[50] Why is it, Corinthians, that you

* * * * *

44 'Assemblies': *conventiculis*, Erasmus' paraphrase here for ἐκκλησίαι 'churches,' as distinct from *conciliabula* 'meetings' in the next clause and *coetus* 'gathering' in the paraphrase on 14:35

45 Modern interpreters have generally reassigned the concluding phrase of 14:33 'as in all the churches of the saints' (RSV) to verse 34 (the directive regarding women's silence). Erasmus' paraphrase agrees with his patristic sources, the Vulgate, and his own Latin translation in reading it as the conclusion of Paul's encouragement of orderly worship in verses 26–33.

46 The same explanation appears in the paraphrase on 1 Tim 2:11 CWE 44 17.

47 This may seem an odd paraphrase for Gen 3:16, '... your desire shall be for your husband' (RSV), but the Vulgate version of the verse reads *sub viri potestate eris*, '... you will be under the power of your husband.'

48 See 1 Cor 11:5–15. Ambrosiaster *Comm in 1 Cor* (on 14:34–5) CSEL 81/2 163:4–6 and 164:4–5 also connects the directive regarding silence with the earlier one regarding head coverings.

49 For the image of women's behaviour as an 'adornment,' see 1 Pet 3:3–5.

50 The perceived absurdity of women's participation in the public assembly formed the basis of Aristophanes' *Ecclesiazusae* 'Assemblywomen.' See also Roger Just *Women in Athenian Law and Life* (London and New York 1989) 13 and 34–6 and Jane E. Gardner *Women in Roman Law and Society* (Bloomington and

think it a burden to observe a practice that all the rest observe?[51] Was it from you that the gospel first proceeded so that the others ought to be compelled to follow your way? Or was it to you alone that the gospel came? But if you are neither the first to hold the religion of Christ nor the only ones, why does it bother you to accommodate yourselves to the practices of others?

If anyone among you seems to be a prophet, or otherwise endowed with spiritual gifts, let him acknowledge that the things I write you are not my directives, but the Lord's. But if anyone through contentiousness acts just as though he does not know, and scorns these directives as if they were human biddings, let him not know at his own peril – to be[52] unknown in turn by God. It is not my part to contend; it is enough to have given warning. And so, brethren (to bring this discourse to an end), strive for the gift of prophecy, which is by far the nobler gift, but in such a way that those who have been granted no other gift may not meanwhile be prevented from speaking in tongues, provided that, just as I have instructed, all things be done in both decent and orderly fashion so that no disgrace or disturbance may arise.

Chapter 15

Now I hear, brethren, that some of you are in doubt about the resurrection of the dead. These are people who cannot yet be persuaded because they

* * * * *

Indianapolis 1986) 264–5. Erasmus' rationalization perhaps draws on Livy's account of Roman women's public demonstration in the early second century BC against the Oppian Law, which restricted their public display of wealth. Cf, in particular, the passage from a speech Livy attributes to Cato in support of the law and other restrictions on women's public conduct: 'What sort of practice is this? Running out into the streets and blocking the roads and speaking to other women's husbands? Could you not have made the same requests, each of your own husband, at home?' (34.2.9–10). Cf also Valerius Maximus 8.3.

51 Cf 11:16 and the paraphrase on that verse.

52 to be ... God] Added in 1532. The addition is apparently a concession to the Vulgate reading at 14:38: 'If anyone does not know [this], he will be unknown.' See Ambrosiaster *Comm in 1 Cor* (on 14:38) CSEL 81/2 162:10: 'That person who does not know that the things the apostle speaks are the Lord's will himself also be unknown by the Lord on the Day of Judgment.' For his Latin translation, Erasmus preferred to read the second verb as active subjunctive ('let him not know'), as Chrysostom and Theophylact had also. See Erasmus' annotation on 14:38 (*ignorat, ignorabitur*). This reading was criticized by Latomus. See Erasmus' reply in *Apologia contra Latomi dialogum* CWE 71 53.

are still swollen with human philosophy.[1] There is no need for me to teach
you anything new; I only recall to your memory the gospel that I first
passed on to you,[2] and that you once embraced, in which also you have been
persevering until now, and by whose help you obtain salvation. It would
consequently be superfluous for me to pass on again what has been once
correctly passed on; at the same time it would be wrong for you, if, through
your wavering, you desert what you once embraced, especially since you
know by experience that our gospel is efficacious for your salvation. Yet
the pre-eminent part of the gospel's teaching is belief in the resurrection
of the dead.[3] About this matter there ought to be no debate unless, God
forbid, you have believed in vain. For what was the use of embracing the
gospel if you deny its chief point, namely,[4] that the dead will some day live
again?

You should have especially remembered what I passed on to you – in
the first place by word, and now once again in a letter – and which you once
received. I mean this: that the Lord Jesus Christ died and by his death freed
us from sins, paying on our behalf the penalty our offences had incurred.
Scripture had said many ages before that it would happen like this: that he
would be led to slaughter like a sheep, that he would heal our wickedness

* * * * *

1. In explaining doubt concerning resurrection as a product of philosophical pre-
tension, Erasmus recalls Paul's earlier criticism of the Corinthians' pride in
human wisdom; cf the paraphrase on 1:18–2:16. A long line of early Christian apologists and polemicists had defended the doctrine of bodily resurrection against philosophic scepticism and opposition. Cf eg Irenaeus *Adversus
haereses* 5.3.2–3 PG 7 1129–32; Athenagoras *De resurrectione mortuorum* 2.1–3.2 in
Athenagoras: Legatio and De resurrectione ed and trans William R. Schoedel, Oxford Early Christian Texts (Oxford 1972) 90–5; Tertullian *De resurrectione mortuorum* 11 CCL 2 933–4; and Origen *Contra Celsum* 5.14, 20–4 PG 11 1201, 1209–
17. See also the paraphrases on 6:14 with n39, also 15:33–4 with n48 below,
and Acts 26:8 CWE 50 142 with n6.
2. Chrysostom *In 1 Cor hom* 38.1 (on 15:1–2) PG 61 322 and Theophylact *Expos in
1 Cor* (on 15:1) PG 124 752C introduce the topic similarly as 'nothing new,' but
needing to be recalled to memory.
3. Similarly both Chrysostom *In 1 Cor hom* 38.1–2 (on 15:1–2) PG 61 321–3 and
Theophylact *Expos in 1 Cor* (on 15:1–2) PG 124 752B–753A identify at this point
the resurrection of the dead as the 'whole point' or 'head' of the Christian
faith. Paul does not introduce the resurrection of the dead as a subject until
15:12. Chomarat I 611 comments on Erasmus' introduction of the subject here
as an example of anticipation for the sake of unity and clarity.
4. namely] Added in 1532

with his bruising,[5] that from the wood of the cross he would reign[6] and break the tyranny of the devil.[7] Besides this, you must hold[8] that not only did he truly die, but he also was buried, and on the third day returned to life.[9] That this as well would happen had already long ago been proclaimed by the oracular words of the prophets so that you might believe all the more that the event has occurred which God through his holy men had promised would happen. For thus Hosea says: 'After two days and on the third day we shall rise again and live in his sight.'[10] And thus David also says: 'You will not abandon my soul among the dead' [Ps 16:10].

* * * * *

5 Paraphrasing Isa 53:7 and 53:5. Ambrosiaster *Comm in 1 Cor* (on 15:3) CSEL 81/2 164:24 similarly cites Isa 53:7. Cf 1 Pet 2:24–5.
6 Ambrosiaster *Comm in 1 Cor* (on 15:3) CSEL 81/2 165:11 cites 'the Lord has reigned from the wood' as the scriptural prediction of Christ's death, apparently referring to Ps 96:10, although the phrase 'from the wood' is not in that verse or in similar ones, such as Pss 93:1, 97:1, and 99:1.
7 For the devil as tyrant, compare the paraphrase on John 12:31–2 CWE 46 155 with n35; also the paraphrase on Rom 5:19 CWE 42 36.
8 you must hold] Added in *1532*
9 'Returned to life': *revixerit. Reviviscere* is one of three Latin verbs Erasmus uses in the paraphrase on this chapter to express 'rising up.' In his Latin translation of 1 Corinthians 15 (as in the Vulgate), the Greek passive or middle ἐγείρεσθαι 'to be raised' or 'to awake' is consistently rendered by the Latin intransitive *resurgere* 'to rise again.' The fuller style of the paraphrase, however, accommodates variety of expression, and Erasmus frequently, as here, substitutes for *resurgere* the intransitive *reviviscere* 'to return to life' or 'to live again,' eg in the paraphrase on 15:12 below. And he regularly employs the transitive *excitare* or *suscitare* 'to raise [or stir] up' or 'to awaken' for ἐγείρειν in its active sense, to express God's agency in the act of resurrection, eg in the paraphrase on 15:15 below. Cf the paraphrase on 6:14. Throughout this translation of the paraphrase on this chapter, I have sought to reflect carefully the variety of Erasmus' verb choices. For an interesting discussion of the active, neutral (or middle), and passive senses of the noun ἀνάστασις 'resurrection,' see Erasmus' annotation on Rom 1:4 ('from the resurrection of the dead of Jesus Christ'). The active and neutral senses apply to Jesus' resurrection (it is equally proper to say 'the Father raised the Son' and 'the Son raised himself'). Only the passive sense, however, is proper in reference to the dead in general, who can only be raised through the agency of God or Christ (CWE 56 23–4 and nn40 and 41). See also the annotation on Rom 13:11 ('to rise from sleep') CWE 56 357–8 and on Rom 14:9 ('he died and rose again') CWE 56 376–7.
10 This is the version of the text of Hos 6:2 quoted in Ambrosiaster *Comm in 1 Cor* (on 15:4) CSEL 81/2 165:23–5. The Vulgate differs slightly.

And so that you might believe more surely, I taught you in addition to this how, when he had been brought back to life, he offered himself to be seen by many, first by Cephas, then by the twelve,[11] and that after this he appeared to more than five hundred brethren gathered together. Most of these are alive to this day, if anyone should doubt the trustworthiness of the report. Some of them have died. After this he was seen by James, who was called the brother of the Lord and was the first to fill the high office of bishop at Jerusalem.[12] Then he was seen by all the disciples,[13] not only the

* * * * *

11 In his annotation on 15:5 (*et posthac undecim*) Erasmus defends the definite article and this number against the Vulgate's reading ('eleven'). He does so on the basis of Greek manuscripts and (after *1519*) the readings of Augustine and Theophylact. Erasmus suggests that the term 'the twelve' is by synecdoche appropriate for the chosen disciples of Christ, even after one of them (Judas) had fallen away and his replacement had not yet been chosen (Acts 1:26). Nevertheless, Béda attacked the paraphrase here for its reference to 'the twelve' and also for Erasmus' failure to explain what he meant by 'the twelve.' In response, Erasmus criticized Béda both for his refusal to read the *Annotations*, where the desired explanation had been provided, and for his failure to understand the nature of a paraphrase, where explanatory comment is not permitted. See *Supputatio* LB IX 684C–685B, *Divinationes ad notata Bedae* LB IX 475A–B, and *Elenchus in N. Bedae censuras* LB IX 507F. See also n13 below.

12 Cf Chrysostom *In 1 Cor hom* 38.4 (on 15:7) PG 61 326: 'That is, it seems to me, his brother, for Jesus himself is said to have laid his hand on him and ordained him and made him the first bishop of Jerusalem'; similarly Theophylact *Expos in 1 Cor* (on 15:7) PG 124 756C. Eusebius *Historia ecclesiastica* 2.23 narrates an account of James' martyrdom and says James was assigned the bishopric in Jerusalem by the apostles. Erasmus does not consider the term 'brother of the Lord' to refer to an actual sibling of Jesus; see chapter 9 n14.

13 disciples] First in *1532*; previously 'apostles.' The change was apparently motivated by a complaint from Béda. In 15:7b Paul cites an appearance of the risen Christ 'to all the apostles' (RSV); at issue is the breadth or narrowness of the designation 'apostles.' See the next note. Béda evidently had criticized Erasmus' use of the term 'apostles' here to designate a group larger than 'the twelve.' Erasmus responded that 'apostles' appeared by mistake in place of the more inclusive 'disciples' because of printers' carelessness 'at least in the Froben edition, which I did not assist.' Erasmus also suggested that he was not so ignorant as to suppose that prior to Christ's ascension there were more than twelve 'apostles' (*Supputatio* LB IX 684E–685A). Even the Martens edition of 1519 reads 'apostles' at this place, as do all editions prior to 1532 that I have seen. And Erasmus' response seems to evade the fact that, whichever term he uses here in the paraphrase, he has still taken Paul's citing of an appearance to 'all the apostles' as a reference to a group larger than the original twelve.

twelve among whom the title 'apostle' originated before it spread to many.[14] After all these, moreover, he was seen also by me, an apostle untimely born, so to speak, who was delivered, at last, after the fully developed offspring, like an imperfect fetus, not so much born as miscarried.

I do not complain because I was the last of all to see the Lord. It is a great thing that I merited seeing him. For I am the least of the apostles and not worthy enough to be called an apostle because I persecuted the church of God, which apostles establish. I was therefore unworthy to be chosen even last for the apostolic rank, but God in his gracious goodness deemed me worthy of this honour although I did not deserve it, so that whatever I am, I am by his gift, not by my own merit. And I have not allowed his kindness towards me to lie idle or unproductive. On the contrary, although I am last in the order of time, nevertheless in the performance of evangelical duty I have proven to be not among the last, but have undergone more labours than any of the other apostles, so that no one may grant me less authority on the grounds that I am the last of the apostles. The very fact that I have laboured, however, I do not claim for myself, but ascribe to the divine beneficence; whatever was done was accomplished by its support.[15]

* * * * *

14 Ambrosiaster *Comm in 1 Cor* (on 15:7) CSEL 81/2 166: 17–23 interprets this resurrection appearance to 'all the apostles' as another appearance to the twelve
   (or eleven) apostles, perhaps as recorded in Matt 28:16 or John 20:26. Erasmus, however, apparently follows Theophylact *Expos in 1 Cor* (on 15:7) PG 124
   756C, who followed Chrysostom *In 1 Cor hom* 38.4 (on 15:7) PG 61 326 in interpreting the term 'apostle' more broadly to include, among others, the 'sev-
   enty' whose mission is recorded in Luke 10:1–20. Béda may have objected to
   this broader understanding of 'all the apostles' in reference to an appearance
   of the risen Christ prior to the ascension. See the previous note. For modern
   opinions regarding this appearance, see Conzelmann 258–9 and Barrett 343.
15 'Support': *praesidio*. The word suggests 'assistance' or 'resources.' Valla *Annot
   in 1 Cor* 15 (I 868) had criticized the scholastic interpretation of 15:10 as a scriptural basis for the category of grace called 'cooperating.' Erasmus noted this
   criticism in early editions of his annotation on 15:10 (*non ego autem, sed gratia
   Dei mecum*), and he (like Valla) corrected the Vulgate's 'the grace of God with
   me' to 'the grace of God which is with me' since Paul assigns 'all the credit
   to God.' In *1527*, however, he added to the note a defence of the scholastic
   position, arguing that 'assistance' is one of the meanings of the Greek preposition σύν 'with' and that God's help does not rule out the individual's effort.
   Jerry Bentley considers this addition to be 'anti-Lutheranizing' (*Humanists and
   Holy Writ: New Testament Scholarship in the Renaissance* [Princeton 1983] 56–7,
   178–9). The paraphrase on 15:10 remained unchanged from the 1519 first edition; it refers to the 'support' of grace not as 'cooperating' with Paul's will,
   but as the means by which Paul's accomplishments come about. For Erasmus'

To return to the issue, therefore, whether they have greater authority in the affairs of the gospel, or I do, we certainly all agree in preaching the same thing, and what we preach with great agreement you have believed as sure and undoubted. We do not disagree [in our preaching]; it remains for you to be constant [in your belief], not now calling back into doubt matters about which you once made up your mind.

But if by the testimony of all the apostles it has been and is being preached that Christ, the prince and author of resurrection, has returned from death to life, with what cheek do some among you say that there is no resurrection of the dead? If there is none, then it follows that not even Christ himself has risen. For to what end was it important for our leader and head to rise again, if he were not going before to prepare the resurrection of his members and to open the way for us all?[16] If Christ did not rise again, then surely our preaching is empty, and empty also is your belief and trust.[17] If we[18] have been persuaded that Christ has returned to life, then it ought to be certain that we also shall return to life, for it was to call us back to life that he returned to life. Otherwise not only will we both have been wasting our efforts – we in preaching, you in believing – but also we will be found out to be guilty of injury against God, about whom we have been wrongly asserting that he raised Christ from death when he did not raise him; and indeed he has not raised him if the rest of the dead do not come back to life. Either both must be believed, or both denied, since the resurrection is the same for the head as it is for the members.[19] If the dead do not rise up, for whose sake Christ was destined to rise, then not even Christ

* * * * *

emphasis on God's grace as support for human efforts, see Sider 'Grace' 23 and 'Χάρις' 251–2. See also Eph chapter 2 n15.

16 Erasmus echoes Theophylact *Expos in 1 Cor* (on 15:13) PG 124 760A: 'Indeed, for whose sake did he arise if he were not intending to be the first fruits of us?' For the metaphor of the head and members, see Eph 4:15–16 and Col 1:18, and cf chapter 6 n25. See also the paraphrase on 15:16 with n19 below.

17 'belief and trust': *credulitas ac fiducia*, Erasmus' paraphrase on πίστις 'faith' (Latin *fides*). See his disquisition on the various shades of meaning conveyed by *fides* and πίστις in the annotation on Rom 1:17 ('from faith unto faith') CWE 56 42–5. The two basic senses involve belief (or assent) and trust (or confidence), here represented by *credulitas* and *fiducia*. Cf n20 below, and CWE 42 xxxvii.

18 we] First in 1532; previously 'you' (pl)

19 Erasmus uses the same clause in the annotation on Rom 1:4 ('from the resurrection of the dead of Jesus Christ') CWE 56 20, where he explains Origen's interpretation of Rom 1:4 and the view that Christ's resurrection would not be complete until the rest of his members had been raised as well and joined to the head. See also the paraphrases on 15:13 with n16 above and 15:20 with n28 below.

has risen up. But if Christ has not risen, you have believed in vain that he arose, and you have believed in vain that through your trust[20] in him you have been made free of your sins. You are therefore still subject to your former sins, and baptism, by which mystically[21] through Christ we come back to life from our sins, for the time being has accomplished nothing.[22]

Indeed, even these who with this confidence have died, and in this hope have offered their necks to the executioners' axes,[23] have utterly perished if there is no hope of restoration to life. But if our entire hope, which we have conceived from Christ, does not extend beyond the end of the present life,[24] not only are we not fortunate, but we are even more wretched than the others, who are strangers to Christ. For they at least enjoy, in some way, the comforts of the present life,[25] while here we are afflicted because of the name of Christ and then after this life shall obtain[26] no reward if we do not return to life fully.[27] But God forbid that anyone should believe so foolishly to his own destruction.

* * * * *

20 'Trust': *fiduciam*, a paraphrase on πίστις 'faith.' See n17 above.
21 'Mystically': *mystice*. On this word, see chapter 10 n7. Erasmus is arguing that believers will in fact be raised from the dead, as Christ was raised, but that, in the meantime, in baptism, they have through Christ come back to life from the spiritual death in which they lived because of their sins.
22 For baptism as an essential, but preliminary, step towards eternal life, cf the paraphrases on 6:8 with n26 and 10:11; also Payne *Theology* 170.
23 Erasmus may have in mind Herod Agrippa's execution of James (Acts 12:2) although the weapon there was not an axe, but a sword or dagger. There may also be an allusion to the beheading of John the Baptist (Matt 14:10); the paraphrase on Acts 12:2 CWE 50 80 associates the two executions. More likely, however, Erasmus is alluding anachronistically to martyrdom in general.
24 Cf the annotation on 15:19 (*si in hac vita tantum in Christo sperantes sumus*), where Erasmus provides a nearly identical paraphrase and cites Theophylact *Expos in 1 Cor* (on 15:19) PG 124 760D–761A in taking 'only' with 'in this life' rather than with 'in Christ' or with 'have hoped.'
25 Cf Ambrosiaster *Comm in 1 Cor* (on 15:19) CSEL 81/2 170:19–20: 'But unbelievers enjoy even this life.'
26 [we] shall ... obtain] First in *1521*; previously 'there will be'
27 'Fully': *toti*, ie 'the whole' of us. Here and in the next two paragraphs (paraphrasing 15:19–24) Erasmus stresses resurrection as a 'full' return to life. Cf the similar emphasis in Chrysostom's commentary, which frequently argues against the Manichaean belief that resurrection involves only an immortal soul's deliverance from sin. See eg *In 1 Cor hom* 39.3 (on 15:19) PG 61 335–6: 'Even if the soul should abide and even if it be infinitely immortal, as truly it is, apart from the flesh it will not receive those secret goods, just as it will also not be punished ... For if the body does not rise, the soul will abide uncrowned outside of that beatitude which is in heaven.' See also Theophylact *Expos in 1 Cor* (on 15:19) PG 124 761A and cf n1 above.

No, indeed, if you believe that Christ has risen – and every godly person does believe this – it follows necessarily that we also shall rise again since in him the resurrection has begun that will be completed in us. And just as he has returned fully to life by taking his body up again, so shall we also return fully to life. The head will not be severed from its members.[28] As prince and leader, he was the first to return to life, as a kind of first fruits of all who die with the hope of resurrection. He has inaugurated the resurrection; others have followed, companions of the Lord's resurrection,[29] and we also shall someday follow. For it must not be doubted that he will fulfil in all his members what he has fulfilled in himself and already in many saints. For we should picture two bodies: one subject to death and deriving from Adam as its head, the other destined for immortality and deriving from Christ as its head.[30] Therefore, just as death once crept in through one man who sinned, spread, as it were, from the head through the members, and now advances against all the rest, so also through one man, free from all sin whatsoever, the resurrection of the dead has been ushered in. Since on account of the offence of Adam alone all we who are descended from him are subject to death, so on account of the innocence of Christ alone all who have deserved to be in his body will be restored to immortality.[31] All will come back to life, but in the order proper for

* * * * *

28 Cf the annotation on Rom 1:4 ('from the resurrection of the dead of Jesus Christ') CWE 56 20: 'His resurrection is completed only when the members of the whole body are joined together with their head. Therefore in Christ resurrection made a beginning, and hope was offered to the members.' See chapter 6 n25 on Christ as 'the head' of the body, and 2 Thess chapter 2 n1.

29 See Matt 27:51–3, where many bodies of saints are said to have arisen during the earthquake at Jesus' death. In his paraphrase on these verses, Erasmus calls these risen saints 'heralds and associates of the resurrection of Jesus' CWE 45 371. In the annotation on Matt 27:52 (*et multa corpora quae dormierant*), he reports the patristic concern to demonstrate that these resurrections were not complete until after Jesus' resurrection, since only then did the bodies exit their tombs. The matter receives fuller treatment in the annotation on Rom 1:4 ('from the resurrection of the dead of Jesus Christ') CWE 56 20, where Erasmus says that Paul's reference to Christ in 15:20 as 'the first fruits of those who have fallen asleep' (RSV) pertains not only to these risen saints, but 'to all the members of Christ in whom Paul is trying to inspire a hope of resurrection.'

30 This paraphrase on 15:21 anticipates 15:44. Ambrosiaster *Comm in 1 Cor* (on 15:22) CSEL 81/2 171:7–12 likewise speaks of Adam and Christ as progenitors respectively of all who are subject to death and all who are granted resurrection.

31 The amplification of 15:21–2 reflects Rom 5:12, 17–19. Cf Erasmus' paraphrase on Rom 5:18 CWE 42 35: 'Just as through the offence of one man sin crept into

each; the first of all is Christ, then those who cling to Christ as members to their head. A considerable number of these have already quit their tombs and risen up together with Christ; the rest will return to life at his last coming.[32]

Once the resurrection of the whole body has been accomplished, nothing will remain except the end of human changes. This will not happen before the tyranny of death has been utterly destroyed and Christ victorious delivers the kingdom, made calm and peaceful, to God the Father, for whom, since the enemies have been vanquished, he claims a dominion that is his own.[33] And [it will not happen] before he has completely driven out from his whole body and reduced to nothing all the authority, rule, and power of his adversaries. For it is necessary that the Son carry on this work of claiming the kingdom for God the Father until such time as he has scattered all his enemies under his feet, overcome in utter destruction, so that there may be no rebellion anywhere, nor fear of evils.[34] It is through sin that death reigns, and through death that Satan reigns. Once sin has been wiped out, death will cease to reign. Although in the meantime we struggle with all our strength to accomplish this, it will nevertheless not happen fully until the final resurrection has vanquished all the power of mortality

* * * * *

the world and rendered all subject to death, so through the righteousness of one man we are made righteous and sharers of life, since his righteousness has been extended to all who believe and submit to the kingdom of life.'

32 See Matt 27:52–3 and the paraphrase on 15:20 with n29 above. Ambrosiaster *Comm in 1 Cor* (on 15:23) CSEL 81/2 172:3–8 similarly gives a twofold interpretation to the resurrection of 'those who belong to Christ' (RSV): the 'many bodies of the saints' that were raised at Jesus' resurrection during 'his first coming,' and the general resurrection of the saints at his second.

33 Cf Chrysostom *In 1 Cor hom* 39.4 (on 15:24) PG 61 337, who explains emphatically that the Son continues to retain the kingdom even after handing it over to the Father, and that the Father possessed it all along as well, for otherwise 15:24 would be understood in a way befitting a human conception of dominion rather than the divine one, and numerous absurdities would arise. From a human perspective, when someone delivers up something into the hands of another, the first one ceases to possess the thing; nor did the other possess it before it was handed over. If we were to understand Paul's text according to this human perspective, we would be left with a Son who ceases to hold dominion once he delivers up the kingdom, and with a Father who did not hold dominion before the kingdom was delivered to him. The absurdities, however, disappear when the verse is interpreted in a way 'befitting deity.' Similarly Ambrosiaster *Comm in 1 Cor* (on 15:24) CSEL 81/2 172.18–173.11. See also the paraphrase on 15:28 with n36.

34 Or 'of evil ones'

– the very last enemy,[35] so to speak, destroyed, the one who was most stubbornly rebelling. For the Father has in this way determined that all things
must be placed in subjection under the feet of the Son, just as it was written
in the Psalms: 'You have placed all things under his feet' [8:6].

And yet when it says that all things will be placed under the feet of
the Son, this ought not to be so interpreted as if, with the Father excluded,
the Son alone is going to possess the kingdom; on the contrary, the kingdom
of the Father and the Son is one and the same. Through the Son the Father
claims for himself this kingdom, which is new and indeed his own,[36] so
that thereby, with passions thoroughly subdued, there may be no rebellion
against the divine will.[37] He holds this kingdom in common with the Son
in such a way that the authority remains in his own power inasmuch as it
is from himself that partnership in the kingdom has proceeded to the Son.
The partnership[38] is so full and complete in the Son that in the meantime he
yields nothing to the Father[39] since the will of both is the same. Therefore,

* * * * *

35 Paul's word for 'enemy' in 15:25–6, ἐχθρός, suggests a relationship of personal hatred. The Latin equivalent, used by the Vulgate, is *inimicus*. For both
his Latin translation and his paraphrase, however, Erasmus prefers *hostis*, a
word whose primary reference is to an 'enemy of the state' or a 'public enemy.' In the annotation on 15:26 (*novissime autem inimica*) he cites Valla's elegant argument for calling death the final *hostis* rather than *inimicus*: death's
nature is not a matter of hatred, but of assault. See Valla *Annot in 1 Cor 15* (I
868).

36 'His own': *peculiare*. In its general sense the word means 'special' or 'singular,' and Erasmus may be referring to the kingdom as 'new and exceptional.'
But since he is concerned throughout this passage with establishing the identity of the Son's dominion with the Father's (cf the paraphrase on 15:24 with
n33 above, I have preferred the more specific meaning, denoting 'one's own
private property.' For *peculiaris*, see also 2 Cor chapter 6 n23.

37 The idea of the passions as rebels to be subdued is a common theme in classical philosophies. See eg Plato *Republic* 439B–443B; Cicero *De officiis* 1.20.68–9;
Seneca *De tranquillitate* 2. For Erasmus' use of the motif, cf *Moria* CWE 27 151
and *Enchiridion* 66 43.

38 Or possibly 'kingdom.' The syntax of the clause would allow either noun to
be interpreted as subject.

39 Or possibly: 'In such a way is the kingdom full and complete in respect to the
Son that nothing meanwhile is taken away from the Father.' The verb *decedere*
'to depart' is often taken with a dative to mean 'to yield' or 'to give way
to,' but the separative dative is also attested with *decedere* in the sense of 'to
be removed from' (Lucretius 2.72; Tacitus *Annales* 15.20; Erasmus *Supputatio*
LB IX 685A). The former sense has been chosen for this translation because
the current sentence seems intended to emphasize the equality of the Son
with the Father, just as the previous sentence (in Erasmus' Latin they are

when all things have been made subject to the Son, then also the Son himself will make himself entirely, that is, with the body, subject to the Father, by whose authority it happened that all things passed into the Son's dominion. As a result, henceforth not even in the members will there be anything that dissents from Christ, and the Son will wholly agree with the Father, upon whom as highest cause all things will depend, and to him as source whatever has anywhere been admirably done will be credited by all.

Since I once passed on these teachings to you, and you received them, why is it that some are once more in doubt whether the dead will come back to life? If there is no hope of this, the ones among you who receive baptism on behalf of the dead (although more from superstition than from piety) have accomplished nothing. They fear that one who has died without baptism will not rise again among the righteous. To prevent this from happening, they provide someone in place of the dead person to answer that he believes and desires baptism. I approve the faith; I do not approve the deed.[40] For although it is absurd to think a dead person may be helped by another's baptism, nevertheless it is quite correct for them to believe there will be a resurrection. For they would not fear for the dead person if they believed he would not return to life. Nay then, even we ourselves act foolishly when we risk our lives everyday for the teaching of Christ, if after the heaviest afflictions no reward will follow. Nor are we merely at risk, but in a way we die day after day, exposed to ever new dangers, and it is not just one kind of death that we undergo. As I am not lying in what I say, so may I always be permitted to glory in this boasting that I have through Christ Jesus our Lord, to whose glory contribute even those very[41] evils we patiently endure. As to the fact that among the Ephesians I have endured such great evils for the gospel of Christ that I have had to do

* * * * *

balanced clauses of the same sentence) emphasizes the maintenance of the Father's authority. Coverdale, however, chose the latter sense: '[The kingdom] is in suche sorte fully and wholy the sonnes, that yet the father loseth nothyng (fol xli recto). On Erasmus' Trinitarian thinking, see the annotation on Rom 9:5 ('who is above all things God') CWE 56 242–9. For the equality of the Son with the Father, compare Erasmus' paraphrase on Col 1:15.

40 Cf Ambrosiaster *Comm in 1 Cor* (on 15:29) CSEL 81/2 175:6–8: 'By this example he does not approve their deed, but shows that their faith is firmly fixed in the resurrection.' Chrysostom *In 1 Cor hom* 40.1 (on 15:29) PG 61 347, however, in ridiculing the Marcionite practice of vicarious baptism, denies that Paul had such a practice in mind; similarly Theophylact *Expos in 1 Cor* (on 15:29) PG 124 768c.

41 even those very] Added in *1532*; previously, 'the' implied in *mala* 'evils'

battle with beasts,[42] as someone bound over to death, what profit will there have been, or what reward, if the dead do not return to life? What madness would it be to be plunged willingly into so many evils if soon after death it should matter not at all how you have lived? If a person's entire hope is bounded by death, what remains except what the wicked say in Isaiah who have lost confidence in promises about a future life and measure the sum total of happiness by the comforts of the present life: 'Let us eat and drink, for tomorrow we die. Whatever we have snatched from life, that alone is ours; after death we are nothing' [22:13]. Perhaps philosophers or false apostles croak old songs of this sort for you,[43] but beware lest they lead you astray by their stories into perilous error, and keep in mind always that true saying of a certain comic poet of yours: 'Bad company corrupts good morals.'[44]

* * * * *

42 Erasmus seems to take Paul's statement in 15:32 literally; most modern commentators assume the language is metaphorical, eg Orr and Walther 336 and 338. In the annotation on 15:32 (*ad bestias pugnavi*), he indicates his surprise that Acts does not mention an incident such as this at Ephesus and declares unsatisfactory the explanation of Theophylact *Expos in 1 Cor* (on 15:32) PG 124 769B–C that Paul refers to his contention with the Jews and Demetrius the silversmith as fighting with 'beasts.' Both Ambrosiaster *Comm in 1 Cor* (on 15:32) CSEL 81/2 176:13 and Chrysostom *In 1 Cor hom* 40.3 (on 15:32) PG 61 350 apparently take Paul to be speaking literally. Erasmus does not appear in the paraphrase on 15:32 to have rendered the curious phrase 'humanly speaking' (RSV).

43 On the twin threat posed by pagan philosophy and false apostles, see the Argument of this *Paraphrase* 19 and 22. There Erasmus identifies the false apostles as 'Judaizers.' In the dedicatory letter (11, 14–15), he describes them more generally as those who teach for their own profit rather than for the glory of Christ and who mix heavenly teachings with human and worldly ones. He proceeds in the letter to lament the corruptions of similarly false apostles in his own day. For Erasmus' critique of ancient and contemporary 'Judaizers,' see chapter 9 n6. Among ancient philosophic traditions Erasmus may have in mind especially the Epicureans, who viewed human nature as completely mortal and argued that after death nothing remained except the constituent atoms now freed for other constructions. See eg Lucretius 3:445–1094. On the corrupting influence of the songs and teachings of pagan poets, prophets, and philosophers, cf Clement of Alexandria *Protrepticus* 1–5 PG 8 49–171. For the term 'false apostle,' see 2 Cor chapter 11 n19.

44 In the annotation on 15:33 (*corrumpunt mores*) Erasmus identifies the comic poet as Menander and the verse as a senarius (iambic trimeter). His Latin translation, repeated here in the paraphrase, attempts to render the verse in a Latin senarius: *mores bonos colloquia corrumpunt mala.* A slightly altered Latin

This distrust arises out of idle and wasteful living. As long as they are uneasy in their conscience, they would rather there not be a resurrection[45] – held by so great a darkness of vices are those who live only for the day. But you, through your zeal not for pleasures, but for righteousness, wake up,[46] and do not lapse with the others into the great evil of distrust. For there are some among you who, although they are puffed up with the arrogance of human wisdom, actually lack the chief part of wisdom because they are unacquainted with God. Although he is all-powerful, they do not believe that by his power the dead can be restored to life. Nor do[47] they notice that it is easier to restore what has fallen into ruin than out of nothing to create what does not exist.[48] It is not with hostility towards you that I say this, but so that out of shame you may be reformed and not listen after this to those who try to make you believe such foolish and such wicked opinions.

Now since it is certain that the resurrection is to come, someone who is too speculative[49] will ask in what manner it will come, or in what sort of body they are going to rise, seeing that these bodies turn into ash or earth or something baser yet. You fool, to marvel that God in raising bodies can perform once that which nature does every day in sprouting a seed![50]

* * * * *

version appears in *Adagia* I x 74: *corrumpunt mores bonos colloquia prava*. Erasmus uses this version also in his paraphrase on the Prodigal Son in Luke 15:13 CWE 48 76. The verse is usually cited as *Thais* fragment 218; see Orr and Walther 336.

45 Chrysostom *In 1 Cor hom* 40.3 (on 15:34) PG 61 351 similarly describes bad conscience as the source for disbelief. See also Theophylact *Expos in 1 Cor* (on 15:34) PG 124 769D.

46 'Wake up': *expergiscamini*. On the meanings of this word, see the annotation on Rom 13:11 CWE 56 357–8. There Erasmus uses *expergisci* to translate ἐγείρεσθαι 'to be raised' or 'roused'; here, to translate ἐκνήφειν 'to return to soberness of mind.'

47 Nor do ... not exist] Added in 1532

48 Erasmus uses a similar comparison between creation and resurrection to prove the credibility of resurrection in the colloquy 'An Examination concerning the Faith' CWE 39 430:5–9 and in *Explanatio symboli* CWE 70 311. See also the paraphrase on Acts 26:8 CWE 50 142 with n6. Cf Chrysostom *In 1 Cor hom* 17.2 (on 6:14) PG 61 141 for an extended version of the contrast. See also chapter 6 n39 and, for the conventional nature of this comparison among the church fathers, n1 above.

49 'Too speculative': *curiosior*. On this term, which suggests the scholastic method, see chapter 2 n30; also CWE 44 66 n15 and CWE 50 8 n38.

50 LB understands the sentence as a question and takes *qui* as the adverb 'why': 'Fool, why do you ... ?' The sentence, however, is not punctuated as a question

You[51] toss a dry, dead seed into the ground; there in turn it seems to have rotted and died, and so at length it springs up out of the ground, as if reborn, and comes back to life. And in no other way does it come back to life unless it has first died and been buried. But the seed is reborn in a form far different from what it had when it was buried in the furrow. A weak, worthless little kernel, black and dry, is dug into the earth; after it has rotted in the mud, in its own time[52] it breaks forth into a tender, young plant, as if coming back to life; next there are stalks, and then a crop of grain. Yet none of these was evident in that tiny kernel that you entrusted to the ground. Each seed has in it its own power, which reveals itself when it has again come forth so that now it seems to be something entirely different even though you are looking at the same thing, but reborn into a better form.[53] Do you see from how small a kernel so great a tree has issued forth? What strength there is in its trunk, what meanderings among its roots, how broad the spread of its branches, what pageantry in its leaves, what loveliness in its blossoms, what richness in its fruits? None of these existed when you were burying that worthless and tiny kernel in the earth. Nevertheless you dared to hope for them all, relying on nature's strength. Do you not dare, relying on God's omnipotence, to hope for the same from God?

It is a kernel that you plant, not a tree, and yet once the kernel has been stirred up, God gives it a body, the kind of body that pleased the very one who has placed deep within the individual kinds of seeds their own special power.[54] By this power, although all things are reborn, yet they are not reborn with the same form. This same thing happens in the race of animate beings. Each has its own seed, and it is not the case that just any animal comes forth from any seed at all. And although it is common to all

* * * * *

in any of the editions published during Erasmus' lifetime, and it seems better to take *qui* as the relative pronoun introducing a characteristic clause.

51 Chomarat I 599–600 uses the passage that follows here to the end of the paragraph (on 15:37) as an example of the detailed and poetic description Erasmus sometimes provides in the paraphrases for the reader's pleasure.

52 in its own time] Added in 1532

53 Chrysostom *In 1 Cor hom* 41.2 (on 15:37) PG 61 356–7 similarly emphasizes that despite appearances the body that springs up is not another body, but the same one that was sown, but now transformed: 'For it is not one essence that is sown and another that rises up, but the same one made better'; likewise Theophylact *Expos in 1 Cor* (on 15:37) PG 124 772C.

54 The paraphrase strengthens the allusion in 15:38 to God's creation of distinct kinds of vegetation in Gen 1:11.

animals to possess a body of flesh, nevertheless there is no little difference
between flesh and flesh. There is one kind of flesh for humans, another for
cattle, another for fish, and another for birds. Likewise in those things that
lack life,[55] although all are said to be bodies, nevertheless there is one form
for heavenly bodies, another for earthly ones, say, for rocks or water or
earth.[56] Indeed, as there is one glory and status for heavenly bodies and
another for earthly bodies, so among the heavenly bodies themselves there
is distinction. First, the glory of the moon is not the same as the sun's, nor
is that of the other stars the same as the moon's.[57] In short, even the stars
themselves have differing degrees of brightness; all do not match the rays
of the morning star.[58]

In the resurrection likewise, all people will come to life again with
their own bodies, but with ones differing in status, undoubtedly in accordance with their individual lot and the merits of their life.[59] The ungodly
will come back to life with one form, the godly with another.[60] And again

* * * * *

55 'Life': *anima*, the vital spirit or breath (Greek ψυχή), the 'soul' in its aspect as
   animating principle, infusing life throughout a body. Cf nn63 and 67 below.
56 In his annotation on 15:40 (*corpora coelestia et terrestria*), Erasmus views Paul
   as referring to the bodies that exist in the heavens (namely, stars, etc) and
   on earth, not to the heavens themselves or to the 'substance of heaven and
   earth.' For more figurative interpretations, see Chrysostom *In 1 Cor hom* 41.3
   (on 15:39–41) PG 61 358; Theophylact *Expos in 1 Cor* (on 15:39–41) PG 124 773B–
   D; and Ambrosiaster *Comm in 1 Cor* (on 15:40–1) CSEL 81/2 179:16–180:19.
57 Cf the annotation on 15:40 (*alia claritas*), where Erasmus (echoing Valla *Annot
   in 1 Cor* 15 [I 869]) also prefers *gloria* 'glory' or *dignitas* 'high status' as a translation for δόξα throughout 15:40–1. He questions why the Vulgate switches
   from *gloria* in 15:40 to the less adequate *claritas* 'brightness' in 41. In the next
   sentence in the paraphrase, however, he finds a use for the Vulgate's *claritas*.
58 In the paraphrase Erasmus is able to express both senses of the Greek διαφέρειν,
   as noted in the annotation on 15:41 (*stella enim differt a stella*): 'differ from' and
   'surpass.'
59 Erasmus' chief patristic sources interpret the opening clause of 15:42, 'So is it
   with the resurrection of the dead' (RSV), similarly as positing differing ranks or
   stations of the blessed in heaven, in strict analogy with the differing degrees
   of glory Paul describes for the heavenly bodies in 15:41. See Theophylact
   Expos in 1 Cor (on 15:39–43) PG 124 773B–776B and Ambrosiaster *Comm in 1
   Cor* (on 15:42) CSEL 81/2 179:22–180:10. Cf also Chrysostom *In 1 Cor hom* 41.3
   (on 15:41–3) PG 61 358–9 and Augustine *De civitate Dei* 22.30 CSEL 40/2 666.
   Cf n56 above.
60 In 15:23 and presumably here in 15:42 Paul speaks about the resurrection of
   those who belong to Christ, and no mention is made of a general resurrection
   of all the dead. See also Rom 6:5–11 and 1 Thess 4:13–17. Chrysostom *In 1 Cor
   hom* 41.3 (on 15:39–41) PG 61 358, however, understands Paul to be discussing

among the godly, just as each one has acted in life, so will each excel in the honour of the body made new. To all the godly,[61] nevertheless, a far more blessed body will be restored than the one they gave up in death. In nature, the planting of a seed in the ground is just like, in the case of resurrection, the burying of a corpse. A sprouting in the former is like a return to life in the latter. Just as in that case what sprouts is far more splendid than what had been entrusted to the earth, so in this, although it is the same body that is raised up, nevertheless it is far different. A body subject to decay is interred in the ground, as if a seed kernel, but the same body will come back to life subject to no corruption at all. A scorned and worthless body is interred in the ground, yet the same body will return to life gleaming with much glory. A body is buried which was feeble even while it was alive, but it will rise up endowed with immeasurable strength. A body is buried which, although it was alive, was nevertheless gross[62] and sluggish, and for this reason often a burden to its governor the soul,[63]

* * * * *

the ends of both the righteous and the unrighteous; similarly Theophylact *Expos in 1 Cor* (on 15:39-40) PG 124 773B-C and Ambrosiaster *Comm in 1 Cor* (on 15:41) CSEL 81/2 179:22-180:19.

61 the godly] Added in 1532. Cf the paraphrase on 15:51 below and the annotation on 15:51 (*omnes quidem resurgemus*), where Erasmus argues that Paul refers here to the transformation only of the godly, not of the ungodly.

62 'gross': *crassum*. Here, as well as two more times in this paragraph and three in the next, Erasmus uses his favourite epithet for the physical body. On Erasmus' use of *crassus*, see chapter 2 n22.

63 This sentence begins Erasmus' elaboration on Paul's distinction between physical and spiritual bodies in 15:44-5 and shows immediately the influence of the Platonist conception of a soul-body duality, perhaps mediated through Cicero, who uses the same term, *moderator* 'governor' or 'guide' for the ideal ruler of his commonwealth in *De re publica* 5.8 (= *Ad Atticum* 8.11.1). In 6.24.26-26.28, moreover, the soul is said to govern (*moderatur*) and move the body as God governs and moves the universe. Here and in *Tusculan Disputations* 1.53-4 Cicero quotes Plato *Phaedrus* 245C-E. Erasmus' discussion of the physical body's obstruction of the soul and the spiritual body's gradual purification recalls descriptions of the soul in *Phaedrus* 246A-256E, *Phaedo* 78C-80A, and Virgil *Aeneid* 6.730-47. Cf Lady Folly's extended treatment of the compatibility of Platonic and Christian views of the soul towards the end of *Moria* CWE 27 150-1. For a discussion of the complex interaction of Platonism and Paul in Erasmus' anthropology, see Payne *Theology* 35-40 or 'The Hermeneutics of Erasmus' 17-23. See also chapter 2 n22.

With the exception of the sentence noted in nn67 and 68 below, Erasmus' word for the 'soul' throughout this passage is *animus*, which designates the 'heart and mind,' the faculties of thought and feeling; its highest part is the rational

but it will rise up a natural body no longer, but a spiritual one, of such a kind that it will nowhere hinder the soul, wherever the soul's impulse takes it. For there is this difference also between bodies: one is natural, and it needs food and sleep; it is worn out by work; it is weakened by diseases; it wastes away with age, and it frequently obstructs the effort of the soul by its gross or infected organs. Because of its inherent affections[64] it often incites to wrongdoing, and when the soul clings to it and complies with it, the soul itself is, as it were, turned into a body, falling away from the mind towards the flesh. But another is spiritual, and in this life it has gradually been cleansed of bodily senses and feelings; then it is reborn through resurrection and is in a way transfigured into soul, to which it had adapted itself in its eagerness for godliness.[65] Thus, just as our soul in conforming to

* * * * *

faculty itself, *mens* 'mind'; cf n55. On Erasmus' anthropological terminology, see Payne *Theology* 37–9.

64 'Affections': *affectus*. On this term, see the annotation on Rom 1:31 ('without disposition') CWE 56 64–5 and n2. Cf CWE 56 204–5 n4, CWE 44 xvii, and the paraphrase on 2 Cor 3:6 with n7. For the body's 'inherent affections,' Erasmus may have in mind the physical emotions and passions which in *Enchiridion* CWE 66 42–3 he associates with the two lower 'mortal parts of the soul,' ie the non-rational parts. These include both honourable emotions, such as courage, compassion, and filial affection, and less honourable passions, such as wrath, envy, and concupiscence. The discussion there, based on Plato *Timaeus* 69C–70E, locates not only these lower parts of the soul and their characteristic emotions and passions but also the higher part (reason) in specific parts of the body. Cf *Moria* CWE 27 151. Erasmus may also have in mind Virgil *Aeneid* 6.730–4, where Anchises teaches Aeneas that it is through incorporation within bodies that souls experience fear, desire, pain, and joy. Cf Cicero *Tusculan Disputations* 3.11. On the intimate connection that Erasmus sometimes emphasizes between body and soul, see Payne *Theology* 38–9.

65 Although in this chapter Paul treats the spiritual body mainly as a future reality of the resurrection, elsewhere his spirit-flesh dichotomy is not primarily a temporal distinction. Accordingly, Erasmus treats the spiritual body as present already in this life and undergoing a kind of gradual purification even before death and resurrection. Cf the paraphrase on 2 Cor 5:3, where Erasmus speaks of a soul which, stripped of its mortal body, is found to have been 'clothed in the hope of immortality as a result of the assurance that comes from a good life.' Cf also Chrysostom *In 1 Cor hom* 41.3 (on 15:44) PG 61 359, where this present body is said to be spiritual too, but incompletely so: it is spiritual insofar as the Spirit dwells within it, but as reborn in the resurrection, the body will be wholly spiritual; also Theophylact *Expos in 1 Cor* (on 15:44) PG 124 776C. Erasmus usually suggests baptism as the initiating moment in this earthly version of the spiritual life. See eg the paraphrase on 15:49, chapters 1 n8 and 6 n26.

the divine Spirit is swept up and to an extent transformed into that Spirit, so our body in complying with the soul may be purified and shake off its grossness, refined into such a body as is most like the mind.[66]

We received this gross and earthly body from the beginning of our race, that earlier Adam, who, since he had been fashioned out of mud, was subject to earthly affections. But there is a second, later Adam, the beginning not of birth, but of the return to life, who since he has a heavenly origin was free from every contamination of earthly desires. So we read also in Genesis: 'The first Adam was created to live by the agency of the soul,'[67] but in such a way that the soul, as it were, bound to a gross body, should do nothing except through the organs of the body, or[68] at any rate through something material. But after him there was given the later Adam, who, since he was conceived from the Holy Spirit, would accordingly bestow life upon his people, not this gross life which for the most part we hold in common with beasts, but a spiritual and divine life. And so through Christ we are reborn in all ways to a better condition. What is earlier in time is also grosser in substance in accordance with the order of nature as well. We now carry around a natural body, but we will one day enjoy a spiritual one. Just as that grosser parent of our race came before, so Christ, the author of a new kind of begetting, followed. The descendants of that parent who

* * * * *

66 Cf *Enarratio allegorica in primum psalmum* CWE 63 50: 'The Holy Spirit, inhabiting our spirit, overflows into it and, being the more powerful, changes our spirit into itself, as it were; similarly this transformed spirit of ours overflows into the body ... and, as far as is possible, changes the body into itself.' Cf *De puero Iesu* CWE 29 69–70.

67 'Of the soul': *animae*. See n55 above. Erasmus paraphrases Gen 2:7.

68 or ... material] Added in 1532. The sentence to which this phrase was added had been criticized by Béda, who apparently considered it degrading to God's creation of Adam to refer to the body as 'gross' (*crassus*; see chapter 2 n22) and cited Aristotle against Erasmus' assertion that the soul acted only through bodily organs. In defending the adjective, Erasmus claims not to be asserting anything about Adam's 'condition' before he sinned, but only to be comparing Adam's 'origin' with Christ's. See *Divinationes ad notata Bedae* LB IX 475B–C and *Elenchus in N. Bedae censuras* LB IX 508A. In a fuller response in *Supputatio* LB IX 685B–687A, Erasmus suggests that Béda had not read Aristotle carefully enough or sufficiently understood Paul's distinction between soul and spirit. On the soul as bound to the body and on the affinity between Christian and Platonist views on this bondage, cf *Moria* CWE 27 150. Erasmus discusses his sense of the Pauline distinctions among body, soul, and spirit in *Hyperaspistes* CWE 76 594–5. See Payne *Theology* 39–40. See also nn63, 64, and 66 above.

was made of clay share his nature in that they are bound over to earthly
desires. Again, those reborn into that Adam who came from heaven share
his nature in that they have at heart the things of heaven. For what will
one day come to pass in completeness must already be practised here. Just
as before baptism we expressed in our wicked behaviour the nature of our
first parent, so once we have been reborn in Christ through baptism, we
shall resemble our heavenly author in our heavenly life. But unless we do
this, neither will we here belong to the body of Christ, nor will we then
enjoy the glory of the resurrection.[69] We have indeed been adopted into the
kingdom of God, but I tell you, brethren, that flesh and blood, that is, people
of the first begetting, cannot come to the inheritance of the kingdom of God;
nor will a life corrupted by vices enjoy the inheritance of immortality.

Look, I disclose to you a secret[70] so that nothing about the manner of
resurrection may be hidden from you. We are not all going to die, for that
day will perhaps catch some of us alive; but yet all of us will be changed to
the glory of immortality,[71] who with zeal for godliness somehow practise
immortality here and keep away from the contagion of sin. This change
will not come about gradually, like the changes we see happening in the

* * * * *

69 In the annotation on 15:49 (*portemus et imaginem coelestis*) Erasmus prefers the
   future tense 'we shall bear,' but allows as well the Vulgate's subjunctive 'let
   us bear.' The conditional and hortatory tone of the paraphrase here suggests
   both readings: the prediction of a future immortality and the exhortation to
   a present innocence. Cf nn65 above and 77 below.
70 'Secret': *rem arcanam*. Erasmus is paraphrasing μυστήριον in 15:51. In his Latin
   translation he renders it by *mysterium* 'mystery.' On *arcanus* and *mysterium*,
   see chapters 11 n38 and 7 n30 respectively.
71 Erasmus' reading of 15:51, 'We shall not all sleep, but we shall all be changed'
   (RSV), based on Greek manuscripts, is now the commonly accepted text, but
   his departure from the Vulgate reading, 'We shall all rise, but we shall not all
   be changed,' gave rise to a notable controversy involving the English theologian Edmund Lee (CEBR II 311–14) and the Carmelite Nicolaas Egmondanus
   (Baechem, CEBR I 81–3). See the annotation on 15:51 (*omnes quidem resurgemus*),
   where Erasmus argues in a note extensively enlarged in successive editions
   that Paul's concern here is only with believers, some of whom will still be
   alive at Jesus' second coming and therefore will not need to be raised before
   their transformation to immortality. See also *Responsio ad annotationes Lei* (Concerning Note 161) CWE 72 280–2 and *Apologia de loco 'Omnes quidem'* LB IX 433–
   42. The paraphrase on this verse also came under attack from Béda and the
   Paris faculty. See *Divinationes ad notata Bedae* LB IX 475D; *Supputatio* LB IX 687A–
   B; and *Declarationes ad censuras Lutetiae vulgatas* LB IX 878E–879A. On the textual
   variants for 15:51, see Metzger 502.

natural world, but in a moment and point of time, at the calling of the last
trumpet. For a trumpet shall sound, and at its call those who will by then
have died will return to life now no more to die. And we whom that day
will find alive,[72] being suddenly changed, shall now live in a new way, that
is, in the same manner as those who will have come back to life. For before
we possess the heavenly kingdom fully, it is necessary for us utterly to
cast off everything that smacks of the earth, and the corruptible body we
now have must be rendered incorruptible; the mortal body we now have
must be rendered immortal. When this has happened, then truly will the
saying of Hosea the prophet be fulfilled, who in predicting what will be
revels in death's utter annihilation: 'Death has been swallowed up through
victory.[73] Where now, O Death, is your sting? Where, Hell, is your victory?'
[13:14].[74] Now the sting of death is sin, but the strength of sin is the Law,
which, when opportunity arises, provokes lust for sinning. When the Law
is abolished, the power of sin languishes; when sin is abolished, the power
of death ceases, for the sting by which it is always striking us has been
removed.[75] We were utterly unequal to such violent enemies, if it had been
necessary for us to wage the battle by our own defences; but now we must
be grateful to God for making it possible that we may, if we wish, possess
through Jesus Christ our Lord so celebrated a victory. By his own death on
our behalf he conquered death and took our offences upon himself to be
purified.

　　Therefore, my dearest brethren, since it is certain that the resurrection
is to come, since it is certain that through it such great happiness is guaranteed[76] although this will come only to those who through innocence and

* * * * *

72　See 1 Thess 4:17. In Erasmus' interpretation, Paul distinguishes in 15:52 the
　　fate of believers who have died (resurrection to an imperishable form) from
　　that of believers still alive (transformation to the imperishable form). See the
　　annotation on 15:51 (*omnes quidem resurgemus*) ASD VI-8 310:779 – 808. See also
　　1 Thess chapter 4 n24.

73　Modern commentaries cite Isa 25:8 as the source of this part of the quotation.
　　The portion that follows has its source in Hos 13:14. On the textual history of
　　these two passages, see Conzelmann 292.

74　This is the form and order of the questions as found in Chrysostom *In 1 Cor
　　hom* 42.2 (on 15:55) PG 61 365 and Theophylact *Expos in 1 Cor* (on 15:55) PG
　　124 784A and which Erasmus preferred for his own Greek text and Latin
　　translation. For Erasmus' understanding of the textual variants here, see the
　　annotation on 15:54 (*in victoria*); also Conzelmann 292–3.

75　Cf Rom 5:13, 7:7–11.

76　Erasmus' amplification here closely parallels that of Theophylact *Expos in 1
　　Cor* (on 15:58) PG 124 784C.

flight from sin will have practised the heavenly life here in this life,[77] do not waver in that belief which you once held. Do not allow yourselves to be moved from right opinion by the talk of evil persons,[78] but rather strive that, advancing every day in such matters as commend you to God, you can[79] every day become inherently better and make yourselves ready for the resurrection to come. Do not shrink from any labour since you hold it as certain that with Christ's help, in return for temporary vexations, you shall gain everlasting joys.

Chapter 16

Now concerning the relief, through your generosity, of the saints who live at Jerusalem: just as I instructed the Galatians to collect money for this purpose, if any wished to contribute voluntarily, I would likewise have it done among you so that in this respect also you may be in accord with the other churches. On the first day of the sabbath, that is, on the Lord's day,[1] let each of you put aside at home and store up as much as seems right to each. My reason in giving this instruction is that whatever each one has decided to bestow may be more readily at hand so that, when I come, the money does not then still need to be scraped together. And when I come to you, whomever you have chosen as emissaries these I shall send with my letters[2] to Jerusalem so that they may convey your munificence. But if it

* * * * *

77 For the necessity of practising innocence now in preparation for the immortality to come, cf the paraphrases on 3:4 with n12, 6:14 with n40, 13:11, and 15:49 with n69 above.

78 Cf Ambrosiaster *Comm in 1 Cor* (on 15:58) CSEL 81/2 187:17–21: 'He urges them to be firm ... so that they could not be turned aside by perverse talk.'

79 you can] First in *1521*; previously 'you take care to'

1 These expressions paraphrase κατὰ μίαν σαββάτων – in Erasmus' translation *in una sabbatorum* 'on [day] one of the week' or 'on Sabbath one.' This with slight variations appears as a designation for the day of Jesus' resurrection at Matt 28:1; Mark 16:2; Luke 24:1; and John 20:1, 19; and for the day of meeting for early Christian worship at Acts 20:7. Citing Theophylact *Expos in 1 Cor* (on 16:2) PG 61 785B, Erasmus remarks in the annotation on 16:2 (*per unam sabbati*) that the phrase here refers to the 'Lord's day.' Cf the annotation on Matt 24:1 (*in prima sabbati*). In the annotation on Matt 12:1 (*sabbato*), he notes that the word 'sabbath' can refer to the whole seven-day period of the week. See also CWE 46 219 n18 and CWE 50 121 n9.

2 The Greek text of 16:3 is ambiguous as to whether the letters are the Corinthians' or Paul's and whether the phrase 'by letters' modifies 'approve' or 'send'

seems worthwhile that I myself proceed there, they will go with me so that
no one can suppose that in any respect I am acting in my own interests.[3]

I am, however, going to visit you, when I have journeyed through
Macedonia, for I shall stop to visit the Macedonians only in passing through.
With you, however, I will remain for some time; perhaps I shall spend the
whole winter, so that upon the arrival of the following spring I may, with
you sending me on my way, proceed wherever the business of the gospel
calls. Otherwise I would have come to you now, but I did not wish to see
you hastily in passing through, for I hope I shall be allowed to remain a
good many days with you, if only the Lord Jesus permits. Meanwhile I shall
remain at Ephesus until the fiftieth day.[4] The situation requires some delay
because, although a huge door is open to me in that place,[5] and ample hope
of spreading the gospel's glory, nevertheless there are many who stand
opposed.[6] But if Timothy should come to you in the meantime, see that he
suffers no peril from certain lofty and wealthy persons.[7] He is a young

* * * * *

(cf AV). Literally, the Greek reads, 'whom you approve through letters these
will I send.' Erasmus' Latin translation leaves the phrase ambiguously between the two verbs, as does the Vulgate. Chrysostom *In 1 Cor hom* 43.2 (on
16:3) PG 61 370 and Theophylact *Expos in 1 Cor* (on 16:3) PG 124 785D, however, both assume the letters to be Paul's, which he will send along with the
messengers so that he may participate with them in the embassy.

3 Theophylact in *Expos in 1 Cor* (on 6:4) PG 124 788A explains similarly that
Paul wants witnesses to the fact that he is not receiving anything from the
collection.

4 In the annotation on 16:8 (*usque ad Pentecosten*) Erasmus argues that by πεντη-
κοστή 'pentecost' or 'fiftieth' Paul refers to an interval of time, rather than to
the festival of Pentecost – whether Jewish or Christian.

5 'In that place': *illic*, although we might expect *hic* 'in this place' since Erasmus
appears to favour the view that Paul is writing the letter from Ephesus. See
the Argument 26.

6 In 16:9 Paul states that he will stay awhile at Ephesus because 'a wide door
for effective work has opened to me, and there are many adversaries.' As the
paraphrase here indicates, Erasmus prefers to interpret the second clause as
concessive or adversative: there is abundant opportunity, yet great difficulty
as well because of the opposition of many adversaries. See the annotation on
16:9 (*et adversarii multi*), where he cites support from Jerome's commentary on
Joel.

7 Chrysostom *In 1 Cor hom* 44.1 (on 16:10) PG 61 373–4 and Theophylact *Expos
in 1 Cor* (on 16:10) PG 124 788D–789A similarly identify wealthy, high-born
persons as the danger to Timothy and emphasize his youth. Cf 4:17, where a
visit from Timothy is associated with Paul's rebuke of wealth and arrogance
among Corinthian Christians; also 1 Tim 4:12.

man, but a partner of mine, and he is engaged sincerely and freely[8] in the evangelical task, just as I am. Therefore, let no one scorn him because he is younger in age; nay, rather send him forth as an apostle and a partner of mine, uninjured and unimpaired, and as a courtesy when he is departing see him off so that he may come to me, for I look for him along with the rest of the brethren who are his companions.

Now as to your request that Apollos rather be sent to you, I indeed did not stand in the way of his going. For I earnestly urged him to go to you with some of the brethren, but in vain, since for definite reasons there was not at all the disposition to go to you now;[9] nevertheless he intends to come as soon as he has time.

Keep alert against the snares of those who give evil counsel. Stand firm in the faith that you have once taken up; may you be unbroken in spirit against whatever stands opposed to the gospel; be vigorous and strong. Moreover, let whatever is done among you be done not through contentiousness, but through charity.[10]

I beseech you, brethren, but what need is there for entreaties? You yourselves know the household of Stephanas, worthy of your regard, either because I won them for Christ as the first fruits from Achaia, or because they have given themselves wholly to supporting the saints by their kindness. It is proper, therefore, that you also in turn hold such people in honour, and not only these, but also whoever assists the evangelical cause with us and shares in our labour. I was pleased that you sent Stephanas, Fortunatus,

* * * * *

8 'Sincerely and freely': *sincere libereque*. The first adverb means 'without falseness or adulteration.' Cf the paraphrase on 1 Tim 1:2 CWE 44 5–6, where Erasmus associates 'sincerity' with Timothy's status as a 'true child' of Paul. See also CWE 44 25–6. By the second, *libere*, Erasmus probably means 'without constraint' or 'under no obligation.' Erasmus elaborates on this sense in the paraphrases on 6:12 and 7:24: apostles who do not accept their living from others may 'freely' admonish, and women who remain unmarried may 'freely' serve Christ.

9 It seems likely that it is Apollos' *animus* 'disposition' that Erasmus has in mind here, but he leaves the construction impersonal as it is in the Greek text. In the annotations on 16:12 (*et utique* and *quum ei vacuum fuerit*), Erasmus passes over the ambiguity as to whether it is Apollos' will or God's that Apollos not go to Corinth, but he cites Theophylact *Expos in 1 Cor* (on 16:12) PG 124 789B in support of the latter. Ambrosiaster *Comm in 1 Cor* (on 16:12) CSEL 81/2 191:6–11 and most modern interpreters assume it is Apollos who was unwilling to visit Corinth at that time.

10 Erasmus echoes Ambrosiaster *Comm in 1 Cor* (on 16:14) CSEL 81/2 192:3–4: 'Where there is contention and division, however, there is not love.'

and Achaicus here since, by coming in the name of all, they have supplied
by their own kindness what I was previously longing for from you.[11] For
they have refreshed my spirit, nay yours, seeing that mine aims at nothing other than your welfare, and is made happier by nothing more than by
your progress. Give recognition to such people, therefore, and wait upon
them with a special show of respect.[12]

The congregations[13] of Asia greet you. Aquila and Priscilla out of their
affection for godliness wish you a hearty greeting along with the rest of
the congregation of Christians they have at their house. All those here who
profess the name of Christ greet you. May you also be joined in mutual
good will among yourselves, and for your part greet each other with a holy
and pure kiss, the symbol of true concord.[14]

I, Paul, greet you and have signed this with my own hand, witnessing
at the same time both to my affection for you and to the fact that this letter
is not counterfeit. If anyone does not cherish the Lord Jesus, let him be
cursed! Maranatha. For he rejects the only one from whom he was able to

* * * * *

11 In the annotation on 16:17 (*quod vobis deerat*) Erasmus identifies what Paul was
longing for simply as the 'presence' of the Corinthians.

12 For attendance upon someone as a sign of respect, cf CWE 44 67 n24.

13 'Congregations': *congregationes*; Erasmus' paraphrase for ἐκκλησίαι 'churches.'
Similarly he uses 'congregation' for the singular 'church' in the next sentence.
In the annotation on 16:19 (*cum domestica sua ecclesia*) regarding this second
case, Erasmus notes a preference for 'congregation' over 'church' since he
thinks the reference here is to a Christian household (*familia*; on this term, see
chapter 7 n63). It is possible then that Erasmus considers the 'churches of Asia'
in the first part of the verse to refer as well to household churches, but this
seems unlikely. Elsewhere in the *Paraphrase*, when representing ἐκκλησία, he
appears to use one or the other of the two Latin terms without significant distinction. See eg the paraphrase on 11:16 with n22. Moreover, in his translation
of 16:19 he uses *ecclesia* in both parts of the verse. See also chapters 1 n3 and
11 n32; 1 Thess chapter 1 n2; and the annotation on Rom 16:5 ('and [their] domestic church') CWE 56 425. On Erasmus' terms for the church, cf CWE 44 71
n7 and CWE 50 40 n20.

14 Cf Ambrosiaster *Comm in 1 Cor* (on 16:20) CSEL 81/2 193:23: 'The holy kiss is
the sign of peace, in which he teaches them, discord having been removed,
to cling to one another.' Chrysostom *In 1 Cor hom* 44.2 (on 16:20) PG 61 376
and Theophylact *Expos in 1 Cor* (on 16:20) PG 124 792D similarly comment that
Paul recommends the holy kiss here because of the evident discord among
Corinthian Christians. Cf the paraphrase on 2 Cor 13:12 with n13. On forms
of kissing in the ancient world and on the 'holy kiss' in Paul and the early
church, see the concise summary and references in Furnish 582–3.

obtain salvation, and denies that that one has come[15] who it is certain did come with great good for believers, but great evil for the unbelieving. The favour and kindness of the Lord Jesus Christ be with you. I pray that just as I cherish you with Christian affection, so may you in turn genuinely cherish each other in the charity with which Christ Jesus has bonded you firmly together.[16] Amen.

The End of the Paraphrase on the First Epistle
of Paul the Apostle to the Corinthians
by Erasmus of Rotterdam

* * * * *

15 Erasmus agrees with his patristic sources in interpreting the Aramaic term *Maranatha* to mean 'Our Lord has come.' See the annotation on 16:22 (*anathema sit*). See also Ambrosiaster *Comm in 1 Cor* (on 16:22) CSEL 81/2 194:4–6 and Chrysostom *In 1 Cor hom* 44.3 (on 16:22) PG 61 377. Modern interpreters often translate *Maranatha* as an imperative: 'Our Lord, come!'

16 'Has bonded ... firmly together': *conglutinavit*. The final verb in the paraphrase recalls the work's initial emphasis on unity and harmony. See chapter 1 n4.

PARAPHRASE ON SECOND CORINTHIANS

In epistolam Pauli ad Corinthios posteriorem paraphrasis

translated and annotated by
MECHTILDE O'MARA
and
EDWARD A. PHILLIPS Jr

THE ARGUMENT OF THE SECOND EPISTLE TO THE CORINTHIANS BY ERASMUS OF ROTTERDAM

First of all he explains to the Corinthians why he had not visited them again as he had promised in his earlier letter.[1] He prefaces this with some remarks about the afflictions he was suffering on account of the gospel of Christ, showing that in the midst of such great evils God had been his comfort.[2] Next he restores to the Corinthians the individual he had, in his earlier letter, ordered to be handed over to Satan,[3] so that they might lovingly receive back, chastened, the one whom they had expelled while he was sinning.[4] These are, for the most part, the topics in the first chapter and the second.

Then he recalls his own zeal in preaching the gospel and, in passing, censures others whom he brands as 'false apostles' serving the interest of their own financial gain, zealots for their own glory, everywhere luring people to the Mosaic law.[5] They were trying to blend it in with Christ, just

* * * * *

1 Modern scholars are convinced of the authenticity of 2 Corinthians as a Pauline text, but unsure of when or where the Epistle was written, or whether what we have is one letter or a compilation of several letters. See Brown *Introduction to NT* 548–51. When Erasmus in paraphrasing 2 Corinthians refers to 'my earlier letter,' he means 1 Corinthians.
  The text of 1 Cor 4:21 contains the question 'Shall I come to you with a rod, or with love in a spirit of gentleness?' (RSV), and it is probably this to which Erasmus refers in the mention of a promise in an earlier letter. Erasmus' paraphrase on 1 Cor 4:21 makes the promise explicit: 'Do you want me to come to you? I shall come indeed.' Paul explains why he has not come in 2 Cor 1:15–2:4.
2 For God's comfort in the midst of sufferings, see 2 Cor 1:3–11.
3 See 1 Cor 5:1–13 for the episode to which Erasmus refers.
4 See 2 Cor 2:5–11.
5 For Paul's zeal, see 2 Cor 2:14–3:6. On false apostles as greedy and prideful exponents of Mosaic law, cf the paraphrases on 2 Cor 7:1 with n4 and 11:13 with nn19, 21, and 22; also the Argument of 1 Corinthians 19.

as if, without its addition, there would be no hope of salvation. Accordingly, he sets the light of the gospel before the shadows of the Mosaic law as he repeatedly exhorts them to follow not the ceremonies of the Law, but a conscience and a life worthy of Christ. Meanwhile he testifies to the sincerity with which he has preached the gospel of Christ and to the magnitude of the evils he has suffered for its sake in hope of a heavenly reward.

In addition, he indicates wherein especially Christian piety lies. These matters are handled at the end of the second chapter, in the third chapter, the fourth, the fifth, and at the beginning of the sixth.[6] In the remainder of the sixth chapter, and likewise at the beginning of the next, he exhorts them to recognize the dignity and holiness of their profession and in every way to abstain from the defilements of the pagans, with whom they had nothing in common.[7]

In the fourth place, he softens the sharpness of his earlier reproach[8] by praising their compliance because in every respect they had obeyed his Epistle, reproachful as it was. And he expresses his pleasure because that temporary sadness brought forth the greatest joy on both sides,[9] just as happens when most-welcome health follows from bitter medicine.

In the fifth place, he challenges each of them not only by the example of the Macedonians,[10] but by various other arguments as well, and by the testimony of the Scriptures,[11] to contribute something, as each was inclined and means allowed, to the help of the saints who were living at Jerusalem.[12] He kept in mind that this had been Peter's mandate to him,[13] and for this business Titus[14] was being sent together with a second colleague (Luke, as most people think),[15] both of whom he commends to

* * * * *

6 See 2 Cor 2:14–6:10.
7 See 2 Cor 6:14–7:1.
8 By 'earlier reproach,' Erasmus may have in mind specifically 1 Cor 5:1–13, but his language in this paragraph is general enough to refer to the praise and blame occurring throughout 1 Corinthians.
9 For the sorrowful letter resulting in joy, see 2 Cor 7:8–16.
10 For the example of the Macedonians, see 2 Cor 8:1–5.
11 2 Cor 8:15 refers to Exod 16:18; 2 Cor 9:9 quotes Ps 112:9 (Vulgate 111:9); 2 Cor 9:10 is reminiscent of Isa 55:10.
12 For the collection for Jerusalem, see 2 Cor 7:4–9:15.
13 See Gal 2:9–10: 'James and Cephas [Peter] and John ... would have us remember the poor' (RSV). The collection for the believers in Jerusalem is mentioned also at Acts 11:29–30, 24:17; 1 Cor 16:1–3.
14 Mention of Titus occurs at 2 Cor 8:17–18, 23.
15 The interlinear Gloss, Theophylact, and Thomas Aquinas all mention both Luke and Barnabas as possibilities. See the *Gloss* (on 2 Cor 8:18); Theophylact

the Corinthians. He treats of these topics in the eighth chapter and in the ninth.

In the sixth place, he openly inveighs against the false apostles whom he had previously attacked indirectly. In pride and arrogance they were vaunting apostolic dignity and majesty, calling Paul into contempt as lowly on the ground that he practised a menial pursuit,[16] as unskilled and unable to speak, and, in addition, beaten and wronged[17] so many times. Against these false apostles he asserts his own authority among the Corinthians, affirming that nowhere is he lacking in the apostolic authority and power, but he does not wish to use it to burden others as the rest have done, but only for their advantage and the glory of Christ.

Then, after proffering an excuse for his folly because he was compelled to speak rather boastfully about himself,[18] he first makes himself the equal of the highest apostles,[19] then he even places himself above them, and that on many grounds: because he has sown the teaching of the gospel more broadly;[20] or because he was the only one to have handed it on free of charge, without burden to the Achaeans from either himself or his representatives;[21] or because he had suffered more for the sake of the gospel than had any of them,[22] turning to his own glory those things on account of

* * * * *

Expos in 2 Cor (on 8:18) PG 124 885D; Aquinas Super 2 Cor lect cap 8 lectio 3.313 (I 510). Erasmus does not mention here the third member of the expedition described at 2 Cor 8:22.

16 'Menial pursuit': cerdonicam, a word derived from cerdo, a contemptuous expression for craftsman. See E. Courtney in A Commentary on the Satires of Juvenal (London 1980) 228–9 (on 4.153). For Paul as tentmaker cf Acts 18:3.
In Greco-Roman society artisans were generally considered of lower caste, and the accusation of being a craftsman, or the son of one, was a recognized weapon of oratory. See Alison Burford, Craftsmen in Greek and Roman Society (London 1972) 156. For Greek aristocratic bias against mechanical trades and commerce, see also Joseph M. Bryant Moral Codes and Social Structure in Ancient Greece: a Sociology of Greek Ethics from Homer to the Epicureans and Stoics (Albany 1996) 113, 118, 131, 355.

17 'Wronged': vexatum iniuriis 'harassed by wrongs.' Iniuria refers not only to physical injury but also to civil injustice and social insult. See OLD iniuria. Paul's sufferings are listed at 2 Cor 11:23–33, a beating at Acts 16:22–3.

18 For Paul's apology for boasting, see 2 Cor 11:1–4.

19 For Paul as not inferior to the highest apostles, see 2 Cor 11:5. On the designation 'highest apostles,' see 1 Cor chapters 3 n15 and 9 n14.

20 For Paul's more extensive mission, see 2 Cor 10:13–16.

21 For Paul's preaching of the gospel without charge, see 2 Cor 11:7–9.

22 For Paul's greater sufferings, see 2 Cor 11:23.

which he seemed to some people rather contemptible. Furthermore, while through modesty he acknowledges the unskilled manner of his speech, he claims for himself knowledge, so that even here they should have nothing to wish for.[23] Finally, since the false apostles were ingratiating themselves among the simple by means of their feigned visions of angels, Paul introduces a remarkable and true vision: that he had been snatched right up to the third heaven and there shown what exceeds the grasp of humans.[24] These are, generally speaking, the topics in the tenth, eleventh, and twelfth chapters.

In the seventh place, so that they might not slip back into their earlier sins through the agency of the false apostles, he affirms that he intends to visit them,[25] threatening them with authority, so that he might not find them in such a condition that he would be forced to be unlike himself, or be compelled to show his anger in their presence just as he had been forced to do in his Epistle. He had not done this previously, although with every right he could have. He deals with these matters at the end of the twelfth chapter and in the thirteenth chapter.

Greek subscriptions[26] testify that this Epistle was sent from Philippi by means of Titus and Luke. But the Arguments (without author, but of convenient brevity) that are contained in the Latin codices affirm that it was sent from Troas through the same individuals, for he makes mention of this place in the second chapter.[27]

The End

* * * * *

23 See 2 Cor 11:6: 'Even though I be rude in speech, yet I am not so in knowledge' (Conf).
24 Paul's vision is recounted in 2 Cor 12:1-6.
25 For Paul's promise to visit a third time and the motivation for such a visit, see 2 Cor 12:14-13:10.
26 'Subscriptions': inscriptiones. Both the Greek and the Latin subscription in all editions of Erasmus' New Testament indicate that the letter was sent from Philippi, and that Titus and Luke were the bearers.
27 The old Latin argumenta were prefaced to the epistles only in Erasmus' 1516 edition of the New Testament; in the case of 2 Corinthians the argumentum states that the letter was sent from Troas. Troas is mentioned at 2 Cor 2:12. On the identification of this city with Alexandria Troas, see Furnish 168-9.

THE PARAPHRASE ON THE SECOND EPISTLE
OF PAUL TO THE CORINTHIANS
BY ERASMUS OF ROTTERDAM

Chapter 1

Paul, discharging the role of an emissary[1] in the name of Christ Jesus under the authority of God the Father, together with Timothy,[2] a brother in the fellowship of religion, a colleague in sharing responsibility,[3] [sends greetings] to the Christian flock that lives at Corinth, and not only [to the flock] at Corinth, but also to all the saints who serve Christ throughout the whole of Achaia in which Corinth is the capital city.[4] We pray that you might have the grace, peace, and harmony[5] that is bestowed by the Lord Jesus Christ and God, his Father, whom we have as Father in common with him.[6]

* * * * *

1 'Role of an emissary': *legatione*. On this term and its cognate *legatus* 'emissary,' commonly employed by Erasmus to paraphrase the Greek ἀπόστολος 'apostle,' see 1 Cor chapter 1 n2 and Phil chapter 4 n8. For Paul's concept of his role as emissary or ambassador, see 2 Cor 5:20 and Eph 6:20. Cf also CWE 46 162 n20 and CWE 50 143 n21.

2 Erasmus elaborates on the background and character of Timothy in the Argument of 1 Timothy CWE 44 4 and in the paraphrase on 1 Tim 1:1 CWE 44 5–6.

3 'Responsibility': *officii*. Erasmus elsewhere distinguishes between the responsibility of office and the mere holding of it. See chapter 2 n18 and Erasmus' annotation on Rom 1:5 ('grace and apostleship') CWE 56 19 n7.

4 Erasmus' paraphrase underlines the importance of Corinth during the Roman administration of Greece when the province of Achaia included most of mainland Greece; so too Aquinas *Super 2 Cor lect* cap 1 lectio 1.6 (I 440). Cf the Argument of 1 Corinthians 19.

5 By adding 'harmony' to the two gifts mentioned in the text he is paraphrasing, Erasmus shows his own concern for the unity of the Church and foreshadows Paul's message that there should be a consensus among believers. He may also be following a rhetorical preference for the rhythm created in a tricolon. On Erasmus' concern for harmony, see 1 Cor chapter 1 n4.

6 In 2 Cor 1:2 the Greek allows, ambiguously, two possible readings: 1/ 'grace ... from God our Father and the Father of our Lord Jesus Christ' and 2/

God, who is also the Father of our Lord Jesus Christ, is to be commended with words of good promise[7] and extolled with praises. He is the source and author of every kindness; a God who does not fill the godly with dread, but from whom comes all our consolation.[8] He does not cease to alleviate and revive[9] us apostles, no matter what affliction has befallen us from any source. This he does not only out of concern for us lest broken by evils we fail, but also for all of you. Indeed, because of our mutual love, just as you are tormented by our misfortunes, so you yourselves also derive solace when we have been refreshed, and, following our example, in the hope of divine refreshment you remain bravely steadfast in enduring afflictions, trusting that God will not fail you when you are afflicted, for you see he has been our help when we were overwhelmed and nearly extinguished.

In proportion to the measure of the misfortunes that oppress us, he mingles his consolation.[10] We are not troubled by the afflictions that we patiently endure on account of Christ and after Christ's example. The harsher the sufferings he endured, the greater the solace he enjoys.[11] In our case, too, the more harshly we have been afflicted for Christ's sake, the greater the solace with which God has refreshed us when we have been freed from misfortunes by the assistance of Christ to give you hope that what you see has happened in our case will happen in your case too. Accordingly, if we are at all cast down by adversities, it serves to encourage you and contributes to your salvation, so that strengthened by our example you bravely

* * * * *

'grace ... from God our Father and from the Lord Jesus Christ.' Erasmus' paraphrase incorporates both interpretations, although for his Latin translation of the verse he chooses the second. See also the annotation on 1:2 (*a deo patre nostro et domino*).

7 'Words of good promise': *verbis bene ominantibus*, literally 'of good omen.' Erasmus is adapting the language of augury used by the ancient Romans to foretell future events. See OLD '*ominor.*' Cf the annotation on Rom 1:25 ('who is blessed') CWE 56 55, where he uses the idiom similarly to describe the pronouncement of a blessing upon someone.

8 Erasmus adopts the Vulgate *consolatio* 'consolation,' and opposes it in this context to 'dread' so as to connote peace, joy, and a sense of confidence. Cf the annotation on Rom 1:12 ('to be comforted together') CWE 56 37.

9 'Revive': *refocillare.* On this term, see CWE 48 101 n32 and CWE 50 29 n33, and cf the paraphrase on 7:6 with n8.

10 The image may be drawn from the mixing of drinks. Cf Horace *Epodes* 17.80.

11 For the notion of a proportional relationship between the amount of suffering and of ensuing consolation, see Origen *Martyrdom* XLII 72: 'Those who share in sufferings will share also in the comfort in proportion to the suffering they share with Christ.'

bear the harshest things, whatever they may be; to endure them, although
it is bitter, is nevertheless salvific. If we are refreshed when the tempest of
misfortunes has been driven away, again God does this too, in order to re-
new your spirits by the support he has given to us, so that you may not
falter because of grief, but, by the alternation of misfortunes and solace,
you too may be able to endure what we are enduring. Indeed, we are confident that, just as you are participants in our afflictions, so you will be participants also in our solace; and, just as formerly you grieved over our ha-
rassment, so you will rejoice at our deliverance, since it is appropriate that
among friends there be a partnership in good things as well as in bad.[12]

You will rejoice all the more if you know fully how great was the
hurricane of evils by which we were blasted in Asia.[13] There we were
oppressed to an amazing extent by a weight of afflictions absolutely too
heavy for our strength. It had come to the point that we were despairing
of life too, truly no match for so many and so great evils that had to be
endured. So great was the violence of the persecutions that not only did
others despair of our ability to stand firm, but in our own mind, despairing
of its strength, we had nothing but death before our eyes;[14] we had no
presentiment of anything but final ruin. God suffered us to be reduced to
this point, so that we might not trust at all in our own strength, but in his
support, which, as a general rule, is most available when human supports
most forsake us.

When he so wills, he not only frees from danger of death, but even
calls back to life those who have been destroyed. So far as pertains to
me, I was already dead, already deprived of life, but from this death God

* * * * *

12 The Greek text at 1:7 is elliptical: Paul affirms his continuing hope in the
   Corinthians for he knows that 'as you share in our sufferings, so also you
   share in our consolation' (NRSV). The Vulgate supplies the future verb *eritis*
   'you will be' to complete the last clause: 'So also will you be sharers in our
   consolation'; cf DV, AV, RSV. In his annotation on 1:7 (*sic eritis et consolationis*),
   Erasmus notes that a present-tense verb should instead be understood, and he
   corrects to *estis* 'you are.' Nevertheless, he makes the clause future in his Latin
   translation of the verse: 'So too you are going to be sharers ...' Here in the
   paraphrase as well, the Vulgate's future reference dominates. On the idea of
   friends sharing all things, see *Adagia* I i 1. For an expansion of Erasmus' views
   on friendship and common property, see Kathy Eden *Friends Hold All Things in
   Common: Tradition, Intellectual Property, and the Adages of Erasmus* (New Haven
   2001).
13 For Paul's troubles and hopes in Asia, especially in Ephesus, see 1 Cor 15:32,
   16:8–9; Acts 19:23–40.
14 For the expression 'death before our eyes,' see Ambrosiaster *Comm in 2 Cor*
   (on 1:9) CSEL 81/2 199:1–2.

delivered and, even now, is delivering me.[15] In him[16] I have confidence that in the future, too, he will deliver, especially if your entreaties are added to win God's favour for me, so that, just as we are saved by the prayers of many and for the advantage of many, so may thanks, in many places,[17] by many people, be offered to God because we have been saved, as though God's kindness, by which it has fallen to my lot to be unharmed, should seem to have been conferred not only on me, the one saved, but on all for whose good I am saved.

In any case, so far as I am concerned, I have within myself that which consoles me even in the midst of afflictions and, indeed, encourages and cheers me even to the point of boasting. I mean this strong consciousness that in all of Greece and especially among you we have been engaged in the work of the gospel, not like some of you, who through a show of human learning hunt for profit, but with a simplicity and sincerity worthy of God. Although for your sake we have endured such great sufferings, nevertheless we have never looked for, or taken, any recompense from you, so that no one might be given a handle for suspecting that we were trying to ensnare you for our profit.[18]

I do not say this with arrogance, but with truth. I am not throwing out empty boasts about myself; you yourselves have made the test. For you have never found us to be other than what we are affirming in this

* * * * *

15 By the phrase 'even now,' Erasmus stresses that the deliverance is not only past, but is continuing in the present, thus paraphrasing the present tense printed in his Greek text and Latin translation, rather than the future tense ('will deliver') he evidently found in the Vulgate text he had at hand. See his annotation on 1:10 (*eripuit et eruet*). The future tense is the preferred reading in both the Greek and the Vulgate text (see Metzger 506 and Weber 1789–90), although in fact the Vulgate text Erasmus printed in the 1527 edition has the present tense.

16 'In him': *de quo*. This translation supports Erasmus' 1527 translation of the text of 1:10, which reads 'on him we have our hope fixed'; grammatically, it could also be translated 'as a result of which,' ie the deliverance.

17 'In many places': *multifariam*, or possibly 'in many ways,' paraphrasing ἐκ πολλῶν προσώπων in 1:11, for which, however, in his Latin translation Erasmus chooses the meaning 'from many persons.' He discusses the full range of possible meanings for this phrase in his annotation on 1:11 (*ut ex multarum personis facierum*).

18 Ambrosiaster *Comm in 2 Cor* (on 1:12) CSEL 81/2 200:5–11 notes that Paul, as he had done in 1 Cor 2:4–5, is here contrasting his preaching with that of false preachers who adapted their preaching to the sensibilities of the world to avoid giving offence. On 'handle' as a metaphor cf 100 n46.

letter that you are reading. Nor in the letter do we represent ourselves with our words other than we have proven ourselves before you by our deeds. Really, I hope that you will always find us by experience to be such as you have, in part, thus far found us to be, so that with good reason we may each be able to boast about the other; and so it will be, if, as I have proven myself to you a sincere apostle, so you, likewise, as beloved and docile children, correspondingly fulfil the duties and embody the attitude of your parent and teacher. Meanwhile, let others who scorn me as a man rejected and afflicted vaunt themselves before men. Certainly, when the Lord comes and there is not any place for pretence, then I shall boast about you because I won you for Christ, and you, in turn, about me since I have handed down to you nothing except what was worthy of Christ.

This assurance of my clear conscience, together with the hope conceived for your progress, was the basis of my intention previously to visit you so that I might bring you joy twofold: first, from the Epistle, then, from my presence. For I had decided that in setting out for Macedonia I would visit you along the way and, again, coming back from Macedonia, I would return to you (a promise I made in my last letter);[19] and thus with you sending me on my way I would set out for Judaea. But meanwhile, it will occur to someone to wonder, since I had my mind set on this, whether I changed my view through inconstancy, or whether, through a plan characteristically human, I am not carrying out what I wished to do, changing my decisions to suit the circumstances, whatever they may be.

Not at all! Rather, I have deliberately not complied with my desire because I realized it would be more to your advantage that, with my return postponed, certain people would be corrected, for I did not wish to see them when they were defiled.[20] I have always been consistent and unchanging in this: that in every situation I serve your welfare, so that in this respect I never waver, but I always do what seems most to your advantage and always avoid what I realize will be disadvantageous to you. This I do,

* * * * *

19 For Paul's promise to visit Corinth on his return from Macedonia, see 1 Cor 16:5–7.
20 With *impuros* 'defiled' Erasmus may refer to the sexual immorality Paul reproves in 1 Cor 5:1–13, which in the traditional view had been identified with the offence of 2 Cor 2:5–11. Ambrosiaster *Comm in 2 Cor* (on 1:12) CSEL 81/2 202:3–5 suggests as a reason for Paul's change of plans, 'that they [the Corinthians] might improve, knowing that he had postponed the visit for this very reason: because some among them had not yet purified (*purificaverant*) themselves from their sins.' For difficulties with this interpretation, see Furnish 163–8.

not because I think it lies in us to do whatever we may have decided is expedient, but God does not deceive, and it is by his assistance that our word, through which we proclaimed his gospel, has not wavered, but has always been consistent. For we – I, Silvanus, and Timothy – did not proclaim to you human things, but we passed on to you consistently and with one voice solid reality, efficacious, and unchangeable, namely, Jesus Christ, the Son of God, whose name has not been without effect among you, but has been powerful and efficacious, not by our assistance but by his kindness.

Having come to know the gifts of the Holy Spirit, you are thus far in possession of the down payment, and what has been promised for the future will not fail. For any promises that have been made are dependable through him, and they are unquestionable because of the very one to whom this glory is due.[21] For the promises that we have set before you are not ours. Their author is God; we are only servants and messengers. It contributes to his glory if what we proclaim in his name is found true and efficacious.

Moreover, it is a matter of God's gift that we have preached Christ unflinchingly, and that you stand firm in the religion of Christ that you accepted. In order that we may rely more on his promises, he has anointed us with his hidden gifts and has impressed his seal, as it were, on our minds. Indeed he has also set his Spirit in our hearts as a down payment and pledge of felicity promised for the future.

Accordingly, so that no one may attribute to inconstancy the fact that I have thus far postponed my return visit to you, I make God my witness: that I have not come to Corinth up to now was not the result of hatred towards you, but rather of a kindly disposition lest, if I had come sooner, I might be forced to show my anger against certain people who had not yet recovered their senses;[22] but I was confident, nevertheless, that they would in the meanwhile be corrected. I preferred to return somewhat later, provided that my coming might be more pleasant both for you and for me, for I did not want it to be sad and gloomy.

These statements should not appear to have been made in a threatening and somewhat imperious manner, but for your correction. We do not exercise power except over those who have sinned. Accordingly, in respect to faith, in which you persevere, we do not rule you. But in respect to your

* * * * *

21 For these commonplaces of Erasmus' thought, see the General Index of CWE 50 under 'God: is true,' under 'promises,' and under 'ministers.'

22 'Recovered their senses': *resipuerant*. Erasmus often uses *resipiscere* in its ecclesiastical sense of 'repent.' See the Argument of 1 Corinthians n15.

life I wanted some improvement. So far are we from threatening them in order to show off our authority over you that, instead, we have in this way taken into consideration your joy. I did not want your joy to be contaminated by any grief on account of the impure morals of certain people and my own unavoidable severity.

Chapter 2

Since I had unavoidably caused you grief by my earlier letter, condemning the incestuous man,[1] I decided not to act in such a way that my coming, too, would bring new grief to me as well as to you. For I should like always to cause you pleasure, never grief, if you let me. But if sometimes, provoked by the transgressions of certain people, I am forced, while correcting the few, to bring grief to all and to grieve myself, who will make me merry again except the very person whom I have touched with grief? That will happen if I see him healed by the bitterness of reproof and see you rejoicing with the one who has been healed, just as previously you participated in his sorrow.[2] In fact, I am writing this Epistle[3] to you before coming, for this very reason: that if I come to you I will not be pained by the very people who ought to be a source of pleasure and solace to me.[4] This is especially

* * * * *

1 See 1 Cor 5:1–5.
2 For healing as Paul's intention in rebuking the incestuous man, see the paraphrase on 1 Cor 5:5 with n9, and cf the paraphrase on 2:6 below. On the power of a reproof to heal, see also Erasmus' paraphrases on Acts 5:6 CWE 50 40 n15 and on Titus 1:13 CWE 44 60. For the theme in early Christianity, see Augustine *De correptione et gratia* 16.49 PL 44 946.
3 In this and in the following paragraph (paraphrasing 2:3–4) Erasmus uses the epistolary perfect tense *scripsi* (literally 'I have written'), used of present time in classical Latin epistles to indicate that the action is thought of as completed before the letter is delivered to its addressee. See Allen and Greenough 301 §479. Erasmus represents Paul as talking about this present letter, for he explicitly states *hanc epistolam.* Cf 1527 Vulgate, Erasmus' translation *hoc ipsum* 'this same' (DV), and Theophylact *Expos in 2 Cor* (on 2:3) PG 124 816C. RSV and modern scholars translate the Greek aorist ἔγραψα (Vulgate perfect *scripsi*) of 2:3–4 as a true past form and insist that Paul must be writing about a former letter, possibly a lost 'tearful letter.' See Furnish 153–4 (note on 2:3) and 159–60.
4 Erasmus' paraphrase on 2:3 corresponds to his annotation on that verse (*tristiam super tristiam*), where he rejects the Vulgate reading, 'that I may not, when I come, have sorrow upon sorrow' (DV). He argues there that 'sorrow upon sorrow' is an interpolation from Phil 2[:27] with the support of neither the Greek manuscripts available to him nor Ambrosiaster and Theophylact.

the case since I believe that you are so disposed towards me that, if I am distressed as a result of correcting certain people, my distress is shared by all of you; or if I rejoice because some have been set straight, my joy is likewise shared by you all.

Nothing would be sadder for me than to see in you what is unworthy of your profession; nothing more gladdening than to perceive that there is nothing in you that can be censured. And so, as I was upset beyond measure by the disgrace of the great outrage discovered in your midst, I am writing you this letter[5] in terrible torment of mind and anxiety of heart and with many tears – not in order to sadden you, but so that you may understand my love and affection towards you. The more my love inclines towards you and the more abundant it is in your regard, the more bitterly am I tormented if anything base appears in you. If anyone has given cause for distress, he has saddened not only me, but to some extent at least, he will have saddened all of you along with me.

But for that person (for I am not reporting his name, and one does not wish to recall an offence[6] for which its author is sorry),[7] it is sufficient punishment to have been reproved thus openly in the sight of all and shunned by all. This was done for his healing[8] and to deter the rest. Now it remains that you add no grief to the one brought low. No, rather you, the very people who bristled at the sinner, pardon the penitent; console the sorrowing so that he may not somehow be consumed by boundless anguish. On this account, I beseech you, since you condemned him out of charity, not hatred, and condemned him only that he might recover his senses[9] and be saved, make sure that you quickly and lovingly welcome, as reformed, the one you expelled with sorrow, so that he may also experience your love as efficacious in his regard.

For this, too, was the cause of my writing you this letter, namely, that I might test whether you comply with my instructions in all matters. You

* * * * *

Erasmus touches upon this point in his response to Zúñiga; see ASD IX-2 192:495–507.

5 'I am writing': again, the epistolary perfect. See n3 above.

6 'Offence': *facinoris*

7 Cf Theophylact *Expos in 2 Cor* (on 2:6) PG 817C–D, who notes that in 1 Corinthians 5 Paul did not wish 'even to name the person, but that here he does not name the person in order to spare him, and nowhere does he mention his offence, teaching us too to be more compassionate to the crushed.'

8 See n2 above.

9 'Might recover his senses': *resipisceret*. On this word, see chapter 1 n22 and the Argument of 1 Corinthians n15.

complied in condemning one I had bidden you condemn; you will comply also in receiving back into favour the person with whom I wish you
to be reconciled, so that in every respect our intentions[10] are in harmony.
Whomever you forgive, I too forgive, thinking amends have been made to
me if I see that they have been made to you. For I, too, if I have forgiven
anybody anything, have done it for your sake – Jesus Christ is my witness and judge – lest as a result of despair, Satan should snatch one of our
people away from us and take possession of him for himself.[11] We are well
aware of the disposition of Satan who lays traps for us, not only through
pleasures, but also through sadness; on the one side offering enticements
to disgraceful actions, on the other hurtling us into the abyss of despair.[12]

But when I had come to Troas to preach there the gospel of Christ[13] and
was being shown,[14] by the kindness of God, the hope of copious fruit, I was
terribly distressed because I did not find there, as I was hoping, Titus, my
brother and colleague, whose assistance I had needed to carry the weight of
the work. Accordingly, I said goodbye to the people there and not without
grave danger went off into Macedonia.

I give thanks to God,[15] who always through us spreads abroad the
triumph[16] of the Christian name and [through us] renders the triumph more

* * * * *

10 Erasmus has been using the first person singular in this chapter up to this
   point; *nostra voluntas* 'our intentions' here refers to the harmony between Paul
   and the Corinthians.
11 Despair is an important theme in Erasmus' spiritual writings. Its dangers and
   its antidote, ie reflection on God's mercy, are the substance of Erasmus' sermon
   De immensa Dei misericordia CWE 70 77–139. See also *De preparatione* CWE 70 408–
   9, 439–46. For the counsel 'there is no reason to despair,' often linked with
   reminders of God's mercy, see eg the paraphrases on Mark 5:36–43, 10:31,
   13:33 CWE 49 71–4, 127–8, 156; on Acts 2:21 and 37, 3:18 CWE 50 19, 22 with
   n88, 28; on James 5:7–11 CWE 44 167–8 nn13 and 14.
12 For the expression 'abyss of despair,' see *De immensa Dei misericordia* CWE 70 82.
13 of Christ] In all editions from 1519 to 1538; in *1540* and LB, 'of Jesus Christ.'
14 shown] In LB, 'shown there'
15 See Erasmus' comments on this expression in his annotations on Rom 6:17
   ('but [let us give] thanks to God') and 7:25 ('the grace of God') CWE 56 180
   and 195–6. A helpful distinction among expressions of gratitude in classical
   Latin is made by T.F. Carney in his commentary on Terence *Hecyra* 583–4. See
   Proceedings of the African Classical Association, Supplement 2 (Pretoria 1963) 96.
16 As his annotation on 2:14 (*qui semper triumphat nos*) shows, Erasmus understands 'triumph' here to refer to the Roman ritual in which the general leads
   in procession both the soldiers through whom his victory was won, so that
   they may share in their leader's glory, and the vanquished over whom the victory was achieved. But he also indicates that it is not clear whether the Greek

illustrious as day by day the glory of the gospel shines more widely.[17]
Everywhere on earth he disseminates knowledge of himself through our
proclamation, using us, so to speak, in the place of sweetly smelling incense.
For in preaching the glory of the gospel everywhere in the world, what else
are we doing but scattering the fragrance of Christ, pleasing even of itself
and salvific for all, but for many, through their own fault, deadly? It is
salvific for those who believe in the gospel and attain salvation, but death-
dealing to those who reject it and double the condemnation of death upon
themselves by adding to their former outrages the offence of ingratitude and
stubbornness. How few are suitable to play such a role as this! Whoever
wishes to discharge this office[18] must look at nothing other than the glory
of Christ. There are people who, teaching the gospel for ambition or gain,
do not so much scatter the fragrances of Christ as their own deceits,[19] and
further their own interests, not Christ's. From the ways of these people
we are far removed. For we do not vitiate the word of God with human
teaching, serving our own gain; but with a sincere heart we teach it as
something that has proceeded from God, not from ourselves. And we do
this – God himself is our witness – to the glory of Jesus Christ.

Chapter 3

But I am afraid that someone may think that we are making these claims
again in your presence in order to be more highly recommended to you

* * * * *

θριαμβεύοντι ἡμᾶς (Vulgate *triumphat nos,* NRSV 'he leads us in triumphal procession') means 'he triumphs concerning us' or 'he triumphs through us.' In
both his translation and paraphrase, Erasmus chooses the latter interpretation. For various modern interpretations of the verse, see Furnish 174–5. For
the concept of the triumph in Erasmus' Pauline paraphrases, see O'Mara 'Triumphs, Trophies, and Spoils' 111–25. See also Eph chapter 4 n17 and 1 Thess
chapter 2 n34.
17 Words connoting 'light' (here *illustris* 'bright,' 'shining,' 'famous' and *corus-
care* 'shine,' 'gleam,' 'flash') are also associated with 'glory' in Erasmus' paraphrases on Eph 3:10; Col 1:8; and 2 Thess 1:12.
18 Erasmus uses *fungi munere* 'to discharge the office,' to ensure that the reader
does not confuse the rank and privileges of officiant with the actual fulfilment
of the duties of that office. Elsewhere, for the same purpose he similarly uses
functio 'service' or 'ministry' with the name of the office in a genitive or ad-
jectival form. See his annotation on Rom 1:5 ('grace and apostleship') CWE 56
18–19. For the expression in Erasmus' paraphrases, see CWE 50 46 n8 and the
references there; also 84 n10. Cf the paraphrase on 1 Cor 9:2–4 with n9. See
also Col chapter 1 n7.
19 deceits] Added in 1532

and to others. What need is there of a recommendation when the situation itself[1] recommends a person? Or do we need the letters of reference that false apostles carry about, whether solicited from others for you, or from you for others? We care not at all for letters of this sort. You Corinthians are a living epistle – sufficient commendation we think – inscribed on our hearts, whereby more easily do I carry it about with me everywhere. It is both recognized and read far and wide by everyone.[2] As a result, there is now no need of other epistles, since your piety has given adequate testimony to all about the sort of apostles we have been.

And we are so confident about your attitude towards us that, self-recommended by our exercise of duty, we do not stand in need of letters of recommendation from people, so long as you show by sincerity of faith and evangelical life that you are the epistle of Christ, written by him indeed, but through our ministry; written, moreover, not with ink like those which humans write when they are teaching human matters, but written by the Spirit of the living God; nor, again, inscribed on the stone tablets on which human laws are inscribed, but on the fleshy tablets of the heart. Your minds, on which we imprinted evangelical doctrine, served as parchment[3] for us, our tongue as pen, but Christ himself dictated through his Spirit what we were to write.[4]

And yet, to the extent that the teaching of the gospel is more excellent than the law of Moses, our work is better than his. We do not claim for ourselves so great a deed, but nevertheless we do speak what is true – as God is our witness, who through Christ, by our ministry, has accomplished

* * * * *

1 'The situation itself': *res ipsa*. On this expression see the paraphrase on 1 Cor 1:6 with n13.
2 Erasmus, in his annotation on 3:2 (*quae scitur et legitur*), complains that the Vulgate fails to reproduce the charm (*venustas*) of Paul's Greek figure here. He translates γιγνωσκομένη καὶ ἀναγιγνωσκομένη as *intelligitur et legitur* 'understood and read' reproducing the homoioteleuton of the Greek in the Latin of both his translation and his paraphrase. On Paul's penchant for this kind of wordplay, see Furnish 181.
3 Erasmus uses the word *membrana* 'membrane', 'parchment,' which is applicable both to the parchment (treated animal skin) that was used for important texts and to the membrane of the heart, here used figuratively. Cf the annotation on 2 Tim 4:13 (*et membranas*). For *membrana* and the associated technology, see Harry Y. Gamble *Books and Readers in the Early Church: A History of Early Christian Texts* (New Haven 1995) 49–66. For the history of the metaphor of the heart or soul as 'book,' see Eric Jager *The Book of the Heart* (Chicago 2000).
4 The perfect tenses of the verbs *impressimus* 'we imprinted' and *dictavit* 'dictated' are taken as referring to the past evangelization of the Corinthians by Paul since he is referring to the process by which they became his 'letter.'

the things of which we speak. Otherwise, who are we, that we would be able by our own powers even to imagine something of this sort, to say nothing of achieving it? But if we have effected or do effect anything, we have and are doing it by God's kindness. As he assists us in our labours, so he has delegated to us this task of administering the new covenant, so that we might impart to you, not the old covenant whose administration was entrusted to Moses, which, as the false apostles teach it,[5] is a carnal[6] thing, placed in the letter, but the new, which is spiritual and heavenly, located in affections,[7] not in ceremonies.[8]

The authority that delegated is not different, but the execution of the task is different, and the apostolic ministry far more excellent. For the letter that was entrusted to Moses promotes death with its prescribed laws, inasmuch as it both stimulates the inclination to sin when occasion offers, and punishes the sinner with the loss of his life.[9] On the other hand, the Spirit that is conferred through gospel teaching offers life to those meriting death after all the transgressions of earlier life have been pardoned. But

* * * * *

5 as the false apostles teach it] Added in 1532. In his paraphrase on 1 Thess 4:2, in much of his *Paraphrase on Galatians*, and especially in the Argument of that Epistle, Erasmus warns against the tendency of the false apostles to mingle Jewish teaching with evangelical doctrine. See CWE 42 94–6. Cf also the Argument of 2 Corinthians n5.

6 'Carnal': *crassum*, literally 'gross', 'thick.' On Erasmus' use of this adjective, see 1 Cor chapter 2 n22. In Erasmus' vocabulary of spirituality, the contrast between the two covenants is often expressed in terms of heavy, carnal, burdensome, and earthly as opposed to light, spiritual, easy, and heavenly. See his paraphrases on Romans 1:9 and Gal 2:18 CWE 42 16 with n9 and 106 with n8; on Acts 2:1, 8:14, 15:1 CWE 50 13 with n4, 59 with n30, 94 with nn6 and 7; on James 1:24 and Heb 7:16 and 19 CWE 44 145 with n31 and 231 with n10. Jerome similarly distinguishes between the old law of the letter and the new spiritual law. See *Comm in Gal* II (on 4:1–2) PL 26:370A–B. Erasmus knew, however, that there was also a valuable, spiritual side to the Hebrew Scriptures and the Mosaic law. See his paraphrase on 2 Tim 3:14–17 CWE 44 51, his *De immensa Dei misericordia* CWE 70 117–8, and his paraphrase on Romans 16:25–7 CWE 42 90 with n6.

7 'Affections': *affectibus*. On this term, see 1 Cor chapter 15 n64.

8 Erasmus insists on an integral morality that values the disposition of the person and his docility to the inspiration of the Holy Spirit above formal observance of legalistic minutiae. See John O'Malley's introduction in CWE 66, especially xi–xxv; also Erasmus' colloquy 'The Godly Feast' CWE 39 181–91 and n157, and his paraphrase on 1 Cor 3:12–13 with nn20 and 22, on Titus 1:14–16 CWE 44 60–1 with n18, and especially on Philippians 3, where he gives a sustained description of the contrast.

9 See Erasmus' paraphrase on Rom 7:7–12 CWE 42 42–3 for his elaboration of the Law as 'the revealer of sin.'

if that previous Law, engraved in letters on stone, which brought death to the transgressor and did not confer grace, had so much majesty and glory that, when Moses was carrying down the tablets a second time, the Hebrews could not look upon his countenance because of a grandeur[10] and majesty that was, nonetheless, destined to pass away in time, why will the evangelical ministry not rather find its own grandeur and majesty, since it confers eternal salvation through faith and the Spirit's kindness?[11] If there was so much esteem for the Law that could condemn, but could not save, far more esteem is merited by the gospel, since through its preaching, not only is sin abolished, but also righteousness is conferred.

So vast is the difference in these things, that if someone wanted to make a rather close comparison with that which was of itself magnificent, the Law would seem to have no grandeur at all, obscured, so to speak, by the extraordinary glory of the gospel's grandeur. For if the Law, which was given for a fixed time only, soon to be rescinded,[12] had so much grandeur among men, much more grandeur has the evangelical law which, as it is given to all, so it is never to be abrogated. Indeed the new testament, by which the old is rescinded, is called everlasting by Christ, as I showed in my earlier Epistle.[13]

Relying on the sure conviction of this fact, we are not keeping the gospel under wrappings, but freely and openly[14] we bring forth the light

* * * * *

10 'Grandeur': *dignitatem*. Erasmus will repeat this word four times before the end of the next paragraph.

11 This is a very long sentence, whose meaning is obscured in LB by the punctuation, which mistakenly indicates a full stop and a new paragraph beginning at *cur non potius* 'why ... not rather.' *1532* shows a colon at that point.

12 'To be rescinded': *antiquanda*. The problematic word *antiquare*, used four times in this chapter, is interpreted in the latter part of this sentence by *abrogare* 'abrogate.' For Erasmus' use of the verb elsewhere in his New Testament scholarship, see 1 Cor chapter 1 n60.

13 If by 'my earlier Epistle' Erasmus is referring to 1 Corinthians, the most likely passage is 1 Cor 11:25, where the context is the institution of the Eucharist. Although Paul did not there describe the covenant as 'everlasting,' Erasmus' paraphrase interprets the cup as 'the new testament,' and the banquet is to be 'the symbol of an everlasting covenant.' See the paraphrase on that verse with n37. In the scriptural accounts of the institution of the Eucharist (Matt 26:26–9; Mark 14:22–4; Luke 22:19–20; 1 Cor 11:23–5), neither Christ nor Paul uses the word 'everlasting.' For the new covenant as an 'everlasting covenant' see Isa 55:3, 61:8; Jer 32:40; Ezek 16:60, 37:26; and for the expression 'blood of the everlasting covenant,' see Heb 13:20.

14 Erasmus here paraphrases the Greek παρρησία, Latin *libertas*, with *libere ac palam* 'freely and openly,' because, as he states in his annotation on 3:12 (*multa fiducia*), 'there is a reference here to Moses, who did not dare to speak openly

of the gospel, trusting both that such is the glory of this law that it should not be hidden, and that you have the strength and purity of mind to be able to look upon it. And so we are not doing what we read was done by Moses:[15] when he was bringing forward the second tablets, after the earlier ones had been broken,[16] he covered his face with a veil so that the Israelites might neither fix their eyes upon it nor stick fast there forever. Even by this sign an indication was given them that the glory of that Law must pass away; for not even then, when it was being introduced, did it shine with extraordinary[17] glory. What cannot be perceived is glorious in vain.[18]

This image[19] was depicting the insensitivity[20] of that people who seeing did not see, and hearing did not hear,[21] inasmuch as what was taking place on the face of Moses was in the truest sense happening in their minds, which were blinded as if covered over by the veil of dullness.[22] What

* * * * *

and clearly (*palam et aperte*) but with a veiled face.' For Erasmus' translations of παρρησία, a frequent New Testament descriptor of Paul's preaching, see CWE 50 33 n36 and 113 n19; cf Eph chapter 6 n40.

15 Moses did not wear the veil when he spoke with God or when he conveyed to the people the commandments of the Lord for the second time; it was immediately after he spoke with them that he put on the veil. See Exod 34:33–5.

16 Moses broke the first tablets at the foot of the mountain when he saw the golden calf. See Exod 32:19.

17 extraordinary] Added in *1532*. Cf Valla *Annot in 2 Cor* 3 (I 871): 'The sense is that the Old Testament, which is the Mosaic law, was not truly glorious because it was glorious in part, and glorious only on this account: that it was a figure of a greater glory, that is, of the New Testament for whose sake the Old itself was ordained.'

18 Cf Theophylact *Expos in 2 Cor* (on 3:13) PG 124 833A: 'Since what was not seen was not glory.'

19 'Image': *typus*. See LSJ τύπος V and VII. For the idiom *typum gerere* 'to be a type of,' see Erasmus' paraphrase on Romans 5:14 CWE 42 34. For other examples of typology, cf 1 Cor 10:1–13 and 15:45–50 and Erasmus' paraphrases on these passages, and 1 Cor chapter 10 nn4 and 10; also the paraphrases on Eph 5:32 and Phil 3:7.

20 'Insensitivity': *crassitudinem* 'thickness,' here 'a lack of subtlety in perception.' On *crassus*, see n6 above and 1 Cor chapter 2 n22. In this sentence, the connotation of *crassitudo* receives explication in the word *hebetudo* 'dullness,' 'lack of sharpness.' See n22 below.

21 See Matt 13:13–15, where Jesus explains why he speaks in parables.

22 'Dullness': *hebetudinis* derived from *hebes, – etis*: 'dull,' 'blunt-edged,' 'faint,' 'sluggish,' 'stupid.' Cf Ambrosiaster *Comm in 2 Cor* (on 3:14) CSEL 81/2 218:9–10, who explicates the text with language of sharpness: 'For the converted, the sharp edge [*acies*] of the mind is honed so that they may see the splendour of the divine light.'

is worse, even today that old blindness continues for this race, so that, although they read the books of the Law, they do not understand them, and in their zeal for the Law they stubbornly reject him at whose coming the Law is to be rescinded,[23] as the Law itself testifies.[24] Therefore, when they read the Old Testament in such a way that they are not willing to embrace the New promised in it,[25] that Mosaic veil even now remains upon them, does it not? Since the veil has not been removed by faith, they do not perceive that the wrapping of that Law is abolished[26] by Christ. They still cling tenaciously[27] to their Moses although the one has come whom Moses bade them heed. They read him in their synagogues, but they read dully,[28] looking for nothing but corporeal things, although the Law is spiritual if anyone brings to it keen-sighted eyes. A veil spread over their hearts hinders them right up to the present day; it is lifted by evangelical faith. But when they, too, having given up the insensitivity of their mind and embraced the faith we share, turn to the Lord, then the veil will be removed, so that they may perceive what is perceived only by the wholly purified eyes of faith.[29]

* * * * *

23 'Is to be rescinded': *antiquandam*. See n12 above.

24 Cf Jer 31:31–4: 'The days are coming, says the Lord, when I will make a new covenant . . . and I will write it upon their hearts' (RSV). Erasmus here includes the whole Old Testament under 'the Law.'

25 Erasmus conceived of the Mosaic law as 'two laws, the one base and carnal, the other spiritual' (CWE 42 45, paraphrasing Rom 8:3). See also n6 above; the paraphrases on Gal 4:21–6, 5:4, and 5:16 CWE 42 119, 122, and 125; and Erasmus' annotation on Rom 8:3 ('for what was impossible for the law') CWE 56 200 n4.

26 'Is abolished': *antiquatur*. See n12 above.

27 'Tenaciously': *mordicus* 'by the teeth' or 'tooth and nail.' Erasmus often uses this word in connection with law and rights. See the dedicatory letter for the *Paraphrase on Ephesians* 287, where he brings out the 'doggedness' of contemporary critics who hang on to old teachings 'with clenched teeth'; also his paraphrases on Eph 4:3 with n5, Acts 19:8 CWE 50 116 with n11, and Rom 4:1 and 8:8 CWE 42 26 and 46.

28 For the reading of Moses in the synagogue, see Acts 15:21. 'Dully': *crasse*. See n20 above.

29 Erasmus likes the expressions 'eyes of faith' and 'eyes of the mind' or 'eyes of the heart,' and uses them elsewhere as an expressed contrast to the 'physical eyes' which can see only what is corporeal. See Erasmus' paraphrases on Acts 1:9 and 9:9 CWE 50 8 with n48 and 64 with n16; on John 1 (preface), 6:41, and 9:1 CWE 46 13 with n3, 84 with n57, and 121 with n2; on Rom 11:7 and Gal 3:1 CWE 42 64 and 108 with n2; also on 1 Cor 3:22 with n36; 2 Cor 4:4 and 18; Eph 1:18 with n45. See also Origen *Martyrdom* xxxvi 67: 'The splendour of the coming of Christ, by illuminating the law of Moses with the radiance of

Moses was corporeal and earthly,[30] but the Lord Jesus is spirit, teaching not what is perceived by the eyes of the body but invisible realities
believed through faith.[31] The Mosaic law, since it held people to observance through fear of punishment, was servile, and the veil is an indication of servitude.[32] But where there is the Spirit of the Lord Jesus, who applies secret goads, so that even without being bidden we are borne along
to observances of piety, there is liberty.[33] No one is driven to faith, but
the person who has truly believed avoids defilement of his own accord
and embraces innocence; indeed, under the impulse of charity, he willingly performs far more than could be beaten out of the Jews by fear of
penalties.[34]

They are blinded, therefore, who lack the eyes of faith; we, with face
unveiled, gaze with sincere faith on the glory of the Lord. While we receive
his radiance as though from a mirror, we are somehow being transformed
into the same image,[35] pouring out upon others the radiance received from
the Lord. Just as long ago, as a result of his conversation with God, the face
of Moses once shone like a mirror reflecting the sun,[36] so our soul is furnished more and more with hidden increases, day after day, and advances
from glory to glory on account of its intimacy with the Lord's Spirit, which
is imperceptibly accomplishing in us, even now, what at some time it will
openly bring to fulfilment.

* * * * *

truth, removed the veil that had been placed over the letter and laid open to
all who believe in him the good things that were hidden within.'
30 'Earthly': *crassus*. On this word, see n20 above.
31 Erasmus develops these ideas in his paraphrase on Gal 4:1–5 CWE 42 115.
32 On servitude to the Law, see Erasmus' paraphrases on Rom 8:14–15 and Gal
4:5–6 CWE 42 47 and 115–16. On the veil as an indication of servitude, see 1
Cor 11:3–15, on which Erasmus elsewhere bases his statement that the wedding
veil (although not the virgin's veil) is 'clearly a sign of subjection, as even Paul
testifies.' See *Virginis et martyris comparatio* CWE 69 179. See also the paraphrases
on 1 Cor 11:6–7, 10, and 15.
33 On freedom derived from the Spirit of Christ, see the paraphrase on Gal 5:13
CWE 42 124–5
34 For the contrast between a voluntary and generous response of love and compliance with law coerced through fear of its sanctions, see eg Erasmus' paraphrases on Gal 5:6 and 13 CWE 42 122–3 and 124–5, and the paraphrase on 1
John 2:3 CWE 44 179.
35 Ambrosiaster *Comm in 2 Cor* (on 3:18) CSEL 81/2 219:15–17 recalls 1 John 3:2:
'We know that when he appears we shall be like him' (RSV).
36 For the radiance of Moses' face, see Exod 34:29–30, 35.

Chapter 4

Accordingly, since the compassion of God willed us to be ministers and heralds of such exceptional felicity, through the apostolic task delegated to us, we do not take up our commission in a lackadaisical manner. Instead, just as we proclaim what is truly glorious, so we have rejected the wrappings that suit disgrace, not glory. We do not live our life under cunning disguises, nor do we treat the word of God insincerely through the crafty subtleties of human learning,[1] but openly, frankly, and without disguise, we expose to everyone's view the whole truth unadorned and veiled by no cloud. In this service we behave in such a way that our life itself, apart from human commendation, commends us before all people, the witnesses and confidants of our sincerity; commends us, indeed, not only before humans, who can be deceived, but also before God, who misses nothing.[2]

Consequently, the truth of the gospel shines out through us, hidden from no one. But if there should still be some to whom it is not clear, and so on this account does not bring salvation, this has occurred through their own fault, not the gospel's and not ours.[3] Actually, just as was said of the Israelites,[4] these too have a veil placed over the eyes of their hearts, so as not to perceive realities that, of themselves, are very clear. They grope about,

* * * * *

1 The paraphrase here on 4:2 ('not ... handling the word of God deceitfully; but by manifestation of the truth commending ourselves ...' [AV]) closely follows Erasmus' Latin translation of the verse and the explanation he offers in the annotation on 4:2 (*nec adulterantes*). The Vulgate had translated the Greek δολοῦντες 'disguising' or 'falsifying [God's word]' by *adulterantes* 'adulterating,' 'falsifying.' Erasmus preferred *dolo tractantes* 'treating with deceit' or 'with cunning,' and he elaborated in his note: 'not courting people's favour through deceit, but through sincerity of preaching.'

2 Cf Theophylact *Expos in 2 Cor* (on 4:2) PG 124 837C: 'Since it is possible to deceive humans, Paul then says "in the sight of God," whom false apostles would not welcome as witness.'

3 Erasmus echoes Theophylact *Expos in 2 Cor* (on 4:3) PG 124 837D: 'It is the unbelievers' fault, not the gospel's.' For Erasmus' concern with asserting human, rather than divine, responsibility for failure, see the paraphrase on Acts 1:25 CWE 50 12 with n105.

4 See 2 Cor 3:15. Erasmus develops an analogy (only hinted at by Paul's use of the participle 'veiled' in 4:3) between the Jews treated in 3:12–15 and the unbelievers treated here in 4:3–4. Theophylact *Expos in 2 Cor* (on 4:3) PG 124 837D made the same analogy: 'For what there related to the Jews in respect to Moses here relates to unbelievers in respect to the gospel.'

to use a phrase, in broad daylight,[5] for they bring with them eyes that are impure and vitiated by worldly desires. Through such desires Satan, who is the god of this age (for those make him their god who listen to him more than to the true God),[6] has blinded the minds of the unbelieving so that the gospel's truth might not be able to dawn upon them, as their eyes are covered over. It is the gospel's truth that makes perfectly evident the glory and majesty, not of Moses, but of Christ, who is the image of God the Father so that, through the Son, who is his equal, the Father, too, may be recognized.

And we do not, after the fashion of certain individuals, preach ourselves, handing down the gospel for our own gain or glory, but we preach Jesus Christ our Lord; his teachings we hand down, not our own; it is for him as Lord we labour, whatever labour we do. Far from arrogating anything to ourselves,[7] we profess to be your slaves, ministering to you in the gospel, not through fear of you or hope for compensation, but on account of Jesus. Although we are free, out of love for him we subject ourselves to all as slaves. We ourselves, too, once laboured under that same blindness under which some individuals are still labouring. Nor did we bring forth this light for ourselves; but God, at whose bidding light was first created, from whom all light proceeds, dispelled the shadows of our soul and in their place bade the light of truth to break forth. Or rather, he himself, as he is

* * * * *

5 'They grope about ... in broad daylight': *in medio sole caligent*; literally 'they are covered in darkness in the middle of sunlight.' For the idiom see L&S *caligo* II A.

6 Cf Erasmus' annotation on 4:4 (*deus huius seculi*): Paul is not in any straightforward way calling the devil a god, but only identifying him 'as a god to those who value him above Christ.' Erasmus argues here against those (Theophylact and Ambrosiaster are named from *1519*; Chrysostom also from *1527*) who interpreted the subject of the sentence to be God and then referred the genitive 'of this age' by a difficult hyperbaton to the unbelievers: 'God has blinded the unbelievers of this age.' Cf eg Theophylact *Expos in 2 Cor* (on 4:4) PG 124 840A–B, who seems to adopt the latter reading, in part to avoid the difficulties of a Manichaean understanding, in which the term 'god of this age' would seem to give Pauline legitimacy to the belief in a powerful, evil creator-deity, standing opposed to the good and just God. Erasmus finds it 'truer and simpler' to read the syntax naturally, and to understand the 'god of this age' – only an apparent god – as Satan.

7 The importance of preserving the distinction between master and steward, between author and minister, is a familiar theme in the *Paraphrases*. See eg the paraphrase on 1 Cor 1:12–13 with n32; also the annotation on Rom 15:19 ('of wonders in the strength of the Holy Spirit') CWE 56 408.

eternal light, dawned upon our heart, so that through us, from then on, his majesty might shine forth more widely among all, becoming clear by the preaching of the gospel wherein we preach the Lord Jesus. In his face the image and glory of the Father shine forth with the greatest radiance.[8]

For the time being, such a great thing is being effected in our souls only, since in respect to physical appearance we seem to be abject and wretched. We are carrying around a treasure so precious in poor earthen pots, that is, in our puny bodies, which are subject to affliction and reproach. So God resolved, and his resolution was not without purpose. For he took that precaution lest perhaps, because of the magnitude of his kindness and the loftiness[9] of the miracles that are being performed through us, we should become proud and claim something from this source for ourselves.[10] Rather he wanted us, aware of our weakness, to understand that the pre-eminent power that has been granted to apostles is not a matter of our own strength, but belongs to God alone; while we ourselves, daily, through our weakness, are afflicted with evils, yet with God's help we persevere unconquered in the evils that have to be endured. While we in all

* * * * *

8 The paraphrase here on 4:6 may reflect Heb 1:3. Cf the paraphrase on that verse CWE 44 215: 'He was (and still is) the eternal brightness of the Father's glory in the way that light emanates from light. He was the express image of his substance, similar and equal in everything to him from whom he is born.' So also in his annotation on 4:6 (*in facie Christi Iesu*) Erasmus says that 'in the face of Christ the glory of God the Father has shone forth brightly, as in a most perfect likeness.'

9 the loftiness] Added in 1532. By this addition, Erasmus appears to be making a minor concession to the Vulgate, while at the same time preserving a distinction he emphasizes in his translation and interpretation of 4:7b. The Vulgate's translation reads *ut sublimitas sit virtutis Dei, et non ex nobis* 'that the loftiness may be that of God's power and not from us.' Erasmus preferred *eminentia* 'eminence' or 'superiority' to *sublimitas* 'loftiness,' and his translation reads instead *ut virtutis eminentia sit dei, et non ex nobis* 'that the eminence of the [or 'our'] power may be that of God and not from us.' In his annotation on 4:7 (*ut sublimitas*), Erasmus cites Augustine in support of *eminentia* and also of the more important syntactical and interpretive difference that distinguishes Erasmus' translation from that of the Vulgate (cf Augustine Ep 175.3 PL 33 761). The force of Erasmus' interpretation is to make clear that the powerful actions are indeed Paul's, while still attributing the source of their power to God. The paraphrase in this sentence and the next appears to accommodate both the Vulgate's and Erasmus' understandings of the verse by adding *sublimitas* after 1532 and by referring both to the 'magnitude of [God's] kindness' as well as to the 'extraordinary power ... granted to apostles.'

10 See n7 above.

ways are indeed oppressed by adversity, yet we are not distressed; we are reduced to penury, but are not in penury destitute; we suffer persecution, but are not in persecution deserted; we are cast down and trampled upon, but not, however, so as to perish; and in this respect we are imitating, to the best of our ability, the Lord Jesus whom we preach.

He died once on behalf of all. We, exposed every day to the dangers of death, carry about, as it were, his death in our body, as we spend this life for you. We do this so that, just as we imitate the death of Jesus by dying on your behalf, so too the life of Jesus, the life through which he lived again after death, might be shown in our body,[11] while either we are snatched by him from death, or while, by showing contempt for the life of the body, we openly bear witness to and affirm the resurrection of bodies. For the life of the body would not be so cheap in our eyes if we believed that once extinguished the body would never live again. And so it happens in a new way that the immortal life of Christ becomes more manifest to you through the affliction of our body, which is subject to death. It is indeed death that makes its assault against our person, but the fruit of life, which is born of our death, redounds to you, for whose sake we expose ourselves to these evils.

However, we do not on that account regret the gospel, for since we ourselves also have the gift of faith – the faith by which you hope for future immortality, the gift that was infused in your souls by us[12] – it happens that just as David testifies in the mystical psalm[13] that he speaks because he has believed, so we, confident in our trust, do not hesitate to preach the gospel truth in the midst of mortal danger. In fact, we are certain that the one who has raised the Lord Jesus from death will, through him, raise us

* * * * *

11 Cf the annotation on 4:10 (*vita Iesu manifestetur in corporibus nostris*), where Erasmus emends the Vulgate's 'in our bodies' and explains that, when Paul speaks of the 'life of Jesus' being manifested 'in our body,' he is referring not to any individual body, but to 'body' as 'that which is opposed to spirit.' For the idea that 'the life of Jesus' here refers to the 'resurrected Jesus,' see Theophylact *Expos in 2 Cor* (on 4:10) PG 124 844A.

12 Cf the paraphrase on 1 Cor 1:24, where Erasmus elaborates in similar fashion on the gift of faith and the transformational power of gospel preaching. For the language of 'infusion,' see 1 Cor chapter 1 n53 and CWE 56 154 n13.

13 'Mystical psalm': *psalmo mystico*, ie a 'prophetic' psalm or one 'requiring spiritual interpretation.' See the paraphrase on 1 Cor 14:1 with n1. On *mysticus*, see also 1 Cor chapters 5 n12 and 10 n7. The passage in question is Ps 116:10, which Paul in 2:13 quotes from the Septuagint (115:1a). See Furnish 258.

also, who have died for him, and will display us along with you in the
shared glory of the resurrection since here a shared faith unites us.[14] But
whether we are in the meanwhile[15] afflicted, or are freed from affliction,
all things are done for your sake in order that the truth of the gospel may
be disseminated more widely among you and that the more there are who
come to their senses and repent, the more there may be to give thanks, not
to us, but to God, for it pertains to his glory that the faith, which he wished
all to share, be propagated as widely as possible.[16]

With this hope and relying on this disposition, we are not worn out by
any evils. No, we grow strong instead, well aware of the fact that although
the body, the exterior part of us, is being gradually worn out by daily
labours, nevertheless, while the body grows weaker every day, the soul,
the interior and better part of us,[17] becomes healthier and more vigorous,
as if it is being rejuvenated by the evils themselves and senses in advance
the immortality to come.[18]

Indeed, the affliction of the body that we sustain for the sake of the
gospel is slight and transitory. But this slight affliction produces in us no
slight consequence, rather the weighty and inexpressible consequence[19] of

* * * * *

14 Ambrosiaster *Comm in 2 Cor* (on 4:14) CSEL 81/2 226:3–11 similarly calls a
    shared faith the basis of a shared resurrection 'so that they may be of one
    faith in one home of peace.'
15 in the meanwhile] Added in *1532*. Here in paraphrasing the beginning of 4:15,
    'For it is all for your sake (RSV),' Erasmus follows Ambrosiaster *Comm in 2 Cor*
    (on 4:15) CSEL 81/2 226:20–2 in identifying 'all [things]' as the persecutions
    Paul was willing to endure.
16 Ambrosiaster, too, *Comm in 2 Cor* (on 4:15) CSEL 81/2 226:22–227:6 explains that
    it is God's glory that is at stake in the success of Paul's mission: 'Paul was to
    preach to all so that more could believe, with the result that the overflowing
    gift of God would not, because few offered thanks, be diminished – with
    insult to God ... It is no small insult, is it, when someone gives an opulent
    banquet and although he invites many, has in the end few [who respond]?'
17 'Better part of us': *melior nostri pars*. This is perhaps an echo of Ovid *Metamor-
    phoses* 15.875: *parte tamen meliore mei super alta perennis / astra ferar* 'Still in my
    better part I shall be borne immortal far beyond the lofty stars.'
18 Cf Ambrosiaster *Comm in 2 Cor* (on 4:16) CSEL 81/2 227:15–17: 'By afflictions,
    blows, hunger, thirst, cold, exposure, the body is ruined, but the soul in hope
    of the reward to come is renewed, because by continual tribulations it is
    cleansed. Indeed under distress, instead of perishing, it advances.'
19 'Consequence': *pondus*, literally 'weight.' In his annotation on 4:17 (*quod in
    praesenti est momentaneum et leve*) Erasmus notes the force of παραυτίκα 'of the
    moment,' 'temporary,' contrasting with αἰώνιον 'eternal' and suggests that by

glory, since on account of the slight affliction sustained for the sake of Christ, we are made worthy of the supreme happiness, while a temporary death met for the sake of Christ begets for us the reward of unending immortality. Supported by this hope, we consider the life of the body worth nothing, looking not at all to such things as are seen with bodily eyes, but to those that are seen only with the eyes of faith. For the things that are perceived here, such as profit, honour, pleasure, life, loss, disgrace, suffering, death, besides the fact that they are neither real goods nor real evils, are not even[20] of long duration. Those that are perceived with the eyes of faith, however, are as true as they are eternal.

Chapter 5

This, indeed, is the assurance upon which we consider even life to be cheap. For we know with certainty that even though it should fall[1] to our lot on earth that the soul be driven out of the dwelling of this poor little body, another home has been prepared, in heaven, from which we are never to be cast out. (I might more truly have called the body a tent than a dwelling since we cannot linger in it for very long, no matter how far off is the one who will force us out.) This house, since it is of clay and of human creation, grows shakier willy-nilly every day although no one is demolishing it. In just the same way we see buildings that are constructed by human hands crumbling with age. What has been fashioned by[2] humans cannot be of long duration; what has been restored by God and already made heavenly does not feel the ravages of time. Far from being reluctant to depart from this poor body, we actually sigh here in the meantime, praying to be relieved of the baggage of the mortal body, by which the soul is weighted down so long as it is on earth.[3] It longs to fly away[4] to another place and to be

* * * * *

leve 'slight' Paul means not 'what is easy to bear,' but 'what passes quickly,' and that 'weight' refers not to 'what weighs down,' but to 'the solid and permanent.'
20 even] Added in 1532

1 it should fall] First in 1521; in 1519 'it falls'
2 LB mistakenly prints ad 'towards' or 'for,' instead of ab 'by.'
3 For the body as a burden weighing down the soul, cf the paraphrase on 1 Cor 15:44 with nn62 and 63; also CWE 50 109 n42.
4 to fly away] Added in 1521, probably to correct an unintended omission in 1519, since both the sense and the syntax of the verb gestire 'long for' or 'desire eagerly' are normally completed by an infinitive (L&s gestio II); moreover, the passage reads harshly without the infinitive.

covered with the dwelling of a glorified body, one that will be given back to us from heaven transformed, if only,[5] after we have been stripped of this present body,[6] we should be found not utterly naked, but clothed in the hope of immortality as a result of the assurance that comes from a good life.[7]

In the meanwhile we groan, weighed down by this body subject to so many ills, not because moving from here is of itself a happy event, but because we wish this body to be restored to something better, and in place of mortality to be given immortality through the resurrection. This we desire so that we might seem not to have been stripped of the body, which we have laid aside for the time being, but better clothed with the same body, which we shall receive back as an eternal body in place of a perishable one.

And there is no reason for us to lack faith that, however incredible it seems, in place of a mortal body an immortal one will rise, subject to

* * * * *

5 'If only': si tamen or 'if at least,' 'if nevertheless,' or 'provided that'; for si tamen = si modo 'if only,' see L&S tamen II B (1). Some English translations represent the Greek of 5:3 as indicating purpose (DV, RSV), some proviso (NRSV). For the interpretive difficulties of this verse see next note.

6 Erasmus' reading of 5:3 here differs from both the Vulgate and his Latin translation. Erasmus knew of the two readings for the participle in the Greek text – ἐνδυσάμενοι 'having put on' or 'clothed' and ἐκδυσάμενοι 'having taken off' or 'unclothed.' See the annotation on 5:3 (si tamen vestiti, et non nudi inveniamur). Erasmus chose the former for his Greek text and Latin translation: 'If nevertheless clothed [ie if we have put on the heavenly domicile], we shall not be found naked.' In the paraphrase, however, he elaborates primarily on the other reading, 'unclothed': the body will be given back to us glorified 'provided that, when we have been stripped [ie of the present body or life], we should not be found naked' – naked, presumably because of the unworthiness of our present life. On this clause, see the next note. The interpretation of the verse as proviso (see previous note) may have been suggested to Erasmus by Theophylact Expos in 2 Cor (on 5:3) PG 124 818C–D (although Theophylact read the participle in question as 'clothed'): '"Provided that we," Paul says, "clothed with incorruption," and receiving an uncorrupted body, "not be found naked" of glory and assurance, as having the deformity of sin. For the resurrection is common to all, but not so the honour.' For the idea that there is a resurrection awaiting the ungodly, and that it will be one lacking in glory, see the paraphrase on 5:9 with n10; also 1 Cor chapters 6 n40 and 15 n60. On the textual problem in 5:3 and the lack of modern consensus, see Metzger 511; also Furnish 267–8, 295–9.

7 Interpreting 5:3 as a proviso clause, Erasmus incorporates a variation on one of his common themes: the necessity of practising goodness in this life to ensure the immortality to come. See 1 Cor chapters 3 n12, 6 n40, and 15 n77.

no harm. It is God who has prepared us for this very thing – that we may enjoy the glory of immortality – and it is he also who has imparted to us for the time being, as a pledge and down payment, his Spirit, which might confirm that hope of the future with its present inspiration. So whatever storms arise, we are always confident in heart. We are quite aware of the fact that, for as long as we are at home in this habitation of the body, we are in a foreign land and separated from God. Death joins us to him more closely, not because God is not present to us in the meantime, but because he is not yet clearly perceived in the way he will be gazed upon then. For in the interim he is in some way perceived through faith, but as if from a distance; then he will be seen close up, as he is, not through a veil.[8]

Therefore, we are confident: even if God should wish us to be afflicted in the body for a while longer, we will readily endure, whatever happens, in the hope of a future reward. But still, from our point of view it is preferable to move from this dwelling, if that should be our lot, so that, separated from the body, we may be united directly with God. For that reason we strive to be acceptable to God, whether we should be forced to carry on in this dwelling, or, as we prefer, should have the fortune to move on, that is to say, whether we live or die. For it is not possible to hope for the reward of immortality unless a person has departed from here pleasing to God (in case someone should suppose that baptism is enough to win him that prize, apart from pious deeds).[9] For indeed the impious, through their own wrongdoing, get back the bodies that here they misused for their own lusts, not using them for the glory of God.[10] In keeping with the merits of life, each person's reward will come to him. These are not yet in the open, but we shall, nevertheless, all have to make our appearance openly before the tribunal of Christ. There, nothing will be covered, so that each person might reap a harvest in keeping with the sowing he did in the body, and when the body has been restored, each might carry off a reward in keeping with the nature of the actions that he performed in the body, whether good or evil.

* * * * *

8 This paraphrase on 5:7 echoes 1 Cor 13:12. Cf the paraphrase on that verse.
9 On the insufficiency of baptism, if not accompanied by godliness, see 1 Cor chapter 6 n26.
10 For the assertion that, at the time of the resurrection, the wicked will take back their former perishable bodies, not transformed and glorified with immortality, cf the paraphrases on 1 Cor 6:14 with n40, 15:42 and 49–58 with nn60 and 61. See also n6 above.

Accordingly, having that dreadful day always before our eyes, we take care that everywhere we may be pleasing both to God and to men. Although we may deceive humans by a false appearance of piety, we are nevertheless clearly visible to God, who, unlike humans, sees through the inmost parts of our minds.[11] However, I trust that I have dealt with you in such a way that in your mind you hold our sincerity well known and clearly obvious. With this glory we are content.

We are not extolling our service again in order to gain more esteem from you, or to court some advantage from you. But since I see others boasting because they have been instructed by exceptional apostles,[12] we are providing you with an opportunity of being able to congratulate yourselves concerning us likewise, over against those who are putting you down on this account, that the apostle you got was worthless and insignificant. Granted that we did not see the Lord in a mortal body as others have done; still we have seen him as immortal, from him we have received the apostolic commission in the same way as the rest, and, through his help, we are no less distinguished than the rest.[13] I am recalling this for your

* * * * *

11 Cf Ps 139, especially 1–6, 13–16, 23–4. Erasmus may also have in mind 1 Cor 4:5. See the paraphrase on that verse. Cf also Luke 16:15; Acts 1:24; Rom 8:27; 1 Cor 2:10–13; Heb 4:12–13.

12 Cf the paraphrases on 11:5 with n11 and 12:11 with n13. On rivalry fostered by followers of one identified sarcastically as even 'the highest apostle' (*summus apostolus*), cf the extended exposition in the paraphrase on 1 Cor 4:6–16 with nn5, 6, and 9. Theophylact *Expos in 2 Cor* (on 5:12) PG 124 852D identifies the opponents who were 'ripping us apart with insults' as 'false apostles.'

13 In defending the legitimacy of his apostolate, Paul charges in 5:12 that his Corinthian critics 'boast in outward appearance' (NRSV; cf RSV: 'pride themselves on a man's position'). Erasmus' interpretation here that by 'outward appearance' Paul means his critics' boast of instruction 'by exceptional apostles' who, unlike Paul, could trace their apostolic commissions back to Jesus' mortal life, may derive from Ambrosiaster *Comm in 2 Cor* (on 5:12) CSEL 81/2 233:11–13: 'They had been taught by [apostles] who were always with the Lord,' ie presumably not latecomers like Paul. Erasmus constructs a similar Pauline defence in the paraphrase on Gal 1:1 CWE 42 97, rejecting any qualitative difference based on whether an apostolic commission came during or after Jesus' mortal life. See also nn15 and 17 below. For Paul's claim to equality with the most eminent apostles, see 11:5–12:13 and Erasmus' paraphrase on that passage. Cf also the paraphrases on 1 Cor 7:25 with n53 and especially 1 Cor 9:1–4 with nn4 and 6. For Paul's call to apostolic service, see Acts 9:3–19, recounted in Acts 22:6–16, 26:12–18. Cf Gal 1:13–17. On Erasmus' description of the apostolic office, see CWE 50 12 n98.

Modern commentators may not follow Erasmus' interpretation of 5:12; Furnish

sake, so that you may have an answer for those who are not content with the awareness of good deeds, but out of arrogance and haughtiness hunt for human praise, although their conscience is uneasy. We say nothing for our own sake. If, in making great claims for ourselves, we seem to be insane, we are insane for God: to his glory we proclaim what we have accomplished through him. Or if, when we say ordinary things about ourselves, we seem sane, we are sane for you: with an eye to your weakness we moderate our speech.[14] It is not out of boasting that we equate ourselves with the rest of the apostles, but the love of Christ compels us to speak openly what avails for his glory. For it contributes to his praise, not ours, if something special has been accomplished – through us, indeed, but by his gift – so that it may be more manifest to everyone that his death has not been fruitless, since it profits all on an equal basis. Hence, through us, too, he exerts his power, and not only through those who saw Christ in the body or who have a physical relationship with him.[15]

In fact, the consideration that weighs more heavily with us is this: that if Christ alone has died for all on an equal basis, all whom he willed to redeem from death by his own death must have been equally subject to death. Furthermore, he has died for all to this end, that he may have all equally bound to him, and that those who by his kindness are alive, reborn through him, may live no longer for themselves, but for him who died for

* * * * *

324 eg suggests that the critics' boast in 'what is outward' probably refers to Paul's rivals' claims of 'ecstatic visions,' for Paul turns next (5:13) to ecstatic experience.

14 For the accommodation of speech to the weakness of hearers, see the paraphrase on 1 Cor 3:1 with n3. Cf also a *1519* addition to Erasmus' annotation on 2 Cor 5:13 (*sive sobrii sumus*): 'For if Paul boasts at all, it pertains not to his own glory, but to God's. If he speaks ordinary things, he yields to the weaker ones, to whose feelings and capacity he accommodates himself.' Cf Paul's instructions in 1 Cor 14:1-25 regarding the gift of speaking in tongues (which pertains only to the speaker's own relationship to God) as opposed to the gift of prophecy (which edifies the whole congregation). See Erasmus' paraphrase on that passage.

15 'Physical relationship': *carnalis affinitas*, probably meaning a family connection, literally 'a relationship (or kinship) of the flesh.' Cf n17 below. Erasmus may have in mind, in particular, the James who is identified as 'the Lord's brother' in Gal 1:19, as a witness of the risen Jesus in 1 Cor 15:7, and as a leader of the Jerusalem church in Acts 12:17, 15:13, and 21:18. Cf 1 Cor chapter 9 n14. On James, see 1 Cor chapter 15 n12 and the General Index in CWE 50 under 'James the Just.' On 'eminent apostles,' see nn12 and 13 above.

them and for them has lived again.[16] It is on the basis of these considerations
that we must be judged, not on a kinship that is physical.[17]

Indeed, although we too can boast of Israelite origin, nevertheless,
since being initiated into Christ, we know no one according to the flesh.
We consider our relatives to be those who are united with us by the fellowship of faith. In vain,[18] therefore, do certain people boast that they share
a common family line with Christ, that they are joined to him by a kinship of blood, that they had a physical association with him. Flesh was seen
for a time. Now, since his body has been lifted up[19] and the Spirit sent,[20]
he wants to be recognized according to the Spirit, and he considers as his
closest relative the person who completely trusts in his promises. There is
no reason for anyone to belittle us later apostles on account of the fact that
we did not know Christ while he was living in his mortal body on earth
since, even if it had been our fortune to know him, we now would have
laid aside that knowledge, which was standing in the way of the Spirit, and
in a spiritual manner we would love him who has become spiritual.

Accordingly, let each one who has been grafted onto Christ through
baptism[21] lay aside the old attitudes and not think 'this one is a Jew, that
one a Greek, this one a slave, that one a free man,'[22] but recall that each and
every one has been reborn into a new person, now changed from carnal

* * * * *

16 'Has lived again': *revixit*. On the language of 'resurrection,' see 1 Cor chapter
   15 n9 and the annotations on Rom 13:11 ('to rise from sleep') and 14:9 ('he
   died and rose again') CWE 56 357-8 and 376-7.
17 'On a kinship that is physical': *ex carnis propinquitate*; literally 'on a kinship of
   the flesh.' Cf nn13 and 15 above. Erasmus may again be alluding to James,
   known as 'the Lord's brother,' or perhaps in general to apostles who knew
   Jesus during his mortal life, or even more generally to Jewish descent. The
   obsolescence of this last distinction is in fact a specific issue in the next paragraph of the paraphrase, as Erasmus takes up the meaning of 'human point
   of view' in 5:16. Cf the paraphrase on 10:7 with n11; also Ambrosiaster *Comm
   in 2 Cor* (on 11:4) CSEL 81/2 282:14-18, who notes that some Corinthians were
   comparing Paul unfavourably to apostles who had seen Jesus in the flesh.
18 In vain ... who has become spiritual] The remainder of the paragraph was
   added in 1532.
19 A reference to Jesus' ascension: Acts 1:9-11. See also Jesus' prophecy in John
   12:32: 'And I, when I am lifted up from the earth, will draw all people to
   myself' (NRSV).
20 A reference to Pentecost: Acts 2:1-4
21 For the image of grafting to represent the result of baptism, see Rom 11:17-24.
   Cf the paraphrase on 1 Cor 6:7-8 with n13.
22 Erasmus alludes to Gal 3:28.

into spiritual. Old things have passed away, and behold, through Christ suddenly all things have been made new! So then,[23] let there be an end to those human expressions: 'this is a Greek, this a barbarian, this a Jew, this one but recently a worshipper of idols, this one a violator of the sacred.' The person has ceased to be what he was, and through the workmanship of Christ he has been changed into a new creature, as different from the old self as any beast differs from a human.

But whatever has been conferred on us through Christ has come from the Father who reconciled us to himself, once sin had been vanquished, through his Son Jesus Christ. And the Father also has entrusted to us the preaching of this reconciliation so that, just as the Son fulfilled for the Father a mission among men, so might we fulfil the mission for Christ. Indeed, when Christ was living, as a mortal among mortals, although he seemed simply a man, still, God the Father was in him reconciling the world to himself through Christ's ministry, and through him[24] restoring to newness the world he had once created through him.[25] With such great mercy did he receive humans into grace, that not only did he not exact punishment for the transgressions of their earlier life, but he did not even impute to anyone the sins committed before baptism,[26] just as if one were now not the same person as before. This grace of reconciliation he willed to confer through the Son to be preached by us.

We, therefore, fulfilling in the place of Christ this mission entrusted by him, beseech you in the name of Christ, as if God were exhorting[27] you

* * * * *

23 So then ... differs from a human] Added in 1532, and expanding the paraphrase on 5:17, this passage further emphasizes the absence, within the new community of believers, of former distinctions. Erasmus here appears to be alluding, in particular, to Col 3:10–11, but reorganizing Paul's distinctions from that passage into two sets of fundamental contrasts: first, the cultured Greek and the uncultured barbarian; and second, the triple contrast of a Jew, a long-time devotee of idols, and a totally irreligious and truly profane person.

24 through him] Added in 1532

25 Erasmus follows Ambrosiaster *Comm in 2 Cor* (on 5:19) CSEL 81/2 237:15–16 in noting that the agent of reconciliation had also been the agent of creation: God reconciled us to himself 'through the very one through whom he had created us.'

26 Erasmus echoes Theophylact *Expos in 2 Cor* (on 5:19) PG 124 856D: 'Not only did he not punish, but he even reconciled; not only did he set free, but he did not even impute their sins.'

27 'Exhorting': *exhortante*. Although in his Latin translation Erasmus chose to render θεοῦ παρακαλοῦντος '[with] God making his appeal' (5:20 RSV) by *deo ... obsecrante* 'with God beseeching' or 'entreating,' for the paraphrase he instead

through us, to give up your old vices and be reconciled to God. For he, in order once and for all to deliver us from our sins, in some manner[28] turned his Son into sin, although he is righteousness itself,[29] so that girded with flesh, which in us is subject to sin, he might become an offering to expiate our crimes. Like a felon[30] among felons, the Son was nailed to a cross so that through him God might change us, who were nothing but sin, into righteousness – not our own righteousness, nor the Law's, but God's. By God's mercy, our transgressions have been forgiven so that henceforth God might regard us who have been grafted onto Christ as righteous, just as he regarded him a sinner in our stead.

Chapter 6

Christ desires this, God desires this: that his kind action may be efficacious in you. And so, as we in these our efforts at the same time both pursue God's will and take thought for your salvation, we entreat you not to act in such a way that you, who have once been freely redeemed from your sins, slip back into your old way of life, for so you have received God's grace in vain.

At the present time we may make amends if we slip in some respect, but this will not always be permitted. For thus God speaks in Isaiah the prophet: 'At the acceptable time I have listened to you, and on the day of salvation I have come to your assistance' [49:8]. See, now is that time promised by God, the time of propitiation, in which God does not turn away the sinner who with full resolve comes to his senses and repents. See, now is that day on which we may attain salvation by living piously. There will follow that dreadful day on which reconciliation will be sought[1]

* * * * *

follows the Vulgate: 'with God exhorting' or 'encouraging.' In his annotation (from 1522) on 5:20 (*tanquam deo vos exhortante per nos*), Erasmus indicates no quarrel with those who prefer the Vulgate's participle, but defends his use of *deo ... obsecrante* in the translation by dismissing the scruple of 'those who think it unseemly for God to beseech.'

28 in some manner] Added in 1532
29 Erasmus follows Theophylact *Expos in 2 Cor* (on 5:21) PG 124 857B: 'him who did not know sin, that is, the one who was righteousness itself.' Theophylact, however, does not complete the parallel, as Erasmus does in noting next that we who were to 'become righteousness' were in fact 'nothing but sin.'
30 Cf Theophylact *Expos in 2 Cor* (on 5:21) PG 124 857B: God 'caused him to die on our behalf, like a sinner and evil-doer.'

1 will be sought] First in 1521; in 1519, 'would be sought'

in vain.[2] Consequently, eager to discharge our duty in this regard, we take care not to be in any respect a stumbling block for anyone,[3] so that no failing of ours[4] may bring censure upon the gospel of Christ, whose ministers we are.

There would be blame, however, if we were living in such a way that we ourselves seemed not to believe what we teach others. But in every way we commend ourselves in actual deed, as is appropriate for those [to do][5] who administer God's business, not their own. By what proofs do we commend ourselves? Not by haughtiness, nor by resources, nor by profit, nor by prescribing ceremonies, as certain individuals do, but by the very means with which Christ commended himself, namely, by much suffering, daily afflictions, necessities, anxieties, by sustaining beatings, imprisonments, by enduring riots,[6] by fastings,[7] purity of life, by truly apostolic knowledge,

* * * * *

2 Paul in 6:2 speaks only of the day of salvation; Erasmus amplifies with the contrasting day of judgment; so also Theophylact *Expos in 2 Cor* (on 6:2) PG 124 860A: 'For at the time of judgment [God] will neither listen nor help nor save. In this time of grace, therefore, we ought to contend, for we will readily attain the prizes.'

3 This clause offers a minor example of Erasmus' frequent habit in the *Paraphrases* of accommodating both the Vulgate's reading of a text and his own differing reading. In his annotation on 6:3 (*nemini dantes ullam offensionem*), he notes that the Vulgate's translator reads here 'not giving offence to anyone,' whereas the manuscripts Erasmus had seen read 'not giving offence in any respect [or 'matter'].'

4 ours] First in *1521*; in *1519*, 'mine'

5 'To do' is not explicit in the Latin, but expresses Erasmus' sense of 6:4. The Vulgate reads, 'but in all things let us exhibit ourselves as ministers of God' (DV), ie show ourselves to be ministers. Erasmus points out, however, in his annotation on 6:4 (*exhibeamus*) that 'as ministers of God' agrees with the subject 'we,' not with the object 'ourselves.' Thus Paul asserts that he is commending himself in the way ministers ought to commend themselves, ie in their deeds and way of life. Erasmus cites Ambrosiaster *Comm in 2 Cor* (on 6:4) CSEL 81/2 240:1–4 in support of this reading.

6 enduring] *tolerandis*, first in *1521*; in *1519 ferendis* 'sustaining.' The change is perhaps simply for the sake of varied expression, since *ferendis* 'sustaining' has just before been used with 'beatings.'

7 'Fastings': *ieiuniis*, which may also simply mean 'times without food.' It is uncertain whether Erasmus (or Paul) has in mind devotional restraint from food or simple lack of food. Cf the paraphrase on 11:27 with n38 for Erasmus' use of *inedia* (which can also mean either 'fasting' or 'lack of food'). The context there ('constant labours and hardships') suggests 'lack of food.' Here in 6:5 the context is less clear: *ieiuniis* follows 'enduring riots,' but precedes 'purity of life.' Note also that in the paraphrase just prior to 'fastings' Erasmus has omitted from Paul's catalogue in 6:5 '[by] labours, [by] vigils [or 'sleepless nights'].'

mildness, pleasantness,[8] the Holy Spirit, a love that is sincere and not at all counterfeit, truthful speech.[9] We are bold to attempt all things, not indeed[10] with human supports, but by the power of God; not equipped[11] with the arms and resources of the world, but hedged about with the arms of righteousness, on this side and on that: on the right, so that prosperity may not elevate those who rest on a principled conscience; on the left, so that adversity may not alarm them.[12]

Relying on this, we are making our way through all things for the accomplishment of the work of the gospel: through glory and disgrace, through insults and praise; taken for impostors, although we are truthful;

* * * * *

8 'Pleasantness': *suavitate* 'sweetness' or 'agreeableness.' Erasmus preserves here in the paraphrase on 6:6 the Vulgate's term for expressing the Greek ἐν χρηστότητι 'in goodness' or 'in kindness.' For his own translation Erasmus preferred *in benignitate* 'in kindness' and in the annotation on 6:6 (*in suavitate*) recommended also *bonitate* 'by goodness' and *comitate* 'by friendliness.'

9 '[By] truthful speech': *sermone veraci*, paraphrasing ἐν λόγῳ ἀληθείας (6:7); Vulgate: *in verbo veritatis*. Although in his translation Erasmus preserved the biblical idiom, *in sermone veritatis* 'by the word [or speech] of truth,' he evidently regarded the biblical phrase as another example of the influence of the Hebrew idiom. Cf CWE 56 17–18 and n3, and see other references in the General Index of that volume under 'idiom – Hebrew.' On Erasmus' preference for *sermo* over the Vulgate's *verbum* to translate λόγος, see 1 Cor chapter 1 n40.

10 indeed] Added in *1521*

11 equipped] Added in *1532* along with the stronger punctuation between 'God' and 'not'; previously: '. . . but by the power of God, not with the arms and resources of the world, but hedged about with . . .'

12 At the end of his *1516* annotation on 6:7 (*a dextris et sinistris*), Erasmus concludes that Paul's expression 'with the weapons of righteousness for the right hand and for the left' is best understood as a proverbial figure meaning 'armed on all sides or against all things.' Earlier in the note, however, he entertains the more allegorical interpretation of Jacques Lefèvre d'Etaples, which builds on the figurative senses of δεξιός (Latin *dexter*) 'right' and ἀριστερός (Latin *sinister*) 'left' as 'favourable' and 'unfavourable.' See Jacobus Faber Stapulensis *S. Pauli epistolae* XIV . . . *cum commentariis* (Paris 1512; facsimile ed Stuttgart-Bad Canstatt 1978) 142 recto. Although Erasmus does not in his annotation endorse Lefèvre's interpretation, he does declare it 'not without merit' to call those arms *dextra* 'which . . . fortify us against the indulgence of good fortune' and those arms *sinistra* 'by which . . . we are protected against the attack of evils and afflictions.' And here, in the fuller expression of the paraphrases, Erasmus does find room for Lefèvre's idea. Cf Theophylact *Expos in 2 Cor* (on 6:7) PG 124 861C, who identifies 'left' with pains or afflictions, and 'right' with things 'more cheerful,' and concludes that in both 'Paul was shown to be blameless – neither cast down by painful things nor swollen by cheerful ones, but making of them the arms of righteousness.'

regarded as unknown, although we are known; like those dying, although, see, we are alive; as if chastened, although we are not cut down; as if grieving, although we always rejoice; as if paupers, although we enrich many; as if having nothing, although we possess all things through Christ, and charity would provide more than a patrimony if we would be willing to use our right.[13]

But to where does the fervour of my speech carry me?[14] I am not restraining myself from pouring out whatever is in my heart. Our mouth is opened towards you, O Corinthians; our heart is widened. So much confidence do I have concerning you, so bold am I to boast about you.[15] I do not regret my lot; you should not regret yours. If you are willing to match my feelings in return, there is reason for me to boast about you, there is reason for you to congratulate yourselves on my account; but there is no reason for you to be narrow in your heart[16] because of me. If there is

* * * * *

13 To Paul's list of the ways in which his life supports his gospel teaching, the paraphrase adds the observation that he has refrained from exercising an apostle's right to be supported financially, a point elaborated in 1 Cor 9:3–18.

14 Erasmus here understands 6:11, 'Our mouth is open to you, Corinthians; our heart is wide' (RSV), as an impassioned flourish concluding a passage (6:2–10) of heightened rhetoric, and not as a simple statement of apostolic frankness. The paraphrase appears in fact to imitate the poet Horace, who presents himself as gripped in the rapture of poetic inspiration: 'Where are you hurrying me, Bacchus, full as I am with you?' (*Odes* 3.25.1–2; for another echo of this Horatian line, see the paraphrase on 12:11). In the annotations on 6:8 (*ut seductores* and *sicut qui ignoti et cogniti*), Erasmus comments on the beauty and especially the forcefulness of Paul's speech throughout this passage and criticizes the Vulgate for falling short. He cites Augustine's discussion of the passage's passion and harmonious balance in *De doctrina christiana* 4.20.42 CSEL 80 151–2, where it is quoted as an example of the grand style of rhetoric, and where 6:11 in particular exemplifies the continuous level of the Apostle's fervour. It is perhaps a sign of Erasmus' admiration for Paul's rhetorical achievement in 6:4–10 that the paraphrase adds very little to the biblical text itself and follows Erasmus' Latin translation very closely, echoing the changes Erasmus makes there in the Vulgate's diction in order to reveal more clearly the Apostle's use of assonance and antithesis, among other rhetorical devices.

15 about you] Added in *1521*

16 'Narrow in your heart': *angusti animi* '[people] of narrow heart [or mind].' In 6:11–12 Paul contrasts his own 'wideness' of heart with the Corinthians' 'narrowness' of heart or affections. His term for 'being narrow' is στενοχωρεῖσθε, nicely caught by Furnish: 'you are cramped.' In his annotation on 6:12 (*non angustiamini in nobis*), Erasmus explains that by 'narrowness of heart' he thinks Paul refers to 'anxiety-ridden adherence to the ceremonies of Mosaic law or

some narrowness of mind in you, it is born of your own attitudes. For the sake of your salvation, there is nothing that I, for my part, do not both do and suffer; you do not in like manner respond to love in kind. There is nothing that I do not endure with heart unbroken because of my hope of the resurrection and my love for you.[17] Since the same reward awaits you, since[18] up until now I have embraced you with fatherly love – for these things are not said as reproaches hurled at foes, but as reminders offered in the midst of very dear children – it is right for you to resemble your father with a great and open heart. Dare[19] to despise the frigid ceremonies[20] of the Jews; dare to despise this world; dare to trust in the good things that are yours.[21] It is the mark of a constricted mind to be content with present things. It is the mark of a constricted heart to have

* * * * *

to human traditions.' Paul's distinction here would then be, in part, once again the contrast between Christian freedom and Jewish legalism. Cf nn19–21 below. On narrowness of heart, see also n18 below.

17 and my love for you] Added in 1532

18 since ... it is right for you to] First in 1532; previously '– I am speaking as to children – you should ...' This expansion, emphasizing Paul's fatherly love for the Corinthians, may reflect Erasmus' reading of Chrysostom, whose homilies on 2 Corinthians had first become available to Erasmus in time to influence the 1527 edition of the *Annotations*. See Robert D. Sider ' "Searching the Scriptures": John Chrysostom in the New Testament Scholarship of Erasmus' in *Within the Perfection of Christ: Essays ... in honor of Martin Schrag* ed Terry L. Brensinger and E. Morris Sider (Nappanee, IN 1990) 89–93. In a 1527 addition to the annotation on 6:13 (*eandem autem habentes retributionem*), Erasmus elaborates, following Chrysostom *In 2 Cor hom* 13.1–2 (on 6:11–13) PG 61 491–2, on a further sense of Paul's contrast between 'wideness' and 'narrowness' (see n16 above). Wideness or fullness of heart is the quality of 'an exceeding love,' while narrowness of heart is that of a 'love that does not respond equally.' Paul requires 'no difficult thing,' only the expectation of a father from his children, that he 'be loved in return,' for then he would consider 'all accounts to be settled.'

19 Dare ... Jews] Added in 1532

20 'Frigid ceremonies': *frigidas ceremonias*. Erasmus uses the expression similarly in the paraphrases on 1 Cor 3:12 and 15. See 1 Cor chapters 3 nn20, 22, and 28, 8 n25, and 9 n6.

21 'Good things ... yours.' As may be inferred from the next two sentences, Erasmus probably means the eternal truths of the gospel, the 'goods' that free believers from their dependence on Mosaic 'shadows' or other false or incomplete goods. Cf the paraphrases on 1 Cor 5:7 and 7:31; also the Argument of 2 Corinthians 201. By 'goods' Erasmus may also be looking forward to the catalogue of Christ's qualities that begins the paraphrase on 6:14, 'Do not be mismated with unbelievers' (RSV), at the beginning of the next paragraph.

no ambition beyond these shadows of good things, shadows that will soon perish.

For you Christ is abundantly rich, abundantly glorious, abundantly powerful, abundantly fortunate. Let him alone suffice for you; embrace him with your whole heart; recognize your greatness; recognize your felicity; consider yourselves too great to have fellowship with the unbelieving. The difference between you is too great to allow you to be joined by the same yoke.[22] For what partnership at all does righteousness have with unrighteousness? Or what communion does light have with darkness? Or what harmony does Christ have with Belial? Conflicting deities, conflicting religion, conflicting morals, conflicting hope. What agreement is there between the temple of God and profane images? For you are the temple of the living God, just as God himself testifies in mystical literature: 'I shall dwell among them, and I shall walk about among them, and I shall be their God, and they in turn will be a people dedicated to me, and [a people] of my very own.'[23] Wherefore, if Jews shudder at a pagan as something impure and profane and even flee from being contaminated by him, you, who have been truly consecrated to the living God, go out from the midst of the profane, separate yourselves from association with them, just as the Lord exhorts through Isaiah: 'Since you are holy,' he says,[24] 'you are not to touch what is polluted. Ungodly morals truly are polluted and carry a dangerous contamination; beware lest your purity be stained by any commixture with them. The flight I advise is not a matter of place but of attitudes.[25] If you

* * * * *

22 In his annotation on 6:14 (*nolite iugum ducere*) Erasmus translates the Greek text similarly, noting that ἑτεροζυγοῦντες means more than simply 'being yoked with' – rather, 'being joined under the same yoke' with a being different in kind from oneself. Erasmus' Latin translation, however, remains close to the Vulgate and fails to indicate this nuance of being 'mis-yoked': 'Do not be yoked with unbelievers.'

23 Paul quotes Lev 26:11–12 and Ezek 37:27. Erasmus does not quote the biblical texts verbatim: 'and [a people] of my own' (*ac peculiaris*) eg is Erasmus' addition. Erasmus uses *peculiaris* 'special,' 'one's own,' 'private' also in the paraphrase on 1 Cor 15:28 (cf n36), and in his Latin translation of Titus 2:14: 'to purify for himself a people of his own.' Cf the paraphrase on that verse CWE 44 63. Erasmus may have remembered *peculiaris* in several Vulgate passages similar to the Leviticus and Ezekiel passages Paul quotes, eg Deut 14:2: '... the Lord has chosen you to be a people for *his own possession* ...' (RSV).

24 he says] Added in *1521*. Cf Lev 11:44 and Isa 52:11.

25 In similar vein, Horace, in distinguishing between physical movement and attitudinal change, warns that 'they change their clime, not their mind, who rush across the sea' (*Epistles* 1.11.27).

do this, not only shall I recognize you and, as the holy one, welcome you as holy, but also you will experience me as a father, and I shall embrace you as children. It is the Lord Almighty who says this, should you distrust at all the author of the promises.'[26]

Chapter 7

Therefore, dearest ones,[1] relying on such promises of God, let us take care to appear worthy of the promises. Let us cleanse ourselves of all filth, not only of the body, but also of the soul, so that we may live innocently before men and at the same time render our conscience acceptable to God, and furnish for ourselves a full and complete holiness for the coming of Christ, as we are in the meantime held to our duty, not by hypocrisy, but[2] by the fear of God, who will reward all persons according to their deeds.

I embrace you wholly with my whole soul, so great is the breadth of my love towards you. You, in turn, welcome me just as I am into your hearts,[3] since in fact you welcome others who, although they love you less,

* * * * *

26 When his paraphrases incorporate Paul's quotations from Scripture, Erasmus typically changes very little, and the quotations are usually easily recognizable. Here, however, the paraphrase is quite loose and expansive. Erasmus appears to be paraphrasing the Pauline text, with an occasional addition from the Old Testament sources, in particular the allusions to Deut 14:2 (cf n23 above) and Isa 52:11c, from where the image of those 'who bear the vessels of the Lord' is transferred to the paraphrase as those 'who have been truly consecrated to the living God.'

1 'Dearest ones': *carissimi*. Here in the paraphrase on 7:1 (as also in his Latin translation), Erasmus follows the Vulgate in using *carissimi*, rather than *dilecti* 'beloved' to represent the Greek ἀγαπητοί 'beloved.' See also 1 Cor chapter 4 n23 and 2 Cor chapter 12 n22.
2 not by hypocrisy, but] Added in 1532
3 In his Latin translation of the imperative in 7:2 Erasmus replaces the Vulgate *capite nos* 'take us,' 'welcome us,' 'understand us' with *capaces estote nostri*, literally 'be spacious of us,' ie 'be roomy or wide enough to contain us'; he explains in the annotation on 7:26 (*capite nos*), 'just as a vessel or a place takes [or 'holds'] something.' Cf Furnish's translation: 'Provide us room!' Erasmus argues that Paul is here renewing (*refricat* 'he rubs again,' 'reopens,' 'irritates') the message of 6:12–13 that the Corinthians not be 'narrowed' or 'cramped' in their hearts, but 'widened.' Modern editors do in fact often see 7:2 as a continuation of Paul's exhortation in 6:13 and interpret 6:14–7:1 as an interpolation from another Pauline letter to the Corinthians, or at least as an inter-

still burden you with arrogance and expenses, weigh you down with ceremonies.[4] We have harmed no one; we have corrupted no one by adulterated
teaching; from no one have we extorted anything. I am not making these
statements in order to condemn and reject you, but to improve you. For indeed, it is quite evident from my words above that I embrace you with my
whole heart and attend you with inseparable love, prepared to share both
death and life with you. With regard to you, I am utterly bold, so great is
my confidence concerning you. I have cause to boast earnestly about you,
for I have found you obedient in every respect.

I did not hesitate to speak frankly in chiding those who were falling
short, but when I see you set straight, I am filled with such great consolation, flooded with such overflowing joy that, in the midst of all my afflictions, it[5] has wiped away the vexation of my soul. At the same time it is
even a pleasure to suffer for such people, for we have been buffeted by
various tempests of evils besides. Indeed, when we came into Macedonia,
no respite from labours was granted to our body; we were harassed on every side. From without, enemies of the gospel were stirring up war;[6] from
within, the risk that the cunning of false apostles might upset some people
was a great worry.[7] By the former we were being pummelled; for the latter meanwhile, we were afraid that, alarmed at our ills, they might lose
faith.

* * *'* *

ruption in thought. See footnotes in RSV, NRSV; for fuller discussion, Furnish
367–83.
4 Erasmus amplifies 7:2, 'Open your hearts to us' (RSV), with his familiar contrast between Paul's authentic ministry and the prideful, self-enriching, and
often Judaizing program of false apostles. The annotation on 7:2 (circumven-
imus) notes that Paul 'is twitting the false apostles indirectly' and cites Ambrosiaster's explanation that false apostles 'load up their purses through the
trickery of their serpentine cunning.' See Comm in 2 Cor (on 7:2) CSEL 81/2
248:1–4. The thematic contrast between Paul and false apostles appeared most
recently in the paraphrase on 6:4. See nn16 and 20; see also chapter 11 n30
and 1 Cor chapters 9 n6 and 15 n43.
5 The subject of 'has wiped away,' although not explicit in the Latin, is presumed
to be the preceding noun, 'joy.' Cf Theophylact Expos in 2 Cor (on 7:4) PG 124
869C–D: 'And so great, he says, was the joy that in all our affliction, great as
it was, the joy prevailed, and it wiped out the affliction.'
6 Erasmus may have in mind Acts 16:19–24, recounting the beating and imprisonment of Paul and Silas at Philippi in Macedonia.
7 Cf Theophylact Expos in 2 Cor (on 7:5) PG 124 872A: he feared 'that the weak
among the believers might be swept away by the false apostles.'

But God restores the humble and afflicted. He has revived[8] and restored us by the coming of Titus: not only because he came (for we were particularly eager to have him with us), but also because he returned from you happy and in high spirits. The pleasure he drew from you flowed back into me, when he reported to me how greatly you longed for me; when he described to me your tears, as you grieved because in my displeasure I had not yet come; when he spoke of the enthusiasm with which you were following my orders. The result was that when I learned these facts from Titus, the pleasure I drew from your obedience, and my correction of you, was greater than the grief I had felt from your transgressions.

I am reluctant to sadden you, but since it has turned out well, I am not sorry that I caused you grief by my earlier letter, even if previously I was somewhat sorry.[9] For indeed, that Epistle was just as sad for me as it was for you. Although[10] it brought grief to you for the moment, nevertheless it is now a source of pleasure for me, not because we made you grieve, but because this grief has led you to repentance. This world has its own grief – but a fruitless and harmful one – when people feel tortured in their minds because of diminution of wealth or loss of pleasures, or because of anger or jealousy. Piety also has its own grief, but it is a fruitful and indeed salvific grief. By it you have been touched in such a way that, so far from experiencing any detriment from me, you have gained a good conscience.[11]

* * * * *

8 'Revived': *refocillavit*, literally 'rekindled.' On this term see chapter 1 n9. Cf the fiery imagery employed by Theophylact *Expos in 2 Cor* (on 7:7) PG 124 872C to describe the new zeal the Corinthians had for Paul: 'For on account of me you have been inflamed and set on fire, so that you carry out my orders.'

9 Erasmus evidently changed his mind about the meaning of εἰ καὶ μετεμελόμην 'although I was sorry' (RSV 'though I did regret it') in 7:8. In the annotation on that verse (*et si poeniteret*), prior to 1527 Erasmus interpreted Paul to admit that 'he did in the past grieve [or feel sorry] because he had grieved the Corinthians,' as the paraphrase here suggests in this concession. In 1527, however, Erasmus revised the annotation to interpret the clause as contrary to fact: 'even if I had been sorry.' In this new interpretation, Paul makes no admission of past regret in 7:8, but only hypothesizes that 'if he had been sorry for the prior action, he would now be ready to cast regret aside.' Most modern translations (as also the paraphrase here, which remained unchanged) assume the earlier of these interpretations. For a brief discussion, see Furnish 387, 394–5.

10 Although] First in 1532; previously 'however much'

11 In his Latin translation as well, Erasmus interprets 7:9b as result rather than purpose; so also RSV, NRSV, NEB. Furnish, however, translates: 'For you were grieved as God willed, that you might not sustain a loss in any way because

For the person who grieves because he has offended God provides proof of a conscience set straight, and sorrow leads to repentance in such a way that it does not allow a person to slip back into former transgressions.[12] On the other hand, the grief that is born of worldly desires brings death; it is harmful equally to body and soul.[13]

Does not the situation itself make this evident?[14] For what great enthusiasm has this same grief, which you have suffered according to the will of God, stirred up in you? Why do I say 'enthusiasm?' No, rather,[15] 'amendment,'[16] for by it you cleared yourselves, as far as I am concerned, when you affirmed that you did not approve that shameful deed; or rather, 'indignation,' for by it you so raged against the profligate that I had to recall you to leniency[17] and moderation; or rather, 'fear,' as if the peril of one were shared by all; or rather, 'longing' that the wrong-doing should be corrected[18] then and there; or rather, 'zeal' and 'ardour' for imitating us in

* * * * *

of us'; similarly AV, DV, Conf. In a 1527 annotation on 7:9 (*ut in nullo detrimentum pateremini*), Erasmus notes that Paul sometimes interchanges the two grammatical constructions. Cf Erasmus' discussion of Greek purpose and result constructions in his annotations on Rom 11:11 ('can it be that they have so stumbled that they fell') and 11:31 ('unto your mercy') CWE 56 298–301, 313, 315, and n10.

12 For Erasmus' views on the stages of repentance, see CWE 44 13 n5. Cf n16 below.

13 Cf Theophylact *Expos in 2 Cor* (on 7:10) PG 124 873B: the worldly kind of grief 'produces death utterly for the soul, often as well for the body.'

14 'Does ... evident': *non hoc ipsa declarat res*. For the expression, see chapter 3 n1 and 1 Cor chapter 1 n13.

15 'No, rather': *imo* [OLD: *immo*]. In his annotation on 7:11 (*sed defensionem*), Erasmus recommends *imo* 'nay rather' or 'no indeed' instead of the Vulgate's *sed* 'but' for expressing the sense in which Paul here uses ἀλλά 'but': 'nay, something more,' for with each new item in this catalogue of Corinthian responses, in a kind of rhetorical crescendo, Paul 'enlarges and, so to speak, corrects.'

16 'Amendment': *satisfactionem* 'satisfaction,' ie 'making amends,' 'reparation.' The word in the Greek text of 7:11 is ἀπολογίαν 'argument in defence,' translated in RSV 'eagerness to clear yourselves.' In his own translation, Erasmus replaced the Vulgate *defensionem* 'defence' with the same word he uses here, *satisfactionem*. In the annotation on 7:10 (*stabilem*), he explains that true repentance (*vera resipiscentia*) 'is accompanied by three things: sorrow, confession (which in my judgment is part of making amends [*pars satisfactionis*]) and amendment [*satisfactio*], which compensates for bad deeds with good deeds.' See also n12 above.

17 leniency] First in 1521; in 1519 'levity.' The change is no doubt the correction of a printer's error.

18 'Should be corrected': *corrigendi*; more literally, 'should be set straight,' as this

the routing out of indecency; or rather, 'punishment' finally, in that he who had sinned paid the penalty then and there. For in all ways you have made evident that in this business you are pure and innocent.

Accordingly, even if I wrote to you on this subject as if it pertained to all, I wrote not only for the sake of the individual who had committed the sin, or the one against whom it had been committed, but rather on this account, that it might be perfectly clear to you how great is my care for you – as God is witness – seeing that I have been so very anxious in case that plague of evil creep into your midst, and the sin of one or two people contaminate the whole body.[19] Then too, I wanted your enthusiasm towards me to become known, for you have obeyed my will with such ready dispositions.[20]

* * * * *

verb's participle has been translated in the previous paragraph (the paraphrase on 7:10): 'a conscience set straight.' In interpreting Paul's purpose in highlighting the Corinthians' 'longing,' Ambrosiaster *Comm in 2 Cor* (on 7:11) CSEL 81/2 253:15–16 evokes a similar image of correction: 'One who knows that through sin he has become deformed [or 'misshapen'] longs to be reformed [or 'reshaped'].' Modern interpreters, however, generally understand the 'longing' Paul praises here in 7:11 to be the same as that which gave comfort in 7:7, ie the Corinthians' longing for Paul himself. See Furnish 389.

19 Theophylact *Expos in 2 Cor* (on 7:12) PG 124 876B similarly interprets Paul's statement that he had written the severe letter 'not on account of the one who did the wrong, nor ... the one who suffered the wrong' (7:12 RSV) to mean that Paul 'in fact did write on their account, but not primarily on their account, rather on your account, making every effort that the whole community not be harmed.' Erasmus notes in a 1527 addition to his annotation on 7:12 (*igitur etsi scripsi*), that 'the Greek commentators advise that the negation here has the force of a comparative,' ie 'not for' means 'not so much for.'

20 The paraphrase accommodates both the Vulgate reading and Erasmus' preferred reading of 7:12b. In the Vulgate reading, Paul states that he wrote the previous letter 'in order that our concern, which we have for you, might be made manifest to [or 'among'] you' (similarly AV, DV). In his annotation on 7:12 (*ad manifestandam sollicitudinem nostram quam habemus pro vobis*), Erasmus, although noting that Ambrose and Theophylact support the Vulgate reading, argues instead, on the basis of Greek sources, that the personal pronouns (ὑμῶν 'of you,' ἡμῶν 'of us') have been inverted (an easy scribal mistake), and that Paul had actually said, 'in order that your enthusiasm towards us might become clear ... among yourselves.' Paul's intent, Erasmus explains, was to show those Corinthians who favoured false apostles in what affectionate regard 'the whole Corinthian church' held Paul. Modern scholarship and translations generally read the text in agreement with Erasmus. See RSV, NRSV, NEB, Furnish 390.

Since this affair has resulted in consolation for you (as people who rejoice because those who needed it have been corrected),[21] I too personally rejoice on account of your joy.[22] But the joy of Titus has increased this pleasure of ours. He was welcomed among you on my recommendation in such a way that his spirit was refreshed by all, when he saw that my authority carried so much weight with you. As a result, if I have boasted at all in his presence about your uprightness and obedience, I have not been put to shame. For this is a risk a person takes when he recommends anyone. I had commended him to you, you to him. On both sides it has turned out well: for just as you have found that Titus, in every circumstance, was the sort of person I told you he was, so he has found that whatever boasts I made about you in his presence are true. Accordingly, neither before you nor before him am I ashamed of empty claims. Although even before this he esteemed you, still now, after experiencing your devotion, he has been more powerfully drawn to you, in his inmost being, while he ponders and reconsiders in his own mind the great alacrity with which you all obeyed our will when he conveyed it, and the great reverence and fear with which you welcomed him at his coming.

I am glad, indeed, that I have found you to be such that there is no regard in which I should not after this be confident about you. And for the future there is nothing I shall be afraid to require of you.[23]

* * * * *

21 Erasmus found a similar explanation in Ambrosiaster *Comm in 2 Cor* (on 7:13) CSEL 81/2 254:23–5, but as a cause of Paul's consolation rather than the Corinthians'. Paul received consolation 'when he learned that those whom he was accusing were willing to correct, so that through repentance they might reform themselves.' See the next note.

22 The Vulgate reads at 7:13: 'Therefore we were comforted. But in our consolation we did the more abundantly rejoice for the joy of Titus ...' (DV). This is essentially the reading accepted by modern scholarship. Cf AV, RSV, Furnish 390. Erasmus, however, reads the verse as follows: 'For this reason we have received comfort from your consolation; nay more fully have we rejoiced beyond this because of Titus' joy ...' See his annotation on 7:13 (*abundantius magis*). The paraphrase here retains Erasmus' preferred punctuation of the verse, as well as the reading of the consolation as 'your' (ὑμῶν; Latin *vestri*) rather than 'our' (ἡμῶν; Vulgate *nostra*).

23 This amplification of Paul's new confidence regarding the Corinthians seems to derive once again from Theophylact *Expos in 2 Cor* (on 7:16) PG 124 877C: 'I am confident ... that such things as I shall either do or say in regard to you you will gladly take up – and with a view to the improvement of yourselves, whether there should be need of reproaching, or of praising, or of enjoining a heavy burden.'

Chapter 8

Therefore, in order that in this respect too you may measure up to our intent and to the godly devotion of the other churches, I am informing you of the way in which God helped me in the churches of Macedonia. They welcomed the gospel with ready and responsive hearts; and so far were they from being cast down by my sufferings and those of Silas that, as they themselves were afflicted along with us, they actually endured all things with boundless joy through their confidence in the gospel. In short, the more grievous the sufferings we endured, the more abundantly did they rejoice when we were released.[1]

Although they are in straitened circumstances and extremely indigent themselves, so ready and well disposed were they that, for the sustenance of the poor, they drew even out of their paltry money boxes whatever was left. Consequently, the poorer and more destitute they became through their holy benevolence, the richer and richer they grew through the sincerity and simplicity[2] of a most ready and willing heart. For indeed, far from finding them reluctant to give generously, as I can truly witness for them, not only did they want[3] to contribute according to their ability, but even beyond

* * * * *

1 With this reference to Paul's suffering and release in Macedonia, Erasmus may have in mind Acts 16:19–40, which tells of the Apostle's imprisonment and miraculous release at Philippi, the chief city in Macedonia. Cf the paraphrase on 7:5 with n6. For joy felt in the midst of affliction, cf Phil 2:17–18 and 1 Thess 1:6–7. In the latter passage, the church at Thessalonica, another centre of Paul's ministry in Macedonia, is congratulated 'as an example to all the believers in Macedonia and in Achaia,' because it had 'received the word in much affliction, with joy inspired by the Holy Spirit' (RSV).

2 'Simplicity': *simplicitate*. The adverbial construction in which this word appears ('through the sincerity . . . heart') is Erasmus' amplification of the Greek term by which Paul defines the poor Macedonians' riches: ἁπλότης, translated by both the Vulgate and Erasmus with the Latin *simplicitas*, which signifies 'lack of duplicity,' 'guilelessness,' 'candour,' but is often rendered in modern translations as 'liberality' (AV, RSV) or 'generosity' (NRSV). Furnish 400 notes that within the context of 2 Corinthians 8–9, ἁπλότης tends 'towards the extended meaning of . . . an open-hearted – and open-minded – concern to do what is right.' Erasmus explains in his annotation on 8:2 (*in divitias simplicitatis*) that 'someone is quite simple [or 'guileless': *simplicior*] who dispenses [alms] cheerfully, and the poorer he is rendered in money, the richer he becomes by virtue of his candour and benevolence.' Cf Theophylact *Expos in 2 Cor* (on 8:2) PG 124 880A: 'the characteristic of an ungrudging and bountiful mind.' On *simplicitas*, see also CWE 44 191 n28. Cf Phil chapter 3 n30 below.

3 The emphasis on the eager will in the passage reflects the Greek αὐθαίρετοι 'self-chosen,' 'voluntary,' which in his translation he renders by *prompti*

their ability, inasmuch as their will exceeded their means. The extent of their willing disposition was revealed in this, that when we, fearing that hardship would lead them to regret after their unrestrained liberality,[4] refused to accept what they wanted to offer of their own accord, they begged us with many an earnest entreaty to allow them, too, to have a share in this glorious enterprise, that by imparting something from their own means to [alleviate] the neediness of the saints, they might in turn partake of their godliness. They not only met our expectations, but even surpassed all our hope, when they did not simply offer their possessions, but also gave their very selves, on their own initiative, first to God[5] and then to us too, as God willed, for it was by his inspiration that they were moved to obey us with such alacrity.

Their disposition pleased me so much that we urged Titus to bring to completion what was begun in you (for it was by his urging that you initiated this munificence[6] towards the saints), so that you might be bound still more closely to him. Through him you will gain this praise, too, for godliness, so that you might not be in this regard at all inferior to the rest. Rather, just as you excel in other endowments – in the gift of faith, the gift of tongues, the gift of knowledge, the gift of diligence in stewardship,[7]

* * * * *

'ready,' 'inclined,' and which he glosses in the annotation on 8:3 (*voluntarii*) as 'spontaneous ... not asked for, not invited.' Cf Theophylact *Expos in 2 Cor* (on 8:3–4) PG 124 880A: 'not admonished by us, but of their own free will.'

4 Ambrosiaster *Comm in 2 Cor* (on 8:4) CSEL 81/2 257:16–17 similarly explains Paul's reluctance to accept the Macedonians' offer 'lest it happen that hardship lead them to regret their good work.'

5 'To God': Ambrosiaster *Comm in 2 Cor* (on 8:4) CSEL 81/2 257:22 also reads 'to God' in this verse, but Erasmus' own Greek text and also his Latin translation, as well as the Vulgate, agree with the accepted reading 'to the Lord.' Furnish 402 notes that the reference is to Christ.

6 'Munificence': *munificentiam*. One of several terms Erasmus recommends in the annotation on 8:6 (*ita et perficiat in vobis*) for expressing the specific sense here of the biblical term χάριν 'grace,' 'gift' – the work that Titus is to bring to completion among the Corinthians; the Vulgate translates with the more general *gratiam* 'grace.' Another term Erasmus recommends (and the one he adopts for his translation) is *beneficentia* 'beneficence,' 'generosity,' citing Cicero's use of this term in outlining the human moral obligations in regard to social order and community. See *De officiis* 1.7.20, 14.42. Thus, Erasmus interprets 'grace' here as the 'gracious act' expressed in the Corinthians' generosity towards less fortunate Christians. Cf NRSV: 'generous undertaking'; also Furnish 402.

7 'In stewardship': *in administrando* 'in administering,' 'in being stewards,' 'in assisting,' ie in carrying out or managing the business of someone else, in this

the gift of charity, which you have shown towards us[8] – so[9] also in this endowment you should be outstanding.

Not that I demand this from you, but I mention the readiness of the Macedonians for this reason that, challenged by their example, you might of your own accord make evident the sincerity of your love, in this way too emulating the Lord Jesus Christ to the best of your ability. Although he was rich and the Lord of all, nevertheless in order to benefit us, of his own accord he made himself poor. He became man, his power concealed, in order that you might grow rich through his poverty, as if an exchange of properties occurred, so that by this exchange, when the poverty of our humanity was taken up into himself, he might impart to us the riches of his divinity.[10] Accordingly, just as in the earlier letter I

* * * * *

case, the gospel of Christ. Erasmus uses the same verb in the paraphrase on 1 Cor 4:2. On the distinction between author (*auctor*) and steward (*minister*), see 1 Cor chapter 1 n10.

8 This relative clause expresses the reading of 8:7 that Erasmus adopted for his Greek text and endorsed in his annotation on the verse (*insuper et charitate*): '[you excel] in your love for us,' literally 'the love from you [the Corinthians] towards us [Paul].' In the annotation, however, Erasmus acknowledges the possibility of an alternative reading in which the pronouns are reversed, reading 'our love for you.' He cites Ambrosiaster *Comm in 2 Cor* (on 8:7) CSEL 81/2 258:23–4 for this reading, but understands Ambrosiaster's interpretation as 'the love which you have learned from us.' Modern scholarship now tends towards the reading 'our love for you' (NRSV). See Metzger 512–13; also Furnish 403.

9 so] *ita*, first in *1521*, possibly in correction of *ut* (*1519*) 'that' or 'in order that.' The *1519* version reflected the Greek conjunction ἵνα (Vulgate *ut*) 'that,' at the beginning of the last clause in 8:7. Erasmus apparently thought the biblical syntax (which he interpreted to mean, literally, 'that you abound in this gift also') was incomplete. In his annotation on 8:7 (*et in hac gratia abundetis*), he notes that some introductory verb like 'I urge' or 'see to it' ought to be supplied before Paul's 'that.' Hence, his translation of the verse reads: 'Take care that [*facite ut*] you abound ...' The emendation to the paraphrase here in *1521*, substituting 'so' for 'that,' seems designed to clarify the exhortative or imperatival nature of the final clause in 8:7. Furnish 403 notes, however, that the 'imperatival' usage of ἵνα is not uncommon in Paul and, thus, that the Greek text as given is not incomplete. See also Maximilian Zerwick SJ *Biblical Greek Illustrated by Examples* translated and adapted from the fourth Latin edition by Joseph Smith SJ (Rome 1963) 141–2.

10 Paul implies in 8:9 that the Corinthians ought to alleviate the poverty of others because they themselves have been 'enriched' by Christ's exchange of his own richness for their poverty. In the paraphrase, Paul's statement is amplified with traditional Christological language and, perhaps reflecting Phil 2:6–11 and John 1:14, affirms a soteriology based on the Incarnation.

did not require celibacy of you, but advocated it, thinking of your welfare,[11] so too in this matter I am advising, not commanding, and I am advising for this reason, because I think it will turn out to your advantage, especially seeing that what I am now advocating you, yourselves, without my persuasion, have begun not only to do, but even to will of your own accord.

Now, therefore, it remains for you to bring to completion what you have begun to do of your own accord. Just as you long since[12] willingly adopted that[13] intent, so, after the example of the Macedonians, you should carry it through, not beyond your ability as they did,[14] but in accordance with each person's means. What is conferred by an unwilling person is not accounted benevolence.[15] But when one has a heart that is ready and willing of its own accord, it is enough if generosity is governed according to the measure of one's resources.[16] For you are not required to give what you do not have. Nor, indeed, is benevolence to be practised in such a way that the recipients of the gift live pleasantly and at ease, while those who confer it are reduced to want.[17] What is required is that there be a kind of equitable reciprocity between you, namely, that from the resources in which

* * * * *

11 See 1 Cor 7:6–8, 25–40. Paul advocates the single life because it allows single-minded devotion to Christ and therefore, ideally, serves the greater good of every Christian (7:35, 40). However, for those whose sexual passions do not permit the ideal of celibate living, Paul allows – and in fact advises – marriage as a proper and sin-free, if not anxiety-free, state (7:9, 28, 36).

12 'Long since': *iampridem*. Erasmus is paraphrasing Paul's 'last year.' On *iampridem*, see CWE 50 55 n64.

13 that] Added in *1521*

14 Paul mentions the Macedonians' extreme poverty in 8:2. Cf the paraphrase above.

15 Paul states only the positive condition in 8:12: 'If the readiness is there, [whatever you are able to give to the poor] is acceptable' (RSV). Erasmus may have borrowed the negative expansion from Ambrosiaster *Comm in 2 Cor* (on 8:12) CSEL 81/2 260:6–7: 'For one who does something under compulsion, does not [gain] the reward.' Cf the variation in Pliny *Epistles* 1.13: in performing service, 'a duty performed deserves no gratitude if a return is expected.'

16 Cf the similar thought and language in Cicero *De officiis* 1.14.42–4, where the second condition of generosity (*benignitas*) is that it should not go beyond the giver's means (*facultates*).

17 Cicero in *De officiis* 2.15.54 urges the same moderation in respect to excessive benevolence: 'For many have squandered their patrimony by indiscriminate giving. But what is worse folly than to do the thing you like in such a way that you can no longer do it at all?'

you abound, assistance in the meantime be given to their neediness, and in turn, that their faith and the piety in which they are superior compensate for any lack in you.[18]

Accordingly, it may come about that while each shares with the other, nothing is lacking to either, but equity exists. Just as we read once happened to our ancestors in the gathering of manna: no more was left over for the person who had collected much than for the person who had collected a little. For thus it was written in the book of Exodus: 'Nothing was left over for him who had much, and to him who had very little, nothing was lacking' [16:18]. Those things are possessed for a time so that on them we may, as it were, live from day to day. No one is to estimate on the basis of long-range[19] calculations what is left over for himself; otherwise, no one will think that he has anything to spare that he may share with someone else. Meanwhile this individual is in need; you have a surplus. What is extra is[20] to be shared with a view to the immediate necessity. If something should happen that you too might be in need in the future, you will be supported by a similar turn of benevolence.

* * * * *

18 Paul suggests in 8:14–15 a principle of reciprocity to the Corinthians: 'a fair balance between your present abundance and [the saints'] need so that their abundance may be for your need' (NRSV). In the paraphrase, Erasmus seems to present two explanations of this reciprocity. First, in the current sentence, he follows Ambrosiaster *Comm in 2 Cor* (on 8:14–15) CSEL 81/2 261:10–25 in seeing the balance as that between the Corinthians' present alleviation of the saints' material impoverishment and the saints' compensation for the Corinthians' (relative) spiritual impoverishment. For, as Ambrosiaster explains, the saints in renouncing all worldly goods are rich 'in their hope for the age to come,' and 'just as the [worldly] hardship of the saints is relieved by the kindness of [the Corinthians], so also, by the kindness of the saints, [the Corinthians] may become rich in the age to come, in which they seem poor.' The result is that 'those who are rich here, but poor there, will be enriched by the support of the saints, who, although situated here, are already there in their minds.' At the end of the next paragraph, however, Erasmus offers another and simpler explanation: the 'fair balance' may be that between the present benevolence of the Corinthians and the like benevolence they might enjoy if they should suffer hardship at some time in the future.

19 'Long-range': *in longum*. The phrase could also have the sense of 'tedious.' See OLD *longus* 9 and 14.

20 What is extra is] Added in 1521; in 1519 this sentence was incorporated into the preceding sentence: '... you have a surplus to be shared with a view to the immediate necessity.'

Then too, I am grateful to God,[21] by whose impulse this concern is just
as dear to the heart of Titus as it is to mine. For since he was so inclined of
his own accord, he readily accepted our appeal, or rather, he came to you
not at my urging, but of his own will (although the more eagerly because
of my urging). Moreover, we sent with him that brother whose faith and
integrity in the work of the gospel[22] is regarded throughout all the churches
– and so well regarded that he was chosen by the churches to be the comrade and colleague[23] of our journeying, in order that he might be our assistant in collecting the money that you kindly bestow for the glory of the
Lord himself.[24] It is by the Lord's inspiration that the action is being undertaken so that the readiness of your[25] heart may be shown to all. But it is
important that men of integrity and proven character[26] be provided for this

* * * * *

21 Paraphrasing the biblical text's 'thanks [be] to God' (8:16 RSV). On expressions
    of thanks, see chapter 2 n15.
22 Ie in preaching the gospel, as Erasmus makes clear in his annotation on 8:18
    (*cuius laus est in evangelio*): 'He is so skilled in the preaching of Christ ...
    that he is praised in the testimony of all the churches.' In the Argument of 2
    Corinthians 201, Erasmus notes that 'most people think' this second colleague
    was Luke. For modern speculation on his identity, see Furnish 435–6.
23 'Comrade and colleague': *comes et collega*. In his Latin translation, Erasmus
    renders συνέκδημος 'fellow-traveller' by *comes peregrinationis* 'comrade of [my]
    journeying,' but in his annotation on 8:19 (*sed et ordinatus est*) he suggests that
    collega 'colleague' could be preferred to *comes* in order to identify better an
    'equal' rather than a 'follower.'
24 'Himself': *ipsius*. Erasmus follows his Greek text in including the intensive
    pronoun in 8:19. The textual tradition is mixed. See Metzger 513, where the
    pronoun is retained, but placed within square brackets and considered the
    'least unsatisfactory' reading.
25 'Your' follows Erasmus' reading of 8:19 (also Theophylact, AV), although Eras-
    mus knows that Ambrosiaster and the Vulgate read 'our,' which is also the
    reading of modern scholarship. In his annotation on 8:19 (*destinatam volun-
    tatem*), Erasmus explains Paul's sense of the double purpose behind his con-
    ducting the charitable collection: 'for the glory of the Lord, and at the same
    time in order to advance and make known the ready and willing heart of
    those who were contributing on their own.'
26 'Proven character': *spectatae probitatis*; a common expression in Erasmus for
    virtue that has been tested and is widely regarded. Cf the same phrase (trans-
    lated 'proven integrity') in the paraphrases on Acts 6:3 CWE 50 46 with n7, and
    15:22 CWE 50 98 with n54. Note that this is the third appearance of the par-
    ticiple *spectatus* 'regarded' or 'tested' in this paragraph; it appears again, in
    the superlative degree (translated 'highly regarded,' ie 'most tested' or 'most
    approved') at the beginning of the next paragraph.

task.[27] Otherwise, some suspicion may arise in the minds of the weak, or it may seem that we are collecting as great a sum of money as your kindness willingly contributes not for others only, but also for ourselves, although in this matter we claim nothing for ourselves except the service of taking the collection and the effort[28] of carrying it through. For it does not escape our notice that money, generally, and especially a vast amount of it, is extremely liable to the suspicion of rapacity.[29] People's minds are corrupted more swiftly by nothing else.

To these two individuals, highly regarded by you, we have added also a third, a brother of ours. Even if he is not as thoroughly known to you, still, we personally have found him diligent and trustworthy time and again in many circumstances, but more diligent in this work than in the other matters. As a result I am entirely confident[30] that you will not hesitate to entrust to them even a sizable amount of money, whether you have in view Titus, my colleague and a sharer in the labours that I am undertaking for your sake, or the others joined to him, who, besides the fact that they

* * * * *

27 Ambrosiaster *Comm in 2 Cor* (on 8:21) CSEL 81/2 263:10–14 similarly connects Paul's intent to do 'what is honourable ... in the sight of men' to the character of the men chosen to manage the collection 'because he sends such [emissaries] ... as would by their character cause no obstacle, but would challenge [the Corinthians] that the good teachings of the Apostle not fall into censure through his careless stewards.'

28 the effort] *studium* 'eagerness,' 'effort,' 'zeal'; added in 1532. The addition creates rhetorical balance and highlights the letter's characteristic emphasis on Paul's earnest performance of apostolic ministries.

29 Erasmus offers a similar explanation in his annotation on 8:20 (*in hac plenitudine*). Cf Theophylact *Expos in 2 Cor* (on 8:20) PG 124 888B: 'For that abundance, he says, ie the ample supply of money, is sufficient cause to rouse suspicion in those who are base.'

30 The biblical text of 8:22 concludes with the phrase 'because of [or 'through'] much confidence in you.' Modern editions and translations generally interpret this as the confidence the unnamed third emissary has in the Corinthians: '[He] is now more eager than ever because of his great confidence in you' (NRSV); similarly NEB, Furnish. Erasmus' paraphrase seems, however, to refer the phrase here to Paul's confidence that the emissary's diligence will result in a generous reception of the emissaries by the Corinthians. In his annotation on 8:22 (*confidentia multa in vos*), Erasmus similarly treats the confidence as Paul's, but provides a somewhat different interpretation: 'The Greek is ambiguous. For the confidence can be referred to Paul, who trusts that [the third emissary] will be more diligent, because he [Paul] hopes that [the Corinthians] will treat the individual well.'

are our brothers, have been chosen by the decision[31] of the churches for this responsibility. Through them the gospel has been made so illustrious that with good reason they could be called not only apostles,[32] but even the glory of Christ.

Accordingly, you will deal with them in such a way that now, above all, you will show with what great love you attend us, and how it was not without cause that we boasted to them about you.[33] Moreover, any service you confer on them, you will confer on all the churches on whose account they are coming as emissaries.

Chapter 9

There is no need for me to make an effort by my writing to goad you on to the generosity that is to be directed towards the saints. The readiness of your disposition is so well known to me and so clearly evident that I do not hesitate to boast of it even among the Macedonians, to the extent that, since a great many people have been challenged by your example, not only Corinth, but almost all Achaea is ready and eager to bestow the same generosity. Although we considered your disposition clearly evident, still it seemed good to send these brothers of ours on ahead lest, by any

* * * * *

31 'By the decision': *suffragiis*; this could also be translated 'by the votes.' Within the specific context of Roman assemblies, *suffragium* refers to a vote cast by voice or ballot. Cf Erasmus' paraphrase on Acts 1:26 CWE 50 12–13 in reference to the election of two nominees to replace Judas as the twelfth disciple: 'The two most approved were elected by vote.' Since the current context does not seem to suggest selection specifically by vote, we have chosen to translate the term by its more general sense of 'judgment,' 'assent,' or 'decision.' For this more general sense in the plural as well as the singular, see L&S *suffragium* II B 2.

32 'Apostles': *apostoli*; this is (in Latin form) the Greek term (ἀπόστολοι) Paul uses in 8:23 as he sums up the 'credentials' of the two unnamed emissaries. Erasmus has just paraphrased the term with what is, in effect, a definition: those 'who ... have been chosen by ... the churches for this responsibility.' For his own translation, Erasmus preferred *legati* 'emissaries' to the Vulgate's *apostoli*. See the annotation on 8:23 (*confidentia multa in vos*). The current sentence in the paraphrase, however, appears to justify the Vulgate's translation *apostoli* for these two emissaries, as well as Paul's use of the title 'the glory of Christ.' On the meaning of ἀπόστολος, see Furnish 99, and cf 1 Cor chapter 1 nn2, 6, and 16; 2 Cor chapter 11 n19; and CWE 50 12 n98. On Erasmus' use of the term, see CWE 50 92 n14.

33 Cf Theophylact *Expos in 2 Cor* (on 8:24) PG 124 889B: 'Show ... how it is also not in vain that we boast about you.'

chance, I may seem to have boasted idly to others about you. For until
now, in this regard at any rate, so far as the other points are concerned,
you have measured up to my praise of you. We have sent them on ahead
that, as we previously wrote you,[1] money might be collected in good time,
and whatever you have decided to contribute may be ready. Let it not
happen somehow that, if the Macedonians, to whom I have boasted about
you, come with me and find you unprepared, I find myself embarrassed,
as if I have boasted idly about you, not to mention that you find yourselves
embarrassed for being in this respect unlike yourselves, although you excel
in the rest of your endowments. For this reason, it seemed worthwhile to ask
these brothers to go there before my visit and to prepare the contribution
you had already previously fixed upon[2] and promised, so that it might
all the more be in readiness. It is with good reason that in Greek we call
this contribution εὐλογία, that is,[3] 'a blessing,' because a benefit ought to be
given and received, not grudgingly, nor with murmuring, but with good

* * * * *

1 Erasmus probably has in mind Paul's instructions to the Corinthians in 1 Cor
  16:1-3. On references to a 'previous letter' in Erasmus' *Paraphrase on Second
  Corinthians*, see the Argument of this Epistle n1. Paul's clause, 'as I said,'
  however, is usually taken as a reference to the boasts Paul has just stated he
  was making about the Corinthians to the Macedonians. Cf RSV: 'as I said you
  would be.'
2 'Fixed upon': *destinatam* 'destined.' On this word see 1 Cor chapter 1 n37. In
  his annotation on Rom 1:4 ('who was predestined') CWE 56 11, Erasmus defines
  the verb *destinare* as 'to fix something firmly in the mind beforehand.'
3 εὐλογία, that is] Added in 1532. Εὐλογία 'gift' is Paul's term in 9:5 for the collection promised by the Corinthians for the relief of the Jerusalem church.
  Literally 'good speech' or 'praise,' the word is translated in the Vulgate by its
  exact Latin equivalent *benedictio* 'benediction,' 'blessing.' Erasmus may have
  added the Greek term here in order to clarify the Vulgate's translation and also
  to indulge his own interest in etymology. In his annotation on 9:5 (*repromis-
  sam benedictionem*), he suggests two explanations for the extended meaning
  of εὐλογία as 'an act of blessing,' 'gift,' 'bounty.' In the first, he denies that
  the term derives from λόγος 'word,' 'reason,' 'account,' and connects it with
  λεγεῖν 'to gather,' 'collect,' from which λογία 'collection [for the poor]' also derives. Thus, he concludes, it makes sense for εὐλογία to be translated 'munificence' or 'generosity.' In the second explanation, which is the one he develops
  here as well in the paraphrase, he does acknowledge that 'gift' is appropriately called εὐλογία or *benedictio* because 'a benefit [*beneficium* 'something done
  well'] ought to be given eagerly and with kind words' just as, by way of contrast, misers give 'as little as possible, and if it happens that they are forced
  to give, their gift is accompanied by ill-omened words.' Cf the annotation on
  Rom 1:25 ('who is blessed') CWE 56 55. In his Latin translation, Erasmus translates εὐλογία as *bona collatio* 'good collection.'

wishes; otherwise it will seem an extortion, not a collection. Let each one contribute voluntarily if he wants to, and as much as he wishes.

But we remind you of this: the more generously each one contributes, the richer is the reward he will bring back. The person who does his sowing sparingly likewise will reap sparingly; the one who sows eagerly and with high expectations will in equal measure reap what he has sown,[4] not as though on my bidding, but as each has voluntarily determined in his own heart.[5] For a person gives more generously and more gladly who gives voluntarily.[6] That one gives quite resentfully who gives with a gloomy spirit, as if compelled. But God loves a cheerful giver. Indeed, in God's eyes a person who does his duty under compulsion does not do his duty.[7]

There is no reason for you to fear lest that kind act of yours be lost to you. God permits whatever is conferred upon the saints out of love for him to be credited as conferred upon him.[8] And he is very well able to bring it

* * * * *

4 what he has sown] Added in 1521
5 The paraphrase preserves the Vulgate's language, 'every one as he has determined in his heart' (DV), despite the reservations Erasmus notes in the annotation on 9:7 (ut destinavit), ie that the verb should be in the present tense and that no possessive modifies 'heart': 'For he is not referring to the mind of this person or that one, but only pointing out that what is given ought to be given gladly and from the heart.'
6 In this paragraph Erasmus amplifies Paul's quotation (in 9:7) of the proverb on the 'cheerful giver' (Septuagint Prov 22:8a) with a number of loosely classical adages. Cf in particular Adagia I viii 91: 'He that gives quickly gives twice' – usually attributed to Publilius Syrus (although by Erasmus to Seneca) – a variant itself of another of Publilius' sayings: 'Twice welcome what we need, when offered free.' See CWE 32 174 n6.
7 A negative variation on the 'cheerful giver' proverb. See previous note and cf, again, Adagia I viii 91, where Erasmus quotes Ausonius, the fourth-century Latin poet: 'Favour slow-footed is favour without favour' (Epigrammata 16 and 17). Cf also Ambrosiaster Comm in 2 Cor (on 9:7) CSEL 81/2 267:17–19: 'The person who does something against his will on account of some impending shame, in order not to be found base in the inference of others, has no reward.' Ambrosiaster's warning about a shame-induced compulsion squares well with Paul's precaution (9:4) against the Corinthians' possible embarrassment at the visit of the Macedonians, and may well underlie Erasmus' treatment here of verse 7. Cf also Theophylact Expos in 2 Cor (on 9:7) PG 124 893B: 'For if [an action] is not voluntary it is not virtuous (ἀρετή, literally 'moral virtue') ... since what is done under compulsion precludes reward.'
8 Cf Matt 25:40. Erasmus uses nearly identical language in the paraphrase on that verse CWE 45 339; also in the annotation on 9:8 (abundare facere in vobis).

about (even if humans give you no thanks at all in return) that your kind act will still return to you with interest, if he grants both that money is always available to you for the necessities of life and, in addition, that you grow luxuriantly rich in all the duties of piety. For a good part of godliness and righteousness is the generosity that assists the saints in their need, just as the Psalmist too attests: '[The righteous person] has distributed freely, he has given to the poor and, on account of this, his righteousness endures forever' [Ps 112:9].[9]

It is my prayer[10] that he who furnishes seed for the sower and supplies bread for food, who has bestowed the fortune[11] from which you now relieve the indigence of the saints, may always replenish your stock so that you may be able to relieve them from time to time. May he multiply what you sow and at the same time increase the yield of your righteousness[12] so that you may be enriched in every kind of virtue and always progress to all simplicity[13] of heart and to sincerity. May you hold money of less worth every day. As long as it is being spent, not on just anyone, but on the saints, it causes your liberality to overflow to the glory of God, while the godly, who have been refreshed by your generosity, give thanks to God through us. As a result, I too, who am tending to this business, lay claim to a bit of the reward for it.

For by carrying out this ministry, not only do we gain this, that godly people are restored again from their need by your open-handedness, but in addition, the more abundant your beneficence, the more there are who

* * * * *

9 This idea of a 'happy exchange,' whereby the generous disposal of one's earthly wealth results in the acquisition of heavenly treasure, is a common theme in Erasmus' New Testament writings. See Sider 'The Just' 13–22.

10 The paraphrase here follows Erasmus' Latin translation and Theophylact *Expos in 2 Cor* (on 9:10) PG 124 895A–B in reading the main verbs of 9:10 as infinitives serving an optative or jussive use and thus expressing Paul's wish that God 'supply bread... multiply seed... increase the harvest'; so also AV. See the annotation on 9:10 (*qui autem subministrat*). This annotation, however, acknowledges Ambrosiaster's support for the Vulgate reading of future indicatives expressing, instead, the certainty that God will supply, etc. Modern texts and translations generally read future indicatives here; so NTGL, DV, RSV, NRSV, NEB. For a brief summary of the textual evidence, see Furnish 442–3.

11 'Fortune': *sortem* 'lot,' 'condition,' ie the prosperous circumstances that allow the Corinthians to contribute alms.

12 'Of your righteousness': *vestrae iustitiae*. On the meanings of *iustitia* 'justice' or 'righteousness,' see 1 Cor chapter 1 n41.

13 'Simplicity': *simplicitatem*, ie candour or guilelessness. On this term, see chapter 8 n2.

give thanks to God. After experiencing your piety,[14] they extol God with praise for your kindness because they realize that you are heeding with such utter unanimity the evangelical admonitions.[15] In compliance with them you gladly and eagerly share your means, not only with these people whose cause we are supporting at present, but with all the rest. For assistance must be brought to those in need wherever they are.

In short, in the prayers that in their gratitude they offer to God for you, they long to see you,[16] so that they may behold in person the extraordinary godliness of those whose extraordinary generosity is restoring them. They perceive from the size of your gift that it is God who has conferred this godliness upon you.[17] But above all, we must offer thanks to God for that

* * * * *

14 'Piety': *pietatem*, often translated as 'godliness' in this volume. On this word see 1 Cor chapter 3 n22.

15 The paraphrase follows Erasmus' translation of 9:13 in interpreting ὁμολογία to mean *consensus* 'agreement,' 'unanimity' rather than the Vulgate's *confessio* 'confession.' In the annotation on 9:13 (*et in oboedientia confessionis*), Erasmus acknowledges the usual understanding of the biblical phrase ἐπὶ τῇ ὑποταγῇ τῆς ὁμολογίας ὑμῶν εἰς τὸ εὐαγγέλιον τοῦ Χριστοῦ '[the destitute saints glorify God] for the obedience of your confession unto the Gospel of Christ' (DV): 'Because by obeying the gospel in bestowing alms, [the Corinthians] were showing that they truly and genuinely confessed the gospel.' Cf AV, JB, RSV, NRSV; but RSV and NRSV understand the Corinthians, not the saints, as the subject of 'glorify.' Erasmus' translation, as well as the paraphrase here, however, follows a different understanding, explained in the annotation in this way: 'that many give thanks to God when they see the Corinthians obeying Paul with such utter unanimity ... for it pertains to the business of the gospel if all Christians agree among themselves in good deeds.'
The reference to heeding 'evangelical admonitions' at the end of this sentence in the paraphrase may have been suggested by Theophylact *Expos in 2 Cor* (on 9:12–14) PG 124 897A: 'They glorify God because you have been made so subject to the gospel that you fulfil its ordinances lavishly. For the gospel teaches alms-giving.'

16 Erasmus notes in his annotation on 9:14 (*desiderantium vos*) that Ambrosiaster *Comm in 2 Cor* (on 9:14) CSEL 81/2 270:21 reads the text's 'longing for you' as 'longing to see you.' Theophylact *Expos in 2 Cor* (on 9:12–14) PG 124 897A–B remarks similarly that they wanted to be 'deemed worthy of seeing you ... because of the grace of God that had been incomparably given' to the Corinthians.

17 Erasmus is paraphrasing '[they are longing for you] because of the surpassing grace of God in you' (RSV). Although in his translation he preserves the Vulgate's *gratiam* to translate the text's χάριν 'grace,' in the annotation on 9:14 (*desiderantium vos*) he suggests instead *beneficium* 'kindness,' 'service': 'So that you may understand that they were eager to see the Corinthians, on whom

gift which defies description: by it, he inspires in you your disposition to give,[18] and in them their readiness to be summoned by your kindnesses, not to ease or extravagance, but to the praise of God.

Chapter 10

But let us set these topics aside and come to other matters. I entreat you – I, not just any apostle but the very Paul who has been amply regarded[1] by you – I, who have suffered and am suffering so many ills for the sake of your salvation. I entreat you, moreover,[2] by the gentleness and compassion and kindness[3] of Jesus Christ, after whose example I abase myself in your presence, behaving, according to outward appearance, as if I were someone worthless and lowly; I do not make a show of the prestige and authority of an apostle, which false apostles think rest in arrogance. And yet (as they slanderously charge), when I am absent, I try to terrify you with bold and

* * * * *

God had conferred such great beneficence towards themselves.' The paraphrase here emphasizes this understanding of God's χάρις as manifest in the Corinthians' godly generosity.

18 Ambrosiaster *Comm in 2 Cor* (on 9:15) CSEL 81/2 271:18–20 similarly describes the 'ineffable gift of God' as that which 'incites towards good work. For the promised hope spurs [them] on towards the ministry [of alms-giving].' Theophylact *Expos in 2 Cor* (on 9:15) PG 124 897B describes the gift as 'the good things themselves that happen through alms-giving – both to the ones giving and to the ones receiving.'

1 'Regarded': *spectatus,* ie 'tested and proven.' On this participial adjective, see chapter 8 n26.

2 The adverb 'moreover' may suggest that Paul's appeal to the meekness of Christ in 10:1 is intended as a contrast to the harsher, bolder approach the apostle hopes to avoid when he visits the Corinthians. Cf Theophylact *Expos in 2 Cor* (on 10:1) PG 124 897D–900A: 'But he inserts the meekness of Christ' partly to show 'why he is sparing them, that is, because he is imitating the meekness of Christ, and not because he is weak.' The subsequent reference in the paraphrase to Paul's status (*dignitas*) and authority as an apostle may also be influenced by Theophylact, who stresses that from the start Paul is engaged in self-defence of his worthiness (ἀξίωμα; Latin *dignitas*) against false apostles who were 'slandering him as being an unversed and brash braggart.'

3 and kindness] Added in *1532*. On *humanitas* 'humanity,' translated 'compassion' here, cf the paraphrases on John 4:27 and 40 CWE 46 59 and 61, and 59 n47. See also the annotation on Philem 20 (*ita frater*), where Erasmus describes Paul as 'a person of a certain singular humanity [*humanitas*], who so passionately commended a fugitive slave ...'

savage letters, confident that you will obey me. And so I entreat you: set
your life in order in such a way that when I come I shall not be compelled
to employ again the same boldness that I seem to have expressed[4] against
certain false apostles. Measuring me by their own attitude, they judge that I
am dealing with you in accordance with carnal affections, as if I flatter you
when I am present – whether to curry favour or because of fear – while
when I am absent I talk big in my letters, and there is nothing I do not dare.

Whatever I do, I do for your welfare and for the gospel, not out of
human affection. For although we are enclosed by this mortal flesh,[5] still we
do not wage war under the auspices and leadership of the flesh, but under
the protection of the Spirit and of God. However lowly and feeble we seem
to you, still we are not defenceless, and we do not lack the strength to hold
in check the foes of the gospel.

The arms of our warfare, which is spiritual, are not powerful in the human way with iron or bronze, but they are powerful through the inbreathing
of God[6] for demolishing whatever defence seems to have been set up against
him. With them we demolish and overturn clever counsels and all the lofty
pretentiousness of the ungodly, which is erected and elevated on the bulwarks of human wisdom,[7] in opposition to the knowledge of God, which we

* * * * *

4 The biblical text of 10:2, paraphrased here, is $\tilde{\eta}$ λογίζομαι τολμῆσαι: '[with the
   confidence] with which I reckon to be bold [against my critics]' – apparently
   an approach Paul contemplates using against his critics in the future. Erasmus,
   both here in the paraphrase and in his translation, presents the bold approach
   as something Paul has already used against his critics. Erasmus may have in
   mind the harsh words Paul directs at factious individuals and detractors of
   himself among the Corinthians in 1 Cor 4:6–21. See also the Argument of 2
   Corinthians 202.
5 Theophylact *Expos in 2 Cor* (on 10:3) PG 124 900C similarly phrases Paul's
   'walking in flesh': 'although clad in flesh . . .'
6 See the annotation on 10:4 (*sed potentia deo*), where Erasmus explains the dative
   'to God' (in Paul's claim that 'the weapons of our warfare . . . are mighty to
   God' [DV]) as instrumental, ie 'as if you should say "strong through God" or
   "by divine agency." ' Cf AV: 'mighty through God'; also Theophylact *Expos in
   2 Cor* (on 10:4) PG 124 900D. On the variety of modern interpretations given to
   this phrase, see Furnish 457. On 'the inbreathing [*afflatus*] of God,' especially
   as the power behind effective preaching, the weapon Paul and Erasmus have
   in mind here, see 1 Cor chapters 1 n53 and 2 n6.
7 The paraphrase reinforces Paul's metaphor of siege warfare. In his annotation
   on 10:4–5 (*consilia destruentes*), Erasmus explains that 'some [of the enemy's
   fortifications] are impregnable because of craft [hence, 'clever counsels' here],
   others because of their height [here 'lofty pretentiousness . . . elevated . . . on
   the bulwarks'].'

profess through the gospel. We not only cast down, but also subdue and take captive all human thinking,[8] so that henceforth it may obey Christ, against whom previously it was in rebellion. But should anyone stubbornly rebel, we have ready a punishment against all disobedience. For your sake we have not used it yet for fear that I might throw the public tranquillity into confusion by raging against people who are interspersed among you: a few are still somewhat well disposed towards them, thinking that they are distinguished apostles. Perhaps I shall use it later on, when I perceive that your obedience has advanced so far towards perfection that you will appear likely to tolerate with equanimity the separation of such people from your fellowship,[9] as you did in punishing the incestuous man.[10] The power and prestige of an apostle is spiritual, not physical.

Do you still judge an apostle from things that are seen, as the common crowd judges a prince from his retinue, or from the ostentatious fanfare of fortune?[11] I shall not say anything, for the moment, about false apostles, but

* * * * *

8 Theophylact *Expos in 2 Cor* (on 10:5) PG 124 901B structures his elaboration similarly: not only 'do we conquer all human thinking, but we also take it captive, which is a more complete victory.'

9 The paraphrase goes far beyond the actual text of Paul in 10:6, 'being ready to punish every disobedience, when your obedience is complete' (RSV). For the ideas that the threatened punishment is being delayed because Paul's critics are still 'interspersed' among the Corinthians, and that this punishment, when it comes, will be a 'cutting off' of the incurable rebels from fellowship with the faithful, cf Theophylact *Expos in 2 Cor* (on 10:6) PG 124 901C.

10 Erasmus assumes that the incestuous man whom Paul in 1 Corinthians 5 urged the Corinthians to cut off from their fellowship is the same as the man who in 2 Cor 2:6–10 has been properly chastened and reformed through the Corinthians' actions, and with whom Paul now urges reconciliation. See 1 Cor chapter 5 n5 and the paraphrase on 2 Cor 2:6–9.

11 The text of 10:7 raises two problems for interpretation. First, the verb βλέπετε can be taken as imperative ('look at,' as in the Vulgate, DV, and most modern commentaries and translations; cf NRSV 'look at what is before your eyes'), as simple indicative ('you are looking at'), or as interrogative ('do you look on things after the outward appearance?' [AV]). Erasmus chooses the interrogative for both his translation and the paraphrase here, and explains in the annotation on 10:7 (*quae secundum faciem sunt videte*) that it is 'as if Paul imagines that thing to be happening which he wants to rebuke,' ie 'Are you Corinthians basing judgments on external characteristics?' Second, the phrase τὰ κατὰ πρόσωπον is typically interpreted as either 'what is before your eyes,' ie 'plain fact' (RSV, NRSV, NEB, Conf) or, as here in the paraphrase, 'according to outward appearance' (DV, AV). In the same annotation, after acknowledging opposing views, Erasmus opts for the second interpretation, citing Theophylact (from *1516*) and Chrysostom (from *1527*): 'This is the speech of one who is

this I shall say in general:[12] if anyone has confidence in himself on account of his belonging to Christ, either because he saw him as a mortal, or because he was related to him by blood,[13] let him ponder carefully the fact that, just as he belongs to Christ, so also do we belong to Christ. In this respect we are equals; he has no grounds for despising us, while flattering himself. For it is not a relationship of the flesh that joins us more closely with Christ, but rather the Spirit.

Meanwhile I am doing nothing more than claiming equality with the rest of the apostles. But if I should claim for myself something of even greater scope, boasting of my power, or rather not mine, but the power entrusted by the Lord, entrusted, however, for this – that I may benefit, not harm you – I would not, I think, be put to shame, as if I have boasted idly rather than truly. Yet I shall be silent about the extent of my power,[14] so that no one may think that I am trying to terrify you with threatening epistles.

Someone, whose name I do not yet mention out of respect, spoke like this: 'Paul sends Epistles that are arrogant and powerful, but when he is present in person, he is a different man; he seems to be weak in body, a body that makes no show of majesty, and his contemptible[15] speech does not recall the authority with which his Epistles thunder and hurl lightning bolts.' I would like whoever despises my authority on this account to be

* * * * *

rebuking them because they were judging a person by externals.' For a concise discussion of the different interpretations, see Furnish 465–6. On preoccupation with ostentatious display, cf the paraphrase on 1 Cor 4:7 with n9.

12 Cf Theophylact *Expos in 2 Cor* (on 10:7) PG 124 904A, who notes that Paul's remarks are addressed as much to the Corinthians who had been deceived as to the false apostles who had deceived them.

13 On such 'visible' criteria, ones that are based on considerations 'of the flesh' and wrongly employed in ranking apostles, see the paraphrase on 5:12–14 with nn13, 15, and 17; also the paraphrase on 11:22. Cf Theophylact *Expos in 2 Cor* (on 10:7) PG 124 904A: 'For false apostles were boasting ... because they themselves perhaps saw Christ.'

14 The transition in Paul's text between 10:8 (Paul's claim of a power to build up) and 10:9 (his wish not to terrify with his letters) is difficult. See Furnish 467–8. Erasmus evidently sees the connection in the idea of power, explicit in 10:8, implied in 10:9. Cf Theophylact *Expos in 2 Cor* (on 10:8) PG 124 903B–C, who observes that the power for building up is implicitly accompanied by a like power to tear down, which Paul can employ if anyone proves intractable.

15 'Contemptible': *contemptibilis*; preserving the Vulgate's word, although in his translation and the annotation on 10:10 Erasmus' corrects to *contemptus* 'vile,' 'despised.'

convinced of the fact that my strength, when I am present, and my authority too (if I decided to use it), is of the same kind as my speech in the Epistles when I am absent, a speech that they say is weighty. To vaunt in words what I cannot perform in fact is a characteristic of others, not one of mine.

We cannot imagine[16] counting ourselves among those people, or even comparing ourselves with the sort who commend themselves not by deeds, but by deceit and, indeed, by pomposity. They do not understand at all,[17] in the meantime, that they are measuring themselves not on the basis of their merits, but as idlers in a comparison with idlers, and they show that they are great solely by singing their own praises and disparaging the merits of others.[18]

Far be it from me to boast without limit, after their example. For, according to that mode, there would be no measure or end to boasting, if each wished to be considered as great as his arrogance makes him. We measure

* * * * *

16 'We cannot imagine': *non possumus animum inducere*. One of the expressions Erasmus recommends in his annotation on 10:12 (*inserere aut comparare*) to replace the Vulgate's *non audemus* 'we do not dare' in translating Paul's οὐ τολμῶμεν 'we do not undertake' or 'endure,' 'have the heart.' Erasmus explains: 'Why would Paul not *dare* to compare himself with false apostles, for he does not hesitate even to prefer himself to honest apostles? No, rather he doesn't *want* to be compared with [them].'

17 not ... at all] *nequaquam*, first in 1532; previously *non* 'not.' Erasmus here departs from the Vulgate and follows his own reading of the Greek text for 10:12b: 'But they do not understand that they are measuring themselves by one another and comparing themselves with themselves.' The Vulgate, following a Western textual tradition, omits 'they do not understand' and makes 'we,' ie Paul, continue as subject of the participles 'measuring' and 'comparing': 'But we measure ourselves by ourselves and compare ourselves with ourselves' (DV). On the textual problem, see Metzger 514 and Furnish 469–71, and cf Erasmus' annotation on 10:12 (*sed ipsi in nobis*). Modern translations largely agree with Erasmus' reading, but many treat the verb 'they do not understand' as absolute. Cf NRSV: 'When they measure themselves by one another and compare themselves with one another, they do not show good sense.'

18 Theophylact *Expos in 2 Cor* (on 10:12) PG 124 905 notes similarly that each one, in praising himself, disparages the other. The Latin word translated 'idlers' in this sentence is *ignavi*. It refers, at its most basic level, to people who are 'physically lazy or indolent,' 'lacking in energy.' It also connotes moral and spiritual lethargy, and this is perhaps also a sense Erasmus has in mind here: 'fainthearted' or 'cowardly.' Cf the paraphrase on 10:15–16 below, where Paul's rivals are termed *ignavi duces* 'faint-hearted captains' and charged with being both lazy and cowardly, in that they 'sing their own praises' by pilfering glory from someone else's conquests, namely, Paul's.

ourselves by our own abilities,[19] not usurping for ourselves another's glory,[20] but according to the measure and limit of what, with God's help, we have accomplished ourselves. We claim for ourselves as much as has been granted by him, and we do not extend this glory of ours beyond the proper limit. Surely we have in no small way expanded the jurisdiction of our commander,[21] we who reached out even as far as to you, not setting out on our own initiative, but sent by God.[22] This is vast enough material for boasting: that we did not come to you in just any way at all, but we came in such a way as to preach to you the gospel of Christ. As a result, there is now no need for us to amplify with words our praiseworthy deeds, as if we did not reach out all the way to you in actual fact, to you who were otherwise absolutely unassailable. For we did not visit you when you had already been persuaded, as the false apostles do, but we were ourselves the first to persuade you. And we are not boasting endlessly about other people's efforts, transferring to ourselves, by words, the praise for other people's achievements. That is what faint-hearted captains are in the habit of doing, when they claim for themselves praise for a citadel captured by someone else's valour.

* * * * *

19 Erasmus' proverbial Latin idiom here (*nos nosmet nostro metimur pede*) recalls Horace *Epistles* 1.7.98: *metiri se quemque suo modulo ac pede verum est* ' 'Tis right that each should measure himself by his own rule and standard [literally 'foot measure'],' ie one should be content with one's own limits. See *Adagia* I vi 89.

20 In 10:13 Paul says he will not boast 'beyond limit.' Here in the paraphrase on that verse, Erasmus looks ahead to 10:15, in which Paul specifies what a boast 'beyond limit' would be, namely, appropriating for oneself 'the labours of others' (NRSV). Throughout the paraphrases in this section, Erasmus makes explicit Paul's criticism of false apostles who boast 'beyond limit,' a criticism that is only implicit in the biblical text of these verses. Cf Paul's similar delineation (Rom 15:17-20) of his ministry to bring the gospel to regions that have not been previously ministered to by others. The paraphrase on that passage (CWE 42 85-6) bears comparison especially with the paraphrase here on 2 Cor 10:13-18.

21 Erasmus elaborates the imperial analogy similarly in the annotation on 10:13 (*qua mensus est*): Paul 'says "even" or "as far as to you" so that we may realize that it is no small thing to reach out to the limit of the Corinthians,' for 'just as ambitious princes are wont to boast if they have extended their rule very far, so Paul, as Christ's general, boasts because he has expanded the jurisdiction of his prince, hoping that he would spread the rule even farther yet.' For Erasmus' elaboration on Paul as a 'conquering warrior' in the *Paraphrases* on Acts and the Epistles, see Sider 'Historical Imagination' 103.

22 Cf Ambrosiaster *Comm in 2 Cor* (on 10:14) CSEL 81/2 277:22-4: 'Not as if we reached you without having been sent . . ., but [we reached you,] having been appointed, with God sending us to you.'

Rather, we hope that, as your faith burgeons and grows greater and greater every day, we will attain through you a greater praise, in keeping with the goal prescribed for us by God, namely, that in other districts, too, which lie beyond you, we should preach the gospel of Christ and carry the standards of Christ still farther forward than we have done up to now – not acting in someone else's war and under someone else's auspices so that, in taking ourselves into a field already prepared, we might arrogate to ourselves the praise obtained through other people's efforts. On the contrary, so far am I from boasting on the basis of other people's deeds that I do not ascribe to myself even the glory of my own achievements. But whoever boasts ought to boast not on his own account, but on that of Christ, whose work he does. For it is not the person who rushes in blowing his own horn who is truly approved, but the one who has been chosen by God as suitable to discharge in good faith the responsibility entrusted; only he has been truly tested and approved as well.[23]

Chapter 11

I do not refrain from making rather grand claims for myself, although I am well aware that boasting about oneself is considered[1] proof of folly. But I would like you to put up with my playing the fool for a bit; actually, I have no doubt that you will.[2] I am compelled to this measure of folly, not by arrogance, not by desire for any recompense,[3] but by a prodigious

* * * * *

23 'Tested and approved as well': *spectatus ac probatus*. On these terms, see chapter 8 n26. For the same idea from the negative perspective, cf Ambrosiaster *Comm in 2 Cor* (on 10:18) CSEL 81/2 279:19–21: 'But the person who preaches without having been sent commends his own self; and in this he is not suitable, but a usurper, and proved counterfeit.'

1 is considered] First in *1532*; previously 'is'
2 The paraphrase seems to skirt the difference between the two possibilities for interpreting the Greek verb in 11:1b (ἀνέχεσθε): either indicative ('you are putting up with') or imperative ('put up with,' so the Vulgate). In his annotation on 11:1 (*supportate*). Erasmus prefers the indicative: 'For he corrects what he had said: "Would that you had put up with," nay, he says: "You are putting up with," and what I wish done, you are doing.' Modern translations vary. See Furnish 485–6.
3 Theophylact *Expos in 2 Cor* (on 11:1–2) PG 124 908B–D explains that it is necessity and fear, not financial gain or glory, that motivate Paul's 'foolish' self-commendation: Paul fears that his disciples will suffer harm 'if [their teacher] himself were denigrated, but the false apostles held in esteem.' Similarly

and impatient love towards you and, indeed, if I may say so, by jealousy. For I am plainly jealous in your regard: there is nothing I do not fear for you because of the tender love and esteem in which I hold you. I esteem you, moreover, not with human affection, but with divine charity, and I am jealous, not for myself, but for Christ.

For by a spiritual union[4] I have joined you, as a chaste and undefiled virgin, to him, as though to your only husband so that from him you may never be separated. Nothing of yours do I claim for myself. He is the spouse. I have merely played the role of 'bridesman.'[5] I handed over to him a bride chaste and pure, but I am afraid that somehow, just as long ago the serpent's wiles seduced the simple mind of Eve, vitiating the purity in which she had been created, so you too, likewise, in your simplicity[6] may be seduced through the cunning of false apostles, and you may deviate from the purity which, thus far, you have practised towards your spouse, Christ Jesus. Both he and you were alike pure when you received him through us.

* * * * *

Ambrosiaster *Comm in 2 Cor* (on 11:2) CSEL 81/2 280:9–10 explores Paul's self-commendation as fostering the Corinthians' advancement, not his own, 'for the vilification of the father is a loss for the children.'

4 by a spiritual union] Added in *1532*

5 'Bridesman': *pronubi*; a curious term, which could also be translated 'groomsman' or 'marriage maker.' All these senses are appropriate for Paul's role in 11:2. As an ambassador for Christ (eg 2 Cor 5:20), he may appropriately play the part of 'groomsman' or 'best man,' attending to the interests of the bridegroom Christ; however, as 'father' of the Corinthian church (1 Cor 4:14–15), he may function equally well on behalf of the 'bride,' and in that role negotiate the marriage and bring her to it. On the roles of fathers and attendants in arranging and executing marriages during biblical times, see *The Interpreter's Dictionary of the Bible* ed George Arthur Buttrick et al (New York 1962) 3 283–5. Erasmus' language may derive from Theophylact *Expos in 2 Cor* (on 11:2) PG 124 908D–909A: '[Paul says:] "I am zealous, therefore, on behalf of [Christ], not on behalf of myself. For I am not the bridegroom, but the leader of the bride [νυμφαγωγός]." Notice how he did not say, "I am your instructor, and for that reason you ought to bear with me," but he puts them in the place of the bride, himself ... in the role of the marriage maker [προμνήστρια 'a woman who woos ... for another' LSJ].' Erasmus' term in the paraphrase, *pronubus* (the masculine counterpart of the *pronuba*), although not used in classical Latin, has in later Latin the sense of either 'bridegroom's friend,' eg in the Vulgate of Judg 14:20: *unum ... ex pronubis* 'one of his ... bridal companions' (DV), or 'marriage maker.' See Alexander Souter *A Glossary of Later Latin to 600 A.D.* (Oxford 1949) 327.

6 'Simplicity': *simplicitas*. On this word, see chapter 8 n2; Phil chapter 3 n30; and CWE 44 191 n28.

Indeed, if that new apostle of yours,[7] who has crept in upon our labours, were preaching another Jesus, one we did not preach to you, or if through him you were receiving another spirit, one you did not receive through us, or if he were handing on another gospel, one that was not handed on by us, with good reason would you be putting up with his self-vaunting and placing himself before us, inasmuch as he would have conveyed what we were unable to convey.[8] But as matters now stand, if nothing is being conferred by those people that has not already been abundantly handed down by us, why is it that you, in a certain manner, have scorned us while you put up with their insolence? Suppose they are[9] ever so great as apostles; certainly,[10] so far as pertains to the fruit of the gospel, I think that I have not been inferior in any regard even to the distinguished apostles of the foremost rank.[11] Suppose they are more elegant in speech; I would certainly not take second place to them in knowledge. There is no need for the alluring niceties of language, when the reality itself is at hand.[12] Let them

* * * * *

7 The paraphrase assumes a single, particular outsider as the reference in 11:4, 'For if someone comes and preaches ...' (RSV). Most modern commentators take the reference as general. See Furnish 488.

8 The paraphrase turns the biblical text's simple fact conditions ('if someone ... preaches ... you submit to it [or 'him'] ...') into contrary-to-fact ('if that new apostle ... were preaching ... you would be putting up with ...'). This interpretation of Paul's intent in 11:4 is partially in agreement with the Vulgate, which produces a mixed condition: '[if someone ... preaches ...], you would be bearing with ...' cf DV: 'you might well bear with ...'

9 Suppose they are] *sint*, first in *1521*, probably to correct a printer's error in *1519*, which reads *sicut* 'just as' and lacks grammatical completeness

10 certainly] Added in *1521*

11 In his annotation on 11:5 (*nihil me minus fecisse*) Erasmus, citing Theophylact (from *1519*) and Chrysostom (from *1527*), names Peter, James, and John as the apostles Paul has in mind. He notes, however, in the *1519* addition, that 'more recent' (ie medieval) interpreters think Paul means apostles 'who pretend they had been sent by Peter and the others.' In a *1535* addition Erasmus observes that, in identifying them as 'surpassingly excellent apostles,' Paul speaks 'with some vexation.' Modern commentators are divided as to whether Paul refers in 11:5 to the leaders of the Jerusalem church or, with considerable irony, to the false apostles active in Corinth. For the arguments on each side, see Furnish 489–90, 502–5. On 'apostles of the first rank' and similar designations – whether used respectfully or derisively – elsewhere in Erasmus' Corinthian paraphrases, see 1 Cor chapter 3 n15; also 2 Cor chapter 5 n12.

12 On the assertion that authentic preaching does not require overly elegant, charming, or cultivated speech, cf Theophylact *Expos in 2 Cor* (on 11:4) PG 124 911A. On Paul's simple style of speaking, see the paraphrase on 1 Cor 2:1–4 with n6. See also Erasmus' annotation on 2 Cor 11:6 (*sed non scientia*): 'In

recommend themselves with the ornamental trappings of words; it is by all our services that we have shown our intent towards you, and our apostolic power. And we have not allowed anything to be wanting in us.

Unless perhaps you are offended by the very thing that should especially have recommended our intent towards you,[13] namely, that I have not, in their manner, oppressed you by my haughtiness, but have humbled and abased myself among you and without any guile, so that through my lowliness you might be raised up in faith.[14] Or is it that I have not, after their example, weighed you down with expenses,[15] but have preached the gospel of God to you free of charge, and paying for my own provisions? So far did I spare you that, although I was hard pressed by the lack of resources, I preferred to plunder other churches in order to serve you without any cost to you. I was not burdensome to anyone, even[16] at a time when I was living among you, and need was pressing hard. For those who had then come from Macedonia supplied my need. Indeed, not only in this matter, but in all circumstances, I have in the past taken care – and will do so in the future – not to be a burden to anyone.

I am not making these statements arrogantly; as surely as the truth of Christ is always with me, this boast of mine that the gospel has been preached free of charge in the districts of all Achaea, not just at Corinth, will never be shattered.

* * * * *

reference to thought, nothing can be more divine than Paul, but his speech, although lacking the solecisms that the [Vulgate] translator adds to him in many places, nevertheless cannot be called polished, according to a human standard, since the Greek interpreters are everywhere wrestling with the inconveniences of his language – which would not have happened if he had spoken to us in the language of Isocrates or Lucian.'

13 With this paraphrase on 11:7, 'Did I commit a sin in abasing myself ...' (RSV), cf Ambrosiaster *Comm in 2 Cor* (on 11:7) CSEL 81/2 284:12–13: Paul's humbling of himself is not a thing 'of sin, but of glory.'

14 Cf Theophylact *Expos in 2 Cor* (on 11:7) PG 124 913A: '"so that you might be raised up," that is to say, that you might be built up in regard to faith.'

15 Cf Ambrosiaster *Comm in 2 Cor* (on 11:7) CSEL 81/2 284:18–20: Paul 'refused the compensation offered so that ... he would not be found similar to the false apostles, who were preaching not for the glory of God, but for their own advantage.'

16 In the same way Erasmus explains the force of the conjunction καὶ 'and' at the beginning of 11:9 in his annotation on that verse (*et egerem*): it is not a simple connective, 'but gives emphasis ... so that the sense is: "So far was I from weighing you down that not *even* when I was in need did I want to [burden you].'"

For what reason am I doing this? Is it out of hatred for you that I spurn your generosity as well? God knows this is not the case. What I am doing and what I intend to do in the future, I do for this reason: that I may steal in advance the opportunity of slandering me from those who are looking for such an opportunity. Thus, they may be found in this matter also to be in no way superior to us. For in this they are looking for false praise, in that, although they are affluent, they pretend in the open to refuse gifts, but in secret they take them,[17] while we, although pressed by need, do not take anything from anyone, not allowing them to surpass us even by this feigned and counterfeit semblance of piety.[18]

As a matter of fact, these men do not preach the gospel sincerely, but for their own profit and pride. Moreover, although they have not been sent by Christ, and do not do his work, nevertheless they falsely claim for themselves the honour of the name 'apostle.'[19] They pretend that they have been hired for the Lord's vineyard,[20] to undertake his cause through their own efforts, although they obstruct his work, and attend to the affairs of their

* * * * *

17 Erasmus makes explicit a charge that is often seen as implicit in 11:12, ie that Paul's rivals accepted remuneration from the Corinthians. Cf Furnish 509. But Erasmus goes further and charges them with doing so on the sly, a charge also explicit in Theophylact *Expos in 2 Cor* (on 11:12) PG 124 916C, where the pretence is upon Satan's instructions: 'Since the devil knows that humans are especially attracted by this practice, that teachers not take payment, he taught the false apostles to dissemble this also ... But, seeming not to take [payment], they did take [it].'

18 Cf Erasmus' explanation in his annotation on 11:12 (*ut in quo gloriantur*): 'That is, if they, too, boast that they preach the gospel free of charge, they will not in this be superior to me, since I myself teach free of charge even [though I am] in need.' Theophylact *Expos in 2 Cor* (on 11:12) PG 124 917A makes the same point, adding the further observation that their show of taking no payment was a sham: 'They did not truly carry this out, but pretended to.'

19 'The name "apostle"': *apostolici cognominis*. On the word 'apostle' and its meaning see 1 Cor chapter 1 n2. Cf the annotation on 11:13 (*eiusmodi pseudo apostoli*): 'For an apostle does the work of the one by whom he has been sent, [whereas] these people serve their own advantage.' The term ψευδαπόστολοι 'false apostles,' quite possibly Paul's own coinage, appears in the Bible only at 2 Cor 11:13. Interestingly, although Erasmus has used the term nine times so far in the *Paraphrases* on 1 and 2 Corinthians, here in the paraphrase on 2 Cor 11:13 he alludes to the term's etymology, but avoids the term itself. On ψευδαπόστολοι, see Ralph P. Martin 2 *Corinthians* World Biblical Commentary 40 (Nashville 1986) 349–52 and Furnish 494.

20 In paraphrasing 'deceitful workmen' (11:13) Erasmus appears to borrow a metaphor from the parable on vineyard labourers in Matt 20:1–16.

belly[21] under pretext of gospel teaching, while foisting in certain dogmas of their own.[22] They are just like people who mix deadly poison with the most exquisite wine, in order the more effectively to deceive. Meanwhile, masquerading as apostles – the better to impose upon the naïve, under the pretext of authority and the shadow of a great name – they are actors more truly than apostles.[23] This, however, is the most pernicious kind of imposture: under the pretence of piety, to implant[24] the poison of impiety.

They allege that their author[25] is Christ, although they take up the cause of Satan. It is not surprising if the disciples copy their teacher. For there is no other device by which even Satan himself, dark as he is, more effectively harms mortals than by hiding his real form and, through a delusion, transfiguring himself into an angel of light.[26] They are truly the ministers of Christ who resemble their Lord in doing nothing through deceit. But it is nothing new if Satan's ministers assume for themselves the persona of another, so as to appear to be ministers of righteousness, although they are slaves of unrighteousness, most criminal traitors, falsely pretending to be a friend, while they play the part of a foe. I am not yet exercising my authority against them, but for the sake of public tranquillity[27] I leave

* * * * *

21 Ambrosiaster *Comm in 2 Cor* (on 11:15) CSEL 81/2 287:24–288:1 similarly introduces the belly as the false apostle's prime motivator. Paul warns against false teachers who are slaves to their own belly in Rom 16:18. Cf the paraphrase on that verse CWE 42 89: 'Nor do they care simply for the work of Christ, but they serve their own stomach and their own gain while they seduce the minds of the simple by smooth speech and by charming ... words.' For the expression 'affairs [or 'work'] of the belly,' see also the paraphrase on 1 Cor 11:22; and for a similar use of the contrast between honest and dishonest workers, cf the paraphrase on 1 Cor 3:9.

22 Cf Theophylact *Expos in 2 Cor* (on 11:13) PG 124 917A: 'For pretending to do such things [announce Christ, introduce the gospel], they secretly bring in ungodly dogmas.'

23 For the negative theatrical image, cf Matt 6:2, 5 and Erasmus' annotation on Matt 6:2 (*sicut hypocritae*); also the paraphrase on Mark 4:2 CWE 49 56 with n4. For a more neutral use of a theatrical metaphor, see 1 Cor chapter 14 n20.

24 The infinitive *inserere* 'to graft,' translated here 'to implant' (from the root verb 'to sow or plant'), is ambiguous. It can also be translated 'to bring in' or 'introduce' (from the root verb 'to interweave or entwine'). See OLD *sero* 1 and *sero* 2. On 'grafting,' see chapter 5 n21; also 1 Cor chapter 6 n13. Coverdale (fol lix verso) translates here 'to sow.'

25 On the term *auctor* 'author' and the contrasting *minister* 'minister,' 'steward,' which Erasmus uses later in this paragraph, see 1 Cor chapter 1 n10.

26 On Satan and deceitful delusions, see CWE 50 58–9 and other references under 'Satan' and 'magicians' in the General Index in that volume.

27 for the sake of public tranquillity] Added in 1532. Cf the paraphrase on 10:6.

them to their malice.[28] However, they will not escape the penalty, since, indeed, evil works will have an evil end.

Again, I have to ask your indulgence to allow me to say something about myself as well, something true, so that no one will attribute to my folly the fact that I myself am trumpeting my own praises. If I do not obtain this, at least bear with my folly (if that is what it appears to be). Since those men say so many things about themselves in your presence, let it be right for me, too, to make some little boast about myself. For what I am now going to say will not smack of the pure spirit of Christ, but rather of human folly. In fact, I shall boast about matters that do not at all make us more pleasing to God – the sort about which the foolish crowd generally brags, although true glory does not spring from such things. What I am doing has the appearance of foolishness, I know. But I am driven to this pass by the ostentation of those whom you tolerate, even while they foolishly boast. Therefore, since there are so many among you who, although they want to be considered apostles, nevertheless brag about things that have nothing to do with apostolic gifts, I personally shall boast a little about myself, too, imitating their folly.[29] Meanwhile, you will kindly excuse this silliness of ours. Since you yourselves are wise, you will not resent another's foolishness. But in the midst of so many who are constantly boasting, it is fair for you to put up with me too for a little while, especially since my boasting will not weigh you down, as theirs does.[30]

In their case you put up with it, if someone forces you into slavery (although Christ wished you to be free); if someone eats you out of house and home and drains you dry from the cost (although we played our role

* * * * *

28 On *malitia* 'malice,' see the Index of Greek and Latin Words Cited in CWE 50 and 56.

29 The 'folly' Erasmus has in mind is boasting of Hebrew ancestry and of adherence to Mosaic law. See the next note. Paul's imitation of this folly begins in 11:22.

30 Although 'weighing down' here refers most directly to the false apostles' draining of the Corinthians' personal resources, Erasmus may also have in mind the imposition of Jewish legalism, which Paul frequently associates with his rivals. On the false apostles as 'Judaizers,' see the Arguments of Galatians CWE 42 94–6, 1 Corinthians 19, and 2 Corinthians 200–1; also 1 Cor chapter 9 n6 and the cross-references noted there. For Mosaic law as 'burdensome,' see the paraphrase on 2 Cor 7:2 with n4; also the paraphrases on 2 Cor 3:6 with nn5 and 6 and Gal 2:18 CWE 42 106 with n8. Both Theophylact *Expos in 2 Cor* (on 11:18–19) PG 124 920A–B and Ambrosiaster *Comm in 2 Cor* (on 11:18–19) CSEL 81/2 289:8–20 similarly find Paul's critique here to be directed at Jewish Christians who prided themselves, among other things, on circumcision and Hebrew ancestry.

as an apostle free of charge); if someone strains your resources by receiving presents and gifts; if someone, puffed up with arrogance, exercises a
tyranny over you, even to the point of slapping you in the face, which is
the ultimate in abuse; and if they do not actually do this, certainly in other
ways they so treat you that the insult is no less. Although they do such
things, they seem to you to be great apostles. You base your esteem for
them on the very things about which it is commonly considered foolish to
boast, just as if we could not have taken advantage of those same titles to
oppress you with our authority, had we not preferred to consider your welfare rather than our power. For what do they boast about, or in what are
they pleased with themselves, in which I could not match them (to speak
for a moment in the manner of fools)?

They want it to seem important that they are Hebrews, just as if it
makes any difference to God from what stock you are sprung; and yet, if it
is something to be born a Hebrew, I too am a Hebrew. They are Israelites;
I am too. They are descendants of Abraham; I am too.[31] For they vaunt
themselves on empty titles of this sort; and yet[32] in such things we are their
equals, if we should like to boast.

Even in regard to those things that truly do contribute to apostolic
glory, we outshine them. They are ministers of Christ – let us grant it –
but I am more so (to speak foolishly, but to speak the truth nonetheless).[33]
I have shown that this is so, not through arrogance, nor by taking gifts,
nor by boasting of family origin, but by the very proofs that truly attest an
apostolic heart. I have endured more labours than they; far more grievously
have I felt the lash; more often have I been cast into prison; more frequently
have I run the risk of death. But if you wish some instances to be recounted[34]
in detail: five times I received forty lashes less one, when I was beaten by
the Jews; three times I was beaten with lictors' rods;[35] once I was stoned;

* * * * *

31 too] Added in 1532
32 and yet] First in 1521; previously 'then'
33 Cf Erasmus' treatment of this passage (11:23) in the *Moria* CWE 27 144–5.
34 to be recounted] First in 1521: in 1519 'to recount' (ie 'if you wish to recount
     some instances in detail'), possibly a printer's error.
35 By identifying the 'rods' in 11:25 as lictors' rods, the paraphrase makes explicit
     Paul's presumed differentiation between his punishment by Romans (10:25)
     and his punishment by Jews (10:24). Lictors were attendants of Roman mag-
     istrates; they carried bundles of wooden rods (often including an ax), called
     fasces, as symbols of the magistrates' authority and as instruments of punish-
     ment. See OLD *fascis* 3 and *The Oxford Classical Dictionary* ed Simon Hornblower
     and Anthony Spawforth 3rd ed (New York 1996) 860, 1279. For the flogging

three times I was shipwrecked; I spent an entire night and day on the high
sea in the greatest despair of life. But why should I go on enumerating
individual instances, since frequently, for the sake of the gospel, I was in
danger, not only in sailing, but also in journeys by land? Repeatedly I
encountered dangers from rivers, dangers from brigands, dangers from the
persecution of the Jews, dangers from the violence of the gentiles, dangers
springing up in the city, dangers in the desert, dangers in the sea when I
came close to being slaughtered by the sailors,[36] dangers from these falsely
called 'Christians' who were resisting our gospel. Not to recall, for the
moment, the constant labours and hardships undertaken for the sake of the
gospel: the frequent nights without sleep,[37] the hunger and thirst endured
times without number, the frequent times without food,[38] the hardships of

* * * * *

of Roman citizens, see Furnish 516. Acts 16:23 records such a flogging of Paul
and Silas by the Roman authorities at Philippi.

36 Paul's catalogue of dangers in 11:26 merely mentions, as a general category,
'danger at sea.' In this elaboration, Erasmus probably has in mind Acts 27:42–
3, which records a plan by soldiers to kill Paul and other prisoners during the
sea journey to Rome. If so, the reference is strangely anachronistic, since the
Corinthian correspondence (however complicated its composition) is generally
presumed to predate Paul's journey to Rome. Erasmus, however, has the firm
precedent of Ambrosiaster *Comm in 2 Cor* (on 11:26) CSEL 81/2 294:23–295:4,
where 'danger at sea' is specifically explained as referring to the incident
reported in Acts 27.

37 'Nights without sleep': *vigilias*. It is uncertain in what sense Erasmus intends
this word or, for that matter, what Paul intends in 11:27 with the Greek ἐν
ἀγρυπνίαις 'in watchings' (AV) or 'through many a sleepless night' (RSV). There
appear to be three possibilities: devotional exercises, ie nocturnal prayer vigils; nights of wakefulness, 'keeping watch' against dangers; and nights that
were sleepless for some other reason, eg the need to preach and teach when
potential hearers were not busy at work, or the need for Paul to earn his living as a tanner during free hours. Ambrosiaster *Comm in 2 Cor* (on 11:27) CSEL
81/2 295:24–296:3 suggests the first and third of these explanations. Modern
interpreters vary: Furnish 518 supports the third; NJBC §50:53 827 attributes
the sleepless nights to difficulties ancient travellers had in reaching inns prior
to nightfall. Cf Furnish 344 (on 6:5), and see also the next note.

38 'Times without food': *inedias*; or possibly 'fastings' (so Coverdale [fol lx verso]).
Again (see previous note) it is not clear whether in 11:27 Erasmus (or Paul)
has in mind voluntary acts of religious devotion (so AV, DV, NEB) or essentially
involuntary exigencies experienced in apostolic service (so RSV, NRSV, Furnish
518). The context of 'constant labours and hardships' would suggest the latter.
Cf the paraphrase on 6:5 with n7. Cf also CWE 50 145 n7, and, for *inedia* as
'going without food,' see Erasmus' annotation on Acts 27:9 (*eo quod ieiunium
iam praeterisset*).

cold and nakedness endured. But what I have recounted thus far pertains only to the affliction of my body.

Indeed, in the meantime, I was experiencing no less severe affliction of spirit. Daily I was pressed and weighed down on every side by the concerns I have on behalf of so many churches. So close are they to my heart that whatever happens to them I count as happening to me. For whose ills do I not grieve as my own? Who is weak, through whose suffering I do not myself become sick? Who is hurt, through whose injury[39] I do not myself suffer the deepest distress? If there must be boasting, I shall boast of what proves my frailty rather than my greatness. Let others boast that through their commendation of the gospel they are considered important, that they are growing rich, that they reign under the pretext of Christ. I personally think it a finer thing to boast that for the sake of Christ I have been cast down and afflicted. The God[40] and Father of our Lord Jesus Christ knows that I am telling no lie.[41]

When I was at Damascus, the man whom King Aretas (Herod's father-in-law)[42] had put in charge of that people[43] had stationed watchmen in the state of the Damascenes, aiming by every means to win favour with the

* * * * *

39 'Injury': *offendiculo*; the word is translated 'stumbling block' in the paraphrase on 1 Corinthians 8, eg on 8:13 in reference to the eating of sacrificial meat. The 'injury' in question here, then, in the paraphrase on 2 Cor 11:29, is an act that might cause a weak Christian to stumble or fall from true faith. Cf NRSV: 'Who is made to stumble, and I am not indignant.'

40 The God ... hands of the prefect] In *1519* this paraphrase on 11:31–3 is printed after the heading for chapter 12 and thus appears as the beginning of the paraphrase on chapter 12. The chapter heading was moved to its proper place in *1521*.

41 The biblical text of 11:31 includes the phrase, 'the one blessed [or 'who is blessed'] forever,' which Erasmus for some reason does not paraphrase. A similar phrase in Rom 9:5 had been involved in a controversy as to whether or not Paul was in that verse calling Christ God. See the annotation on Rom 9:5 ('who is above all things God') CWE 56 243, where, however, Erasmus notes in passing that the 'similar passage' in 2 Cor 11:31 'can be referred only to the Father' and presumably therefore involves no controversy. Cf Furnish 521. Erasmus' Latin translation of 11:31 reads: 'The God and Father of our Lord Jesus Christ, who is to be praised for ever, knows that I am not lying.'

42 Theophylact *Expos in 2 Cor* (on 11:32) PG 124 928A also makes this identification. Aretas, king of Nabatea (9 BC to about AD 40), was father-in-law to Herod Antipas, son of Herod the Great. On Aretas and his relationship to Damascus, see Furnish 522. On Herod Antipas and Erasmus' confusion of him with Herod Agrippa I, see CWE 50 80 n1.

43 Erasmus explains Paul's reference to the 'ethnarch of Aretas' similarly in his annotation on 11:32 (*Damasci praepositus*).

Jews by arresting me and putting me to death as the instigator of a public uprising. What was I to do? I had learned from the Lord the precept that sometimes we were to avoid the rage of persecutions.[44] My soul kept saying that it was not yet time to undergo martyrdom, but rather to preach the gospel more widely. The tyrant, however, was hemming me in from every side, and there was[45] no other escape except that, enclosed in a basket, I was lowered by a rope[46] from the fortifications through a window, and in this way I slipped through the hands of the prefect.

Chapter 12

Thus far I have recounted evidence demonstrating that I have been beset with calamities and woes, evidence which, according to human judgment, makes a person despicable rather than glorious. But whether I should also recall further events, I have not yet decided – although others falsely boast about such things. Is one to boast or not? Yet it is sometimes expedient to boast, especially when the tenor of our talk has led us to visions and revelations of the Lord Jesus.[1] Although those 'apostles' of yours fabricate many such revelations and vaunt them insolently, I shall recount only one so that I may not seem even here to be their inferior. I shall do so under compulsion and against my will, and not for my glory, but for God's.[2]

* * * * *

44 Jesus enjoins his disciples in Matt 10:23 to escape persecution in one town by fleeing to another. Ambrosiaster *Comm in 2 Cor* (on 11:23) CSEL 81/2 299:8–9 and Theophylact *Expos in 2 Cor* (on 11:33) PG 124 928B similarly note this justification for Paul's escape. The latter notes that 'he was preserving himself for preaching the gospel.' On flight in persecution, see CWE 50 67 n34.

45 'Was': *est*, literally 'is'; first in the 1523 folio edition; prior to that the verb was only implied.

46 'By a rope.' Erasmus also adds this detail to his paraphrase on this incident in Acts 9:25. See CWE 50 67 with n33.

1 The paraphrase here, in stating the occasional usefulness of boasting, appears to differ both from the Vulgate reading of 12:1 ('if it is necessary to boast, it is indeed not useful') and from Erasmus' own Greek text and Latin translation ('boasting is certainly not useful for me'). Cf AV: 'It is not expedient for me to glory.' In his annotation on 12:1 (*si gloriari oportet*), however, Erasmus explains Paul's intent this way: '[Although any boasting I may do about revelations is dangerous and inexpedient for myself,] for you [Corinthians] it is indeed useful, so that you may learn what sort of apostle you have, one far different from those haughty ones.'

2 Theophylact *Expos in 2 Cor* (on 12:1) PG 124 928C similarly notes that Paul reports here only one of the many possible visions and revelations he could report, and that he reports this one only against his will. For the contrast with

I know someone who, fourteen years ago, was caught up, whether in the body or out of the body, I do not know – God knows – but nevertheless he was caught up all the way to the third heaven; from here, again, he was caught up into paradise. In both places he heard certain ineffable words that it is not right for a mortal to utter.[3] On behalf of a person of this sort, I shall boast, since such great felicity has come to him by God's kindness. About myself, meanwhile, I shall make no boast, except to recall the events that show me afflicted and abased.[4]

Besides, if I wanted in this regard, too, to speak about myself, since I am not going to say anything falsely or for personal display, I could not be condemned for folly, even though I acknowledge the charge of folly. Nevertheless, I restrain myself from describing these events, not for my sake, but for yours, so that no one may attribute more to me and suppose that I am somewhat greater than my deeds and my speech attest.

Yet perhaps it would not be quite safe for me to boast about these things that make us important and border on the danger of arrogance. Accordingly, so that I might not be too exalted by the loftiness of the revelations, or more highly regarded among people than is good, the gracious will of God permitted a goad and affliction of the body to be given me. Its purpose is both to remind me forcibly of myself and to prove to all that I am mortal, subject to ills we all share. Moreover, to afflict me as I do Christ's work, a messenger and servant of Satan was given, in order to hinder my gospel and to harass me with the most savage persecutions, just as if, hurling me down and pressing upon me, he were to beat me on the head, so that I should not be unduly elated. Since the situation was fiercely annoying for me, three times I asked the Lord to free me from this affliction.

* * * * *

other apostles, see Ambrosiaster *Comm in 2 Cor* (on 12:1) CSEL 81/2 299:19–20: Paul's purpose in reporting the incident is 'that he might not be thought inferior to the other apostles.'

3 'To utter': *eloqui*. The related noun *eloquium* has for Erasmus the connotation of human, rather than divine speech. See CWE 56 91–2 n12.

4 Most modern interpreters consider Paul to be speaking in 12:2–5 indirectly about himself and about a vision he himself has had. See Furnish 524, 542–4. In his annotation on 12:5 (*pro huiusmodi gloriabor*) Erasmus, too, follows Theophylact in assuming the vision is Paul's own: 'For Paul tells this event as if about some other person ... as if hiding the fact that he himself is that person about whom he is speaking.' Furnish 544 concludes that Paul hides this fact because he is unwilling to boast about his own ecstatic experience or 'to claim it as an apostolic credential.'

But he, having my interest at heart more than I myself, responded after this fashion: 'Paul, be content with my kindness towards you; you are not to press your demands any further. The fact that you are being pummelled by afflictions pertains, at the same time, both to making my glory illustrious[5] – for while you are safe under my protection you cannot be conquered, no matter how great the storms – and to your salvation, inasmuch as the more you are afflicted by the evils of the body, the richer you grow in the goods of the spirit.' Thus it happens that God's[6] strength finds its true end in human[7] frailty, and weakness completes power. For since[8] it is through the lowly and powerless that the gospel stands firm against Satan and a world menacing with every kind of savagery, and indeed flourishes, it becomes evident that this task is being accomplished not by human assistance, but by the power of the godhead. Moreover, the greater the ills with which we are afflicted, the more illustrious becomes the glory of God as he acts and expresses his power through us.[9]

Since I received this reply from the Lord, henceforth I shall boast of nothing more gladly than of the afflictions through which I appear feeble, rather than mighty. Even if any element of greatness or sublimity is evident in them, the whole of it contributes entirely to God's glory, so that I, who appear weak for Christ's sake, through him may seem powerful and strong. Consequently, I am especially pleased and congratulate myself on account of afflictions, insults, indigence, persecutions, and anxieties borne for Christ. For when in this way I am especially destitute and have no confidence in my own resources, then I am truly powerful by reason of Christ's assistance.

But to where does the force of my speech carry me?[10] I see that by boasting I have clearly returned to obvious folly.[11] But you are the reason;

* * * * *

5 Cf the annotation on 12:9 (*nam virtus*): 'Divine power is made especially illustrious [when the one it helps], aware of his weakness, claims nothing from it for himself, but assigns all the praise to God alone.'

6 God's] Added in 1532

7 human] Added in 1532

8 For since ... through us] Added in 1532

9 Cf Theophylact *Expos in 2 Cor* (on 12:9) PG 124 934C: 'For the more [infirmities] there have been, the more lavish is the power of God that is supplied me ... [and I rejoice and boast] as if drawing to myself a greater power of God through the vehemence of the afflictions.'

10 An echo of Horace *Odes* 3.25.1. For the same expression, see the paraphrase on 6:11 with n14.

11 The paraphrase follows Erasmus' Greek text and Latin translation of 12:11 in reading 'I have become a fool by [or 'in'] boasting'; so also Chrysostom, Theophylact, AV. The Vulgate and modern editions and translations read simply 'I

you have driven me to this point. For when I had any strength, it was for your good; it was your duty to say about me what now I am compelled in unseemly fashion[12] to say about myself. I do not claim for myself praise for a service that I have not provided; but if I have provided it to the same extent as someone else has, why are the others preferred to us? I am insignificant, I am lowly, I am afflicted and cast down, I have no eloquence; none of these charges do I deny or refute. Whatever disadvantage they imply pertains to me. But however worthless I am, still, so far as you are concerned, you have found me in no respect inferior to the rest of the apostles – I shall not say of the common sort, but not even those of the highest rank.[13]

I am not bringing up anything about myself[14] that you have not found in me;[15] for by genuine proofs I have demonstrated that I am an apostle, as you can testify.[16] The first and foremost proof of an apostolic heart is to suffer anything gladly for the sake of the gospel;[17] by this index surely I have shown myself to be an apostle. Nor were those things lacking by which God, because of the incredulity of some, for the time being brings to our words the grounds for trust, for example, wonders, portents, and deeds of power.[18]

* * * * *

have become [or 'am'] a fool.' By 'returned to,' Erasmus makes explicit the connection of 12:11 with the theme of folly developed in 11:1, 16 and 21.

12 'In unseemly fashion' qualifies 'I am compelled,' suggesting that it is the Corinthians who have been unseemly in not being gracious enough to commend Paul themselves.

13 This reference to apostles 'of the highest rank' in the paraphrase on 12:11 is probably intended as ironic. Cf Erasmus' annotation on the verse (*supra modum apostoli*): '[Paul identifies them this way] with some vexation, not because they were such, but because they wanted to be regarded as such – lest he seem to have meant Peter and James.' On such designations as 'the highest apostles' (whether used ironically or in straightforward fashion) in the Corinthian paraphrases, see 1 Cor chapter 3 n15.

14 about myself] Added in 1532

15 in me] Added in 1532

16 'As you can testify': *vobis testibus* (literally 'with you as witnesses') paraphrases the Greek ἐν ὑμῖν 'among you' in 12:12: 'The signs of a true apostle were performed among you in all patience' (RSV). In his annotation on this verse (*facta sunt super vos*), Erasmus corrects the Vulgate's *super vos* 'upon you' with *inter vos* 'among you' and explains that the expression is equivalent to *vobis videntibus* 'as you saw' or 'in your sight.'

17 This clause paraphrases 'in all patience' in 12:12. Cf Theophylact *Expos in 2 Cor* (on 12:12) PG 124 936D: 'The first mark of an apostle is patience, and the bearing of all things nobly.'

18 On the temporary usefulness of such extraordinary proofs of apostleship, cf the paraphrase on Acts 5:10 CWE 50 40 and especially n19.

In any case, cite an example, if there is one, in which you have been inferior to the rest of the churches. Or what was conferred on any church by those great apostles that I did not confer on you? You will find nothing wanting in me except the one thing you do miss: the fact that I have not burdened you with expenses, as the other apostles have. If I have hurt you in this matter – precisely because I have not hurt you – pardon me the offending deed, even if I do not regret the attitude.

Now I have been with you twice, and I have not been troublesome to anyone. And, see, my intention is to visit you a third time; however, I shall not be a burden for anyone, any more than I was before. I am not doing this rashly (although I am not yet bringing forward my earnest reason), but whatever the reason for my action, I am serving your interests and playing the part of a true father. For offspring are not obligated to heap up riches for their parents, but on the contrary, parents for their offspring. The affection of parents has this characteristic: that they not only spend their hard-earned resources, but they spend themselves also for their children.[19] Well then, far from extorting anything from you, I am ready and most willing to spend my possessions for you, and even myself in addition, if that is what the welfare of your souls requires. It is enough for me to make this provision as a father for his children, even though I am quite aware that I am finding in you the same thing parents generally find in their children, namely, that although I love you very dearly, I am not equally loved by you in return, but am ranked behind those who are not as well disposed to you as I.

But let us assume I personally did not burden you through fear of odium; still [you say], clever and astute as I am, I caught you by a trick, accomplishing through hirelings what I was ashamed to do in person.[20] Perhaps someone will level that charge, judging me on the basis of other people's character. Come now! Did I extort anything from you, through any of those who came to you in my name? I asked Titus to go to you. As his colleague I added that brother esteemed by all the churches. Surely Titus did not extort anything from you, did he? Was his attitude not the same as ours? Or did we not walk in the same footsteps? For I do not object to have imputed to me whatever those did whom I dispatched to you.

* * * * *

19 For the proverbial extravagance of parents towards their children, cf *De pueris instituendis* CWE 26 302.
20 Theophylact *Expos in 2 Cor* (on 12:16–17) PG 124 940B similarly paraphrases Paul's statement in 12:16 of the charge made against him: 'I suborned others ... to seek something from you as if on their own behalf, so that I craftily received without seeming to receive.'

Again[21] you think that we are saying this to plead our cause; on the contrary, whatever we say, whether we abase or extol ourselves, or expostulate with you, we are speaking, my dearest ones,[22] for your benefit.

God, who knows our heart, is witness; Christ too, whose work we are doing, is witness: there is nothing I do not attempt, no stone I leave unmoved. I turn myself into all things,[23] in order to set you quite straight. There is nothing for me to dread from those counterfeit[24] apostles. But I fear that, if I should happen to come to you, somehow I may not find you such as I would wish, and you, in turn, may find me other than you wish. My prayer is to look upon you purified in every respect, so that you may see me joyful and gentle. But my fear is that, if you go on giving ear to certain people, I may find among you quarrels, rivalries, rage, controversies, disparagements,[25] murmurings, vainglory, disorder. And if I come, it may again[26] happen that the Lord will cast me down[27] once more in your presence, when I ought to appear merry and cheerful because you are blameless. For I have been saddened quite enough up to now because of your disgraceful actions. Instead of a triumph, I may be compelled to feel sorrow on account of many people who have been defiled by sins now for

* * * * *

21 'Again': *rursus*. Modern editors generally read πάλαι 'for a long time now,' 'all along' at the beginning of 12:19. See Metzger 518, Furnish 560. cf RSV: 'Have you been thinking all along . . . ?' Erasmus, however, reads πάλιν 'again.' See his annotation on 12:19 (*olim putatis*), where he rejects the Vulgate's *olim* 'formerly' or 'for a long time now.'

22 'My dearest ones': *carissimi*. Erasmus again follows the Vulgate's custom in translating the Greek ἀγαπητοί 'beloved' by *carissimi* instead of *dilecti* 'beloved.' Although he recommends *dilecti* in the annotation on 12:19 (*omnia enim*), his Latin translation also uses *carissimi* here. Cf the paraphrases on 1 Cor 4:14 with n23 and 2 Cor 7:1 with n1; also CWE 56 311 and 342.

23 Cf 1 Cor 9:22, and see Erasmus' amplification of this Proteus-like quality of Paul in the paraphrase on that verse. For the image of Proteus elsewhere in Erasmus, see 1 Cor chapter 9 n33.

24 'Counterfeit': *personatis*, literally 'masked,' that is, 'in an assumed part.' For other uses of theatrical imagery, see the General Index under 'metaphors and figurative language.'

25 'Disparagements': *obtrectationes*. On this word, see CWE 56 62.

26 Erasmus seems to intend *rursus* 'again' to modify 'it may happen,' as also apparently in his translation of this verse (12:21): 'Lest again, when I come, God make me humble' (similarly DV, Furnish 562). 'Again,' however, could modify 'I come' instead. Cf NRSV: 'I fear that when I come again' (similarly AV, NEB).

27 cast me down] First in *1521*; previously, 'humble me'

some time. They have not yet recovered their senses,[28] so as to repent of the unclean, lustful, and licentious actions which they have committed.

Chapter 13

This will be my third time of coming to you; everyone should prepare for it. For I will not shut an eye to your offences any further; the case will be settled according to strict[1] and exact law. Whoever has been denounced will be acquitted or condemned on the testimony of two or three people.[2] I have already warned you previously; I warn you a second time. What I said to you in person the second time I came, I am now writing from a distance not only to those who had already sinned at that time, but even to all who have become guilty of sin.[3] If I find you unreformed, when I have already admonished you twice, I shall not hold back, as I formerly have done.

In any case, what do you have in mind? Are you trying to find out, to your own hurt, whether what I am saying I say from myself, or from the Spirit of Christ speaking to you through me? Or do you despise him, too, as weak? He was not weak in regard to you, even if he was once weak before the Jews and Pilate. On the contrary, he proved himself powerful among you: at his name you have seen the dead come to life again, demons flee, the sick be healed.[4] For although once, because of the weakness of the

* * * * *

28 'Recovered their senses': *resipuerunt*. On this word, frequently used by Erasmus to express repentance, see the Argument of 1 Corinthians n15. Note here that Erasmus uses the word in conjunction with the more familiar *poenitere* 'to make sorry,' 'to cause to repent' in order to explicate the biblical μετανοεῖν 'to repent.'

1 strict ... law] First in 1521; previously, 'the rigour of the law'
2 Ambrosiaster *Comm in 2 Cor* (on 13:1) CSEL 81/2 309:20–1 paraphrases Paul's reference to Deut 19:15 similarly: 'that with two or three witnesses someone either be cleared or condemned.'
3 Erasmus uses two words meaning 'sin' in this sentence: the verb *peccare* 'to sin' and the noun *delictum* 'sin,' 'offence.' On possible distinctions in meaning between *peccatum* 'sin,' and *delictum* 'sin' see CWE 56 163 n14; cf CWE 56 300 and 301 n3.
4 Erasmus draws on Ambrosiaster's longer catalogue of evidence for Christ's power. Cf *Comm in 2 Cor* (on 13:3) CSEL 81/2 310:12–15: 'Christ is powerful among Corinthians because they saw that in [Christ's] name the dead had been raised, demons had been routed, the paralysed restored to health, that the deaf had heard, the mute been granted [the power of] response, the lame had run, the blind had seen. These are all [evidence] of power, not of weakness.'

nature he had taken on, he willed to be fixed to the cross, nevertheless he ought not on that account to be considered weak. He died through the infirmity of the body he had assumed, but he lives through the strength of God the Father. Likewise, we apostles, who follow in the footsteps of Christ our teacher, although we may be feeble to the unbelieving, as we are beaten by them, cast into prison, and abused with insults,[5] still, through the strength of God, we shall with him be powerful towards you, if your stubbornness overcomes our gentleness.[6]

Do not seek to put us to the test; rather[7] test yourselves: are you standing firm in the gift of the faith, or have you fallen away from it? You, yourselves, examine one another. You have perceived in performing wonders, perceived from such manifold gifts, that not even in you has Christ been weak. If that force has deserted you, it is a proof that your faith has grown faint, or else that Christ, offended by your behaviour, has been estranged from you.[8] Or are you unacquainted with yourselves, and wish to put me on trial, since you yourselves do not understand that Christ is in you? For he is, if the vigour of faith remains in you; unless, perchance, although faith is somehow intact, you have, because of an impure life, deserved to be rejected by Christ. However matters stand with you, I hope that you will discover in actuality that we are not spurious.[9] Faith flourishes in me, and through it Christ will have the strength in me

* * * * *

5 Ambrosiaster *Comm in 2 Cor* (on 13:4) CSEL 81/2 310:28–311:3 similarly notes that 13:4b 'pertains to the person of the apostles, who in preaching him, ie Christ, were weakened, while they were being assailed with wrongs, imprisoned, beaten.'

6 Cf Theophylact *Expos in 2 Cor* (on 13:4) PG 124 945C, interpreting the implicit threat in Paul's assertion that 'we shall live ... by the power of God towards you' (AV): 'For if you also think us weak, [know that] we are powerful towards you, ie for punishing you if you have not been set right.' See also n8 below.

7 rather] Added in *1521*; *1538* and *1540* (followed by LB) strengthened the adversative: 'but rather ...'

8 Erasmus' paraphrase on 13:5 seems influenced by Theophylact *Expos in 2 Cor* (on 13:5–6) PG 124 945D–947A: 'that is, unless you have fallen away from the grace of the signs you received. He hints that they have also been corrupted in regard to their life ... [But he hopes they will find that] we have not been corrupted in our life to the extent that Christ has departed from us.'

9 'Spurious': *reprobi*. The word suggests being tested and proved unfit or a failure. It also appears at the end of the next paragraph and is the word used three times in both Erasmus' Latin translation and the Vulgate of 13:5–7. On its positive counterpart, *probatus* 'approved,' see chapters 8 n26 and 10 n23.

to chastise those who are unwilling to come to their senses of their own accord.[10]

But why did I say 'I hope'? No, on the contrary, I pray rather, and beseech God that, through his kindness, it may turn out that I am not forced by your offences to manifest my power; not because we are afraid that, if power had to be used, we might be found weaklings (as some people declare concerning us), but rather, we desire this: that you be approved through the noble character of your life, although we be regarded as spurious.

For if you persevere in the faith and in moral purity, there will be no reason for me to exercise my power against you, and I do not object to looking weak, to this extent anyway, that if I am judged to have little strength, the reason is that you have not given me the opportunity to exercise power. For we can do nothing against the truth. Whatever power we have, we have on behalf of truth. We are not mighty against innocence; we are mighty against transgressions. But if there is nothing in you that deserves censure, you will have disarmed us, so to speak. You will show yourselves powerful through your innocence, while I, like a weakling, will have been deprived of the power of showing anger.

Those disparagers among you will continue to pin a false charge of weakness on me, quibbling that it was through a failing of mine that I could not do what, in fact, I was unable to do on account of your integrity. But it gives me pleasure to be judged feeble, as often as you are strong according to that standard; or rather, not only do we rejoice if that happens,[11] but we even desire, with the most fervent prayers, that I may appear to lack something, provided that you are made perfect.

This is the reason I thought that you ought to be admonished rather severely through a letter: so that when I come, I may not be compelled to be severe in person. I prefer to have you corrected by threats rather than to exercise against you my power of punishment, a power the Lord has

* * * * *

10 Theophylact *Expos in 2 Cor* (on 13:6) PG 124 948A similarly explains the implicit threat in 13:6. See also n6 above. On 'come to their senses' (*resipiscere*), see chapter 12 n28.

11 Erasmus' Vulgate at 13:9 reads, 'for we rejoice that [or 'since'] we are weak and you are strong' (DV). Erasmus corrected to '... *when* we are weak and you are strong.' Cf his annotation on 13:9 (*gaudemus enim quoniam nos infirmi sumus, vos autem potentes*): 'For [Paul] does not affirm [that he is weak and the Corinthians are strong], but says that he rejoices if it is so.'

given me for your good, not ill. Against the innocent I can do nothing. But it is important for you that those who are contaminating your assembly by disgraceful actions not always[12] be left unpunished.

I have discharged my responsibility; it remains for you to discharge yours. Take care that when the causes of your distress have been removed, you rejoice chastely; and that, as you advance always towards better things, you be made perfect, repairing those things that damage your integrity; and that, when the correction of your ills has been completed, you derive solace from your amendment. Be of the same mind, and do not contend with one another by reason of differing opinions. Let there be peace among you and mutual charity. If you do this, God, the author of charity and peace, will be present to favour and befriend you. Greet one another with a holy kiss, not the sort the common crowd gives, but one that is from the heart.[13] All the saints who are here greet you.

May the favour of our Lord Jesus Christ, and the love of God the Father, and the communion[14] of the Holy Spirit be with you all. Recognizing the kindness of the Son, the charity towards you of the Father, who has so loved you as to give his only Son for you, and the goodness of the Holy Spirit, through whom he always shares his gifts with us, may you live according to the example of this indivisible Trinity and yourselves be of one mind and, indeed, pure and perfect.

The End[15] of the Paraphrase on the Second Epistle of Paul
to the Corinthians by Erasmus of Rotterdam

* * * * *

12 always] Added in 1532
13 Cf Theophylact *Expos in 2 Cor* (on 13:12) PG 124 949D: 'not with a feigned and treacherous [kiss], like that of Judas.' Cf similar descriptions of the 'holy kiss' in the paraphrases on Rom 16:16 CWE 42 88; 1 Pet 5:14 CWE 44 108 with n19; 1 Cor 16:20 with n14; and 1 Thess 5:25. On forms of kissing in the ancient world, including the 'holy kiss' in Paul and the early church, see the concise summary and references in Furnish 582–3.
14 'Communion': *communio* 'fellowship.' In his Latin translation Erasmus uses *communicatio* 'an imparting,' 'a sharing' for the Greek κοινωνία 'a sharing,' and explains in the annotation on 13:13 (*gratia domini*) that 'the distribution of gifts is done through the Holy Spirit.' The paraphrase here similarly describes the role of the Spirit.
15 The End ... Rotterdam] First in 1522. In 1519, 'The End, to the Glory of Jesus Christ and of Paul the Apostle. 30 January 1519'; in 1521, 'The End of the Paraphrase on the Second Epistle of Paul by Erasmus of Rotterdam'

PARAPHRASE ON EPHESIANS

Paraphrasis epistolae Pauli Apostoli ad Ephesios

translated and annotated by
MECHTILDE O'MARA

DEDICATORY LETTER

TO THE MOST REVEREND FATHER IN CHRIST, LORENZO CAMPEGGI, TITULAR CARDINAL OF SAN TOMMASO IN PARIONE, FROM ERASMUS OF ROTTERDAM, GREETING[1]

Whenever I survey the mutability of human affairs, *my lord Lorenzo,*[2] *brightest ornament of the college of cardinals,* I seem to see precisely some Euripus[3] *or whatever*[4] *may be more inconstant than that,* so incessant are the changes as affairs surge *this way and that,*[5] up and down, and cannot long continue in one position. They reach[6] a climax and swing back to what was left behind, until once more they come to such a point that we are obliged to *turn away*[7] our course from some excess that has now become intolerable; and what is

* * * * *

1 The translation of the dedicatory letter (Ep 1062 CWE 7 195–201) to Cardinal Campeggi is by R.A.B. Mynors with minor revisions by M.T. O'Mara. Peter G. Beitenholz's notes on the letter have been incorporated and supplemented below. Cardinal Lorenzo Campeggi (1474–1539), the dedicatee of the *Paraphrases* on Ephesians, Philippians, Colossians, and 1 and 2 Thessalonians, played an important role in papal diplomacy especially on missions to Germany and England. His connection with Erasmus was that of a patron and advocate among the influential members of the Roman curia. For a biographical sketch and for Erasmus' correspondence with him, see CEBR I 253–5.

2 my Lord Lorenzo ... cardinals] First in *1521*; previously 'most reverend Father.' For the *1520* texts of this letter, see the Translators' Note xvii, and 475–8.

3 Cf *Adagia* I ix 62: *Euripus homo* 'Man's a Euripus.' The water in the Euripus, a narrow gulf between Boeotia and Euboea, was said to rush in and out seven times every twenty-four hours. Erasmus elsewhere alludes to the Euripus as a symbol of flux and inconstancy. Cf *De copia* I 19 ASD I-6 66:848–53 / CWE 24 337:10–15 where 'Euripus' is translated as 'channel' with a reference to Cicero's *Pro Murena* 17.35.

4 or whatever ... than that] Added in *1521*

5 this way and that] Added in *1521*

6 they reach] *ventum est*, first in the 1520 8° edition; in the 1520 4° edition (only) *vectum est* 'they are carried to.' The change from *vectum est* to *ventum est* may be a printer's error.

7 turn away] First in *1521*; previously 'turn back'

more, were one to try to stand against the sea or bend its course a different
way, one could never do this without putting all things in serious jeopardy
and *immense*[8] upheaval. It was thus that in olden days the kings of Rome
gave place to a democracy *or*[9] *at least an oligarchy*, which in its turn reached
such a pitch of licence that there was need of *tribunes*[10] *of the people and* dictators[11] and after that even of *emperors*,[12] whose power then rose to enormous
heights and provoked once more a desire for *earlier*[13] *forms of commonwealth*.
But it would be an infinite task to collect in this way the many different
shapes that things have taken *as they rise*[14] *and fall in turn, and flourish and*

* * * * *

8 immense] Added in *1521*

9 or ... an oligarchy] Added in *1521*. Erasmus is correcting the facts in his historical analogy, influenced perhaps by his reading of Livy, a new edition of
which, accompanied by a prefatory letter from Erasmus, had appeared early in
1519. See Ep 919. The royal family of the Tarquins was expelled from Rome in
510 BC and replaced by the republic that lasted (with modifications) for nearly
five hundred years. This government had three distinct layers: two annually
elected consuls; the senate (originally an advisory council of about three hundred city fathers), the most important deliberative body, from which were
elected the consuls and most other magistrates who made up the aristocratic
'oligarchy' of privilege, magisterial experience, and power to which Erasmus
refers; the common people (*plebs*), who could vote on issues put before them
by a magistrate and serve in the army, but who could not themselves speak
in a public meeting. Cf Livy 1.58.1–2.33.11. On the underlying theory and the
development of Rome's constitution, see Andrew Lintott *The Constitution of
the Roman Republic* (Oxford 1999).

10 tribunes ... and] Added in *1521*. The Roman *plebs* 'common people' attempted
in 494 BC to secede from the city but were persuaded to return by the speech
of Menenius Agrippa. Henceforth, the plebs could elect tribunes of the people
to speak in their defence and to challenge the senatorial government in cases
of abusive behaviour. On senatorial arrogance, see Livy 2.3.3–4, 2.23.2; on the
granting of tribunes, see Livy 2.33.2–3.

11 At Rome the dictator was mandated by the senate to exercise sole authority
for a specific time or a specific crisis. See Livy 2.18.4–19.13, 2.29.9–30.7.

12 emperors] First in *1521*; previously 'kings.' Erasmus may have been thinking
of Julius Caesar when he wrote 'kings.' For Caesar's adoption of regal and
divine attributes and the attempts to invest him as king, see Stefan Weinstock
Divus Julius (Oxford 1971) 270–86, 318–41.

13 earlier ... commonwealth] First in *1521*; previously 'democracy.' There is, however, little evidence of any attempt to establish a full democracy in Rome. This
reference to the people's desire for 'earlier forms of government' may be a
generalization.

14 as they rise ... new shape] Added in *1521*

decay, and bloom once more and shoot again from time to time in a new shape.
What is more surprising is that even *sacred*[15] studies, *which ought*[16] *to be the*
most consistent thing there is, have their own ebb and flow.

In olden days the Christian *philosophy*[17] was a matter of faith, not of
disputation; men's simple piety was satisfied with *the oracles of*[18] Holy Scripture, *and charity,*[19] *spontaneously responsive, had no need of complicated rules, be-*
lieving all things, nowhere hesitating. Later, *the management*[20] *of theology was*
taken in hand by men nurtured in humane learning, but mainly in those fields of
learning which today we commonly call rhetoric. Gradually philosophy came to be
applied more and more, Platonic first and then Aristotelian, and questions began
to be asked about many points *which*[21] *were thought to pertain either to morals*
or to the field of speculation about heavenly things. At first this seemed almost
fundamental; but it developed by stages until many, neglecting *the study*[22]
of the ancient tongues and of polite literature and even of Holy Writ, grew old
over questions meticulous, needless, and *unreasonably*[23] minute, as if drawn
to the rocks on which some Siren sang.[24] *By now theology*[25] *began to be a*
form of skill, not wisdom; a show-piece, not a means towards true religion; and be-
sides ambition and avarice it was spoilt by other pests, by flattery and strife and
superstition.

Thus at length it came about that the *pure*[26] image of Christ was almost
overlaid by human *disputations;*[27] *the crystal*[28] springs of the old gospel teaching

* * * * *

15 sacred] Added in *1521*

16 which ought ... there is] Added in *1521*

17 philosophy] First in *1521*; previously 'teaching'

18 the oracles of] Added in *1521*

19 and charity ... hesitating] Added in *1521*. For the attributes of charity that
'believes all things,' see 1 Cor 13:7.

20 the management ... Aristotelian and] First in *1521*; previously 'humane learning was applied'

21 which ... heavenly things] First in *1521*; previously, with a stop after 'points,'
'much was swept into controversy'

22 the study ... and even of] Added in *1521*

23 unreasonably] Added in *1521*

24 The Sirens were sea nymphs who lured voyagers to destruction by their song.
See Homer *Odyssey* 12.39–54, 158–200.

25 By now theology ... superstition] Added in *1521*

26 pure] First in 1521; previously 'heavenly'

27 disputations] First in *1521*; previously 'subtleties.' Erasmus complains of the
scholastic philosophers and Scotist niceties. See Epp 1183:128–36, 1211:70–75,
462–83.

28 the crystal ... that point] Added in *1521*

were choked with sawdust by the Philistines;[29] *and the undeviating rule of Holy Scripture, bent this way and that, became the slave of our appetites rather than of the glory of Christ. At that point* some men, *whose intentions*[30] *certainly were religious,* tried to recall the world *to the simpler studies*[31] of an earlier day and *lead*[32] it back from pools *most*[33] *of which are now* sullied to those pure *rills*[34] *of living*[35] water. To achieve this end, they thought a knowledge[36] of the tongues and liberal studies (as they call them) were of the first importance, *for*[37] *it was neglect of them, it seemed, that brought us down to where we are.*

And here at once there is a great uproar at the very outset, one party cleaving with clenched teeth[38] to things as they are, the other *breaking in*[39] *with undue violence, more like an enemy than a guest. Both sides are wrong; both suffer. So it was in the olden days, when the Jews rejected the new wine of the gospel teaching, accustomed as they were to the old wine of the*

* * * * *

29 Cf Gen 26:14–18 for the description of the Philistines choking the wells of Isaac. This is a favourite image of Erasmus. See Epp 384:51–62, 858:191–217, 916:256–61.

30 whose intentions ... religious] Added in *1521*. Erasmus probably means the humanists. Valla had demonstrated the importance of Greek for scriptural studies by persistent reference to the Greek reading as a corrective to the Vulgate. See his *Annot in Eph* 1 (I 875). Erasmus himself (cf Epp 396:277–305, 1007:68–90, 1010:39–42) and other scholars, eg Johann Reuchlin, Johannes Cono of Nürnberg, Beatus Rhenanus, as well as printers such as the Amerbachs and Froben (see Ep 335:319–26 and CWE 61 233–6), helped make available the correct reading of the Scriptures and the teachings of the church Fathers. See eg Epp 335:311–38 (re Jerome), 1001:95–101 (re Cyprian). Erasmus may also refer to men like Jean Vitrier and John Colet, praised not for their knowledge of Latin, Greek, and Hebrew, but for scriptural exegesis that departed from the scholastic methods. See Ep 1211:16–273 (on Vitrier), Epp 1211:273–686 and 1053:579–90 (on Colet).

31 to the simpler studies] First in *1521*; previously 'of studies to the simplicity'

32 lead] First in *1521*; previously 'draw'

33 most ... now] First in *1521*; previously 'now excessively'

34 rills] First in *1521*; previously 'springs'

35 living] Added in *1521*. For 'living water,' see John 4:10.

36 a knowledge ... studies] First in *1521*; previously 'expertise in tongues and knowledge of liberal studies'

37 for ... where we are] Added in *1521*

38 For other examples of Erasmus' use of *mordicus* 'with clenched teeth,' 'doggedly,' see the Index of Greek and Latin Words Cited.

39 breaking in ... tenants side by side] First in *1521*; previously 'preferring to dislodge its opponent, once and for all, from the height, rather than escorting him down by degrees'

Mosaic law,[40] *and saw as a disgrace to their earlier code what really filled out and beautified it; they thought it novelty and hated it, when they were really recalled to the original truth. In this way a kindness can turn into an injury, if the physician applies his remedy without sympathy and tact, and the patient sees the man whose concern is about his health as though he were an enemy. How much more fitting that those who profess the learning that is commonly called new and is therefore unpopular, although it is very ancient, should effect their entrance courteously and not break in like enemies;*[41] *not instantly throwing any man over sixty off the bridge,*[42] *as the old custom was, but gradually taking root, the new guests and the ancient tenants side by side.* The humanities are not brought in to do away with *subjects*[43] *which are taught, to the great benefit of the human race, in all our universities,* but to purify them and make them more reasonable than they have been hitherto in some men's hands. *Let theology*[44] *by all means be the queen of sciences: no queen is so effective that she can dispense with the services of her handmaidens. Some she allows to counsel and some to adorn her, and she believes it part of her glory that those who serve her should be honourable women.* If only *those*[45] *who are keen to enliven traditional learning with all that the humanities can offer would contribute their services courteously and peaceably, and* those who have grown grey in *the ancient subjects*[46] *would not*[47] *be so grudging towards themselves and their juniors but would welcome the new arrivals to share the rights of citizens in a generous spirit,* we should see each group bring ornament and profit to the other, *for both*[48] *will share their advantages and the benefit will be doubled.* As it is, while we bespatter each other

* * * * *

40 On new wine, see Luke 5:33–9. On the juxtaposition of the new wine of the gospel with the old wine of Mosaic law, see also Erasmus' paraphrases on John 2:11 CWE 46 40 and Acts 2:13 CWE 50 16.

41 For the same idea expressed to Campeggi again in some of the same words, see Ep 1167:15–19. That the debate had moved from courteous exchanges to satire and bitter acrimony between polarized positions is demonstrated by Erika Rummel *The Humanist-Scholastic Debate in the Renaissance and Reformation* (Cambridge, MA 1995), summarized on 194.

42 Cf *Adagia* I v 37: *Sexagenarios de ponte deicere* 'To throw the sexagenarians off the bridge'

43 subjects ... universities] First in *1521*; previously 'scholastic discipline'

44 Let theology ... honourable women] Added in *1521*

45 those ... peaceably, and] Added in *1521*

46 the ancient subjects] First in *1521*; previously 'them'

47 would not ... spirit] First in *1521*; previously 'would embrace them civilly, and the professors of the liberal studies would accommodate themselves to the former group in turn'

48 for both ... doubled] Added in *1521*

with mud or, it would be truer to say, throw stones at one another,[49] both parties lose the advantage that was theirs and both leave the field having suffered great loss. In the pamphlets in which each side tears the other to pieces there is more abuse than argument.[50] In their *academic*[51] discourses there is more spite than scholarship, more bad language than good judgment, *more prejudice than liberty.*[52] In their sermons the gospel teaching, which ought to appear in its purest form, is infected with human emotions. It is a sin to declaim in offensive language *against*[53] *the studies which have been accepted hitherto, inarticulate though they may be.* But it is *a more grievous*[54] sin to climb into the pulpit, from which one ought to hear the gospel trumpet-

* * * * *

49 Elsewhere Erasmus characterizes his critics as stone-throwers. Cf Ep 1126:207 where he describes the charges of his ruthless critic, Standish (on whom see CEBR III 279–80, Rummel *Catholic CriticsscM I* 122–7) and also Ep 1225:171 where he describes attacks made on him by Carmelite and Dominican theologians at Louvain. Cf Ep 597:63–5.

50 Erasmus distinguishes three forms of attack:
   1/ Pamphlets: *libelli*. These were short, quickly composed, inexpensive, printed documents meant to win support for the author's ideas and values. Pamphlets were often focussed attacks on the doctrine or person of a specific opponent that had prompted them. Erasmus' *apologiae* against his critics fall into this category. Erasmus speaks of pamphlet wars in Epp 1060:16, 1132:18, 1225:117–20, 143–5. See 'pamphlets' in OER 3 201–3; and Ep 1083 introduction. For examples see Erasmus' *Manifesta mendacia* CWE 71 116–31, and the lampoon attributed to Konrad Nesen of Nastätten, *Dialogus bilinguium ac trilinguium* CWE 7 334–7.
   2/ Academic discourses: *scholasticae diatribae*. The 'diatribe' was a dialogic didactic discourse with a long history in the philosophical and rhetorical schools. See ABD 2 190–3. Ideally it was a rational, 'temperate debate . . . with the aim of eliciting the truth.' Cf Erasmus' *De libero arbitrio* CWE 76 6, and 5 n1, 89 n405; also Erika Rummel *The Confessionalization of Humanism in Reformation Germany* (Oxford 2000) 54–61.
   3/ Sermons: *conciones*. Sermons in ecclesial contexts were understood as pastoral reflections intended to inform an assembly about the truth to be believed, the charity to be practised, and the state of beatitude to be desired. Erasmus uses *concio* in some titles, eg *In psalmum quartum concio* CWE 63 169 and *Concio de immensa Dei misericordia* CWE 70 69. Although these two 'sermons' were probably not delivered orally, Erasmus refers to sermons in which he was attacked from the pulpit. See eg Epp 541:92–7, 948:108–13, 1144:43–8, 1147:76–81.

51 academic] Added in *1521*

52 more prejudice than liberty] Added in *1521*

53 against . . . they may be] First in *1521*; previously 'that inarticulate scholastic studies are of no benefit'

54 a more grievous] First in *1521*; previously 'on the other side a'

call that heralds the glory of Christ, and there cry, *in words*[55] *designed to stir up strife,* 'Keep[56] *your children away from* Greek! Greek is the mother of heresies.[57] *Touch not*[58] *the books of this man or that man*' (for they do not refrain from mentioning names) 'who corrects the Lord's Prayer, *criticizes the Magnificat,*[59] and *emends*[60] the Gospel of St[61] John. Do your duty, ye magistrates! Back them up, citizens! *Keep*[62] *this great plague far from the world of men!*'

If words like these are used before the inexperienced public, *what*[63] *can be imagined* more subversive? If before people *of education*[64] and intelligence, *what*[65] could be more crazy? And yet the men who do this in public wish to pass for pillars of the Christian religion.[66] They do not stop to reflect that, *while*[67] *they profess Christ's teaching, as they do,* their attacks on the reputation of those who do them good service, *or*[68] *who at least strive to do so,* are diametrically opposed to *their professions.*[69] *Besides*[70] *which, they forget that all*

* * * * *

55 in words ... strife] Added in *1521*

56 Keep ... from] First in *1521*; previously 'Don't let your children learn'

57 heresies.] First in 1521; previously 'heresies and the Antichrist.' See the reports of the Carmelite Nicolaas Baechem's attack on Erasmus 'claiming that I [Erasmus] was the Antichrist,' Epp 1581:265, 878:15n, 948:141–9, 1153:148–51, 1196:128–35, and Erasmus' complaint to Pope Leo x that critics of the new scholarship were using words like 'heresy,' 'Antichrists.' See Ep 1007:47–53.

58 Touch not ... names)] First in *1521*; previously 'There is a certain individual.' 'Touch not' reflects a biblical idiom; cf 2 Cor 6:17, Col 2:21.

59 criticizes the Magnificat] First in *1521*; previously 'and the Magnificat as it is called.' Erasmus reports specific instances of such carping against him in Epp 948:101–21, 1196:423–5.

60 emends] First in *1521*; previously 'criticizes'

61 St] Added in *1520 8°*

62 Keep ... of men!] Added in *1521*

63 what ... imagined] First in *1521*; previously 'nothing is'

64 of education] First in *1521*; previously 'of training'

65 what] First in *1521*; previously 'nothing'

66 Cf Gal 2:9 which describes James, Cephas, and John as 'pillars.' In Ep 1153:20–244 (18 October 1520) Erasmus complained to the rector of Louvain University against Baechem, who had attacked him at parties, in public academic lectures, and from the pulpit on 9 and 14 October. Ep 1162 describes in detail the resulting confrontation with Baechem, on whom see CEBR I 81–3, Rummel *Catholic Critics* I 135–42.

67 while ... they do] Added in *1521*

68 or ... so] Added in *1521*

69 their professions] First in *1521*; previously 'to the doctrine of Christ which they profess'

70 Besides ... time] First in *1521*; previously 'and that'

the time a great[71] *part of their efforts is wasted, both*[72] *for them and for the common people*, as long as this behaviour loses them all their credit with *their audience.*[73] Who would put his trust in a man who manifestly betrays his spite *and hostility?*[74] *And on the other side,*[75] *the works of those who are keen that their labourious nights should advance both learning and true religion to the best of their power are less profitable when such men read them – unless we suppose it makes little difference whether you take up a book with an open mind or a mind already occupied by hostile convictions or, at best, suppositions. Last*[76] *but not least, what is sown is*[77] not the gospel but the pestilent tares[78] of strife and hatred; and when these have once seized upon the *minds of*[79] men, they are not easily weeded out.

Nor[80] *is it easy to credit what small sparks, as they gradually spread, can often start an immense conflagration.* Nothing in human affairs is so flourishing that discord cannot turn it into disaster. And nowhere should discord be more strictly *avoided*[81] than in scholarship, and in sacred studies above all, *the authority*[82] *of which ought to be specially effective in quelling the tumults of men's appetites. What does he teach if not peace, who teaches Christ? If the salt*[83] *has lost its savour, what is there left with which to season this tasteless mess? If the light of Christian philosophy is darkened by the appetites of men, what will be left to lighten the darkness of our minds? Everyone*[84] *knows that a great part of our*

* * * * *

71 great] First in *1521*; previously 'good'
72 both ... common people] Added in *1521*
73 their audience] First in *1521*; previously 'the people'
74 and hostility] Added in *1521*
75 And on the other side ... suppositions] Added in *1521*. On *lucubrationes* 'works,' a word that became 'almost a signature' of Erasmus, see Mark Vessey 'Erasmus' Lucubrations and the Renaissance Life of Texts' ERSY 24 (2004) 23–51, especially 41–9.
76 Last but not least] First in *1521*; previously 'And indeed'
77 what is sown is] First in *1521*; previously 'they sow'
78 Cf Matt 13:24–30, 37–43; also Epp 1053:515–7, 1061:364, 876–9
79 minds of] First in 1521; previously 'pursuits of'
80 Nor ... conflagration] Added in *1521*. For the same idea, see Epp 1007:107–10, 1061:848–60. Cf also Erasmus' paraphrases on Eph 4:25–32 and James 3:5–6 CWE 44 155.
81 avoided] First in *1521*; previously 'watched' (*servatam*), ie 'guarded against,' but the ambiguous sense led to the clarification of *1521*.
82 the authority ... our minds?] Added in *1521*
83 For the images of salt and light here, see Matt 5:13–15.
84 Everyone ... system of study] First in *1521*; previously 'On scholarship a great part of our Christian commonwealth depends.'

religion depends *upon our system of study. And now here*[85] *too the Eden of our life has been ruined with his venom by that cunning old serpent so that it seems to me far*[86] *preferable to cultivate any*[87] *garden rather than scholarship;*[88] *for chives*[89] *and cabbages will bring more profit to the man who grows them than nights of toil spent by the lamp.*

But for some time now *your mind*[90] has been silently protesting, '*What*[91] *can be the object of all this?*' Why, in hopes that on the advice of you and others like you our beloved *Pope Leo*[92] will complete the *circle*[93] *of immortal glory* which he has so prosperously begun *to*[94] *form. Long ago*[95] he rendered a more than human service to the Christian world; for when kings and peoples were in confusion, warring wickedly on one another, he brought them into agreement,[96] and perhaps he will confer *a no less eminent benefit*[97] on us,

* * * * *

85 here ... so that] First in *1521*; previously 'we see that the situation has come almost to the point of madness so that if it continues after this fashion.' For the depiction of the life of scholarship as paradise, see Ep 1053:544–51.
86 to me far] Added in *1521*
87 any] Added in *1521*; previously 'a' understood
88 For the image of cultivating scholarship, see also Ep 1043:1–8.
89 for chives ... by the lamp] Added in *1521*
90 your mind] First in *1521*; previously 'I know, your reverend Lordship'
91 What ... this] First in *1521*; previously 'How does this relate to me? Or how to the *Paraphrase*?'
92 our beloved Pope Leo] First in *1521*; previously 'his Lordship, our beloved Leo x'
93 circle ... glory] First in *1521*; previously 'very splendid and laudable work'
94 to form] Added by the translator
95 Long ago] Added in *1521*
96 From the time of his election in 1513, Leo x attempted to do by diplomacy what Julius ii had done by military force, ie to secure peace and the unification of Italy under papal authority, free from the threat of intervention by Austria-Spain or France-Venice, forming two axes of rival power. Leo x had made treaties with both sides in an attempt to maintain the balance of power. Erasmus repeatedly expresses gratitude for the concord established among princes in 1518 by Leo x and supported by Henry viii of England, Francis i of France, and Charles v the Hapsburg crowned emperor in 1520. See Epp 964:30–46, 967:21–4. Leo further attempted to build harmony among the Christian princes of Europe by directing their united forces against the Turks (see Ep 729:56n and *Querela pacis* cwe 27 311, 314); and he tried to secure the allegiance of the fractious Italian states through Medici family connections, treaties, even purchase. For his attempts to reach a lasting peace, see M. Gattoni *Leone x e la geo-politica dello stato pontificio (1513–1521)* (Vatican 2000) 143–74, 267–336. See also Epp 1007 n14 and 964:35–9 and n49.
97 a no less eminent benefit] First in *1521*; previously 'no less.' There were precedents for the attempt made here to have Leo silence the critics of humanistic

if in the same way he restores to our studies the tranquillity that should be theirs. For *in them*[98] *so bitter is the hostility, so venomous the language, so bloody the fighting, that* it is not yet clear to me which is the greater evil for the human race, the armed conflicts of which I spoke or these feuds among the learned. His most serene majesty the king of England, Henry, eighth *of that name,*[99] with the support of his Achates,[100] the reverend *Lord Thomas,* cardinal of York, *and*[101] *no doubt with advice from you,* has done this for his native country; and Leo *ought to*[102] do the same for the world *at large,*[103] *of which*[104] *he is head, acting as viceregent of Christ, who loved nothing more than concord. I doubt whether any monarch or emperor of antiquity was ever honoured with a more splendid tribute than the inscription*[105] *lately set up, they say, in honour of our Leo:* 'To Leo x,[106] who gave peace back to Christendom.'

And[107] *further, it is not only in theory and in general that this duty belongs to him, to whom belongs all that belongs to the advancement of religion and piety; it is particularly his affair not to leave the ancient languages and humane letters exposed to assault from any quarter, seeing that he himself, whose judgment carries supreme*

* * * * *

studies in the universities. Erasmus had written directly to Pope Leo in August 1519 with such a request (Ep 1007:117–27), and on Feb 1 1520 he asked Wolsey to urge the pope to 'suppress the passion for attacking other people' (Ep 1060:48–61).

98 in them ... that] Added in *1521*. Erasmus describes the bitterness of the academic disputes in his correspondence. See eg Ep 1053:525–42.

99 of that name] Added in *1521*

100 The translation follows the Latin closely; cf Mynors' somewhat freer translation in CWE 7 199:141, 'with the support of his *fidus* Achates, the cardinal of York ...' In *1521* 'Lord Thomas' was added. 'Achates' refers to Aeneas' faithful friend and companion in Virgil's *Aeneid.* His characteristic ephithet is *fidus* 'faithful.' Cardinal Thomas Wolsey was archbishop of York, the chancellor of England 1515–29. See CEBR III 460–2. For Erasmus' claim that Henry and Wolsey forced the learned to stop feuding see Epp 968:14–17, 969:10–15, 970:16–22, 990:1–28; on Wolsey and the humanities see Ep 967:31–51.

101 and ... from you] Added in *1521*. Cf Ep 968:14–20. On a curious textual change of uncertain significance introduced in the 1534 edition, see Bateman 'Textual Travail' 245.

102 ought to] First in *1521*; previously 'can.' Cf Erasmus' advice to Pope Leo x Ep 1007:117–27.

103 at large] Added in *1521*

104 of which ... in honour of our Leo] First in *1521*; previously, 'When he has done this, then at last that inscription, by far the most handsome, will bring full praise'

105 The inscription reported here is otherwise unknown.

106 Leo x] First in *1521*, previously 'Pope Leo x'

107 And ... the glory Leo's] Added in *1521*

weight, sets so high a value on them that he engages men from every land at great personal expense to teach them in Rome,[108] *in the conviction that the Eternal City with all its famous monuments will gain no small further distinction thereby. That most intelligent mind of his perceives, of course, that a knowledge of these tongues is necessary, not only for the teaching of academic disciplines but, beyond that, to extend or fortify the boundaries of Christendom. What kingdom ever became united or long endured without the cement of languages which all men shared? Consider now for yourself how greatly it concerns him if the New Testament,*[109] *which I undertook with his encouragement, revised with further encouragement from him, and dedicated to Christ and to him, is to be misrepresented by any ignorant and worthless fellow before men no less ignorant. For my own part, the loss of my reputation moves me little, provided (as is right) the gain is Christ's, the glory Leo's.*[110]

And[111] *if the question is asked how concord can be re-established, I think it can be done very easily if he proclaims*[112] with all the authority of an oracle that every man should promote and promulgate[113] his own convictions without offensive criticism of those of others, so that[114] *on both sides this frenzy of tongue and pen is restrained, by those especially of whom this moderation is most to be expected. But if there is*[115] *a difference – and often enough, just as tastes differ, so do attitudes of mind – let all dispute be confined to courteous* confrontation, and[116] *never issue in frenzy. Furthermore, if anything seriously*

* * * * *

108 For Leo's patronage of learning, and especially of a college of Greek studies founded in the first year of his pontificate and directed at first by Janus Lascaris, see Ludwig von Pastor *The History of the Popes from the Close of the Middle Ages* ed and trans R.F. Kerr et al, 3rd ed (London 1938–53) VIII 258–80. On Lascaris, see CEBR II 292–4. The following lines appear to be alluding both to the Greek college and to Leo's hope for a crusade. See Epp 729:56n, 785:22–41.
109 For Leo's approval of Erasmus' New Testament scholarship, see Epp 843:369–74, 543–7; 950:43–7; 961:10–14. Erasmus dedicated his *Novum instrumentum* to Leo (Ep 384). See also the introductions to Epp 835 and 864.
110 Erasmus' letters show that he was profoundly distressed by criticsm. See Ep 843.
111 And ... very easily] First in 1521; previously 'Moreover, the policy of concord will easily stand firm'
112 if he proclaims] First in 1521; previously 'if he refuses permission to certain sycophants and if he proclaims'
113 promote and promulgate] First in 1521; previously 'promulgate and promote'
114 so that ... expected] Added in 1521
115 there is ... mind] First in 1521; previously 'their attitudes of mind differ, as happens'
116 and ... Christians or not] Added in 1521. For the proposal outlined in the remainder of this paragraph, see *Consilium* CWE 71 108–12, a document un-

concerns the integrity of the faith – for all things should not be dragged here by the scruff of the neck[117] *– let the question be discussed above all by those who really*[118] *know the mysteries of the faith; secondly by such as will not under cover of the faith pursue their own personal ends; last but not least, let it be done with judgment and moderation and not with subversive clamour. It is not perhaps to all men's liking that some persons, no matter who, should decide whether they are Christians or not.*

I had no doubts of my ability to convince you of this, for I well know how your *marriage*[119] of learning and fairness of mind abhors all virulence. Nor will it be hard for your Eminence to persuade our Holy Father Leo, whether because he rightly values you so *highly*[120] for your distinguished gifts or because of his very own nature he is so wonderfully disposed towards peace and concord. *The aid*[121] *I ask is not great; but* in case it should seem an inadequate reward to have *the name of Lorenzo Campeggi*[122] exalted by the whole company of educated people *for all time to come,*[123] here is a small[124] addition offered on my own account: a paraphrase on

* * * * *

signed but now attributed to Erasmus and recommending an independent inquiry into the doctrine contained in Luther's writings by 'men of outstanding knowledge, proven virtue, and unstained honour, whom no one could possibly suspect of wishing ... to flatter the pope and forget the truth of the Gospels, or of favouring the other party from some purely human motive' (CWE 71 111). See Ep 1156:108–14 where Erasmus describes the plan as that of Johannes Faber. It is mentioned by Erasmus also in Ep 1225:208–21 and defended in Ep 1217:16–63.

117 Cf Ep 916:310–14: 'But disputes ... of this sort ... multiplied even during Paul's lifetime – disputes not about indulgences or applications or other questions of the kind, which we now drag by the scruff of the neck into the substance of the faith, but about the resurrection of the dead, which is the foundation and crown of our belief.'

118 really] *vere*, omitted from Mynors' translation

119 marriage ... mind] the Mynors translation here is free; literally 'your learned open-mindedness and your open-minded learning,' first in *1521*; previously 'your learned open-mindedness.' Cf similar language in Ep 996 to Campeggi, 'a capital marriage of learning and wisdom such as yours.'

120 highly] *plurimi*, first in *1532*; previously *maximi*; Allen prints *maximi*. The change does not affect the translation.

121 The aid ... but] First in *1521*; previously 'for this help'

122 the name of Lorenzo Campeggi] First in *1521*; previously 'your name'

123 for all time to come] Added in *1521*

124 'Small': *qualecunque*, literally 'of whatever sort,' the self-depreciatory term used by classical poets to describe their work, eg Catullus 1.9, in the dedication of his *libellus* 'little book of poems' to Cornelius Nepos, and Ovid *Tristia* 1.7.11 to describe his *carmina* 'poems'

the *five*[125] *Pauline Epistles which remain*[126] *out of all his genuine letters,*[127] completed in one recent spell of work. *For*[128] *I did not finish this task in the right order or all at the same time or with one burst of energy; and thus it has come about that the various parts are dedicated to different names.*[129] *I have good hopes that this work at least will live, seeing that it wins approval even from those who criticize everything of mine as though by avowed intent.*[130] At the same time I *thought to*[131] pay off, at any rate in part, the debt *I owe*[132] to your Eminence; for I have forgotten neither what I owe to your unheard-of generosity[133] nor what I have promised you *in writing.*[134] Pray accept therefore this payment on account,[135] until I can scrape together the means to pay in full.

When[136] *I dined with your Eminence at Bruges,*[137] *your last words to me at parting, I remember, were that in whatever court Lorenzo Campeggi might be*

* * * * *

125 five] First in *1520* 8°; *1520* 4° (only) prints 'four' epistles, probably a slip. This is one of several corrections which taken together indicate that the *1520* 4° roman-font edition is the earlier of the two.

126 remain ... letters] First in *1521*; previously 'which I'

127 Erasmus offers here five new *Paraphrases* (on Ephesians, Philippians, Colossians, 1 and 2 Thessalonians); the *Paraphrasis in Hebraeos* remained to be written and published in 1521. See Ep 1181. For Erasmus' reluctance to ascribe Hebrews to Paul, see CWE 44 212 n3.

128 For ... intent] Added in *1521*

129 The different dedicatees of the *Paraphrases* on the other Pauline epistles are as follows: on Romans, Domenico Grimani (Ep 710, November 1517); on 1 and 2 Corinthians, Erard de la Marck (Ep 916, February 1519); on Galatians, Antoine de la Marck (Ep 956, May 1519); and on 1 and 2 Timothy, Titus, and Philemon, Philip (I) of Burgundy (Ep 1043, late 1519).

130 Evidence that Erasmus' *Paraphrases* initially met with general approval is of four kinds: expressions of gratitude from readers (Epp 755:4–7, 762:48, 1255, 1333:79–80); exhortations to provide more *Paraphrases* (Epp 937:14–39, 953:60–1, 988:22–5, 995:11–20, 1171:48–57, 1333:1–15); popular acclaim (Epp 762:48, 806:19–21, 835:2–4, 910:19–20, 970:33–5, 1171:54–6, 1253, 1255:20–4); frequent reprints / revisions in various formats to the extent that the *Paraphrases* 'provoked more re-editions than any other writing of Erasmus, with the exception of the New Testament itself.' See Peter G. Bietenholz 'Edition et réforme à Bâle, 1517–1565' in *La Réforme et le livre: L'Europe de l'imprimé (1517–v.1570)* ed Jean François Gilmont (Paris 1990) 251, and Erasmus Ep 1017:3–4.

131 thought to] First in *1521*; previously 'would'

132 I owe] Added in *1521*

133 Cf Ep 995 n9.

134 in writing] Added in *1521*. For the promise, see Ep 996:62–4.

135 Payment on account: *arrabo.* Cf Eph 1:14 and the paraphrases on Eph 1:14, 17, 2:16. See also 1 Cor chapter 1 n23.

136 When ... devoted servant] Added in *1521*

137 For this meeting in late summer 1519, cf Epp 1025:6 n3, 1029:30, 1031:3–5.

found, I could be sure to find a friend who sincerely wished me well. May I say in my turn that in whatever country Erasmus may be found, you may believe you have there a most devoted servant. My respectful best wishes to your Eminence.[138]

Louvain, 5 February [1519][139]

* * * * *

138 Eminence] So concluded the text of the letter first in *1521*; previously the title was followed by the words 'to whom I wish to be commended as highly as possible.'

139 Although the dedicatory letter for the *Paraphrases in Ephesios . . . Thessalonicenses* (Ep 1062) appears with the date Nones [5th] of February 1519 in all Froben editions from 1520 to 1540, the correct date is February 1520. For the anomaly see CWE 2 xii–xiii.

THE ARGUMENT OF THE EPISTLE OF PAUL
THE APOSTLE TO THE EPHESIANS
BY ERASMUS OF ROTTERDAM

Ephesus was once the chief city of Asia Minor, a city superstitiously dedicated to the worship of demons and especially to the worship of Diana.[1] For this reason, too, in Acts[2] it is called the temple-warden[3] of Diana, not of Diana the huntress, to whom the poets assign arrows and arms, but of Diana the many-breasted, whom the Greeks call Polymastos. They meant she was the nurse of all living things, as Jerome has indicated.[4] Diana's Ephesian temple, the most celebrated in all the world, is also mentioned here and there by pagan writers.[5]

* * * * *

1 In this paraphrase Erasmus is heavily indebted to Jerome, who describes Ephesus in similar terms in his *Comm in Eph* Prologue §537–44 PL 26 441 / Heine 77. I have generally cited Jerome in Heine's translation, but, since he worked from a different (unpublished) text, my translation will sometimes follow the text of PL, eg in chapter 3 n20. On the city and its goddess, see Rick Strelan *Paul, Artemis, and the Jews in Ephesus* Beihefte zur Zeitschrift für die neutestamentliche Wissenschaft und die Kunde der älteren Kirche 80 (Berlin 1996). Erasmus connects demons with false or pagan gods elsewhere in the *Paraphrases*. See 1 Cor Argument n10; Col chapter 1 n15; 1 Thess chapter 1 nn22, 23; but see Eph chapter 3 n14.
2 Acts 19:35
3 'Temple-warden': *neocoros*. Theophylact *Expos in Eph* Hypothesis PG 124 1033A also mentions that Ephesus is called νεωκόρος. A.N. Sherwin-White notes that the title appears on provincial proconsular coinage first in AD 65–6; cf *Roman Society and Roman Law in the New Testament* (Oxford 1963) 89.
4 See Jerome *Comm in Eph* Prologue §541 PL 26 441 / Heine 77. The Greek goddess Artemis (Roman Diana) is a maiden huntress. The Anatolian deity called Artemis by the Greeks was in fact different in both character and ritual from the Greco-Roman deity. See Merrill M. Parvis 'Ephesus in the early Christian Era' in *Biblical Archaeologist* 8 (1945) 61–73 and Floyd V. Filson 'Ephesus and the New Testament' ibidem 73–80.
5 Eg Xenophon *Anabasis* 5.3.4–13; Dionysius of Halicarnassus *Archaeologia* 4.25.4; Strabo *Geography* 14.1.22–3; Pausanias *Description of Greece* 4.31.8, 7.2.6–9, 7.5.4;

The people of Ephesus were fascinated by the study of recondite arts.[6] Whence we read that at the preaching of the apostles, books on magic were gathered up by the Ephesians and consigned to the fire, and when the value of these books was calculated it was found to be fifty thousand in cash, as is reported in the nineteenth chapter of Acts.[7] To lead them away from such great errors, Paul spent a three-year period in their midst. In the meanwhile he left undone nothing that was conducive to their salvation, although many people with great feeling shouted contradictions and clamoured in opposition, just as he personally testifies somewhere;[8] and here he was even thrown to the beasts, as he himself recalls[9] in the Second Epistle to the Corinthians.[10] But on his departure he bade Timothy remain with them. That city, moreover, abounded not only in superstitious[11] folk and people dedicated to magic, but also in very learned men. Consequently, Paul, inasmuch as he accommodates himself to the character and intellectual abilities of all, frequently makes mention of demons and spirits, indicating the difference between the good and the evil. In addition, he opens up some things that were concealed. For no other epistle has such hidden meanings. As a result it is especially on account of this letter, it seems, that Peter has written, 'Just as our most dear brother Paul also, according to the wisdom given him, has written to you, as indeed he did in all his Epistles, speaking in them of these things. In these Epistles there are certain things difficult to understand, which the unlearned and the unstable distort, as they do the rest of the Scriptures also, to their own destruction' [2 Pet 3:15-16 Conf].[12]

* * * * *

Caesar *De bello civili* 3.33; Pliny *Naturalis historia* 36.21.95; Aulus Gellius *Attic Nights* 2.6.18

6 'Recondite': *curiosarum* ; cf n11 below.

7 Acts 19:19

8 See Acts 20:29-30.

9 recalls] First in 1532; previously 'testifies'

10 Erasmus is mistaken; the reference is to 1 Cor 15:32.

11 'Superstitious': *curiosis*. The syntax of the passage indicates that Erasmus is using *curiosus* to mean 'superstitious.' Elsewhere *curiosus* generally describes people who give too much time and energy to idle speculation. Cf 1 Cor chapter 2 n19 and 2 Thess chapter 3 n13.

12 Erasmus clearly took Ephesians to be a genuine Epistle of Paul. In his first annotation on the Epistle (*idem in hac epistola*), Erasmus comments that in this Epistle Paul has the same fervour, depth, spirit, and energy as in his other Epistles, but nowhere else is his expression more difficult because of hyperbata and other rhetorical figures, 'whether this is caused by the amanuensis (*interpres*) whom he used for this Epistle or whether facility in expression did

Therefore, since they had stood firm in the faith, he urges them to continue on and advance towards perfection. He reminds them forcefully both of the sort of people they were when they were addicted to vices, the slaves of evil spirits, and of the sort they have now become, grafted onto Christ. Meanwhile he teaches that by the divine plan the grace of the gospel, although it had been promised to the Jews, was rightly extended to the gentiles also, and that he had been established by God as a minister of this gift. But since he wrote from prison, he exhorts them not to lose heart on account of his afflictions, but rather to consider them their glory. This he treats in the first chapter and the second.[13]

In the remaining three,[14] he prescribes a plan of life for them, showing what ought to be followed, what ought to be avoided; what are the responsibilities of husbands to wives, of wives to husbands; of parents to children, of children to parents; of masters to slaves, of slaves to masters.

The Epistle was written from the city of Rome through Tychicus, a deacon, of whom he makes mention at the end, calling him a faithful minister.[15] Ambrose adds that it was written from prison when Paul, who had

* * * * *

not match the sublimity of its contents. Certainly, the style differs so much from the other Epistles of Paul that it could seem to be the work of another person did not the heart and soul of the Pauline mind assert clearly his claim to this letter.' Debate on the authorship of Ephesians dates from the late eighteenth century. For representative views of modern scholars, see Barth *Ephesians* I 36–51 who argues for Pauline authorship of Ephesians and sets 'Rome, about 62 [as] the best guess for the origin.' See also Paul J. Kobelski in NJBC §55:3–13 883–5. Kobelski places the Epistle among the Deutero-Pauline works and dates it 'late in the 1st century (AD 80–100).'

13 With this sentence, Erasmus covers what is included in the first three chapters according to our division of the text.

14 By our count, there are four remaining chapters in Ephesians and this is probably what Erasmus intended. The varied divisions in the commentaries he was following may have led to Erasmus' confusion. There is no indication in the *Paraphrase* itself or in the text as printed with the *Annotations* that Erasmus' chapter divisions differed significantly from what is ordinarily printed in modern editions.

15 That the letter was sent from Rome to Ephesus by Tychicus is part of the subscription to be found in Erasmus' text. See LB VI 859B–860B. Tychicus appears as a companion of Paul in Acts 20:4, a faithful minister in Eph 6:21, a very dear brother and fellow slave in Col 4:7, and an emissary in 2 Tim 4:12 and Titus 3:12. See also 1 Thess Argument n8. For 'subscription' see *Paraphrase on Colossians* Argument n13; on the idiom cf ibidem n10.

been taken under escort from Jerusalem to Rome, was living under a guarantor outside the camp in his rented lodging.[16]

The End of the Argument

* * * * *

16 Ambrosiaster *Comm in Eph* Argument CSEL 81/3 71:10 mentions these details with the disclaimer 'it is understood.' On Ambrosiaster, whom Erasmus calls 'Ambrose,' see Translators' Note xxi n19. On Paul's escort, see Acts 27:1–28:16; on his rented lodgings, see Acts 28:30.

THE PARAPHRASE OF THE EPISTLE[1] OF PAUL THE APOSTLE TO THE EPHESIANS BY ERASMUS OF ROTTERDAM

Chapter 1

I, Paul, the ambassador not of Moses nor of any man but of Jesus Christ in whose interest I act, an ambassador, moreover, not as a result of usurping the office myself, nor by human appointment,[2] but by the authority and bidding of God the Father who, through his Son, bade me be the herald of the gospel teaching among the gentiles. As such, I am writing this Epistle to all who live at Ephesus,[3] and who live in such a way that they are zealous to keep themselves clear of this world's foul vices, and that with a sincere heart they believe[4] in the gospel of Jesus Christ, while they hope for the reward of innocence and holiness from no source other than from the model they have chosen, and await the culmination of their happiness from none other than the source from which it began.

Meanwhile I desire for you not what is generally desired by the people who measure their happiness by the security this world provides, but I desire that God may daily increase in you the kindness by which he has gratuitously freed you from the offences of your former life and changed wicked people into cultivators of innocence and justice, for he is the author of all good things, whom now we too are able to call 'our

* * * * *

1 The Paraphrase of the Epistle] *Paraphrasis epistolae*, first in 1532; previously *Paraphrasis in epistolam* 'Paraphrase on the Epistle,' conforming to Erasmus' normal usage
2 For Paul's divine appointment see Gal 1:1 and 11–12 and Acts 9:15 and 13:47. For Paul as ambassador see Eph 6:20 and 1 Cor chapter 1 n2.
3 Erasmus is paraphrasing a text that includes in 1:1 the words 'in Ephesus.' On the biblical text, see Metzger 601. For Erasmus' vision of Paul as 'the divine agent of the providential merger of Jews and gentiles in a single Church' see Roussel 'Exegetical Fictions?' 71.
4 believe] Subjunctive mood first in 1532; previously indicative

Father,'[5] not only for the reason that[6] we were created by him, but much more because, grafted onto the body of Christ, we have been co-opted into the rights and privileges of sons. May he guard the harmony of your relationship so that you may be of one mind with each other. Once and for all you have been reconciled to God; may you be on your guard, lest by sinning again you shatter the covenant entered with him, entered indeed[7] through Jesus Christ his Son, through whom and with whom he bestows all things on us. Deservedly shall we henceforth call him our Lord after he has rescued us from the tyranny of the devil at the price of his most sacred blood, has claimed us for himself, and has received us, emancipated from servitude to the devil, into his own jurisdiction.[8] Happy servitude by which we are firmly bonded to Christ!

This happened to us not by chance nor by our own merit. With every kind of praise we ought to extol God, the very Father of our Lord Jesus Christ, who by his gratuitous good will has poured out on us every kindness, not only bestowing on us the benefits that pertain to our enjoyment of this life and to the support of the body, but also those gifts that contribute to the salvation of the soul and to the immortal life that awaits us in heaven[9] – awaits us through Christ, through whom the Father has opened for us an approach to those above.[10]

* * * * *

5 For 'our Father' as creator see *Explanatio symboli* CWE 70 266; also the paraphrase on Matthew 6 CWE 45 119, where 'our Father' is explained as 'the heavenly Father to whom you owe your creation, to whom you owe your redemption. 'We too' invites a reference to God the Father of Jesus Christ, as paraphrased above.

6 for the reason that] First in *1532*; previously 'because'

7 Erasmus frequently uses the interjection *idque* 'and that' (here translated 'entered indeed') to summarize the preceding clause.

8 The interlinear *Gloss* (on 1:7) explains redemption in similar terms: that we may be able to be restored from the captivity by which we were enslaved to the devil, after we had been sold under the reign of sin.

9 Erasmus' paraphrase includes both corporeal and spiritual blessings. In this he departs from his chief guides through Ephesians, Theophylact and Jerome. Theophylact *Expos in Eph* (on 1:3) PG 124 1033D–1036A sees in 'every spiritual blessing' a deliberate contrast with the mundane and corporeal blessings promised in the Hebrew Scriptures. Jerome *Comm in Eph* I §546–7 (on 1:3) PL 26 445 / Heine 82–3, although he acknowledges that there are earthly blessings, sees an emphasis here on the spiritual.

10 Erasmus here anticipates 2:18 and 3:11–12. But cf also Ambrosiaster *Comm in Eph* (on 1:3) CSEL 81/3 72:26–8, who quotes John 12:26 and interprets the words as a promise that those who believe in Christ 'will be filled with heavenly glory and carried above the powers of the heavens,' that is, above the ranks of the faithful angels.

But let no one inquire, 'Whence such great good will as this? Whence such unheard of kindness?' By his goodness it had been determined thus through an eternal plan even before the foundations of the created world were set in place.[11] Already at that time he had chosen us so that through his Son (through whom he created, governs, and restores all things), when the vices of our former life had been obliterated we might become holy and blameless[12] not only in the eyes of men, but also before God himself who appraises a person according to the hidden dispositions of the heart. And that[13] not by the fear characteristic of the Mosaic law whose severity has been found ineffectual for this objective but by evangelical faith and[14] charity, which obtain more from those who are willing than the Law used to extort from those who acted under compulsion.[15] Moreover, perfect service is not what the fear of punishment or the wrath of a lord extorts from slaves, but what voluntary charity and piety obtain from sons.

This could not be done by our power unless by his eternal decree he[16] had adopted us for himself into the place[17] and with the rights and responsibilities[18] of his sons, and that through Jesus Christ. To him God has so firmly bonded us by faith and charity that having become members of Christ we are one with him through whose fellowship we attain what was not owed to our merits. There is no reason for us to attribute any praise[19] to ourselves on this account; he willed it this way – he who by nature is good

* * * * *

11 Erasmus is intent on emphasizing both God's initiative in choosing those who are called and his power to do what he wills. With *aeternum consilium* 'eternal plan,' cf Oberman *Harvest* 43 on *potentia ordinata*.

12 Cf Jerome *Comm in Eph* 1 §549–50 (on 1:4) PL 26 447–8 / Heine 87: 'Paul and those like him were not chosen because they were holy ... but they were chosen ... that in their following life they might become holy ... by works and virtues.' See his *Apologia adversus libros Rufini* §478 1.22 PL 23 (1845) 415–16, where Jerome is defending his discussion of Origen. Erasmus notes that although we have sinned, the vices of our former life have been obliterated; so too Augustine *De praedestinatione sanctorum*, especially chapters 17.34–20.42 PL 44 985–91.

13 'And that': *idque*. See note 7 above.

14 faith and] Added in *1532*

15 For a similar expression, see Erasmus' paraphrase on Gal 5:6 CWE 42 122–3.

16 he] First in *1521*; previously 'he first'

17 Erasmus articulates his understanding of adoption in his annotation on Rom 8:15 ('the spirit of adoption of the sons of God') CWE 56 209–10. See also his annotations on Eph 1:5 (*in adoptionem filiorum* and *in ipsum*).

18 'Rights and responsibilities': *ius*

19 any praise] Added in *1532*. Previously this entire clause was appended to the preceding sentence in a syntactically deficient construction.

– in order to render his gratuitous kindness towards us more resplendent
and more evident to the world. So far as pertained to our own power we
could be nothing else but enemies of God, worthless slaves, but he, through
the one whom he loves beyond words,[20] has reconciled us to himself and
has changed us from slaves[21] deserving of hatred into sons, pleasing and
dear.[22]

As long as we were members of the devil, guilty of crimes, we were
capable neither of loving God nor of being cherished by him. But when
his very precious Son at the price of his most sacred blood redeemed us
from the slavery of vices and bonded us firmly to himself as members, it
is impossible for the Father not to love those whom he has willed to share
in the inheritance[23] of the Son.[24]

* * * * *

20 Erasmus' annotation on 1:6 (*in dilecto filio suo*) recognizes that the Greek texts
read only 'in [ie through] the Beloved' without adding, as the Vulgate does,
'his Son.' Jerome also *Comm in Eph* 1 §552 (on 1:6) PL 26 450 / Heine 90 comments that '"in his beloved Son" ... written in the Latin codices is not to be
considered, but simply "in the Beloved."'

21 The mention of redemption in 1:7 underlies the introduction of the idea of
slave here. See Jerome *Comm in Eph* 1 §553 (on 1:7) PL 26 450–1 / Heine 91,
who defines redemption in terms of Christ's snatching us from servitude and
forgiving us. See also Theodoret, fifth-century bishop and exegete, whose work
Interpretatio XIV *epistularum sancti Pauli Apostoli* Erasmus evidently found ex-
cerpted in a 'catena-like commentary' he calls the 'Greek Scholia.' Cf CWE 44
70 n1 and ASD IX-2 194:540n. For the reference here see Theodoret *Interpretatio
epistulae ad Ephesios* (on 1:7) PG 82 512A: 'The death of the Lord made us worthy of love. For by it the stains of our sins were laid aside, and, freed from
the servitude of a tyrant, we received the character of the divine image.'

22 On sonship as compared with slavery, see Erasmus' paraphrases on Rom 8:14–
17 and Gal 4:1–7, CWE 42 47–8and 115–16. Cf Theophylact *Expos in Eph* (on
1:6) PG 124 1037C, who paraphrases the Greek ἐχαρίτωσεν ἡμᾶς ἐν τῷ ἠγαπημένῳ
'he freely bestowed on us in the beloved' (RSV) as 'he made us pleasing and
lovable.'

23 'To share in the inheritance': *consortes esse*. In describing the interrelationship
of Christians with Christ and with each other, Erasmus uses *consortium* 'fellowship,' 'share,' 'participation' or its cognate *consors* 'fellow inheritor,' 'associate,' 'partner' thirty-four times in his *Paraphrases* on Ephesians, Philippians,
Colossians, and 1 and 2 Thessalonians, and once in the dedication to Cardinal
Campeggi. An institution of archaic Roman law, *consortium* created joint own-
ership between brothers through inheritance; later it developed as a concept
of idealized cooperation within a partnership granting equality to all members. For the legal texts and an extended interpretation, see Cynthia J. Bannon
The Brothers of Romulus: Fraternal Pietas *in Roman Law, Literature, and Society*
(Princeton 1997) 12–61.

24 of the Son] First in 1532; previously 'of his Son'

Incalculable benefit! But such was the will of our excellent God's rich liberality, a liberality that is poured out everywhere, although it has been especially abundant towards us in particular,[25] while[26] he is now revealing to us, as a gracious father to his own sons, the secret[27] of his eternal will, concealed from the world for so many ages past. To know it[28] is the highest wisdom and the highest prudence,[29] far superior to that by which you have excelled all other mortals up to now, exceptionally skilled as you are in human disciplines.[30] Nature's secrets are investigated by human talent, and yet when they have been thoroughly investigated they do not instantly make people blessed. This secret the human mind could not grasp however great its power of reasoning, had God himself not disclosed it to us; once understood, it leads to true happiness.

If anyone should ask why what has been hidden for such a long time is now at last revealed, I have no reply but that this seemed right to the most excellent mind of God, a mind that can will nothing except what is

* * * * *

25 The *Gloss* (on 1:8) notes that up to this point the writer has in mind the blessings granted to the whole human race; now he turns to blessings conferred in a special way on the apostles.

26 while he is now revealing] First in *1521*; previously the passage read, 'now revealing.'

27 'The secret': *arcanum*. Erasmus used *arcanum* in his translation and three times in his paraphrase on 1:8–9 in preference to the Vulgate *sacramentum* 'sacrament' for the Greek μυστήριον. See Erasmus' annotation on 1:9 (*sacramentum*). With this substitute for *sacramentum* Erasmus emphasizes the hitherto unpublished nature of the mystery, avoids a word whose specific ecclesiastical interpretation as sacrament would be quite inappropriate in the context, and follows the lead of Valla *Annot in Eph* 1 (I 877). On *arcanum*, see 1 Cor chapters 11 n38 and 12 n15; the paraphrases on 1:8–9, 3:3–4 and 9, 5:32 with n38, 6:19; on Col 1:27 with n48, 2:2 with n3; see also Phil chapter 1 n34.

28 To know it] First in *1532*; previously 'knowledge of it'

29 In his annotation on 1:9 (1:8 DV, NRSV) (*in omni sapientia et prudentia*), Erasmus acknowledges that 'in all wisdom and insight' (RSV) may be taken with what precedes: 'With all wisdom and insight he has made known to us' (1:8–9 NRSV) or with what follows: 'For he has made known to us in all wisdom and insight' (RSV). Although Erasmus' translation favours the former, the paraphrase here adopts the latter reading, in which Erasmus interprets 'wisdom and insight' as that which the elect come to possess rather than that with which God acts.

30 In the Greek world, the Ephesians were noted for their learning. See Erasmus' Argument above. Greek Hypotheses prefacing the expositions of Chrysostom and Theophylact note that famous philosophers had lived in the city; Chrysostom refers specifically to Pythagoras and Parmenides. Cf Chrysostom *In Eph hom* PG 62 9 and Theophylact *Expos in Eph* PG 124 1033A.

best since it is goodness itself. What to us now is new with him is not new. What he has disclosed to the world now through the Son he sent had been ordained from eternity by the Father and the Son. But in accordance with his fixed and ineffable plan, he willed it to be secret and hidden until the time previously determined by him for the disclosure of this secret to mortals should be fulfilled. In this way, the sum total of all that pertains to real innocence and real blessedness might be gathered together into the one Christ[31] – once the costly but ineffective efforts[32] of earlier times had been abolished, efforts through which happiness was being sought in vain (in some cases, through the observance of the Mosaic law, in others, through the study of philosophy, in still others, through superstitious religion and the worship of demons). Apart from Christ nothing was now to be desired by anyone, since from this unique source could be sought any good that heaven or earth contains. For God the Father has willed that Christ be the head of all;[33] he has willed that on him alone all depend, that whatever might truly be desired be hoped for from him, that he be credited[34] with whatever the Father bestows upon us in his kindness.

* * * * *

31 Erasmus' annotation on 1:10 (*instaurare*) refers to Jerome *Comm in Eph* 1 §556 (on 1:10) PL 26 453–4 who found *instaurare* 'to take up again,' 'restore,' 're-new,' 're-establish' in Latin codices of Ephesians and laments this imprecise translation of the Greek ἀνακεφαλαιώσασθαι, preferring the Latin *recapitulari* 'to sum up' or 'gather into the main headings.' The term is borrowed from Greek rhetoric to describe the practice of the orators, who would sum up briefly in the epilogues of their speeches what they had previously argued more discursively, in order to help the judges remember the main points of the argument. Erasmus found the expression problematic. See his annotation on Rom 9:28 ('bringing to completion the word') CWE 56 272. For discussion of ἀνακεφαλαιοῦται, see also his annotation on Rom 13:9 ('it is restored in this word') CWE 56 354–5. The concept of recapitulation is central in the theological discourse of Irenaeus (c 140–c 202), who frequently appeals to Eph 1:10, especially in book 5 of *Adversus haereses*, for which text Erasmus provided the Latin *editio princeps* in 1526. See eg 5.1.2, 5.19.1, 5.21.1 PG 7 1127, 1175, 1179.

32 'The costly but ineffective efforts': *dispendia*. See OLD *dispendium* 1 'expense,' 'cost' and 2 'losses.' For a comparable statement of the 'partly treacherous and vain, partly weak and ineffectual' gospel taught by the lawgivers and philosophers, and the propaedeutic nature of Mosaic teaching, see Erasmus' paraphrase on Mark 1:1–3 CWE 49 13–14.

33 Cf Theophylact *Expos in Eph* (on 1:10) PG 124 1040C–D who, after noting the division between things heavenly and things earthly, explains, 'The Father proposed to recapitulate [Greek ἀνακεφαλαιώσασθαι] ... [them], that is to set Christ as one head for all.'

34 Erasmus uses here a term from bookkeeping. See OLD *acceptum* 2.

It is through him that we also have found a felicity so great that we are adopted into the portion[35] and inheritance of immortality, not as a result of our own merits, but because we were long ago destined for it through the ordinance of the one by whose pleasure and might all things, by a plan inscrutable[36] to us, are administered and regulated according to his will, the one who can will nothing except what is both best and most wise, since he is best and most wise.[37] Thus, then, it was his pleasure that we should be called to this inheritance and partnership with Christ, not through merits of our own but through his gratuitous generosity, we who, admonished by the predictions of the prophets, had in some measure pinned our hope on the Christ promised to us even before the truth of the gospel began to dawn. Thus, this benefit might not be attributed to observance of the Mosaic law, but the entire praise might redound to the glory of divine goodness. Thus it pleased the divine goodness to lavish these graces on us freely through his Son.

But we Jews were not the only ones called to the promised partnership with Christ, we who, distrusting the shadows of the Mosaic law, have embraced the gospel truth from which we hope for true salvation even outside the protection of the Law. No indeed; you too, although uncircumcised, were, nevertheless, adopted into the same partnership after you came to believe in the same gospel. For it is not to circumcision that we owe the fact that we are admitted to the hope of immortality, but to our ready belief,[38]

* * * * *

35 Erasmus again uses the Vulgate word *sors*, which Jerome *Comm in Eph* 1 §557 (on 1:11) PL 26 454 / Heine 98 defines as including both 'inheritance and lot.' Max Zerwick and Mary Grosvenor *A Grammatical Analysis of the Greek New Testament* 2 vols (Rome 1974–9) 2 579 lists three possible translations of the Greek phrase ἐν ᾧ καὶ ἐκληρώθημεν: 'in whom we were chosen,' 'in whom we were allotted' (namely, an inheritance), or 'in whom we have been made his heritage,' ie 'claimed as God's own.' Erasmus has incorporated these ideas into his paraphrase on 1:11. See also Theophylact *Expos in Eph* (on 1:10–11) PG 124 1041: 'It is the mark of a fortunate person to be chosen by lot, just as if it happened without effort and by divine grace, even if it happened to worthy people.'

36 See the paraphrase on 1:9 where Erasmus develops the idea that the secrets of nature are subject to human scrutiny; the divine secret, on the contrary, is unsearchable. See also Erasmus' paraphrase on Rom 11:33–4 CWE 42 68, and his annotation on Rom 11:33 ('untraceable') CWE 56 317–18.

37 Erasmus is writing in the context of medieval theology in which the question of whether God can will anything but what is good was quite alive. See Oberman *Harvest* 96–103.

38 For the contrast between the observance of Jewish regulations and Christian faith, which proclaims universal access to God, see 1 Cor chapter 9 n6; 2 Cor chapter 11 n30; Eph chapter 2 n26 and n38.

and if you share this with Jews, what reason is there for you to be strangers to God's kindness?

A little bit of cut-off foreskin is a sign by which you may distinguish a Jew from a gentile.[39] But the gospel's sign extends further and is impressed not upon the body but on the spirit. By it in equal degree are sealed all the people of any nation who embrace the gospel teaching and believe the gospel's promises.[40] Someone will ask: 'But what is this seal that sets Christians apart from the wicked?' It is the Holy Spirit and the disposition not of a slave, but such as is generally found in loyal sons, acting[41] in us so that with our whole heart we trust the gospel's promises, even though they are not yet evident here. The inheritance into which we have been grafted is entirely executed only when the resurrection of the body takes place; nevertheless in the meantime he imparts to us his own Spirit as a pledge and a down payment on the promised inheritance.[42] By this sign we are certain that God regards us as his sons; and there is no doubt but that he will claim for himself his own people whom he has redeemed by the death of his Son. The divine generosity desires to gain as many as possible; it desires its own magnificence to be as resplendent and as well known to the race of mortals as it can be. For the more widespread it is, the more numerous will be the people by whom it will be praised. At one time the Jews in a special way were God's concern because he had liberated them from Egyptian servitude. But it was not enough that the goodness of God be celebrated in one race; he wishes to be praised by all since he has redeemed

* * * * *

39 Circumcision is described in the same pejorative terms elsewhere in the *Paraphrases* to emphasize its inadequacy; cf eg the paraphrases on Rom 4:11 CWE 42 28 and Acts 7:51 and 11:2 CWE 50 54 and 76. Theophylact *Expos in Eph* (on 1:13) PG 124 1041C–D similarly mentions the Jews and circumcision in his exegesis.

40 On the equal access to righteousness available to Jew and gentile, see Erasmus' paraphrase on Rom 3:27–31 CWE 42 25–6; also Sider 'The Just' 18.

41 'Acting': *qui hoc agit*, preserves the ambiguity of Erasmus' Latin: the referent of *qui* may be either the Holy Spirit, or the disposition described, or the two taken as one, perhaps suggesting the Spirit as seal, the disposition as the imprint of the seal. On the Spirit and the attitude of loyal sons, see also Erasmus' paraphrase on Rom 8:11–7 CWE 42 46–8.

42 Erasmus' paraphrase on 1:14 includes both the Vulgate *pignus* 'pledge,' 'security for a loan,' and his own translation / transliteration of the Greek ἀρραβών, 'both the sign and the assurance of future possession which strengthens the obligation in a contract between a buyer and seller'; cf the annotation on 1:14 (*qui est pignus*), where Erasmus criticizes '*pignus*' as inadequate. See also Jerome *Comm in Eph* 1 §560–1 (on 1:14) PL 26 457–8 / Heine 104.

all, free of charge, from the slavery of sins. And he thinks it pertains to his
glory if not only the Jews but all the nations of the whole world become,
through evangelical faith, sharers in salvation.

For these reasons I, for my part, have nothing to say on the subject
of circumcision in your case, since I see clear indications of evangelical
salvation: first, because you have placed your confidence in the Lord Jesus;
then, because you publicly manifest your truly Christian charity towards
all the saints, Christ's members.

Accordingly, I do not cease giving thanks on your behalf. For gospel
piety has this effect: that we rejoice in other people's blessings no less than
in our own. And I always make mention of you in the prayers with which
I daily appeal[43] to God to advance the work of the gospel, asking that he –
the one who is equally God of all peoples and also of Jesus Christ according
to human nature, who is the source too from which Christ has his status
as God, to whom as to the author and fount of all good things the sum
total of all glory is owed – may more and more impart to you the down
payment about which I have spoken. I pray, that is, that he may impart his
Spirit to inspire your minds with this heavenly wisdom and the knowledge
of this secret, so that you may recognize him who is the one and only
bestower of salvation and, in some measure, may perceive him for the time
being[44] with the eyes, not of your body, but of your heart and mind,[45] eyes
sharpened by the light of faith. By these eyes even events yet to come are
experienced, events which cannot be perceived by dull[46] eyes. In this way
you may be able to know what no human philosophy teaches,[47] namely,
how happy is the inheritance to whose hope he has admitted you, how

* * * * *

43 'Appeal': *interpello*. See Erasmus' annotations on Rom 8:26 ('the Spirit makes
request') and 11:2 ('in what way he appeals to') CWE 56 222 and 292.

44 For the effect of this heavenly wisdom on present and future cf Ambrosiaster
Comm in Eph (on 1:17–18) CSEL 81/3 76: Paul prays for the Ephesians 'that
they may [in the present] know the hope of their faith in the heavenly reward,
because ... if they are so devout before they know the glory of the promise,
they will, of necessity, be even more inclined to goodness when they know it.'

45 The contrast between physical eyes and eyes of the heart recurs in Erasmus.
See for example 1 Cor chapter 3 n36 and 2 Cor chapter 3 n29. Cf Jerome *Comm
in Eph* I §562–3 (on 1:15) PL 26 458–9 / Heine 106–8. For Origen on the 'eyes
of the heart,' see Heine 57–8.

46 'Dull': *crassis*. These 'dull' eyes are contrasted with the 'sharp' eyes of the
mind and the heart described in the preceding clause. On *crassus*, see 1 Cor
chapter 2 n22 and Col chapter 2 n18.

47 On the limits of human philosophy, see Erasmus' paraphrases on Mark 1:1
CWE 49 13; Acts 17:18–21 CWE 50 107–8; and Rom 1:20–4 CWE 42 18.

great the value of this magnificent inheritance which the saints are destined to receive, how ample is its grandeur, and how extraordinary the greatness of its power.[48]

Even now he is revealing this power in us. By a kind of hidden and ineffable energy it has so transformed us from our old way of life that, despising all else, we trust in him alone and, disdaining what we see, we look to him for what we do not see. Previously he revealed it openly in Christ, our head. By his own power God summoned Christ from the dead to immortal life and paid him the great honour of placing him at his own right hand in the heavenly realm, exalted above every remaining principality, authority, force, and domination,[49] or other title of status or power, if there is any that can be uttered more splendid even than the ones I have mentioned, whether in this age or in the age to come, so that he may preside not only over all that is corporeal and terrestrial, but also over the spiritual and celestial. Indeed, without any exception he has set all things under Christ's feet. And to make more certain our hope that we too shall come to the fellowship of this glory, he has willed that this same Christ, exalted above all things, be the head of the whole flock of believers, which adheres to Christ just as the whole body is connected to its head and the one cannot be torn away from the other.

Furthermore, the glory of the head is shared, likewise, with the rest of the members over which the head presides, in such a way that it transfuses its own goods into the individual parts. Nor is the body complete unless the head be attached; and the head is deemed to be missing something unless the body is attached,[50] perfect in all its members. Into these individual members Christ transfuses his own gifts in such a way that he also fills them

* * * * *

48 'Power': *potentiae*. In his annotation on Rom 1:4 ('in power') CWE 56 15–17 Erasmus distinguishes among Latin words for power: *potentia* 'ability,' 'power' (so below, in the expression 'title of status or power'); *potestas* 'authority,' 'power' (so below in the expression 'every remaining principality, authority'); *virtus* he sees as ambiguous, sometimes 'virtue' as the opposite of vice, sometimes 'strength,' 'force,' or 'might' as the opposite of weakness (so below in the expression 'force, and domination'). See the annotation on Eph 1:21 (*et virtutem et dominationem*); cf also the annotation on Rom 1:16 ('for it is the power of God') CWE 56 41–2.

49 For this list Erasmus adopts the language of the Vulgate of 1:21. The list appears with some variations at Col 1:16 and Rom 8:38–9. See the annotation on Rom 8:38 ('nor things to come, nor might') CWE 56 237–8.

50 Erasmus, in describing the union of Christ as head with his members, the church, uses the future perfect tense, here translated by the present according to idiomatic English.

all, and now, whole and entire, he lives and reigns with all the members bonded closely to him.

Chapter 2

And yet, I ask you, consider this: how the Father even now has begun to manifest in you in a certain way what has been brought to fulfilment in Christ and is later to be fulfilled in you. Christ died and came to life again, never to die henceforth. He indeed was not subject to sin, but still, on account of the body he had assumed, he was subject to mortality. Furthermore, as sin is a kind of death of the soul,[1] a prelude[2] to eternal death, so innocence is a kind of life of the soul, the first beginning of eternal life. But the originator[3] of this life is God imparting his Spirit to us. The author of death is the devil; he too has his spirit and those who are inspired by it are carried away to the advantages of this world, no doubt distrusting the promises of eternal life. Christ died on account of our offences and he came to life again to give us confidence in a future immortality. Meanwhile, after his likeness you too, who were grafted onto Christ through baptism, have died to sins and also to your vices.[4] While you were living wickedly in your sins, you truly were dead, loving nothing except the lethal shadows of good things by which, for the time being, this world deceives those who are without the Spirit of God and are driven by the spirit of Satan, who has now been granted a temporary[5] tyranny over this lower atmosphere.[6] Satan's spirit itself, I say, is also putting forth a sort of power

* * * * *

1 Cf both Jerome *Comm in Eph* 1 §571 (on 2:1–5) PL 26 465 / Heine 120: 'But clearly sin is said to be the death of the soul,' and Theophylact *Expos in Eph* (on 2:1) PG 124 1049C–D.

2 On 'prelude' or 'rehearsal,' see 1 Cor chapter 10 n10.

3 'Originator': *princeps*. Erasmus preserves the Vulgate reading *princeps* commonly used for 'prince,' which, for Erasmus' contemporary readers, may have suggested the political structures of the day and conveyed the sense that God is Lord of life in all respects.

4 On conversion as 'dying to sin' and on the effect of baptism as the grafting of a shoot onto the Body of Christ, see Erasmus' paraphrases on 1 Cor 6:5 and 10:2, and on Rom 6:1–10 and 11:17–24 CWE 42 36–7 and 65–7. See also his annotations (with their arboricultural images) on Romans 6:3 ('we have been baptized in Christ Jesus') and 6:5 ('for if we have become planted together') CWE 56 175–6.

5 a temporary] First in *1521*; previously 'for a second time'

6 In his annotation on 2:2 (*potestatis aeris huius spiritus*) Erasmus notes that the

of its own in those who, as they have distrusted the evangelical promises, place the culmination of their happiness in what is visible and perishable. They do not hear God the Father inviting them to real happiness, for they prefer to be slaves to the wicked and cruel lord whom at one time you served.

And yet not only you, but all of us also. For although the Law kept[7] us from the worship of idols, nevertheless all of life was contaminated by harmful desires for material things at whose whim we used to live, doing not what that heavenly Spirit was prescribing, but what our own mind, given up to base passions, used to prescribe for us. By this means it came about that, just as those who are closely bonded to Christ through faith belong to the inheritance promised to obedient sons, so we, like insubordinate sons, belonged to a different inheritance, indeed, sharing in the lot of him to whom we had been joined. This is the eternal death that is owed to the wicked. To this death, therefore, we too, like the rest, had been delivered, so far, at least, as it was in our hands. Of our own accord we had delivered ourselves to it, nor was it within our power to be disentangled from that servitude, by far the most wretched of all.

You have heard our death, you have heard our ruin, but whence life, whence salvation? Not at all from our merits, nor from the benefit of the Mosaic law.[8] Whence then? From the gratuitous liberality of God the Father, of course. So rich is his kindness and so great his devotion towards the human race that not only did he not punish us as we had deserved, but, when we were dead on account of our sins, he even summoned us back to life along with Christ. This was not, I repeat, a matter of our merit: what he bestows is freely given. And not only did he

* * * * *

devil 'reigns only in this lower part of the world, not as a lord, since Christ is Lord of all, but as a tyrant with power only because of our vice.' The exegetical tradition stressed that the term *aer* here limited the Satanic power to the 'lower part' of the universe; 'heaven' was left free from its influence. See eg Ambrosiaster *Comm in Eph* (on 2:2) CSEL 81/3 79:7–15; Jerome *Comm in Eph* 1 §572 (on 2:1–5) PL 26 466 / Heine 121. Cf the paraphrase on Mark 8:12 CWE 49 100–1.

7 kept] First in *1521*, previously 'restrained'

8 On the relationship of Law to faith, and on the nature of the true Israelites, see Erasmus' paraphrase on Rom 9:6–24 CWE 42 53–7. For detailed discussion of Erasmus' paraphrase on Eph 2:5–6 showing that 'the paraphrase is much richer in theological harmonics than the translation, which is itself slightly at odds with the annotation,' see B. Roussel, 'Exegetical Fictions?' 62–5, 73–4.

summon us back to life with his Son but he also raised[9] us from these low estates[10] to the heavenly and he placed us there through Christ Jesus, through whom we hold in common whatever he, our head, has. Indeed we possess now in hope whatever we are soon going to possess in reality.[11]

He resolved to do so in order that at the time of the resurrection, when what he has promised will appear, he might make evident the heaped-up generosity he willed to lavish on us in virtue of his gratuitous kindness; not on account of our good deeds,[12] but on account of the merits of Christ Jesus. For lest you be possessed by the error of some Jews[13] who promise themselves salvation by observing the prescriptions of the Mosaic law,[14] what must be very deeply impressed upon your heart has to be repeated over and over again: it is gratuitous, I repeat, that out of the death by which you were held, you have attained salvation. You owe your salvation to the faith whereby you believed in the gospel and yet there is no reason for you to arrogate to yourselves even that faith. He loved you first, and

* * * * *

9 raised] *evexit* first in 1532; previously *revexit* 'carried back'

10 Erasmus does not define what he means by *humiles res* 'low estates.' Cf Jerome *Comm in Eph* 1 §576 (on 2:7) PL 26 469 / Heine 127 (adapted): 'But let us, who once were regarded by the Law as belonging to the lower world even on account of our vices and sins, as we had been destined for the works of the flesh so also for punishments, now reign in Christ and take our seat with him. Moreover let us not sit in some lowly place [*in humili quocumque loco*] but above every principality and power.'

11 Cf the similar interpretations of Augustine *Contra Faustum Manichaeum* 11.8 PL 42 252, and Theophylact *Expos in Eph* (on 2:5) PG 124 1053B–C: 'For he made him [Christ] and us to live: him in actuality, us in potency for the present, but a little later also in actuality ... this is the hope of our calling.'

12 Cf Jerome *Comm in Eph* 1 §577 (on 2:7) PL 26 470 / Heine 128 and n40 quoting Apollinaris of Laodicea (c 315–92): 'because we have been saved not by our merit but by his grace.'

13 In the paraphrases on chapters 3, 4, 9 and 11 of Romans CWE 42 22–32 [especially 27], 52–9 and 63–9, Erasmus develops at length the idea that some Jews have nothing but circumcision in common with Abraham, while others, in addition to being circumcised, imitate Abraham's faith. Paul identifies only the second group as true sons of Abraham. See also John B. Payne 'Erasmus on Romans 9:6–24' *The Bible in the Sixteenth Century* ed David C. Steinmetz (Durham NC 1990) 119–35.

14 With this allusion to the Jewish observance of the Law, Erasmus paraphrases the text of 2:8b, 'and that not of yourselves' (DV). Cf Nicholas of Lyra (on 2:8), who adds briefly to the biblical text the phrase 'and not through the law of Moses.'

when you had been drawn[15] close he freely granted[16] that you love him in return. Likewise gratuitously, he showered on you that gift of faith by which you might perceive the light of evangelical truth when the mist had been dispelled. Therefore, the whole must be ascribed to his munificence; nor is there any reason for anyone to boast as if about a personal achievement.[17]

The fact that we have been created we owe to God. Again, we owe to him the fact that we have been reborn through faith and baptism[18] and, so to speak, created again in another way: separated from the inheritance of our parent Adam, a sinner,[19] and grafted onto Christ, the author of innocence, so that henceforth by his aid and example, we may be available for the duties of true piety and, putting off the old man, we may reveal the new man by our new actions.[20] Thus we will be so unlike ourselves that anyone will have good reason to say we are not the same persons. For through evangelical teaching, God shows us the prize of immortality on this account: that we may strive for it by innocence of life and by right deeds. For evangelical faith is no idle thing,[21] but it has as an inseparable companion char-

* * * * *

15 Cf John 6:44: 'No one can come to me unless the Father who sent me draws him' (RSV), quoted by Nicholas of Lyra (on 2:8). This quotation will appear also in Erasmus' 1524 work *De libero arbitrio* CWE 76 66–7, where it is explicated as a non-violent drawing which moves us to cooperate willingly with actual grace. In his paraphrase on Ephesians 2, Erasmus articulates his belief that God respects free will in human creatures, offering to them the opportunity to draw near, but leaving them free to turn a deaf ear to the invitation. Erasmus also stresses the responsibility to cooperate actively with grace so that faith with its companion charity is expressed in charitable living. For the relation of faith and charity see the paraphrases on 6:23 and 1 Cor 13:13 with n21. See also 1 Cor chapter 15 n15.

16 'He freely granted': *dedit*. For this sense, see OLD *do, dare* 1.

17 Cf Aquinas *Super Eph lect* cap 2 lectio 3.96 (II 26): 'The whole glory is to be referred to God' with references to Ps 115:1 (Vulgate 113B:1) and 1 Cor 1:29.

18 With the mention of baptism in this context, cf Theophylact *Expos in Eph* (on 2:10) PG 124 1056D: 'You have become a new creation, your old self [literally 'man'] having died in baptism.' The paraphrase at this point evokes images from a variety of New Testament passages: John 3:4–6; 1 Pet 1:23; Rom 6:1–11; 2 Cor 5:17; Eph 4:22–4. On faith and baptism in the wider context of Erasmus' thought, see Payne *Theology* 155–78.

19 Cf 1 Cor 15:21–2, 42–9.

20 With the 'old man' / 'new man' contrast Erasmus anticipates 4:22–4; cf also Col 3:9–10 and Rom 6:6.

21 Cf Theophylact *Expos in Eph* (on 2:10) PG 124 1056D: 'And you were made not to be idle but to work.' Erasmus recurs to the idea that genuine faith is accompanied by charity and expresses itself in work ie the services of Christian charity.

ity, which obtains more services from the willing than any prescription of the Law could extort from those who are constrained.[22] The yoke of Mosaic law is not being imposed upon you; the law of Christian charity is sufficient in itself for the performance of every duty. The Jews do not owe this salvation to their Law; you, however, are in greater debt to the divine kindness to the extent that you were farther from the worship of God and from true religion.

Accordingly, so that you may better understand how completely you are in debt to the generosity of God for being the sort of people you now are, you ought to remember the kind you once were.[23] For you were at one time gentiles (at least according to the physical distinction of racial descent);[24] and the nation of the Jews, taking pride in circumcision, a matter of the flesh, an operation performed by hand, calls you by a humiliating designation 'the foreskinned,' considering you profane and abominable, and thinking that this good fortune, promised indeed in times past by the oracles of the prophets, pertains in a special way to themselves.[25] Nor do they understand that, in God's eyes, only they are held to be unclean who have a mind uncircumcised. But at that time you, whose bodies as well as souls were uncircumcised,[26] were more despicable and deplorable than the Jews because you were not looking for the Christ for yourselves inasmuch as you were utterly alienated from the rights and the inheritance of the Jewish race to whom in a special way he seemed to have been promised. You were excluded from the terms of God's agreement by which he had given an assurance when he said to Abraham, author of the race, 'Through your

* * * * *

22 For the contrast between love and fear see the paraphrase on 1:4 with n15.
23 This paragraph paraphrases 2:11–12, stressing the alienation of the pagan gentiles from Israel; similarly Nicholas of Lyra (on 2:11) who summarizes 2:11–12: the gentiles were strangers because as idolaters they were separated from God, separated from Israel who worshipped the one true God, and separated from the promises.
24 Jerome, too, notes *Comm in Eph* 1 §579 (on 2:11) PL 26 471–2 / Heine 131 the special emphasis of the words 'gentiles in the flesh' and distinguishes between gentiles uncircumcised in the flesh but circumcised in the spirit and 'Israelites' circumcised in the flesh but uncircumcised in the spirit.
25 Cf Ambrosiaster *Comm in Eph* (on 2:11–12) CSEL 81/3 82:26–7: 'The Christ was promised to the Jews, not to the gentiles.'
26 'Circumcision' for Erasmus serves as a kind of shorthand for 'purification through the works of the Law.' For Erasmus' understanding of the absolute necessity of faith in this context, see n13 above and nn30 and 31 below.

seed all nations shall be blessed'[27] [Gen 22:18].[28] And it seemed that there was no hope left for your salvation, since as worshippers of demons in this world you were ignorant of the true God, while the Jews called God their own, and he in turn said they were his people.[29]

But as soon as the truth of the gospel shone out, Christ turned things upside down, bringing it about that you, who seemed at one time to have no relationship to God, are now very closely joined to him, not through circumcision of the foreskin, but through the blood of Jesus Christ. Freed from the sins of your former life at the cost of his blood, you have been reconciled to God the Father. Previously there was a split between you and the Jews, between you and God, but Christ, the author of peace and harmony, has removed every distinction of circumcised and uncircumcised; he has removed the ceremonies of the Mosaic law[30] – a sort of wall, so to speak, breaking the harmony of gentiles and Jews – so that the two races, previously quite disconnected from each other, have now combined and grown together into one, with the old hostility abolished. For before Christ, the gentiles vehemently abhorred as superstitious the minutiae of Jewish observance, and by reason of these observances the Jews were so pleased with themselves that they detested all who had no part in them. Therefore, by a marvellous plan Christ abolished and rescinded the hated Law expressed in the precepts of fleshly ceremonies:[31] he would neither alien-

* * * * *

27 Erasmus quotes *per semen tuum benedicentur omnes gentes* 'through your seed all nations shall be blessed'; the Vulgate reads *et benedicentur in semine tuo omnes gentes* 'and in your seed all nations shall be blessed' (cf Weber 30). For Erasmus on 'in' as 'through' in the New Testament, see CWE 56 16 and n8.

28 Gen 22:18] In Froben editions of the *Paraphrase* from 1520 to 1523, the quotation appears without the attribution to Genesis 22 that was introduced as a marginal note in *1532*. 'Gen 22' is omitted in the paraphrase in *1534*, reappears in *1540*, and is incorporated into the text of LB, whose margins contain only the biblical text being paraphrased.

29 Cf 2 Cor 6:16, 'I will be their God and they shall be my people,' with its echoes of Lev 26:12; Jer 31:33; Ezek 37:27; Heb 8:10.

30 Cf Ambrosiaster *Comm in Eph* (on 2:14) CSEL 81/3 83:20–84:5, who likens the wall to the ceremonies of the Hebrews: circumcision, the observances of foods, sacrifices, sabbaths.

31 In his annotation on 2:15 (*decretis evacuans*) Erasmus reviews at some length the exegetical tradition on the difficulties of the Greek text in the verse: τὸν νόμον τῶν ἐντολῶν ἐν δόγμασιν καταργήσας (literally 'rendering void the law of the commandments in teachings'). He subscribes to the view of Ambrosiaster *Comm in Eph* (on 2:15) CSEL81/3 83:11–18, who says that the Law that Christ

ate the Jews nor oppress the gentiles with its burden. He himself, although
he was God and also man, observed according to the flesh the precepts of
the Law, and yet he bore witness that the salvation that he was bringing
according to the spirit[32] pertained to the gentiles no less than to the Jews,
so that now the prepuce in you should not be abhorred, nor circumcision
in them be a matter for boasting, but, with the past of both races abolished, from the two he might fashion one new race that would grow together into one new man, Christ, the common saviour of both on an equal
basis.[33]

And just as he had united the Jews and gentiles with one another, so
likewise did he reunite[34] both with God in order that there might not be
anything anywhere to destroy peace, but that heavenly as well as earthly
realities might be fitted together as if into a single body.[35] The death Christ
paid for our sins has joined us to God, with whom no one who is guilty
of sins has peace.[36] Since that was paid out equally for the gentiles and the
Jews, there is no reason for the one race to prefer themselves to the other,
especially since the pledge also and the down payment of the Holy Spirit,
about which I spoke a little earlier,[37] has been granted to both together
without distinction.[38]

Now we see accomplished what the inspired Isaiah long ago foretold
would happen:[39] for Christ offered the gospel teaching not only to the Jews,

* * * * *

rescinded is 'the one that was given to the Jews with regard to circumcision,
new moons, foods, sacrifices, and sabbaths; he ordered it to cease because it
was a burden.' Ambrosiaster goes on to quote Acts 15:10 where Peter describes
the Law as a burdensome yoke. Cf also Acts 15:28. For an outline of diverse
interpretations of Eph 2:15, see Peter T. O'Brien *The Letter to the Ephesians* The
Pillar New Testament Commentary (Grand Rapids 1999) 196–9.

32 The language 'according to the flesh ... according to the spirit' reflects the
idiom of Rom 1:3–4.

33 Cf 2 Cor 5:17.

34 Erasmus uses the verbs *conciliare* 'unite' and *reconciliare* 'reunite' or 'reconcile.'
The prefix of the second verb implies that the act of reconciliation with God
is the renewal of a previous relationship.

35 Jerome *Comm in Eph* 1 §584–5 (on 2:19) PL 26 475–6 / Heine 139–40 records an
opinion interpreting the union as pertaining not only to Jews and gentiles but
to heavenly and earthly realities.

36 Cf Rom 5:1–10; 2 Cor 5:18.

37 Cf the paraphrase on 1:14 with n42.

38 On access to God, available equally to Jew and gentile, see Erasmus' paraphrase on 1:11–14 with n40.

39 See Isa 45:20–2, 49:6.

to whom, it seemed, this happiness had been specially promised and who already, in their own way, were worshippers of the true God, but also to you, who were far away both from kinship with the Jewish race and from worship of the true God. He taught that through his death both flocks of sheep would come together into one fold and would recognize one and only one shepherd.[40] He made possible for us an approach to the Father who had previously been angry because of our offences. The one who made the approach possible for the Jews was the very one who made it possible also for the gentiles. It is to the same person that we all, both Jews and gentiles, owe the fact that we dare now to draw near to the gracious Father, relying indeed on the Spirit held in common, who inspires this confidence in our souls equally.

Accordingly, you are not to be at all uneasy because according to physical relationship you are not descended from the stock of David or of Abraham, or because you are not subject to the Mosaic law, since according to the Spirit you are citizens and associates of the saints belonging to the house[41] of God which is constructed not of Jews only, but of all who believe simply in the gospel. Its foundations are the apostles – heralds of the gospel – and the prophets, who already, long ago, showed by their predictions that the gift[42] of the gospel would be shared by all on an equal basis. On this foundation you, too, rest. Moreover, Jesus Christ is the principal[43] stone of this building; inserted at the corner, he joins and holds both walls; by his powerful embrace the whole structure of believers, fitted together from whatever source,[44] daily increases and rises up into a spiritual temple, truly holy, indeed consecrated by the Lord himself. And you too, like living stones built upon these same foundations and fastened together by the same

* * * * *

40 See John 10:14–16.
41 house] The reading of all editions from 1520 to 1538; 1540 and LB erroneously print *donum* 'gift.'
42 gift] *donum*, first in 1521; both 1520 editions read *domum* 'house,' which fits the paraphrastic context and is appropriate to the imagery of 2:19–22.
43 'Principal': *summus*. Cf the annotation on 2:20 (*angulari lapido*), where Erasmus explains that the Greek word signifies the principal (*summus*) stone in the corner of the building, which is usually the strongest stone. For a concise discussion of the meaning in 2:20 of ἀκρογωνιαίου as 'cornerstone' (RSV), or 'keystone,' see Barth *Ephesians* I 270–1, 317–22.
44 Cf Nicholas of Lyra (on 2:21): 'from Jews as well as from gentiles,' and Jerome *Comm in Eph* I §585 (on 2:19–22) PL 26 476 / Heine 140: 'The chief cornerstone which holds the two peoples together or, if we take the second interpretation, [which] joins heavenly and earthly beings, is Christ our Lord.'

cornerstone, are part of this sacred structure while in purity of mind and spirit you furnish God with a holy dwelling free from all the defilements of vices and of lusts. Moses' temple[45] received none but the Jews; to this temple[46] belong, on an equal basis, all who embrace evangelical faith.

Chapter 3

So that you may believe this even more firmly, know that I, Paul, have been loaded down with these fetters, not for an evil deed, but solely because of the love of the Lord Jesus Christ. I am eager to win you gentiles for him (although the Jews resent it), if, as I hope, you have heard that the sphere of responsibility assigned to me by Christ himself is this: to dispense especially among the gentiles, to whom you belong, the good news of salvation[1] which, until now, some people used to think belonged to the Jews alone.

　　This secret, formerly hidden from the other apostles, Christ has revealed especially to me, a point I started to mention briefly before when I was writing to other peoples.[2] By reading those letters you will be able to recognize[3] that the secret plan of Christ was not unknown to me, for he not only foretold to Ananias[4] that I would publish his name abroad among the gentiles, but Christ himself also bade me play the part of his ambassador by going to the gentiles far off.[5] Formerly it seemed abhorrent that ungodly people and devotees of idol worship should be called to the fellowship of the gospel, although that is what had been decided by God long before the world was created, and through divine inspiration it was in some manner

* * * * *

45　Erasmus continues to make explicit the implied contrast between the Old Law and the New. There is no mention of Moses in the text Erasmus is paraphrasing. 'Moses' temple' metaphorically suggests the whole Israelite tradition. See Jerome *Comm in Eph* 1 §582 (on 2:15–17) PL 26 474 / Heine 137: he 'withdrew the commandments of the law in consequence of those teachings which were to be fashioned in the tabernacle whose type and image Moses saw (Exod 25:40).'
46　temple] Added in 1532

1　Cf Acts 22:21.
2　Erasmus seems to be referring to 2 Cor 12:1–4; Gal 1:11–16.
3　recognize] First in 1523 2°; previously 'know'
4　Theophylact *Expos in Eph* (on 3:2) PG 124 1068A similarly cites the example of Ananias (Acts 9:15).
5　For Paul's commission as ambassador, see 2 Cor 5:20; for one sent to those far off, see Acts 13:47 (= Isa 49:6) and Acts 22:21.

revealed to the prophets.[6] However, that gentiles attain the good news of salvation by faith alone and without the help of the Mosaic law had not been revealed to the race of mortals in the way it is now being revealed through me.[7] So true is this that even the leaders of the apostles did not dare to admit the uncircumcised to baptism.[8]

Now, however, by the inspiration of the Holy Spirit, it has been made clear to the holy apostles of Christ and to his prophets[9] that the gentiles have been so firmly bonded to the Jews by faith that they have come into partnership in the same inheritance and have grown together into the same body, rejoicing in Christ their common head; and through this, at the same time, they have become participants in all the promises that await those who have faith in the gospel of Christ.

The authority to preach his gospel has been assigned to me; nor am I neglecting the responsibility entrusted to me – even to the point of undergoing chains and imprisonment – thus far labouring constantly in the work of the gospel. Not that I myself by my own strength am equal to so lofty a responsibility; but the very one who assigned this office to me is also of his own accord adding his assistance. Thus it happens that, although by my own defences I am feeble and frail, by his kindness I am strong and fearless against the gales of all ills. I am not boasting of my lofty status. I acknowledge that I am the least of the saints. But nevertheless to me, who am the least, it has pleased the divine goodness to entrust a task by far the greatest, namely, that among gentiles (who have been until the present completely ignorant of God), I should promulgate and proclaim

* * * * *

6 Cf Jerome *Comm in Eph* II §588–90 (on 3:5) PL 26 479–80 / Heine 144–6, who wonders how Paul could say that the mystery was unknown to previous generations when the prophets foretold the coming of Christ and the mission to the gentiles. He postulates that Paul spoke in general terms that did not exclude the view that the prophets knew in some manner, but not as Paul knew now. For Ambrosiaster's solution, see the next note.

7 Ambrosiaster *Comm in Eph* (on 3:5) CSEL 81/3 87:20–88:5 similarly explains that, while many passages of Scripture revealed that the gentiles would share in the promised grace, until Paul it was still hidden that they would be saved without the practices of the Jewish religion.

8 See Gal 2:11–13.

9 For example, to Peter in the incident with Cornelius and the other gentiles on whom the Spirit was poured out as recorded in Acts 10:44–8; cf Theophylact *Expos in Eph* (on 3:5) PG 124 1069A. On prophets, see the paraphrases on 1 Cor 12:27–31 with n30 and 14:1–25.

the unsearchable[10] riches of Christ which he is offering abundantly to all; and that what up to now lay hidden, I should bring to light, I mean the fact that the benefit of the gospel is to be dispensed now to all nations.[11] Previously it was thought to have been conferred on the Jews alone, although from eternity[12] it had been determined otherwise by God, both the creator and the director of the universe.

This plan of his own divine mind he willed to be secret until now, because it was precisely in these times that he willed it to be published, and published through his church. Into the church he is pouring spiritual gifts in such abundance that his manifold wisdom, which regulates all things by a wondrous design – bestowing life through death, leading to glory through disgrace, shedding light on God's majesty through humility,[13] a design once unimaginable – this wisdom is now becoming known, not only to the whole earth, but also to the first and foremost of angelic minds and also to the foremost of the demons that dwell in the heavens and the highest part of the atmosphere.[14]

* * * * *

10 unsearchable] *investigabiles*, first in 1523 2°; previously *impervestigabiles* 'thoroughly unsearchable.' Thus Erasmus returned in the 1523 folio edition to the Vulgate reading (for variants, see Weber 1811), although he himself translated *impervestigabiles* (all editions) and defended his translation in his *Annotations*. See his annotation on 3:8 (*investigabiles*) and on Rom 11:33 ('untraceable') CWE 56 317–8. Cf Jerome's explanation of *ininvestigabiles* in *Comm in Eph* II §593 (on 3:8–9) PL 26 482 / Heine 148–9. For these words in patristic writings, see O. Hiltbrunner 'Der Schluss von Tertullians Schrift Gegen Hermogenes' *Vigiliae Christianae* 10 (1956) 215–28.

11 It is unclear whether the text of 3:9 originally read φωτίσαι 'to bring to light' or φωτίσαι πάντας 'to enlighten all men' (Conf). See Metzger 534. As his annotation on the verse (*et illuminare*) makes clear, Erasmus preferred the former, although in his translation he printed *in lucem proferam omnibus* 'to bring to light for all.' In this sentence the paraphrase incorporates both readings.

12 Cf Theophylact *Expos in Eph* (on 3:9) PG 124 1072A, who explains that the mystery of the calling of the gentiles to such great blessings is not recent but had been decided '"from the ages," that is, "from farther back" and "from the beginning."'

13 Cf Theophylact *Expos in Eph* (on 3:10) PG 124 1072C–D who includes the paradoxes of the three parallels (life/death, glory/disgrace, majesty/humility) and his acknowledged source, Gregory of Nyssa *Commentarii in Canticum canticorum* Homilia 8 PG 44 948B–949B.

14 Although elsewhere (see Ephesians Argument n1) Erasmus acknowledged the *daemones* 'demons' as satanic (cf indexes of CWE 49, CWE 50), here he uses the term to designate the 'principalities and powers' of the biblical text whom he evidently regards as obedient to God; cf Col chapter 1 n23. In this interpreta-

Even if they could have imagined that the human race might at some time be redeemed, still hidden was the process by which the divine wisdom had determined from eternity to redeem mankind. This he made known only after he had sent his Son into the world to take on a human body and by ineffable means to claim the church for him and bind it to him, with Jesus Christ our Lord himself as its head. Just as it is through him that innocence has come to us (that is to say, our sins have been abolished), so through him confidence has come with the result that, like sons, we do not fear to approach the Father, although previously we would not have dared to look at the Father's angry countenance. For what would we not dare when we rely on such a head who certainly does not allow any of his own members to perish, however much affliction we may suffer here in the meantime?

Since I am boldly proclaiming this secret plan of God everywhere, I am greatly afflicted by those who cannot yet be persuaded of it. But I beseech you not to be disturbed at all or discouraged by the afflictions that I am suffering for your sake. There is no reason that you should be ashamed of this apostle laden with shackles. For just as the cross of Christ is our glory,[15] so my shackles, which I am wearing not because of scandalous behaviour but because of the integrity of the gospel, are your glory, not your shame.[16] The more evils we endure with unbroken spirit on account of the gospel of Christ, the fuller the confidence we inspire that the promises of Christ are not empty; bolstered by the hope of these promises, we are not shaken by any evils of this life. And not only for me is it glorious to be afflicted on account of the work of the gospel, but also for all who have been initiated into Christ it would be a fine thing to follow the example of their source and their head.

Indeed, for this reason, on bended knee, from the depth of my heart,[17] I earnestly entreat God our Father and the Father also of our Lord Jesus

* * * * *

tion he follows Jerome, although Jerome recognizes that some understand the expression to refer to 'the prince of the air and his angels,' ie the satanic powers. See *Comm in Eph* II §594 (on 3:10) PL 26 483 / Heine 149–50. In the paraphrase here, the *daemones* are said to dwell in the 'highest part of the atmosphere'; in the paraphrase on 2:2 the satanic power is said to operate rather in 'this lower atmosphere.' But cf the paraphrase on 6:12, where the 'powers' are the 'demonic powers besieging us from on high.' Cf also 1 Cor chapter 4 n20.

15 Cf Gal 6:14.

16 Cf 1 Pet 4:14–16.

17 Erasmus interprets the 'bended knee' as an exterior sign of a mind and heart bowed down; so also Jerome *Comm in Eph* II §598–9 (on 3:14) PL 26 486–7 / Heine 155–7 and Aquinas *Super Eph lect* cap 3 lectio 4.166 (II 42).

Christ, on whom, as on the supreme head, depends all spiritual kinship[18] by which both the angels in heaven and the faithful on earth are firmly bonded, and from whom alone as source proceeds whatever pertains to true happiness. Just as he has begun to make his abounding glory evident in you, so may he increase[19] more and more his generosity towards you, so that you, who have been grafted onto Christ through baptism and born anew, as it were, may with daily increments gather firmness and strength, not of the body but of the mind and heart.[20] And may this be accomplished by the ever-increasing gift in us of the Father's Spirit, through whom we are made brave and invincible against all the bogies of our persecutions. May the constancy of your faith be such that you think that Christ will be present to you everywhere, or rather that he dwells in your inmost hearts on account of the confidence with which you entrust yourselves entirely to him. For he is present to help especially those who distrust their own resources and depend entirely on his assistance. That will happen all the more if to evangelical faith you join evangelical charity and if you add it in such a way that it settles deeply in your hearts and puts out roots so that, resting on and supported by this firm foundation, you begin to grow in your spirit and, in a way, correspond to the infinite Spirit of God.

And now mature, may you advance to such a measure of capacity that, not only with the Jews but also with the whole multitude of the saints, which is bonded closely to the body of Christ through evangelical faith, you

* * * * *

18 Erasmus follows his own translation 'from whom all kinship [cognatio] from a common father is named,' avoiding the Vulgate's 'from whom all fatherhood [paternitas] is named.' In his annotation on 3:15 (omnis paternitas), he indicates that the Greek word πατριά (Latin familia 'family' [RSV]) expresses the sense that from one source arises the multitude that constitutes a tribe or race. Cf Jerome Comm in Eph II §599–602 (on 3:15) PL 26 487–490 / Heine 157–9. On Erasmus' view of the exclusive paternity of God, see Pabel Conversing with God 116. For Lee's criticisms and Erasmus' response, see Responsio ad annotationes Lei (Concerning Notes 186, 187) CWE 72 294–6.

19 Here begins the lengthy series of prayers (3:16–19) that constitutes the 'earnest entreaty' that 'Paul' makes to 'God our Father.'

20 With Erasmus' paraphrastic explication of the biblical clause 'be strengthened with might through his Spirit in the inner man' (RSV) compare Jerome Comm in Eph II §602 (on 3:16) PL 26 490: 'For we are not asking for powers [vires] of body, but of soul [animae]; we desire not that the exterior man be strengthened but the interior man, so that after Christ has taken up his dwelling in the interior man, he may dwell in the inner sanctum of this man, that is in our hearts [cordibus] ... dwelling in its rational [rationabili] part.'

may be able to comprehend how the goodness of God the Father stretches to infinity, how it is not restrained by narrow limits: in height reaching all the way to the angels, in depth penetrating all the way to hell,[21] in length and in breadth spreading to all regions of this world. At the same time may you be able to understand the inestimable love of Christ towards the race of mortals. Knowledge of this surpasses all human[22] knowing,[23] however excellent.

And what is more, with these gifts may you grow in such a way that as strong and perfect members you correspond to a head so distinguished, to a Father so sublime. For just as corporeal birth has stages of life, has its own spurts of growth, has also a turning point[24] up to which it is allowed to mature, so also this spiritual begetting has its own infancy, has its adolescence, has also the firmness of an age that is already complete and mature.

These gifts, I repeat, I frequently beg on bended knee from God the Father. They are great indeed and far beyond human strength, but I beg them from him whose power is so great that he can far exceed anything that can be imagined by us. So good and gracious is he that by his generosity he not only keeps pace with our prayers but surpasses even our hope. For there is not any question here of our merits or our strength. We are nothing else but the instrument[25] of divine power that shows its strength in us. To his liberality, therefore, must be assigned all the glory which shines out in

* * * * *

21 'Hell': *inferos*. Cf Jerome *Comm in Eph* II §603 (on 3:18) PL 26 491 / Heine 161 (adapted): 'We ... understand "height" as the angels and the powers above, and "depth" as inhabitants of the infernal regions [*inferos*] and what are below them; "length" and "breadth" as whatever stands between those above and those below.' On *inferus*, see the paraphrases on Rom 8:39 CWE 42 52 and 1 Cor 8:5 with n10; see also Eph chapter 4 n15.

22 Cf Theophylact *Expos in Eph* (on 3:19) PG 124 1077A: 'Since it surpasses all knowing, how are we to know it? First he says that this surpasses knowing, meaning human knowing. You, however ... know this through the Spirit.'

23 knowing] Latin *scientiae* in all Froben editions to 1540; LB in a footnote records an alternate reading 'wisdom.'

24 'Turning point': *metam*. Erasmus borrows a word from the racetrack, where the *meta*, a 'cone-shaped goal' or 'turning-point,' marked the beginning of the backstretch, the limit set to forward movement. Aristotelian teleological theory requires that any being grow and develop only up to a certain point beyond which it decays and/or becomes something else. Cf Aristotle *De anima* 432b21–5, 434a24–5.

25 'Instrument': *organum*. Erasmus uses *organum* elsewhere to designate a minister of the gospel. See eg CWE 50 65 n21 and CWE 42 85.

the church through Christ Jesus by whose interchange[26] she possesses such great gifts. And of his glory there will be no end; it will persist forever through every generation, just as the church of Christ, too, will have no end, ever. What I have said is certain and without doubt.[27]

Chapter 4

Therefore, since you understand from how vile a condition you have been called to such an exalted position, from what great hopelessness you have been called to such extraordinary rewards, I implore you by these chains[1] with which I am bound – not because of my misdeeds, but because of the glory of God[2] and your salvation – that, as for the rest, you show yourself, by the innocence[3] of your character, worthy of your profession and of God's kindness towards you. That will happen if the lofty status of your profession does not make you rather haughty and contentious, but if the whole tenor of your life manifests in all circumstances a genuine sobriety of spirit, mildness, and gentleness. No one should despise another through pride, but through mutual charity you are to support each other.[4] It is preferable to go along, for the time being, with another's weakness rather than to see a split in harmony and concord as each one doggedly

* * * * *

26 'Interchange': *commercium*. Erasmus adopts a term of commercial exchange. Here the word implies a theology of divine self-communication enabling human self-transcendence whereby the Son's sharing in humanity gives humanity a share in divinity and becomes the source of the church's possessions. See Erasmus' paraphrase on 1:7–8 and the *Carmen heroicum* 32–8 (in CWE poem 112) CWE 85 307–8 with CWE 86 627 n36.

27 With this last sentence, a paraphrase apparently on the word 'amen' (3:21), compare the paraphrases on *fidelis sermo* in 1 Tim 4:9–10 and Titus 3:8 CWE 44 25 and 65–6. For the 'amen' as an affirmation of a prayer, cf the paraphrase on 1 Cor 14:16.

1 Erasmus amplifies the Vulgate of 4:1 *vinctus in Domino* 'bound in the Lord' by calling attention to literal chains; Jerome *Comm in Eph* II §606 (on 4:1) PL 26 492–3 / Heine 164 prefers to emphasize an allegorical meaning, 'bound in the love of Christ.'

2 Cf Theophylact *Expos in Eph* (on 4:1) PG 124 1080A: 'not on account of some wicked deed but on account of the Lord.'

3 'Innocence': *innocentia*. For Erasmus, 'innocence' is the fruit of baptism's purifying grace. On innocence, see 1 Cor chapters 1 n41 and 3 n12, and Payne *Theology* 164.

4 On the responsibility for sustaining one another in need, see Erasmus' paraphrase on Gal 6:1–15 CWE 42 126–9.

defends a personal prerogative.[5] By harmony and concord you have been connected and cemented together with the bonding of peace. It is not right that people who have so many interests in common should be torn asunder by a disagreement.

You are all one body; on one head you depend. You have all imbibed the same Spirit of Christ and, indeed, you have all been equally called to the same hope of inheritance.[6] Jesus Christ is the one Lord of all. The profession of faith is the same for all. There is one baptism for all which, as a result of the death of Christ, is equally efficacious for all who believe in the gospel,[7] whether they are uncircumcised or circumcised.[8] Finally, the God and Father of all is one. As the originator and author of all things without exception, he presides over us all in such a way that for the present, he is, by his Spirit with which he governs us, diffused through all and dwells in all, ever present to us with his aid.[9]

* * * * *

5 By *mordicus* 'doggedly,' 'tooth and nail' Erasmus characterizes the person who persists in opposition to the truth. See his use of the word in the dedication to Campeggi n38, and see 2 Cor chapter 3 n27.

6 The metaphor of the interdependence of limbs and body in the imagery of Erasmus has an obvious source in Paul's writing on the mystical body, but may also derive from classical Latin literature. See M. Adinolfi 'Le Metafore greco-romane della testa e del corpo e il corpo mistico di Cristo' in *Studiorum Paulinorum Congressus Internationalis Catholicus 1961*, Analecta biblica: Investigationes scientificae in res biblicas 17–18 2 vols (Rome 1963) 2 333–42. On the Body of Christ as the church, see Erasmus' paraphrase on Rom 12:4–6 CWE 42 70; and also the paraphrases on 1 Cor 10:16–17 and 12:12–31; Col 1:18 and 2:19. See Joseph A. Fitzmyer 'Pauline Theology: Body of Christ' NJBC §82:122 1409–10. For the influence of Augustine, see Stanislaus J. Grabowski 'St. Augustine and the Doctrine of the Mystical Body of Christ' *Theological Studies* 7 (1946) 72–125.

7 Here and throughout his paraphrases, Erasmus expresses, often with some ambiguity, his views on baptism. See eg 1 Cor chapter 1 n35 and the paraphrases on Acts 8:36–9 CWE 50 62–3; 1 Pet 3:21 CWE 44 99; and Hebrews 10:22–3 CWE 44 241.

8 Here as elsewhere Erasmus distinguishes somewhat rudely between the uncircumcised *praeputiati* 'the foreskinned' and the circumcised *recutiti* 'the pared back.' For other disparaging references to circumcision, see chapter 1 n39 and the paraphrase on 2:1–15 with nn26 and 30.

9 In his annotation on 4:6 (*qui super omnes et per omnia*) Erasmus is concerned, as Valla had been (cf *Annot in Eph* 4 [I 877]), with the gender of the substantives in the Greek ἐπὶ πάντων καὶ διὰ πάντων καὶ ἐν πᾶσιν 'above all and through all and in all' (RSV), represented in the Vulgate by *super omnes et per omnia et in omnibus nobis* 'above all [persons] and throughout all [things] and in us all' (Conf). Erasmus said that he preferred to read all three as neuter or

From one source, therefore, arises whatever there is in us of good. The fact that his gifts[10] do not appear identical or equal in all persons should not stand in the way of our harmony, any more, assuredly, than we see the concord of the body's members disrupted[11] because they all are not equally efficacious for the same end and do not feel the influence of the head in the same degree. Instead, this very diversity ought rather to invite to harmony. For as long as no one of the members is independently, entirely self-sufficient, individual members stand in need of each other's service, and there is no reason for one to be able to despise another.

This division of gifts, however, depends not on us, but on the will of God, who distributes his benefits to each one more lavishly or more sparingly just as he views suitable.[12] There is no reason to disdain the person who has less, and no reason for the one who has more to plume himself. The former case is a matter of God's distributing, the latter of his lavishing – granted that all these gifts come through Christ who, together with the Father, imparts them.[13] Actually, it was this that the Psalmist[14] long ago predicted under the inspiration of divine power. For when Christ had

* * * * *

as masculine, and to avoid mixing persons and things. Nevertheless, in his translation he did mix the genders (the first two neuter, the third masculine). Here in the paraphrase he represents all three as masculine, without, however, excluding the neuter entirely (cf 'all things ... dwells in all').

10 Here and eight other times in this *Paraphrase*, Erasmus has used *dos* 'gift' (Ep 1062:82; and the paraphrases on Eph 1:3 and 23, 3:10, 19, and 21, 4:7, 11, and 12). In classical literature, the primary meaning of the word is 'dowry' (see OLD *dos*); it is also used for a marriage gift from husband to wife. Here Erasmus may be anticipating the relationship of Christ to the church described in 5:25–33.

11 Classical authors record the image of discord between the body's members in rhetorical pleas for civic harmony. Cf eg Livy 2.32.9–12 (the appeal to the Roman plebs by Menenius Agrippa in 494 BC); Seneca *Epistulae morales* 92.30, 95.52; Josephus *Jewish War* 1.507.

12 Cf Jerome *Comm in Eph* II §611 (on 4:7) PL 26 497 / Heine 171 who notes that God's boundless generosity is tempered by the capacity of the recipient, and Theophylact *Expos in Eph* (on 4:7) PG 124 1084A who similarly emphasizes the total gratuitousness of the gifts according to God's pleasure and the measure of Christ's giving.

13 Although the text that Erasmus is paraphrasing (4:7) refers only to Christ, his paraphrase assigns Christ an instrumental role because it is still emphasizing the unity of God as the background for the functions of the equal persons of the Trinity. See his annotation on 4:7 (*et in omnibus vobis*); also Sider 'Χάρις' 249–51.

14 Psalmist] In all editions from 1520 to 1540; LB adds 'Ps LXVII' (ie 67:19 Vulgate / 68:18 RSV).

already vanquished the infernal powers in war,[15] alive again, he ascended
to the Father's realm on high, leading with him the trophy of his victory:
the flock of captives freed from the tyranny of sin and the devil. And from
that place, in keeping with the Father's generosity he gave[16] various kinds
of gifts through the heavenly Spirit, distributing them among men just as
those who are celebrating a triumph normally scatter presents, tossing them
among the people from on high.[17] From heaven he sent gifts, and heavenly
were the gifts he sent.

* * * * *

15 The victory of Christ over the *inferi* 'infernal powers' was won when he conquered death through the cross. See chapter 3 n21; also the *Carmen heroicum*
   55–219 (in CWE poem 112) CWE 85 308–21 with CWE 86 668–70. On the doctrine
   of Christ's freeing of the souls of the just by his descent among the dead immediately after his death, see J.N.D. Kelly *Early Christian Creeds* 3rd ed (New
   York 1972) 378–83. For Erasmus' picture of Christ in the infernal regions, see
   his colloquy 'An Examination concerning the Faith' CWE 39 426:25–37 and n58;
   his *Explanatio symboli* CWE 70 306–10; also his paraphrases on 1 Pet 3:18–20 CWE
   44 98–9 and Acts 2:27 CWE 50 21 with n78.
16 In his annotation on 4:8 (*adscendens in altum*), Erasmus notes that Paul has
   adapted the psalm by changing 'received gifts' to 'gave gifts.' Cf Jerome *Comm
   in Eph* II §612–13 (on 4:8) PL 26 498 / Heine 172 and Theophylact *Expos in Eph*
   (on 4:8) PG 124 1084D.
17 A Roman triumph was the formal honour conferred by the senate on a general who had defeated the army of a significant foreign enemy of the Roman
   state in a declared war. The paraphrase on 4:8 suggests certain features of the
   triumph, for example, the procession of the victorious general with his troops,
   their spoils and captives, through the city and up to the temple of 'Jupiter Best
   and Greatest' on the Capitoline Hill. For the Roman triumph in its context, see
   H.S. Versnel *Triumphus: an Inquiry into the Origin, Development and Meaning of
   the Roman Triumph* (Leiden 1970), especially 56–8 (the triumphator) and 95–6
   (the procession), also W. Ehlers 'Triumphus' in *Realencyclopädie der classischen
   Altertumswissenschaft* ed August Friedrich von Pauly and Georg Wissowa VII A
   1 (1938) 493–511. In connection with the celebration, the triumphator called an
   assembly of his soldiers, addressed them, and distributed rewards for service,
   both money and gifts, eg armlets or crowns. Sometimes, in addition, gifts from
   the spoils of war were distributed among the general populace. See Zonaras
   Epitome 7.21. The indiscriminate scattering of presents is no recorded part of
   the triumphal procession. Erasmus may have introduced a feature from another kind of celebration. His language in this passage echoes Suetonius' description of a theatrical festival at which the emperor Nero watched proceedings from the roof of the stage building and 'there were scattered (*spargere*)
   for the people (*populus*) presents (*missilia*) of all kinds.' See Suetonius *Nero*
   11.2. On the image of the triumph in the *Paraphrases*, see also 2 Cor chapter 2
   n16; Col chapter 2 n50; CWE 44 14 n11; CWE 48 147 n45; CWE 50 57 n11; also
   O'Mara 'Triumphs, Trophies, and Spoils' 115–20.

Furthermore, that word 'ascended,' does it not imply that at some time he descended? And there is no descent except from a height. The descent is first, the ascent afterwards. For only humility and self-abasement deserve exaltation. Moreover, the greatest exaltation follows upon the greatest humiliation. Christ stooped down from the highest heaven (than which there can be nothing more exalted) to the infernal regions (than which there can be nothing lower). Accordingly, on this account he deserved to be carried up again beyond the pinnacles of all the heavens, withdrawing from us the presence of his body so that from on high he might fill all things with heavenly gifts and that now, in some other way, he might be present to us more efficaciously than he had been when he was living with us on earth.[18] He did not abandon[19] his body but divided his own gifts among the individual members in such a way that in the whole there might be nothing missing – granted that some gifts are more distinguished than others. For he wished some people to be pre-eminent, as apostles, the founders and authors of evangelical preaching; some, however, prophets,[20] who would know how

* * * * *

18 Erasmus is referring in a conveniently indefinite manner to the 'heavenly gifts' promised together with the Spirit (cf eg John 16:7). The thought that we see Christ better with spiritual eyes than did the disciples with their physical eyes is very common in Erasmus. See CWE 50 8 n48 and the allusions there to CWE 66 73 and CWE 25 162. For the efficacious presence of Christ 'in some other way' cf the *Paraclesis* Holborn 146:22–6, 149:11–13: 'What he [Christ] promised, that he would always be with us until the end of the world, he provides especially in these Scriptures [ie the Gospels and Epistles] in which even now he lives for us, breathes, speaks, almost more efficaciously, I would say, than when he lived among men ... These [Scriptures] recall for you the living image of his most holy mind, and Christ himself speaking, healing, dying, rising; in short, they render him so wholly present that you would see less if you caught sight of him face to face with your eyes.' See Ep 384:47–51 and the paraphrase on 6:18–19 with n36; also 1 Thess chapter 2 n21; and CWE 46 16. On the living reality of the text, see Mark Vessey 'Erasmus' Lucubrations and the Renaissance Life of Texts' ERSY 24 (2004) 23–51.

19 did ... abandon] *deseruit* in all editions; in LB *deservit*. By way of exception, LB prints the vocalic 'u' as 'v,' although its usual practice is to print 'u.' See Erasmus' paraphrase on John 14:18, 'I will not leave you orphans' (Conf) CWE 46 172. On the church as the Body of Christ, see 1 Cor 12:27–31 with Erasmus' paraphrase on those verses.

20 'Prophets': *prophetas*. In response to criticism that he departs from the customary practice of the Latin church in the language of his *Paraphrases*, Erasmus in his *Declarationes ad censuras Lutetiae vulgatas* LB IX 880A–B distinguishes *fatidici* 'oracular' (which he admits to using 'once or twice at most') from *prophetici* 'prophetic.' *Propheta* 'prophet,' he says has a narrower scope than *fatidicus*, 'for

to unfold the wrappings[21] of Mosaic law; some, evangelists, who, doing the work of apostles, would travel around to proclaim the gospel; some, again, pastors and teachers, for example, the bishops, who would feed the flock of Christ with the nourishment of sacred discourse and the salutary example of their lives.[22] In the same way he equipped the rest – some with some gifts, some with others – so that, as a result of all these gifts gathered together into one, the assembly of the saints might be made perfect, equipped in this way for the discharge of every duty. [He did this] so that the complete body of Christ, connected together through all its members, might for a time be fostered with mutual supports, and for a time the stronger member might accommodate the weaker and the weaker strive after the example of the hardier, until at last[23] we all come to equal hardiness of faith and with similar perfection know the Son of God. By his assistance may we grow

* * * * *

[*fatidicus*] is properly used only of one who predicts the future.' In the *Paraphrases*, however, he gives to the prophets of the early church the primary role of discerning and interpreting the hidden meanings of Scripture in the light of the gospel. See his paraphrases on 1 Cor 12:28 with n30, 13:2, 14:3–4; and CWE 50 99 n64. Cf Ambrosiaster *Comm in Eph* (on 4:11) CSEL 81/3 98:20–4 who acknowledges that in the New Testament, prophets like Agabus (Acts 21:10) foretold the future, 'but now prophets are expositors of the Scriptures ... now, interpreters are called prophets.'

21 'Wrappings': *involucra*. In Erasmus' view, expressed in *Elenchus in N. Bedae censuras* LB IX 504, the full meaning of biblical texts is not immediately evident: 'No, indeed, the Holy Spirit allowed obscurity to remain in sacred literature in order to give us scope for hard work just as Augustine teaches.' Cf Augustine *De doctrina christiana* 2.6.7–8 CSEL 80 36–7. See also Erasmus' paraphrase on Gal 4:24 CWE 42 119: 'This is usually the case with the law of Moses; just as in man the mind, as ruler of the body, lies hidden under the heavy cover of the body, so under the story something deeper and more sublime lies concealed.' There is a veil, or wrapping, which prevents the hard-hearted from penetrating to the meaning of the Scriptures, a veil being removed by Paul's preaching to those who are capable of receiving it. Cf the paraphrase on 2 Pet 1:19–21 CWE 44 115: 'The prophetic part of Scripture is obscure because of its cloak of figurative speech and cannot be understood without interpretation.' See the paraphrase on 2 Cor 3:13–16 with nn22 and 29.

22 In his annotation on 4:11 (*alios autem pastores et doctores*) Erasmus notes that Paul has deliberately joined these two offices because every pastor should also be a teacher. On the teaching responsibility of the bishop, see also Erasmus' paraphrases on 1 Tim 3:1–3 and Titus 1:9 CWE 44 18–20 and 59.

23 until at last ... God] In Froben editions from 1520 to 1540, this clause is clearly tied to what precedes. In LB, 'until ... God' is separated by a full stop from what precedes.

through hidden spiritual increments[24] so that at last we turn out to be the complete man[25] and in our own way measure up to our completely perfect head in whom there was no element of weakness, error, or vice.

There is a stage of physical development that adds full hardiness to all the members and drives out all the softness of childhood. Similar to this, in the advancement of piety there is a progress towards which we all must put forth every effort not to be in the future what we once were: like children, wavering with unsure views, relying on no fixed principles about achieving happiness but void of truth and carried about by any wind[26] of doctrine now into one opinion, now into another; offering ourselves with childish naïveté to the crafty cleverness of certain people whose purpose is not to teach us Christ sincerely, but to attack us with their clever skills and catch us in the snares of their deceits, whether the syllogisms[27] of the philosophers with which they call into question what should be certain by reason of our faith, or the shadows of the Mosaic law, which they palm off on us as evangelical truth. Instead, once we have embraced evangelical truth let us join to it sincere love towards all mortals, striving with indefatigable zeal for this: that by continually progressing both in the knowledge of truth and in the duties of charity alike, we may achieve the result that all the members correspond to their head. Our head, in fact, is Christ who is truth itself and who has so loved us that he has paid out his life to save us.

* * * * *

24 For a similar description of spiritual growth, see Erasmus' paraphrases on 3:19 and 1 Tim 3:6 CWE 44 20: 'Baptism to be sure grafts a person into the body of Christ, but this person does not instantly acquire perfect godliness … it is still left to us to gain stature and strength over an extended period of time by growing to maturity through daily increases in godliness'; cf also the paraphrase on 1 Pet 2:1–2 CWE 44 88–9.

25 'Man': *virum*. Erasmus adopts the Vulgate word but cf the *Gloss* (on 4:13), which points out that 'man' is to be interpreted 'not according to sex but according to the perfection of virtue, for at present we are little children as far as the powers of body and soul are concerned.'

26 'Any wind': *quovis vento*. Erasmus adopts his own translation. Cf his annotation on 4:14 (*et circumferamur*), where he corrects the Vulgate *omni vento*, which, he says, could mean either 'any wind' or 'every wind.'

27 'Syllogisms': *ratiocinationibus*. For the negative connotations of the word, see the annotation on Romans 1:5 ('for his name') CWE 56 28 (where the verb analogue *ratiocinor* is translated 'spin out syllogisms'). For the word as a rhetorical term cf CWE 56 291 and n3. Erasmus frequently expresses his distrust of 'subtle argumentation.' See eg the paraphrase on 1 Tim 1:4 CWE 44 7–8, and *Paraclesis* Holborn 144:35–145:1 where Erasmus contrasts the Christian philosophy with the philosophy based on syllogisms and reasoning (*ratio*).

The members must be fitted to him, our head, for from the head that life-giving Spirit has flowed down into the whole body.[28] As the various members in their proper order cling to each other, the body is closely joined and fitted together and the Spirit penetrates all the joints of the limbs.[29] This would not happen unless the parts of the body were joined together in mutual harmony[30] so that the Spirit could flow in them from member to member. For a hand or a foot that has been amputated could not share in the strength coming from the head at the top.[31] But so long as all the body is firmly bonded together, the Spirit of Christ expresses its own power in individual members according to each one's capacity and proper order; and so long as all the members are eager to be of use to one another through mutual love, the whole body grows and is rendered hale and hearty, not at all disposed to yield to the winds of false opinions that buffet it from this side and that, making it veer away from the truth.

Of all these things, therefore, which I wanted to convey by so many metaphors,[32] the sum total is this: I not only advise but, through the Lord Jesus to whom you owe your salvation, I even beg and beseech you, that after you have once been grafted onto him, you be like him not only in sincerity of faith and in truth of dogmas,[33] but also in integrity of life. When

* * * * *

28 Erasmus' annotation on 4:16 (*secundum operationem*) explains: 'He refers to the life-giving Spirit which, proceeding from the head, imparts its 'energy' [Latin *vis*, reflecting the Greek ἐνέργεια] not in equal measure to all [members], but, to the extent that is helpful, to the whole body.'

29 Cf Heb 4:12.

30 Cf Livy 2.32.9–12 describing how Menenius Agrippa brought about *concordia* 'civic harmony' through a speech that drew a similar analogy. Cicero employs the same analogy with reference to the body politic at *De officiis* 3.5.22, 32.

31 Theophylact *Expos in Eph* (on 4:16) PG 124 1089B–C mentions as an example that 'the hand torn from the body could not have feeling.'

32 'Metaphors': *involucris*. On this word as 'wrappings,' see above n21. Cf Jerome *Comm in Eph* II §620 (on 4:16) PL 26 503–4 / Heine 181, who comments that the ideas expressed metaphorically in the Greek cannot be literally translated into Latin. Modern scholars similarly find the diction and syntax of 4:16 difficult because of syntactical ambiguity and confusion of images from the realms of architecture, the physiology of the head and body, and marriage. See Barth *Ephesians* I 445–51.

33 'Dogmas': *dogmatum*. Erasmus speaks here of dogmas, not *doctrina* 'teaching.' Cf Erasmus' account of 'dogma' in *Detectio praestigiarum* ASD IX-1:575–83:
There are three kinds of dogmas. The first is the class of those that the Catholic church holds without controversy and with widespread consensus, the sort that are explicitly contained in Holy Scripture and in the Apostles' Creed. To these I would allow to be joined those that are decreed in councils

you belonged to the gentiles you were consistent with their breed; now other behaviour becomes you since you have been changed and born again into Christ. The gentiles, since they have not grasped the truth of the gospel, are led by groundless opinions, worshipping dumb idols[34] in place of God and measuring happiness by the transitory goods of this world. Indeed, they worship dead things and gape with longing upon things about to perish for this reason, that they do not know the real and eternal life which is God.[35] And since he cannot be perceived except by the purified eyes of the soul, he is not, therefore, perceived by those people who have a heart darkened, or rather blinded, by the shadows of evil desires and the clouds of distrust.[36] Abandoned to their own vices, at last they have come to such a depth of evil that, as if despairing of a return to a more honourable life and rendered deaf to the clamour of their own unhappiness,[37] they have hurled themselves into every kind of wickedness with an insatiable lust to

* * * * *

duly convoked and conducted. The second is the class of those on which the authority of the church has not yet made a clear pronouncement and about which theologians are still debating among themselves. The third is the class of those that are palmed off onto us as oracles of the church, although they are the opinions of men, frequently very conducive to quarrels and disagreements, very little or not at all to piety.
In this paraphrase on 4:17 'dogmas' appear to be understood as articles of the faith: the content of core beliefs. On the other hand, 'doctrine' in the *Paraphrases* generally implies the active 'teaching' that is the work of a preacher or teacher. Cf eg the paraphrase on 1 Tim 1:2 CWE 44 5: 'Timothy ... so resembles and reflects his parent in the constancy and sincerity of his faith and in the purity of his evangelical doctrine.'

34 Cf 1 Cor 12:2: 'When you were gentiles you went to dumb idols according as you were led' (Conf).

35 Cf 1 John 5:20: 'He is the true God and eternal life' (Conf). On pagan gods characterized in early Christian apologetic as lifeless statues and dead men, see Erasmus' paraphrase on Acts 14:14 CWE 50 92 with n18.

36 Erasmus' paraphrase suggests personal responsibility for the darkness in which the unconverted walk. Cf Jerome *Comm in Eph* II §621 (on 4:17–19) PL 26 505 / Heine 184, who notes the implications of the clause 'they have given themselves up' (Conf): 'No one is called ignorant and "blind," except one who has the possibility of knowing and seeing. We do not say that a stone is "blind" and that a brute animal is ignorant, for we do not look for such things in them nor does it belong to the nature of the one to know or to the other to see.'

37 unhappiness] In all editions from 1520 to 1538; in *1540* and LB 'happiness.' Cf Erasmus' annotation on 4:19 (*qui desperantes semetipsos*), which acknowledges two possible meanings in this context for the Greek word ἀπηλγηκότες: *indolentes* 'they have become callous' (RSV) and *desperantes* 'despairing' (Vulgate, DV). The paraphrase includes both meanings.

perpetrate any and every shameless deed,[38] falling into forms of immorality that are repulsive even to name.[39]

But quite different from them is the gospel teaching from which you have learned not human and foolish opinions but Christ himself, the source and pattern of all innocence, if, that is, you have truly listened to him speaking from within[40] and have truly been taught through his Spirit to imitate carefully, to the best of your ability, what was truly in Jesus. That is to say, that just as he was guilty of no vice and now, victorious over death, enjoys a glorious immortality, so you, too, reborn into him, are to strip off the old man, who resembles in his evil and deadly appetites that first progenitor; and now,[41] grafted through baptism onto the new man, Christ, you, too, are to be renewed with him. This renewal is, in fact, not according to the body, but according to the mind, the realm into which, above all, the Spirit of Christ leads.[42] And indeed, after setting aside the decrepitude[43] of your former life, you are to clothe yourself with the new man who in some spiritual manner has recently been fashioned[44] in

* * * * *

38 This passage echoes two themes common in Erasmus. 1/ Moral blindness is voluntary – an unwillingness to believe. Cf the paraphrase on John 16:8–11 CWE 46 185–7, and n36 above. 2/ God allows people to plunge themselves into dreadful sins. Cf the paraphrase on Rom 1:21–32 CWE 42 18: 'He has allowed them to rush headlong into the gratification of the desires of their own hearts ... he has allowed these to sink into filthy and shameful desires ... God has allowed them, blinded by their own darkness, to turn aside into a false way of thought.' Cf CWE 50 56 n1 on wilful perversity. For 'blindness' elsewhere in the *Paraphrases* see 'metaphors' in the General Index CWE 45 and CWE 50.

39 Erasmus' anticipates 5:3: 'But immorality and every uncleanness or covetousness, let it not even be named among you' (Conf). With the language of this paragraph, compare the paraphrase on Rom 1:20–8, a passage to which Jerome refers. See *Comm in Eph* II §620–1 (on 4:17–20) PL26 504 / Heine 182–3.

40 Cf Jerome *Comm in Eph* II §623 (on 4:20) PL 26 506 / Heine 186–7, who similarly notes that Christ himself sometimes speaks to us in our minds; the words that he pours forth are the Holy Spirit's. Erasmus deals with the interiority of the Spirit's teaching in his paraphrase on John 16:7 CWE 46 187.

41 and now] First in *1521*; 'but' in the editions of *1520*.

42 Cf Rom 12:2: 'Be transformed in the newness of your mind' (Conf).

43 'Decrepitude': *vetustate*. See OLD *vetustas* 3: 'age' as bringing destruction, wear, decay. Cf Jerome *Comm in Eph* II §624–5 (on 4:22) PL 26 507 / Heine 189: 'I think the old self, whom he directs to be put off, is called old [*inveteratum*] on the basis of wickedness. For that self, always erring and indulging in the work of corruption in accordance with his former manner of life and the desires of error, "is being corrupted" and violated.'

44 'Fashioned': *conditus*. The paraphrase evokes the creation story of Genesis 1–2. For the 'new creation,' see 2 Cor 5:17–18; Gal 6:15; Eph 2:10; Col 3:10. Jerome observes *Comm in Eph* II §627 (on 4:24) PL 26 509 / Heine 191 that the Greek

you by divine artistry. He has been fashioned, moreover, as if through a kind of metamorphosis, so that when injustice had been abolished its place would be taken by innocence, and when the uncleanness of human appetites had been removed its place would be taken by the holiness of evangelical truth.

Therefore, pursue this truth eagerly everywhere. Do not cheat each other with lying pretences; each one is to discern personally what is true and to deal in truth with his neighbour, mindful that we are all members of the same body so that now no one can harm another without at the same time harming himself. To be perfect is to be untouched by anger, but if on account of the frailty of human nature some outburst of anger seizes your soul, be mindful of what the holy Psalmist advises:[45] so restrain your anger when it longs to burst out, that it does not result in wrangling or injury or hatred. Let your anger not only do no harm, but let it also be short lived, the sort that leaves your hearts sooner than the sun the earth. When the earth, at the coming of night, has ceased to be torrid, you should not continue meanwhile to burn with wrath. Let harmony, by itself, make you safe against the scoffing of the devil; if it is torn apart by hatreds and mutual affronts, there will be laid open to the foe a fissure[46] through which he may burst in,[47] to your destruction. Against those who are of one mind he is feeble; against the divided, powerful. To him you will be giving a place if a place is given to hatred.

The person who, following the old way of life, used to plunder others by stealing should now not just abstain from what belongs to others, but even share personal resources voluntarily. If means are lacking he should not take it amiss to provide by the honest labour of his hands the wherewithal to assist a person in need.[48]

And it is not sufficient to have temperate hands unless the tongue, too, is blameless. An evil tongue tends to be destructive in various ways: it stains with off-colour talk, ruins reputations by disparagement, cuts throats

* * * * *

here implies a major work, like the creation of the world, or the founding of a city, rather than a minor one, like the building of a house.

45 Cf Ps 4:4 Vulgate (4:5); LB adds '[Ps. IV]' here.

46 fissure] *rima*, first in 1521; previously *ruina* 'collapse'; perhaps a printer's error.

47 'Burst in': *irrumpat*. Cf Jerome *Comm in Eph* II §630 (on 4:27) PL 26 511 / Heine 196, who, alluding to 1 Pet 5:8, likens the adversary to a roaring lion seeking a place through which he can 'burst in' (*irrumpere*).

48 Cf the paraphrase on 2 Thess 3:8–12, where Paul becomes an emphatic example of the admonition given here.

with denunciations, deceives by falsehood and perjury.[49] Accordingly, let no evil conversation proceed from your mouth. Speech is the mind's reflection. If you are of pure mind it is unsuitable for impure talk to come out.[50] It is not enough that the conversation of a Christian person be harmless; no, it should be the sort that, produced[51] at the proper time and occasion, brings fruit to the hearers.

If you act otherwise, it is not only humans you will offend with your useless, unseasonable, or harmful conversation, but also the Holy Spirit of God, who dwells in Christian minds. By the Spirit your souls and your bodies have been sealed, so to speak, for God. But it is fitting that you show this seal, clear and undamaged on the day when, set apart from the herd of evil doers, you accept the reward of your innocence.[52] Moreover, this Spirit is offended and put to flight by all vileness and permits no dealings with anger, with vengeance, with obscenity. It is peaceful, kind, and beneficent; if you have truly drunk it in, all bitterness, insolence, and ferocity should be far removed from your character. Wrathfulness, shouting, wrangling should be so far removed that there remains in your soul no leaven of the malice from which these evils generally grow.[53] Instead you are to be affable with one another, good-natured, and inclined towards compassion, mutually forgiving, and pardoning[54] one another, if some offence is

* * * * *

49 deceives by falsehood and perjury] First in 1532; previously 'deceives by falsehood and even commits perjury.' For Erasmus' views on sins of the tongue, see also the paraphrases on James 3:3–10 CWE 44 154–7 and Acts 2:3 CWE 50 14 with n17, and see especially *Lingua* CWE 29 315–67.

50 Cf Luke 6:45.

51 'Produced': *depromptus*, a word sometimes associated with good wine brought out on a special occasion for the *fructus* 'enjoyment' and 'profit' of the company. Cf eg Horace *Odes* 1.9.7 and 3.21.8.

52 For the separation of evildoers on the Day of Judgment, see Matt 25:32–3. On the character of the seal, cf Jerome *Comm in Eph* II §632 (on 4:30) PL 26 514 / Heine 200: 'He . . . who is sealed is sealed so that he may preserve the seal and show it pure, genuine, and unmutilated on the day of redemption and on that account be considered worthy to be numbered with those who have been redeemed.' A wax seal imprinted with a distinctive and recognized signet guaranteed in ancient Rome the authenticity of significant documents: for financial agreements, see Pliny *Naturalis historia* 33.6.28; for marriage contracts, see Juvenal 2.119; for letters or official communications, see Cicero *In Catilinam* 3.5.10. For a discussion of whether sacrament or seal is meant in Eph 1:13–14 and 4:30, see Barth *Ephesians* I 135–43.

53 For the 'leaven of malice,' see 1 Cor 5:8.

54 In his paraphrase on 4:32, Erasmus follows an exegetical tradition that understood the Greek χαριζόμενοι (Vulgate *donantes*) as 'forgiving' 'pardoning'; so

committed through error and human frailty; pardoning, I repeat, on account of Christ, since once and for all, through Christ, God has forgiven you all your transgressions. Indeed on this condition has the Lord forgiven his servants: that following his own example[55] we[56] in turn should pardon our fellow servants.[57] For harmony can last among mortals only if they put up with one another in their human faults.

Chapter 5

Well then, since through the Holy Spirit you are sons of God, see that you resemble your parent by the holiness of your life[1] so that you may be worthy of his constant love. For thus he will preserve a constant love towards you, if you preserve mutual love with one another. The extent of the Father's love towards us has been revealed by his Son, who loved us so dearly that not only did he freely forgive all sins, but he even laid himself open to the punishment of the cross so that by this sacrifice and by a victim with a fragrance truly pleasing to God the Father,[2] the Father although

* * * * *

Ambrosiaster *Comm in Eph* (on 4:32) CSEL 81/3 109:11–18; Theophylact *Expos in Eph* (on 4:32) PG 124 1101A; Nicholas of Lyra (on 4:32). But as his annotation on 4:32 (*donantes invicem*) indicates; Erasmus preferred an explanation of Jerome *Comm in Eph* III §639 (on 5:1) PL 26 518/Heine 208: 'We too pour forth our goodness on all persons,' and so his translation reads *largientes* 'giving generously.'

55 'Following Christ' is a key element in Erasmus' spirituality. See eg the paraphrases on John 13:15 CWE 46 163; 1 Cor 11:1; Phil 2:5–11 and 3:17–21; 1 Pet 2:21 CWE 44 93. See also the 'sixth rule' in the *Enchiridion* CWE 66 84: '[The Christian's] model of piety should be Christ alone and no other.

56 we] First in *1521*; previously, 'we fellow servants': 'we fellow servants in turn should pardon our fellow servants.' In his annotation on 4:32 (*donavit vobis*) Erasmus advocated a change from the Vulgate 'you' to 'us' although his Greek codices were divided. See Metzger 538 in support of 'you.'

57 Cf Matt 18:23–35; the parable of the unforgiving fellow slave is introduced into the interpretation by Ambrosiaster *Comm in Eph* (on 4:32) CSEL 81/3 109:16–18.

1 For the importance of the parent-child resemblance, see the paraphrase on Phil 2:15: 'You are to be ... in your behaviour so pure and blameless that no one can rightly complain about you, and that it will be evident to all that you are not bastards or counterfeits, but truly sons of God resembling your heavenly Father by your heavenly life.' See also the paraphrases on 1 Tim 1:2 CWE 44 5 and John 8:37 CWE 46 115 with nn60 and 61. Cf 1 Cor chapter 4 n31.

2 Although the English translation is not affected, the order of words was changed: *victimaque fragrantiae vere suavis apud deum patrem* first in *1521*; previously *victimaque vere suavis apud deum patrem fragrantiae*.

formerly displeased might be reconciled to us and favourably inclined once
again. If, as is fitting, we emulate this love, not only will we be good-
natured, if any fault is committed against us, but also, for the welfare of
our neighbour (if matters come to such a pass), we will not hesitate to risk
our life.[3]

But now, what need is there to deter you from those filthier and grosser
vices,[4] I mean, dealing with prostitutes and anything else that is base; likewise, the insatiable attachment to money. Christian behaviour should be so
far removed from such monstrosities[5] that it is disgraceful for Christians
even to name them. There are certain matters so detestable that a disposition pure and chaste shrinks even from mentioning them.

But for the saints it is fitting not only that their life be pure and free
from all foulness, but that they also have a mouth that is chaste and pure.
Nor should we think it sufficient for life and speech to be free from foulness, unless in our conversation we shrink from stories that are foolish as
well as[6] frivolous, and from inane jokes as well as witticisms.[7] Although

* * * * *

3 Cf Erasmus' paraphrase on John 3:16 CWE 46 48–9; also Nicholas of Lyra (on
   5:2), who comments that, since Christ has handed himself over for us, so should
   we, when necessary, lay down our lives for the salvation of our brothers.
4 'Grosser vices': *crassioribus vitiis*. On 'vice' in Erasmus' paraphrases, see CWE
   44 141 n16.
5 Cf Nicholas of Lyra (on 5:3): 'from such actions you are to be distanced.'
6 as well as] *ac*, first in *1521*; previously 'and.' The change improves the style,
   making this and the following phrases parallel.
7 Social graces in the teacher that increase the attractiveness of the gospel teaching are endorsed by Erasmus, eg in his paraphrase on Col 4:5–6. Witticisms,
   however, and frivolous tales that serve merely to display the speaker's brilliance he considers a species of self-indulgence for which a true Christian has
   no time. See the paraphrases on 1 Tim 1:6–7 CWE 44 8 and James 3 CWE 44 153–
   60, especially 155 n6. See also, on the Christian use of the tongue, *Lingua* CWE
   29 402–12. Erasmus (who was himself a wit) explicates the text of this passage
   in his annotation on 5:4 (*aut scurrilitas*). He says, 'I for my part allow jokes,
   provided that they are learned and seasoned with salt [*sal* 'salt' or 'wit'].' He
   finds particularly offensive what he has seen some monks or priests doing,
   ie twisting the words of Sacred Scripture and hymns of the liturgy to make
   a clever or offensive point in order to seem smart and sophisticated.For an
   example of a monk twisting the words of the liturgy in an obscene manner,
   see the account of an incident Erasmus witnessed in Italy reported in *Lingua*
   CWE 29 392–3. See also the further annotation on 5:4 (*quae ad rem non pertinent*),
   where Erasmus adumbrates his notion of the kind of joking appropriate to the
   servant of Christ. Jerome *Comm in Eph* III §641 (on 5:4) PL 26 520 / Heine 211–
   12 thinks jokes that have no other purpose than to raise a laugh are unworthy
   of Christians.

these may be tolerated in others or even praised,[8] certainly they are inappropriate for Christians as they hasten towards heaven, engaged in a constant war with vices, a war so dangerous that there is no leisure to indulge in jesting and similar[9] nonsense. There should be weeping[10] instead or, if a soul must be glad on account of some prosperous issue, the gladness should be expressed in hymns with which we give thanks to God.[11]

But it is no secret to me that there are philosophers who teach that sexual intimacy[12] outside of marriage is not a shameful act since it is not punished by human laws;[13] that attachment to money is not a crime since

* * * * *

8 Aristotle eg in *Nicomachean Ethics* 1128a1–33 praises appropriate social grace including playful conversation.

9 similar] First in *1521*; previously 'scurrilous.' The change connotes an increased emphasis on the notion that one must render an account for every idle word, not merely for words that are inherently wicked. Ambrosiaster *Comm in Eph* (on 5:4) CSEL 81/3 111:26–8 cites Matt 12:36.

10 There is no mention of weeping in the text Erasmus is paraphrasing, but see Jerome *Comm in Eph* III §641 (on 5:4) PL26 520 / Heine 212: 'For holy men ... weeping and mourning are more appropriate.' Cf also Theophylact *Expos in Eph* (on 5:4) PG124 1104C–D: 'But if you want to say something, let your every word be thanksgiving; and if you grow accustomed to giving thanks, you will remember the extent to which you have been changed, grieve over your sins, and be astounded at the one who has valued you so much; and you will have no time to say anything else.'

11 These last two clauses are a paraphrase on the words, 'but rather thanksgiving' (5:4 Conf). On 'hymns,' see Erasmus' annotation on 5:19 (*in psalmis*) which notes praise as the distinguishing feature of hymns. Cf the interlinear *Gloss* (on 5:19). See also the paraphrases on Acts 16:25 CWE 50 103–4 with n41 and Col 3:16, where the hymn singers are described as *hilares* 'cheerful.'

12 'Sexual intimacy': *veneris usum*. The Latin is a euphemism for sexual love. In some editions both *Venus* and *Pecunia* 'money' in the following clause have initial capitals, as though both are to be regarded as idols. Cf Luke 16:13, 'You cannot serve God and Mammon.'

13 In his paraphrase on Acts 15:20 CWE 50 98 (cf n48), Erasmus explains that the prohibition against fornication arose because 'certain people do not think it a sin since it is commonly done and is not punished by human laws.' The 'philosophers' to whom Erasmus refers here in the paraphrase on Eph 5:3 may include the 'Cynic philosopher' and those 'sages' who agreed with his 'filthy and shameful heresy' mentioned by Jerome *Comm in Eph* III §640 (on 5:3–4) PL 26 519 / Heine 209. Erasmus comments on the moral philosophy of the Stoics and Peripatetics in the *Enchiridion* CWE 66 44, acknowledging their view that 'we must live according to reason and not according to the passions.' See also Juha Sihvola 'Aristotle on Sex and Love' in *The Sleep of Reason: Erotic Experience and Sexual Ethics in Ancient Greece and Rome* ed Martha C. Nussbaum and Juha Sihvola (Chicago 2002) 200–21. On the latitude afforded Greek and

there is no penalty for this evil.[14] However, I want you to know this: that whoever runs after prostitutes, or is stained by any other sort of lust, or is given up to avarice, since he places the main defence of his happiness in a mute manufactured object, is not very far from the worship of idols.[15] That person will not be admitted to the inheritance of immortal life which God has promised to his own to share with Christ. If this penalty seems light to you, believe those people who are trying to persuade you that these are slight sins! Do not allow yourselves to be cheated by empty and frivolous conversations of that sort; rather give ear to the gospel's teaching, since indeed, even if they are not punished[16] by human laws on account of vices of this kind, still, the divine vengeance is wont to rage against disobedient sons who, having lost confidence in the Father's promises, place the defence of their happiness in things of this kind.

When you professed Christ you removed yourselves once and for all from such dealings with people. You must take care, then, that your life does not match the vices of those whose profession is at variance with their mode of life.[17] Until now the world has wandered in the shadows of ignorance

* * * * *

Roman men to engage in sexual activity beyond marriage see Kathy L. Gaca *The Making of Fornication: Eros, Ethics, and Political Reform in Greek Philosophy and Early Christianity* (Berkeley 2003) 97 n8. For discussion of the second century transformation of ancient philosophical principles in the light of Pauline doctrine under the influence of Tatian, Clement, and Epiphanes, see Gaca ibidem 221–91.

14 The ancients saw excessive attachment to wealth as *stultitia* 'folly' if not crime. On 'meanness,' see Aristotle *Nicomachaean Ethics* 1121b37–1122a15; on 'sponging,' 'pennypinching,' and 'chiselling' see Theophrastus *Characters* 9, 10, 30; on 'love of wealth,' see Plutarch *Moralia* 523C–528B. The *avarus* 'miser' was often the butt of satire. See eg Horace *Satires* 2.3.82–159, which purports (2.3.44) to be a lecture on Stoic dogma derived from the philosopher Chrysippus.

15 Cf Jerome *Comm in Eph* III §643 (on 5:5) PL 26 521 / Heine 214–15 who reports that both avarice and fornication are called idolatry. Ambrosiaster *Comm in Eph* (on 5:5) CSEL 81/3 112:14–113:1 offers a detailed explanation of the similarity between avarice and idolatry. Theophylact *Expos in Eph* (on 5:5–6) PG 124 1105B notes that 'the more sophisticated Hellenes deny that they worship idols,' and yet 'the greedy person worships an object of his own making.' In *Explanatio symboli* CWE 70 365, Erasmus writes: 'Every crime is connected with idolatry.'

16 they are not punished] All editions from 1520 to 1540; LB alone has the present subjunctive *puniantur* 'they may not be punished.'

17 Occasionally, as here, *professio* 'profession' can be taken in the *Paraphrases* as referring to the promises or vows of a monk or religious. The contrast between profession and behaviour is familiar in pagan and Christian antiquity. Cf Tertullian *Apologeticum* 46 CCL 1 160–2. It is also a contrast Erasmus makes

that have all been dispersed by the truth of the gospel which has dawned; you too once used to dwell in the night and perform shameful deeds by night.[18] Now, through the gospel's light, God has illumined your mind so that you now perceive how detestable are the practices that previously seemed sweet. Night has no sense of decency and it covers over many deeds that no one would have the audacity to do in broad daylight.

Therefore, arrange all your life so as to remember that you are living in the light, always visible to the eyes of God. The person who journeys by night frequently stumbles[19] for he does not perceive what he ought to avoid. Light has[20] this effect: that it indicates what should be followed, what avoided. It shows us that everywhere we must avoid malice, abuse, and pretence, and in place of these we must pursue goodness, justice, and truth, and, in general, always have an eye to this: not what pleases people, not what is sweet or what is expedient for ourselves, but what is acceptable to the divine will at whose nod[21] all our life is to be governed. He is the source of our light. By always clinging to him you will be available for the duties of piety, duties that are fruitful, honourable, and worthy of the light. After this you will be ashamed to be associated with the fruitless works of darkness.

* * * * *

in relation to Christians of his own day, especially to the monks, eg in his criticisms of some of them, evidently Dominicans and Carmelites, in the dedicatory letter to Cardinal Campeggi: 'They do not stop to reflect that, while they profess Christ's teaching, as they do, their attacks on the reputation of those who do them good service, or who at least strive to do so, are diametrically opposed to their professions.' For the identification of the monks, see the dedicatory letter nn57 and 66, and Ep 1167:39–54. For criticism of monks see *Moria* CWE 27 130–5; Ep 858:530–611; *De contemptu mundi* CWE 66 172–5. On 'profession' in the *Paraphrases*, see 1 Cor chapter 1 n8.

18 Cf 1 Thess 5:4–8; Rom 13:11–13; and Erasmus' annotation on Romans 13:12 ('the night has preceded') CWE 56 359–61. This paraphrase on 5:8 clarifies the metaphorical nature of the light/darkness imagery as does Jerome *Comm in Eph* III §645 (on 5:8) PL26 523 / Heine 218–9. Ambrosiaster *Comm in Eph* (on 5:8) CSEL 81/3 113:20–2 suggests that Paul refers to the mystery rites celebrated by pagans in a cave with their eyes covered.

19 Cf John 11:9–10.

20 Light has] In editions from 1520 to 1538; *1540* and LB read *enim* 'For light has.' Bateman notes that *enim* 'for' 'changes the apodictic statement into an explanation of what it means to stumble in the night.' The author of the change is uncertain. See 'Textual Travail' 248–9.

21 'Nod': *nutum* is a classicizing touch. The word is used to symbolize the slightest indication of an authority figure's wishes (cf Horace *Satires* 2.2.6), the absolute power of Jupiter, and the terror which it inspires. Cf Virgil *Aeneid* 9.106.

Far from sinking back again into your former darkness, you should rather, by your light, expose and censure the shameful deeds those people perpetrate in their own darkness. Since they do not revere God, the deeds they commit, when night or secrecy has taken away their sense of decency, are too vile even to mention. As long as they sin and no light exposes them, they sin freely and with impunity. But when a light has appeared exposing these actions, then the vileness of the situation begins to be recognized. When their shame is exposed, they are changed for the better and are corrected, that is to say, night has been turned into day and the soul's blindness dispelled. But if your life is light, the perception of your innocence will make them ashamed of their foulness, and so it will come about that, stimulated by your chaste and moral behaviour, they will be awakened to innocence, if they see shining in you the light of Christ.[22]

Presumably that is what is meant by the prophecy: wake up, sleeper and arise from among the dead, and Christ will shed his light upon you.[23] It is a fatal sleep, or rather death, to be buried under the pleasures of this world and not to raise the eyes to real, eternal goods. They cannot otherwise wake up, they cannot otherwise be restored to life, unless Christ, breaking like dawn on their minds, dispels the thick darkness of ignorance.

You Ephesians, on the other hand, on whom Christ our sun[24] shines brightly, consider carefully again and again the ways in which you are to walk. Live now not like the gentiles, who on account of the blindness of their mind do not have a sense of what is honourable; live rather as befits those who truly discern evangelical doctrine; at the cost of all things make the most of your opportunity to obtain salvation. You must seize[25] salvation all

* * * * *

22 Cf Theophylact *Expos in Eph* (on 5:13) PG 124 1108C: 'If you are virtuous, the wicked will not be able to escape notice; for just as a thief will not enter when a lamp is lit so … when the light of your virtue shines, the wicked will be caught.'

23 LB inserts here a reference to Isaiah 60. In a *1535* addition to his annotation on 5:14 (*et illuminabit te*), Erasmus suggests that the Apostle here mingles words from Isaiah 60:1 with words that are his own. In another annotation on Eph 5:14 (*surge qui dormis*), Erasmus notes Jerome's view that this prophecy is not to be found in Sacred Scripture. Cf Jerome *Comm in Eph* III §648 (on 5:14) PL 26 525 / Heine 223.

24 Cf Jerome *Comm in Eph* III §650 (on 5:16) PL 26 527 / Heine 225: 'you Ephesians, on whom Christ, the sun of justice, has risen.'

25 The Latin verb *rapere* 'to seize' denotes violent action. Cf Matt 11:12: 'But from the days of John the Baptist until now the kingdom of heaven has been enduring violent assault and the violent have been seizing [Vulgate *rapiunt*] it by force' (Conf).

the more eagerly because this is a troubled age and from all sides there are many attacks that could drive away from the purity of Christian doctrine people who are heedless and not prudent enough. Therefore, you ought even more to pay attention lest through a lack of prudence you give the impious the occasion either for raging against the gospel themselves or for calling you aside from what you have professed. This is the sum total of your salvation, and on this point it is necessary for you to be prudent, turning a blind eye to all else and making it evident that you understand what the will of the Lord is. For he desires all to be led to evangelical salvation if it can be done.

For those who are pursuing this course sobriety is appropriate; drunkenness is senseless and improvident, and not only senseless, but even rash and hazardous. Therefore, do not be inebriated on undiluted wine (such inebriation pertains to overindulgence,[26] not to necessity), but be filled with the unfermented wine[27] of the Holy Spirit. For this is a happy inebriation,[28] the sort which goads you on, not to wanton dances, or to the silly little songs with which the gentiles call upon their demons[29] but to the psalms, the hymns, the spiritual canticles with which you express great joy among yourselves, which you sing, and in which you raise psalms to the Lord, not with the unbecoming shouts usual with intoxicated people, but inwardly,

* * * * *

26 Erasmus, in a long annotation on 5:18 (*in quo est luxuria*), insists that here ἀσωτία (Vulgate *luxuria*) refers to overindulgence particularly in food and drink, not to sexual sins. Cf 'debauchery' (RSV, Conf). He excoriates Aquinas who wrote that *luxuria* denoted primarily sexual sins and only secondarily other forms of indulgence. See *Super Eph lect* cap 5 lectio 7.307 (II 72). Cf Jerome *Comm in Eph* III §651 (on 5:18) PL 26 528 / Heine 227: 'One who is filled with wine possesses foolishness, rage, shamelessness, and lust.' Erasmus agrees with Theophylact *Expos in Eph* (on 5:18) PG 124 1112B that ἀσωτία is immoderation that has the capacity to destroy.

27 For the ancient Greeks and Romans *vinum* 'wine' was normally served mixed with water; *merum* 'undiluted wine' was a sign of extravagance (cf eg Horace *Odes* 1.9.8, 1.18.8, 2.14.26, 3.29.2); whereas *mustum* 'fresh, unfermented wine' was the drink available to the poor. Cf Acts 2:13: 'They are full of new wine' (*mustum* Vulgate).

28 For a picture of this 'happy inebriation,' see Erasmus' paraphrase on Acts 2:13–14 CWE 50 16–18.

29 Cf Theophylact *Expos in Eph* (on 5:19) PG 124 1112B: 'The psalm-singers are filled with the Holy Spirit just as the singers of satanic songs are filled with an unclean spirit.' For a description of the place of wine, dance, and song in pagan orgies, see Jasper Griffin 'Of Wines and Spirits' in *Latin Poets and Roman Life* (Chapel Hill 1986) 65–87; see also Apuleius *Metamorphoses* 11.3–4.

in your hearts and souls.[30] This is the pleasure, this the gladness,[31] this the revelling worthy of Christians. Let them not envy the gentiles on account of their drunken parties. Their drunken joys are followed by sadness and sometimes, too, by physical illness. Your pleasure is perennially fresh.

Whatever comes to you, whether happy or sorrowful (the happy from God who is gracious, the sorrowful from God who cares about your welfare), you must always give thanks for all things, certain that all that happens yields an increase of eternal happiness. Moreover, it is God who must be thanked, for he is the author of all good things for everyone, but he is also the Father and God of our Lord Jesus Christ, through whom he showers all things upon us; with him God wishes to share the praise that comes from all.

Christ subordinated himself to the Father; it is appropriate for us likewise to be subject to him, not because it is appropriate for one Christian to be the cause of dread to another Christian, but those who revere Christ on an equal footing are not reluctant to yield to each other since the one who is highest of all has lowered himself before all. Let the lower in rank recognize the authority of the higher. In turn let the higher adapt himself to the measure of the lower, so that he may be all the more able to be of service. I say this because among Christians the person who is superior in honour is not superior for any other reason except to be of more productive service.[32]

Let wives, therefore, recognize the authority of their husbands and be subject to them just as the church is subject to the Lord Jesus.[33] For just as Christ is the head of the church so is each husband the head of his own

* * * * *

30 Erasmus much preferred inward singing to the extravagances of contemporary church music and the expense of providing for the musicians. See his annotation on 1 Cor 14:19 (*quam decem milia*). For an extended treatment of Erasmus' comments on church music, see J-C. Margolin 'Erasme et la musique' in *Recherches érasmiennes* (Geneva 1969) 85–97.

31 gladness] All Froben editions from 1520 to 1534; *1538, 1540* and LB print *caritas* 'love,' probably by error. See Bateman 'Textual Travail' 249.

32 Cf Jerome *Comm in Eph* III §653–4 (on 5:21) PL 26 530 / Heine 231–2 (adapted): 'Let the bishops hear these words, let the priests hear them, let every order of teachers hear them: that they are subjects of their subjects . . . just as Christ was subject to his servants, so also these who appear to be greater are to be subject to their inferiors in doing the services that are appointed.'

33 Jesus] Added in *1532*. For marriage in the wider context of Erasmus' writings, see the introduction to *Institutio christiani matrimonii* CWE 69 203–13 and Payne *Theology* 109–25.

wife.[34] But just as the head has dominion over the body in such a way that the welfare of the body depends upon it, so the husband takes precedence over his wife not in such a manner as to exercise tyranny over her,[35] but to take thought for her well-being, doubtless being more prudent and more steadfast. And a wife ought not to rise up against her husband just because he shows himself lovable more than formidable. Rather, this is all the more reason why she should be subject to him in all things, just as the church has subjected itself to Christ – all the more as he lowered himself for the salvation of his betrothed.

In your turn, husbands, do not abuse your authority over your wives in tyrannical fashion. You are rather to bestow on them with that love that Christ has bestowed and continues to bestow on his church. So far was he from repudiating her as adulterous and rebellious that he surrendered himself to death to purchase her salvation, making the defiled pure and holy, the filthy and unclean attractive and pure, not reproaching her for her foulness but washing her in the wave of his blood and cleansing her with a life-giving bath by the efficacious invocation of the divine name. By this means, through his own kindness, he might prepare for himself a glorious spouse, namely, the church, which now would have neither spot nor wrinkle, nor anything else of the kind that could offend the spouse's eyes, but would be pure and blameless in all respects.

It is fitting for husbands to have a similar affection for their wives so that they will do everything to make them worthy of Christ, just as anxious for their well-being as the head is anxious for the well-being of the body, since, indeed, the wife is her husband's body. A wife is peevish, she is shameless or addicted to other faults; you are not to destroy her by your harshness, but with gentleness correct and cure. Cure the faults in such a way that you love your wife all the while. For what would the head do, if it were to perceive that its own body had some illness or fault? Would it begin to hate and to turn away or would it rather begin to cure, if it could; to bear and to cherish, if it could not cure? Would it not seem absurd for the head to wish ill to its own[36] body? Whoever loves his wife loves himself, seeing that she is a part of himself. Who was ever so insensitive to feeling that he considered his own body hateful? Who does not rather nourish and cherish his body to improve it and make it more vigorous, regardless of the

* * * * *

34 Cf 1 Cor 11:3.

35 Cf Theophylact *Expos in Eph* (on 5:25) PG 124 1116A: the husband 'is not to behave despotically.'

36 its own] All editions from 1520 to 1538; omitted in *1540* and LB

kind of body he was born with? This is effected in pagans by the force of nature; why does Christian love, the love that summons us to such care by the example of Christ, not accomplish this much more in you? He did not turn away his spouse, the church, although previously she was loathsome, indeed in many ways a prostitute, but he cleansed her, made amends for her, and strengthened her.

We are members of Christ's body, which is the church, just as a wife is the body of man from whose flesh and bones she was created. Therefore, husbands, offer your wives what Christ has offered to us, to make it evident that what is one and the same reality ought not to be torn apart. For so do we read in Genesis:[37] for his wife's sake a man shall leave father and mother more quickly than he would desert his own wife; to her he shall cleave in such a way that the two become one by the closest union of their bodies and their souls. After God, to no one do we owe more than to parents, and yet a wife is preferred to them.

There lies here some remarkable and ineffable secret:[38] how what happened in Adam and Eve typologically is mystically brought to completion in Christ and in the church.[39] Anyone who carefully examines the indivisible

* * * * *

37 Cf Gen 2:24; editions from 1532 to 1540 print 'Gene 2' as a marginal note; LB incorporates into the text 'Cap II.'

38 In his paraphrase on 5:32 Erasmus carefully avoids the Vulgate *sacramentum* for a number of reasons (see chapter 1 n27) and especially because of his opposition to the use of 5:32 as a proof text for marriage as a sacrament. He follows his translation in using the word *mysterium*, whose explication he offers in this sentence: an ineffable secret (*arcanum*), an Old Testament type completed in the saving events recorded in the New Testament. See his annotation on 5:32 (*sacramentum hoc*), where he does not deny that marriage is a sacrament, but intimates that it is the least of the sacraments, and argues that this passage in Ephesians does not offer grounds for calling it a sacrament. On the basis of his treatment of 5:32, both Lee and López Zúñiga accused Erasmus of denying that marriage was a sacrament. See *Responsio ad annotationes Lei* 2 (Concerning Note 188) CWE 72 296–303 where, in the course of a very long defence, Erasmus states (298): 'I believe that matrimony is a sacrament, not because it is called a mystery here [Eph 5:32], but because the church lists it among the seven.' See also *Apologiae contra Stunicam* (1) ASD IX-2 210–13, and *Apologia ad Caranzam* LB IX 429. On Erasmus' understanding of the dignity of marriage with special relevance to his paraphrase on Eph 5:32, see Pabel 'Exegesis and Marriage' 178–9.

39 Although the text of Ephesians 5 does not explicitly mention Adam and Eve, the allusion to Gen 2:24 (at Eph 5:31) justifies Erasmus' reference to the context of that passage. Erasmus interprets the Adam and Eve event 'typologically' *quod . . . sub typo gestum est*, ie he attempts to see in this event recorded

bond between them[40] will understand that a great mystery lies concealed in it. For just as he himself was one with the Father, so also he wished all his own to be one with him. Granted, this secret may be too concealed to be unfolded at present; nevertheless it is sufficient to have introduced an example for this end: that each may esteem his wife as he esteems himself and may remember that he and she are one and the same, just as Christ loved his church and joined her to himself most intimately. Moreover, the role of a wife will be not only to respond with love to her husband as her life's companion, but also to revere[41] him as pre-eminent in authority. Harmony will best be maintained if responsibilities are upheld on both sides.

Chapter 6

Authority should be tempered with love lest somehow it turn into tyranny and, again, weakness should be held in check by reverence lest it rise up into rebellion.[1] For no unanimity and tranquillity can exist when order has been thrown into confusion. Over his wife the husband alone has absolute power.[2]

* * * * *

in the Old Testament what was to transpire *mystice* 'mystically' in the New Testament. On this 'mystical sense' of Scripture, see 1 Cor chapters 5 n12 and 10 n4; 2 Cor Chapter 3 n19; and 1 Thess chapter 5 n18. On Adamic typology in Pauline Epistles, see Jean Daniélou *From Shadows to Reality: Studies in the Biblical Typology of the Fathers* trans W. Hibberd (London 1960) 11–21. See also the paraphrase on Rom 5:14 CWE 42 34.

40 'Between them': *huius*, literally 'of this.' The referent of the demonstrative is the bond between Christ and the church. Cf Jerome *Comm in Eph* III §661 (on 5:32) PL 26 535–6 / Heine 241.

41 'To revere': *revereri*. Cf Jerome *Comm in Eph* III §662 (on 5:33) PL 26 537 / Heine 243, who, in distinguishing among kinds of 'fear,' interprets the fear required of a woman towards her husband as that 'which the philosophers call εὐλάβεια [caution, discretion] and which we [ie Latin speakers] can call "reverence" [*reverentia*].'

1 Ephesians begins 'Children obey your parents.' To effect a smoother transition in the paraphrase, Erasmus inserts this generalizing paragraph linking the instruction on the husband-wife relationship (5:21–33) with precepts governing that between children and their parents. Erasmus insists elsewhere on gentleness in the exercise of authority if it is to be effective. See eg *De pueris instituendis* CWE 26 331: 'When corporal punishment is applied too harshly the more spirited children are driven to rebellion.'

2 'Absolute power': *imperium*. Erasmus distinguishes *imperium* from *auctoritas* 'authority,' the term used above and just below in the following sentence.

Children ought to recognize the authority of both parents.[3] In confor-
mity with this rule, therefore, you sons should be compliant and heed your
parents' bidding when they enjoin honourable things,[4] worthy of the profession of Christ. At the same time our natural sense of fairness also makes
this demand: that we show honour to those to whom we owe life's origin
and be grateful to those by whose kindness we have been nurtured and
reared. Finally, the law of God prescribes the same thing:[5] 'Show honour,'
it says, 'to your father and your mother' [Exod 20:12]. And it did not think
it enough to have instructed as in the other commandments: 'You shall not
kill, you shall not steal' [Exod 20:13, 15]; it added also a reward to enhance
the invitation to duty. In the other cases, good actions are to be done even
without recompense. But what reward does it promise? 'That it may be well
with you,' it says, 'that you may be long-lived on the earth'[6] [Exod 20:12],
since indeed it seems that a person is unworthy to enjoy a long life if he is
ungrateful and rebellious against those through whom he has received the
gift of life.

Fathers, on the other hand, you are not to abuse your power and the
obedience of your children, thinking that you can do anything you like
to them. They are sons, not slaves.[7] Let godliness mitigate your absolute
power. You must be careful lest, with the peevishness that comes from age,
either by your harsh commands or unrestrained severity you do not heal
them, but make them worse. If they commit any sin by reason of their
age, they are to be admonished in such a way that they are taught rather
than demoralized. Let the first of your concerns be so to form them from
their early years by your admonitions and training,[8] so to invite them by

* * * * *

3 Cf Theophylact *Expos in Eph* (on 6:1) PG 124 1120D who mentions that the
husband alone governs his wife, but the wife too governs the children.

4 Cf Theophylact *Expos in Eph* (on 6:1) PG 124 1121A who similarly interprets 'in
the Lord': 'when what they command you is in accordance with the Lord.'

5 Finally, the law of God prescribes the same thing] First in *1532*; previously
'and the law of God prescribes'

6 Erasmus quotes from the Vulgate with minor adjustments. The translation of
the quotations in this paragraph is Conf (slightly modified).

7 Cf Jerome *Comm in Eph* III §666 (on 6:4) PL 26 540 / Heine 247: 'It is their
children whom they command and not their slaves.'

8 The Vulgate had translated the Greek ἐν παιδείᾳ καὶ νουθεσίᾳ (6:4) *in disciplina
et correptione* 'in discipline and correction' (DV). Jerome *Comm in Eph* III §666
(on 6:4) PL 26 540 / Heine 248 observed that νουθεσία should be understood
as *eruditio* 'education' and *admonitio* 'admonition' rather than *austeritas* 'severity.' The paraphrase reflects Jerome's comments, as does the annotation on 6:4
(*in disciplina et correptione*), where Erasmus defines the two Greek words as,
respectively, 'training' and 'admonition.'

examples of your piety, that it will be evident that they have been reared by Christian parents according to the teaching of Christ. For if they are taught, not merely forced, they will be guided to the good more swiftly than by threats or harshness.

Slaves, show that you have been improved as a result of your profession of the gospel and made more agreeable. The service that others provide for the masters[9] to whom they are subject in accordance with their transitory condition of servitude, do you provide in far greater measure. For baptism ought not to effect this for you, that you cease to serve, but that you serve more conscientiously; or this, that you wish to disdain your masters inasmuch as they have now become brothers by your profession, but that you revere them more for this very reason and fear to cause them offence. And you should not (as the common run of slaves does)[10] do your duty through fear, mentally cursing them and laying traps for them,[11] but you should be obedient to them with a simple and sincere heart, silently considering the fact that you are providing this service to Christ whose will you obey, if, perhaps, they do not deserve your obedience. Thus it will happen that you will differ from the common run of slaves, who comply with their masters when they are present, through fear of punishment, but again, when they hope to escape notice, revert to their natural disposition. Indeed, this is to

* * * * *

9 Although in the *Paraphrases* Erasmus generally uses the Vulgate's *dominus* 'master,' he occasionally uses *herus*, also 'master,' eg twice in the paraphrase on Ephesians 6 and several times in the parallel passage in Colossians (3:22–5). The connotation of *herus* is more limited than that of *dominus*: *herus* implies a master-slave relationship, while *dominus* suggests a much broader range of proprietorship and authority. In Erasmus' society *dominus* 'lord' or 'master' was used as a common noun to designate the powerful both in church and state. For Erasmus, the slave-master relationship is to be understood in terms of the relationship of the human master to the Lord from whom all authority comes. For the master as fellow slave, see the paraphrase on Col 4:1 with n4.

10 Cf Theopylact *Expos in Eph* (on 6:5) PG 124 1124B–C, who notes that many slaves fear their masters but whenever they are out of sight they plot against them and wrong them.

11 See also Erasmus' paraphrase on Col 3:22–5. Conditions of slavery in ancient Rome are reflected in legislative arrangements (see Alan Watson *Roman Slave Law* [Baltimore 1987]) and in Roman comedy (see George E. Duckworth *The Nature of Roman Comedy: A Study in Popular Entertainment* [Princeton 1952] 249–53). On slavery in Roman society, see also 1 Cor chapter 7 n45. For a discussion of the context of the domestic rules regarding slavery in Eph 6:5–9 and Col 3:2–4:1, see J. Albert Harrill *Slaves in the New Testament: Literary, Social and Moral Dimensions* (Minneapolis 2006) 87–117.

serve for the sake of appearances, not from the heart; this to want to please men, not Christ, for whom nothing is pleasing that is falsified or forced. But, as is suitable for Christ's slaves, in services towards your masters you should be obedient from your heart in good faith and conscientious, not because necessity compels, but because the divine will is thereby pleased.

Nor should you be turned aside from your duty if you have capricious or wicked masters. It is expedient for the work of the gospel that you be obedient to them, too, provided that compliance does not border on wickedness. Consider that you are offering to Christ what you offer to them for the gospel's sake; that you are paying to God, not men, what you are paying to men for the love of God,[12] because if you gain them for Christ by your compliance, your service will be rightly invested.[13] But if they show themselves ungrateful, understand nevertheless that no one loses the reward for his good deeds.[14] If anyone – not just a slave but a free man too – does not receive a reward from men, certainly he will receive it at some time from the Lord if, with good intent, he has invested any service with an ungrateful person.

Furthermore, just as it is fitting that slaves who have professed Christ show themselves more agreeable towards their masters,[15] so it is right that Christian masters should be gentler in governing their slaves and show that they are the sort to be loved rather than feared;[16] that from their heart they are benevolent towards their slaves received now into the fellowship of brothers, and are not on the brink of threats and floggings,[17] as is commonly the case with masters. Let the slaves feel that you have become gentler through the gospel, so that they, too, may be the more attracted to the profession we share, if, perhaps, they have not yet made their profession.

* * * * *

12 See the account of the Last Judgment (Matt 25:31–46) and Erasmus' paraphrase, especially on Matt 25:40, where the language of commerce is clear: *quiquid unicuilibet fuerit impensum* 'whatever has been expended on anyone' CWE 45 339.
13 'Invested': *collocatum* continues the commercial language of the preceding verb, 'paying.' Cf the paraphrase on 1 Cor 9:17–18.
14 loses the reward for his good deeds] First in *1521*. The 1520 editions print 'loses his reward for good deeds.'
15 'Masters': *heris*
16 See also Erasmus' paraphrase on Col 4:1.
17 Erasmus' interpretation (*praecipites ad minas ac verbera* 'on the brink of threats and floggings') is close to that of Jerome *Comm in Eph* III §669 (on 6:9) PL 26 542 / Heine 251: *promptus ad verbera* 'quick to flog.' Erasmus' language is more vivid.

Remember that a master's power is something transitory and indeed a matter of human right which, still, for the time being, should not be upset by us. Just the same, with God there is no consideration of persons; with him no one is of less value because he is subject to slavery, nor greater because he was born of free parents. According to human laws, you have, while on earth, the right of a master over slaves, but in the meanwhile you share a Lord in heaven, none the less.[18] His will is that you care for the well-being of slaves through a temperate exercise of authority, not oppress them by despotic rule.

The advice we have given thus far has this as its object: that you correspond to your head, Christ, in holiness of life and that you agree with one another in mutual harmony.[19]

Now for the rest, fortify yourselves with a courageous and unbroken spirit against the ungodly since they assail your peace by various stratagems.[20] Rely not at all on your own defences but on your champion, the Lord Jesus, who will not desert his own body. The members indeed are feeble, but the one who has taken us under his protection is powerful and strong. From him, therefore, request the spiritual panoply, so that, fortified on every front, you may be able to stand firm against the assaults of the devil. For we do not have a war with human beings whose injuries must be overcome by endurance. No, our struggle is with wicked spirits, enemies and foes of Christ; it is their accomplices and instruments who are attacking us. Through them, principalities and demonic powers are besieging us from on high, seizing for themselves a tyranny over those who are enslaved to this world's vices and laying traps in this present dark-

* * * * *

18 With regard to the ethics of slavery, see Erasmus' annotation on Eph 6:7 (*cum bona voluntate*):

> He [Paul] wishes the Christian slave through love of Christ to serve his master faithfully, just as he wants Christian citizens to obey the commands of idolatrous princes. And if it is not right for slaves to demand that [Mosaic] liberty, still it seems unchristian for Christian masters not to grant to their slaves what that [Mosaic] law, far harsher than the law of Christ, concedes to its own [that all slaves be manumitted every seventh year]. On the contrary, it seems a shame for the word 'master' or 'slave' to be heard at all among Christians. Since baptism makes everyone brothers, how is it right for a brother to be called a 'slave' to a brother?

19 With this brief summary, Erasmus concludes his paraphrase on household relationships advised in 5:21–6:9.

20 'Stratagems': *machinis*. Theophylact *Expos in Eph* (on 6:11) PG 124 1128A–B observes: 'See how it does not say "battles" or "wars," but μεθοδείας "wiles," whose characteristic is to deceive and to capture διὰ μηχανῆς "by stratagems."'

ness for people who love the gospel's light.[21] Against these, I repeat, we must wrestle, for they are not only powerful in their strength, but they are also equipped with a spiritual cunning, and this too in the region of heaven, to make it easier for them to attack us and harder for us to get a hold on them.

Against this kind of enemy, human weapons are of no use; only with the weapons of God will protection[22] be granted. Accordingly, always do what energetic soldiers generally do in dealing with a dangerous enemy whenever a conflict with adversaries erupts. Fortify yourselves with every kind of armour;[23] do everything to enable you to protect your position when a terrible battle breaks out and to stand firm and immovable on the solid rock,[24] Christ. When soldiers are about to contend with a man, they first cover themselves on every side so that they are nowhere exposed to the shafts of the enemy. Then they prepare to strike the assailant. They cover the middle of the body with a girdle interlaced with metal strips, since the midriff is rather vulnerable. They reinforce the upper parts with a breastplate. They protect their calves as well as their feet with greaves.[25] They enclose[26] their head in a helmet. In addition, on their left side, a shield is wielded against every assault of weapons.

For you, therefore, as you constantly contend with wicked spirits in a spiritual war, let truth be the girdle that encircles the loins of your mind,[27] so that you may always stand upright and immovable against all

* * * * *

21 Cf the paraphrase on Rom 8:38–9 CWE 42 52.
22 Cf in the preceding paragraph, 'the one who has taken us under his protection.' In both sentences, Erasmus uses forms of the verb *tueri* 'to protect.'
23 Erasmus gives an extended treatment of the spiritual armour in his *Enchiridion* CWE 66 30–46.
24 Cf Jerome *Comm in Eph* III §677 (on 6:13) PL 26 549–50 / Heine 262 (adapted): 'Let him know that he can then "stand firm" if, full of all virtues, he has "done everything" to plant his feet firmly and not be moved from the battle line ... as the Psalmist says: "He has set my feet upon a rock"' (cf Ps 39:3 DV/40:2 RSV). For Christ, the rock, cf 1 Cor 10:4.
25 with greaves] Added in 1532
26 they enclose] First in 1521; previously *tegunt* 'they cover,' probably for the sake of variation, since the latter verb had already been used twice in this paragraph
27 'Loins of your mind': *lumbos animi vestri*. For the paraphrastic qualification 'of your mind,' see 1 Pet 1:13 'loins of your understanding' (Conf). Cf Theophylact *Expos in Eph* (on 6:14) PG 124 1129D: 'But by "loins" he means "strength of mind" and the power to endure everything.'

the enticements of false goods and false doctrines.[28] In place of a breast-plate may you have innocence and justice to fortify the heart of your under-standing[29] with the scales[30] of all the virtues. In place of greaves to cover your calves and feet may you have a pure affection, seeking nothing but heavenly things, fearing nothing but what is vile, so that you can always be prepared to protect the gospel which is defended, not by violence, but by endurance and tranquillity. Whence it is also named the gospel of peace.[31] Its preachers have the beautiful feet once marvelled at by the prophet.[32] But the shield of faith is to be held at the ready everywhere to keep us from distrusting in the slightest the divine promises. Any terrors that attack will be intercepted by it, any fiery missiles the wily foe hurls against us will be repelled by this shield[33] and it will not allow anything to penetrate the vitals.[34] For what would wound a soul that despises even death? If there be added to it the helmet of a mind that is watchful and anticipates everything, there is no reason for you to fear for your salvation. Finally, let your right

* * * * *

28 For Erasmus' understanding of Christ as the one true good, see eg the 'fourth rule' in the *Enchiridion* CWE 66 61–5. Cf also the paraphrase on 1 Pet 1:2 CWE 44 82: 'I shall not pray for the goods whose acquisition and accumulation make the worshippers of this world think they are happy, but rather for those goods which make us worthy of Christ ... These goods are grace ... and secondly, peace.'

29 'The heart of your understanding': *mentis praecordia.* Cf Ovid *Metamorphoses* 11.149. Technically the *praecordia* are the parts of the body immediately below the heart, more generally the whole chest, corresponding to the vulnerable sec-tion which would be covered by the breastplate of an armour-clad soldier. In *Lingua* CWE 29 266 Erasmus comments: 'We need not investigate here whether the seat of the human mind is in the brain or the heart, because their re-lationship is so close that if one is damaged the other instantly fails.' In the *Enchiridion* CWE 66 43 Erasmus recalls Plato who wrote 'with divinely inspired knowledge,' assigning physical locations to reason (in the brain); to passions like courage and wrath (between the brain and the midriff); to appetites for food, drink, and sex (below the midriff near the liver and belly). Cf *Timaeus* 69C–75C.

30 Erasmus is thinking of the overlapping pieces of metal plate used in the con-struction of scale armour.

31 For a fuller treatment of the gospel of peace by Erasmus, see *Querela pacis* CWE 27 293–322.

32 See Isa 52:7 quoted in Rom 10:15, and Erasmus' paraphrase on the Romans passage CWE 42 61.

33 will be repelled by this shield] Added in *1532*

34 penetrate the vitals] First in *1534*; previously 'penetrate to the vitals of the soul'

hand always be armed with that spiritual sword which both lops off the soul's deformed desires as it penetrates to the inner recesses of the heart and repels those who resist evangelical truth as it slaughters falsehood so that truth may flourish. This is the word of God penetrating with the constant vigour of faith, not grazing with human twaddle, but rather smiting. For the human word is watered down, seeing that it discourses on matters that are without substance and in flux; but the word of God is efficacious, savouring only of what is heavenly, penetrating even to the joints of the soul and making its way through[35] the inmost parts of bone and marrow.[36]

These are the foes with whom Christians are at war;[37] with men, Christians are at peace; with these weapons they defend themselves and even conquer – not, indeed, by their own powers but by the resources of Christ, their commander, under whose auspices this war is being waged. He, therefore, must be solicited at all times and with unremitting prayers; this must be our request made with supplications offered tirelessly night and day[38] in accordance with the heart's deepest affection: that this spiritual sword may prevail among all the saints.

And, what is more, you ought to support me, too, with your supplications, asking God himself to provide me with the evangelical word, as often as it needs to be spoken, and to employ the instrument of my mouth for his glory and your salvation, so that I may bravely and fearlessly reveal[39] to all people the hidden teaching of the gospel to which all are equally summoned. Ask too that I not be blocked by those who in every way offer active opposition to prevent the spreading of the gospel's glory. I am fulfilling my mission on behalf of the gospel even while burdened with chains,

* * * * *

35 'Making its way through': *perlustrans*. The verb *perlustrare* appears to be used here primarily with the meaning 'to traverse through' but in connection with religious rituals the word can also mean 'to purify.' Erasmus may have intended some ambiguity.

36 Cf Heb 4:12, a passage quoted by Jerome *Comm in Eph* III §681 (on 6:18–19) PL 26 552/Heine 267 (adapted). Erasmus adopts here his explanation, and even his words: *vivens quippe sermo Dei et efficax ... et penetrans usque ad artus animae, et ossium, et medullarum* 'the word of God is living and efficacious ... and penetrating even to the joints of the soul, the bones and the marrow.' On the 'efficacy' of the word of God as a theme in Erasmus, see chapter 4 n18.

37 As he had done at the end of his paraphrase on 5:21–6:9 (the household rules cf above n19), so again Erasmus inserts a concluding summary, here of 6:11–17, regarding the foes to be faced, and the weapons to be used.

38 For the imagery, see Luke 2:37 (Anna in the temple) and 1 Tim 5:5 (the pious widow).

39 reveal] First in 1532; previously 'divulge'

steadfastly enduring everything in order to discharge with courage the responsibility assigned to me. Pray also that this purpose remain in me and that, relying on Christ, I speak frankly as I ought to speak. For it is not fitting that the gospel's herald be deterred by any fear from carrying out the gospel's work.[40]

You will learn from Tychicus everything about the state of my affairs and how I am getting along. He is a beloved brother, and not only a brother on account of the family resemblance of faith, but also, in the work of the gospel, a helper and a minister. I am sending him there for this very reason: that you may not be without knowledge of the position we are in, and that from his presence you may derive some comfort so that you should not be dismayed on account of my afflictions. For I have been fettered, but in such a way that from prison, none the less, the gospel of Christ triumphs.[41]

On behalf of all the brethren I am praying for peace and mutual charity joined with sincere faith. From faith, charity is born; by the latter, harmony is fostered. Accordingly, may this happy triad be graciously conferred upon you by God the Father and the Lord Jesus Christ. May divine favour and beneficence ever attend all who love the Lord Jesus Christ with sincere affection and uncorrupted life, spurning these present ephemeral things as they eagerly pursue the eternal and the heavenly. I pray that he may be willing to fulfil this entreaty of mine.

The End of the Paraphrase on the
Epistle of Paul the Apostle to the Ephesians

* * * * *

40 Cf Nicholas of Lyra (on 6:20): 'That is, that the tribulations I am experiencing may not frighten me away from preaching.' In his *Paraphrase on Acts*, Erasmus stresses the importance to the preacher's mission of frank speech, cf παρρησία and παρρησιάζομαι in the Index of Greek and Latin Words Cited in CWE 50. Cf also 2 Cor chapter 3 n14.

41 Triumphs: *triumphet*. Erasmus may intend some irony in having Paul, a prisoner in chains, describe the success of his work with this word.

PARAPHRASE ON PHILIPPIANS

Paraphrasis in epistolam Pauli Apostoli ad Philippenses

translated and annotated by
MECHTILDE O'MARA

THE ARGUMENT OF THE EPISTLE OF PAUL
TO THE PHILIPPIANS
BY ERASMUS OF ROTTERDAM

The Philippians dwell in the first region of Macedonia, as is described in the sixteenth chapter of Acts,[1] a Roman settlement established in the city of Philippi, named after Philip, its founder.[2] The capital of their province is Thessalonica. Since they had persevered in the faith once received,[3] without admitting the false apostles to whom the Corinthians and Galatians gave ear, they are deservedly praised by the Apostle.[4]

Prompted by the Spirit,[5] Paul had set out for the Philippians, then spent several days in their midst, not without trouble. For here Paul was lashed with scourges and, together with Silas, cast into prison; this was the occasion on which the prison guard with his whole family was baptized.[6] Here also was Lydia, a purple-dye dealer; first to be converted, she

* * * * *

1 the sixteenth chapter of] Added in 1521. See Acts 16:12 and its paraphrase by Erasmus, CWE 50 102.
2 So Theophylact also reports in his introductory Argument *Expos in Phil* PG 124 1140A. On the city and the province of Macedonia, see Erasmus' paraphrase on Acts 16:12 CWE 50 102 with nn24 and 25. Philippi, the site of Paul's first extensive missionary activity in Europe, was a walled city of Macedonia towards the eastern end of the Via Egnatia, Rome's main land route to the East. Its population of approximately 10,000 was a mixture of Thracians, Greeks, Macedonians, and Romans, with the Romans in control. See Holland L. Hendrix 'Philippi' ABD 5 313–17.
3 Erasmus uses the expression 'the faith once received' also in his Argument prefacing 1 Thessalonians, where see n2. Cf 'the faith which was once for all delivered to the saints' in the paraphrase on Jude 3 CWE 44 125. See also the paraphrase on 1 Cor 15:1–2.
4 Specific reference to the lapse of the Galatians and Corinthians may be derived from Ambrosiaster *Comm in Phil* Argument CSEL 81/3 129:7–13.
5 A reference to Paul's obedience to the Spirit and his response to a vision described in Acts 16:6–10
6 For the arrest of Paul and Silas and its consequences, see Acts 16:19–34.

welcomed Paul with hospitality.[7] Here too, when it was recognized that Paul was a Roman citizen, the soldiers of their own accord asked him to go away wherever he wished,[8] and the name of Christ became famous under quite happy auspices.[9]

Moreover, while Paul was living at Rome[10] in chains, the Philippians sent him the things that pertained to the necessities of life through Epaphroditus.[11] They had done this previously too, when Paul was living in Thessalonica as he himself attests in this Epistle.[12] Then, after praising them, he exhorts them to persevere and go forward, pointing out that they should glory even in afflictions, for their afflictions would make the gospel of Christ more radiant. Indeed, so far was he from shrinking from death, that he would even desire it, if, Christ willing, it should fall to his lot. Then he exhorts them above all to mutual harmony, which cannot exist among the proud; and in order to put their minds at rest, he promises that Timothy and, indeed, that he himself will return to them in a short time. Meanwhile Epaphroditus, who had recovered from a very dangerous illness, had been sent ahead.

He treats these matters in the first two chapters. In the third he reassures them against the false apostles who were tempting them to Judaism from every side. These false apostles he calls 'dogs,' 'workers of iniquity,'

* * * * *

7 On Lydia, see Acts 16:14–15, 40.
8 In Acts 16:35–9 it was not soldiers but the magistrates, first through the lictors, then in person, who asked Paul to leave their city.
9 Erasmus' use of *auspicia* 'auspices' includes both meanings familiar to English readers: 'beginnings' and 'indication of divine blessings.' The word itself is derived from the Roman augural practice in which the heavens were watched for some sign of divine approval, eg the flight of birds or lightning, before any major decision such as the founding of a city, the undertaking of a war, or any important administrative plan was made. See Cicero *De divinatione* 1.16.28 and A.H.J. Greenidge *Roman Public Life* (London 1911) 36–40. In his paraphrase on Eph 6:18, Erasmus envisions the Christian warrior fighting not by his own strength, but with the assistance of his general, Christ, 'under whose auspices this war is being waged.'
10 Although scholars have suggested Rome, Corinth, Caesarea, and Ephesus as the locus of composition for the Epistle to the Philippians, Erasmus assumes that it originated in Rome, as appears in the Greek subscription to some manuscripts. See Metzger 'Subscription' 551. For a concise summary of the arguments that have led most modern scholars to accept Ephesus, see NJBC §48:5–6 792.
11 For Epaphroditus, see 2:25–30 and 4:18.
12 For the generosity of the Philippians, see 4:15–18.

'enemies of the cross of Christ,' who worship their belly in place of God.[13] Nowhere does he fume more openly against them. The fourth chapter he fills with commendations and greetings, except that he mixes in some warnings incidentally, and he thanks the Philippians for their generosity towards himself.

He wrote the letter from the city of Rome through Epaphroditus,[14] when he was in prison a second time; for after his first defence he was taken back to prison again. He himself recalls this fact in the Epistle to Timothy.[15]

The End of the Argument

* * * * *

13 See Phil 3:2, 18–19.

14 As the Greek subscription states in some versions. See Metzger 551. For subscription, see the *Paraphrase on Colossians* Argument n13; on the idiom cf ibidem n10.

15 See 2 Tim 4:16: 'At my first defence no one came to my support' (Conf) and Erasmus' paraphrase on it CWE 44 53: 'When I had to plead my case the first time before Caesar's courts, no one stood by me.' The belief that Paul was twice tried by Nero, mentioned also in the Argument of 2 Timothy, is found in Eusebius *Historia ecclesiastica* 2.22. See CWE 44 40 n2. Cf Theophylact *Expos in Phil* Argument PG 124 1140A: 'He wrote the Epistle while he was in chains, for after his first defence he was put in bonds again as he reminds us in the Epistle to Timothy.' Cf *Saint Jerome On Illustrious Men* trans Thomas P. Halton (Washington 1999) 12–13. But contemporary scholars are agreed neither on the chronology of Paul's life, nor on the authorship of the Epistles to Timothy. For a convenient summary of the four main positions affecting the 'second imprisonment' of Paul, see Brown *Introduction to* NT 672–5.

THE PARAPHRASE ON THE EPISTLE OF PAUL
THE APOSTLE TO THE PHILIPPIANS
BY ERASMUS OF ROTTERDAM

Chapter 1

Paul and Timothy, colleagues in the work of the gospel and servants of Jesus Christ, to the whole assembly of the saints,[1] who profess wholly and purely the name of Jesus Christ, and also to those who preside over the Christian flock and minister[2] to it at Philippi. We wish you grace and peace from God our Father and from the Lord Jesus Christ.

As often as I appeal[3] to God in my prayers – and this I do without ceasing – I never fail to mention all of you. At the same time, I give thanks and rejoice greatly for all of you because hitherto, from the beginning of your profession right up to this day, you have shown yourselves to be sharing in the gospel by supporting me through your services and your generous spirit. I pray constantly that you may abound more and more in those virtues of yours. And I trust that God, who has bestowed on you those first elements of piety, may bring to completion what he has begun in you, right up to that day on which Christ Jesus shall come and requite deeds well done with an eternal reward.

It is right that I should feel about you as I do, relying on the divine assistance, since up to this time I have experienced your unwavering, truly

* * * * *

1 Ambrosiaster *Comm in Phil* (on 1:1) CSEL 81/3 130:11–14 notes that Paul is addressing the common people, not just the prelates.
2 Erasmus' annotation on 1:1 (*et diaconibus*) indicates that his Latin sources used the third declension (as printed in the 1527 Vulgate). For his own translation he corrects the spelling to *diaconus*, the more usual second declension (masculine) form. He admits that the word *diacon* in the third declension can sometimes be found in the works of Augustine, because, in his opinion, the word was commonly used that way, like 'baptism,' which was sometimes Latinized in the neuter as a concession to the normal usage of the common people.
3 On *interpello* 'appeal,' see Eph chapter 1 n43.

evangelical charity towards me. Consequently, it is easy to infer from excellent beginnings an excellent conclusion.[4] For these reasons, my regard for you is such that I have always felt extraordinary goodwill towards you, even in these chains, and before Nero's tribunal where I had to plead my case on a capital charge, and in the rest of my sufferings, which do not lessen or overshadow the vigour of the gospel but rather confirm it and add to its lustre.[5] I have always had you all as fellow participants in this joy[6] which I am experiencing: that through my adversity[7] the proclaiming of Christ gains renown. For God, himself, from whom nothing lies hidden, knows how much I miss you all.

I miss you, not from any human desire either to gain something from you, or to flatter you because of your generous spirit towards me. Rather, I love you thus from a purely Christian affection, and simply because I see that you love Jesus Christ with enduring constancy and unfeigned sincerity. I congratulate you on those gifts of his, and I pray that your charity may grow richer and richer with the increase of all knowledge and all understanding, so that you may know on whom you ought to bestow[8] the services of charity.

Charity guarantees that you wish to confer a benefit; prudence points out suitable subjects for your beneficence.[9] Moreover, whatever is conferred

* * * * *

4 Cf Theophylact *Expos in Phil* (on 1:6–7) PG 124 1144C–1145A: 'For from the past I conjecture about the future ... so that it is right for me to make these conjectures about you, and from the beginnings to estimate the end.'

5 Erasmus here is punning on *obscurare* 'overshadow' and *illustrare* 'to shed light on,' 'to add lustre.'

6 Erasmus here adopts the reading of the Vulgate, *gaudii* 'of joy,' found also in the lemma of Ambrosiaster at *Comm in Phil* (on 1:7) CSEL 81/3 131:18, although Erasmus' annotation on 1:7 (*socios gaudii*) points out that the Greek reading, supported by Theophylact *Expos in Phil* (on 1:7) PG 124 1145B calls for *gratiae* 'of grace.'

7 adversity] First in 1521; previously 'adversities'

8 'Bestow': *collocare*, a verb translated just below as 'invested.' See the paraphrase on Matt 10:40 CWE 45 180, where the word has the sense of both 'bestow' or 'confer' and 'invest,' and is used as here with *officium* 'service,' 'kindness': '... if any kindness has been conferred on you ... has been invested in you.' See OLD *colloco* 10b, and Eph chapter 6 n13.

9 Generosity and the way it is to be exercised – with sensitivity to the feelings of the recipient, attention to the resources of the donor, and in proportion to the recipient's deserts – is discussed by Cicero *De officiis* 1.14.42–56. See 2 Cor chapter 8 nn16 and 17. For an examination of ancient social conventions surrounding gift-giving or 'social reciprocity' as they are reflected in Philippians, see Gerald W. Peterman *Paul's Gift from Philippi: Conventions of Gift-Exchange and Christian Giving* (Cambridge 1997).

for the love of Christ on preachers and promoters of the gospel is very wisely invested and will return to you with much interest. Therefore I pray that both prudence and charity may increase in you always in order that you may be able to discern the best course of action and live with purity of intention, having nothing in view but Christ and bestowing by the integrity of your life such honour on the gospel you have professed that you are not a stumbling block for anyone,[10] but rather attract all people to the worship of God. And, what is more, [I pray] that you may persevere right up to the day of Christ's coming[11] in such a way that you may then appear rich, with a superabundance of pious works.[12] Here, now, with these you are as it were planting a crop; then you will reap a very fruitful harvest.[13] And this will occur thanks to the kindness of Jesus Christ, not for your glory or mine, but for the glory and praise of God to whom, as to the source of all that is good, all things ought to be referred.[14]

Furthermore, brothers, that you may share even more in my joy,[15] I want you to know that imprisonment, fetters, tribunals, and the other misfortunes that have befallen me on account of the gospel of Christ, have not stood in the way of spreading and confirming the gospel teaching. On the contrary, they have even contributed to its advancement. Far from deterring believers from the profession they have made, they have instead even confirmed them and brought an increase of strength and courage – certainly to those who understand that what I preach is an absolute certainty for which I do not hesitate to suffer, and who challenge themselves, through the example I have set, to acts of similar daring. For in practice it generally

* * * * *

10 For the image of the stumbling block, see Theophylact *Expos in Phil* (on 1:10) PG 124 1148C. Cf 1 Cor 8:9: 'Take care lest this right of yours become a stumbling-block to the weak' (Conf).

11 For the 'day of Christ,' see 1:10 and 2:16.

12 Cf Nicholas of Lyra (on 1:11), who writes, *ut in die iudicii appareatis pleni bonis operibus* 'that on the day of judgment you may appear full of good works.'

13 Cf 2 Cor 9:6 and Gal 6:8–10, especially 6:8: 'Who sows in the spirit, from the spirit will reap life everlasting' (Conf); also Erasmus' paraphrase on Gal 6:9 CWE 42 128: 'In due time we will receive from God fruit which will never perish, and for temporary services an eternal reward will be given to us.'

14 The absolute gratuitousness of God's love as the source of every blessing is a frequent theme in this paraphrase. See Sider 'Grace' 21–2.

15 'Joy': *gaudii*. Cf n6 above. In paraphrasing 1:7 Erasmus, disregarding what he found in his Greek sources, placed the theme of 'joy in adversity' in the forefront of the Pauline narrative. Beginning now to paraphrase 1:12, he recalls the theme as he describes in more detail Paul's adversities, and he will return to the theme in the paraphrase on 1:18.

happens that what is honourable and renowned becomes stronger and more brilliant to the extent that it undergoes oppression and affliction. As a result, the attempt of wicked men turns out contrary to their intention.

My chains, for example, have provided an opportunity for the proclamation of the gospel to reach not just a few people, and those of the lower class,[16] as was previously the case, but even to become well known throughout the court of Nero, and throughout the entire city,[17] to the extent that several of the brothers who used to profess somewhat timidly the gospel teaching, now, since the Lord Jesus is arranging matters in this way,[18] have taken heart from my bonds. After my example, they have also begun to profess the gospel message with greater freedom and boldness, all anxiety set aside.

Although not all have done this with a sincerity to match their enthusiasm, still, the situation brought glory to the gospel through the opportunity it provided. For among these there were some individuals who acted out of a perverse zeal in order to kindle a more savage animosity and to sharpen more keenly Nero's feeling against me as he saw this sect being propagated more widely (a sect he erroneously judges destructive of his empire). They reckoned that in this way he would the more swiftly destroy me.[19] Others, perhaps jealous of my glory (and yet I do not claim it for myself, but sign it over entirely to Christ) have tried to put my

* * * * *

16 'Lower class': *plebeios*, evoking a contrast with the patricians, the city fathers, whom Erasmus has identified with the officials of the praetorium. (See next note). His paraphrase introduces the theme of the gospel call to the poor and lowly, expressed for example at 1 Cor 1:26–9.

17 Because Erasmus has accepted the view that Philippians was written in Rome, he amplifies *praetorium* in its meaning of the court of the emperor, Nero. In a provincial setting, *praetorium* referred to the local headquarters of the Roman *praetor* 'governor.' See eg Cicero *In Verrem* 2.4.28.65 and Erasmus' annotation on Phil 1:13 (*in omni praetorio*). Theophylact *Expos in Phil* (on 1:13) PG 124 1149A also emphasizes the wider audience Paul's arrest has brought his preaching of the word 'now to the praetorium, that is, the royal palace, and in all the city.' Cf Haymo, who writes, 'So many believed, as St Jerome says, that he made the house of his persecutor, Nero, a church of the Redeemer. Then it was obvious in all the praetorium, that is, to the emperor and to all the consuls and leading men and in all places, that he was enduring such things for Christ's sake.' See *In divi Pauli epistulas expositio* PL 117 (1852) 737A. On the range of meanings for πραιτώριον see BDAG.

18 Ie so as to provide the opportunity for evangelization that Paul's 'chains' afford.

19 Theophylact *Expos in Phil* (on 1:15) PG 124 1149B similarly explains the motivations of Paul's antagonists as wishing to 'kindle the wrath of Nero against him so that he would more quickly destroy him.'

excellence[20] in the shade through their rivalry,[21] in the hope that they might appear even to surpass our zeal.

Again, there are in their number some, along with me, who preach Christ with a good and sincere intent, even if an imperfect one. For from natural good-will they are unwilling to fail me, whom they love and see endangered because I steadfastly perform the duty delegated to me of up-holding the gospel against the ungodly.

And yet even those who preach with the worst intention have, nev-ertheless, increased the glory of the gospel. For they proclaim Christ, but with a disposition not at all Christian, doing this not from a sincere motive, but to add affliction to one who is a captive and in chains. They hope, by defending the gospel more vigorously, to drag us into greater odium.

However this turns out for me, it will not make much difference, provided it contributes to the glory of Christ. To him I am so devoted with my whole heart that I rejoice at his being made known to everyone through every opportunity. In the eyes of God, those who preach the gospel with the same attitude as I deserve the fullest praise. Those are to be tolerated who take the side of the gospel through a certain private love of us. But with respect to those who preach Christ to bring hatred on me: the fact that they are harming themselves causes me pain; the fact that they are endeavouring to hurt me I consider unimportant; the fact that their perverse intention results in the glory of the gospel brings me joy provided that they teach Christ truly, although with an insincere heart. I rejoice in the present, as I shall rejoice also in the future, if, through hatred of me, they continue to publish abroad the teaching of Christ.

It does not disturb me that they are attempting these things to destroy me, since I know that, through the help of your prayers and with the Spirit of Jesus Christ to aid and direct this undertaking, the situation will con-tribute to my welfare whether I live or die. Nor will my confidence in him[22] betray me. I am absolutely convinced that in preaching the gospel which he assigned,[23] I am not going to be abandoned in any situation, or made

* * * * *

20 'Excellence': *laudem* 'praise,' 'reputation,' 'excellence.' See OLD *laus*.
21 'Rivalry': *aemulatio*. See Erasmus' discussion of the root meaning of *aemulari* in his annotation on Rom 11:11 ('that they may emulate them') CWE 56 302 n7.
22 The Latin *illo* is problematic. Here translated 'him' and understanding a ref-erence to the 'Spirit of Jesus Christ' or more simply 'Jesus Christ,' it could be translated 'it' and refer to *negotium* 'the undertaking.'
23 assigned] *delegavit*, first in 1532; previously *declaravit* 'made manifest.' For uses of *delegare* and its cognates in contexts of the apostolic appointment, see Eras-mus' paraphrases on Acts 22:14 and 26:14 CWE 50 130 with n15 and 143 with n16. See also the Index of Greek and Latin Words Cited.

ashamed so that I would be compelled by any torment to retract as vain or to keep silent what I know to be unquestionably true. On the contrary, just as the bodily afflictions that I have hitherto patiently endured at the hands of men have turned into gain for the gospel – whether I was being stoned or beaten with rods or thrown to wild animals[24] – so also this affliction, in which I risk even my civic rights[25] and life itself, will be transformed into the praise and glory of Christ, whether I happen to live or die. For just as previous winds of affliction, although they affected this poor body of mine, have never deprived me of my courage or undermined[26] my constancy in preaching Christ, so neither will this storm take them from me now.

If life is granted, I shall bravely defend the gospel truth; if it falls to my lot to die, my death itself, which I shall willingly undergo for the work of the gospel, will add lustre to[27] the glory of Christ. Whichever way it turns out, as far as I am concerned my safety is assured. So far am I from fearing this death that I think it ought the more to be hoped for, if in this way it should prove useful to the gospel. For I am not wearied of this life however afflicted; I measure all its happiness by the success of the gospel. Nor do I shudder at a death that would be to my gain,[28] that will pay me back with a heavenly[29] reward, then, at last, truly to live. However, even this ephemeral bodily life does not lack fruit of its own while, by accumulating godly deeds, the reward of immortality is also accumulated[30] and in the meantime the gospel of Christ is being extended and strengthened by our effort. It is up to Christ whether he prefers me to live or to die. So ready am I for either alternative that I do not know which I prefer. There is reason why I wish to die; there is reason why I do not refuse to live. When

* * * * *

24 For these sufferings of Paul, see eg 2 Cor 11:24–9 (stoning, beating, and other torments), Acts 14:19 (stoning), 1 Cor 15:32 (fighting with wild beasts). For the significance of being 'beaten with rods,' used by magistrates to punish criminals, see CWE 50 132 n30.

25 For Paul's consciousness of his rights as a Roman citizen (Latin *caput*), see Acts 22:25–9. A Roman citizen always had the right to appeal to the people from a death sentence. On the importance of citizenship to a Roman, see Cicero *In Verrem* 2.5.64.165–72.

26 undermined] Added in 1532

27 'Will add lustre to': *illustrabit*. Cf n5 above.

28 The two relative clauses describing *mortem* 'death' are not parallel: the former is a relative clause of characteristic with its verb in the subjunctive; the latter a simple descriptive clause with its verb in the future indicative.

29 heavenly] Added in 1532

30 Erasmus differs markedly from Luther in his emphasis on the reward due good deeds. See Erasmus *Hyperaspistes* 2 CWE 77 431–7; also Sider 'The Just' 22.

the account of my own personal advantage is calculated and I look within, I see that it is far preferable for me, freed from the tribulations of this life, to be joined more closely with Christ and to return to that ineffable happiness tasted in some measure when I was swept up into the third heaven.[31] Again, when I ponder what contributes to your advantage, I realize that it is useful, or rather necessary, for me to engage for a while yet in this service of mine.

And so I know this for certain: that I shall tarry for the present in this life, and tarry so as to enjoy you all one day and to give you access to me, in order that, simultaneously, you may the more fruitfully advance in the faith and I may the more abundantly rejoice over the growth of your faith; and that you, in turn, will be able to rejoice still more over me after I return to you, and you see once again that through the help of Christ I have not only not yielded to these evils, but have also been kept safe for your own increased advantage.[32] Do you see how great a personal happiness I am sacrificing for your gain? Who that desires the third heaven would not despise this life's concerns?[33] Who that misses the higher paradise would not long to fly from these ills? Who that remembers the secret words[34] would not disdain human conversation? Who would not choose a tranquil immortality in place of so many means of destruction, so many dangers, so many deaths? But brotherly love carries such weight with me that I prefer the advancement of others to what I so ardently long for.

All the more diligently must you struggle that your intent correspond to mine. That, however, will happen if you take care to have your life appear worthy of the gospel of Christ, for which I am patiently enduring all these sufferings in order that I may not be cheated of this very fruit,[35] for which alone I tolerate being dragged away from the fellowship of Christ

* * * * *

31 Cf 2 Cor 12:2–4.

32 This sense of mutual advantage goes well beyond the text of Philippians, but Erasmus regards this kind of *captatio benevolentiae* as characteristic of Paul. See his annotation on Rom 1:12 ('to be comforted together') CWE 56 36–7.

33 Beginning with 'Who that desires?' the series of questions parallels that of Ambrosiaster. See *Comm in Phil* (on 1:22–6) CSEL 81/3 136:24–137:1. The questions look further back to 2 Cor 12:2–4 with its mention of 'third heaven ... paradise ... secret words' (Conf).

34 On 'secret words,' cf in 2 Cor 12:4 *arcana verba* (Vulgate) 'secret words' (Conf), 'things that cannot be told' (RSV). See 1 Cor chapters 2 n2 and 11 n38; Eph chapters 1 n27 and 5 n38.

35 'Fruit': *fructu*. Erasmus exploits several meanings of the word that are relevant to this chapter of the *Paraphrase*: the pleasurable enjoyment [of their company], the metaphorical uses of fruit (cf 'more fruitfully advance in the faith' [above]); the return on an investment; see OLD *fructus*.

I so eagerly desire. Take care, then, that if I visit you I shall find you to be such as I hope; or if something stands in the way to prevent my seeing you again, still, from a distance I shall hear of you that you are persevering as you have done hitherto in the one Spirit that you have imbibed in common, and that you are united in the same mind and are bringing the assistance of both your prayers and your work to the faith of the gospel as it contends with the wicked.

May no fear of persecution deter you from bravely opposing everywhere the enemies of Christ. Their wickedness will accomplish nothing else but to prepare destruction for themselves and salvation for you, while the glory of the gospel blazes out ever more and the wicked attempts of those men continually come to ruin. It is an excellent thing to suffer patiently for Christ, glorious to conquer adversaries through him.

In all of this there is nothing we may claim for ourselves. It was God who bestowed on you the gift not only of believing promptly in Christ's gospel, which I preach, but also of being ready to suffer for it. In this, clearly, you have followed my example. May you not decline to accept for the sake of the gospel the same struggle as you once saw also in me when I was afflicted in so many ways while I was living there, and as you now hear about in my case, when I am held in confinement as a defendant on a capital charge. These[36] do not come about by chance but are bestowed by our gracious God only on those whose piety he wishes to be made more proven and esteemed by the afflictions of this life.

Chapter 2

Accordingly, if there is any mutual consolation among those who have blended together[1] into the same Christ; if there is any solace derived from brotherly love, which makes sorrows as well as joys to be felt in common; if the Spirit of Christ common to you all has any power; if there are any feel-

* * * * *

36 The referent of *haec* 'these' may be the afflictions, the events, the gifts, or perhaps all three. Theophylact *Expos in Phil* (on 1:29) PG 124 1157B notes that Paul calls suffering for Christ a gift. See also Peterman *Paul's Gift* (note 9 above) 111 n96.

1 'Have blended together': *conspirarunt* 'to act (or 'to be') in harmony.' See OLD. Erasmus is attending to the etymology of the word; it has the same root as *spiritus* 'Spirit,' which will appear later in the sentence.

ings through which people are touched in the sufferings of their friends;
if there are any sympathies through which, from natural feeling itself, we
groan aloud or feel pain over the ills of those whom we genuinely love and
who are suffering with patience for our sake – by all of these I beseech
you, Philippians, to bring to completion in me this pleasure that I have conceived from your progress. Whatever you owe me on any account I shall
consider paid, if you are bonded to one another[2] with minds and hearts
united, if love is mutual among you all, if you are of one mind, if you are
in accord.[3]

Peace and harmony cannot last among the headstrong and the exalted,
for a headstrong and puffed up spirit begets contention, ambition, a propensity to anger. But[4] these are poisons that quickly have their effect on brotherly love and mutual good will. Therefore, among you, who are bonded
together[5] by the Spirit of Christ and profess the philosophy of Christ,[6] let
nothing be done by means of contention or empty boasting, with one person
fiercely challenging another, while no one wishes to yield to the other. From
these attitudes quarrels, brawls, and divisions arise among the disciples of

* * * * *

2 'You are bonded to one another': *conglutinemini*. This is a favourite image
Erasmus uses when the text being paraphrased emphasizes unity – here in
the paraphrase on 2:2–3, and especially in the *Paraphrase on Ephesians*, where
conglutino occurs seven times, ie in the paraphrases on 1:2, 5, and 7, 3:6 and
15, 4:3 and 16; *adglutino* four times, ie on 1:23, 2:3, 3:11 and 18. See also 1 Cor
chapter 1 n4.
3 Cf Theophylact *Expos in Phil* (on 2:2) PG 124 1160B, 'as if being of one mind,
not in substance but in judgment and concord.'
4 But] First in 1521: *atqui* replacing *atque* 'and'
5 'Bonded together': *conglutinatos*
6 'Philosophy of Christ': *Christi philosophiam*, a recurrent motif of Erasmus in
which he includes the clear and simple teaching, exemplified by the apostles
and evangelists, of a piety imbued with peace; originating with God it leads
to a happy immortality. See 1 Cor chapter 3 nn1 and 4. See also Ep 858:144–
65; *Explanatio symboli* CWE 70 237 n6. Cf in the *Paraphrase on John*, the preface
to chapter 1 and the paraphrase on John 1:39 CWE 46 14 and 34 with n131. The
same circle of ideas is embraced by such phrases as 'evangelical philosophy'
(cf eg the paraphrases on James 3:14 CWE 44 158 with n23 and Acts 1:1 CWE 50
5 with n7), 'philosophy of the gospel' (cf eg the paraphrases on Mark 1:16 and
3:12 CWE 49 23 and 50), and 'Christian philosophy' (cf eg the dedicatory letter
[Ep 1062] for the *Paraphrase on Ephesians* 286 n17). See also Chantraine 85, 111–
13, 364–7, and Cornelis Augustijn *Erasmus: His Life, Works, and Influence* trans
J.C. Grayson (Toronto 1991) 71–88.

the world.[7] Consequently, in your council[8] let there be no anger, ambition, or pride – very bad counsellors – but rather brotherly love and its companion, the modesty of spirit by which no one prefers himself to another, but each one considers the other more important than himself, arrogating nothing to himself, and promoting the gifts of others in a generous and sincere manner. Let no one look to his own private advantage, because where that happens public harmony is in jeopardy; but through Christian charity, which does not seek its own interests, let each one place other people's advantages before his own. Indeed, no one of you should have the impious thought: 'Why should I, with full knowledge and awareness, yield – I, the better man – to one who is my inferior?'

Do not be ashamed to follow the example of Jesus Christ. For why does it not suit you, who are equals and partners, to be disposed towards one another as he was disposed towards us? If he claimed primacy for himself, if

* * * * *

7 'Of the world': *mundi*. Throughout his work Erasmus frequently undertook to elucidate the semantic complexity of the word *mundus* 'world.' In its negative sense, he understands the 'world' as a source of error. With the expression 'disciples of the world,' compare the phrases 'slaves of the world' in *Explanatio symboli* CWE 70 276, 'philosophers/sophists of this world' in the paraphrase on Col 2:3 and 4, and 'the cultivators of the world' in the paraphrase on Col 3:5. So too *apud mundum* 'in the eyes of the world' is juxtaposed to 'in the eyes of the Lord Jesus Christ' in the paraphrase on 1 Thess 2:19. Cf also the paraphrase on Col 3:11, where the standard of judgment *apud mundum* 'in the eyes of the world' is contrasted with that 'in the eyes of God.' Elsewhere in these *Paraphrases* we have 'the care of the world' (on Phil 4:8), 'the vices of this world' (on Eph 1:1), 'the pleasures of this world' as opposed to 'true and eternal goods' (on Eph 5:14), and 'those who are drunk with the desires and enticements of the world' (on 1 Thess 5:7). In each of these examples 'the world' is all that is opposed to what is heavenly, spiritual, pleasing to God. The word does, however, have, infrequently, a positive meaning, eg in the paraphrase on 2:16, when it quotes Matt 5:14, 'You are the light of the world' and explains this as 'luminaries of the world,' and when it is used in such neutral expressions as 'the whole world' in the paraphrases on Col 1:6 and 27. For 'elements of the world,' see Erasmus' Argument of Colossians and the paraphrases on Col 2:8 and 20. For other characteristic analyses of the word, see the *Enchiridion* CWE 66 57–8 and *Hyperaspistes* 2 CWE 77 683–5. Cf also the Argument of the *Paraphrase on 1 John* CWE 44 173; Ep 1538:50–2; and CWE 44 155 n9.

8 'Council': *consilio*. The word can also mean 'deliberation.' With this word Erasmus seems to invite a play on the word *consultores* 'counsellors' in the next line.

he grasped at his own advantage, then among you, too, it would be proper to struggle for these things. But Christ, although he was by nature God, and, moreover, by his very deeds demonstrated that he was God – restoring the dead to life[9] at will,[10] changing natural elements,[11] commanding the demons, with a word driving out all sorts of[12] illnesses – still, in order to provide for us an example of perfect modesty, he did not demand for himself through vainglory that he be considered equal to God, but he humbled himself and lowered himself in the eyes of men, awaiting from his Father the glory, the path to which he showed lies not through ambition, but through humility. To such an extent did he lower himself, although he was most high, that not only did he dwell as a man among men, needing sleep, thirsty, hungry, weary,[13] poor, and exposed to the other hardships of our condition, but he even took upon himself the appearance of a slave, and of a guilty slave although he was innocence itself.

What do I mean? Is a wicked slave not seized, bound, flogged, spat upon? And yet he abased himself not only to this extent, but he lowered himself even to the punishment of death, like a criminal, and to a death that is by far the most ignominious, the death of the cross.[14] Thus it seemed

* * * * *

9 Ambrosiaster *Comm in Phil* (on 2:7–8) CSEL 81/3 141:4 similarly lists proofs of Christ's divinity. This item, the first in both lists, is the same.

10 Erasmus clearly means 'at will.' His word is *nutus* 'nod.' Here he is employing the religious language of classical antiquity to express the concept of God's omnipotence. See Eph chapter 5 n21.

11 Eg the miracles of changing water into wine at Cana (John 2:1–12) and of the multiplication of the loaves and fishes (Matt 14:19–21). Ambrosiaster *Comm in Phil* (on 2:7–8) CSEL 81/3 141:10–13 mentions Christ's walking on the water and the apostles' consequent acknowledgment of him as the Son of God (Matt 14:26–33).

12 all sorts of] Added in 1532. For miracles of healing, see eg Mark 3:1–5 (man with a withered hand); Luke 4:38–9 (Peter's mother-in-law); Luke 7:21 (many with diseases, plagues, evil spirits, blindness); Luke 8:43–4 (woman with a haemorrhage); Luke 8:40–56 (daughter of Jairus); and Luke 17:12–19 (lepers).

13 weary] Added in 1532. Erasmus frequently recurs to the weaknesses of Jesus, which prove his humanity by calling attention to its limitations. See Ep 109:100–8, 115–44; *De taedio Iesu* CWE 70 13–67; and his *Apologia ad Fabrum* CWE 83 31–4.

14 Erasmus' Paul may be thinking of his Roman setting. Cf Cicero *In Verrem* 2.5.66.170: 'To bind a Roman citizen is a crime, to flog him is an abomination, to slay him is an act of murder [literally 'parricide']: to crucify him is – what? There is no fitting word that can possibly describe so horrible a deed.' For the paradox, see also 1 Cor 1:23–4: 'We … preached a crucified Christ – to the

good to the Father that he should in this way pay for our sins,[15] and he willingly showed himself obedient in all respects, refusing nothing that might be conducive to our salvation.

Those who are of a worldly disposition force their way up to a counterfeit glory through[16] ambition and striving, to the detriment of other people. But the Christian, who seeks true and everlasting glory, ought to strive for it by the pathway Christ walked. Through false[17] disgrace is the way to true glory; through temporary losses is the approach to eternal gains. It is not right to seize glory, but to deserve it.

Do you want to hear what the humility of Jesus Christ merited?[18] Indeed, Christ did not assume among men the right to make a show of his majesty before the proper time,[19] but God the Father raised his Son to the loftiest height, and, when he was glorified[20] through humility and the disgrace of the cross, he bestowed upon him a name that excels all human glory.[21] God did so in order that now, at the name of the Jesus who was spat upon and crucified, every knee should bend low, not only every knee on earth, but also every knee that is below the earth or above in the heavens, and that there should be no tongue anywhere, whether of men, of angels, or of demons, that does not acknowledge that Jesus, Prince and Lord of all things, sits at the right hand of God the Father, as one who shares equally in a common kingdom and in all glory – and all this[22] to the glory of God

* * * * *

Jews indeed a stumbling-block and to the gentiles foolishness, but to those who are called . . . Christ, the power of God and wisdom of God' (Conf). In the paraphrase on Phil 2:5–11, Erasmus follows the interpretation he developed in his annotation on verse 6 (*esse se aequalem deo*) – a highly controversial reading of the text. Cf Ep 554 and the *Apologia ad Fabrum* CWE 83 33–9, 60–1.

15 On the expiatory power of Christ's suffering, see Erasmus' *Explanatio symboli* CWE 70 302–4. For further evidence of Erasmus' characterization of God's justice in terms of punishment and reward, see Sider 'The Just' 9–11.

16 through] In 1532 *per* replaces the less emphatic 'with' (an ablative of manner).

17 Ie through apparent disgrace, which is no disgrace at all

18 Ambrosiaster speaks of the nature and extent of what Christ merited through humility. See *Comm in Phil* (on 2:9–11) CSEL 81/3 142:1–10, 23–143:6, 21–26.

19 to make a show of his majesty before the proper time] First in 1532; previously 'of demonstrating what he was.' The clause is an interpretation of the problematic image of 2:6: '[Christ] did not count equality with God a thing to be grasped' (RSV). See n14 above.

20 Here 'glorified' represents Erasmus' *illustrato*.

21 There is a sharp distinction between the actions of Christ and of God the Father.

22 With *idque* 'and [all] this,' Erasmus summarizes what has gone before.

the Father from whom arises and to whom flows back all the glory of the Son.[23]

What ambition of mortals, what resources, what kingdom, what human enthusiasm ever gained for anyone such glory before all[24] as his humility gained for Christ? Moreover, he has done all this for our sake, not his own. For he did not deserve to be cast down, nor did he need to be glorified.[25] All the more should you demonstrate a similar modesty. Without it you cannot be safe.

Accordingly, my beloved brothers, in this area, too, continue to be true to yourselves, and just as, following the example of Christ, you have always obeyed our gospel,[26] do so also for the future, not only when we are present, but much more now, when we are absent. Transfer to yourselves the care I would devote to you if I were there. Attend to the business of your salvation, not in a listless fashion,[27] but with all solicitude and trembling, well aware of how much is at stake, and of the foes with whom you are engaged. There is no place for sleep or negligence, but, on the other hand, there is no reason for you to lose confidence. It is your part to strive with all your might; it is God, however, who is working this in you, namely, that, as far as your salvation is concerned, you both wish for and bring to completion what the mind's good purpose[28] suggests to you. I say this so

* * * * *

23 On God as the source and end of glory, see the paraphrase on Phil 1:11 with n14.

24 all] *omnes*, in all Froben editions from 1520 to 1534; *1538, 1540* and LB read *homines* 'men.'

25 'To be glorified': *illustrari*. Ambrosiaster *Comm in Phil* (on 2:9–11) CSEL 81/3 142:16–23 emphasizes, against the Arians, that Christ needed nothing. Ambrosiaster, Theophylact *Expos in Phil* (on 2:6–8) PG 124 1161A–1165A, the Greek scholiasts in *Catenae graecorum Patrum in Novum Testamentum* ed J.A. Cramer [Oxford 1844] VI 246–56 (on Phil 2:5–8) and Aquinas *Super Phil lect* cap 2 lectio 2.62 (II 102) argue extensively in their comments on chapter 2 against heresies concerning the humanity and divinity of Christ. For this passage in the dispute with the Arians, see Erasmus' annotation on 2:6 (*esse se aequalem deo*).

26 While emphasis on the obedience of Christ is a prominent feature of chapter 2, Erasmus may have in mind also Paul's exhortation at 1 Cor 11:1: 'Be imitators of me as I am of Christ' (RSV).

27 Ambrosiaster *Comm in Phil* (on 2:14–18) CSEL 81/3 146:28 warns that if anything is done 'carelessly and contumaciously' it does not accomplish its objective.

28 Erasmus observes in the annotation on 2:13 (*pro bona voluntate*) that the Greek ὑπὲρ τῆς εὐδοκίας is ambiguous, 'for the good will can be understood to be either God's or that of the Philippians.' In Scripture εὐδοκία has several meanings: purpose, design, desire; or satisfaction, contentment, happiness; or benevolence, good will. See Lightfoot (on 1:15) 89. At 2:13, Erasmus had translated

that you should be aware who ought to be given the credit, if your good will has suggested[29] something to you.

You should see to it that your behaviour commends the gospel's teaching to those also who are strangers to it. This will happen if they perceive that you live in the greatest harmony and in mutual trust, and that whatever you do is done without grumbling, without disputes; the former is characteristic of those who are not whole-hearted in what they are doing; the latter of those who lack confidence.[30] But instead, you are to be transparent[31] in all circumstances, and in your behaviour so pure and blameless, that no one can rightly complain about you, and that it will be evident to all that you are not bastards or counterfeits, but truly sons of God, resembling your heavenly Father by your heavenly life. Thus, in the present time in the midst of a rough and twisted generation,[32] a generation without integrity, you will lead your life in such a way that your sincerity is not compromised,[33] but by the innocence of your life you shine[34] out amid their

* * * * *

εὐδοκία as *bonum animi propositum* 'the mind's good purpose,' thus interpreting the good purpose as human. In the paraphrase Erasmus exploits the ambiguity of the biblical text: human good will has its origin in the divine good will.

29 if your good will has suggested something to you] First in *1523*; previously (and probably by mistake) *successerit* in place of *suggesserit*, with a different meaning, 'if anything has turned out well for you'

30 Erasmus' annotation on 2:14 (*et haesitationibus*) explains the biblical διαλογισμοί as *disceptationes* 'disputes': 'For a person lacking confidence disputes and argues.' Cf AV: 'Do all things without ... disputings (RSV 'questioning'). For fuller explanations and definitions of διαλογισμός and *disceptatio*, see Erasmus' annotation on Rom 1:21 ('but became vain') and 14:1 ('not in disputes of thoughts') CWE 56 51 and 367.

31 'Transparent': *sinceri*, the word with which Erasmus translates the Greek ἀκέραιος (Vulgate *simplex*), and which he paraphrases in his annotation on 2:15 (*et simplices*) as *absque fuco* 'without pretence' or 'without colouring.'

32 At Phil 2:15 in the Vulgate, in Erasmus' translation, and in his paraphrase, *natio* 'generation' (Conf) is used. The word can mean 'a people.' See OLD. The passage incorporates a reference to Deut 32:5, where, however, *generatio* is found in the Vulgate. Erasmus may intend to suggest a reference to his contemporaries.

33 See Erasmus' annotation on 2:15 (*et simplices*), 'that is, sincere and without pretence.'

34 Erasmus' annotation on 2:15 (*inter quos lucetis*) referring to the Greek φαίνεσθε notes: 'It is ambiguous whether indicative or imperative.' His translation opts for the imperative; in his paraphrase he uses a subjunctive. This translation assumes that Erasmus intends the two clauses to depend on 'you will lead your life in such a way that.'

shadows, like luminaries of the world, so to speak, set out before the eyes of all. For you are the people Christ spoke about in the gospel: you are the light of the world; on a lofty height you are upholding the life-giving message of the gospel, expressing also, by your very behaviour, the teaching of Christ.[35]

As a result, I am confident, while you persevere, that I, too, will boast at the coming of Christ that I have not laboured in vain, nor run[36] to no purpose in the stadium of the gospel, since I have gained such disciples for Christ. So far am I from regretting the efforts through which I have presented you to God as a most pleasing victim, that if, in addition to the offering and the sacrifice of your faith, I, too, should be made a sacrificial offering, I would rejoice as much on my account as on yours: on your account[37] since I have offered you to Christ, a most pleasing victim,[38] as converts to the gospel; on mine, seeing that when such a sacrifice has been completed, I myself, too, must be entirely immolated. For just as I see that my afflictions have resulted in your advancement, so I know that my death will be advantageous for the gospel, and for this reason death, too, when it comes, will be pleasing to me. But if it is right for you in all circumstances to be associates in my joy, my death, which is going to bring me delight, should not be a source of grief to you.

* * * * *

35 Cf Matt 5:14. As an indication of the brightness intended here in 2:15, note that the Vulgate, Erasmus' translation, and his paraphrase all use *luminaria* 'luminaries,' the word used in the Vulgate to describe the sun and the moon in Gen 1:14–17. In the context of the paraphrase, *mundus* is to be taken as the 'world' in the sense of the whole cosmos (cf n7 above).

36 run] First in 1522; previously *concurrisse* 'to have striven,' 'competed.' The image of the race and athletic competition as a metaphor for the spiritual life appears in 3:12–14; also in 1 Cor 9:24–7; Gal 2:2; 1 Tim 6:12; cf especially 2 Tim 4:7: 'I have fought the good fight, I have finished the race, I have kept the faith' (RSV).

37 on your account ... immolated] Added in 1532

38 For the faith of Paul's converts as a sacrificial victim, see also the paraphrase on Rom 15:16 CWE 42 85, and Erasmus' annotation on Phil 2:17 (*supra sacrificium*): [Paul] means that his own death and his bonds are a kind of sacrificial victim, of which he is himself the minister and the one who offers the sacrifice, immolating himself for their faith and rejoicing on that account ... For he makes, as it were, two sacrificial victims: one, the faith of those whom he has offered to Christ, and of this he represents himself as the minister and liturgist; the other, himself, if in his eagerness to offer duly their faith to God as a sacrifice, he should be sacrificed and become a victim. Cf the annotation on Rom 15:16 ('sanctifying the gospel of God') CWE 56 404–5.

Now you know on what score you should rejoice over my situation, but I hope, with the help of the Lord Jesus, that I may visit you soon in the person of Timothy, since I am not yet allowed to come myself. I shall send him, therefore, as my *alter ego* so that, just as you rejoice now to know my situation, I, too, may rejoice when I have learned your situation from Timothy on his return here. Certainly, I think him eminently suited for this mission, since there is none of the rest who so matches my way of thinking in the work of the gospel[39] and, in looking after your concerns, will bring before you more whole-heartedly the faith and the diligence of Paul, for he is one whom I consider, with good reason, a genuine son.[40]

There are people whose service here I could do without at less cost, but I did not wish to send anyone except a person of proven integrity. For the rest generally hunt out missions of this sort, not so much in order to help others, as to look out for their own gain rather than that of Jesus Christ – a way of thinking you know I have always abhorred.

I think it unnecessary for me to commend him to you since, indeed, he has for a long time now actually enjoyed your esteem. You can remember how he conducted himself with me in the work of the gospel and how he resembled me in all respects as a true son resembles his father.[41] Him then, as I hope, I shall send to you as soon as I see what turn my affairs will take. In fact, I am confident that, the Lord willing, I personally will also come to you at an early date.

In addition, I thought that this, too, would be worthwhile: that Epaphroditus also should go to you as Timothy's companion. To me he has been a brother, colleague, and companion-at-arms, but to you an apostle, so that he should be commended to you both on my account and on your own. Finally, he is the one who delivered to me the kindly gifts with which you usually assist me in time of need. For a long while he has been possessed by a burning desire to visit you, worried lest you were overly anxious because you had heard that he was dangerously ill. That was no idle rumour; he has been so ill that his life was in danger – close to death. But God has restored him, having mercy on his servant, and indeed not only on him but also on me. For I was in danger along with him, lest, to the distress that his illness caused me, there be added, as a result of his death, the sense of loss

* * * * *

39 Cf Theophylact *Expos in Phil* (on 2:20) PG 124 1172B: ' "There is no one else who is so like-minded," that is, so caring for your concerns as I am, so "genuine," that is, one who will be anxious about your affairs in fatherly fashion.'
40 For the implications of Timothy's being a 'true child in the faith,' see Erasmus' paraphrase on 1 Tim 1:2 CWE 44 5–6.
41 On the resemblance between father and son, see Eph chapter 5 n1.

for such a faithful comrade.[42] Hence I was the more eager to send him to you: first, that you might receive pleasure from his visible presence, when you see that he has recovered and thus are not, perhaps, so ready to believe the report; secondly, in order that all my distress may be banished, if I feel that you are rejoicing with a sure joy over his health. Welcome him, therefore, in a Christian attitude, with all joy, and hold not only him, but all like him, in esteem.

Indeed, when he was sent here by you, so little did he fear the savagery of Nero, whom he knew to be hostile to me, that for the sake of Christ's gospel he exposed himself to such danger that he was very close to death. But he preferred the advancement of the gospel teaching to his own safety, so that he might make up for what, on account of your absence, seemed to be lacking in your service towards me, and so that you might be present to me, in a certain sense, through him, seeing that he has both conveyed your generosity to me and has been attentive to me through his own services when[43] I was in danger.[44] Thus he alone by himself, in a way represented all of you to me.

Chapter 3

Therefore, brothers, since you realize how matters stand here, and since Epaphroditus has been restored to you unharmed, it remains that you be cheerful and, disregarding the afflictions with which the world has harassed

* * * * *

42 Theophylact *Expos in Phil* (on 2:27) PG 124 1173D–1176A offers the same explanation of Paul's additional sadness: 'Lest along with the grief that came to me because of his illness, I grieve again because of his dying.'
43 when ... to me] Added in *1532*
44 Much of this paragraph seems to have been influenced by Theophylact *Expos in Phil* (on 2:30) PG 124 1176B–D who writes that Epaphroditus
    found Paul in Rome amid dangers, for it was dangerous for anyone to approach him since the emperor was hostile towards him. Then, disregarding every danger, he [Epaphroditus] ministered to Paul ... And notice, he does not say, 'on my account,' but 'on account of God's work, he exposed himself to, that is, he threw himself at, death.' But what if, since God disposes, he did not die? Still, he did show clearly his choice ... [Paul] says, you [the Philippians] were not present at Rome to minister to my corporeal needs even if you did send necessities. This deficiency of yours, the liturgy [ie service] of your hand and your body, he himself fulfilled in place of you all by ministering to me ... he was the only one to bring what pertained to all of you.
    See also Erasmus' annotations on 2:30 (*quod ex vobis deerat* and *erga meum obsequium*).

us, that you rejoice because the work of our Lord Jesus Christ is always making progress. I do not fear for the gospel so much from the gentiles, who openly assail the gospel, as from those half-Christians who preach Christ in such a way that they sometimes mix in Judaism.[1] In view of my concern I have frequently given you advice on this subject, but nevertheless I will not consider it a burden to drive home the same message in my letter, so that you may be the safer.

There is hardly ever enough caution exercised against those people who are setting snares everywhere – a baneful, wicked, and shameless group of men. They are jealous of your freedom; they bark out[2] at authentic doctrine; they cling doggedly to[3] a way of life that is foreign [to the gospel]; they labour in the work of the gospel, but in such a way as to corrupt it. They boast about the bit of skin[4] cut from the prepuce although they have an uncircumcised heart.[5] Watch out, brothers, lest they impose upon you; beware of dogs of this kind; beware of wicked operators; beware of the uncircumcised circumcised, or to put it more truly, the mutilated.[6] Without cause, they commend themselves, carrying about on their body the obscene mark of their nobility, while in their soul they are impure and impious.

Deut 30:6
Rom 2:25-29

* * * * *

1 Cf Ambrosiaster *Comm in Phil* (on 3:2) CSEL 81/3 151:10–12: 'He designates those who had upset the Galatians by persuading them to be circumcised.'

2 Cf Ambrosiaster *Comm in Phil* (on 3:2) CSEL 81/3 151:12–14: 'He teaches that they should be avoided and spurned like dogs that first bark, and then harm by their savage bite into the flesh.'

3 'They cling doggedly to': *mordent*. With this use of *mordere* 'to bite,' 'to grasp firmly,' 'to criticize,' cf the cognate adverb *mordicus* 'doggedly,' 'tooth and nail,' used in similar circumstances. See 2 Cor chapter 3 n27 and Eph chapter 4 n5. For Erasmus' views on the Jews and on judaizing Christians, see 1 Cor chapters 8 n25 and 9 n6; Col chapter 2 nn59 and 62; and 1 Thess chapter 2 n26; also the Argument of the Epistle to the Hebrews CWE 44 214 n1. Erasmus' attitude seems part of the medieval tradition. See eg Augustine Ep 140.16.39, 42 PL 33 555, 556.

4 'The bit of skin': *pellicula*, a diminutive frequent in Erasmus, eg in his paraphrases on Eph 1:13 and Col 2:11, and on Rom 2:28 and 4:10 CWE 42 22 and 28.

5 Reference to ritual circumcision in Paul typically evokes from Erasmus denigration of what he understands as a material element in the Jewish religion. See his paraphrases on Eph 2:11–22 and Col 2:11 with n28.

6 Erasmus' annotation on 3:2 (*videte concisionem*) notes the play on words in both the Greek and the Vulgate: κατατομή / *concisio* 'mutilation' and περιτομή / *circumcisio* 'circumcision.' His paraphrase 'uncircumcised circumcised ... mutilated' continues the play. His annotation explains *concidere* 'pull asunder,' verb analogue of *concisio*, in terms of *discerpere* 'tear apart' and *distrahere* 'break up' and points to Jerome, who explains the word as *vastare* 'ravage.' See Jerome *Commentarii in Michaeam prophetam* II §487 (on 5:1) PL 25 (1845) 1195.

If circumcision is worth boasting about, we are the truly circumcised, we are truly Jews,[7] we are the genuine sons of Abraham,[8] we who worship God not with the blood of cattle, but with the Spirit,[9] for he is glad to be worshipped in this way. We glory not in a bit of the body's skin,[10] not in Moses, but in Christ Jesus who, through his Spirit, has pruned all vices from our souls, who has stamped upon our hearts his beautiful brand-mark[11] from which it is clear that we are the children of God. This, and only this, is the true and glorious circumcision.

Henceforth God does not value man by the condition of his body. But these people do not care about the mind. They place their whole reliance on the flesh, in which, if there is any boast to be made, I, at any rate, shall not yield to anyone of them on this ground, in case they would have any reason to allege that circumcision is a trifle in my eyes because I do not have it.[12]

If anyone else takes pride in this, I could take even more pride: properly circumcised, in fact, on the eighth day, according to the precept of the Law;[13] an Israelite, not by grafting,[14] but by birth; not a proselyte,[15] but a Jew originating from Jews; and not just from any tribe at all, but from a

* * * * *

7 Cf Paul's boasts at 2 Cor 11:22–33.
8 Cf 2 Cor 11:22: 'Are they descendants of Abraham? So am I' (RSV). For Erasmus' explication of what it means to be descendants of Abraham, see his annotation on Rom 4:12 ('not to those only who are of the circumcision') CWE 56 113–16.
9 Cf John 4:23.
10 Ie *pellicula*. See n4 above.
11 'Brand-mark': *notam*. The word picks up the 'mark of nobility' in the previous paragraph. There the word referred to the circumcision of Jews; here it refers to the invisible, indelible character impressed on the soul of a Christian by baptism. See Erasmus' paraphrase on Eph 1:13. For a summary of medieval doctrine on the sacramental 'character,' see Thomas Aquinas *Summa Theologiae* III 63:1–6 (in David Bourke ed Latin Text and English Translation volume 56 [London 1975] 76–99).
12 Cf Theophylact *Expos in Phil* (on 3:4) PG 124 1180B who interprets Paul to mean: 'It is clear that I am not belittling circumcision because I have been deprived of the very thing in which you think your nobility lies, but because of the true [spiritual] circumcision.'
13 Circumcision as required by Gen 17:12, Lev 12:3
14 For the analogy of gentiles grafted onto the root of Judaism, see Rom 11:17–24. For the image of grafting, see also the paraphrase on 1 Cor 6:7–8 with n13.
15 Both Augustine in *Sermones* 169.3.5 PL 38 917 and Theophylact *Expos in Phil* (on 3:5) PG 124 1180C interpret Paul's circumcision on the eighth day as evidence that he was no proselyte.

special one, in fact that of Benjamin, which[16] was always joined to the tribe of Judah, whence kings, and Levites,[17] whence too the priests are appointed, for the majority think themselves Israelites because they draw their origin from the concubines of the Israelites;[18] a Hebrew of the Hebrews according to birth; according to the faction interpreting the Law a Pharisees,[19] the sect to which the highest prestige always belonged.[20]

* * * * *

16 which ... Levites] Added in 1532 in response to a criticism of Noël Béda. See *Divinationes ad notata Bedae* LB IX 477C–D, where Erasmus blames the omission of these words on the negligence of the compositor, probably to cover his own error. 'Everyone knows,' Erasmus says, 'that the tribe of Levi alone was designated for the priesthood and the sacred services.'

17 For the association of Benjamin with Judah see Neh 11:4, 7, 31–5. See also 'Benjamin' ABD 1 671–3. In Neh 11:36 'certain divisions of the Levites' (RSV) are said to have been 'joined to Benjamin.' Nehemiah 11 also attests that after the exile priests and Levites were in Jerusalem and Judah (cf 11:3, 10–18, 20). However, on the origins of the tribe of Benjamin, the priests, and the Levites and on their relation to Judah, see the articles 'Levi' and 'priests and priesthood' in *Encyclopaedia Judaica* 2nd ed, ed Fred Skolnik (Detroit 2007) 12 682–4 and 16 513–26.

18 Ambrosiaster explains Paul's reference to Benjamin as a means of underlining the superiority of the descendants of that tribe compared with those who draw their origin from the sons of Jacob's concubines. See *Comm in Phil* (on 3:5–7) CSEL 81/3 152:15–17. Beginning with Jacob's four sons born of concubines, Dan and Naphtali, Gad and Asher, there is much evidence of sons born to the patriarchs from unsanctioned unions (cf Gen 46:8–27). See also Aquinas *Super Phil lect* cap 3 lectio 1.110 (II 110) regarding the tribe: '... because in the tribe of Israel there were certain ones [descended] from slave girls, namely, from Bala and Zelfa, certain ones from free women, namely, Leah and Rachel; and among the latter some who were always [involved] in the worship of God, namely, Levi, Judah, and Benjamin. And on that account the tribe of Benjamin was privileged.' Cf the blessing spoken by Moses at Deut 33:12.

19 At the feet of the Pharisee Gamaliel (Acts 6:34), Paul had been instructed accurately in ancestral law (Acts 22:3). The Sadducees were divided sharply from the Pharisees in their teaching. Paul is represented as exploiting their differences in his speech before the people (Acts 23:6–10). Josephus *Jewish Antiquities* 13.5 reports: 'At that time there were three sects of the Jews which held different opinions about human affairs: the first was called Pharisees, the second Sadducees, the third Essenes.' See also Brown *Introduction to NT* 75–82.

20 Augustine notes the distinctiveness of the Pharisees in *Sermones* 169.3.5 PL 38 917. Theophylact *Expos in Phil* (on 3:5) PG 124 1180D identifies them as the most honoured sect. Josephus acknowledges their exact skill in the law of their fathers, and sees them as respected for their care in religious worship and in the virtue of their lives. For the distinctive beliefs of the three sects, see Josephus *Jewish Antiquities* 17.1, 41, 18.11–22; *Jewish War* 2.119–66. Nevertheless,

But if someone should like to judge one's worth on the basis of zeal for and observance of the Law, not even on these grounds would they have a reason for preferring themselves to me. For I was possessed of such great enthusiasm for our ancestral Law that in the interests of safeguarding it by any means I used to persecute the church of Christ. So steadfast was I in the matters which the Law prescribes, that there was no respect in which I could deservedly be blamed as a transgressor. If such things had anything remarkable, I could boast with better reason than those who want to be thought of as demigods because they lack a prepuce. And indeed, at that point in time, since I had not yet been taught Christ,[21] I thought myself wonderfully fortunate in the nobility of my birth, the status of my sect, and my observance of the Law.

But when I learned through the gospel of Christ the matters in which true righteousness[22] consists and, in addition, came to know that in these types and shadows of the Mosaic law realities far more remarkable are signified, I rejected what earlier I used to pursue as things eagerly to be sought. And I abandoned them, considering pernicious whatever might hinder even the slightest from the teaching of Christ. Not that I condemn the Law if anyone uses it as it should be used.[23] But I attribute so much to the gospel of

* * * * *

the Pharisees were not *always* held in the highest regard. At one time they were expelled from membership in the Sanhedrin. See 'Pharisees' *Encyclopaedia Judaica* (n17 above) 16 30–2.

21 Cf Eph 4:20: 'But you have not so learned Christ' (Conf). Nicholas of Lyra paraphrases 3:7, 'according to my view before my conversion.'

22 'Righteousness': *iustitia*. In 3:9 the Greek δικαιοσύνη appears twice, qualifying in the first case the Law ('the righteousness of the Law'), in the second faith ('the righteousness of God by faith'). In both cases Erasmus followed the Vulgate in translating *iustitia*. In the paraphrase here the meaning of the term is amplified by the contrast between the prescriptions of the Law and the teachings of Christ. Of the former, Paul could 'in no respect deservedly be blamed as a transgressor,' while he would permit 'nothing to hinder him even in the slightest' from following the latter. If *iustitia* here has its chief focus in the notion of obedience to 'prescriptions' and 'teachings,' the word in this context nevertheless evokes the broader connotations of the intellectual framework of such obedience. On *iustitia* see 1 Cor chapter 1 n41.

23 That is, in the spiritual sense which finds fulfilment in Christ. See Erasmus' paraphrases on Rom 8:3, 10:4, 16:25–7 and Gal 4:8–9 CWE 42 45 with n2, 60 with n4, 90 with n6, and 116 with n10; and his annotation on Rom 8:3 ('for what was impossible for the Law') CWE 56 201 n4. Theophylact *Expos in Phil* (on 3:7–8) PG 124 1181B–D also explains that the Law is profitable by its nature in that it frees men from superstition and bestial tendencies and leads to a life worthy of Christ, but compared with the excellence of grace it pales in significance.

Jesus Christ, my Lord, that I not only prefer the surpassing knowledge of him to the carnal Mosaic law[24] in which they glory, but I also regard as a liability whatever this world anywhere holds as worthy or welcome.

Therefore, as soon as I began to have a taste[25] of this, there was no profit in anything however splendid that I do not consider a loss, or indeed that I do not regard as rubbish or something more despicable than rubbish,[26] if only at its expense I am allowed to gain Christ, the source of all the goods that truly are good. I consider as nothing the reputation for righteousness[27] that observance of the Mosaic law used to claim for me among men,[28] provided only there comes to me the true righteousness.[29] I cannot call it mine, since it is not, in any way, obtained through our merits, but is given freely to those who, distrusting themselves, rely on Christ in simplicity.[30] A kind of righteousness springs also from the Law, but it is not efficacious for securing salvation.[31]

The righteousness that is given by God, however, while it is not ours,[32] nevertheless confers true salvation upon us, provided that believing in the

* * * * *

24 For criticism elsewhere of the ceremonial details of the Law, eg circumcision, dietary regulations, sabbaths, see the paraphrase on 3:18 below; also the paraphrase on Rom 4:15 CWE 42 30. For 'the burdensome and carnal part of the Mosaic law' as opposed to 'the spiritual part' cf the paraphrase on Gal 5:4 CWE 42 122.

25 Cf Ps 34:8 (Vulgate 34:9) 'O taste and see that the Lord is good' (RSV); also 119:103 (Vulgate 118:103).

26 With this decorous paraphrase Erasmus avoids the Vulgate *stercora* 'excrement,' which he acknowledges to be the real meaning of the Greek σκύβαλον. See his annotation on 3:8 (*ut stercora*).

27 See n22 above.

28 For a fuller treatment of the righteousness that comes from the Law, see Erasmus' annotation on Rom 10:5 ('for Moses wrote') CWE 56 278–80.

29 See n22 above.

30 'In simplicity': *simpliciter*. On simplicity as a qualification of faith see the annotation on Rom 1:5 ('to the obeying of the faith') CWE 56 27: '[Faith] is not obtained by a painful process of logical reasoning, but by simple obedience and quiet compliance ... today [Paul's expression] applies to the convoluted labyrinths of the questions of the scholastics concerning those matters of which it is pious to be ignorant.' For *simplicitas* 'simplicity' and *simplex* 'simple' in the paraphrases see chapter 2 nn31 and 33; Col chapter 2 nn7 and 9; 1 Cor chapter 1 n40; and the annotation on 1 Thess 2:3 (*neque ex munditia*).

31 On the true righteousness, see n22 above.

32 The Latin is elliptical and adds a nuance obscured in idiomatic English: the righteousness that is a gift of God is far from being ours, yet for that very reason it confers salvation if we believe.

gospel through faith we come to know Jesus Christ. His birth[33] is too won-
derful to be understood by any mortal wisdom; the power[34] of his resurrection is too great to admit of persuasion by any human arguments. Faith
alone[35] can persuade us of these truths. Indeed it has persuaded us so well
that, relying on the hope of the promises, I rejoice to enter into the partnership of his afflictions – in my turn bound and dying for the sake of his
gospel just as he for our sake was beaten and crucified – if only it may come
about that, just as I imitate his death, so I may arrive at the glory of the resurrection, raised up through him. This most certain hope comforts me in these
afflictions because I rely on the promises of Christ, who has promised a partnership in his kingdom to those who have not refused a share in the cross.

I should not have said these things as though it depended upon me to
attain so great a prize.[36] I have not yet arrived at the goal of the race; I have
not yet attained the award; the contest is not yet completed; but nevertheless,
I am striving towards it with all my strength in order to attain what I am
pursuing. For the prize does not come to a person who runs just any old way
at all, but[37] to the person who presses on keenly, the one who puts forth
effort consistently. There is good hope that I shall lay hold of the prize,
since for this very purpose Christ took hold[38] of me and drew me back

* * * * *

33 Paul mentions only the resurrection here but cf Ambrosiaster *Comm in Phil*
(on 3:8–11) CSEL 81/3 154:7–8 who also mentions at this point the mystery
of the incarnation. Theophylact *Expos in Phil* (on 3:10) PG 124 1184B–C asks:
'[In comparison with the resurrection] how will what is greater, namely, his
nativity, be grasped by reasoning? But how is it greater? Because there are
many examples of resurrection: for many rose even before Christ; but from
a virgin no one else was born.'
34 Erasmus' interest in terms denoting power is evident here: *vis* 'power' paraphrases the Vulgate *virtus* 'virtue,' 'excellence,' 'strength' (3:10), which Erasmus'
translation had rendered *potentia* 'ability,' 'strength.' See Eph chapter 1 n48.
35 'Faith alone': *sola fides*, a Lutheran watchword. In this context, however, Erasmus is not arguing that faith alone suffices for salvation, but that faith, pure
and simple, is the teacher of these truths. He discusses the expression in two
annotations on 1 Cor 13:2 and 13:13; see 1 Cor chapter 13 nn8 and 21. See also
1 Cor chapter 15 n17.
36 For other analogies based on the athletic training of the runner and on the
single-minded pursuit of one's God-given calling, cf the paraphrases on 1 Cor
9:24–7; Eph 2:10; and Heb 12:1–4 CWE 44 252–3. See also Theophylact *Expos in
Phil* (on 3:12–14) PG 124 1185B–1188A.
37 but ... consistently] First in 1532. Previously, 'but to the one who puts forth
effort consistently, keenly.'
38 Erasmus' paraphrase *me apprehensurum ... reprehensus sum a Christo* 'I shall
lay hold ... Christ took hold' approximates the play on words in the Vulgate

from the midst of the course I had once badly begun against his church:[39] that by running well in the gospel stadium, I might deserve the reward of immortality. [I say this] so that confidence in the promised prize might not make you lazy and careless.

Brothers, I, personally, do not think that I have as yet attained what I strive and hope for. What I pursue is very great and no one attains it without set purpose. I know that Christ is truthful, but the frailty and fickleness of human nature does not yet allow me to be careless. Accordingly, with a hope that is great indeed, and considering everything else secondary, I attend to this one objective: namely, that in the gospel race, as though forgetful of all that is left behind, I move forward with every effort towards what is still in front. And yet[40] I do not proceed without design to any place at all – for he who runs badly loses – but I head straight for the evangelical goal set before us, and for the prize of immortality to which we are called by God, our umpire at the games,[41] who carefully watches our attempt from heaven,[42] while Christ Jesus brings assistance. So then, what else do those who mingle the Law with the gospel desire but to delay our course?

All of us who are perfect, then, should be disposed in such a way that we set for ourselves nothing except the gospel target.[43] But if there are

* * * * *

(*comprehendam ... comprehensus sum*), which in turn mirrors the play on the Greek καταλαμβάνω.

39 As a persecutor of the Christians (Acts 7:58–8:3, 9:1–2). See also Theophylact *Expos in Phil* (on 3:12) PG 124 1185B: 'When I was one of the persecutors ... Christ pursued me and while I was fleeing from him he lay hold of me and turned me around.'

40 And yet] Added in 1532

41 'Our umpire at the games': *agonotheta*. Erasmus uses the word in his paraphrases on 1 Cor 9:24 (see n34 there) and 1 Tim 6:12, and in *Concionalis interpretatio in psalmum 85* CWE 64 114–15 (cf nn551, 556). Although it does not appear in the New Testament, the word, familiar from classical Greek authors, is used also by patristic writers in the context of the athletic contest as a metaphor for the Christian life, eg Jerome *Adversus Iovinianum* 1.12 PL 23 (1845) 228A: 'The agonothete proposes the prize, invites [you] to the race, holds the trophy ... in his hand.' For the allegory in the Fathers, see further CWE 44 37 n12; on Erasmus and Jerome, see Alan W. Reese 'So Outstanding an Athlete of Christ: Erasmus and the Significance of Jerome's Asceticism' ERSY 18 (1998) 104–17.

42 Cf Heb 12:1–4 and Erasmus' paraphrase on the verses in CWE 44 252–3.

43 'Target': Latin *scopum*, Greek σκοπός. The word is found in the paraphrases on 3:14 and 19, and 1 Cor 1:13 (cf n30). The Vulgate had translated *ad destinatum* 'towards the goal' (Conf). See the annotation on 3:14 (*ad destinatum*): 'Jerome

any among you who are somewhat weaker, who cannot entirely disregard the ancestral Law to which they have grown accustomed,[44] let them be tolerated until they, too, make progress. To you God has revealed that the protections of the Law are in no way necessary; perhaps he will make the same revelation to them also.

But for the time being, by all means let us go forward according to the rule prescribed on that course which we have already begun. In this, at least, let us be of one heart: that we not allow ourselves to be deterred from our purpose; to the best of our ability let each of us hasten towards the prize of immortality. There are people who do not take the direct course; to follow them would not be safe. Instead, imitate me as I hasten by the direct route towards the gospel prize[45] and pay close attention to those whom you see walking after our example. Christ has provided us with an excellent pattern; in accordance with it you see me straining towards the same goal at which he has arrived.

Not all who run in this stadium attain the prize. Nor would it be safe for you to follow just any of those who run before you. There are many – I have frequently talked to you about them before, and now again I say with tears – who preach Christ in such a way that they are all the while enemies of the cross of Christ. For they are unwilling to imitate his life and death so that with him they may live forever. With an eye to their own gain and glory they teach, instead of true piety, petty Jewish

* * * * *

notes that the Greek word has greater significance [than the phrase in the Latin Bible]. For σκοπός properly is a sign set up for archers.' In 1519 Erasmus added to the note: 'Hence, what we settle on in our mind and set up in advance is a *scopus.*' Cf Erasmus' translation of 3:14 κατὰ σκοπόν *iuxta praefixum signum* 'according to the sign set up in advance.' Tertullian uses the word *scopus* quoting Phil 3:14 in *De resurrectione mortuorum* 23.9 CCL 2 950. D.F.S. Thomson mentions *scopus* as a favourite word of Erasmus, 'The Latinity of Erasmus' *Erasmus* ed T.A. Dorey (London 1970) 117, 129. See also Marjorie O'Rourke Boyle *Erasmus on Language and Method in Theology* (Toronto 1977) 72–81 and Manfred Hoffmann *Rhetoric and Theology: the Hermeneutic of Erasmus* (Toronto 1994) 84 n104.

44 Cf Romans 14; Gal 4:1–14. Erasmus understands the weaker in faith as the Christian converts from Judaism who were not yet able to set aside the Law. See his annotation on 3:15 (*aliter sapitis*). See also his paraphrases on Romans 14 and Gal 3:24–4:11 CWE 42 77–83 and 113–17, and his several annotations on Rom 14:1–2 CWE 56 366–70.

45 Erasmus uses *brabea* 'prizes' plural, because more than one person is intended, each to receive his own prize.

observances[46] – circumcision of the foreskin,[47] choice of foods, distinctions among days – so that, while others are burdened by these observances, they themselves in the meantime live like kings[48] and have a pleasant life, just as though they do not look forward to another life after this.

May the end of those people deter us from their conduct. For just as we push our way towards eternal glory through disrepute on the human level, and through passing afflictions strain towards imperishable happiness, so they, through momentary pleasures, appropriate to themselves everlasting destruction, having in place of God a belly that will not be able to come to their aid; and through a counterfeit glory before men, a glory they place not in Christ but in shameful things, they hurry towards eternal disgrace. Whatever is of the earth is temporary and counterfeit; whatever is of heaven, true and everlasting. Yet they care about nothing other than earthly concerns. In these they place their glory, in these their pleasure, in these their riches, straying far from the target[49] of the gospel.

But we who follow Christ truly, although we are detained upon earth by our bodies, nevertheless in our spirits we live in heaven, aspiring constantly to the place to which our head has gone in advance, and from which also through faith we await our Lord Jesus Christ. When the dead have been raised again, he will show without concealment the realities he promises, about to transform meanwhile this poor body, lowly and subject to all ills, and restore it in the likeness of his own glorious body, in order that the members that here shared in his afflictions, there may be called to share in his happiness. And that will not seem incredible to anyone who has pondered the strength[50] of the one through whom this will be done. There is nothing that he cannot fulfil; for it is in his power[51] to subject all things to himself whenever he pleases. That capability he will then reveal to all, however much he often hides it in the meantime.

* * * * *

46 Diminutives are frequent in Erasmus' writings; *observatiunculae* 'petty observances' is one of the pejorative category. See Jean-Claude Margolin *Erasme: Declamatio pueris statim ac liberaliter instituendis: étude critique, traduction et commentaire* (Geneva 1966) 604.

47 of the foreskin] Added in 1532

48 'Live like kings' represents Erasmus' *regnent* 'reign.' The context suggests luxury and self-indulgence, not simply monarchical power.

49 Again Erasmus uses *scopus* 'target' to complete the archer analogy. See n43 above.

50 Or 'power'; Erasmus uses *vis* here again. See n34 above.

51 'Power': *in manu.* Cf OLD 16d 'within one's grasp' (in phrases expressing possession or control).

Chapter 4

Braced, then, with the hope of such great things, my brothers, loved and longed for, whose success I consider my joy, whose victory I judge my crown, continue as you have begun, and do not allow yourselves to be turned aside from Christ Jesus.

Again and again,[1] my beloved brothers, I beg Evodia and I beg[2] Syntyche, individually, to be in heartfelt agreement in promoting the gospel of Christ.

What is more, I ask you also, my true and genuine partner,[3] since you are in sympathy with me in the work of the gospel, to assist those women who have been associates of my labours and dangers in the gospel, along with Clement and the rest as well, who were co-workers with me in the gospel. What is to be gained by my repeating their names, when they have been written in the book of life indelibly? There are written the names of

* * * * *

1 Cf the annotation on 4:2 (et Syntychen obsecro) where Erasmus points out that the repetition of the verb παρακαλῶ 'entreat' (RSV) signifies Paul's strength of feeling in his entreaty.

2 Erasmus deliberately repeats the word obsecro 'I beg.' The Vulgate had varied the verbs – rogo and deprecor – demonstrating a 'love of variety' that Erasmus deplored. See his annotation on the verse (cited in the preceding note).

3 'Partner': coniunx, usually 'wife' or 'help-mate.' Coniunx is formed from cum + iugum and is therefore the etymological equivalent of the Greek σύζυγος, literally 'with yoke,' ie yoke-mate. Of common grammatical gender, Erasmus modifies it with feminine adjectives. It is clear, then, that Erasmus is interpreting the request as addressed by Paul to a woman. His paraphrase, however, is conveniently ambiguous. In his 1519 annotation on 4:3 (germane compar), he reports that many Greek commentators think that Paul is referring to his wife, that the context makes a woman an appropriate recipient of instructions that affect women, and that a true wife is one united to her husband in intimacy, in profession of faith, in zeal for goodness, and in similarity of life. The annotation, and then the paraphrase, provoked much controversy and were severely criticized especially by Noël Béda and López Zúñiga. Ultimately Erasmus states that he does not know Paul's marital status, and in fact considers it irrelevant, particularly in light of the fact that Peter, chief of the apostles, was known to be married. See Erasmus Apologiae contra Stunicam (1) ASD IX-2 214:845–216:864, and Supputatio LB IX 692–3. For discussions of various interpretations of the individual intended by Paul, see Lightfoot 168–71, and Peter T. O'Brien The Epistle to the Philippians: a Commentary on the Greek Text (Grand Rapids 1991) 480–1. See also Erasmus' annotation on 1 Cor 7:8 (dico autem non nuptis) and his paraphrase on that verse with n14, and on 1 Cor 9:5–6 with n12.

all who assist the evangelical task by their services and you too are of their number.

Therefore, rejoice always, even in the midst of afflictions. Again and again I bid you to be cheerful. No matter how much the iniquity of the wicked rages against you, still let your equity[4] and your moderation be recognized and approved by all mortals, not only by the brothers but even by those who are strangers to Christ, so that challenged more quickly by your goodness, they may be enticed to a share in the gospel.[5] Gentleness of character wins over and softens[6] even the impious. You should not wish to take vengeance on them or begrudge them their trivial delights.[7] For the coming of Christ is at hand. He will bestow immortality on you in compensation for this world's advantages which you have scorned; those people will pay the penalty for their madness.

Live a day at a time, anxious about nothing, acting with only this in mind: that he at his coming may find you ready. Rely on him with your whole heart. If there is need of anything, do not trust in the assistance of the world, but importune God with incessant entreaties, making known to him by ardent prayers whatever you require; giving thanks to him whatever happens, whether prosperity or adversity, certain that through him even adversities will be turned to your advantage. That one [being God] indeed knows, even if you make no request, what is profitable for you, but nevertheless he loves to be addressed by embassies[8]

* * * * *

4 The translation represents the wordplay in the Latin: *iniquitas* 'iniquity' and *aequitas* 'equity' or 'fairness,' linked here with *moderatio* 'moderation,' an aspect in Erasmus of *humanitas* 'humaneness,' although he does not use that word here. For the concept of 'humaneness'; see also 2 Cor chapter 10 n3; Col chapter 4 n14; 2 Thess chapter 3 nn15 and 16; and the paraphrase on John 4:27 CWE 46 59 with n47. From his annotation on Phil 4:5 (*modestia*), we know that Erasmus is following Ambrosiaster's interpretation *Comm in Phil* (on 4:5) CSEL 81/3 159:7–12 to the effect that Paul is calling for rational, uncontentious behaviour.

5 Ambrosiaster *Comm in Phil* (on 4:5) CSEL 81/3 159:9–10 also suggests that the possibility of winning others to imitate their way of life is the reason for allowing their good qualities to be seen.

6 'Softens': *frangit*, on which see OLD 10.

7 'Trivial delights': *delicias*, on which see OLD *delicia*. The feminine form is derived from the neuter plural of *delicium* 'pet' or 'darling,' used by Erasmus in his annotation on Rom 10:1 ('the will indeed of my heart') CWE 56 276 n6. See also 1 Thess chapter 5 n5.

8 'Embassies': *legationibus*. In this context *legationes* may stand, by metonomy, for 'requests' of a public, communal nature. Together with its cognates, *legatus* 'ambassador' and *delegare* 'delegate,' it is a favourite word of Erasmus, of-

of this kind; he loves to be solicited and, as it were, compelled by pious prayers.[9]

In this way it will happen that peace, by which you have been reconciled to God – a reality too happy for the human mind[10] to perceive – will fortify your hearts as well as your souls against all the horrors that can occur here. For what would a person dread, if he knows that he is dear to God through Christ Jesus?[11]

Well then, as I want you to be free from the care for the things on which this world fawns, or which it fears, so you must be vigilant with all your power of mind in order to grow rich in the virtues that will commend you to God. And so whatever things are true and free of subterfuge, whatever are decent and honourable and worthy of people who despise what is petty and silly, whatever are just, whatever are pure and holy, whatever cater to harmony, whatever win a good reputation, if there is any virtue, if there is any ground for praise, the companion of virtue, let these be your care and concern, let these be kept in your hearts. These, I say, and considerations like them, are what you learned long ago, and received from us. Not only did you hear them from me, you have also seen them in me. For I did not teach you what I myself did not practise. Therefore you are not only to keep these same teachings in mind, you are also to practise them and model yourselves on us. To people who live out these instructions, God,

* * * * *

ten used in connection with Paul's role in the early church and serving to paraphrase or elaborate the Greek ἀπόστολος 'apostle.' See eg his paraphrases on 2 Cor 5:20 and Eph 6:20 (in both passages translated as 'mission'). See also 1 Cor chapter 1 n2 and 2 Cor chapter 1 n1.

9 That importunity in prayer is pleasing to God is a prominent theme in Erasmus' paraphrase on Luke 11:5–9 CWE 48 7–9. With this sentence Erasmus seems to be correcting Theophylact *Expos in Phil* (on 4:6) PG 124 1193C who says that we should make known our requests with grateful prayers because otherwise God does not acknowledge them. On this point, see Pabel *Conversing with God* 39–42.

10 Erasmus, in his annotation on 4:7 *(omnem sensum)*, clarifies the meaning of the Vulgate *sensum* lest the reader think it apply only, or mainly, to physical feeling. Cf Ambrosiaster *Comm in Phil* (on 4:7) CSEL 81/3 159:6, 24 and 160:2 whose lemma reads *mens* 'mind.'

11 Although he uses much of the language of Ambrosiaster *Comm in Phil* (on 4:7) CSEL 81/3 160:4–5: *quis enim non metuat eum, quem scit dei esse amicum?* 'For who would not dread the person he knows to be a friend of God?' Erasmus twists the question into a reflection on the subject's relationship with God: *quid enim metuat, qui se norit Deo carum esse ?* 'For what would a person dread if he knows that he [himself] is dear to God?

the author of peace, will be present; he is at peace with none but those who cultivate virtue.

Moreover, I derived extraordinary pleasure from the fact that your love's customary affection for me, interrupted now for some time, has at last renewed its strength and, so to speak, flowered again. No, it was not the affection that was interrupted, but although it had not changed you had no opportunity to send what you wanted. And so I rejoice not so much over the advantage I have received as over your love; I rejoice that by it you have been made worthy of God. I am not so greatly moved by the fact that your generosity has come to the aid of my penury, for I am not unacquainted with these circumstances or unaccustomed to them. On the contrary, as the result of already extensive experience, I have been hardened to the suffering of these ills. I have learned to be content with present fortune, whatever it may be. I know, indeed, how to be poor and lowly amid the needy; I know also how to shine amid the wealthy. If there is a lack, I place restraint upon myself; if there is abundance, I pour it out for the use of others and play the role of a bountiful donor. Indigence is safer, abundance more kindly.[12] I know how to adapt myself to every place, every time, every occasion, so thoroughly am I prepared and good for either fortune. Satiety does not corrupt me if an abundance is at hand; nor does hunger make me downcast if something to eat is lacking. Riches do not make me haughty if something beyond necessity comes my way; nor does the lack of resources terrify me if there is less than the conduct of life requires. Why would these disturb my spirit when for the sake of the gospel I scorn fetters and scourges? There is none of these that I would not endure with spirit unbroken while I am confirmed and strengthened[13] by Jesus Christ, by whose help I am strong, since of myself I am nothing.[14]

I should not say this because I despise your munificence; on the contrary, I earnestly praise your devotion, seeing that you have enrolled yourselves in the fellowship of my afflictions; in rewards, also, you shall be my partners in the presence of God. I embrace the spontaneous prompti-

* * * * *

12 For wealth and poverty contrasted elsewhere in Erasmus' works, see the paraphrase on James 5:1–6 CWE 44 165–7; *De contemptu mundi* CWE 66 140–2; and *Institutio principis christiani* CWE 27 262, where he describes generosity as 'the special glory of good princes.'

13 The paraphrase on 4:13 reflects Erasmus' own translation, replacing the Vulgate *confortare* 'to comfort' with *corroborare* 'to strengthen.' See his annotation on the verse (*qui me confortat*).

14 Cf 2 Cor 12:11.

tude of your heart. For I personally am not in the habit of soliciting from anyone the favours you have conferred.[15] You yourselves are also the witnesses, Philippians, that[16] when I was first preaching the gospel of Christ in the neighbouring regions and I was leaving Macedonia, no church shared with me (at least by way of giving and receiving). Those people did not donate anything, nor was I eager to receive. You alone, of your own accord, brought to me – not only when I was living among you, but even when I was absent at Thessalonica, you sent me, once and then again a second time – what you thought I needed. In riches Thessalonica had the advantage, but yours was the more generous attitude.

I do not find fault with them, but I congratulate you on your profit; I rejoice in[17] your gain more than in my own. For a person makes a huge gain if on account of the gospel of Christ he diminishes his temporal estate and exchanges wealth that belongs to others for real and lasting riches.[18] I am not looking for a gift, but I am looking for the interest that accrues to you as the result of your prompt and voluntary munificence. There is a little decrease in your financial accounts; there is some impairment of your household estate, but very much is credited to the account of your heavenly rewards.

And yet, insofar as it pertains to me,[19] there is no reason for you to feel sorry that your generosity was not quite welcome. I have recovered[20] everything and now, through your munificence, I am rich; I have been filled to the brim with the delivery Epaphroditus brought me from you, so abundantly have you sent.

* * * * *

15 An echo of 1 Cor 9:1–18 where Paul insists on the gratuitousness of his ministry. Cf 1 Cor 4:12: 'We toil, working with our own hands' (Conf).

16 that] Explicit in the early versions, *quod* 'that' is omitted in 1532 and subsequent editions. The omission does not change the meaning of the sentence.

17 I rejoice in] First in 1521, replacing a repeat of *gratulor*, which connotes both congratulation and rejoicing.

18 Erasmus also adverts to the happy exchange of temporal for eternal goods in his paraphrase on the parable of the unjust steward in Luke 16:1–12 (CWE 48 92–3), discussed in Sider 'The Just' 23 and n79. See also the paraphrase on Col 1:15.

19 Erasmus has represented Paul pointing out that the profit of the Philippians' generosity flowed back to the donors; now he notes that it has also enriched his, ie Paul's, life.

20 Erasmus adduces Theophylact's support for his interpretation that the Greek ἀπέχειν means 'to recover what is owed,' as in collecting a tax or a land rental fee. See Erasmus' annotation on 4:18 (*habeo autem omnia*) and Theophylact *Expos in Phil* (on 4:18) PG 124 1201B.

However, I have received this not so much as a gift sent by men to a man, but as a victim most pleasing to God, for whom no odour of sacrifice is more pleasing than the spontaneous service of gospel charity.[21] Moreover, to the extent that you impair your fortunes in order that I may lack nothing, so may my God, in turn, make up for you whatever will have been wanting in this life. Since he is wealthy, he will not allow you who are becoming poor for the sake of his gospel to lack anything you need. This pertains to his own glory and to that of Christ. May all glory be[22] to God our Father for ages unending. Amen.

Greet all who strive after sanctity and purity of life according to the teaching of Jesus Christ.

Greetings to you, in return, from those in Rome who along with me are openly acknowledging Christ, not only those who have a rather close association with me, but also all the rest, above all, the members of Caesar's household who have embraced the teaching of Christ and have not been deterred from the public acknowledgment of Christ even through the fear of such a savage prince and lord. May the favour and kindness of our Lord Jesus Christ be always with your spirit. Amen.

The End[23]

* * * * *

21 Cf Eph 5:2; Matt 9:13, 12:7.
22 May ... be] Latin *sit* in all Froben editions to 1540; *sic* 'thus' in LB only.
23 The End] In editions from 1522 to 1534. Earlier editions printed a version of the characteristic longer form of this concluding notice (cf eg 197, 356). *1540* and LB omit it entirely.

PARAPHRASE ON COLOSSIANS

In epistolam Pauli Apostoli ad Colossenses paraphrasis

translated and annotated by
MECHTILDE O'MARA

THE ARGUMENT OF THE EPISTLE OF PAUL
THE APOSTLE TO THE COLOSSIANS
BY ERASMUS OF ROTTERDAM

The Colossians live in Asia Minor, neighbours to the Laodiceans.[1] The Apostle had not seen them,[2] for they were converted to Christ by the preaching of Archippus, or, as Ambrose adds, of Epaphras,[3] to whom this task had been assigned.[4] They were being seriously menaced by false apostles attempting to seduce them into the worst possible dogma, for they were teaching that the Son of God was not the author of salvation, but that through the angels a path lay open to the Father.[5] They alleged that the Son of God had not come into this world nor would he come in the future, since in the Old Testament all things were administered through angels.[6] Next, they were

* * * * *

1 In a prefatory annotation on Colossians Erasmus sets forth the classical evidence for the existence of the city of Colossae in Phrygia not far from Laodicea and Hierapolis in Asia Minor. Cf Col 2:1, 4:14. He expresses amazement that some think the letter is addressed to the Rhodians on account of the Colossus, a thirty-two metre statue the Rhodians had erected to the sun god Helios. Erasmus is correcting an entry in the frequently reprinted Latin dictionary (24 editions between 1502 and 1520) of Ambrogio Calepino (c 1435–c 1510) which identified the Colossians with Rhodians, a point taken up by his Spanish antagonist López Zúñiga. Cf *Apologiae contra Stunicam* (1) ASD IX-2 218–19. For Calepino, see CWE Ep 1725:13–14 with n3 and CEBR I 244.
2 See Col 2:1.
3 See Ambrosiaster *Comm in Col* Argument CSEL 81/3 167:2.
4 For Archippus, see Col 4:17 and Philem 2; for Epaphras, Col 1:7, 4:12 and Philem 23. Ambrosiaster similarly mentions them. See *Comm in Col* Argument CSEL 81/3 167:4: 'after the preaching of Epaphras or Archippus.' Modern scholars are of the opinion that there is no way of knowing the precise ministry of Archippus (Col 4:17). See Lohse 175 and Ralph Martin *Colossians and Philemon* New Century Bible (London 1974) 139. Similarly, it is clear that Epaphras works tirelessly for the community but it is not clear at what he is working. On Col 4:12–13, see Lohse 173–4.
5 The identification of these false apostles continues to exercise modern scholars. See NJBC §54:8 877–8.
6 See Col 2:18–19 and Theophylact who writes in his 'Hypothesis' (ie Argument) *Expos in Col* PG 124 1205B: 'For they thought that not through the Son, but

mixing Judaism and the superstition of philosophy[7] in with the teaching of Christ, adhering to certain ordinances of the Law and superstitiously observing the sun, the moon and the stars, and the elements of this world to which, according to their teaching, we are subject.

Accordingly, he reminds them of their profession, showing that they owe whatever they have attained thus far not to the angels but to Christ, the creator of the angels; that he alone is the head of the church, and that they are not to seek salvation from any other source. In the meantime Paul asserts his own authority. But he warns them carefully not to allow themselves to be deceived by the pompous speech of false apostles and by feigned visions of angels, nor to slide into Judaism or philosophical superstition.[8] He deals with these topics in the first two chapters.

In what remains he exhorts them to the duties of piety, prescribing in detail what sort of person a wife should be in relation to her husband, a husband to his wife, parents to children, children to parents, slaves to masters, masters to slaves. The final part is taken up with greetings, except that he reminds Archippus of his duty.[9]

Furthermore, he wrote from the prison at Ephesus, through Tychicus, as he openly attests in this Epistle.[10] In our Arguments,[11] Onesimus is added

* * * * *

through angels they would be brought to God the Father, thinking it absurd to believe that the Son of God would appear in the last times, since in the Old Testament all things were done by angels.' For a brief summary of 'Angels in Scripture,' see Steven Chase *Angelic Spirituality: Medieval Perspectives on the Ways of Angels* (New York 2002) 8–14. See also chapter 2 n64.

7 We find a similar reference to philosophy in Ambrosiaster *Comm in Col* Argument CSEL 81/3 167:3–5: 'The false apostles . . . would ensnare the simplicity of their [the Colossians'] minds by philosophical disputations.' Theophylact *Expos in Col* Argument PG 124 1205B mentions 'many Jewish and Greek practices' but does not mention philosophy specifically.

8 For the character of the religion advocated by the 'false apostles' see especially Col 2:8, 16, 18, 21–3; cf Eph 5:6. See also NJBC §54:8 877–8 'The Opponents.'

9 See Col 4:17.

10 Col 4:3 and 10 attest to the fact of Paul's imprisonment but not to the place, which must be inferred from the study of the corpus of Pauline Epistles. Information about the place of composition and letter bearers was generally given in the Greek subscriptions, and usually included in the old Latin Arguments, occasionally with minor variations from Greek precedents. Erasmus typically offers such information in his own Arguments. In the *Paraphrases* on Ephesians, Philippians, Colossians, and the two Thessalonians he adopts the idiom of the old Latin Arguments, apparently carried over from the Greek subscriptions, 'written from . . . through . . .' evidently meaning 'written from . . . conveyed by.' My translation reflects Erasmus' idiom. See also n13 below.

11 By 'our Arguments' Erasmus intends the traditional Latin Arguments found in Vulgate Bibles. See Translators' Note xvi.

to Tychicus as a colleague, just as[12] Paul attests in chapter four; while the Greek subscriptions affirm that it was sent from the city of Rome,[13] certainly it was from Rome that he sent back Onesimus whom he had begotten for Christ when he was in chains in that place.[14]

The End of the Argument

* * * * *

12 just as ... four] First in *1532*; previous editions, '(and I don't know on what evidence).' Cf Col 4:9.
13 Many Greek texts add at the end of the Pauline Epistles 'subscriptions,' ie short notes identifying the addressee, the place of writing, and the bearer of the letter. See Metzger 560 and the Argument of 1 Corinthians n29. In his 1516 edition of the New Testament, Erasmus included some of these subscriptions, and in subsequent editions included them for all Pauline Epistles.
14 Cf Philem 10–12: 'I plead ... for my own son, whom I have begotten in prison, for Onesimus ... I am sending him back' (Conf).

THE PARAPHRASE ON THE EPISTLE OF PAUL
THE APOSTLE TO THE COLOSSIANS
BY ERASMUS OF ROTTERDAM

Chapter 1

Paul, the ambassador of Jesus Christ, and that not by human appointment[1]
but in accordance with the will of God the Father, and also Timothy, who
is like a brother to me on account of our perfect agreement in the gospel,
to those who live at Colossae trusting in Christ Jesus and eagerly pursuing
holiness of life in accordance with his teaching, now our[2] very dear brothers
in the fellowship of our profession. May grace be to you and peace from
God our Father, so that, just as you have been freely reconciled to him,
you may always foster mutual harmony with one another as befits brothers
glorying in a common father.

 Even though it has not fallen to my lot to see you, still in the prayers
with which we incessantly address God and the Father of our Lord Jesus Christ on your behalf, we both give thanks for his gifts bestowed
on you and at the same time entreat him to increase his benefits day by
day and to protect the increase given. [We have been doing this ever]
since we learned through Epaphras of your faith. Relying on it we are
confident that you will be kept unharmed, not by the help of angels,[3]
but by the freely given kindness of Christ Jesus through whom the Father has been pleased to bestow all things on us. He wanted him to
be named both Christ and Jesus, Christ so that all might draw salvation
from him, Jesus so that no one would hope for salvation from any other

* * * * *

1 For 'not by human appointment,' see Gal 1:1 and the paraphrase on Eph 1:1.
2 our] First in 1521; previously 'your'
3 Angels are explicitly mentioned first at Col 2:18; in the paraphrase, however,
  Erasmus introduces them repeatedly from the beginning. Cf Theophylact *Expos in Col* (on 1:1–4) PG 124 1208A–C who mentions angels five times in his
  commentary on the first four verses.

source.[4] And we have learned not only of your trust[5] towards him, but also of its companion, the charity, which, after Christ's example,[6] you have towards the saints, on whom you are eager to bestow kindness; not through any hope of a benefit to be returned to you with interest from time to time, but in the hope of the immortality that you know is stored up in heaven for your piety. For thus you have been truly persuaded through Christ's gospel, which is so truthful that, although it makes vast promises and offers what has never been heard of, still, since it depends on God as author, it cannot lie. As it is extended throughout the whole world more and more each day, so it has come to you, too, daily growing and increasing, spreading more widely and, at the same time, bearing fruit in the pious works that Christian charity spontaneously begets. The same thing is happening in you, who have always been advancing to better things since the day on which you first heard and came to know that, through the freely given kindness of God, sins are truly remitted for all who believe the gospel, if sincere charity is joined to correct belief.

For so you learned from Epaphras, my very dear fellow slave and a genuine apostle. In fact, he has sincerely acted as my deputy among you while he carried out the work[7] of the gospel on behalf of Jesus Christ in such a way that he has behaved irreproachably in all circumstances. Accordingly, just as I have taught you through him, so through him too we know of your

* * * * *

4 On the significance of the double name: Christ 'the anointed one' and Jesus 'Saviour,' cf Theophylact *Expos in Col* (on 1:4) PG 124 1210A: 'These names, "Christ" and "Jesus," are symbols of beneficence. For he was anointed for us and he saved the people from their sins.' Erasmus explains at greater length the significance of the name 'Christ' in his *Commentarius in psalmum* 2 CWE 63 88: 'The term "anointed" befits him because of the full store of divine grace which "dwelt in him bodily" as St Paul says.' See also *Explanatio symboli* CWE 70 281–3.

5 'Trust': *fiduciam*; Erasmus describes the meaning of πίστις by distinguishing its various nuances as expressed in Latin terms: *fides, fidelis, fiducia, fidere* (and its compounds and antonyms) in his annotation on Rom 1:17 ('from faith unto faith') CWE 56 42–5. See 1 Cor chapter 15 n17.

6 Cf John 13:1–17, especially verse 15, and John 13:34. On Christ as example in Erasmus' writing, see also Eph chapter 4 n55; Payne *Theology* 68–9; and Chomarat 1 639–65.

7 Erasmus uses in this sentence both *fungi* 'to act,' 'to function,' 'to fulfil,' and *functio* 'work,' 'function,' 'fulfilment.' In part Erasmus is emphasizing the service or duties of the apostle as opposed to an office with rank. See 2 Cor chapter 2 n18 for other examples of this distinction.

benevolence towards us; not that common sort by which people as a general rule[8] are benevolent towards friends and acquaintances,[9] but the spiritual and evangelical kind by which we love all those through whom the glory of the gospel is illuminated and confirmed, even if we have never looked on them with our bodily eyes.

We, likewise, in response to your disposition towards us, even without seeing you, have loved you from that very day on which we were informed about your readiness to believe and about your charity. With unremitting prayers we have been importuning God on your behalf and beseeching with ardent supplications that the gifts he has begun to confer he may perfect and complete in you, so that you recognize his will even more fully when you have been thoroughly instructed, not by human philosophy or by the superstitious opinion of certain individuals,[10] but by the spiritual wisdom and prudence of which you have already attained a good portion. I want you to lack no element of spiritual wisdom, so that when you have been perfected you may lead all your life in such a way that it seems worthy of God, and you are pleasing to him in everything, omitting no good work, for in these his pleasure lies. To have believed in the gospel is the first beginning of salvation; salvation is completed and perfected, however, by godly actions.

It is not enough to have learned through the gospel that God is the author of salvation through Jesus Christ his Son unless through this same knowledge you grow to maturity in the duties of Christian charity and bring forth fruit, progressing continually from better to better, and unless you persevere steadfastly in these ways, confirmed by all firmness of purpose,[11] so that no violence or storm of persecution[12] drives you from the straight course. To this end there is need of strength that is truly great. There is no reason for us to promise ourselves this strength out of our own resources. God must be the one to supply it so that all the glory of deeds valiantly performed by us returns to him. By his kindness we are empowered to sustain with the greatest endurance and the greatest gentleness

* * * * *

8 as a general rule] Added in 1521
9 Erasmus is exploiting the etymology of *benevolentia* 'benevolence' from *bene velle* 'to wish well,' 'to be benevolent.'
10 The contrast is between Hellenism and Judaism.
11 'Firmness of purpose': *robur*. The Latin word has a range of meanings: 'the hard wood of the oak tree,' 'physical strength,' 'military force,' 'strength of purpose.' See OLD *robur*. On *virtus* see Eph chapter 1 n48.
12 With Erasmus' explicit mention of persecutions, compare Theophylact *Expos in Col* (on 1:11) PG 124 1213C: 'For what purpose? Against trials and persecutions.'

whatever cries out against us, from time to time, on account of the gospel of Christ.[13]

It is not enough in these circumstances for us to be brave and fearless. No, it is fitting, rather, that we should even welcome sufferings eagerly, joyfully giving thanks to God the Father because he deemed you worthy of this honour: that, although previously you had been worshippers of images and demons, he saw fit to enrol you in the company of the Jews,[14] who were holy (in contrast with you)[15] on account of their worship of the true God, and to admit you to the same inheritance of immortality. In hope of this we ought to despise whatever here is terrifying or enticing. He saw fit also to impart the light of evangelical truth to you, who were previously enveloped in the thickest darkness of ignorance; and when he had ransomed you, who previously were subject to the most degrading, and at the same time the most miserable, servitude under the tyranny of the devil,[16] Prince of Darkness, he saw fit to transfer you into the kingdom of his Son, than whom he holds nothing more precious. In this way, adopted into his body, you might along with him have a share in his kingdom. In it there is no room for those who are under the domination of sin,[17] and for this reason freedom has been granted through God's Son, through whom the sins of our former life have been remitted. You have come under the authority of him, therefore, through whose kindness you have been restored.

And just see what a happy exchange! Previously you belonged to the body of the devil. Now you are grafted onto the body of Christ. So worthy is his excellence that he is the image of God the Father who dwells in light inaccessible[18] and cannot be perceived by anyone even though he is

* * * * *

13 Erasmus' theology of grace holds in tension both God's generosity in providing all that is requisite for us to act and the continued need for the Christian's generous response in action. Cf Theophylact *Expos in Col* (on 1:12) PG 124 1216C: 'God both honoured us and made us suitable to accept the honour.'

14 Erasmus identifies 'the saints' with the Jews. Cf Ambrosiaster *Comm in Col* (on 1:12) CSEL 81/3 170:4–6: 'He saw fit to summon and lead the gentiles into the promise of the Jews, which is light eternal.'

15 For the very reason that the Colossians ('you') had previously worshipped images and demons, ie false gods.

16 Theophylact *Expos in Col* (on 1:13) PG 124 1217B similarly explains: 'They then were under the power of darkness, that is, of error and of the tyranny of the devil.'

17 For a similar statement concerning the exclusion of sinners from the kingdom of God, see Gal 5:21 and Erasmus' paraphrase on it CWE 42 126.

18 For the expresssion 'who dwells in light inaccessible,' see also 1 Tim 6:16 and Erasmus' paraphrase on it CWE 44 37.

somehow perceived by us through the Son,[19] inasmuch as the Son is so like the Father as to be even his equal. For he is no less wise, or less powerful, or less good than the Father;[20] nor have these attributes been conferred upon him recently, but before anything was created, he was, from eternity, the image of the eternal Father, not created, but born of him from whom all things exist and who alone has no beginning. The Father of himself begot the Son, and through the Son and at the same time with the Son he created and fashioned[21] all things: whatever exists anywhere whether in the heavens or on the earth, visible as well as invisible, not even excepting the angels,[22] even the eminent ones, whether you would call them thrones or dominations

* * * * *

19 This paraphrase on Col 1:15 attempts to articulate how the Son has revealed God – whom no one has seen. In his annotation on 1:15 (*imago dei invisibilis*) Erasmus points out:

> Just as the Father alone is said to be immortal and wise, so the Father alone is said to be invisible – not that the Son is visible according to his divine nature, but that he has his invisible nature from the Father. The Father therefore, as the source, remains invisible. But the Father somehow manifests himself through his image, the Son, inasmuch as he created this world through him, inasmuch as he becomes known to us through the Son made man.

See Ambrosiaster's note *Comm in Col* (on 1:15) CSEL 81/3 170–2, which cites John 1:18 ('No one has at any time seen God' [Conf]) and John 14:9–10 ('Philip, he who sees me sees also the Father. How canst thou say, "Show us the Father"? Dost thou not believe that I am in the Father and the Father in me?' [Conf]). Ambrosiaster also notes: 'By an understanding of the divine works [creation, incarnation], they have seen the Son, not with their bodily eyes ... For this reason, then, he is said to be the image of the invisible God, so that it would be understood that he is God who is seen by the understanding.'

20 On wisdom, power, and goodness as the particular attributes of God in Erasmus, see CWE 50 109 n36; *De immensa Dei misericordia* CWE 70 82–3; *Explanatio symboli* CWE 70 276, 281; and *Responsio ad annotationes Lei* 1 (Concerning Note 61 and Concerning Note 72) CWE 72 167 and 180.

21 Erasmus paraphrases 'the first-born of every creature' (Col 1:15) in such a way as to include two meanings of a Greek word depending on the position of its accent: that Christ was πρωτότοκος 'first-begotten,' and that he was the πρωτοτόκος 'first-begetter.' Erasmus' paraphrase employs the language of the Nicene Creed. Similarly, Theophylact *Expos in Col* (on 1:15) PG 124 1220A– 1221B directs his comments against the deceptions of the Arians. In his annotation on 1:15 (*primogenitus omnis creaturae*) Erasmus noted that the translation 'begotten before all creation' would counter the Arian argument that Christ was a creature. But Edward Lee demurred. See Erasmus *Responsio ad annotationes Lei* 2 (Concerning Note 190) CWE 72 304–5.

22 For the inclusion of 'angels' among 'things created ... invisible' (1:16), cf Theophylact *Expos in Col* (on 1:15) PG 124 1221A: '[Paul refutes] the opinion of the

or principalities or powers.[23] These do excel all other created things, but in such a way that they are still far beneath the excellence of him to whom you have been closely bonded. For what has been created must necessarily be inferior to its own creator. Through Christ not only have all things been created, but they are also all governed and preserved by him, the equal and associate of the Father in this respect too. Truly, he himself is second to none, but he excels all created things which continue to exist through him and would be likely to perish did they not depend on him.[24] You see what the excellence and pre-eminence of Christ is, in case anyone should attribute too much to the angels.

But lest his majesty deter you, hear of his goodness so that you will not think that you have to seek another through whom to have access to the Father.[25] For so pre-eminent is he among angelic minds that he does not disdain also to be head of the church, which he bonded to himself so firmly that it adheres to him in just the same way as the body is attached to the head. In just the same way must we share in common whatever has preceded us in the head. He was the first to rise from the dead, not that he might be the only one to enjoy immortality, but that he might raise us, his members, to share in his immortality. What is granted to the first fruits must be shared in common by the whole mass.[26] He indeed is the prince and author of the resurrection, but through him we, too, shall

* * * * *

Colossians ... so that they would not think that he [Christ] is younger than the angels.'

23 On thrones, dominations, principalities, or powers (1:16), see also 2:10 and 15; Eph 1:21, 3:10, 6:12; 1 Cor 15:24; Rom 8:38; and 1 Pet 3:22. Erasmus' understanding that these belong to the nine ranks of angels follows the tradition of the medieval church as outlined, for example, by Aquinas *Super Eph lect* cap 1 lectio 7.61 (II 16). See also Pierre Benoit 'Pauline Angelology and Demonology: Reflexions on the Designations of the Heavenly Powers and on the Origin of Angelic Evil according to Paul' *Religious Studies Bulletin* 3 (1983) 1–18. Recent scholarship looks rather for wider, socio-political interpretations of these titles. See Barth *Colossians* 200–3. On Erasmus' interpretation of 'principalities and powers' see Eph chapter 3 n14.

24 For a similar explanation of what is meant in 1:17 by 'in him all things hold together' (RSV), see Theophylact *Expos in Col* (on 1:16) PG 124 1221D: 'And he not only created them but he also holds them together, so that if they were plucked from his providence, they would perish.'

25 On Christ as the way to the Father, see John 14:6; Rom 5:2; and 1 Tim 2:5. See also Augustine *De civitate Dei* 9.15 CSEL 40/1 428–31.

26 For the language, see 1 Cor 15:20 and 23, and Erasmus' annotations on Rom 11:16 ('but if the first portion') and Rom 16:5 ('who is the first of the church of Asia') CWE 56 305–6 and 425–6.

rise.[27] Just as he holds the first place among created things without detract-ing from the fact that he himself was not created, so, too, in the restoration of created things he holds the first place. As we owe to him the fact that we were born, we owe to him also the fact that we have been reborn to salva-tion. For thus the Father was pleased to pour into the Son all the plenitude of divine power and goodness, which should so remain in him that there is no need, ever, to seek anything from elsewhere, since the Father neither can nor will do anything but what the Son also can and will do.[28]

Nor is it our business to investigate why the Father was so resolved, since it is certain that whatever he has decreed is the very best.[29] Thus, I repeat, he considered it conducive both to our salvation and to his glory to reconcile everything to himself, not through the angels but through his own Son, who, by his blood and the suffering of the cross, would pay the penalty for our sins. By the wiping away of the sins that were destroying the peace and harmony of those in heaven and those on earth, all things, whether in the heavens or on the earth, would now be joined in friendship, drawing together, of course, into the one Christ.[30]

You, too, are of their number although you were once so estranged from God that you worshipped likenesses of demons instead of him. Not only of your own will[31] were you at variance with him, but by impious works you played the part of foes.[32]

* * * * *

27 On Christ as the 'prince and author' of the resurrection, who, as such, guar-antees our resurrection, see the paraphrase on 1 Cor 15:12 with n19.
28 On the Son's full sharing in the Father's power and their complete harmony of will, see also Erasmus' paraphrases on John 5:30 and 6:38–9 CWE 46 70–1 and 83.
29 Theophylact *Expos in Col* (on 1:19) PG 124 1224D similarly refuses to speculate on why this course of action pleased God: 'It is impossible to give any other reason except for the glory and the good pleasure of God.' On the goodness of God's will according to the medieval tradition, see Oberman *Harvest* 90–103.
30 On 'friendship' with God available to the just, see Sider 'The Just' 10–12.
31 In his translation of διάνοια 'understanding,' 'way of thinking' in 1:21, Eras-mus substitutes *mens* 'mind,' 'understanding' for the Vulgate *sensus* 'feeling,' 'inclination.' In his paraphrase he draws out the connotations of 'will' *volun-tas*, inherent in both the Greek and the Latin Vulgate. Cf the next note. Cf also Theophylact *Expos in Col* (on 1:21) PG 124 1228A: 'We, [Paul] says, were not unwilling nor were we being forced, but turning aside from him willingly and spontaneously, and being wholly unworthy, he reconciled us ... For you were enemies ... by intent, that is by deliberate choice ... and not only this, but you ... did the works of enemies.'
32 Erasmus adopts the Vulgate's *inimici* 'enemies' (Conf) for his translation, but his paraphrase uses the stronger *hostes* 'foes.' See his annotation on 1:21 (*in-imici sensu*) where he asks: 'But enemies to what?' He prefers to understand

Nevertheless, he has now reconciled you to himself although you neither looked for it nor deserved it, and out of enemies he has made you friends, and even sons. He did this, not by the ministry of angels but through the physical death of his Only-Begotten[33] whom he willed to assume a mortal body for this very purpose. And since the guilty can have no peace with God, he has freely remitted all the offences of your former life so as to present you holy, blameless, and without fault in his sight. For who would impute to you your earlier debts if he counts them as paid to him? That will be the case if, once freely admitted to the gospel faith, you always persevere in the profession you have made and, resting on the solid foundation, you show yourselves so steadfast that neither by men nor by angels will you be parted from Christ, from whom you[34] ought to hope for whatever the gospel has promised. Once you heard it, you believed[35] what has been preached not only[36] to you, but also openly to all the world's peoples whom the circumference of heaven embraces.[37] It is characteristic of a fickle person to abandon what has been demonstrated once and for all. It is characteristic of a shameless person to consider pointless a belief on which the whole world agrees, and, finally, a belief of which I, Paul, am[38] the preacher: in no way would I have abandoned our paternal law and replaced it with the gospel of Christ, if I did

* * * * *

'enemies to your mind' since 'those who serve the flesh fight against reason,' thus stressing that it is of one's own will that one is estranged from God.

33 his Only-Begotten] The reading of all Froben editions from 1520 to 1534; in 1538, 1540, and in LB *filii* 'son' replaces *sui* 'his' of the earlier editions to read 'the Only-Begotten Son.' Bateman suggests that this may be a case of the 'expected formula' replacing the harder reading. See 'Textual Travail' 247. For examples of Erasmus' substantive use of 'Only-Begotten,' see CWE 56 127, 144, 244.

34 you] So the Froben editions from 1520 to 1534; 'we' in 1538, 1540, and LB.

35 On the readiness to receive Paul's teaching, once heard, interpreted as a sure sign of faith, see also Erasmus' Argument of Philippians n3 and of 1 Thessalonians n2.

36 only] *modo* of the early editions was changed to *tantum* first in 1532. The change does not affect the translation.

37 It is clear from Erasmus' annotation on 1:23 (*quod praedicatum est in universa creatura*) that he considered Paul to be speaking here in an hyperbole that 'indicates that the gospel of Christ has already been published everywhere so that the Colossians might not think of changing a faith that had already been accepted by all.' The Greek, the Vulgate, and Erasmus' translation are all more inclusive than Erasmus' paraphrase, which refers specifically to 'all the world's peoples,' whereas the Greek and the Latin texts include all creation.

38 am] *sum* 'I am' indicative, first in 1532; previously *sim* subjunctive

not regard as certain that it is a heavenly work and one that originated with God.

As matters now stand, I am so persuaded that the gospel is true that not only do I feel no regret or shame, but I even suffer joyfully and count as my glory the scourges, the prisons, the fetters that I endure not for my crimes but for your salvation.[39] For although the Jews protest, I teach that you belong to the gospel grace no less than the Jews themselves. Why should I not say that I am suffering for your salvation, for which Christ suffered? Why should an apostle be reluctant to do what our leader was not loath to do? He not only suffered in his own body on our behalf, but he also suffers in ours, somehow, as if filling up through his deputies[40] what could appear to have been inadequate in his afflictions; not[41] that his death of itself does not suffice, but that in some way the affliction of head and members, of prince and deputies, is one; the more abundant it is, the more it overflows to add to the full measure of your salvation, indeed, not only of yours but of Christ's whole body, which is the church.[42]

* * * * *

39 For Paul's sufferings, see 2 Cor 11:23-7 (prisons, scourges); Eph 4:1 and Philem 1, 10-14 (prisoner); Eph 6:20 and Phil 1:13-18 (chains). For his attitude towards suffering, see Gal 6:14; 2 Cor 4:8-15.

40 'Deputies': vicarios. For the concept, see also Theophylact Expos in Col (on 1:24) PG 124 1229C: '... when the general is away, his deputy [ὑποστράτηγος] ... stands in for him and personally receives the wounds intended for him.' For the example of a subordinate officer substituting for a commander in his absence, see Chrysostom In Col hom 4.2 (on 1:24) PG 62 327.

41 not ... suffice] First in 1521; previously, 'not that his death did not suffice for the salvation of the whole world.'

42 Erasmus is careful to deny the simplistic and heretical interpretation that the sufferings of Christ are insufficient for redemption (cf 1:14, 2:13-14). He paraphrases 1:24 in line with the tradition that identification with Christ in his sufferings (Phil 3:10) is part of the challenge of the Christian life. See his paraphrase on Mark 8:34-8 CWE 49 107-8: 'The man who wants to be my true follower, the true companion of my happiness and glory, must prepare in his mind to be a companion in suffering and death.' In his annotation on 1:24 (et adimpleo ea quae desunt passionum), Erasmus attributes to Ambrosiaster the view that 'the suffering of Christ and the martyrs, that is, of head and members, is one'; he attributes to Theophylact the explanation that 'Christ was still suffering in his apostles on behalf of his body, not because Christ's sufferings were insufficient, but because of his great love towards us.' See Theophylact Expos in Col (on 1:24) PG 124 1229C. Ambrosiaster, however, does not make, at Comm in Col (on 1:24) CSEL 81/3 175:23-177:2, the assertion Erasmus has indicated. On the exegetical problems in this passage see Barth Colossians 254-8 and his commentary 289-95.

I am carrying out[43] the task assigned; the care of the church has been entrusted to me. Christ has assigned his own responsibilities to me; he has handed over the care of his body, especially that portion of the care that is directed towards welcoming the gentiles[44] to the gospel, so that I may fulfil by my work what he seemed to lack, and might divulge what has been concealed from many past generations and from the gentiles, namely, that not only for Jews but also for gentiles an approach lies open, through faith,[45] to gospel salvation.

This had already been decided by God long ago, but nevertheless it has been hidden thus far from the world; now by my preaching it has been revealed especially to those who, abandoning their former life, are embracing the teaching of Christ. To them God has been pleased to reveal how glorious is his[46] richness[47] towards us; since, with the publication of the secret[48]

* * * * *

43 Erasmus again uses the verb *fungi* 'to carry out, perform' of the apostolic task. See n7 above.

44 Erasmus anticipates by a few verses the explicit reference to Paul's mission to the gentiles as does Theophylact *Expos in Col* (on 1:25) PG 124 1232A.

45 Theophylact *Expos in Col* (on 1:25) PG 124 1232A introduces a similar emphasis on faith: 'He seeks not works, nor virtues, but faith and baptism.'

46 The precise referent of 'his' (*illius* genitive singular, common gender, literally 'of that one') in Erasmus' paraphrase is unclear. Most probably the referent is either Christ or the mystery. If 'mystery' read 'its.' See Erasmus' annotations on 1:27 (*verbum dei mysterium* and *quod est Christus*).

47 Although NTGL prints the word 'richness' as neuter τὸ πλοῦτος, followed by the neuter relative pronoun ὅ 'which,' Erasmus' annotation on 1:27 (*quod est Christus*) notes that in Greek ὁ πλοῦτος 'the richness' is masculine singular and is followed by the masculine relative pronoun ὅς to read 'which is Christ in you' – a clause paraphrased in the next paragraph. In this reading 'which' indubitably refers to 'richness'; in the preferred reading (neuter) 'which' can refer either to 'richness' or to 'mystery.'

48 The 1527 Vulgate transliterates μυστήριον as *mysterium* in 1:26, but translates it as *sacramentum* in 1:27. Erasmus paraphrases μυστήριον/*mysterium* (1:25–7) with the expressions: *quod ... fuit absconsum* 'what has been concealed'; *id ... fuit hactenus celatum* 'this has been hidden thus far.' See his annotation on 1:27 (*verbum dei mysterium*), where he affirms his view that *mysterium* means 'secret,' 'hidden.' Because μυστήριον in Erasmus' view usually conveys some element of 'hiddenness,' he often translates it as *arcanum* 'something secret,' as eg in his paraphrases on 1:27 and 2:2 and on Eph 3:3–4. On 'mystery,' see 1 Cor chapter 7 n30 and Eph chapter 1 n27. For a close study of the word and theme in Erasmus' writings on the New Testament see Georges Chantraine 'Le mustèrion paulinien selon les *Annotations* d'Erasme' *Recherches de science religieuse* 58 (1970) 351–82.

that previously lay hidden,[49] the whole world understands that free salvation, which at first they believed was conferred on[50] Jews only, is equally shared by all the gentiles; and that observance of the Mosaic law is not required, but only the faith by which they have no doubt concerning the gospel's promises.

In place of all that the Jews foolishly believe in, Christ alone suffices for you. If he is in you there is no reason for you to regret your hope, a hope that is quite steadfast and glorious through him who, without any doubt, will of himself fulfil his promises. It is he that we preach (not Moses or the angels) admonishing not only the Jews but the whole race of mortals, and, without omitting anything at all, teaching what pertains to the gospel's wisdom: that all people, whether they have been circumcised or not,[51] may understand that perfect salvation is not to be based on anything but Christ Jesus.

So eagerly am I striving to persuade everyone of this gospel wisdom that for its sake I am not reluctant to throw myself in the way of a great many dangers and evils, too severe, assuredly, for me in my weakness to bear. But he is powerful; with his inspiration and help, these things are accomplished through me,[52] since, when the situation calls for it, belief in our preaching is won even by miracles.[53]

* * * * *

49 I have translated an ablative absolute (literally 'the secret ... having been published') by the prepositional phrase 'with the publication of the secret.'

50 conferred on] Latin *delatam* is the reading of all the Froben editions from 1520 to 1538 (see OLD *defero* 11a); *1540* and LB print *delegatam* 'entrusted to.'

51 There is no explicit reference to circumcision in the Pauline text at this point, but see Ambrosiaster *Comm in Col* (on 1:27–8) CSEL 81/3 177:16–21: 'The gentiles also were to be admitted, without circumcision of the flesh, to the faith of the Christ who had been promised to the Jews. For before the preaching of the faith, it was mandated that the nations (the gentiles) be circumcised if they wished to draw near to the Law; but now, by the mercy of God they are invited to be welcomed to the faith.'

52 By using the passive voice 'these things are accomplished,' Erasmus emphasizes God's initiative and Paul's instrumentality in accomplishing effective persuasion in the midst of adversaries. Cf Theophylact *Expos in Col* (on 1:29) PG 124 1233D: 'For he makes me strong enough for this, clearly it is his plan.' See also Aquinas *Super Col lect* cap 1 lectio 6.73 (II 139): '... because God does this in me.'

53 Both the importance of miracles as a proof of Paul's apostolic mission and Paul's humility in acknowledging them as a gift from God are mentioned by Erasmus in his annotation on Rom 15:19 ('of wonders in the strength of the Holy Spirit') CWE 56 407–8; in his paraphrase on that passage CWE 42 85–6; and in *Ecclesiastes* I ASD V-4 50:288–316. He also reflects, in his paraphrases on

Chapter 2

People of Colossae, I have said these things, not so that I may boast before you, but because I want you to know how great is the anxiety that grips me, the extent of the dangers I am approaching, not only for the sake of those to whom I have passed on the gospel's teaching when personally present, but also for those to whom I am not known by sight, especially for you[1] and the Laodiceans. Even if I have not looked upon you with bodily[2] eyes, still with the eyes of the mind I gaze upon you constantly, rejoicing over your progress, alarmed if I perceive that some danger lurks or that your uncompromised soundness begins to waver.

That those who have not seen me should know these things is not as important to me as it is to them. For by my concern and by my dangers and sufferings they are goaded on to experience greater harmony and to be more united in evangelical charity, bonded and fitted together like limbs; also to understand better and more surely to believe the rich kindness of God the Father as it is generously poured out on all the race of mortals, or rather on absolutely everything in the heavens and on the earth. This secret,[3] which had up to this point been kept hidden, is now laid open through Jesus

* * * * *

Acts 5:12–16 and 10:26–8, on the humility of Peter and the place of miracles in his ministry when the need arose. See CWE 50 40 n19, 41 n28 and 72 n36. But Erasmus believed that the gift of miracles was unnecessary for those preaching to his own contemporaries. See his colloquy 'The Well-to-do Beggars' CWE 39 474:29–41 and n41 with further references. Aquinas *Super Col lect* cap 1 lectio 6.73 (II 139) had amplified the text *in virtute* 'with power' (cf Conf 'mightily') by adding *miraculorum* 'of miracles.'

1 for you] First in *1532*; previously *de vobis* 'concerning you.' Erasmus' translation (*1516*) reads: 'What a struggle ['anxiety' from *1519*] I have concerning [*de*] you'; the Vulgate gives 'what anxiety I have for [*pro*] you.' See the annotation (*qualem sollicitudinem*) on 2:1, where Erasmus rejects the Vulgate translation *pro vobis* 'for you' and affirms *de vobis* 'concerning you' as the correct translation of the Greek. But while 'anxiety concerning you' and 'anxiety for you' are equally idiomatic, 'approaching dangers concerning you' is unacceptable. In *1532*, therefore, Erasmus followed the Vulgate, evidently for stylistic effect.

2 bodily] *corporeis* is the reading of the Froben editions from 1520 to 1538; *1540* and LB print *corporis* 'of the body.' The distinction of bodily eyes from the eyes of the mind or heart is frequently used in Erasmus' paraphrases. See 1 Cor chapter 3 n36; 2 Cor chapter 3 n29; Eph chapter 1 n45.

3 For μυστήριον (Vulgate *mysterium*) paraphrased by *arcanum* 'secret,' see chapter 1 n48.

Christ, namely, that apart from him alone we should look nothing of human wisdom – whether some promise made by the philosophers of this world[4] or some offer made by the teachers of the Mosaic law or by others who boast that they have been instructed by the conversations of angels[5] – since in him alone are stored up and kept from view all the treasures of wisdom and of fruitful[6] knowledge. From this source one may draw summarily whatever pertains to authentic salvation.

Now these statements of ours have this objective: that you should take care again and again that no one, armed with human skills against the simplicity[7] of gospel doctrine, should play a trick on you and deceive you with talk that is false, but to all appearances plausible and consistent with the facts. It is the custom of this world's sophists[8] to ensnare the minds of

* * * * *

4 Erasmus' language is similar to that of Ambrosiaster. See *Comm in Col* (on 2:4) CSEL 81/3 180:12: *sapientes mundi* 'philosophers of the world.'

5 See Nicholas of Lyra (on 2:4) for the idea that Paul is persuading the Colossians to be on their guard against the deceptions of false apostles who try to deceive in three ways: 'One, by the arguments of the philosophers, for some of them [the Colossians] were instructed in philosophy; another, by the authority of the Law, on the ground that it had been given by God; third, by the pretence of a holiness by which simple folk are frequently deceived.' See also 'The "Threat" to the Colossian Community' in Barth *Colossians* 378–87.

6 fruitful] First in *1521*; previously 'salvific.' Erasmus amplifies the text's simple 'knowledge' by the addition of an adjective, and thereby prepares for a discussion of the kinds of false knowledge that lead away from Christ.

7 'Simplicity': *simplicitatem*. The word here refers to the straightforward, unadulterated; its opposite is the devious, deliberately confused, and confusing. See Phil chapter 3 n30. For the word in the sense of 'naive and credulous,' see n9 below.

8 In his annotation on 2:4 (*in sublimitate sermonum*) Erasmus notes that Ambrosiaster *Comm in Col* (on 2:4) CSEL 81/3 180:10–14, whose sense he follows here, twists this passage to apply to sophists. In fact, it is Theophylact *Expos in Col* (on 2:4) PG 124 1236D who explicitly mentions sophistries at this point, probably with the Arians in mind.

In late fifth-century BC Athens, the Sophists were stereotyped by Aristophanes in his *Clouds* as those who could make the worse cause seem the better. By teaching their students the tricks of clever speech, the Sophists could enable men educated in their skills to defraud honest Athenians. The bias of the Platonic dialogues against the Sophists (an aspect of the quarrel of the philosophers with the rhetors) is reflected in Erasmus' use of the word, which here designates those who mislead by clever speech devoid of significant content. The abstract theorizing of the scholastic theologians comes in for similar criticism from Erasmus. See the dedicatory letter to Campeggi 286–7.

simple people[9] with some legal quirks and the clever arguments of human thinking. It is no secret to me that there are some people of this kind among you craftily aiming at the simplicity of your faith. For even if I am physically absent and do not see face to face what is happening among you, still, in spirit I am present,[10] looking with joy upon the order and circumstances of your life and at the same time observing the firmness and strength of the confidence you have in Christ Jesus, to whom, once and for all, you have entirely entrusted yourselves.

It remains for you to persevere and make progress on the course rightly begun. Just as you have once learned and believed that Jesus Christ our[11] Lord is the sum of all our blessings, the source and origin of our felicity, so may all your life correspond to your profession and your faith. Just as you were once planted in him through baptism, so with your roots fixed in him may you gather strength. Just as once a solid foundation of evangelical doctrine was laid among you,[12] so may you build superstructures worthy of such a foundation. May you not bend now in this direction now in that,[13] wavering at every wind of new doctrine,[14] but instead, persist, firm and immovable,[15] in what you have once learned. May you not only persist but daily abound more and more,[16] so that as you daily increase in the growth of your faith and religion you may always have reason to give thanks to God. To him must go the credit for whatever is rightly accomplished.

* * * * *

9 'Simple people': *simplicium*. Erasmus uses the adjective *simplex* 'simple' here as a substantive, to include the naive and gullible victims of those who engage in duplicitous argumentation. Cf n7 above.

10 Compare the interpretation of Nicholas of Lyra (on 2:5), who cites 2 Kings 5:26, a passage in which Elisha the prophet claims to have been present in spirit to Gehazi when he accepted gifts from the healed Naaman.

11 Although in his annotation on 2:6 (*Dominum nostrum*) Erasmus criticizes the Vulgate translator for adding a redundant 'our' when it is not justified by the Greek, here his paraphrase follows the *1527* Vulgate.

12 For other examples of the architectural image in the Epistles, see 1 Cor 3:10–11 and Eph 2:20.

13 The language is appropriate to the plant imagery preceding. For the linkage of the plant and building imagery found here in 2:7, see also 1 Cor 3:5–9, 'I have planted, Apollos watered, but God has given the growth ... you are God's tillage, God's building' (Conf).

14 Cf Eph 4:14: 'no longer children, tossed to and fro and carried about by every wind of doctrine' (Conf).

15 Cf 1 Cor 15:58: 'Be steadfast and immovable' (Conf).

16 more and more] The Froben editions from 1520 to 1540; LB omits 'and more.'

Those who set traps for your simplicity keep watch. You must keep watch in return so that you are not, once captivated by some splendid guise of philosophy, seduced from the solidity of faith to the inane, petty comments of men,[17] and become prey for the foe. That will happen, if, led astray from the precept of evangelical truth, you begin to be influenced by human precepts and regulations, which are based on visible realities and on the gross[18] elements of this world. The doctrine of Christ, on the contrary, is heavenly; it propounds true piety located in souls, not in food or drink, not in personal attire, not in the observance of days or in the washing of hands.[19] These latter are not conducive to true religion. Instead, they summon away from Christ and draw away from the source whence all things are to be sought. For it is not as if a few gifts have been channelled off into him like water into a pool; but in him all the fullness of the deity[20] remains and dwells corporeally,[21] so that having him, there is no reason for you to

* * * * *

17 'Petty comments': *commentatiuncula*. See Ep 1053:515–17 where 'petty comments' describes scriptural studies of the kind Erasmus deplores: 'I saw the teaching of the gospel almost overlaid with the petty comments of men, and the Gospel texts buried in mistakes as though in brambles and in tares.' For Erasmus' critique of traditional studies, see the dedicatory letter to Campeggi 286–7.

18 'Gross': *crassis*. *Crassus* appears repeatedly in this chapter in a range of meanings defined by context: here 'gross elements of this world' are the human precepts that attend to the body in contrast to the heavenly doctrine of Christ propounding a piety located in souls. Cf nn30, 39, 57, 66 below. See also 1 Cor chapter 2 n22 and Eph chapter 1 n46.
   On the 'elements of this world' (2:8), see Gal 4:3 and 9 and Erasmus' paraphrases on those verses in CWE 42 115–16 with n2. For the variety of possible meanings and modern interpretations of the phrase, see 'The "Elements of the World" ' in Barth *Colossians* 373–8.

19 Erasmus interprets 'human tradition' (2:8 RSV) in terms of the requirements of Mosaic law, a theme common elsewhere in Erasmus. See eg CWE 42 115 with n2, 58 n25, 78 n5, 90 n6, 116 n10; CWE 50 94 n5, 95 n13.

20 'Deity': *deitatis*, representing the Greek of 2:9 θεότητος 'the essence of God.' Erasmus' annotation on 2:9 (*divinitatis corporaliter*) indicates that the Vulgate *divinitas* 'godhead' or 'divinity' should be corrected to *deitas* 'deity,' the word he chooses for his paraphrase. Cf Ambrosiaster whose lemma at *Comm in Col* (on 2:9) CSEL 81/3 181:16 shows *deitas* 'deity.'

21 Erasmus' annotation on 2:9 (*divinitatis corporaliter*) explains 'corporeally' by noting the opposition between 'body' and 'the shadows of Mosaic law.' In his annotations on 2:9–23, Erasmus frequently refers to the interpretations of this passage in Augustine (specifically to Ep 149.25–6 PL 33 640–1), whose work he had undertaken to edit. Cf Epp 581:22–4, 922:40–1, 1144:80 n17. Augustine, in his response (Ep 149 just cited) to Paulinus' request (Ep 121 PL 33 462–70) for

follow the shadows of Mosaic law or the illusions of human philosophy. Truth[22] has been clearly manifested to all the senses; there is no reason now for you to look to types or ambiguous promises. Accordingly, once you have been grafted onto Christ[23] and fitted together into one body, there is no reason for you to long for anything from any other source. Since he lacks nothing and wishes all that is his to be shared equally with you, you[24] too ought to be abundantly supplied through him whether you long for wisdom[25] or for power. For just as he is the inexhaustible source of all wisdom, so also is he the head of every sovereignty and power. Nor is there any power among even the highest of the angels that does not kneel before him.[26]

Perhaps a Jew might try to persuade you as though it were something important that, following his example,[27] you should amputate a bit of foreskin,[28] as if we were commended to God by the body's condition! Rather, all who have Christ have also the glory of circumcision;[29] for those who

* * * * *

an exegesis of the passage, interprets the word 'corporeally' as a metaphor. Augustine explains this metaphorical sense more fully in *De Genesi ad litteram* 12.7 CSEL 28 388–9 / *St. Augustine: The Literal Meaning of Genesis* trans and ann John Hammond Taylor, 2 vols, Ancient Christian Writers 41–2 ed Johannes Quasten, Walter J. Burghardt, Thomas Comerford Lawler (New York 1982) 42 187:

> Now the Godhead is not a body; but because St. Paul calls the religious observances of the Old Testament shadows of what is to come (using the analogy of shadows in the physical world), he says that the fullness of the Godhead dwells in Christ corporeally; for in Him was fulfilled all that was prefigured by those shadows, and thus in a certain sense He is the embodiment of the shadows; that is, He is the truth of those figures and symbols. The figures, therefore, are called shadows in a metaphorical rather than proper sense of the word; and similarly, in saying that the fullness of the Godhead dwells corporeally, Paul is using a metaphor.

Various interpretations are presented by Erasmus in *Apologia ad Caranzam* LB IX 409–11.

22 Truth . . . promises] Added in *1532*
23 Christ] First in *1532*; previously 'him'
24 you] 1520 8° and subsequent editions; 'you all' is the reading of the 1520 4° edition only.
25 While the text itself suggests the theme of power, emphasis on the image of wisdom may be introduced from Augustine Ep 149.24 PL 33 640. Cf n21 above.
26 See Phil 2:10: 'At the name of Jesus every knee should bend' (Conf).
27 Ie the example set by the Jew
28 Erasmus' typical way of referring to ritual circumcision. See Eph chapters 1 n39 and 2 n26, and Phil chapter 3 n5.
29 See the paraphase on Eph 2:11–22 on spiritual and unspiritual circumcision.

have him not, circumcision is useless. A shadow of circumcision is what they have, the reality itself is yours. Since Jewish circumcision denotes that gross and earthy[30] desires are to be pruned away from souls now destined to behold nothing but heavenly realities, people are absolutely uncircumcised who are tortured by the desire to possess, who are slaves to the belly, who are being wasted away[31] by envy, who are hunting glory among men, who are without hope of heavenly rewards. You, on the other hand, are truly circumcised through Christ, not indeed by the circumcision that is accomplished by hands, but by a spiritual one.[32] And it is not just a little part of the fleshly man that has been pruned away in you, but your whole body, contaminated by sins and vitiated[33] by carnal desires, has been removed from you by the spiritual circumcision of Jesus Christ. Just as he, in dying, laid aside the body subject to death and, in rising, received an immortal body,[34] so you, through a baptism according to the Spirit,[35] have died along with him, after all the sins of your former life have been set aside; and not only have you died with him but you have been buried together with him at the same time.[36] For[37] when the affections have been mortified a very deep serenity of mind follows.

Accordingly, after thus laying aside the body that was subject to sin (and indeed sin is the soul's death), through Christ you have risen along with him, free from sins not through your own merits, but only because you simply believe that God, who by his power raised Christ from the dead, is by his might doing the same in you so that since all sins have been freely remitted through the Son's death, you may henceforth live with him, not guilty of any sins, but hastening towards true immortality in unflagging zeal for innocence. Therefore, to God the Father are owed all the things that are generously bestowed on you[38] through the Son.

* * * * *

30 For 'gross and earthy' *crassus ac terrenus*, see CWE 50 13 n4.
31 wasted away] First in 1521; in the 1520 editions 'tortured'
32 Nicholas of Lyra (on 2:11) offers a similar interpretation: 'circumcision given through Christ, is spiritual, for the remission of sins.'
33 vitiated] Added in 1532
34 Cf Augustine *Contra Faustum Manichaeum* 16.29 PL 42 335. Augustine understands Col 2:11, paraphrased here, to mean that Christ divested himself of the 'body of the flesh,' and explains the 'body of the flesh' as 'mortality,' which Christ put off, rising again with an immortal body.
35 For the distinction between baptism by water and baptism by the Spirit, see Acts 1:5 and 11:16, and Erasmus' paraphrases on these passages CWE 50 7 and 78 with n23.
36 The paraphrase amplifies the text with imagery from Rom 6:1–4.
37 For ... follows] Added in 1532
38 you] First in 1521; previously 'us'

To lack the foreskin was of no use to the Jews, nor for you was the bodily foreskin a hindrance. But the foreskin was death-dealing because, bound over to gross and impious desires,[39] you were subject to death; or, rather, you were dead in the spiritual sense, lacking God who is the life of minds. This foreskin, I repeat, was common to us and to you; this he has amputated by his Spirit, all our sins forgiven for us,[40] once and for all, and forgiven in such a way that there is no danger that they might be imputed to us in the future because we had sworn in formal terms to obedience of the Mosaic law, no danger that on this account the adversary might be able to bring us to trial for non-observance of the Law, as if bound by a written document.

On the contrary, that long-standing, binding contract[41] on account of which the devil was pressing us hard,[42] Christ has annulled[43] by the profession of gospel faith, on account of which the offences of our former life

* * * * *

39 Here the contextual contrast between spiritual and physical points to the 'carnal' nature of the 'gross' desires. As the paraphrase implies in the next sentence, the 'foreskin' is a metaphor for 'gross and impious desires.' For circumcision associated with evil desires, see the paraphrase on Rom 12:1–2 CWE 42 69–71; cf also next note.

40 Cf the interlinear *Gloss* on the words 'putting off the body of flesh in the circumcision of Christ' (2:11 RSV): 'when all vices have been amputated – something Christ alone effects.' Erasmus has understood 'in the circumcision of Christ' as a circumcision performed by Christ; some modern scholars prefer to understand it as the circumcision undergone by Christ, not as an infant but in his crucifixion. See eg C.F.D. Moule *The Epistles of Paul the Apostle to the Colossians and to Philemon* (Cambridge 1957) 96 and James D.G. Dunn *The Epistles to the Colossians and to Philemon: A Commentary on the Greek Text* (Grand Rapids 1996) 158.

41 In his annotation on 2:14 (*chirographum decreti*) Erasmus explains the difference between *syngrapha* 'written document' and *chirographum* 'autographed contract': the latter is the more strongly binding in that it is personally signed. See συγγράφω and χειρόγραφον in BDAG; also χειρόγραφον in Kittel-Friedrich IX 424–5; and Lampe *Patristic Greek* 1522.

42 In the annotation on 2:14 (*chirographum decreti*) Erasmus explores various patristic interpretations of the *chirographum* 'contract' that 'stood against us' through its dogmas ie its decrees, 'legal demands' (NRSV) – demands 'either of the Mosaic law or of the divine law.' This contract was, however, annulled by the decree [*decreto*] of evangelical faith. Since human beings proved unable to fulfil the contract, Christ took on himself the penalty owed from the pact, paid it, and tore up the contract, changing the obligation of death into a pact of eternal salvation. Here in the paraphase, the devil is portrayed as the creditor dunning (ie 'pressing hard') a debtor. See OLD *urgeo* 8b.

43 'Annulled': *antiquavit*. Cf 1 Cor chapter 1 n60.

are not being imputed to anyone. Whatever[44] could be exacted from us on the terms of this binding contract, Christ has paid on the cross on which the contract was torn to pieces[45] and completely destroyed. Nor is there any reason[46] for us to fear the tyranny of Satan after Christ on the cross conquered, through his own death, death's source, by recovering us like glorious spoils[47] snatched away from demonic principalities and powers over which he triumphed when he had conquered them. For then did he frankly and openly display them not only to men but also to angels when he had vanquished and indeed despoiled them,[48] carrying them in a triumph, as it were; and displaying his adversaries ruined and shattered, not through the help of angels[49] or men, but by his own power, he hung upon

* * * * *

44 In this non-specific term Erasmus includes the interpretations of both Ambrosiaster *Comm in Col* (on 2:14) CSEL 81/3 186:3–8, who refers to the decree against all humankind incurred by the sin of Adam, 'to dust you shall return' (Gen 3:19 RSV), and Theophylact *Expos in Col* (on 2:14) PG 124 1244B, who paraphrases both the Israelites' response to God's offer of a covenant: 'All that God has said we shall do and we shall obey' (cf Exod 19:8), and the treaty God struck with Adam saying: 'Whatever day you shall eat [of the forbidden tree] you will die' (cf Gen 2:16).

45 There is an interesting difference between the annotation and the paraphrase here. The latter implies that the chirograph was torn up on the cross but an addition to the annotation in 1527 describes the image in 2:14 in more detail: 'Christ tore up and mangled the chirograph, destroying it and fixing it to the cross, on which he hung for us what we owed and turned the obligation of death into a pact of eternal salvation.' The addition may be a refinement of ideas expressed in the paraphrase; but cf n50 below. For the tendency of the 1527 annotations to reflect the earlier paraphrases, see CWE 50 xvii.

46 Nor is there any reason] First in 1521; previously 'nor is there any reason after this'

47 'Glorious spoils': *opima spolia* (literally 'rich spoils'), a technical term applied in classical Latin to the armour that the victorious Roman leader (king or consul) fighting under his own auspices had captured on the field of battle from the enemy supreme commander whom he had slain by his own hand. The armour was then dedicated in a formal ritual in the temple of Jupiter Feretrius. In the history of the Roman state this supreme military achievement was acknowledged in the case of only three heroes before the end of the Republic: Romulus, Cossus, and Marcellus. See Livy 1.10, 4.20; Servius on *Aeneid* 6.855; O'Mara 'Triumphs, Trophies, and Spoils' 119–21.

48 vanquished ... angels] In 1532 three occurrences of *et* 'and' were replaced with *atque*, *cum*, and *tum* 'and indeed ... not only ... but also.'

49 Cf Theophylact *Expos in Col* (on 2:15) PG 124 1245C, who writes: 'Then if the angels did not suffer for you, but Christ did, how do you say that you were saved by them?'

the cross such a magnificent trophy[50] that from high above it was visible to all.

Only see that you do not slip back into former sins. There is no danger of anyone condemning you on account of having neglected the ceremonies of Mosaic law, for instance, on account of food or drink that is clean or unclean, on account of the distinction between a feast day or ferial, on account of non-observance of the new moon, on account of the violation of sabbath rests,[51] since in fact these were[52] shadows that once presaged and traced the outline of realities that afterwards were to be truly exposed to view by Christ.

But after we possess the body itself, after truth has openly shone upon us, why do we still fear shadows?[53] The person who clings to Christ, our head living in heaven, cares only for heavenly things and by a direct route makes for the prize of immortality.[54] Beware, then, lest anyone, calling you back to earthly things, defraud you of the prize you have begun to pursue: in place of sublime realities teaching ignoble things, in place of the true religion of Christ introducing a sort of superstitious cult of angels. Such a person boasts among the simple of certain feigned visions, puffed up by

* * * * *

50 In Greek and Roman warfare a trophy was a commemorative display of captured armour set up on the battlefield at the point where the enemy turned back. Originally the trophy was simply a tree trunk hung with captured shields or other weapons. For Erasmus, the trophy seems to be the contract itself, nailed to the cross. Origen *Homiliae in librum Iesu Nave* 8.3 PG 12 865 describes the cross as a 'trophy over the devil on which the Son of God incarnate was crucified visibly, but invisibly the devil with his principalities and powers was fixed to the cross.' See also Theophylact *Expos in Col* (on 2:15) PG 124 1245C: 'The Lord, setting up the trophy on the cross ... triumphed over the demons.' On the image of the trophy in the paraphrases, see O'Mara 'Triumphs, Trophies, and Spoils' 115–20.

51 Ambrosiaster *Comm in Col* (on 2:16) CSEL 81/3 188:8–14 lists (in the same order) the neglected ceremonies on which Jewish criticism directed against the early Christians is based: '... because they eat from foods forbidden by Moses when God has made all [foods] clean ... because we disregard their holy days, or because we do not observe the beginnings of the months which they call new moons, but especially because we do not keep the day of the sabbaths.'

52 were] First in 1521; previously 'are'

53 Cf Theophylact *Expos in Col* (on 2:17) PG 124 1248A: 'The former things are shadows, the body, that is, the truth, belongs to Christ ... what need is there to hold onto shadows when the body is present?'

54 Into this paraphrase on 2:17–18 Erasmus introduces the imagery of the Christian athlete developed eg in 1 Cor 9:24–7; Phil 3:12–14; and 2 Tim 4:7. See the paraphrases on those passages, and 1 Cor chapter 9 n34.

his own base passion[55] to hunt glory among people, teaching things he has fabricated from his own imagination as though they were from the oracles of angels. Not bold in Christ,[56] compared with whom all things, however sublime, may properly be despised, he relies so much on angels that he deserts Christ, the heavenly head on whom the whole body of the church depends. By Christ, too, the church is nourished, as every spiritual gift flows down into individual members through the joints of limbs and members, and by him the body grows right up to the highest spiritual perfection, a perfection worthy of God, to whom we are joined through Christ.

If Christ has died to this gross[57] and visible world and lives in heaven, and if, so far as concerns your attachment to life, you have died along with him to the elements of this world[58] as you gaze on nothing but heavenly realities, to what end are you subject to human decrees that prescribe not the things that suggest Christ but the elements of the world, as if you were not already dead to such things but were still living in the world?

Why is an audience granted to the Jew[59] issuing the following precepts according to the carnal sense of the Mosaic law? 'Do not touch this body: it is impure.[60] Do not taste this food: it is impure.[61] Do not handle this object: it is holy and the profane are not permitted to touch it.'[62] As if the teaching

* * * * *

55 Augustine Ep 149.28 PL 33 642 describes the danger of a false humility in similar terms: 'In a surprising way . . . it happens that the soul of a person is more puffed up by false humility than it would be if he were openly arrogant.'
56 For the phrase 'bold in Christ' (RSV), see Philem 8.
57 'Gross': *crasso*
58 On 'elements of the world,' see n18 above. From the context it is clear that Erasmus contrasts 'the elements of the world' with the teachings of Christ.
59 The text of 2:16–23 does not explicity name the Jews; the paraphrases on those verses, however, mention them both at the beginning and the end. Erasmus often describes contemporary legalism in terms pertaining to Jewish religion. His annotation on 2:21 (*ne gustaveritis*) explicitly relates this text to 'some priests of our time who heap regulations on regulations.' The examples in the text of regulations governing eating and drinking, festivals, the new moon, and the sabbath incorporate terms that stem from prescriptions of the Torah. Modern scholars see not a reference to the Jews but to the syncretistic Hellenistic 'philosophy,' which had assimilated some Jewish traditions with taboos arising from ascetical disciplines of various philosophical schools. See Lohse 115–16.
60 For prohibitions regarding the touching of bodies, see eg Lev 11:24–32.
61 For clean and unclean foods, see eg Lev 11:2–23, 34–8; Deut 14:3–21.
62 The paraphrase clarifies that these are the words of Judaizers whom Paul quotes. But see Erasmus' annotation on 2:21 (*ne gustaveritis*), in which Erasmus describes the interpretations of some unnamed priests of his own time who

of Christ does not suffice for you, you attend to such precepts in keeping with the regulations and teachings of people who argue persuasively that piety is located in the selection of foods, in the observance of days and the rest of the Jewish precepts. Food, drink or clothing does not commend us to God, but they are provided for the body's necessity and are spent in the very act of consumption; they do not stay behind in the soul. But the people who teach these doctrines exhibit a false appearance of wisdom among foolish and inexperienced individuals; indeed they are more highly esteemed the more they fill people's minds with a superstitious and faulty humility.

For it is clearly superstition to equate the angels with Christ. It is a twisted[63] humility to expect through an angel what ought to have been sought from Christ himself, or, at any rate, through Christ from the Father.[64] Foods and the rest of visible things have not been given so that we may be compelled to abstain from them to our body's harm,[65] but rather that our body may be supported by the assistance they render: that by clothing, of whatever kind, it may be defended against injury from winds or the cold; by food, of whatever sort, it may be satisfied, and be furnished without distinction whenever, wherever, whatever, however much present need demands. Those other concerns belong to the Jews who do not yet have a

* * * * *

out of pride multiply rules in order to tyrannize Christians, whom Christ wanted to be free. In support of his interpretation, Erasmus cites Augustine (to Paulinus) Ep 149.23 PL 33 640.

63 The humility coupled with the worship of angels mentioned in 2:18 is only an apparent and inauthentic humility aimed at misleading the gullible among the Colossians. See the Argument n6. This is noted also by Theophylact *Expos in Col* (on 2:18) PG 124 1248C. Erasmus follows Paul and insists on a Christocentric spirituality. He endeavours also to correct superstitious practices of sixteenth-century popular religion that would substitute angels or saints for Christ. On praying to the angels in Erasmus' writings, see Pabel *Conversing with God* 100–1.

64 Erasmus interprets in line with the early Christian view that 'the role of the angels is bound up with the Old Testament's preparatory mission and it ceases with the coming of Christ, who takes the history of salvation directly into his own hands,' Jean Daniélou *The Angels and their Mission according to the Fathers of the Church* trans David Heimann (Westminster 1957) 9.

65 Cf Nicholas of Lyra (on 2:23), who mentions those who 'boast to the simple of not sparing themselves physical labour in order to secure the salvation of the neighbour ... such pretensions frequently deceive the simple and it is on this account that the Apostle warns them to be on guard against such teachings ... heretics deceive the simple in the same way.'

mind freed by circumcision from a gross and carnal[66] understanding of the Law.

Chapter 3

Those concerns are base, and unworthy of genuine members of Christ. If you are truly dead to earthly things and have risen along with Christ to an ardour for the sublime and everlasting, despise base things; seek what is sublime and worthy of heaven where your head, Christ, sits at the right of God the Father. For it is proper for the interests and concerns of the members to tend towards the place where the head is already situated[1] and where the members themselves, together with their head, are destined to reign later on. Each person lives in the place where he loves.

To this world you seem dead, you who find no pleasure in worldly felicity, nor are your cares those that disturb the cultivators of the world. Accordingly, you are not alive here among humans; still, before God you are alive with Christ,[2] even if in the meanwhile your life has been hidden away as the world judges.[3] But when Christ has returned again he will show to the world his own glory and that of his whole body; then you too, along with the head, will be perceived as sharers in his glory. Meanwhile you must see to it that the whole body corresponds to its sublime and heavenly head; his members, unless they are completely dead to earthly desires here, cannot live in heaven with Christ.

The devil too has his own body, which I have elsewhere called the body of sin.[4] Its members are these: fornication, which the cultivators of the world regard as even praiseworthy,[5] uncleanness, effeminacy and the

* * * * *

66 On 'gross and carnal understanding of the Law,' see n18 above.

1 Nicholas of Lyra on 3:1 also notes that 'the members ought to follow their head.'

2 The expression is reminiscent of Gal 2:20, 'It is now no longer I that live but Christ lives in me' (Conf). See Erasmus' paraphrase on Gal 2:20 CWE 42 107.

3 Ambrosiaster *Comm in Col* (on 3:3) CSEL 81/3 192:27–193:2 similarly specifies: 'From carnal and worldly people, the life of Christ and of those who belong to him is hidden in God beyond the world in his heavenly realm in which they live.'

4 Ambrosiaster *Comm in Col* (on 3:5) CSEL 81/3 193:16–17 also recalls the phrase from Rom 6:6.

5 Cf Phil 3:19: 'Their god is their belly, their glory is in their shame, they mind the things of earth' (Conf).

other kinds of lust too vile even to be named, desires for harmful things like glory, sovereignty, vengeance, but especially for money, an evil that comes very close to the most criminal[6] impiety of all – the worship of images.

People who are subject to these cannot be sharers in the glory of Christ. If you are stained by such sins you are very far from being able to be sons of God, inasmuch as it was on account of such actions that he raged even against his own sons, the Jews, disowning and destroying them as disobedient.[7] By these iniquities your life too was once stained, when you had not yet died with Christ through baptism, but were alive to evil desires. Now, reborn through him, it is right for you, also, to cast aside all that belongs to your former life,[8] since Christ has left behind no remnant of anything mortal[9] or earthly. And not only should you cast aside those enormities about which we spoke just now, but also the following,[10] in regard to which people as a whole make excuses for themselves. These are the sort: wrath, arrogance, spite, slander. Not only is the mind to be free of these desires, but the mouth too is to be pure of all obscene speech.

Christ is truth itself;[11] it is not fitting for you, his members, to lie to one another. And – not to list every particular – after you have put on Christ, slough off[12] the whole old earthly man[13] along with his actions and

* * * * *

6 The language suggests Ambrosiaster *Comm in Col* (on 3:5) CSEL 81/3 193:26– 194:2, who notes that Paul 'compared avarice to idolatry to show that there is nothing more criminal than avarice.' See also Ovid *Metamorphoses* 1.131: *amor sceleratus habendi* 'a criminal love of possessing.' In Erasmus' *Paraphrase on Acts* the dangers of avarice constitute a prominent theme. See CWE 50 xiii, 11 n88, 38 n2; see also Eph chapter 5 n15.

7 For God's 'raging against and destroying his own sons' see 1 Cor 10:1–10, in which many commentators see allusions to Numbers 11:4, 33–5, 21:5–6, and 25:1–9.

8 Cf 1 Pet 1:14: 'Do not conform to the lusts of former days' (Conf).

9 of anything mortal] First in 1532, replacing 'of anything of mortality'

10 The interlinear *Gloss* (on 3:8) similarly notes that the text intends 'not only the above mentioned great vices, but all the others as well.'

11 Cf John 14:6: 'I am the way, and the truth, and the life' (Conf).

12 López Zúñiga defended the Vulgate *exspoliantes* 'stripping off' against Erasmus' translation (and by extension, his paraphrase) of ἀπεκδυσάμενοι as *exuistis* 'you have sloughed off,' by reference to Cicero *In Verrem* 2.4.40.86, where, however, modern editions read *spoliatum* (for *exspoliare* cf *In Verrem* 2.4.54.120). In his response Erasmus notes that 'Paul is not speaking here of clothing torn away by force, but laid aside willingly.' See his *Apologiae contra Stunicam* (1) ASD IX-2 218:894–9 and 897n.

13 The interlinear *Gloss* (on 3:9) identifies the 'old man' with the 'old life lived in sin according to Adam.' Ambrosiaster *Comm in Col* (on 3:5) CSEL 81/3 193:17

desires;[14] put on the new who does not know the feebleness of age. On the contrary, as the knowledge of God increases in him day by day, he flourishes and grows up into something better and greater, after the likeness of Christ. Christ himself, the new man, has fashioned in us too a new man, once the old died.

All of us who have been grafted onto the body of Christ have so completely ceased being what we were, as though created anew in another way, that at this point there is no distinction between pagan and Jew, between circumcised and uncircumcised, between barbarian or Scythian and Greek or Athenian,[15] between slave and freeborn. By these standards are people evaluated in the eyes of the world; before God there is no consideration of these, but Christ, who is equally common to all, alone supplies everything for everyone. For the slave he is freedom, for the poor, riches, for the barbarian, civilization, for the uncircumcised, circumcision. In short, through him all things are made equal among you so that no one may disdain the other.

Accordingly, in place of the members you have cast off as unworthy of Christ, put on other members, different from those vile ones we have enumerated above. In their place put on what befits people whom God has chosen for holiness and deemed worthy of his love. Someone will say, 'What are they?' Indeed, what Christ taught us and what he has shown,[16]

* * * * *

refers to Rom 6:6. A connection with Rom 6:6 and Eph 4:22–4 is noted by Aquinas *Super Col lect* cap 3 lectio 2.154 (II 154).

14 Theophylact *Expos in Col* (on 3:9) PG 124 1248A goes into great detail, interpreting the passage to mean 'slough off the will with the works [of the old man].'

15 In his translation of 3:11 Erasmus 'corrected' the Vulgate at two points: he omitted the Vulgate's introductory pair, 'male and female' (attested in the *Gloss*, in Nicholas of Lyra, and in the *1527* Vulgate, but not cited even as a variant in Weber 1823 or Metzger); he changed the Vulgate's *gentilis et Iudaeus* 'gentile and Jew' to *Graecus et Iudaeus* 'Greek and Jew,' following closely his Greek manuscripts. In the paraphrase it is the explanation of 'Greek' that is most extensive. Erasmus interprets *Graecus et Iudaeus* as *ethnicus et Iudaeus* 'pagan and Jew,' then at the end of the list he recalls the word 'Greek' to reflect its connotation of 'cultured,' hence the contrast between 'barbarian or Scythian and Greek or Athenian,' 'Scythian' and 'Athenian' representing the epitome respectively of uncultured and cultured. See Erasmus' annotation on 3:11 (*barbarus*): 'Compared to the Scythian, the rest of the barbarians are not barbarians.'

16 See Erasmus' paraphrase on Luke 2:40 for his articulation of the way in which the young Christ showed the virtues by his manner of living, also *Ratio* Holborn 210:4–15; 222:4–13.

I mean[17] a compassionate disposition so that you may be ready to relieve another's weakness, affability so that you may be adaptable in our common social intercourse, a modest spirit so that you may not put yourselves ahead of anyone through arrogance, gentleness so that you may not rage against those who err, patience and calmness of mind so that you may not rush headlong to vengeance. But you are to support one another and mutually pardon each other if, through human weakness, something should come up between you for which one person could blame another. It is right that you in your turn forgive those who sin, since Christ, who harmed no one, has forgiven us all our sins.

Beyond all else, let Christian charity adorn your souls; far from harming anyone, charity is eager to help everyone, requiting injury with kindness. This is that perfect and indissoluble bond by which the body of Christ holds together, and the members, otherwise likely to fall apart, are firmly bonded to one another. Charity's companion will be harmony and peace, not, indeed, the ordinary sort,[18] but one that remains steadfast through the bond of Christ. May it always prevail and win out in your hearts; may it carry off the palm[19] against envy, pride, wrath, and contention. God has summoned you to harmony and he has reconciled all of you to himself and co-opted you into one body with this intent: that you may live in unanimity with one another, just as members of one body.

You are not to be ungrateful and unmindful of the divine clemency towards you. We would not have peace with him unless of his own accord he had pardoned us all our outrageous offences. And, forgetful of this, does brother stir up war against a brother on account of a slight injury?[20] You are not to fight to the death with one another over the pre-eminence of a worldly philosophy.[21] May the word of Christ, which teaches what pertains

* * * * *

17 I mean] Added in 1532
18 For a distinction in kinds of peace, see the *Gloss* (on 3:15), which notes that there is a peace without charity but charity always brings peace.
19 For an exposition of the proverbial expression *palmam ferre* 'to bear the palm,' its origin, and the reason for its metaphorical use, see *Adagia* I iii 4.
20 Erasmus was a passionate advocate for peace among Christians. See eg his description of Philip 'the handsome' (later Philip I of Spain), as peace-loving, and his praise for the benefits of peace in *Panegyricus* CWE 27 50, 53–4; his argument on behalf of peace attributed to Peace herself, *Querela pacis* CWE 27 293–322; and his letter on peace, Ep 288, which would be expanded into the adage *Dulce bellum inexpertis* 'War is a treat for those who have not tried it' *Adagia* IV i 1.
21 Although he does not name it here, Erasmus advocates instead the 'philosophy of Christ,' a pious learning based on the Scriptures, directed towards the moral edification of the Christian and leading to the imitation of the peace-loving

to authentic piety, abide and continue in you abundantly so that you may have such a feel for it that you yourselves not only can know what is pleasing to Christ but you can also teach one another in turn if anyone should err, offer an admonition if anyone is remiss,[22] all the while being cheerful in the hope of future bliss, with psalms and hymns and spiritual canticles, singing to the Lord his praises and his kindnesses, singing, however, not only with your physical voice, but especially in your heart. For God is delighted by songs precisely of this kind, so no one should think it a great thing to raise a din with his mouth to the powers above.[23]

Finally, whatever you do, whether speaking or taking some action, do it in such a way that all your life relates to the glory of the Lord Jesus, smacks of him, rings of him, breathes him forth. Moreover, no matter what happens to you meanwhile when you are acting thus, whether it be prosperous or adverse, let nothing deject or exalt you, but for all things give thanks to God the Father through the Son; through him there is nothing that fails to turn into good for us.[24]

Wives,[25] be subject to your husbands, as is proper to those professing Christ who must be more perfect than the rest in all responsibilities. Conversely, husbands, love your wives. Remember that they are subject to

* * * * *

Christ rather than the study of abstruse theories which leads to quarrels. See Phil chapter 2 n6; also *Ratio* Holborn 296:12–304:27 where the quarrelsome nature of 'worldly' philosophy is contrasted with the philosophy of Christ. See also Hilmar M. Pabel 'The Peaceful People of Christ: the Irenic Ecclesiology of Erasmus of Rotterdam' in *Erasmus' Vision of the Church* ed Hilmar M. Pabel, Sixteenth Century Essays and Studies 33 (Kirksville, Missouri 1995) 57–93.

22 The interlinear *Gloss* (on 3:16) amplifies the text in similar fashion, 'so that there may be teaching (*doctrina*) for those who do not know and warning for those who do.'

23 Theophylact *Expos in Col* (on 3:16) PG 124 1248A interprets 'singing in your heart' as 'singing to God ... alternatively it means not for show.' For singing to God as an expression of joy, see also Erasmus' paraphrase on Acts 16:25 CWE 50 103–4. For further evidence of Erasmus' preference for inward singing, see his paraphrase on Eph 5:19 with n30.

24 Cf Rom 8:28: 'For those who love God all things work together unto good' (Conf).

25 Erasmus translates *uxores* 'wives,' a word he retains in the paraphrase, as more appropriate to the context than the Vulgate *mulieres* 'women.' As Valla *Coll* (on 3:18–19) Perosa 236 had noted: 'Because the word [γυναῖκες 'women' or 'wives'] is ambiguous in the Greek, the translator [of the Vulgate] wished to translate ambiguously, but *uxores* "wives" would be better in both instances.' That a fuller version of the precepts for good order within the household is to be found in Eph 5:21–6:9 is noted by Nicholas of Lyra (on Col 3:18 and 19).

you on the assumption, however, that you are not to be full of bitterness towards them. Children, show yourselves compliant and obedient to your parents without any exception even if they prescribe rather harsh measures, provided only that the measures are not evil,[26] for this is pleasing to Christ. Conversely, fathers, do not abuse your authority towards your children and do not so irritate them by your fierceness that they lose heart.

Slaves, obey in all things the masters to whom, according to human law, you owe service, not eager now to please for appearances' sake as the common run of pagan servants generally are, for they consider it sufficient if they do not give offence to their owner, a human being; but with a simple and sincere heart do your duty, not through fear of a human being, but of God, who regards the disposition with which you act. And do not ponder what your master, a human being, deserves, but whatever service you render him, whatever kind of man he is, regard it as a service you are rendering to Christ, not to human beings, certain that you will receive from him the prize of an eternal inheritance, even if a thankless owner gives you no spending money and fails to recognize you among his children. Really, while you serve unworthy masters on account of Christ, it is Christ you are serving. For just as an owner, if he commit any sin against a slave, even if he be not punished in the presence of men, still will not go unpunished before God, so too, a slave who behaves rightly, even if he earn no payment in the presence of men (who do not think any thanks is owed to slaves who discharge their responsibility),[27] still will not lose his reward before God, with whom there is distinction not of persons but of intentions, and there is a reckoning not of rank but of service.[28]

Chapter 4

Again, masters, do not abuse your right – a right given you by human laws, not by the true principles of nature[1] – to exercise a tyranny over slaves, but

* * * * *

26 Theophylact *Expos in Col* (on 3:20) PG 124 1265B inserts a similar proviso: 'When he says "in all things" he is speaking to the children of pious parents, since it is not necessary to heed impious parents in all things. For they are not to be obeyed when they force impiety from them.'

27 See eg the treatment of the servant described in Luke 17:7–9.

28 Erasmus is also careful to distinguish between service and rank within the church. See above chapter 1 n7.

1 The arbitrary and sometimes transitory status of slavery is a theme of Roman Stoic philosophy, which advocated life according to nature. See *Epistulae morales*

grant them what is just and fair, providing them with nature's needs.[2] And do not, at a whim, keep some as favourites while oppressing others with intolerable servitude.[3] Be aware that you are now more truly their fellow slaves[4] than their masters, since you too have a master in heaven you share with them. You will find that he is, deservedly, the same to you as[5] you prove to be to your slaves.

In order to succeed better in being worthy members of Christ's body, be insistent in prayers, not slothful or weighed down with excessive wine-drinking, but sober and watchful. At the same time blend into your prayers thanksgiving, so that, in addition to requesting of God the things that are conducive to salvation, you also give thanks for his daily acts of kindness towards you, in order that he[6] may be more generously kind towards you if he sees that you remember and are grateful.

In the meanwhile, beseech God for us, too, that he may see fit to remove all hindrances and grant freedom in the preaching of the

* * * * *

47 of Seneca, a contemporary of Paul. On the human laws governing aspects of slavery, see Alan Watson *Roman Slave Law* (Baltimore 1987). In spelling out the human laws, Ambrosiaster *Comm in Col* (on 4:1) CSEL 81/3 203:10–15 notes: 'God had not created them slaves and free (*liberi*), but all free-born (*ingenui*). But this [enslavement] happened through the wickedness of the world as, while one invades another's boundaries, he takes free-born men as captives ... the same condition still holds, some are redeemed, others remain slaves.' See also 1 Cor chapter 7 n45 and Eph chapter 6 nn11 and 18.

2 The requisite food, drink, and clothing to be allotted to slaves for pragmatic reasons is set out by eg Cato in *De agri cultura* 5.2, 56–9.

3 Servitude was rendered intolerable in Paul's world by dreadful punishments and by the demeaning services that might be demanded. Some of these are outlined by Seneca in *Epistulae morales* 47.5–7, and depicted by Petronius in the *Satyricon* 27.5–6, 45.8, 53.3. Some slave owners, however, behaved in a more kindly manner to at least some of their slaves; Cicero eg shows affection and concern for the comfort and health of Tiro (his slave, then freedman-secretary) in the letters addressed to Tiro gathered in Cicero's *Ad familiares* 16.

4 For mention of fellow slaves, compare ὁμοδούλοις in Theophylact *Expos in Col* (on 4:1) PG 124 1268D, also *conservi* in Seneca *Epistulae morales* 47.1 and the parable of the unmerciful servant, Matt 18:23–35.

5 as you] *qualem* ('you' singular implied) in the Froben editions from 1520 to 1538; *quales* 'as you' ('you' plural implied) in 1540 and LB. Since the referent of the pronoun is plural, the 1540/LB reading is grammatically correct; the singular, however, makes sense in the context of moral teaching.

6 he ... towards you] First in 1521. In 1520 4° 'the kindness may be more generous towards [1520 8° 'in'] you.'

gospel[7] so that, while[8] God opens the hearts of men and women through faith, the mystery[9] may steal into all their minds. Although[10] it has been concealed up to this point, now the Father has willed the mystery concerning Christ to be made known to all. Through him, without the support of the Law, he offers salvation to all. It is because I preach him that I am bound by these shackles. Pray that nothing may stand in the way of my publishing the gospel of Christ in the presence of all; I long to publish it freely and fearlessly just as he has bidden me.

With those who are alien to the profession of Christ, you must deal prudently so that nothing is evident in your[11] behaviour that might provoke them to the cruelty of persecution or alienate them from the gospel.[12] Since you cannot help having some[13] dealings with the pagans and cannot escape the ordinary association of your common life with them, let them find you

* * * * *

7 Cf 'freely and fearlessly' just below. Theophylact *Expos in Col* (on 4:3-4) PG 124 1269B comments that Paul prays, 'in order that he [God] may give me freedom of speech, not that I may be freed from the bonds.'

8 while ... through faith] Added in 1532. In his paraphrases generally, Erasmus made many additions of this sort after 1524, emphasizing the import of faith. See John B. Payne 'The Significance of Lutheranizing Changes in Erasmus' Interpretation of Paul's Letters to the Romans and the Galatians in his *Annotationes* (1527) and *Paraphrases* (1532)' in *Histoire de l'exégèse au XVI siècle: textes du colloque international tenu à Genève en 1976* ed Olivier Fatio et Pierre Fraenkel, Etudes de Philologie et d'Histoire 34 (Geneva 1978) 312-30.

9 In his paraphrase on 4:3 Erasmus retains the Vulgate's *mysterium* for the Greek μυστήριον, a word he paraphrases in the immediately subsequent 1532 addition (see n10) emphasizing its hiddenness. He is propounding here a profound conviction expressed also in the *Paraphrase on Ephesians* (see Roussel 'Exegetical Fictions?' 71) that the *mysterium Christi* 'mystery of Christ' (Conf) is the revelation of Christ's salvific action to all men and women irrespective of observance of the Law. On 'mystery,' see also 1 Cor chapter 7 n30; Eph chapters 1 n27 and 5 n38; and Col chapter 1 n48.

10 Although ... point] Added in 1532

11 your] First in 1521; previously 'our'

12 For winning others to the gospel by acts of kindness, see also Erasmus' paraphrase on Luke 6:27-35 LB VII 347B-348C, especially 348C. Erasmus is even more explicit in Ep 858:112-16, the preface to the 1518 revised edition of his *Enchiridion*. See also Ambrosiaster *Comm in Col* (on 4:5) CSEL 81/3 203:22-7: 'Since it is necessary to walk among the infidels ... this is the warning he gives: that the association be characterised by wisdom because of the [likelihood of] scandal to the gentiles so that they may not receive from us an occasion for blaspheming nor be incited to persecution.'

13 some] Added in 1532

more agreeable and more humane[14] as the result of your profession of a new religion whenever an opportunity arises to gratify them without the loss of piety.[15] Now especially this should be done so that all may be enticed to the profession of the gospel. The opportunity for this should not be lost on account of silly contentions; rather, it ought to be bought at the cost of jettisoning all things. Concede honour, concede money, let go of vengeance. Judge it a huge profit if, at the cost of these, the impact of the gospel[16] has increased. Let your conversation in their presence not be abusive and harsh, but let it be flavoured with human graciousness joined with the salt of prudence. For affable speech more swiftly bends fierce spirits, and prudence teaches what reply ought to be made, to whom, and with what moderation. Princes of the world ought to be dealt with in one way, people of some means in another way, lowly people in another way; the gentle in one way, the wrathful in another;[17] the learned in one way, the uneducated in another. Speech should be so[18] adapted to each person's station that it is of service to the gospel. There is a time when it is preferable to give way: as often as the person you are preparing to instruct shouts out protestations with furious abuse, or while the one you are speaking with is out to catch you in your teaching.[19]

* * * * *

14 'More humane': *humaniores*. The humanists picked up from authors of the Roman Republic the meaning of *humanus* as 'pertaining to all that is human' (cf Terence *Heauton Timorumenos* 77), 'cultured,' or 'civilized.' See OLD. See also Phil chapter 4 n4, and Craig R. Thompson 'The Humanism of More Reappraised' *Thought* 52 (1977) 231–48, especially 231–9.

15 On accommodating oneself in all that is not sinful, see Erasmus' paraphrase on Rom 14:13–21 CWE 42 80–2. For the importance of winning the respect of pagans, see his paraphrase on 1 Tim 3:6 CWE 44 21.

16 Literally *res evangelica* 'the business of the Gospel.' See Pabel 'Promoting the Business of the Gospel' ERSY 15 (1995) 53–70.

17 Thus far the list seems to have been drawn from Ambrosiaster *Comm in Col* (on 4:6) CSEL 81/3 204:3–6. Erasmus adds the further classes of the learned and the uneducated, distinctions that, though they reflect a preoccupation of humanists, appear also in the interlinear *Gloss* (on 4:6).

18 so] In all Froben editions from 1520 to 1534; omitted in *1540* and in LB

19 Cf Proverbs 15:1, 'A soft answer turns away wrath' (RSV), and Ambrosiaster *Comm in Col* (on 4:6) CSEL 81/3 204:6–8: 'For when you give way before a person *out to catch* the Lord's words, and before the *furious* boldness of the time, you turn the wrongs of a troublesome time into gain.' In the paraphrase here Erasmus has twice used a form of the same Latin word as Ambrosiaster: (indicated above by italics): *insidiare* 'to be out to catch,' 'to lie in ambush,' and *furiosus*. Cf *furere* 'to rage' or 'to be furious.'

About the state of my own affairs I am not writing to you, but Tychicus will inform you about them all when he delivers this letter.[20] He is my beloved brother on account of our common profession, and likewise both a reliable minister and a fellow slave in the work of the gospel. I am sending him there for this: that from him you may know what is happening with us, and that I may learn from him, likewise, what is happening with you; that your hearts may be refreshed by his conversation, and mine[21] may be restored by his words about you.[22]

As a companion for Tychicus I am also sending Onesimus.[23] I would not have you judge him on the basis of his former condition or life since he is now my reliable and, indeed, beloved brother. He ought to be more estimable in your eyes on account of this: that he is of your race, a convert from the uncircumcised to Christ.[24] These two will report to you in good faith whatever is of consequence for you to know about our affairs here.

Greetings to you from Aristarchus. Even if he is of the Jewish race, still, because of his brotherhood in the faith, he ought to be commended to you.[25] Certainly I consider him the ally[26] and associate of my captivity for the gospel of Christ. Greetings, too, from Mark, the cousin of Barnabas

* * * * *

20 letter] Expressed in *1520*; in *1521* and subsequently the word *literas* was suppressed but the meaning of the sentence remains unchanged.

21 mine] *meus*. First in *1521*; previously *mens* 'mind'

22 See also Erasmus' paraphrase on Phil 1:25–6 which in similar fashion goes beyond the text in emphasizing the mutual consolation to be derived from the visit announced in the letter. Erasmus is filling out his picture of Paul as a kindly teacher, as in his annotation on Rom 1:12 ('to be comforted together') CWE 56 37 n15. In his paraphrase on Philem 9 CWE 44 72, Erasmus similarly amplifies the text: 'I want to ask as a brother does a brother, rather than to order it as a teacher does a pupil. You will not spurn an intercessor like me.'

23 Onesimus, described at Philem 10–18 ('no longer a slave but instead of a slave a brother most dear' [Conf]), has generally been identified with the Onesimus of Colossians. See eg Eduard Schweizer *The Letter to the Colossians: A Commentary* trans Andrew Chester (Minneapolis 1976) 298: 'Onesimus can hardly be taken to mean anyone else except the person mentioned in Philemon'; so too Lohse 171.

24 Nicholas of Lyra (on 4:12) explains the expression 'who is one of you' as 'very closely joined to you by charity and perhaps he was of the gentile nation and from the region of the Colossians, but he became a disciple of Paul.'

25 See 4:11 for Aristarchus, Mark, and Jesus Justus as converts from Judaism.

26 Cf Ambrosiaster *Comm in Col* (on 4:10) CSEL 81/3 205:6–7: 'Aristarchus has been designated as the participant and ally of the Apostle's labours.'

whom you know well.[27] We have recommended him[28] to you elsewhere[29] with the instruction that we now repeat: if he comes to you, you are to welcome him graciously. Greetings too from Jesus, surnamed Justus. These people are, to be sure, from a different race, namely, the Jewish, but still they are deserving of your support because they are my only allies in my efforts to preach the kingdom of God. And in these evils with which I am afflicted they have been a consolation to me.

Greetings to you from Epaphras;[30] not only does he share with you in worshipping Christ, but he is joined with you also in the kinship of race. So sincerely does he foster your interests that with anxious earnestness he never stops beseeching God on your behalf that with God's help you may persevere in what you have begun and be not half-Christians,[31] but complete and perfect in doing all that is pleasing to God. For in his regard I testify to this: that he feels passionately about you; and not about you only, but also about your neighbours, the Laodiceans and the Hierapolitans. Greetings to you from Luke,[32] a doctor by profession, especially

* * * * *

27 Barnabas is often mentioned: as an outstanding and generous Christian (Acts 4:36), as an envoy to Antioch from the church in Jerusalem (Acts 11:22–6), and as a companion of Paul (Acts 12:30–15:38) until in disagreement about Mark they separated (Acts 15:39). See Erasmus' paraphrases on these passages in CWE 50 38, 79–80, 95, and 100.

28 From the word order of the Latin in this paraphrase on 4:10 we conclude that 'him' here refers to Mark, though the Greek is ambiguous. It is also unclear in the Greek whether the 'instruction' the Colossians have received is undefined or specific, ie 'to welcome Mark if he comes.' English translations tend to retain in some measure the ambiguity (cf DV, AV, RSV, NEB). In his translation Erasmus allowed the ambiguity of the Vulgate to remain; here in the paraphrase the instruction is specific. See his annotation on 4:10 (*de quo accepistis mandata*).

29 The precise meaning of 'elsewhere' in regard to these instructions cannot be determined. The Pauline text of 4:10, 'concerning whom you have received instructions' (Conf), does not attribute to Paul any such instructions.
Acts 15:37–9 records a disagreement between Paul and Barnabas because of Mark, who had 'withdrawn from them in Pamphylia and had not gone with them to the work' (Conf), but it is clear from Col 4:10, Philem 24, 1 Peter 5:13, and Tim 4:11 that Mark's earlier failing had been forgiven.

30 Epaphras is mentioned at 1:7 and included in the list of those sending greetings at Philem 23.

31 For the importance that Erasmus attached to being a 'true Christian,' see eg his *Institutio principis christiani* CWE 27 216–17 and 'Christian' in the General Index of CWE 50.

32 Luke is named also at Philem 24 as a fellow worker and at 2 Tim 4:11 as Paul's sole companion. The third Gospel is anonymous, as also is Acts. But according

dear to me, and, along with him, from Demas, who is still staying with me.[33]

Greet all the other brothers who are at Laodicea, but especially Nymphas together with that man's[34] household assembly. When this letter has been read in your presence see that it is read likewise in the assembly of the Laodiceans, and that you, in turn, read[35] the letter that was written to Timothy[36] from the city of the Laodiceans so that both letters may benefit

* * * * *

to traditions dating to the second century Luke is named as the author of Luke-Acts both in manuscript headings and in Irenaeus *Adversus haereses* 3.1.1 and 3.13.3–14.1 PG 7 845 and 912–14. For a summary of this and later evidence, see Joseph A. Fitzmyer *The Gospel According to Luke (I–IX): Introduction, Translation and Notes* The Anchor Bible Commentaries 28 (New York 1981) 35–53.

33 2 Tim 4:10 reports Demas' departure.

34 Erasmus clearly refers to Nymphas in the words *viri eius* 'of that man.' So, too, does Theophylact *Expos in Col* (on 4:15) PG 124 1276C, who refers unambiguously to Nymphas as 'a great man.' Valla *Annot in Col* 4 (I 881) also notes that the pronoun αὐτοῦ 'of him' in his Greek text refers to Nymphas as a man, in opposition to 'certain people' who had assumed that the person was a woman. For the opposite view, see the Latin commentaries on 4:15, eg the *Gloss*, referring to Nympha as a woman 'who [feminine singular] welcomes preachers'; and Nicholas of Lyra, who reports: 'She was taking care of the expenses for the preachers out of her own resources.' Depending on its accentuation the Greek name here could be either feminine Νύμφαν or masculine Νυμφᾶν. The gender of the Latin accusative, *Nympham*, is likewise ambiguous; the ambiguity is intensified by the possessive pronoun *eius* 'of him/her/it.' On the variants in the Greek text of 4:15, see Metzger 560, and Lohse 174 n44. Cf RSV 'to Nympha and the church in her house'; similarly NEB.

35 read] Froben editions from 1520 to 1538 print the subjunctive *legatis*, preferable here in the context of an indirect command; *1540* and LB print the future *legetis* 'will read.'

36 Erasmus is paraphrasing a problematic phrase in the Pauline text of 4:16: 'You yourselves read the letter from Laodicea' (Conf). Erasmus supposes that the letter may be identified with 1 Timothy. Cf Theophylact *Expos in Col* (on 4:16) PG 124 1276D: 'What was the [letter] from Laodicea? The First to Timothy, for it was written from Laodicea.' In a lengthy annotation on 4:16 (*et cum lecta fuerit*), Erasmus castigates his learned friend Lefèvre d'Etaples, who had included in his pioneering commentary on the Epistles of St Paul (cf 2 Cor chapter 6 n12) a letter attributed to Paul written to the Laodiceans (an early forgery meant to explain the allusion in 4:16). See Eugene F. Rice Jr *The Prefatory Epistles of Jacques Lefèvre d'Etaples* (New York 1972) 295–302, especially 300 n9. On the 'Epistle from Laodicea,' see J.B. Lightfoot *Saint Paul's Epistles to the Colossians and to Philemon, a revised text with introductions, notes and dissertations* (London 1879; repr 1987) 274–300. For an English translation and more recent scholarship on 'The Epistle to the Laodiceans,' see *New Testament Apocrypha*

more people. To Archippus, your prefect, say this in my words: See what a province you have taken on.[37] It is the Lord's work that has been delegated[38] to you, not man's. See that you accomplish what you have undertaken, as one who will render an account to the Lord.[39]

So that this letter may be more trustworthy in your judgment, I shall add again a greeting to all of you in my own hand, that is, Paul's, not unknown to you.[40] Be mindful of my bonds which I bear for your sake, and live in such a way that I will not regret them.[41] May the favour of Jesus be always with you. Amen

The End of the Paraphrase on the Epistle of Paul
to the Colossians by Erasmus of Rotterdam

* * * * *

rev ed Wilhelm Schneemelcher, English translation ed R.McL. Wilson, 2 vols (Louisville 1991) 2 42–6.

37 For the proverbial expression *capere provinciam* 'to take on a department,' see *Adagia* II iv 41.

38 delegated] *delegatum* in Froben editions from 1520 to 1538; *1540* and LB print *delatum* 'conferred.' For the exchange of these forms in the opposite direction, see chapter 1 n50.

39 See Rom 14:12: 'Everyone of us will render an account for himself to God' (Conf), and Erasmus' paraphrase on the verse CWE 42 80.

40 There is no external evidence that the Colossians would recognize Paul's handwriting, but note that the interlinear *Gloss* (on 4:18) makes that assumption, 'that you may know the letter was sent by me.'

41 Cf Ambrosiaster *Comm in Col* (on 4:18) CSEL 81/3 207:3–5: '[He reminds] them to keep in mind the fate he was suffering for the salvation of the nations, and to show themselves such that he would not be sorry to suffer wrongs for them.'

PARAPHRASE ON FIRST THESSALONIANS

In epistolam Pauli Apostoli ad Thessalonicenses paraphrasis

translated and annotated by
MECHTILDE O'MARA

THE ARGUMENT OF THE FIRST EPISTLE
OF PAUL TO THE THESSALONIANS
BY ERASMUS OF ROTTERDAM

Thessalonica is the capital of Macedonia;[1] hence also the district's inhabitants are called Thessalonians. These people persevered with such great constancy in the faith once received,[2] that, following the example even of Paul, they endured persecutions from their fellow citizens with an unflagging and cheerful heart; and they could not be turned aside from their instruction[3] in the gospel by any persuasion of false apostles. Having feared precisely this, and well aware of the wickedness of the false apostles, Paul sent Timothy[4] to visit the Thessalonians because he was not himself able to visit them. When on Timothy's return he had learned of their constancy, he praises them, giving thanks to God. And this is what he does in the first and second chapters.

In the remaining two,[5] he instructs them in the various duties of piety, hinting that there were among them some who were not yet entirely free from all lust and that those were not lacking who had given themselves up to idleness and so were a burden on others; likewise, there

* * * * *

1 See F.F. Bruce 'St. Paul in Macedonia' *Bulletin of the John Rylands University Library of Manchester* 61 (1979) 337–54. Thessalonica (now Salonica), on the Via Egnatia in north-east Greece, was the capital city of the Roman province of Macedonia from 146 BC. According to Acts 17:1 the city was evangelized during Paul's second missionary journey. Erasmus uses the word *metropolis* with which medieval annotators on 1 Thess 1:1 identify Thessalonica as the capital of Macedonia. See eg Peter Lombard *Collectanea in omnes D. Pauli Apostoli epistulas* PL 192 287–8; the *Gloss*; and Nicholas of Lyra (on 1:1).
2 With the phrase 'faith once received' cf the Argument of Philippians n3 and Col chapter 1 n35; also the paraphrase on 1 Cor 15:1–2.
3 'Instruction': *institutione*. See OLD 4.
4 See Acts 16:1, 1 Thess 3:2, also Heb 13:23 and its paraphrase CWE 44 260 n23.
5 two] Froben editions from 1520 to 1538; *1540* and LB print 'three,' evidently because there are five chapters in the epistle, a necessary correction 'overlooked through nine successive editions.' See Bateman 'Textual Travail' 252.

were some people who, restless themselves, were upsetting the tranquillity of the church; these he bids the Thessalonians to correct. In addition, there were some whose belief in the resurrection was not yet sufficiently established, for they were grieving for the deceased as if they had perished and had not, rather, moved on to better things. These he instructs and strengthens. Again he hints that others had argued about the day of the Lord's coming as if it could be foreknown and foretold, although it was unknown to all.[6] But he says that it will come suddenly and contrary to everyone's expectation so that we might the more be ready at every moment.

He wrote from Athens[7] through his assistant Tychicus,[8] according to the Greek subscription; the Arguments – of uncertain authorship[9] – which are read in our printed copies[10] attribute Onesimus[11] to him as a colleague.

* * * * *

6 Cf Matt 24:36; Mark 13:32; also CWE 50 8.
7 Erasmus follows a widespread tradition when he declares that 1 Thessalonians was written from Athens. The subscription in many Byzantine witnesses affirms this (see Metzger 566), and Erasmus printed the subscription in his own Greek text. It is likewise stated in the Greek Hypothesis that preceded his Latin Argument (LB VI 899–900), as well as in the traditional Latin Argument of Thessalonians as found in Erasmus' *Novum Instrumentum*. Most modern scholarship, however, points to Corinth as the place of composition. See Rigaux 42–51, and Best 7–13, 211.
8 On Tychicus, see the Argument of Ephesians n15. Neither Tychicus nor Onesimus is named in 1 Thessalonians, in the subscriptions or in the Greek Hypothesis for this letter. Erasmus may have mistakenly transferred into his Argument (LB VI 898) part of the Colossians' subscription ('written through Tychicus and Onesimus') which immediately precedes 1 Thessalonians. See Metzger 560. For 'subscription' see Col Argument n13; on the idiom cf ibidem n10.
9 For these Arguments, see Translators' Note xvi; on their uncertain authorship cf Ep 894:45–6.
10 'Printed copies': *vulgatis exemplaribus*. According to Chomarat 1 486–7 Erasmus used this expression to signify printed books without distinguishing them from manuscripts. Modern critical editions of the Vulgate, eg Weber, do not print Arguments.
11 Onesimus is the subject of Paul's letter to Philemon, mentioned also in Col 4:9 in connection with Tychicus. See n8 above.

THE PARAPHRASE ON THE FIRST EPISTLE
OF PAUL THE APOSTLE TO THE THESSALONIANS
BY ERASMUS OF ROTTERDAM

Chapter 1

Paul, Silvanus, and Timothy,[1] to the congregation[2] of the Thessalonians that unites together in God the Father and in our Lord Jesus Christ. From them[3] may grace and peace be granted to you.

Rejoicing as is right in your progress,[4] we always give thanks to God on behalf of all of you whenever we speak with God in holy prayers, because the extent to which you have excelled[5] in safeguarding the profession of your faith never fails to come to our mind. Then too, we are aware of how much effort you have spent on account of the charity you have towards the heralds of the gospel,[6] how courageously and firmly you have put up

* * * * *

1 Paul is linked with Silvanus and Timothy again in 2 Thess 1:1 and in 2 Cor 1:19.

2 Erasmus paraphrases 1:1 using *congregatio* 'congregation' rather than the Vulgate transliteration *ecclesia* of the Greek ἐκκλησία 'church.' In the tradition, exegetes had stressed the significance of the word *ecclesia*. See Chrysostom *In 1 Thess hom* 1.1 (on 1:1) PG 62 393 and Theophylact *Expos in 1 Thess* (on 1:1) PG 124 1280B. For Erasmus' use of *congregatio* and *ecclesia* in the paraphrases, see 1 Cor chapters 1 n3 and 16 n13, and 2 Thess chapter 1 n1.

3 'From them' seems to be a paraphrastic compromise between Erasmus' Greek text, which included in 1:1 the words 'from God the Father and our Lord Jesus Christ' and the Vulgate, which generally omitted them. Cf av. See his annotation on 1:1 (*et pax*). For the evidence of the witnesses, see Metzger 561.

4 Ambrosiaster *Comm in 1 Thess* (on 1:2) CSEL 81/3 212:4 also noted in his commentary the 'progress' (Latin *profectus*, as here in the paraphrase) of the Thessalonians.

5 excelled] *praestiteritis* in all editions; LB however, reports in a footnote an alternative reading: *perstiteritis* 'persisted'

6 Erasmus' paraphrase specifies 'the labour of love,' observing that it has been directed to the preachers of the gospel. Cf Theophylact *Expos in 1 Thess* (on

with everything, relying on the hope and expectation[7] of the rewards[8] that our Lord Jesus Christ has promised in the life to come to those who disregard the disadvantages of this life[9] for the sake of his name. You will not lose the reward for deeds rightly done; he will repay who has seen in what spirit you have acted – our God and Father.

You yourselves know,[10] beloved brothers, that you were not transformed by human persuasion but you had been chosen for this by divine will.[11] For we did not preach the gospel to you in such a way that we brought you nothing but words; on the contrary, the power of God strengthened our preaching with miracles.[12] The Holy Spirit was given through us[13] also, and nothing at all was lacking that was conducive to complete faith in the gospel teaching, since indeed through our gospel you gained whatever the Jews gained at the preaching of others.[14] And, what is more, on

* * * * *

1:3) PG 124 1281C who, referring to Acts 17:1–15, reminds his readers that it was Paul to whom the Thessalonians showed charity.

7 The Vulgate follows closely the Greek of 1:3 in reading, 'remembering ... the steadfastness of hope in our Lord Jesus Christ' (RSV); Ambrosiaster's text *Comm in 1 Thess* (on 1:3) CSEL 81/3 212:10, however, reads, 'remembering ... the expectation of the Lord Jesus Christ.' In the phrase 'hope and expectation,' Erasmus apparently combines the two readings.

8 Cf Nicholas of Lyra (on 1:3), who explains the word 'hope' (RSV) as 'the hope of the reward to be received from the Lord Jesus Christ.'

9 life] In the 1520 editions 'life here'; the subsequent editions from 1521 to 1538 and LB omit 'here.'

10 The paraphrase reflects Erasmus' annotation on 1:4 (*scientes fratres*) and his own somewhat ambiguous translation, which can be read '[you] knowing.' As Erasmus observes in his annotation, Theophylact *Expos in 1 Thess* (on 1:4) PG 124 1281D understood 'we (Paul and his colleagues) knowing' – the commonly accepted interpretation. Cf RSV, Conf.

11 Erasmus discusses the divine choice and foreknowledge in his annotation on Rom 8:29 ('whom he had foreknown') CWE 56 225–6. See also the paraphrase on 2 Thess 2:13 with n23.

12 Miracles as evidence of the strength of Paul's preaching are mentioned in the interlinear *Gloss* (on 1:5) and by Ambrosiaster *Comm in 1 Thess* (on 1:5) CSEL 81/3 212:28–30, who in this connection mentions signs and prodigies.

13 through us] Added in 1532

14 In his annotation on 1:5 (*in plenitudine*) Erasmus explains the phrase 'with full conviction' (RSV) as meaning 'with full persuasive power.' Cf Aquinas *Super 1 Thess lect* cap 1 lectio 1.13 (II 166), who suggests that Paul intends to assure the Thessalonians 'that they should not think that they had received less than the Jews.' The 'others' who preach authentically to the Jews are the apostles and their disciples. For Paul's vocation as 'Apostle to the Gentiles,' see Acts 11:1–3; Gal 2:7–10; 1 Tim 2:7; 2 Tim 1:11.

this point, you yourselves are the witnesses of how simply, how humbly,[15] how assiduously,[16] we behaved among you. There is nothing we did not endure in order to win you for Christ.[17]

Nor did you prove to be unworthy disciples, but you have imitated our example, or rather not ours but the Lord Jesus', who subjected himself in this way, who suffered all things in this way, to win us for himself. Far from rejecting our gospel, for its sake you have endured many severe afflictions not only bravely, but even with much joy, a joy produced in your souls by the Holy Spirit, whom you received at our preaching, a pledge, for the time being, of happiness to come. In the hope of this felicity any evil inflicted here on account of Christ's gospel is even a source of delight.

So remarkable was the strength of your faith that you were an example to all believers in the rest of Macedonia and Achaia.[18] For to such an extent did the example of the capital city[19] move the hearts of all, that the fame of the gospel echoed widely like a sounding trumpet,[20] spreading abroad not only in Macedonia and Achaia but in all the other regions as well[21] the ardour of the faith that you have towards God, so that now there is no need for us to proclaim your piety. For whenever we try to tell the story of these events, the people themselves, informed by a report often repeated even before we speak, rather, of their own accord, tell us how we first came to you to preach the gospel's doctrine, and with what great readiness

* * * * *

15 The scriptural text of 1:5 represents Paul saying: 'You yourselves know what manner of men we have been among you for your sakes' (Conf). Erasmus paraphrases the passage in line with Ambrosiaster *Comm in 1 Thess* (on 1:4–5) CSEL 81/3 212:26–7, who mentions that Paul and his fellow preachers were humble.

16 'Assiduously': *laboriose*, which may refer to Paul's working with his hands, or it may mean 'painfully,' 'suffering much hardship.' See OLD *laboriose* and *laboriosus*.

17 Cf Theophylact *Expos in 1 Thess* (on 1:5) PG 124 1284B: 'We did everything earnestly for your sake.'

18 'Achaia' was the name of the Roman province that comprised the isthmus of Corinth and the Peloponnesus. Corinth was its administrative centre in the first century AD. See also 1 Cor Argument n1.

19 Namely, Thessalonica

20 Exegetes before Erasmus had noted the trumpet image suggested by the Greek ἐξήχηται 'sounded forth' (1:8 RSV): so Valla *Annot in 1 Thess* 1 (I 880) and Theopylact *Expos in 1 Thess* (on 1:8) PG 124 1285A, following Chrysostom *In 1 Thess hom* 2.1 (on 1:8) PG 62 399.

21 as well] Added in 1521

you received us, despising the dangers that seemed to threaten you on our account; and with what ease you were brought over to the worship of God from the superstition of your ancestors in which you used to worship the images of demons.[22] Henceforth, renouncing false and dead gods,[23] you were to serve the living and true God. Relying on his promises you reckon as nothing the advantages of this life and equally its disadvantages, while you wait for his Son Jesus to come again from heaven to display openly to the world what he has promised. Through Jesus he has claimed us for salvation and promised us the rewards of the life that is to be. Indeed, he raised him to life for this, that through him we too might be restored to life again to enjoy with him immortal blessings, just as here we endure the evils of this world for his sake. Nor will his coming then be a source of terror for us, for having cleansed us from our sins by his blood, he has reconciled us to God, and set us free from the eternal punishment that was due our offences.[24]

* * * * *

22 What Erasmus meant by 'images of demons' (part of his paraphrase on 'idols'), may be grasped by consideration of the illustrations of evil powers in fifteenth-century books. See eg Norbert H. Ott 'Facts and Fiction: the Iconography of Demons in German Vernacular Manuscripts' in *Demons: Mediators between This World and the Other, Essays on Demonic Beings from the Middle Ages to the Present* ed Ruth Petzoldt and Paul Neubauer, Beiträge zur europäischen Ethnologie und Folklore: Reihe B: Tagungsberichte und Materialien 8 (Frankfurt am Main 1998) 27–50. For *daemones* 'demons' defined as those who 'rejoice in every sin, especially, however, in fornication and idolatry,' see the *Gloss* on the expression *contaminatae sunt* found in the Vulgate of Lev 18:24. In the context of New Testament writings, 'demon' designates hostile powers opposed to the message of Christ, see CWE 50 92 n18, 107 n24, and 'Demons' in EEC 325–7. For demons in the Bible, their names, characteristics and the biblical evidence, see *Dictionary of Deities and Demons in the Bible* ed Karel van der Toorn, Bob Becking, Pieter W. van der Horst, 2nd ed rev (Leiden 1999). On demons in the paraphrases, see 1 Cor Argument n10 and Eph Argument n1.
23 Erasmus develops the antithesis of Paul's statement, which adverts only to the service of the living and true God. Erasmus' paraphrase on 'idols' includes 'superstition ... demons ... false and dead gods.' Ambrosiaster *Comm in 1 Thess* (on 1:9) CSEL 81/3 214:16 also speaks of 'abandoning dead gods.' Worshipping idols associates the worshipper with demons (1 Cor 10:19–21), but these idols are false gods, inert and lifeless (Ps 115:4–8), as opposed to the living God who is the source of all life. Early Christian apologetic also interpreted false gods as dead men eg Tertullian *Apologeticum* 10–11 CCL 1 105–9.
24 In Erasmus' scheme, cleansing ie restored innocence is a necessary prerequisite for reconciliation. See Sider 'The Just' 20–1.

Chapter 2

What is the point of recalling, since you yourselves know perfectly well that even if we did not come to you with pride and arrogance, weighing out certain big words or professing some grand philosophy, still our approach to you was not without effect. On the contrary, although previously too at Philippi we had endured much[1] (as you yourselves know), and had been subjected to many insults along with Silas because we expelled a spirit of divination from the girl it possessed,[2] nevertheless, relying on the aid of our God, we were not afraid to preach freely[3] the gospel of Christ in your presence too, although not without serious risk. If we had been preaching an empty fabrication, we never would have risked our lives for its sake. For people who teach on their own authority what they have not received from Christ, and teach with a view to their own gain, do it to deceive others to their own profit. These have no authority and they withdraw straightaway when they fear risking their life or possessions.[4]

* * * * *

1 The paraphrase follows some Vulgate Bibles (including 1527) which read 'having suffered much.' However, in his annotation on 2:2 (*sed ante passi multa*), Erasmus notes that the reading 'much' had no support in the Greek codices, in Ambrosiaster, or in the oldest Latin manuscripts. In fact, the word represents a minor variant, and does not appear in the *apparatus* of Weber 1825. Certainly, the account of Paul's sufferings recorded in Acts 16:16–24 and outlined in the remainder of this sentence justifies the word here in the paraphrase.

2 For the narrative of the expulsion of the spirit of divination and the consequent sufferings of Paul and Silas, see Acts 16:16–40. 'Spirit of divination' represents Erasmus' single word '*Pytho*' in the paraphrase here; in his translation of Acts 16:16 he followed the Vulgate in writing *spiritus Pythonis* 'spirit of Pytho.' In his annotation on that verse (*habent ... spiritum Pythonem*), he notes that 'Pytho' was the name of the serpent slain by Apollo at Delphi and that the term was later applied to those who foretold the future. Substantially the same account of the word is given by BDAG 896–7. Jerome referred to such ventriloquistic spirits as 'pythons' in his *Commentarii in Isaiam prophetam* III (on Isa 8:19–22) PL 24 1845) 122A–123B. Both Ambrosiaster *Comm in 1 Thess* (on 2:2) CSEL 81/3 215:3–5 and Aquinas *Super 1 Thess lect* cap 2 lectio 1.24 (II 169) identify this expulsion of the divining spirit as the cause of Paul's sufferings at Philippi.

3 Cf Ambrosiaster *Comm in 1 Thess* (on 2:1–2) CSEL 81/3 215:6–10: '[Paul] dares to preach and he does not fear to speak' – proof, says Ambrosiaster, of the devoted preacher.

4 Ambrosiaster *Comm in 1 Thess* (on 2:3–6) CSEL 81/3 215:18–216:3 also notes that false apostles teach for gain and, being without authority, are weak in the face of danger.

But the teaching to which we invited you was not fabricated and counterfeit or drawn up to deceive.[5] We neither concealed impure arts[6] under its
cover as false apostles do, nor did we do anything through trickery, publicly declaring one thing while aiming at something else and, on the pretext
of Christ, carrying out our own business, like those who make themselves
apostles. But just as God through his Son has assigned us to this duty,[7] that
we should sincerely preach the gospel entrusted, so we preach to all, not
in order to win honour or curry favour with men, but to make our performance acceptable to God, who sees deep into our hearts[8] and on this basis
assesses each person. We did not fawn on anyone – you yourselves are the
witnesses of this fact – nor did we turn to our gain the word[9] of the gospel
and your readiness to believe. God himself is the witness of this intent of
ours. We did not hunt for human renown from the gospel whether among
you or any others, although we could have used our authority and arrogance just as much as false apostles do. Although they teach idle tales[10] for

* * * * *

5 'To deceive': *ad imposturam*. The Vulgate had translated πλάνη by *error* 'error';
  Erasmus by *impostura* 'deception' as here in the paraphrase. In his annotation
  on 2:3 (*non de errore*), Erasmus explained that the Latin word *error* is used
  of one who has been deceived while the Greek word πλάνη is used both of
  one who has been deceived and one who deceives; hence his preference for
  impostura 'deceit.' In commenting on the Greek word πλάνη, Theophylact *Expos
  in 1 Thess* (on 2:3) PG 124 1288B observes that it is not characteristic of those
  who deceive to put themselves in danger.
6 The clause paraphrases *inmunditia* 'impure motives' (Conf), 'uncleanness' (RSV)
  in 2:3. Erasmus' annotation on the word (*neque ex munditia*) explains his
  thought: magical arts are called 'uncleanness' because they take place by 'impure and sordid methods to deceive simple folk.' Cf also the paraphrase on
  Acts 8:9-24 CWE 50 58, in which Erasmus paints a graphic picture of Simon
  who, 'with counterfeit miracles and prodigies, had deluded the Samaritan populace with his magic arts.'
7 Erasmus is careful in describing the work of the apostle; here he uses *munus*
  'service.' See his annotation on Rom 1:5 ('grace and apostleship') CWE 56 19,
  and his paraphrase on Col 1:7 with n7.
8 Erasmus is fond of this image of God seeing into the heart. Cf CWE 50 60; CWE
  56 97 n32.
9 'Word': *sermonem*. See n20 below.
10 'Idle tales': *inania*. Cf both Cicero *De oratore* 1.51, who describes as *furiosus*
  'mad' the speaker who produces *sonitus inanis* 'hollow thundering' without
  thought or knowledge, and Erasmus' paraphrase on 1 Cor 13:1, which mentions the *inanis strepitus* 'hollow clatter' of the person who speaks without
  love.

their own profit, nevertheless they demand honour and compliance from you.[11]

We, on the other hand, mindful of what befits apostles of Christ, who lowered himself for the sake of our salvation, have not laid claim to pride and arrogance, but have shown ourselves peaceable and mild[12] in your midst, not ranting and raging as if against pupils,[13] but with all gentleness accommodating your weakness. Just as a nursing mother would foster the young and tender life of her children, so too we were affectionately inclined towards you and sincerely longed, not only to impart to you the gospel of God as nourishment for your souls, but even to devote our own life[14] – not that we hoped for any reward from you, but because we sincerely considered you precious – just as a mother cherishes her children. We are not complaining about the responsibility, but testifying to our affection. I say this because you yourselves, brothers, remember how for your sake we avoided no labour, no effort, thirsting for or catching at nothing else but your salvation.[15] So far were we from hunt-

* * * * *

11 In this and the previous sentence Erasmus paraphrases 'might have been burdensome' (AV, DV) in 2:6–7, understanding it as 'exercising the authority to demand obedience.' Cf RSV 'might have made demands.' Ambrosiaster understood the phrase similarly. See *Comm in 1 Thess* (on 2:6–7) CSEL 81/3 216:18–20.

12 Erasmus follows his own Greek text in 2:7, which reads ἤπιοι 'mild.' Some Greek texts read νήπιοι 'little children,' the reading followed by the Vulgate, translating *parvuli*. Cf DV 'little ones.' Erasmus defended his reading in a long annotation on 2:7 (*sed facti sumus parvuli*), where he observed that the word 'mild' is especially appropriate to a bishop, for no gift 'more graciously adorns ... than ... mildness ... which ... accompanies wisdom.' Paul deserves the glory of this praise as the outstanding example of apostolic humility. Among his own contemporaries, Erasmus knew none to approach the ideal more nearly than William Warham, archbishop of Canterbury. At this point the note takes on a life of its own and moves through a eulogy of Warham to praise all Erasmus' patrons in a context, liberally illustrated by the careers of other humanists, describing the benefits to be won through patronage of the liberal arts. Several names were eliminated from the roll-call in the 1535 edition of the *Annotations*. See LB VI 903D–905D.

13 For another Erasmian portrait of a foolish teacher, see *Moria* CWE 27 122.

14 Erasmus' expression, literally 'we longed to impart to you not only the gospel of God ... but even to devote our life,' betrays over-hasty composition by his misplacement of the correlatives, 'not only ... but even.' The translation reports what Erasmus intended to say.

15 'Thirsting': *sitientes* and 'catching at': *captantes*. On the idiom cf Horace describing the tortures of Tantalus in *Satires* 1.1.68–9: *Tantalus a labris sitiens fugientia*

ing any bounty from you that we provided a livelihood for ourselves by the work of our hands,[16] night and day, in order not to be a burden to any one of you. False apostles inflict their gospel upon you and extort as much as they can; we have preached the gospel of God to you free of charge.[17]

You are my witnesses and God himself is the witness of how reverently, how justly, how blamelessly, we behaved towards you who believed. In fact, you know full well how we have done everything with genuine affection, so that we felt affection towards each of you as any father feels towards his children, now entreating, now consoling, now imploring not that you should give us something, but that you should lead a life worthy of God. Although you were formerly strangers to all piety, he has called you through faith to the pursuit of true piety,[18] and, through afflictions lasting but a moment, he has admitted you[19] into his kingdom and into the glory that never dies.

It is well that you recognize God's kindness. We, too, therefore, give thanks to him unceasingly because, when we had come to you in our lowliness recommended by no outward show of status, he inspired your hearts to accept the gospel's teaching as soon as you had heard it from us, not as if it were human discourse or a human tale, but as if it were a word come from God himself, as in fact it was. For it[20] was speaking to you through

* * * * *

captat / flumina 'Thirsting Tantalus catches at the streams that fly from his lips.' Erasmus quotes these lines from Horace in *Adagia* I vi 22 and II vi 14.

16 For Paul's efforts to earn his livelihood by manual labour, see 1 Cor 4:12; also Acts 18:2–3, and Erasmus' paraphrase on these verses CWE 50 112.

17 Cf Christ's instruction to the apostles (Matt 10:8): 'Freely you have received, freely give' (Conf).

18 to the pursuit of true piety] Added in *1532*

19 he has admitted you] Added in *1532*

20 Possibly 'he.' The masculine Latin pronoun *ille* could refer to either of the immediately preceding masculine singular nouns *Deus* 'God' or *sermo* 'discourse' or 'word.' Erasmus preserves the ambiguity in the Greek of 1 Thess 2:13 in his translation. Cf eg 'the word of God *who* works in you' (Conf), with 'God's word *which* is at work in you' (RSV): In his annotation on 2:13 (*qui operatur*), Erasmus favours the latter interpretation, as does Ambrosiaster *Comm in 1 Thess* (on 2:13) CSEL 81/3 218:9. Here, as elsewhere in his translation, Erasmus replaced the Vulgate's *verbum* by *sermo* as a translation of λόγος. Erasmus' New Testament scholarship shows a persistent interest in the semantics of the term 'word.' See 1 Cor chapter 1 n40 and CWE 44 223 n5, CWE 50 73 n49 and 76 n1. See also the annotations on Rom 9:9 ('for the word of promise') CWE 56 255 n1 and Rom 9:28 ('bringing to completion the word') CWE 56 272 n3.

us. Human discourse is weak and without effect, but the word of God is
efficacious.[21] As soon as you drank it in, it was not idle but began to exert its power in you[22] so that it was quite evident that you had received the
Spirit also.[23] For at once you began to imitate the other churches of God in
Judea which acknowledge Christ Jesus.

What Christ, what we, what the rest of the Jews who embrace the
gospel teaching have suffered from the people of their own race, who find
this doctrine hateful, you too have suffered from your fellow countrymen.
For as they, intolerant of the truth,[24] killed the Lord Jesus and slaughtered
their prophets before him, so also are they persecuting us too, the heralds
of evangelical truth. They do so with such great blindness of heart[25] that
they both call forth upon themselves the wrath of God against whose will
they rebel, and are opposed to all men, as if they are enemies of the human
race, envying all for the salvation offered through faith and desiring to
drag all to destruction along with themselves.[26] It is not because of any
private hatred that they resist us in this way; rather they begrudge the
good of all races and for this reason stir up trouble for us so that we may
not preach to the gentiles the gospel through which they could be saved. It
is as if it were too little to have previously slaughtered the prophets, then
after the prophets, Christ, unless by afflicting us, too, and eliminating us,
they put the finishing touch on the culmination of their crimes and place
this colophon,[27] so to speak, on their impiety. They are always the same.

* * * * *

21 For examples of Erasmus' attention to the 'efficacy' of God's word, see his
   annotation on Heb 4:12 (*et efficax*). See also Eph chapters 4 n18 and 6 n36.
22 in you] 'in us' in the octavo editions of 1521 and 1523
23 For the potentially medicinal effect of the gospel, see eg Erasmus' paraphrase
   on Luke 23:5 CWE 48 209.
24 For the expression cf Theophylact *Expos in 1 Thess* (on 2:15) PG 124 1293C κατὰ
   τῆς ἀληθείας λυττῶντες ' raging against the truth.'
25 On the perversity of those who are deliberately blind, see Erasmus' paraphrases on John 12:37–43 CWE 46 156–7 and Acts 2:40 CWE 50 23 and n101.
26 For Erasmus' interpretation that a spiteful unwillingness of the Jews to share
   salvation with the gentiles lies behind their resistance to the gospel, see eg his
   paraphrases on Acts 13:9–11 and 22:22 CWE 50 85 and 131, and the entry 'Jews'
   in the General Index of CWE 44, 46, 48, 50. For an assessment of Erasmus'
   treatment of Jews in the *Paraphrases*, see also Hilmar M. Pabel 'Erasmus of
   Rotterdam and Judaism: A Reexamination in the Light of New Evidence' *Archiv
   für Reformationsgeschichte* 87 (1996) 9–37.
27 Borrowed from the Greek, 'colophon' meant to Erasmus 'the finishing touch.'
   In Erasmus' interpretation, the slaughter of Paul and the Christians is all
   that the enemies of the faith think they need to complete their victory. See

They never recover from their madness.[28] By these means, they provoke the divine wrath against themselves to such an extent that we must despair of them, seeing that with malice aforethought they drive from themselves the mercy of God and attack in every way the gospel by whose help alone they could have been saved.

But the more I love you, brothers, on account of the keenness and the readiness of your faith, the more grievous was our longing for you because, torn from you for a little while, we were not allowed the pleasure of looking upon you.[29] An amazing desire to be with you possessed us, although indeed we had never been sundered in spirit.[30] And yet this was not enough for our love towards you, unless present in your presence I should see you with my physical eyes also. Consequently, I did not think it sufficient to send someone to you, or to converse with you through a letter, but I myself, Paul, repeatedly tried to go to you so that I might further strengthen your spirits. Satan, however, obstructed me in the attempt. For it was he who, through wicked Jews,[31] hindered my setting out for you.

But what wonder if I am possessed by such a longing for you? For what else is there in this world for me to take pleasure in, for me to boast of,[32] for me to rely on in order to promise myself happiness? All things I

* * * * *

Colophonem addidit 'He added the colophon' Adagia II iii 45 with its introductory note. The Oxford English Dictionary 2nd ed, ed J.A. Simpson and E.S.C. Weiner, 20 vols (Oxford 1989) 3 496–7 reports that the specialized use of 'colophon' to designate the final note set by the printer at the end of a book is an eighteenth-century development.

28 The Latin word resipiscere 'to recover' (in classical Latin 'to come to one's senses') is doubly appropriate here in the context of insania 'madness.' Since Erasmus often uses resipiscere to connote repentance, it is clear that the 'madness' referred to here is the sin of perversity. See nn25 and 26 above and 1 Cor Argument n15.

29 Paul had preached in Thessalonica on three sabbaths, but some Jews stirred up trouble and the brethren sent Paul away hurriedly. See Acts 17:1–10.

30 Cf Ambrosiaster Comm in 1 Thess (on 2:17) CSEL 81/3 219:13–14: non animo sed corpore divulsos 'sundered not in spirit but in body.'

31 Cf Ambrosiaster Comm in 1 Thess (on 2:18) CSEL 81/3 220:1–5: 'The minds of the treacherous ones were kindled so as to detain the apostles with whips and chains lest they speak the word of God. For the elders of the Jews said to the apostles: "Did we not warn you with the instruction that you should not speak in this name (Jesus) to anyone?"'

32 Erasmus paraphrases the Greek στέφανος καυχήσεως 'crown of boasting' (2:19 RSV) in accordance with his own Latin translation 'corona gloriationis' correcting the Vulgate corona gloriae 'crown of glory' (Conf); Valla Coll (on 2:19) Perosa 239 had also insisted on gloriationis here.

despise in comparison with the gospel of Christ.[33] What hope, therefore, is ours? Or what is our joy? Or what is our crown? Is it not you also among the other gentiles I have won for Christ, if not in the eyes of the world, certainly in the eyes of the Lord Jesus Christ? After the foes of the gospel have been defeated, when the triumph[34] is openly celebrated at his coming, what trophies then, what souvenirs of victory will I exhibit in that procession except you and others like you?[35] Meanwhile, I enjoy the sure hope of these rewards. You, therefore, in this life are the food and fuel of our renown.[36] You are our joy, if only you persevere in what you have begun.

Chapter 3

Accordingly, since we were already unable to bear our longing for you, and no opportunity of coming to you was arising, we decided to do through a close associate, one very faithful to me, a second self so to speak, what we were not permitted to do in person. Therefore, we stayed behind alone in Athens and from there sent Timothy, a brother of ours and God's proven servant, our ally and assistant in the obligations we discharge in the gospel of Christ.[1] We preferred for the time being to do without the comfort of a colleague so unique and so close to us, rather than act in such a way that we seem to have been careless at any time in looking out for your interests.

* * * * *

33 An allusion, perhaps, to Phil 3:8
34 'Crown' seems to have suggested to Erasmus the analogy between Paul and the Roman general who celebrated a triumph. On the triumph see Eph chapter 4 n17.
35 Erasmus follows his own Greek text and Latin translation of 2:19. The Vulgate reads: 'What is our hope ... if not you' (Conf); Erasmus reads 'What is our hope ... Is it not you also?' and in his annotation (*nonne vos ante dominum*) observes that the addition of the Greek καί 'also' points to all the gentiles who were converted to Christ, including the Thessalonians, as Paul's hope and crown. In support of this view, he cites Theophylact *Expos in 1 Thess* (on 2:19) PG 124 1297A.
36 For the phrase *segetem ac materiem ... gloriae* 'the food and fuel of ... renown,' see Cicero *Pro Milone* 13.35.

1 Erasmus' paraphrase on 3:2 reflects the reading of his Greek text, 'minister of God and our co-worker in the gospel of Christ' (so AV). The Vulgate reads 'minister of God in the gospel of Christ' (so DV, RSV). The preferred reading is 'co-worker with God in the gospel of Christ' (NRSV). See Metzger 563.

It was not, however, for our sake that we sent Timothy, but principally for yours, precisely that he might give strength and solace to your hearts.[2] He was to do this by showing you that, despite these sufferings with which I am buffeted on every side, my spirit is not at all shaken, and that the renown of the gospel is even enhanced. Consequently, none of you should be upset on account of those sufferings of mine about which you have heard. For it should not seem strange to you, if such things befall heralds of the gospel, since you already knew that I was chosen by God for this very task: that by the sufferings of my body I might make the name of Christ illustrious, resembling in this respect my preceptor and Lord. For even then when we were present among you we used to predict this very thing: that we would undergo suffering on account of the gospel. What we predicted at that time, you now see happening, just as you know has happened also before.[3] Nothing happens to me that is unexpected, and all has been foretold to you, so there is no reason for your spirit to be shaken.

Accordingly, in response to my boundless anxiety about you, which makes me fear even where there is no danger,[4] since I could not endure my longing for you, I sent Timothy, as was mentioned above, for this purpose: that being in some sense present myself, I might ascertain through him the constancy of your faith and seek to discover whether the one who is always alert to overwhelm the good had tempted any of the feebler[5] among you, and my labour over them had been lost.

Recently, however, Timothy had returned to us from you bringing us joyful news and reporting both that your faith, strong as oak, was unshaken and that your charity remained unchanged from the beginning; that our separation had not erased your memory of us but that it is ever fresh and never failing among you, and that you are always possessed by a reciprocal

* * * * *

2 For *confirmare* 'to strengthen' and *consolari* 'to offer solace' used together, see Rom 1:11–12 and Erasmus' annotation on Rom 1:12 ('to be comforted together') CWE 56 36–8.

3 A reference to the sufferings of Paul, of Christ, and of the prophets

4 Cf Theophylact *Expos in 1 Thess* (on 3:5) PG 124 1300A: 'Those who love are anxious even when things are safe.' If Erasmus' thought here reflects Theophylact, his words reflect Virgil. Compare Erasmus here, *tuta etiam timeo*, literally 'I fear even safe circumstances,' and the description of Dido *Aeneid* 4.298 *omnia tuta timens*, 'fearful when all was safe.'

5 Cf Ambrosiaster *Comm in 1 Thess* (on 3:5) CSEL 81/3 221:17–19 who notes that in every group some are strong and some weak; Paul is concerned here about the weaker part.

longing to see us, just as the longing to see you dominates us. In consequence of this report, there is none of the necessities or the evils that press upon me that I shall not bear with equanimity now that I know your faith is safe.[6] In my fear for your faith, I was not afraid for myself: I think myself safe if your faith is safe. Now we live and seem to have been plucked from every danger if, with the help of Christ Jesus, you are continuing steadfast in the course you have begun. I do not regret these evils if commensurate profit accrues to you for whose sake I am suffering them.

Since I see that this is so, and that day by day the gospel is spreading more widely among the gentiles, what thanks could we return to God to match so great a benefit? It is by his kindness that such an extraordinary joy has come to us in the midst of these very evils. With this joy we sincerely rejoice over your progress, as God is our witness, to whose goodness you owe the fact that you have stood firm. Let us importune him unremittingly in prayers night and day with greater intensity for this, too: that by his kindness we be permitted the joy of seeing you at some time. Presence confers something that neither a letter nor a messenger, however faithful, could confer. For this reason, therefore, I desire to see you so that, if anything is still lacking in gospel discipline, I may restore and repair it.[7]

But I pray that, since wicked men do not allow it, God himself, our Father, and his Son, Jesus Christ our Lord, will remove all hindrances and open for me a path to you, and that also in the meantime he will enrich[8] you with his gifts, so that I may be able to look upon you with great joy. That will be the case if he makes you rich and overflowing with mutual charity towards one another, and not only towards each other but towards all people, just as we too have a sort of extraordinary love towards all of you, prepared even to die for your salvation.[9]

Accordingly, may he so strengthen your hearts that your integrity may not be faulted in any respect, not only in the eyes of men, but, far more,

* * * * *

6 This and the preceding sentence are, in the Latin, a single sentence variously punctuated in the lifetime editions.

7 'I may ... repair': *sarciam*. Cf the metaphorical use of *sarcire* 'to mend,' 'to repair' in the title of Erasmus' exposition of Psalm 84: *De sarcienda ecclesiae concordia* 'On Mending the Peace of the Church.' See ASD V-3 245.

8 enrich] In all editions from 1520 to 1540 and LB, excepting only the 1520 quarto edition, which reads *cingat* 'surround'

9 For Paul's readiness to die for the gospel, see Acts 21:13 and 2 Cor 7:3. For the sentiment, see John 15:13: 'Greater love has no man than this, that a man lay down his life for his friends' (RSV).

before God and the Father (whom nothing deceives) at the coming of our Lord Jesus Christ when, in the sight of all the saints, it will be evident not only what each has done, but even in what spirit each has acted.[10]

Chapter 4

As for the rest, brothers, since you have already been thoroughly taught by us how you ought to behave and with what zeal you ought to please God, we ask and exhort you through the Lord Jesus to take care not only to persevere in what you have learned but even to surpass yourselves in the progress you make each day. For you know, and indeed recall,[1] what instructions I have handed on, not on my own authority, but on the authority of our Lord Jesus Christ. I laid down none of those precepts that false apostles din[2] into you about ceremonies of the Mosaic law, about the excellence of the angels, and about the visions of angels who give access to salvation,[3] but only those instructions that I knew were pleasing to God. For this is the will of God: that you keep yourselves holy and undefiled; that you be chaste not only in soul but also in body; that you abstain from fornication,[4] by which bodies are defiled.

* * * * *

10　Theophylact *Expos in 1 Thess* (on 3:13) PG 124 1304C–D commenting on the phrase 'establish your hearts unblamable in holiness' (RSV), contrasts the sinful deeds of some with others who are evil whatever their actions: 'For out of the heart come evil thoughts' (Matt 15:19 RSV). In his annotation on 3:13 (*sine querela*), Erasmus notes that Paul's language emphasizes blamelessness of heart.

1　Theophylact *Expos in 1 Thess* (on 4:2) PG 124 1305B–C comments that Paul here wishes merely to recall and not to repeat instructions given previously with threats and much fear.

2　Erasmus uses *inculcare* most often with the sense of 'to inculcate,' 'to drive home,' or as here 'to din.' See eg the Argument of 2 Thess and the paraphrase on Phil 3:1 where the verb is translated 'impresses on' and 'drive home' respectively.

3　Literally 'about the excellence and visions of angels' *de praecellentia visisque angelorum*. For parallel treatment of the false teaching that access to salvation depends on the mediation of angels, see the paraphrase on Col 2:18 with n63, which is further illuminated by his annotation on Col 2:18 (*nemo vos seducat*).

4　Both in his translation of 4:3 and here in the paraphrase Erasmus chooses *scortatio* to translate the Greek πορνεία (Vulgate *fornicatio*) 'prostitution,' 'fornication.' For explicit justification of this translation, see Erasmus' annotation on 1 Cor 5:1 (*inter vos fornicatio*) and CWE 50 98 n48. Cf 1 Cor chapter 5 n22.

Bodies are dwellings of the soul; the soul is the guesthouse of God.[5]
Therefore, as the soul must be pure on account of God, its guest, so it is
fitting for the body to be pure because of its resident, the soul. Accordingly,
each person should know how to show this honour to his own poor body,
a little earthenware vessel[6] as it were, that he keep it pure and untainted
and not allow it to be contaminated[7] by the disease of vile desires and
lusts, a thing so unworthy of Christians that it is not even characteristic
of all the pagans, but only of those who do not know God. These people,
however, can be in some measure excused, because they think that everyone
is allowed whatever he pleases and that whatever is pleasant to the body is
honourable.[8]

But the evil of lust is doubled if it is combined with injury to a brother,
as when someone wrongly takes another's wife. Therefore, let no one cheat
his brother either in this or in other matters by taking for himself more
than he should, because God will leave none of these acts unavenged. The
perpetrators of such deeds will not benefit from their baptism; quite the
contrary, they will be punished even more severely, as we have told you
previously and demonstrated. For God did not call us[9] from the practices
of our former way of life so that, once washed, we might roll back again

* * * * *

5 For the image of the indwelling of God's Spirit, see 1 Cor 3:16–17.
6 Erasmus understands σκεῦος as 'vessel' (Latin vas) here in 4:4 to mean the body,
  as it is plainly used in 2 Cor 4:7. This is the interpretation of the interlinear
  Gloss (on 4:4) and of Theophylact Expos in 1 Thess (on 4:4) PG 124 1305D. The
  exegetical tradition also supported an alternative view, that the 'vessel' is
  one's wife. See eg the Gloss; also Aquinas Super 1 Thess lect cap 4 lectio 1.80
  (II 180).
7 With the imagery here compare Horace Satires 1.3.55–6: at nos virtutes ipsas in-
  vertimus atque / sincerum cupimus vas incrustare 'But we turn the virtues themselves upside down and desire to dirty a clean vessel'; Epistles 1.2.54 sincerum
  est nisi vas, quodcumque infundis acescit 'unless the vessel is clean, whatever you
  pour in turns sour.' See also Adagia II iv 20.
8 'Honourable' here represents Erasmus' honestum, a term used in classical
  sources to describe the upright or virtuous person. It appears in Latin translations of the Greek Stoic maxim μόνον τὸ καλὸν ἀγαθόν ἐστιν, eg Seneca Epistulae morales 76.6: unum est enim bonum quod honestum 'for there is but a single
  good – namely, that which is honourable,' and is translated as 'morally noble,'
  'moral goodness,' and 'moral worth' in the Loeb editions of Cicero Paradoxa
  Stoicorum 1.6; De officiis 3.3.11 and 3.4.15, 18; and De finibus 2.21.68, 3.11.36,
  3.22.75, 5.23.64–6. See P.G. Walsh Cicero On Obligations (De Officiis) (Oxford
  2000) liv for reasons to prefer 'honourable' as a translation of honestum, over
  'morally upright.'
9 call us] First in 1523; previously 'call us away'

into the same filth,[10] but in order that we might guard our innocence, once freely given, by the holiness and purity of our way of life. Let us not, by the foulness of lust, drive from us the Holy Spirit, the lover of chastity. I have solemnly declared and I declare again that these are not, I say, my precepts but God's.[11] Accordingly, the person who rejects them does not reject the man who propounds them, but he rejects God,[12] their author, who has communicated his own Holy Spirit to you so that by its inspiration you may embrace holiness. The person who defiles his own body with vile lust is insolent against God.

Concerning the charity of Christians towards Christians, I think it unnecessary to advise you in this letter, for you of yourselves, providentially inspired, have been taught to love one other by Christ's Spirit, which you have imbibed. You show it, in fact, by bestowing Christian charity on all the brothers, not only those who are in Thessalonica, but also those in the whole of Macedonia. I will not urge you, therefore, to do[13] what you are doing of your own accord, but rather to surpass yourselves in what you are doing at the prompting of the Spirit, as you move forward always to what is better.

However, you should take care that your tranquillity be not disturbed by idlers and busybodies, but that each person look after his own business. If anyone does not have sufficient means, let him provide for himself with his own hands resources both to support himself and to share with others in need, just as we have instructed you previously also.[14] In this way you will be able to behave with dignity towards those who are outsiders to the profession of faith in Christ, for to beg for alms among them,[15] or to act

* * * * *

10 For the proverbial image of a filthy pig implied here, see 2 Pet 2:22 and Erasmus' paraphrase on that verse CWE 44 119 with n22; also *Adagia* III v 13 and IV iii 62.

11 Cf 1 Cor 7:8–26, where Paul distinguishes between God's commands and his own advice.

12 Cf Luke 10:16: 'He who hears you hears me; and he who rejects you rejects me; and he who rejects me, rejects him who sent me' (Conf).

13 to do what you are doing of your own accord] First in 1532; previously, 'to do of your own accord what you are doing'

14 Although the paraphrase here apparently follows the biblical text of 4:11 in referring to instruction during Paul's earlier visit to the Thessalonians, the injunction is also found elsewhere in the Epistles. Cf 1 Cor 4:12 and Eph 4:28. For Paul's own example, see 2:9; 2 Thess 3:8–12; and Acts 18:3, 20:34.

15 Erasmus' 1516 annotation on 4:11 *(ut vestrum negotium agatis)* betrays hostility to the mendicants: 'He [Paul] dissuades them from seeking what belongs to others, and from idleness to which many, even then [in Paul's day], were

shamelessly on account of need would bring dishonour on your profession. Instead of this, let each person provide for himself with his own hands so that there be no need. And there will easily be enough for the one who is content with a little.[16]

Moreover, so far as concerns the mystery of the resurrection, I would not allow anything to escape your notice lest you mourn with uncontrolled grief[17] for those who have fallen asleep relying on the promises of the gospel, as if they have perished; lest you mourn, I repeat,[18] after the example of the pagans who mourn the death of their kin because they have no hope that they will ever live again. But the death of Christians is nothing other than sleep.[19] They will awaken[20] from it at the coming of Christ to live then in a far happier way. Indeed, why should we not hope that the members will experience what we know has happened in the head?[21] For if we truly believe that Jesus died according to our human manner and has come back again to deathless life, we ought to believe that God the Father, who raised Jesus to life, will also, at the coming of the Son, bring back along with Christ and alive again those who have acknowledged Jesus[22] and have fallen asleep relying

* * * * *

inclined under the pretext of religion. Now the world is crammed full of this sort of fellow.' In a 1535 addition, Erasmus goes on with biting sarcasm to implicate monks in the charge of mendacity. For Erasmus on beggars, see CWE 50 26 n5. Theophylact *Expos in 1 Thess* (on 4:12) PG 124 1309D also criticizes Christians who live by begging.

16 To be content with a little is praised also by Horace *Satires* 2.2.110.

17 Erasmus warns not against feeling grief, but against immoderate or inconsolable grieving; so too Augustine *Sermones* 172.1 (on 4:13) PL 37 936; Aquinas *Super 1 Thess lect* cap 4 lectio 2.93 (II 182); and Nicholas of Lyra (on 4:13).

18 lest you mourn, I repeat] Added in 1532

19 Erasmus follows the exegetical tradition in his development of the 'waking' theme. See eg Aquinas *Super 1 Thess lect* cap 4 lectio 2.93 (II 182) who notes three ways in which the analogy is appropriate: a person goes to bed in the hope of rising again; the soul keeps awake while the person sleeps; and people rise from sleep more refreshed and more energetic. Elsewhere in his New Testament scholarship, Erasmus describes death as falling asleep; cf eg CWE 50 56.

20 For Erasmus' understanding of the implications of *expergisci* 'to awaken,' see 1 Cor chapter 15 n46.

21 Ambrosiaster *Comm in 1 Thess* (on 4:15–18) CSEL 81/3 227:21 reminds the reader that Christ is the head of all. For the image of head and body, see 1 Cor 11:3 and Eph 5:23; for the image used, as here, in reference to the resurrection, see CWE 56 20.

22 Cf Zech 14:5: 'Then the Lord your God will come, and all the holy ones with him' (RSV).

on his promises, so that the members may not be lacking to their head.

We are not reporting to you a human story but what we have learned from Christ himself,[23] namely, that we whom the coming of the Lord will find alive and remaining here,[24] will not be made to appear in the presence of Jesus before those who have died are made to appear there together with us. Someone might say: 'How can people who have been buried and reduced to dust[25] be made to appear?' The Lord Jesus himself, through an angel's voice ringing out from heaven with a divine trumpet, will arouse them, urging them, now awake, to hasten, and straightaway those who had fallen asleep in this hope will be restored to life and will rise up out of their tombs. When that has happened, we, who will be found alive[26] and remaining behind, at the coming of Christ will suddenly be swept through the clouds along with those restored to life to meet the Lord in the air, and thence he will bear us with him into heaven to live eternally with him. Accordingly, comfort one another with these words so that the death of the godly may not torture you too grievously, for it deserves to be accompanied by expressions of joy and thanksgiving rather than lamentations.

Chapter 5

I have acquainted you with the manner and order of the resurrection, since it was important for you to know it. But of the times and the critical

* * * * *

23 Theophylact *Expos in 1 Thess* (on 4:15) PG 124 1312D also interprets the phrase 'in the word of the Lord' (Conf) as 'what I have learned from Christ.'

24 In his annotation on 4:17 (*nos qui vivimus*) Erasmus says that 'Paul seems to be writing as if the resurrection would happen in the age in which he was writing.' But Erasmus notes that Greek syntax invites the interpretation, not 'we who are alive' but 'we who will be alive,' and he observes that Paul wrote in such a way that his readers would always assume the imminence of the day. See n26 below. The paraphrase here does not explain how the living who are 'caught up to meet the Lord in the air' (RSV) will be 'changed,' but for the controversy surrounding this question, see 1 Cor chapter 15 n71.

25 and reduced to dust] Added in *1532*. Cf Theophylact *Expos in 1 Thess* (on 4:15) PG 124 1312D–1313A, who mentions that it is just as easy for God to restore those who are whole as those who have been reduced to dust.

26 In his annotation on 4:15 (*nos qui vivimus*) Erasmus prefers to interpret Paul as talking literally about his being alive at the coming of the Lord, but he acknowledges the view expressed by Theophylact *Expos in 1 Thess* (on 4:15) PG 124 1313A: 'Paul is not speaking of himself (for he was not going to live until the resurrection), but he means the faithful.'

moments[1] when these events will take place, it is of no use to write to you. So far is it from being helpful that not even the Lord was willing to reveal any such thing to his disciples although they petitioned him earnestly.[2] And indeed, you yourselves know plainly, since I earlier taught you,[3] that the day of the Lord will creep up on the world unexpectedly, as a thief in the night steals up on those who are sleeping, and will catch them napping, precisely when least expected.[4] For when those who do not believe the gospel have said in the midst of their pleasures,[5] 'There is no danger, but all things are peaceful and secure; the Lord will not come,' then, without warning, the end will come upon them, just as the sudden pain of childbirth seizes a pregnant woman before the day expected.[6] And there will be no escape for those who are overtaken before they realize it.

The day is to be feared by those who, blinded now by their offences, lead their life by night. You, brothers, ought not to fear that it will catch you unprepared, for you all who are following Christ do not belong to the dominion of darkness[7] but to the dominion of light and day; especially if we[8]

* * * * *

1 In his annotation on 5:1 (*et momentis*) Erasmus distinguishes between χρόνος and καιρός, preferring for καιρός the translation *articulus* 'juncture,' 'critical moment' (cf OLD 5), or *opportunitas* 'opportuneness,' 'the quality of happening at the right moment' (cf OLD 2). 'For χρόνος simply denotes time, as a year or a month; but καιρός the critical moment of time at which something has to be done.' Erasmus makes a similar distinction among expressions for time in his annotation on Acts 1:7 *(tempora vel momenta)*. See CWE 50 8 n39; also CWE 56 133–6, 356. On καιρός see Erasmus' *Adagia* I vii 70: *Nosce tempus* 'Consider the due time' and Peter Bietenholz *History and Biography in the Work of Erasmus of Rotterdam* (Geneva 1966) 40–2.

2 See eg Matt 24:3 and 36–44, 25:13; Mark 13:4 and 32–7; Luke 12:40; Acts 1:6–7.

3 This clause serves as a gloss on ἀκριβῶς (5:2) 'well' (Conf), translated *plane* by Erasmus, *diligenter* in the Vulgate.

4 See Matt 24:43; Luke 12:39; 2 Pet 3:10.

5 'Pleasures': *deliciis*. See Phil chapter 4 n7. In the plural, the word often means 'pleasures,' 'luxuries.'

6 Theophylact *Expos in 1 Thess* (on 5:3) PG 124 1316D similarly elaborates the childbirth image to explain the unexpectedness of the day of the Lord: 'A woman certainly knows that she will deliver, but she may be caught unawares by giving birth unexpectedly after the seventh month, perhaps even when she is on a journey.'

7 For Erasmus' similar treatment of 'darkness' as the dominion of the devil at war with those who love the evangelical light, see his paraphrases on Eph 6:12 and Col 1:13.

8 As his annotation on 5:5b *(non estis noctis, neque tenebrarum* 'you are not of night nor of darkness') indicates, Erasmus was obviously aware of the variant

measure up to our profession[9] by the zeal of our piety and live so that it is evident we are keeping awake in the light, not snoring in the darkness. So then, if we do not want to be caught, we should not sleep as do the others who know not the light of Christ. But we should be watchful and sober, always on the lookout to see that we do not, through thoughtlessness, do anything that would offend the eyes of men and, what is more, of God. For those who sleep in body, sleep at night, and those who are drunk with wine are drunk at night. So those who nap and sleep in their vices live in spiritual darkness, and those who are drunk with the desires and enticements of the world are enveloped in murkiness of the mind.[10] But as for us on whom the day of the gospel has dawned, it is fitting that we be sober and watchful,[11] always girt for action and prepared against the sudden assault of the foe who is ever watching for our destruction; and that we be furnished with spiritual arms: having put on faith and charity as a breastplate, and the hope of eternal salvation as a helmet.[12]

There is no reason why you should lose confidence. God himself will be present as defender for those who keep watch. For he did not call us to the gospel's teaching that by living in disregard of what it so clearly demands we should double God's wrath and vengeance upon us. Rather, he called us to the gospel that by obeying it we may attain salvation through the help of our Lord Jesus Christ who died for us. Consequently, if it is our lot to live, we live with him through piety and the hope of immortality,

* * * * *

reading 'you are.' This reading is not, however, reflected in his paraphrase here, which follows the generally accepted reading 'we are,' the reading found both in his own translation and in the 1527 Vulgate.

9 Theophylact *Expos in 1 Thess* (on 5:7) PG 124 1317C comments: 'You are not the sons of night and darkness but of the day, through baptism and the taking on of God's mandates.' On *professio* 'profession,' see the paraphrase on 1 Cor 1:2 with n8.

10 Theophylact *Expos in 1 Thess* (on 5:7) PG 124 1317B notes that when Paul speaks of inebriation here he means not only that which is caused by wine, but also that which results from the emotions and disturbances of the mind and clouds reason.

11 With the images associated here with sobriety, compare 1 Pet 1:13: 'Gird up your minds, be sober (RSV), 4:7: 'Keep sane and sober' (RSV), 5:8: 'Be sober, be watchful. Your adversary the devil prowls ... seeking someone to devour' (RSV). See also Erasmus' paraphrases on these passages CWE 44 86, 102, 107. Aquinas *Super 1 Thess lect* cap 5 lectio 1.117 (II 186) cites 1 Pet 5:8.

12 With the armour imagery, compare Eph 6:10–17 and Erasmus' paraphrase on those verses; also Wisd of Sol 5:17–20 and Isa 59:17–18.

or if death is our lot, we shall live with him immortal. That you may do this more and more, hearten each other with mutual encouragement and challenge one another in turn to make progress, just as you are doing on your own initiative.

Indeed, brothers, this too we ask of you: have regard for those who are working among you, who preside over you in evangelical teaching, and who advise you how you ought to please Christ. Although one must show honour to all, still you should hold these precious beyond the rest, returning to them the love they show for you by enduring so many toils and dangers for your sake. And if ever they reprove you for your failures, still keep peace with them;[13] for the person who reproves in order to benefit does not deserve hatred.

I entreat you also, that each of you as far as you can assist them in their duties. Admonish those who throw your good order into confusion by living according to their own whim, comfort the faint-hearted, support the weak, be gentle and patient towards all, not only to Christians but also to those who are strangers to Christ. Take care that no one repay an injury with an injury or retaliate with evil for an evil. For it is not proper to imitate the wicked in wickedness and become like them. Rather, you ought to strive all the more to show kindness to all, not only Christians to Christians, but to absolutely everyone whether deserving or not in the certainty that the service is not without its reward for you, since Christ is the guarantor.[14] Wherefore, whatever happens to you, secure in godliness[15] rejoice always;[16] without ceasing call on God in your prayers. Whatever your fortune give thanks, for thus it is pleasing to God that you may always have cause to give thanks for the Father's kindness towards you through Jesus Christ.

* * * * *

13 In his 1527 Greek text, Erasmus reads at 5:13b: 'Be at peace' ἐν αὐτοῖς 'with them' (so Conf; cf 1527 Vulgate *cum eis*, Erasmus *cum illis*), rather than ἐν ἑαυτοῖς 'among yourselves,' ie 'with one another' (so NTGL 537, RSV; cf Ambrosiaster *Comm in 1 Thess* [on 1:3] CSEL 81/3 230:12). Cf Theophylact *Expos in 1 Thess* (on 5:13) PG 124 1320D–1321A whose lemma reads: 'Be at peace among yourselves,' but who notes: 'It is also written "towards them," that is, to the teachers,' who 'because they reproach ... are hated.' Erasmus, in his annotation on 5:13 (*et pacem habete cum eis*), also observes that the manuscripts are divided.

14 For similar instructions on the inclusiveness of Christian love, see Matt 5:43–7 and Luke 6:32–5.

15 The translation 'secure in godliness' takes Erasmus' expression *incolumi pietate* (literally 'with piety intact') as an ablative of description applied to the Christian whose godliness cannot be shaken whatever external events may befall. Cf Rom 8:35.

16 See Phil 4:4: 'Rejoice in the Lord always, again I say, rejoice' (Conf).

Moreover, you must guard against this also: that no division arise
among you as the result of your differing talents. One person happens to
have the gift of tongues so as to sing in the Spirit. Although the gift is very
small,[17] still, do not extinguish, but rather foster it so that he may advance
to better things. Another has received the gift of prophecy so as to explain
the mystical sense of Scripture.[18] Do not reject whatever is said: tolerate him
that he may advance; listen to him, but with discrimination,[19] in such a way,
however, that no troublesome clamour is raised while he is speaking.[20] Let
no one favour his own gifts in such a way as to despise other people's. Test
all things, but let each judge what is suitable for himself and embrace that.
Whatever has the appearance of good is not to be rejected. As for the rest,
you must so abhor evils that you abstain even from things that present the
outward appearance of evil. But it will be your business to strive for these
goals with all your efforts.

God himself is the author of peace.[21] To him is pleasing the harmony
and concord of the whole person in things that are honourable.[22] May he
cause you to be entirely holy and complete;[23] so that your soul may measure
up to your spirit, your body[24] to your soul, and your spirit itself measure

* * * * *

17 In comparison with charity, or even with prophecy, the gift of tongues is the
least of gifts. See 1 Cor 12:31–14:33.

18 Erasmus here limits the Epistle's reference to 'prophecy' to the interpretation
of the 'mystical' sense of Scripture. See 1 Cor chapters 10 n7, 12 n30, 13 n4,
14 n1, and Eph chapter 5 n39. Erasmus sometimes names this the 'spiritual'
sense of Scripture, eg in *Enchiridion* CWE 66 35. He recommends the patristic
exegetes who depart as much as possible from the literal sense: after Paul,
'Origen, Ambrose [ie Ambrosiaster], Jerome, and Augustine' (ibidem 34), and
he contrasts, especially in his expositions of the Psalms, the mystical sense with
the 'Jewish custom' of strictly historical criticism. On Erasmus' understanding
of the mystical sense of Scripture, see also CWE 44 115 n28 and 216 n12; CWE
50 22 n84 and 99 n64; CWE 63 xxiv–xlix.

19 For examples of discriminating listeners, see Erasmus' letter to Campeggi Ep
1167:291–9.

20 See in the dedicatory letter to Campeggi (287–90) Erasmus' complaint against
the harsh and unchristian denunciations against writers and speakers.

21 Cf Nicholas of Lyra (on 5:23), who interprets 'God of peace' as *actor et dator
pacis* 'agent and giver of peace.'

22 On 'honourable,' see chapter 4 n8. For similar ideas regarding the necessity of
harmony for a virtuous life, see Cicero *De finibus* 5.9.26, 5.23.66.

23 Jerome Ep 120.12 CSEL 55 512:20–513:22 explains the Greek ὁλοτελεῖς in 5:23
as 'complete in all its parts: spirit, soul, and body.'

24 The triple division into spirit, soul, and body is Paul's. On Erasmus and this
division, see M. Screech *Ecstasy and the Praise of Folly* (London 1980) 96–112. For

up to God, so that there is nothing in which you can be blamed; and may
he cause you to persevere in this holiness right up to the coming of our
Lord Jesus Christ. There is no reason for you to lose confidence. He is of
good faith who has called you to this holiness and its rewards. Likewise,
he will bring to completion what he has begun; he will fulfil what he has
promised.

Brothers, assist our attempts, too, with your prayers. Greet all the
brothers with a kiss – not the sort that the common crowd of greeters
customarily offers, but one that is holy and worthy of Christian love.[25]

I solemnly entreat you by the Lord that this epistle be read to all the
holy brothers. May the favour and kindness of our Lord Jesus Christ be
ever with you. Amen.

The End of the Paraphrase on the First Epistle
of Paul the Apostle to the Thessalonians

* * * * *

a Platonizing tendency in some of Erasmus' work, see Payne 'The Hermeneutics of Erasmus' 17–23, and 'Erasmus: Interpreter of Romans' in *Sixteenth Century Studies* ed Carl S. Meyer (St Louis 1971) II 6–10.

25 With Erasmus' paraphrase on *osculo sancto* 'holy kiss,' compare Ambrosiaster
Comm in 1 Thess (on 5:26) CSEL 81/3 234:14–16, who argues that kisses in a
Christian greeting are holy, while any kiss that is given 'without Christ' is
carnal. See also Erasmus' paraphrase on Rom 16:16 CWE 42 88: 'Greet one
another with a kiss worthy of Christians, that is, one which is both pure and
sincere and which is certain evidence of true concord.'

PARAPHRASE ON SECOND THESSALONIANS

*Paraphrasis in epistolam Pauli Apostoli
ad Thessalonicenses posteriorem*

translated and annotated by
MECHTILDE O'MARA

THE ARGUMENT OF THE SECOND EPISTLE
OF PAUL TO THE THESSALONIANS
BY ERASMUS OF ROTTERDAM

Since Paul did not have an opportunity of visiting the Thessalonians again,[1] he encourages them through an Epistle,[2] so that they may bravely endure sufferings inflicted on account of Christ: they will not fail to receive a reward, nor their adversaries punishment. Again, concerning the day of the Lord's coming, on which he had touched to some extent in the earlier Epistle, he warns them not to be disturbed at all by the statements of certain people who were emphatically asserting that it was already upon them, secretly, as they imagine. He indicates that the Roman empire will have to be abolished first, and that then the Antichrist will come.[3] More carefully still he impresses on them the necessity of restraining people who disturb the peace and public order by their idleness and curiosity, and of compelling them to work since Paul himself toiled with his own hands in their midst.[4]

* * * * *

1 Paul had already expressed his desire to see the Thessalonians again and attributed his failure to do so to the hindrance of Satan (1 Thess 2:17–18, 3:10).
2 Erasmus expresses no hesitation in attributing 2 Thessalonians to Paul. Some modern scholars, however, have questioned the authenticity of Pauline authorship. For a list of those engaged in the debate together with their principal arguments, see Rigaux 124–52 and Robert Jewett *The Thessalonian Correspondence: Pauline Rhetoric and Millenarian Piety* (Philadelphia 1986) 3–18.
3 For this interpretation, see Ambrosiaster who refers, however, to the Roman *regnum* 'realm' rather than the *imperium* 'empire' in *Comm in 2 Thess* Argument (and on 2:2–9) CSEL 81/3 235:7–8, 239:18–240:13 and 25, and 241:5 and 8.
4 This toil is mentioned at 1 Thess 2:9 and 2 Thess 3:7–8.

He wrote from Athens,[5] through the same people[6] by whom he sent the previous Epistle, as our Arguments, at any rate,[7] show.

The End of the Argument

5 The traditional Latin Argument and the subscription in some Greek manuscripts state that the letter was written from Athens. Erasmus printed the subscription in his own Greek text and it appears after 3:18 in AV. If the letter is by Paul, it was more probably written from Corinth. See Best 59; also NTGL 542 *Subscriptio*.

6 On the expression 'wrote ... through,' see Col Argument n10.

7 *quidem* 'at any rate'] Added in 1532

THE PARAPHRASE ON THE SECOND EPISTLE OF PAUL THE APOSTLE TO THE THESSALONIANS BY ERASMUS OF ROTTERDAM

Chapter 1

Paul, Silvanus, and Timothy, to the assembly[1] of believers who live in harmony at Thessalonica and are of one mind towards God our Father and the Lord Jesus Christ.[2]

We should always give thanks to God generously for his generous liberality towards you. For by his aid you are not only continuing steadfast in what you have begun, but day after day you are even growing richer and richer in faith and mutual charity towards one another, so much so that I think it unnecessary now to kindle your enthusiasm for piety by the example of others. Instead, we ourselves boast of you before the other churches of God, inflaming the rest to virtue through your example.[3] We recall before them your patience and the constancy of your faith in all the persecutions and sufferings you are enduring, so that in you, later on, the judgment of God might be proven just, when he admits into the fellowship of his realm you who have been harassed for the glory of his name, while on the

* * * * *

1 In his paraphrase on 2 Thess 1:1 Erasmus chose *coetus* 'a coming together,' 'an assembly' in place of the Greek ἐκκλησία (Vulgate *ecclesia*). On the significance of the translations for 'church,' see 1 Cor chapters 1 n3 and 16 n13, and 1 Thess chapter 1 n2.

2 Christ] At this point LB adds *a quibus contingat vobis gratia et pax* 'from whom be grace to you and peace.' These words are evidently taken from the paraphrase on 1 Thess 1:1 and inserted as the paraphrase on 2 Thess 1:2. The Froben editions from 1520 to 1540 carry no explicit paraphrase on 1:2.

3 Nicholas of Lyra (on 1:4) similarly introduces, as the motive for Paul's boasting, his intention to provide the other churches with an example. Ambrosiaster *Comm in 2 Thess* (on 1:4) CSEL 81/3 236:13–17 notes Paul's hope that by imitating the Thessalonians the others may grow in dedication to suffering for Christ.

contrary he hands over to eternal punishment those who have persecuted you out of hatred for him. Actually, it will be characteristic of the divine justice to pay to both sides the recompense deserved by their deeds: to give suffering to those who cause the innocent to suffer, and to grant to you who are suffering with us, along with us also, refreshment[4] and consolation.

This will happen on that day when the evangelical promises are made visible and the Lord Jesus reveals himself to the world openly from heaven, no longer lowly as he appeared in his first coming, but surrounded by an angelic entourage as befits a powerful prince; no longer mild and peaceable in order to heal the wicked, but armed with a dreadful flaming conflagration, ready to inflict vengeance on those who were not willing here to know God and did not heed the gospel of our Lord Jesus Christ. As a result they will experience as just and powerful the one whom they despised when he was merciful and mild; and, taught even by their punishments, they will confess that what the gospel has preached is true. Since they have set no limit to their wickedness, they will pay the penalty forever, once they have caught sight of that divine face of the Lord and the majestic strength[5] of the one they spurned here as weak and lowly. The first time he came to save all; then he will come to show himself glorious, not only in himself, but also in all his members (these are the godly), so that he may be wonderfully visible in all who believed in his gospel. For then, openly to all, there will be revealed in you the things you believed when we were bearing witness to Christ, but which the wicked distrusted and rejected.

We want that day to be favourable and happy for you. We do not cease, therefore, to beseech the Lord on your behalf that since he has been pleased to call you to the hope of this glory he may likewise deign to assist you as you strive to reach that goal; that your life may be consistent with your profession; and that he may bring to fulfilment and perfection what he has begun in you because of his own goodness.[6] May he add

* * * * *

4 'Refreshment': *refrigerium*. On *refrigerium*, see CWE 50 29 with n33. The Greek ἄνεσις (1:7) suggests a relaxing of tension (cf the Vulgate *requies* 'rest,' Erasmus *relaxio* 'relaxing'). The word *refrigerium* adds the connotation of coolness in anticipation of the 'flaming conflagration' that will accompany the day of vengeance in the paraphrase on the following verse.

5 'Strength': *fortitudinis*, as in Erasmus' translation, in place of the Vulgate's *virtutis*. In his annotation on 1:9 (*gloria virtutis* ['the glory of his power' DV]) Erasmus explains the Greek ἰσχύος by the Latin words *robor*, connoting physical strength and power, and *potentia*. Cf Eph chapter 1 n48.

6 Erasmus' annotation on 1:11 (*omnem voluntatem*) calls attention to the word εὐδοκίαν, rendered here in the Vulgate by *voluntatem* 'will' (elsewhere by *bona*

strength to your souls so that by bravely enduring the sufferings imposed by the wicked, you may show how strong in you is the sure hope of everlasting happiness, for the sake of which you disregard even your bodily[7] life.

As Christ by his death has given lustre to the Father's glory and in turn has been made illustrious by him through the resurrection, so may the name of the Lord Jesus Christ now be glorified by[8] your endurance and may you, in turn, be glorified by him on the day of his coming, not according to your merits,[9] but according to the kindness of our God and of the Lord Jesus Christ, without whose aid your attempt would be futile.

Chapter 2

Through this coming of our Lord Jesus Christ, about which we have just now spoken, and through the participation in glory by which we members shall then be attached to him as head,[1] we entreat you, brothers, not to be easily shaken from your considered judgment should his coming be postponed.[2] Do not be thrown into confusion, whether by a counterfeit

* * * * *

voluntas 'good will') and translated by Erasmus *bonum propositum* 'good purpose.' Erasmus thought that the word referred to God's good pleasure, and that with this word 'Paul and the evangelists generally exclude human merits.' For evidence of Erasmus' interest in this word, see also his annotations on Rom 10:1 ('the will indeed of [my] heart') CWE 56 276; Phil 1:15 (*propter bonam voluntatem*), 2:13 (*pro bona voluntate*) LB VI 864E, 869D; and especially Luke 2:14 (*hominibus bonae voluntatis*).

7 bodily] Added in 1532

8 Compare Theophylact *Expos in 2 Thess* (on 1:12) PG 124 1337C: 'The name of the Lord will be glorified in you even in this life.'

9 Criticism of this phrase by theologian Noël Béda provoked defence of it from Erasmus in *Divinationes ad notata Bedae* LB IX 477E, in *Elenchus in N. Bedae Censuras* LB IX 509C, and in *Supputatio* LB IX 693F–694A. Erasmus' treatment of merit was also censured by the Faculty of Theology at Paris as approaching the teaching of Luther regarding faith and works. Erasmus defended it again in *Declarationes ad censuras Lutetiae vulgatas* LB IX 883D–884A. For a similar emphasis on the divine initiative, see Theophylact *Expos in 2 Thess* (on 1:12) PG 124 1337D.

1 For the image of the Church as union of head and members, see the paraphrases on 1 Cor 15:20–3 with n28 and Eph 1:19–23 with n50; cf also 1 Cor chapter 6 nn25 and 41.

2 In addition to the commentaries of Best and Rigaux, on this chapter see Charles H. Giblin *The Threat to Faith: an Exegetical and Theological Re-Examination of 2*

prophecy,[3] a plausible avowal, or an epistle sent in our name,[4] claiming that the coming of the Lord[5] is already upon us. Let no one impose upon you in any way. The Lord is not about to arrive unless a defection[6] has preceded and not before that evil man, the son of perdition,[7] has appeared. As he differs vastly from Christ so is he his adversary, exalting himself not only above the Son of God but above everything whatsoever that is said to be god or a divine power to be worshipped,[8] so that he sits in the temple

* * * * *

Thessalonians 2 Analecta biblica: Investigationes scientificae in res biblicas 31 (Rome 1967).

3 'Counterfeit prophecy' paraphrases 'spirit' (2:2), which both Theophylact Expos in 2 Thess (on 2:2) PG 124 1339A and Ambrosiaster Comm in 2 Thess (on 2:1–4) CSEL 81/3 239:5–6 interpret as 'prophecy.'

4 Erasmus in his annotation (1516) on 2:2 (tanquam per nos missam) explains that the phrase 'attributed to us' (Conf) modifies each of the three possible sources of confusion: prophecy, avowal, and epistle. However he himself made the phrase modify only epistola 'epistle' in the first four editions of his translation as in the Vulgate and the paraphrase here. It was only in the 1535 translation that he follows his own note.

5 Both Ambrosiaster Comm in 2 Thess (on 2:1–4) CSEL 81/3 239:15–24 and Theophylact Expos in 2 Thess (on 2:2) PG 124 1339B equate the 'day of the Lord' with the coming of Christ.

6 Erasmus uses the word defectio 'defection,' 'rebellion' (OLD 3), which he found in Ambrosiaster's citation of the biblical text in Comm in 2 Thess (on 2:3) CSEL 81/3 238:24. Cf Vulgate discessio 'separation' (OLD 3) or 'apostasy' (Conf). In his annotation on 2:3 (nisi venerit discessio), Erasmus explains it in terms of a revolt from one's advocate or prince. Theophylact Expos in 2 Thess (on 2:3) PG 124 1340B–C equates the Antichrist with the ἀποστασία 'defection' as its cause, and emphasizes the separation from God. The paraphrase can be taken to include both interpretations: a political overthrow and apostasy from God.

7 Erasmus' annotation on 2:3 (homo peccati) calls attention to the phrase homo ille peccati 'that man of sin' found in the lemma of Ambrosiaster Comm in 2 Thess (on 2:3) CSEL 238:24–5, and notes that ille 'that' shows the force of the Greek definite article and indicates some individual known to Paul's readers whom Paul does not name. Erasmus includes the demonstrative both in his translation and here in his paraphrase. The individual to whom reference is made is sometimes identified with the Antichrist of 1 John 2:18, 22 and 4:3; 2 John 7; and Rev 12:9. See, for example, Augustine De civitate Dei 20.19.2– 4 CSEL 40/2 471–4, who says that 2 Thess 2:1–11 refers indubitably to the Antichrist but the precise meaning of the mystery of iniquity is the subject of many theories, some of which he then reports. See also Ambrosiaster Comm in 2 Thess Argument CSEL 81/3 235:7–8, and Theophylact Expos in 2 Thess Argument (and on 2:3 and 7) PG 124 1329A–1330A, 1340B–D, 1341C.

8 Erasmus' paraphrase follows the Vulgate supra omne quod dicitur deus 'above everything [neuter] that is called god' (Conf), even though he finds that the

as a god, displaying himself in place of God. Or do you not remember[9] that I told you these things when I was still with you?

And now you know what stands in the way of Christ's coming: really, it is the fact that the evil one,[10] concerning whom I have spoken, is to exercise his tyranny over the saints openly in his proper time. For now the power of wickedness is secretly at work through him; and through wicked people the devil rages against those who profess the gospel. Nor, as you know from me,[11] is there anything to hinder the adversary of Christ[12] from revealing himself openly, except that for a time each one is keeping

* * * * *

Greek manuscripts would be better translated 'above every one [masculine] who is called god,' and this masculine form is what we find in his own translation. However, in his 1535 addition to the annotation on 2:4 (*supra omne quod dicitur*) Erasmus reports that he thinks παν 'everything' [neuter] had been the original reading of the Greek text. Cf Theophylact *Expos in 2 Thess* (on 2:4) PG 124 1341C.

9 Erasmus adopts here the word used in his own translation *meministi* 'remember' rather than the Vulgate's *retinetis* 'retain,' which he severely criticized in his 1516 annotation on 2:5 (*non retinetis*). Thus he provoked an insulting response from Zúñiga. For Erasmus' long and aggressive response to the ill-advised criticism of Zúñiga see Erasmus' 1522 annotation on 2:5, and *Apologiae contra Stunicam* (1) ASD IX-2 222–3.

10 'The evil one': *ille scelerosus*. Cognates of *scelus* 'crime,' 'villainy,' 'accursedness' are distinguished in the OLD under *scelerosus*: *sceleratus* describes the person who is polluted and infamous because of some crime of his own; *scelestus*, the person who is guilty of committing villainies; *scelerosus*, the person who is steeped in villainy.

11 For references to Paul's earlier, personal instruction, in addition to 2:5 here paraphrased, see 1 Thess 3:4 and 2 Thess 3:10.

12 Erasmus' exegetical sources distinguish the 'man of sin ... the son of perdition' (2:3 Conf) from 'the wicked one' through whom the 'mystery of iniquity' works (2:7 Conf). In this way they interpret 2:3–6 as referring to the Antichrist and 2:7 as referring to one or more of the Roman emperors who precede the Antichrist but embody his spirit. Erasmus, however, has used the same word *adversarius* 'adversary' in paraphrasing both expressions. See Theophylact *Expos in 2 Thess* (on 2:7) PG 124 1341C–1344C, who thinks that 2:7 is directed against Nero (AD 37–68) as a τύπος 'figure' of the Antichrist. Ambrosiaster *Comm in 2 Thess* (on 2:7) CSEL 81/3 240:16–26 includes among the agents of the 'mystery of iniquity' the emperors from Nero to Diocletian (c AD 54–305) and, closer to his own time, Julian (AD 360–3). Erasmus reports these views in his annotations on 2:7 (*mysterium iam operatur iniquitatis* and *tantum ut qui tenet nunc*), but his paraphrase preserves the vagueness of the text of 2:6–7. For a history of the exegesis of 'the Antichrist,' 'the wicked one,' and 'the mystery of iniquity,' see Rigaux 259–80.

possession of what he holds[13] until that realm,[14] by which all the others are held in check, is abolished. When this happens, that evil one will come out into the open, equipped with every kind of illusion and deceit for the destruction of the human race. But while he is storming under diabolical inspiration, the Lord Jesus will destroy him with the powerful breath of his mouth.[15] And while he vaunts himself with a false show of divinity, the Lord will completely eclipse him and obliterate him with the brilliance of his coming, just as nocturnal apparitions and vanishing reflections yield to the splendour of the rising sun. For that deceiver will come equipped with the spirit of Satan. Through Satan will he exert his force, and in order to rage more cruelly he will be armed not only with vast power to terrify human souls, but also with the lying illusions of signs and wonders. With these he will imitate Christ, just as the sorcerers among the Egyptians once imitated Moses.[16] In short, there is no kind of deceit aimed at impiety with which he will not be armed.

But he will effect nothing[17] except to contribute to the punishment[18] of those who, in any case, are perishing on account of their own lack of belief. For their stubborn rebellion against Christ deserves this. They are worthy of this reward, inasmuch as they have not received Christ, through whom

* * * * *

13 In his annotation on 2:7 (*tantum ut qui tenet nunc*) Erasmus acknowledges that there is an ellipsis in the Greek which makes the translation of this verse problematic, but in the paraphrase Erasmus makes some attempt to clarify the biblical text. For a summary of analyses of interpretations of the Greek text for 2:6–7, a passage described as 'the most problematic ... in the whole of the Pauline corpus,' see Wanamaker 249–52.

14 Reference to the political world is avoided in the biblical text of 2 Thessalonians, but in the paraphrase on 2:7 Erasmus identifies the reality that has to be removed with a *regnum* 'realm.' By speaking only of 'realm' in keeping with the cryptic style of apocalyptic, Erasmus is somewhat less explicit than other exegetes. In his annotation on 2:7 (*tantum ut qui tenet nunc*) he notes that some have understood that what must be removed is the Roman empire (so Ambrosiaster *Comm in 2 Thess* [on 2:7] CSEL 81/3 240:17–26 and Theopylact *Expos in 2 Thess* [on 2:6–7] PG 124 1341A–1343B).

15 The Epistle seems to be alluding to Isa 11:4: 'And with the breath of his lips he shall slay the wicked' (DV), a passage cited in connection with 2 Thess 2:8 by Theodoret *Interpretatio epistulae II ad Thessalonicenses* PG 82 665C. On Theodoret as a source for Erasmus' exegesis, see Eph chapter 1 n20.

16 For the miracles performed by Moses to convince Pharaoh of his mission, and replicated up to a point by the magicians of Egypt, see Exod 7:11–8:18.

17 effect nothing] First in 1532; previously, 'accomplish nothing with these [prodigies]'

18 'Punishment': *malum*

they could have been saved, since he desires to save all by virtue of his love; and by virtue of his truth he reveals what pertains to salvation.[19] Now with God's leave,[20] let falsehood prevail among them instead of truth; tyranny prevail instead of charity; the destroyer prevail instead of the Saviour. And now let them believe the lies of an evil man,[21] for they have refused to believe the Son of God preaching what is true. Thus, it will then be obvious to everyone that those who, even at some other time were going to perish on account of their obstinate unbelief, perish with good reason since they turned away from Christ and shortly afterwards gave their approval to an evil deceiver.[22] Just as this storm will show them worthy of destruction, it will make your constancy shine through even more.

On this account, my brothers beloved with Christian charity, we should always give thanks to God because he did not suffer you to persist in error but chose you from the beginning[23] to be saved, not through

* * * * *

19 In his annotation on 2:10 (*charitatem veritatis*) Erasmus notes that the phrase 'love of truth' (Conf) is difficult, and adds that the Greek here means either *amor veri* 'love of the true' or *charitatem veram* 'true love,' or, 'if we believe Theophylact, "Christ himself, who was both *charitas et veritas* [love and truth]."' The paraphrase amplifies the biblical text to include all these meanings. See Theophylact *Expos in 2 Thess* (on 2:10) PG 124 1344D.

20 Here as elsewhere Erasmus is careful to show the wicked as responsible for their sins, distinguishing God's permissive will, which allows humans to exercise free will even when sin is the result, from his ordaining will, which could not cause anyone to sin. The distinction is prevalent in the medieval tradition. See, for example, Aquinas *Super 2 Thess lect* cap 2 lectio 3.54 (II 202) who explains the words 'God shall send' (2:11 Conf) as 'he will allow to come.' See Oberman *Harvest* 90–102. Cf Erasmus' paraphrase on Rom 1:24, 'God has allowed them' (paraphrasing 'God has given them up') CWE 42 18 with n20, and his annotation on the same verse ('to the desires of their hearts') CWE 56 53–4. For a fuller treatment of free will, see Erasmus *De libero arbitrio* CWE 76 1–89, especially 9, 46–50.

21 'Of an evil man': *hominis scelerati*. Cf n10 above. Here Erasmus omits the demonstrative *ille* 'that.'

22 'Evil deceiver': *impostorem ac sceleratum* by hendiadys

23 Erasmus follows his own translation of 2:13 'from the beginning,' a correction of the Vulgate 'the first fruits.' Cf Conf 'as first-fruits'; RSV 'from the beginning.' The Greek manuscripts provide evidence for both readings: ἀπ᾽ ἀρχῆς 'from the beginning,' and ἀπαρχήν 'first fruits.' Both Best 312–4 and Rigaux 683–4 argue for the reading 'from the beginning' adopted by Erasmus. In his annotation on 2:13 (*primitias in salutem*) Erasmus explains that he understands the expression to refer to divine predestination, and cites Theophylact (cf *Expos in 2 Thess* [on 2:13] PG 124 1345D) for the same interpretation. Ambrosiaster *Comm in 2 Thess* (on 2:13–14) CSEL 81/3 242 17–26 comments that 2:12–14

the Mosaic law but through his Spirit, the bestower of holiness, and through
the obedience by which you have believed without reservation in the truth.
Besides, as he had chosen you from eternity, so he has called you through
our gospel in order that your salvation might add to the glory of our Lord
Jesus Christ, for you believed while the Jews lacked faith. The true and
genuine[24] gospel I have handed on to you. There is no reason for you to
seek another.[25] Accordingly, persist in it, brothers, and hold on to what we
have handed on to you and what you have learned from us, whether by
word of mouth or by letter.

It will be your responsibility to strive earnestly towards these objectives with all vigilance. But the Lord Jesus Christ himself and our God and
Father – who of his own accord has loved us who are called to salvation,
and through his Spirit has given us, for the time being amidst these sufferings, an everlasting solace, while we await with good hope the rewards
of heavenly life, relying not on our merits but on his gratuitous kindness
– may he more and more comfort your hearts and make you strong and
steady so that you may persevere not only in every good word but also in
every good deed.

Chapter 3

As for the rest, brothers, just as[1] we are helping the work of your salvation
by our prayers to God, so it is fair that you in your turn should advance
my endeavours by your petitions to him, in order that, just as the gospel
teaching swiftly and successfully gained ground with you, so it may speed
out in every direction and gain wide circulation among all people. That
this may be done more promptly, pray that with God's help we may be
set free from the senseless, wrong-headed individuals who in every way
are throwing up obstacles to prevent us from disseminating the teaching

* * * * *

pertains to the 'foreknowledge of God, who knows the minds of all before
they are born, for it is not hidden from him who will believe. On that account
he knows from the beginning that they will be faithful.'
24 and genuine] Added in *1532*
25 With this sentiment cf Theophylact *Expos in 2 Thess* (on 2:15) PG 124 1348B: 'It
is the tradition, seek nothing further.' Erasmus similarly warns the Galatians
against the preaching of certain pseudo-apostles who preach the ceremonies
of the Old Law in order to subvert the 'gospel received.' See his paraphrase
on Gal 1:6–9 CWE 42 98–9.

1 just as] First in *1532*; previously 'since'

of Christ without hindrance. For not all who hear the gospel believe in the gospel. And yet there is no reason for you to lose faith on account of their wicked efforts.

They assail the gospel, but they do not overcome it, since, in fact, its trusty champion is the Lord Jesus. He will strengthen you against their wickedness, keep you from evil, and bring to perfection what he has begun in you, since he is truthful in his promises.[2] His assistance will not fail you, provided only that you are attentive to his goodness; he will bring support, but to those who are trying.

And indeed we are not making these remarks because we doubt your constancy; on the contrary, we are confident about you that with the help of the Lord Jesus, as you are presently doing what we have instructed you, so will you also in the time to come.[3] In addition, may the Lord Jesus by his favour direct your hearts so that you may always journey by the direct route[4] and make progress in the love of God and in the expectation[5] of Jesus

* * * * *

2 in his promises] Added in 1532. Ambrosiaster *Comm in 2 Thess* (on 3:3) CSEL 81/3 244:7–13 also introduces the notion of God as faithful 'in his promises.'

3 Erasmus' annotation on 3:4 (*quoniam quaecumque*) points to an ambiguity occasioned by the repeated καί in the Greek which could be translated either as 'we are confident that *just as* you now observe our teachings, *so also* you will observe them in the future' or 'we are confident that what we have taught, you *both* are observing now *and* will observe in the future.' The paraphrase seems to adopt the first, but Erasmus' translation is ambiguous. In his annotation Erasmus notes that Theophylact *Expos in 2 Thess* (on 3:4) PG 124 1349D–1352A follows the first interpretation, Ambrosiaster *Comm in 2 Thess* (on 3:4) CSEL 81/3 244:16–18 the second. For the phrase ἐν κυρίῳ 'in the Lord' (RSV) Erasmus adopts Theophylact's interpretation, ie 'with divine help.' Theophylact emphasizes the careful balance here between the divine initiative and the individual's cooperation. This is to be distinguished from the alternative offered by Ambrosiaster that the Thessalonians deserved Paul's confidence because he did not doubt that what he had prescribed in the name of the Lord was presently being observed and would be in the future.

4 In the paraphrase Erasmus elucidates the verb κατευθῦναι by a play on words: *dirigat* 'direct' (past participle *directus*) ... *recto* 'direct.' Theophylact *Expos in 2 Thess* (on 3:5) PG 124 1352A similarly plays on the Greek word κατευθῦναι 'direct,' 'make straight,' which he interprets: 'Make them come by a straight road and not to go astray,' and he lists many distractions from the direct path to charity.

5 In his annotation on 3:5 (*et patientiam Christi*) Erasmus observes that Ambrosiaster *Comm in 2 Thess* (on 3:5) CSEL 81/3 244:20 read *exspectationem* 'expectation,' and in his paraphrase he adopts Ambrosiaster's word in place of the Vulgate's *patientiam* 'patience.' The notion of patient endurance is then transferred to the next sentence of the paraphrase. Theophylact *Expos in 2 Thess* (on 3:5) PG 124 1352B notes both interpretations: expectation and endurance.

Christ. Love will give you boundless[6] enthusiasm for showing kindness to everyone, just as God is generous towards all; the expectation of Christ's coming will ensure that you endure all sufferings bravely.

But if there is any among you that lives according to his own inclination, scorning the pattern of living we have set out for you according to the rule of the gospel; and if such a person, idle himself, is destroying your public peace, and what is worse, is prying into the actions of other people while he does nothing himself, we instruct you on the authority of our Lord Jesus Christ to separate yourselves from association with this person, if he is a Christian.

It will not irk others to imitate our example: although we took on both the distinction and the responsibility of an apostle, we were not reluctant to be reduced to the ranks[7] among you. And so far from making any claim for ourselves beyond the rest, we did not even accept[8] bread from anyone. On the contrary, forgetful of our status, by our toil night and day, and by the work of our hands, we provided for ourselves what life's necessities demanded so that no one might find us a burden. Not that we judged we had no licence to do what the rest of the apostles are doing,[9] but we were unwilling to make use of our prerogative in order that we might serve as a pattern and model that the rest might not be reluctant to imitate. What we

* * * * *

6 boundless] First in 1521; previously 'tireless'
7 'To be reduced to the ranks': in ordinem cogi. Cf the Vulgate 3:7 non inquieti fuimus 'we were not unruly' (Conf). In his annotation on 3:7 (non inquieti fuimus), Erasmus explains that the Greek ἀτάκτως 'irregularly' (Conf; 'in idleness' RSV) and its cognate οὐκ ἠτακτήσαμεν 'we were not unruly' (3:8 Conf; 'we were not idle' RSV) represent a metaphor derived from military service. For the classical associations of the Greek words, see LSJ ἀτακτέω 'of a soldier, to be undisciplined.' Cf the adverb 'in an irregular, disorderly manner, of troops.' For the Latin idiom, which applies to civic magistrates as well as to military officers, see Livy 3.35.6, 3.51.13. Erasmus further clarifies the Greek in the annotation just cited. The Greek, he says, should be interpreted 'we were not out of line' or 'we were not disorderly,' and he explains that 'to be reduced to the ranks means they are bound by the common law and are in no way different from the rest.'
8 Erasmus follows a reading he found in Greek codices ἐλάβομεν 'take' or 'accept,' and which he thinks squares better with the syntax of the rest of the sentence than does the ἐφάγομεν 'eat ' that lies behind the Vulgate and behind the lemmata of both Theophylact Expos in 2 Thess (on 3:7) PG 124 1352D–1353A and Ambrosiaster Comm in 2 Thess (on 3:8) CSEL 81/3 245:10. See Erasmus' annotation on 3:8 (neque gratis panem manducavimus).
9 On Paul's abstention from the right of the apostle to be fed at the expense of the community, see also 1 Cor 9:1–18; 2 Cor 11:7; 1 Thess 2:9; and Erasmus' paraphrases on these passages.

exhibited in deed, we taught in word also:[10] that if anyone were unwilling to work that person should not eat.[11] They are entitled to sustenance, who are on sentry-duty[12] day and night for your salvation. But idle curiosity and laziness that indulges curiosity are not entitled to support.[13]

We have heard[14] that there are among you certain people who are disturbing your good order by their idleness, shrinking from work, and having no business of their own, so that in the meantime they concern themselves with other people's. Thus far I spare their names. But for all people of this sort we are prescribing and, if they prefer, we call to witness our Lord Jesus Christ, that they are not, through their idleness, to disturb the public tranquillity, nor are they to cry out against other busy people while they themselves do nothing; but they, too, working quietly with their own hands are to secure provisions for themselves instead of causing trouble for others by their outrageous demands. Indeed, they deserve to be refused what they seek, but nevertheless it is characteristic of Christian humaneness[15] to

* * * * *

10 For preaching as characteristic of Paul, see 1 Thess 2:9–12; as marking the 'good teacher,' cf CWE 50 5 with nn7 and 8. Ambrosiaster interprets similarly *Comm in 2 Thess* (on 3:10) CSEL 81/3 246:2–13: 'Not only did he teach in words but he encouraged them also by his deeds.' Ambrosiaster then develops the importance of the teacher's example.

11 On the importance of work for a Christian, see also Eph 4:28; 1 Thess 4:11; and Erasmus' extensive paraphrases on these passages.

12 Erasmus is repeating here in the paraphrase on 3:10 an image he had paraphrased in 3:8. Theophylact *Expos in 2 Thess* (on 3:8) PG 124 1353A had noted the forceful intensification of thought: 'We worked night and day in labour and toil' (Conf). Erasmus intensifies the force of the verse both by echoing the image here in his paraphrase on 3:11, and by evoking a military image (*qui . . . vigilant* 'who . . . stay awake,' 'are alert') used often of sentries on duty. See OLD *vigilo* with examples.

13 The paraphrase on 3:10 reflects Erasmus' continuing interest in the destructive nature of curiosity unaccompanied by piety. See 1 Cor chapter 2 n19; Eph Argument nn6 and 11; 2 Thess Argument. For the ramifications of 'curiosity' in both the intellectual and moral spheres as understood in medieval moral teachings, see Richard Newhauser 'The Sin of Curiosity and the Cistercians' in *Erudition at God's Service* ed J.R. Sommerfeldt, Studies in Medieval Cistercian History 11 / Cistercian Studies Series 98 (Kalamazoo 1987) 71–95.

14 we have heard] First in 1521; previously 'we hear.' Erasmus' annotation on 3:11 (*audivimus enim*) recognizes the present tense ἀκούομεν in the Greek text and he himself had translated *audimus* in 1516. The Vulgate of 1527 and some other witnesses to the Vulgate have the perfect tense *audivimus* although *audimus* is the preferred reading.

15 Erasmus may have adopted the concept of *humanitas* 'humaneness' in his paraphrase on 3:12 from Ambrosiaster, who remarks *Comm in 2 Thess* (on 3:13) CSEL

hasten to the assistance even of the undeserving, for the simple reason[16] that they are human and perhaps at some time they will improve. Therefore, brothers, do not grow tired of doing good to the deserving and the undeserving alike.[17]

If anyone disdains to obey our admonitions, which I passed on to you when I was present and which I am writing about now that I am absent, let this be punishment enough as far as Christian charity is concerned: that the person of this sort[18] be nourished indeed, but nonetheless censured, separated from close association with you only for this object: that when he has been corrected by embarrassment, he may come to his senses. You are not to cast him off directly like a foe, but rather warn him as you would an erring brother, one whom you wish healed not destroyed, shunning his company in such a way that you still esteem him in your hearts. For this is characteristic of love, that a separation is undertaken only for a period in order that the one who has transgressed may come to his senses.[19]

May the Lord Jesus himself, the author of peace, grant you perpetual peace in all your affairs. May the Lord be always with you all.

Again, I add a greeting to you in my own hand, namely, Paul's. This token you will notice in all my Epistles whether written to you or to others.[20] For I write in this way so that no one may deceive you with spurious

* * * * *

81/3 247:17–23 that Paul adds 'Do not grow tired of well doing' (3:13 Conf) to prevent anyone from seizing the opportunity to be stingy or inhumane. Erasmus calls for a specifically Christian humaneness: generous assistance even to the undeserving, tireless, courteous, and compassionate. See Phil chapter 4 n4.

16 for the simple reason ... improve] Added in 1532. The addition, offering a motive for coming to the assistance of the otherwise undeserving, calls to mind the famous line from Terence 'I am human and nothing human is alien to me' (*Heauton Timoroumenos* 77). See Col chapter 4 n14.

17 Cf Matt 5:45.

18 of this sort] Added in 1521. The phrase refers only to the idle.

19 'May come to his senses': *resipiscat*, both here in the paraphrase on 3:15 and just above in the paraphrase on 3:14. The biblical text (ἐντραπῇ, Erasmus' translation *pudore suffundatur* 'may be ashamed') provides a background that enlarges the connotation of the verb *resipiscere*, used normally in Erasmus' New Testament scholarship in the context of 'repentance.' On *resipiscere*, see also 1 Cor Argument n15; 1 Thess chapter 2 n28; CWE 50 22 n90, 44 n53, 111 n53; and Payne *Theology* 195–209.

20 For other references to the personal signature of the Apostle, see 1 Cor 16:21; Gal 6:11; Col 4:18; and Philem 19. Theophylact *Expos in 2 Thess* (on 3:17) PG 124 1357B points out that 'every letter' (Conf) could mean 'those that are to be sent to you or simply every Epistle no matter to whom it was sent.'

Epistles.[21] May the favour and kindliness of our Lord Jesus Christ be continually present to you all. Amen

The End of the Paraphrase on the Second Epistle
of Paul the Apostle to the Thessalonians

* * * * *

21 That Paul's signature is intended as a guarantee of authenticity is an explanation found in both Theophylact *Expos in 2 Thess* (on 3:17) PG 124 1357B and Ambrosiaster *Comm in 2 Thess* (on 3:17) CSEL 81/3 248:18–21.

DEDICATORY LETTER [1520]
TO CARDINAL CAMPEGGI

DEDICATORY LETTER [1520]

TO THE MOST REVEREND FATHER IN CHRIST
HIS EMINENCE LORENZO CAMPEGGI
TITULAR CARDINAL OF SAN TOMMASO IN PARIONE
FROM ERASMUS OF ROTTERDAM, GREETING[1]

Whenever I survey the mutability of human affairs, most reverend Father, I seem to see precisely some Euripus, so incessant are the changes as affairs surge up and down and cannot long continue in one position. They reach a climax and swing back to what was left behind, until once more they come to such a point that we are obliged to turn back our course from some excess that has now become intolerable. And what is more, were one to try to stand against the sea or bend its course a different way, one could never do this without putting all things in serious jeopardy and upheaval. It was thus that in olden days the kings of Rome gave place to a democracy which in its turn reached such a pitch of licence that there was need of dictators and after that even of kings, whose power then rose to enormous heights and provoked once more a desire for a democracy. But it would be an infinite task to collect in this way the many different shapes that things have taken. What is more surprising is that even studies have their own ebb and flow.

In olden days the Christian teaching was a matter of faith, not of disputation; men's simple piety was satisfied with Holy Scripture. Later, humane learning was applied; questions began to be asked about many points; much was swept into controversy. At first this seemed almost fundamental; but it developed by stages until many men, neglecting Holy Writ, grew old over questions meticulous, needless, and minute, as if drawn to the rocks on which some Siren sang. When it had come about that the heavenly image of Christ was nearly overlaid by human subtleties, some men tried to recall the world of studies to the simplicity of an earlier day and draw it back from pools now excessively sullied to the pure springs. To this end, they thought expertise in tongues and

* * * * *

1 For the 1520 version of the dedicatory letter see Translators' Note xvii, and cf the version that appeared first in 1521, 284–97 above.

knowledge of the liberal studies (as they call them) were of the first importance.

And here at once there is a great uproar at the very outset, one party cleaving with clenched teeth to things as they are, the other preferring to dislodge its opponent once and for all from the height rather than escorting him down by degrees. The humanities are not to be brought in to do away with the curriculum of the schools but to purify them and make them more reasonable than they have been hitherto in some men's hands. If only those who have grown grey in them would embrace the others civilly, and the professors of the liberal studies would accommodate themselves to the former group in turn, we should see each group bring ornament and profit to the other. As it is, while we bespatter each other with mud or, it would be truer to say, throw stones at one another, both parties lose the advantage that was theirs and both leave the field having suffered great loss. In the pamphlets in which each side tears the other to pieces there is more abuse than argument. In their discourses there is more spite than scholarship, more bad language than good judgment. In their sermons the gospel teaching, which ought to appear in its purest form, is infected with human emotions. It is a sin to declaim in offensive language that inarticulate scholastic studies are of no benefit. But on the other side it is a sin to climb into the pulpit, from which one ought to hear the gospel trumpet-call that heralds the glory of Christ, and cry: 'Don't let your children learn Greek! Greek is the mother of heresies and of the Antichrist. There is a certain individual who corrects the Lord's Prayer and the Magnificat, as it is called, and criticizes the Gospel of John. Back them up, citizens! Do your duty, ye magistrates!'

If words like these are used before the inexperienced public, nothing is more subversive; if before people of training and intelligence, nothing more crazy. And yet, the men who do this in public wish to pass for pillars of the Christian religion. They do not stop to reflect that their attacks on the reputation of those who do them good service are diametrically opposed to the doctrine of Christ which they profess and that a good part of their effort is wasted for them while they are also losing all their credit with the people. Who would put his trust in a man who manifestly betrays his spite? And indeed they sow not the gospel but the pestilent tares of strife and hatred; and when these have once seized upon the pursuits of men, they are not easily weeded out.

Nothing in human affairs is so flourishing that discord cannot turn it into disaster. And nowhere should discord be more strictly watched than in scholarship, and in sacred studies above all. On scholarship a great part of our Christian commonwealth depends. And now we see that the situation has come almost to the point of madness, so that, if it continues after this fashion, it seems to me preferable to cultivate a garden rather than scholarship.

But for some time now, I know, your reverend Lordship has been silently protesting: 'How does this relate to me? Or how to the paraphrase?' Why, in hopes that on the advice of you and others like you his Lordship, our beloved Leo x, will complete the very splendid and laudable work which he has so prosperously begun. He rendered a more than human service to the world, for when kings and peoples were in confusion, warring wickedly on one another, he brought them into agreement, and perhaps he will confer no less on us, if in the same way he restores to our studies the tranquillity that should be theirs. For it is not yet clear to me which is the greater evil for the human race, the armed conflicts of which I spoke or these feuds among the learned. His most serene majesty the king of England, Henry the Eighth, with the support of his Achates, the reverend cardinal of York, has done this for his native country; and Leo can do the same for the world. When he has done this, then at last that inscription, by far the most handsome, will bring full praise: 'To Pope Leo x, who gave peace back to Christendom.'

Moreover, the policy of concord will easily stand firm if he refuses permission to certain sycophants and if he proclaims to all, with all the authority of an oracle, that every man should promulgate and promote his own convictions without offensive criticism of those of others. But if their attitudes of mind differ, as happens, let all dispute be confined to courteous confrontation.

I had no doubts of my ability to convince you of this, for I well know how your learned fairness of mind abhors all virulence. Nor will it be hard for your Eminence to persuade our Holy Father Leo, whether because he rightly values you so highly for your distinguished gifts or because of his very own nature he is so wonderfully disposed towards peace and concord.

For this help, in case it should seem an inadequate reward to have your name exalted by the whole company of educated people, here is a small addition offered on my own account: a paraphrase on the four Pauline Epistles which I have completed in one recent spell of work. At the same time I would pay off, at any rate in part, my debt to your Eminence; for I have forgotten neither what I owe to your unheard-of generosity nor what I have promised you. Pray accept therefore this payment on account, until I can scrape together the means to pay in full.

My respectful best wishes to your Eminence, to whom I wish to be commended as highly as possible.

Louvain, 5 February [1519]

THE SEQUENCE AND DATES OF THE
PUBLICATION OF THE PARAPHRASES

WORKS FREQUENTLY CITED

SHORT-TITLE FORMS
FOR ERASMUS' WORKS

INDEX OF SCRIPTURAL REFERENCES

INDEX OF CLASSICAL REFERENCES

INDEX OF PATRISTIC AND MEDIEVAL
REFERENCES

INDEX OF GREEK AND LATIN
WORDS CITED

GENERAL INDEX

The indexes refer primarily to the Preface, the Translators' Note,
the dedicatory letters, and the notes. An index of all the names
and theological terms in the paraphrases themselves
is beyond the scope of this volume.

THE SEQUENCE AND DATES OF THE PUBLICATION OF THE PARAPHRASES

The Epistles

Romans	November 1517
Corinthians 1 and 2	February 1519
Galatians	May 1519
Timothy 1 and 2, Titus, Philemon	November / December 1519
Ephesians, Philippians, Colossians, and Thessalonians 1 and 2	January / February 1520
Peter 1 and 2, Jude	June / July 1520
James	December 1520
John 1–3, Hebrews	January 1521

Gospels and Acts

Matthew	March 1522
John	February 1523
Luke	August 1523
Mark	December 1523 / February 1524
Acts	February 1524

The Epistles were originally published by Dirk Martens in Louvain, except for Timothy, Titus, and Philemon, which were published by Michaël Hillen in Antwerp. The Gospels and Acts where all originally published by Johann Froben in Basel. On the publisher and date of the set 'Ephesians to Thessalonians,' see the Translators' Note.

WORKS FREQUENTLY CITED

This list provides bibliographical information for works referred to in short-title form in this volume. For Erasmus' writings see the short-title list following.

ABD	*The Anchor Bible Dictionary* ed David Noel Freedman (New York 1992) 6 vols
Allen	*Opus epistolarum Des. Erasmi Roterodami* ed P.S. Allen, H.M. Allen, and H.W. Garrod (Oxford 1906–1958) 11 vols and index
Allen and Greenough	*Allen and Greenough's New Latin Grammar for Schools and Colleges* ed J.B. Greenough, G.L. Kittredge, A.A. Howard, Benj. L. D'Ooge (Boston 1916)
Ambrosiaster *Comm in 1 Cor* etc	*Ambrosiastri qui dicitur Commentarius in epistulas Paulinas* CSEL 81/1–3 ed H.J. Vogels (Vienna 1966–9)
Aquinas *Super 2 Cor lect* etc	St. Thomas Aquinas *Super epistolas S. Pauli lectura* ed Raffaele Cai OP 8th ed rev (Rome and Turin 1953) 2 vols
ASD	*Opera omnia Desiderii Erasmi Roterodami* (Amsterdam 1969–)
AV	*The Holy Bible ... Authorized King James Version* (London 1611; repr 1969)
Barrett	C.K. Barrett *A Commentary on the First Epistle to the Corinthians* Harper's New Testament Commentaries (New York 1968)
Barth *Colossians*	Markus Barth and Helmut Blanke *Colossians: A New Translation with Introduction and Commentary* trans Astrid B. Beck, The Anchor Bible Commentaries 34B (New York 1994)
Barth *Ephesians*	Markus Barth *Ephesians: Introduction, Translation, and Commentary* The Anchor Bible Commentaries 34 and 34A (Garden City, NY 1974) 2 vols
Bateman 'From Soul to Soul'	John J. Bateman 'From Soul to Soul: Persuasion in Erasmus' Paraphrases on the New Testament' *Erasmus in English* 15 (1987–8) 7–16
Bateman 'Textual Travail'	John J. Bateman 'The Textual Travail of the *Tomus Secundus* of the *Paraphrases*' in Pabel and Vessey *Holy Scripture Speaks* 213–63

BDAG

A Greek-English Lexicon of the New Testament and Other Early Christian Literature 3rd ed revised and edited by Frederick William Danker based on Walter Bauer's *Griechisch-deutsches Wörterbuch zu den Schriften des Neuen Testaments und der frühchristlichen Literatur* 6th edition, ed Kurt Aland and Barbara Aland with Viktor Reichmann, and on previous English editions by W.F. Arndt, F.W. Gingrich, and F.W. Danker (Chicago 2000)

Best

Ernest Best *A Commentary on the First and Second Epistles to the Thessalonians* (London 1972)

Brown *Body*

Peter Brown *The Body and Society: Men, Women and Sexual Renunciation in Early Christianity* Lectures on the History of Religions ns 13 (New York 1988)

Brown *Introduction to NT*

Raymond E. Brown *An Introduction to the New Testament* The Anchor Bible Reference Library (New York: Doubleday 1997)

CCL

Corpus christianorum, series Latina (Turnhout 1953–   )

CEBR

Contemporaries of Erasmus: A Biographical Register of the Renaissance and Reformation ed P.G. Bietenholz and T.B. Deutscher (Toronto 1985–7) 3 vols

Chantraine

Georges Chantraine *'Mystère' et 'Philosophie du Christ' selon Erasme* (Namur and Gembloux 1971)

Chomarat

Jacques Chomarat *Grammaire et rhétorique chez Erasme* (Paris 1981) 2 vols

Chrysostom *In 1 Cor hom* etc

Joannes Chrysostomus *Opera omnia quae extant* X PG 61 9–610 (1 and 2 Corinthians) and XI PG 62 9–500 (Ephesians–2 Thessalonians)

Conf

The New Testament ... A revision of the Challoner-Rheims Version (Paterson, NJ 1947)

Conzelmann

Hans Conzelmann *1 Corinthians: A Commentary on the First Epistle to the Corithians* trans James W. Leitch (Philadelphia 1975)

Coverdale

The Second Tome or Volume of the Paraphrase of Erasmus upon the Newe Testament (London 1549)

CSEL

Corpus Scriptorum Ecclesiasticorum Latinorum (Vienna 1866–   )

CWE	*Collected Works of Erasmus* (Toronto 1974–)
DV	*The Holy Bible* ... Douay-Rheims Version, rev Bishop Richard Challoner (New York 1941)
EEC	*Encyclopedia of Early Christianity* 2nd ed, ed Everett Ferguson with Michael P. McHugh and Frederick W. Norris (New York 1997) 2 vols
ERSY	*Erasmus of Rotterdam Society Yearbook* (1981–)
Furnish	Victor Paul Furnish *II Corinthians: Translated with Introduction, Notes, and Commentary* The Anchor Bible Commentaries 32A (Garden City, NY 1984)
Gloss	*Biblia Latina cum Glossa Ordinaria* Facsimile reprint of the *editio princeps* by Adolph Rusch of Strasbourg 1480/1 with an introduction by Karlfried Froelich and Margaret Gibson (Turnhout 1992) 4 vols
Heine	Ronald E. Heine *The Commentaries of Origen and Jerome on St Paul's Epistle to the Ephesians* Oxford Early Christian Studies (Oxford 2002)
Holborn	*Desiderius Erasmus Roterodamus: Ausgewählte Werke* ed Hajo Holborn with Annemarie Holborn (Munich 1933; repr 1964)
JB	*The Jerusalem Bible* (New York 1966)
Jerome *Comm in Eph*	S. Eusebius Hieronymus Stridonensis *Commentariorum in epistulam ad Ephesios libri tres* PL 26 (Paris 1845) 439–554
Jerome *Comm in Gal*	S. Eusebius Hieronymus Stridonensis *Commentariorum in epistulam ad Galatas libri tres* PL 26 (Paris 1845) 306–438
Kelly *Early Christian Doctrines*	J.D.N. Kelly *Early Christian Doctrines* 5th ed (San Francisco 1978)
Kittel-Friedrich	*Theologisches Wörterbuch zum Neuen Testament* begründet von Gerhard Kittel. In Verbindung mit zahlreichen Fachgenossen herausgegeben von Gerhard Friedrich. (Stuttgart 1933–73) 10 vols
Lampe *Patristic Greek*	*A Patristic Greek Lexicon* ed G.W.H. Lampe (Oxford 1961)
LB	*Desiderii Erasmi Roterodami opera omnia* ed J. Leclerc (Leiden 1703–6) 10 vols

Lightfoot   J.B. Lightfoot *St. Paul's Epistle to the Philippians: A Revised Text with Introduction, Notes and Dissertations* (London 1885; repr 1987)

Lohse   Eduard Lohse *Colossians and Philemon: A Commentary on the Epistles to the Colossians and to Philemon* trans William R. Poehlmann and Robert J. Karris ed Helmut Koester (Philadelphia 1971)

L&S   Charlton T. Lewis and Charles Short *A Latin Dictionary* (Oxford 1879; repr 1975)

LSJ   *A Greek-English Lexicon* compiled by Henry George Liddell and Robert Scott, revised and augmented by Sir Henry Stuart Jones with the assistance of Roderick McKenzie, 9th ed with revised supplement (Oxford 1996)

McConica 'Erasmus and the Grammar of Consent'   James K. McConica 'Erasmus and the Grammar of Consent' in *Scrinium* II 77–99

Metzger   Bruce M. Metzger A *Textual Commentary on the Greek New Testament* 2nd ed rev (Stuttgart 1994)

NEB   *The New English Bible with the Apocrypha* Oxford Study Edition (New York 1976)

Nicholas of Lyra   Nicolaus de Lyra *Postilla super totam Bibliam* (Strasbourg 1492; facsimile ed Frankfurt am Main 1971) 4 vols

NIGTC   *The New International Greek Testament Commentary* ed Howard Marshall and Donald A. Hagner (Grand Rapids, Mich 1978–   )

NJBC   *The New Jerome Biblical Commentary* ed Raymond E. Brown ss, Joseph A Fitzmyer sj, Roland E. Murphy O. Carm (Englewood Cliffs, NJ 1990)

NRSV   *The Holy Bible … New Revised Standard Version* (New York 1989)

NTGL   *Novum Testamentum Graece et Latine.* Textum Graecum post Eberhard Nestle et Erwin Nestle communiter ediderunt Kurt Aland, Matthew Black, Carlo M. Martini, Bruce M. Metzger, Allen Wikgren; Textus Latinus Novae Vulgatae Bibliorum Sacrorum Editioni debetur; utriusque textus apparatum criticum recensuerunt et editionem novis curis

elaboraverunt Kurt Aland et Barbara Aland una cum
Instituto studiorum textus Novi Testamenti Monasteriensi
(Westphalia) 3rd ed (Stuttgart 1999)

Oberman *Harvest*

Heiko Augustinus Oberman *The Harvest of Medieval Theology:
Gabriel Biel and Late Medieval Nominalism* (Cambridge, Mass
1963)

OER

The Oxford Encyclopedia of the Reformation ed Hans J.
Hillerbrand (New York 1996) 4 vols

OLD

Oxford Latin Dictionary ed P.G.W. Glare (Oxford 1982)

O'Mara 'Triumphs,
Trophies, and Spoils'

Mechtilde O'Mara 'Triumphs, Trophies, and Spoils: Roman
History in some Paraphrases on Paul by Erasmus' in Pabel
and Vessey *Holy Scripture Speaks* 111–25.

Origen *Martyrdom*

Origen *An Exhortation to Martyrdom, Prayer, First Principles
Book IV, Prologue to the Commentary on the Song of Songs,
Homily XXVII on Numbers* trans and intro Rowan A. Greer,
preface Hans Urs von Balthasar, The Classics of Western
Spirituality (New York and Toronto 1979)

Origen *De Principiis*

Origen *On First Principles* trans, intro, and annot G.W.
Butterworth (New York 1966)

Orr and Walther

William F. Orr and James Arthur Walther *I Corinthians: A
New Translation with Introduction with a Study of the Life of
Paul, Notes, and Commentary* The Anchor Bible Commentaries
32 (Garden City, NY 1976)

Pabel *Conversing
with God*

Hilmar M. Pabel *Conversing with God: Prayer in Erasmus'
Pastoral Writings* Erasmus Studies 13 (Toronto 1997)

Pabel 'Exegesis and
Marriage'

Hilmar M. Pabel 'Exegesis and Marriage in Erasmus'
Paraphrases on the New Testament' in Pabel and Vessey *Holy
Scripture Speaks* 175–209

Pabel and Vessey
Holy Scripture Speaks

*Holy Scripture Speaks: the Production and Reception of Erasmus'
Paraphrases on the New Testament* ed Hilmar M. Pabel and
Mark Vessey, Erasmus Studies 14 (Toronto 2002)

Payne 'The Hermen-
eutics of Erasmus'

J.B. Payne 'Toward the Hermeneutics of Erasmus' in
Scrinium II 13–49

Payne *Theology*

John B. Payne *Erasmus: His Theology of the Sacraments*
(Richmond 1970)

PG   *Patrologiae cursus completus ... series Graeca* ed J.-P. Migne
                            (Paris 1857–66) 161 vols. Indexes F. Cavallera (Paris 1912)
                            and T. Hopfner (Paris 1928–36) 2 vols

PL   *Patrologiae cursus completus ... series Latina* ed J.-P. Migne, 1st
                            ed (Paris 1844–55, 1862–5; repr Turnhout) 217 vols plus 4 vols
                            indexes; Chadwyck-Healey *Patrologia Latina Database* (1996–
                            2006). In the notes, references to volumes of PL in which col-
                            umn numbers in the first edition are different from those in
                            later editions or reprints include the date of the edition cited.

Rawson *Family*   B. Rawson ed *The Family in Ancient Rome: New Perspectives*
                            (Ithaca, NY 1986)

Rigaux   B. Rigaux OFM *Saint Paul: Les épitres aux Thessaloniciens*
                            (Paris 1956)

RSV   *The Oxford Annotated Bible with the Apocrypha: Revised
                            Standard Version* ed Herbert G. May and Bruce M. Metzger
                            (New York 1965)

Roussel 'Exegetical   Bernard Roussel 'Exegetical Fictions? Biblical Paraphrases
Fictions?'   of the Sixteenth and Seventeenth Centuries' in Pabel and
                            Vessey *Holy Scripture Speaks* 59–83

Rummel *Catholic*   Erika Rummel *Erasmus and His Catholic Critics* I: *1515–1522*
Critics   and II: *1523–1536* (Nieuwkoop 1989) 2 vols

Rummel *Erasmus'*   Erika Rummel *Erasmus' Annotations on the New Testament:
Annotations*   From Philologist to Theologian* Erasmus Studies 8 (Toronto
                            1986)

Scrinium   *Scrinium Erasmianum: Mélanges historiques publiés ... à
                            l'occasion du cinquième centenaire de la naissance d'Erasme* ed
                            J. Coppens (Leiden 1969) 2 vols

Sider 'Χάρις'   Robert D. Sider 'Χάρις and Derivatives in the Biblical
                            Scholarship of Erasmus' in *Diakonia: Studies in Honor of
                            Robert T. Meyer* ed Thomas Halton and Joseph P. Williman
                            (Washington 1986) 242–60

Sider 'Historical   Robert D. Sider 'Historical Imagination and the Repre-
Imagination'   sentation of Paul in Erasmus' Paraphrases on the Pauline
                            Epistles' in Pabel and Vessey *Holy Scripture Speaks* 85–109

Sider 'Grace'   Robert D. Sider '"In Terms Quite Plain and Clear": The
                            Exposition of Grace in the New Testament Paraphrases of
                            Erasmus' *Erasmus in English* 15 (1987–8) 16–25

Sider 'The Just'   Robert D. Sider '"The Just and the Holy" in the New
                            Testament Scholarship of Erasmus' ERSY 11 (1991) 1–26

Theophylact *Expos in*   Theophylactus *In omnes epistulas Pauli expositiones* PG 124
1 Cor etc   559–952 (1 and 2 Corinthians), 1031–1358 (Ephesians–2
                            Thessalonians)

Thomas Aquinas   *See* Aquinas

Valla *Annot*   Laurentius Valla *Annotationes in Novum Testamentum* in
                            Opera omnia 2 vols (Basel 1540; repr Turin 1962) I

Valla *Coll*   Laurentius Valla *Collatio Novi Testamenti* redazione inedita
                            a cura di Alessandro Perosa (Florence 1970)

Wanamaker   Charles A. Wanamaker *The Epistles to the Thessalonians: A
                            Commentary on the Greek Text* NIGTC (Grand Rapids 1990)

Weber   *Biblia sacra iuxta vulgatam versionem* adiuvantibus B. Fischer,
                            I. Gribomont, H.F.D. Sparks, W. Thiele recensuit et
                            brevi apparatu critico instruxit Robertus Weber 4th ed
                            emendatam cum sociis B. Fischer ... preparavit Roger
                            Gryson (Stuttgart 1994)

SHORT-TITLE FORMS FOR ERASMUS' WORKS

Titles following colons are longer versions of the same, or are alternative titles. Items entirely enclosed in square brackets are of doubtful authorship. For abbreviations, see Works Frequently Cited.

Acta: Acta Academiae Lovaniensis contra Lutherum *Opuscula* / CWE 71

Adagia: Adagiorum chiliades 1508, etc (Adagiorum collectanea for the primitive form, when required) LB II / ASD II-1, 2, 4, 5, 6, 7, 8 / CWE 30–6

Admonitio adversus mendacium: Admonitio adversus mendacium et obtrectationem LB X

Annotationes in Novum Testamentum LB VI / ASD VI-5, 6, 8 / CWE 51–60

Antibarbari LB X / ASD I-1 / CWE 23

Apologia ad Caranzam: Apologia ad Sanctium Caranzam, or Apologia de tribus locis, or Responsio ad annotationem Stunicae ... a Sanctio Caranza defensam LB IX

Apologia ad Fabrum: Apologia ad Iacobum Fabrum Stapulensem LB IX / ASD IX-3 / CWE 83

Apologia adversus monachos: Apologia adversus monachos quosdam Hispanos LB IX

Apologia adversus Petrum Sutorem: Apologia adversus debacchationes Petri Sutoris LB IX

Apologia adversus rhapsodias Alberti Pii: Apologia ad viginti et quattuor libros A. Pii LB IX / CWE 84

Apologia contra Latomi dialogum: Apologia contra Iacobi Latomi dialogum de tribus linguis LB IX / CWE 71

Apologia de 'In principio erat sermo' LB IX

Apologia de laude matrimonii: Apologia pro declamatione de laude matrimonii LB IX / CWE 71

Apologia de loco 'Omnes quidem': Apologia de loco 'Omnes quidem resurgemus' LB IX

Apologiae contra Stunicam: Apologiae contra Lopidem Stunicam LB IX:
(1) Apologia respondens ad ea quae Iacobus Lopis Stunica taxaverat in prima duntaxat Novi Testamenti aeditione ASD IX-2; (2) Apologia adversus libellum Stunicae cui titulum fecit Blasphemiae et impietates Erasmi; (3) Apologia ad prodromon Stunicae; (4) Apologia ad Stunicae conclusiones; (5) Epistola apologetica adversus Stunicam [= Ep 2172]

Apologia qua respondet invectivis Lei: Apologia qua respondet duabus invectivis Eduardi Lei *Opuscula* / ASD IX-4 / CWE 72

Apophthegmata LB IV

Appendix de scriptis Clithovei LB IX / CWE 83

Appendix respondens ad Sutorem LB IX

Argumenta: Argumenta in omnes epistolas apostolicas nova (with Paraphrases)

Axiomata pro causa Lutheri: Axiomata pro causa Martini Lutheri *Opuscula* / CWE 71

Brevissima scholia: In Elenchum Alberti Pii brevissima scholia per eundem Erasmum Roterodamum CWE 84

Carmina LB I, IV, V, VIII / ASD I-7 / CWE 85–6

Catalogus lucubrationum LB I / CWE 9 (Ep 1341A)

Ciceronianus: Dialogus Ciceronianus LB I / ASD I-2 / CWE 28

Colloquia LB I / ASD I-3 / CWE 39–40

Compendium vitae Allen I / CWE 4

Concionalis interpretatio (in Psalmi)

Conflictus: Conflictus Thaliae et Barbariei LB I

[Consilium: Consilium cuiusdam ex animo cupientis esse consultum] *Opuscula* / CWE 71

De bello Turcico: Consultatio de bello Turcico (in Psalmi)

De civilitate: De civilitate morum puerilium LB I / CWE 25

Declamatio de morte LB IV

Declamatiuncula LB IV

Declarationes ad censuras Lutetiae vulgatas: Declarationes ad censuras Lutetiae vulgatas sub nomine facultatis theologiae Parisiensis LB IX

De concordia: De sarcienda ecclesiae concordia, or De amabili ecclesiae concordia (in Psalmi)

De conscribendis epistolis LB I / ASD I-2 / CWE 25

De constructione: De constructione octo partium orationis, or Syntaxis LB I / ASD I-4

De contemptu mundi: Epistola de contemptu mundi LB V / ASD V-1 / CWE 66

De copia: De duplici copia verborum ac rerum LB I / ASD I-6 / CWE 24

De esu carnium: Epistola apologetica ad Christophorum episcopum Basiliensem de interdicto esu carnium LB IX / ASD IX-1

De immensa Dei misericordia: Concio de immensa Dei misericordia LB V / CWE 70

De libero arbitrio: De libero arbitrio diatribe LB IX / CWE 76

De praeparatione: De praeparatione ad mortem LB V / ASD V-1 / CWE 70

De pueris instituendis: De pueris statim ac liberaliter instituendis LB I / ASD I-2 / CWE 26

De puero Iesu: Concio de puero Iesu LB V / CWE 29

De puritate tabernaculi: De puritate tabernaculi sive ecclesiae christianae (in Psalmi)

De ratione studii LB I / ASD I-2 / CWE 24

De recta pronuntiatione: De recta latini graecique sermonis pronuntiatione LB I / ASD I-4 / CWE 26

De taedio Iesu: Disputatiuncula de taedio, pavore, tristicia Iesu LB V / CWE 70

Detectio praestigiarum: Detectio praestigiarum cuiusdam libelli germanice scripti LB X / ASD IX-1

De vidua christiana LB V / CWE 66

De virtute amplectenda: Oratio de virtute amplectenda LB V / CWE 29

[Dialogus bilinguium ac trilinguium: Chonradi Nastadiensis dialogus bilinguium ac trilinguium] *Opuscula* / CWE 7

Dilutio: Dilutio eorum quae Iodocus Clithoveus scripsit adversus declamationem suasoriam matrimonii / *Dilutio eorum quae Iodocus Clithoveus scripsit* ed Emile V. Telle (Paris 1968) / CWE 83

Divinationes ad notata Bedae LB IX

Ecclesiastes: Ecclesiastes sive de ratione concionandi LB V / ASD V-4, 5

Elenchus in N. Bedae censuras LB IX

Enchiridion: Enchiridion militis christiani LB V / CWE 66

Encomium matrimonii (in De conscribendis epistolis)

Encomium medicinae: Declamatio in laudem artis medicae LB I / ASD I-4 / CWE 29

Epistola ad Dorpium LB IX / CWE 3 / CWE 71

Epistola ad fratres Inferioris Germaniae: Responsio ad fratres Germaniae Inferioris ad epistolam apologeticam incerto autore proditam LB X / ASD IX-1

Epistola ad graculos: Epistola ad quosdam imprudentissimos graculos LB X

Epistola apologetica de Termino LB X

Epistola consolatoria: Epistola consolatoria virginibus sacris, or Epistola consolatoria in adversis LB V / CWE 69

Epistola contra pseudevangelicos: Epistola contra quosdam qui se falso iactant evangelicos LB X / ASD IX-1

Euripidis Hecuba LB I / ASD I-1

Euripidis Iphigenia in Aulide LB I / ASD I-1

Exomologesis: Exomologesis sive modus confitendi LB V

Explanatio symboli: Explanatio symboli apostolorum sive catechismus LB V / ASD V-1 / CWE 70

Ex Plutarcho versa LB IV / ASD IV-2

Formula: Conficiendarum epistolarum formula (see De conscribendis epistolis)

Hyperaspistes LB X / CWE 76–7

In Nucem Ovidii commentarius LB I / ASD I-1 / CWE 29

In Prudentium: Commentarius in duos hymnos Prudentii LB V / CWE 29

Institutio christiani matrimonii LB V / CWE 69

Institutio principis christiani LB IV / ASD IV-1 / CWE 27

[Julius exclusus: Dialogus Julius exclusus e coelis] *Opuscula* / CWE 27

Lingua LB IV / ASD IV-1A / CWE 29

Liturgia Virginis Matris: Virginis Matris apud Lauretum cultae liturgia LB V / ASD V-1 / CWE 69

Luciani dialogi LB I / ASD I-1

Manifesta mendacia ASD IX-4 / CWE 71

Methodus (see Ratio)

Modus orandi Deum LB V / ASD V-1 / CWE 70

Moria: Moriae encomium LB IV / ASD IV-3 / CWE 27

Novum Testamentum: Novum Testamentum 1519 and later (Novum instrumentum for the first edition, 1516, when required) LB VI / ASD VI-2, 5, 6, 8

Obsecratio ad Virginem Mariam: Obsecratio sive oratio ad Virginem Mariam in rebus adversis, or Obsecratio ad Virginem Matrem Mariam in rebus adversis LB V / CWE 69

Oratio de pace: Oratio de pace et discordia LB VIII
Oratio funebris: Oratio funebris in funere Bertae de Heyen LB VIII / CWE 29

Paean Virgini Matri: Paean Virgini Matri dicendus LB V / CWE 69
Panegyricus: Panegyricus ad Philippum Austriae ducem LB IV / ASD IV-1 / CWE 27
Parabolae: Parabolae sive similia LB I / ASD I-5 / CWE 23
Paraclesis LB V, VI
Paraphrasis in Elegantias Vallae: Paraphrasis in Elegantias Laurentii Vallae LB I /
    ASD I-4
Paraphrasis in Matthaeum, etc (in Paraphrasis in Novum Testamentum)
Paraphrasis in Novum Testamentum LB VII / ASD VII-6 / CWE 42–50
Peregrinatio apostolorum: Peregrinatio apostolorum Petri et Pauli LB VI, VII
Precatio ad Virginis filium Iesum LB V / CWE 69
Precatio dominica LB V / CWE 69
Precationes: Precationes aliquot novae LB V / CWE 69
Precatio pro pace ecclesiae: Precatio ad Dominum Iesum pro pace ecclesiae LB IV,
    V / CWE 69
Psalmi: Psalmi, or Enarrationes sive commentarii in psalmos LB V / ASD V-2, 3 /
    CWE 63–5
Purgatio adversus epistolam Lutheri: Purgatio adversus epistolam non sobriam
    Lutheri LB X / ASD IX-1

Querela pacis LB IV / ASD IV-2 / CWE 27

Ratio: Ratio seu Methodus compendio perveniendi ad veram theologiam (Methodus
    for the shorter version originally published in the Novum instrumentum of 1516)
    LB V, VI
Responsio ad annotationes Lei: Responsio ad annotationes Eduardi Lei LB IX /
    ASD IX-4 / CWE 72
Responsio ad collationes: Responsio ad collationes cuiusdam iuvenis geronto-
    didascali LB IX
Responsio ad disputationem de divortio: Responsio ad disputationem cuiusdam
    Phimostomi de divortio LB IX / CWE 83
Responsio ad epistolam Alberti Pii: Responsio ad epistolam paraeneticam Alberti
    Pii, or Responsio ad exhortationem Pii LB IX / CWE 84
Responsio ad notulas Bedaicas LB X
Responsio ad Petri Cursii defensionem: Epistola de apologia Cursii LB X / Allen
    Ep 3032
Responsio adversus febricitantis libellum: Apologia monasticae religionis LB X

Spongia: Spongia adversus aspergines Hutteni LB X / ASD IX-1
Supputatio: Supputatio calumniarum Natalis Bedae LB IX

Tyrannicida: Tyrannicida, declamatio Lucianicae respondens LB I / ASD I-1 / CWE 29

Virginis et martyris comparatio LB V / CWE 69
Vita Hieronymi: Vita divi Hieronymi Stridonensis Opuscula / CWE 61

Index of Scriptural References

This index cites biblical verses quoted in the text and verses that are identified as possible sources or that are commented upon in the notes. References to the *Annotationes* and *Paraphrases* are found in the General Index under 'Erasmus, works.'

Genesis

1–2	335 n44
1:1–2	152 n16
1:11	186 n54
1:14–17	375 n35
2:7	142 n14, 153 n17, 190 n67
2:16	415 n44
2:24	83, 347 nn37 and 39
3:16	88 n8, 172 n47
3:19	414 n44
17:12	379 n13
18	39 n49
22:18	317 n28
24:62	11 n43
26:12–22	11 n43
26:14–18	287 n29
46:8–27	380 n18

Exodus

3:2–4:17	39 n48
5:22–6:13	39 n48
7:11–8:18	467 n16
10:8	131 n14
12:1–24	72 n13
12:34	72 n14
12:39	72 n14
13:1–13	72 n13
13:21–2	129 n3
14	72 n13
14:16	129 n6
14:19–20	129 n3
14:19–22	129 n6
16:18	201 n11, 249
19:8	415 n44
20:12	349
20:13	349
20:15	349
25:40	320 n45
32	131 nn12 and 14
32:19	218 n16
32:27–8	131 n12
32:28	131 n14
32:35	131 n12
33:12–23	39 n48
34:29–30	220 n36
34:33–5	218 n15
34:35	220 n36

Leviticus

7:6	135 n33
7:15–18	135 n33
10:1–2	131 n12
11:2–23	417 n61
11:24–32	417 n60
11:34–8	417 n61
11:44	238 n24
12:3	379 n13
18:24	439 n22
19:18	161 n20
26:11–12	238 n23
26:12	317 n29

Index of Classical References

Aeschylus *Eumenides* 142 n17
Appian *Bella civilia* 140 n5
Apuleius *Metamorphoses* 141 n10
Aristophanes
– *Acharnians* 11 n41
– *Clouds* 409 n8
– *Ecclesiazusae* 172 n50
Aristotle
– *De anima* 325 n24
– *De generatione animalium* 88 n6, 142 n17
– *Nicomachean Ethics* 340 n8, 341 n14
– *Politics* 142 n16
Ausonius *Epigrammata* 254 n7

Caesar *De bello civili* 299 n5
Cato *De agri cultura* 425 n2
Catullus 295 n124
Cicero
– *Ad familiares* 425 n3
– *Brutus* 157 n1
– *De divinatione* 170 n38, 359 n9
– *De finibus* 450 n8, 457 n22
– *De officiis* 84 n44, 106 n65, 151 n9, 168 n28, 182 n37, 246 n6, 248 nn16 and 17, 333 n30, 362 n9, 450 n8
– *De oratore* 151 n9, 157 n1
– *De re publica* 19 n2, 79 n21, 151 n9, 156 n32, 188 n63 (=*Ad Atticum* 8.11.1)
– *In Catilinam* 337 n52
– *In Verrem* 364 n17, 366 n25, 371 n14, 420 n12
– *Orator* 134 n26, 157 n1
– *Paradoxa Stoicorum* 450 n8
– *Pro Milone* 446 n36
– *Pro Murena* 284 n3

– *Tusculan Disputations* 188 n63, 189 n64

Dionysius of Halicarnassus *Archaeologia* 298 n5

Gellius, Aulus *Attic Nights* 299 n5

Herodotus 53 n11
Homer *Odyssey* 286 n24
Horace
– *Epistles* 238 n25, 262 n19, 450 n7
– *Epodes* 206 n10
– *Odes* 34 n28, 104 n60, 236 n14, 275 n10, 337 n51, 344 n27
– *Satires* 9 n34, 114 n18, 341 n14, 342 n21, 442 n15, 450 n7, 452 n16

Josephus
– *Jewish Antiquities* 380 nn19 and 20
– *Jewish War* 328 n11, 380 n20
Juvenal 11 n46, 57 n26, 103 n55, 141 n10, 202 n16, 337 n52
Livy 57 n26, 170 n38, 173 n50, 285 nn9–11, 333 n30, 473 n7
Lucretius 20 n6, 88 n6, 182 n39, 184 n43

Martial 80 n28, 141 n10
Menander *Thais* 184 n44
Musonius Rufus 142 n16

Ovid
– *Metamorphoses* 32 n20, 225 n17, 354 n29, 420 n6
– *Tristia* 295 n124

Index of
Patristic and Medieval References

Ambrose *De viduis* 10 n38

Ambrosiaster *Ambrosiastri qui dicitur Commentarius in epistulas Paulinas* xxi n19, 8 n30, and passim

Aquinas, Thomas
- *Super epistolas S. Pauli lectura* 201 n15, 205 n4, 315 n17, 323 n17, 326 n26, 344 n26, 373 n25, 380 n18, 402 n23, 407 nn52 and 53, 421 n13, 437 n14, 440 n2, 450 n6, 452 nn17 and 19, 455 n11, 468 n20
- *Summa theologiae* 379 n11

Athenagoras *De resurrectione mortuorum* 174 n1

Augustine
- *Confessions* 87 n5
- *Contra Faustum Manichaeum* 77 n8, 314 n11, 413 n34
- *De bono coniugali* 9 n33, 86 n2, 90 n16
- *De civitate Dei* 34 n29, 187 n59, 402 n25, 465 n7
- *De correptione et gratia* 211 n2
- *De doctrina christiana* 37 n40, 161 n20, 236 n14, 331 n21
- *De Genesi ad litteram* 412 n21
- *De haeresibus* 13 n54
- *De praedestinatione sanctorum* 304 n12
- *Enarrationes in psalmos* 54 n19
- *Epistulae* (47) 8 n32; (55) 11 n45; (140) 378 n3; (149) xxii, 411 n21, 412 n25, 417 nn55 and 62; (153) 6 n22; (175) 223 n9
- *Sermones* (169) 379 n15 and 380 n20; (172) 452 n17; (262 *De poenitentia*) 7 n26

Chrysostom, John
- *In epistulam primam ad Corinthios homiliae* xxii n21 and passim
- *In epistulam secundam ad Corinthios homiliae* xxii n21 and passim
- *In epistulam ad Ephesios homiliae* 306 n30
- *In epistulam ad Colossenses homiliae* 405 n40
- *In epistulam primam ad Thessalonicenses homiliae* 436 n1, 438 n20

Clement of Alexandria *Protrepticus* 184 n43

Dionysius the Pseudo-Areopagite *Hierarchies* 4 n9

Eusebius *Historia ecclesiastica* 6 n21, 120 n12, 176 n12, 360 n15

Glossa ordinaria xxii n22; (on 2 Cor 8:18) 201 n15; (on Eph 1:7) 303 n8; (on Eph 1:8) 306 n25; (on Eph 4:13) 332 n25; (on Eph 5:19) 340 n11; (on Col 2:11) 414 n40; (on Col 3:8) 420 n10; (on Col 3:9) 420 n13; (on Col 3:11) 421 n15; (on Col 3:15) 422 n18; (on Col 3:16) 423 n22; (on Col 4:6) 427 n17; (on Col 4:15) 430 n34; (on Col 4:18) 431 n40

Gratian *Decretum* 10 n39, 12 n49

Gregory of Nyssa *Commentarius in Canticum Canticorum* 322 n13

Haymo *In divi Pauli epistulas expositio* 364 n17

Index of
Greek and Latin Words Cited

This is a selective index to words discussed in the notes to this volume. It includes those words that Erasmus undertakes at some point and in some manner to explain.

GREEK WORDS

ἀγαπητοί 239 n1, 278 n22
ἀγαπητός 67 n23
ἀγαθός 450 n8
ἀγρυπνίαις 271 n37
ἀδελφήν 120 n12
αἰώνιον 225 n19
ἀκέραιος 374 n31
ἀκούομεν 472 n14
ἀκριβῶς 454 n3
ἀκρογωνιαίου 319 n43
ἀληθείας 235 n9, 444 n24
ἀλλά 242 n15
ἀναγιγνωσκομένη 215 n2
ἀνακεφαλαιώσασθαι 307 n31, n33
ἀνάστασις 175 n9
ἄνεσις 463 n4
ἀνέχεσθε 263 n2
ἀξίωμα 257 n2
ἀπ' ἀρχῆς / ἀπαρχήν 468 n23
ἀπεκδυσάμενοι 420 n12
ἀπέχειν 391 n20
ἀπηλγηκότες 334 n37
ἁπλότης 245 n2
ἀπολογίαν 242 n16
ἀποστασία 465 n6
ἀπόστολοι 252 n32
ἀπόστολος 27 n2, 205 n1, 252 n32
ἀριστερός 235 n12
ἀρραβών 309 n42
ἀσχημονεῖ 159 n11
ἀσωτία 344 n26

ἀτακτέω, ἀτάκτως, ἠτακτήσαμεν 471 n7
αὐθαίρετοι 245 n3
αὐτοῖς 456 n13
αὐτόν, αὐτῶν 132 n16

βλέπετε 259 n11

γῆς 112 n10
γιγνωσκομένη 215 n2
γλῶσσα 165 n10, 166 n12
γυναῖκα 120 n12
γυναῖκες 423 n25

δεξιός 235 n12
διαλογισμοί, διαλογισμός 374 n30
διάνοια 403 n31
διαφέρειν 187 n58
δικαιοσύνη 381 n22
δόγμασιν 317 n31
δολοῦντες 221 n1
δόξα 187 n57
δρᾶμα 167 n20

ἑαυτοῖς 456 n13
ἐγείρειν 175 n9
ἐγείρεσθαι 175 n9, 185 n46
ἔγραψα 211 n3
εἴδωλον 109 n1
εἴθε 74 n21
εἰ μή 97 n37
ἐκδυσάμενοι 227 n6
ἐκκλησία 27 n3, 196 n13, 436 n2, 462 n1
ἐκκλησίᾳ 27 n3

General Index

The General Index covers references and topics of interest in the Preface, the Translators' Note, and in our notes on the translation of the Arguments, Dedicatory Letters, and *Paraphrases* contained in this volume. For citations from Classical, Patristic, and Medieval authors see the preceding indexes. An index of the text of the Paraphrases translated here is beyond the scope of this volume.